Justice in the Marketplace

Collected Statements of the Vatican and the United States Catholic Bishops on Economic Policy, 1891-1984

General Introduction and Document Introductions by
Rev. John T. Pawlikowski, OSM, Ph.D.

Edited by
David M. Byers

In its 1985 planning document, as approved by the general membership of the NCCB in November 1984, the Department of Social Development and World Peace was authorized to develop materials to educate members of the Church on issues of justice and peace. This present document was prepared under that authorization. The specific text was approved by Rev. J. Bryan Hehir, the Secretary for the Department of Social Development and World Peace, and was authorized for publication by the undersigned.

Monsignor Daniel F. Hoye
General Secretary
NCCB/USCC

July 3, 1985

Selections from Pope Pius XII's *Christmas Messages* were taken from the NCWC News Service file copy and are used with permission.

Pope John Paul II's addresses in Canada are reprinted from L'OSSER-VATORE ROMANO.

Contents

Appendix

Index / 501

Preface

The Catholic bishops of the United States will soon issue a pastoral statement on Catholic social teaching and the U.S. economy. This document will have many sources: study, expert testimony and spirited discussion among the bishops themselves, to name a few. It will also have another kind of source, less immediate perhaps but just as influential. The Church's teaching over the past century on economic matters has given the bishops a framework of ideas and a context for their deliberations. Familiarity with this teaching is essential to interpreting the pastoral and applying it to our economy, our way of life.

This volume brings the economic teaching together in readily usable form. The first section presents, in whole or in excerpt, all the major messages on economics that have emerged from Vatican City since Leo XIII's *Rerum Novarum*, the first *social encyclical*. These documents are a mixed lot, including a decree of the II Vatican Council, encyclicals, papal addresses and the statement of a Synod of Bishops. The second section presents the much less extensive comments the United States Catholic bishops have made on economic issues, starting with the 1919 *Program of Social Reconstruction* and ending with *The Economy: Human Dimensions* in 1975.

This body of teaching is both repetitious and developmental. Certain fundamental themes appear, fade, reappear in somewhat altered form, and assume a different place in the galaxy of ideas that make up the whole. The General Introduction and the Introductions to the various documents enable readers to trace these themes from origin to current formulation. At the same time, a careful use of the index will provide access to the themes, and a host of subsidiary concepts, in the documents themselves. The roots of most of the key ideas in the upcoming pastoral statement may be uncovered in this way.

This book is the product of many hands. Special thanks are due to Father John Pawlikowski, OSM, Professor of Social Ethics at the Catholic Theological Union in Chicago, for his willingness to write the general and particular introductions. I would also like to thank Ron Krietemeyer, Director of the Office of Domestic Social Development, USCC, who originated the idea for this compendium and guided its early development. Richard O'Keeffe supplied the meticulous index.

Finally, my thanks to the staff of the Office of Publishing and Promotion Services, USCC, who managed production of the text from beginning to end.

June 1985 David M. Byers

General Introduction

Catholic social thought has taken multiple turns since biblical times. For many centuries, however, the theological vision articulated by St. Thomas Aquinas shaped the Church's approach to social questions. Aquinas primarily emphasized the duties a responsible Christian is required to carry out in the social sphere.

Medieval Catholic social policy was based on a recognized set of duties that were an integral part of the major institutions of the state. Establishing social duties as the cornerstone proved extremely effective in forging organic unity within society. As long as all members of society responsibly fulfilled their roles, tranquility was assured. Medieval social thought was confined largely to discussing the *a priori* obligations attached to various community functions.

In Aquinas' world, humanity was integrated into a hierarchically ordered universe whose ultimate sovereign was God. Such a perspective left little room for theories of individual or group rights. Social obligations held clear priority over personal desires or wants. Hence there existed little or no basis for claims against society except in those instances where the state might prevent someone from fulfilling socially assigned duties. The modern discussion of social justice based on human dignity and the consequent claim of every human being to a structural recognition of that dignity by the state was still far off.

These premodern ecclesial attitudes help explain Catholicism's somewhat tardy entry into the struggle for economic rights. The medieval vision died slowly and grudgingly. The Enlightenment with its heightened sense of the individual's self-worth apart from and beyond any social calling precipitated its demise, as did the challenge presented by Marxism and other forms of European socialism.

These latter movements were growing in influence in the final decades of the nineteenth century and the opening decades of the twentieth. Marxism and socialism were not mere subjects of academic debate. Their societal perspectives, often hostile to religion, affected the working classes of Europe, giving people a much greater sense of personal dignity. This burgeoning self-awareness was starting to lead the working classes, frequently heavily Catholic, to question seriously their assigned place in the economic sphere. Many were tempted by the Marxist vision and abandoned their faith.

As such departures from Catholic observance escalated, the Church felt great pressure to respond to the legitimate concerns of European workers in a constructive way. The social encyclicals, beginning with Pope Leo XIII's *Rerum Novarum*, are that response.

The social encyclicals have broken down barriers. Never before had the Church spoken on social matters in such an official and comprehensive fashion. Also, Catholicism in Europe had strong ties to the economic and political elites in many places. It now began to move away from this intimate and sometimes exclusive relationship to a greater identification with all of God's people. A shift was occurring in the status of working people in the Catholic Church.

While the transformation at this early period could not be called earthshaking, it set into motion new patterns of thought and relationship that have deepened over the years. It became theologically conceivable for the individual worker and organized groups of workers to make claims against the state and its ally, private enterprise. Though the medieval emphasis on assigned social duties was not clearly repudiated, the initial encyclicals dealt it a fatal blow. In the same way, they laid the groundwork for the strong emphasis on the Incarnational basis for human dignity that one finds in more recent documents, especially the encyclicals of John Paul II. Themes like the "preferential option for the poor" that have emerged so powerfully in our time represent the ultimate outgrowth of the Church's new orientation.

The first social encyclicals had a profound impact in the United States. They enabled the American Catholic leadership firmly to support workers' rights and unionization. This little-known support represents one of American Catholicism's brightest moments. Through official statements and at times even through prophetic witness, church leaders stood up for the workers in the factories and the miners in the coal fields.

Some historians attribute the American labor movement's relative immunity to Marxist sympathizers to the influence of Catholicism on trade unionism. The working classes in the United States did not become as alienated from the Church as they did in Europe. In part this was due to the absence of close Catholic ties to the political and economic elite. The Church in this country was freer than in Europe to forge an identity with working people, and it did so. Only recently, as Catholics move into positions of greater power in American society, is this relationship between American Catholicism and American trade unionism experiencing some tension.

While early Catholic teachings on economics focused primarily on the problems of European and American workers, later statements have stressed the poverty of people in the Third World and of minority groups. The children and grandchildren of the workers whose lives were significantly improved by church support are now being asked to respond to others. Increasingly, the Church is trying to transform the consciousness of affluent Catholics in Europe and North America, fostering a deep and abiding commitment to economic justice for all in the name of the Gospel. John Paul II has sounded this note in an especially forceful way.

The initial social teachings had considerable success in relieving the distress of European and American workers. Whether the more recent documents will prove as effective in addressing the remaining inequalities in this country (which often have a racist and/or sexist base) and the massive inequalities present in the Third World remains to be seen.

The documents in this volume provide an overview of official church thinking, both internationally and in the United States, on economic questions. (The recent papal speeches in Canada and the Canadian bishops' statement on economic justice have been included because they were given "within earshot" of the United States and have obvious relevance to the situation in this country.) They should serve to dispel any misconception that the pastoral statement on economics the American bishops are currently preparing represents a totally new venture for the Church. The pastoral has behind it close to a century of reflections on Catholic ethics and economic life. Through such reflections, the Catholic Church continues to make constructive confrontation with economic injustice a challenge in faith for all its members.

Reverend John T. Pawlikowski,
OSM, Ph.D.

I
VATICAN DOCUMENTS

Introduction to Rerum Novarum

The path that culminated in the first social encyclical, *Rerum Novarum,* began with a prophetic address given in 1868 to an upper-class audience in Paris by the future Cardinal Mermillod. In his remarks Mermillod tried to sensitize the ruling elites to the awful situation in which most working people found themselves. He warned that the newly emerging proletariat movement might seriously undercut the established political order in Europe unless the Catholic Church could find ways of directing the workers' outrage into constructive channels. A similar message was being voiced at the same time by other Catholic leaders like Frederic Ozanam, Augustin Cochin and Maurice Maignen.

The years 1870-71 marked a decisive turning point in the growth of Catholic social consciousness. The Franco-Prussian War and the worker insurrection known as the *Commune de Paris* threatened major destabilization in Europe. Both heightened the Church's awareness of the need to respond to the deteriorating conditions that workers faced; failure to do so might lead to massive defections to socialism. Thus, conditions were right for the development of a social doctrine that identified the Church more deeply than ever before with the struggles of the working classes.

One early influential group founded in France to address this need was the Committee for the Formation of Catholic Workers' Clubs in Paris. The *Oeuvre des Cercles* quickly attracted considerable attention throughout France, and soon inspired kindred circles in other countries. Cardinal Mermillod became a leader in one such group. In 1881 Pope Leo XIII summoned him to Rome to act as a consultant on church-state issues. Part of his task was working with a new Vatican-supported circle studying economic questions. The ideas expressed in *Rerum Novarum* first saw the light of day in this group.

Mermillod and Count Franz Kuefstein of Austria went on from this Vatican study circle to help form a new organization called the Fribourg Union in 1884. Its members shared a firm commitment to address the social crisis of the period and an equally firm loyalty to Catholic teaching and papal authority. They pledged to study the nature of work, property and society itself within the context of Thomistic thought. The Union was aware that intellectual reflection alone could do little to better the condition of the working classes. They, therefore, committed themselves to pursue the enactment of international legislation reflecting the spirit of their deliberations.

Mermillod emerged as the spiritual leader of this essentially lay Catholic group. Their annual meetings between 1885 and 1891 brought together a diverse collection of Catholic thinkers from every part of Europe. While they shared some basic social ideals, the participants' political philosophies were of many shades. Staunch supporters of the aristocratic tradition rubbed shoulders with those whose allegiance lay with progressive democratic theories.

Certain questions assumed importance in the Union's discussions. The first had to do with the nature of a just wage and the proper role of the state in securing it. The Fribourg Union argued unequivocally that work is far more than a commodity. It represents a personal act of the laborer. People faithful to their work acquire a moral right to a wage sufficient to sustain themselves and their families in decency. No rigid formula was offered for defining a just wage, nor did the Union favor direct state intervention to establish one. Its members preferred freely negotiated contracts, believing that a contract that took all production costs into consideration would inevitably produce a just wage.

One clear implication of this doctrine was that workers must have the freedom to organize for collective bargaining on contracts. Only if the bargaining process broke down and workers were deprived of basic subsistence did the state have a responsibility to get involved. The Fribourg Union wished to preserve the greatest possible latitude for private initiative.

The members of the Union steered a middle course regarding state intervention and the just wage. They were open to greater intervention than liberal theorists were. They distinguished themselves from the socialists, on the other hand, by insisting on the contingent and limited nature of such intervention. *Rerum Novarum* adopted this stance almost exactly.

The Union walked the middle road on the highly controversial question of private property as well. It strongly reaffirmed the right to private ownership, laying special stress on the inviolability of the principle of private property in rural areas. In so doing, the members clearly repudiated the socialist position. Nonetheless, they did not see private property as a totally unqualified right. The right of every human being to subsistence has *primordial* status in their eyes, taking precedence over property, as fundamental as the latter remains. This analysis represented a definite break with the liberal perspective, which raised property rights to the pinnacle of social morality.

Ambiguities remained in the Union's position, and they carried over into the text of *Rerum Novarum*. Do poor people have the right to seize the property of the rich out of desperation? Does the state have the right to take over private property, with or without compensation, if such property is being used in a manner not conducive to the general welfare? The encyclical does not answer these questions.

The Fribourg Union addressed capitalism itself on many occasions. For a time, capitalism came in for harsh criticism, but in the end a more moderate outlook prevailed. Eventually the Union turned to the creation of its own distinctive social model called the *regime corporatif*. This model proposed grouping people on the basis of natural interest and social function. These groups would in turn be joined together in a larger social organism.

The Union fervently hoped that this corporate social model, which shared the organic tendencies prevalent in the medieval social vision, would end the social chaos rampant in Europe at the time, chaos the Union attributed to the influence of Enlightenment rationalism, Protestantism (which the Union felt undermined authority and encouraged irresponsible individualism) and capitalism. Fribourg's solution represented social reform rather than social revolution. Its corporate social model tried to recapture values deeply embedded in the scholastic tradition as a response to the exploitation of the working classes. Here lay the basis of its eventual appeal to Leo XIII, whose natural instincts were conservative and whose principal advisors remained committed to preservation of the aristocratic tradition. The Union's model retained the medieval spirit, even while jettisoning many of its institutions in favor of more participatory ones that benefited the working classes.

The Fribourg model, which served as the basis for *Rerum Novarum*, made a critical contribution to social thought. It recognized that social viability requires that natural and permanent groupings be endowed with some form of legal status in order to ensure the rights of all people. It is also necessary that such groups be free to express their views and that they have representation in the public domain.

This perspective laid the groundwork for Catholic commitment to the principle of union organizing. Especially in the United States, where little attention was paid to the corporate social model, the most direct and lasting effect of *Rerum Novarum* was the impulse it gave to unionization. Although a few American bishops like Cardinal Gibbons and Archbishop Ireland had already given their blessing to unionization and Catholics were already active in union leadership, the encyclical opened the doors for a much more massive and intensive collaboration between American Catholicism and the labor movement.

A dimension of the Fribourg Union's model that has taken on new importance today is its firm rejection of class struggle. The clash of social classes has become a crucial point of discussion in Catholic circles with the rise of liberation theology, especially its Latin American versions. The Vatican's concern about a "sanctification" of class struggle in such theologies has its roots in the first formulations of modern Catholic social thought.

This brief overview of the work of the Fribourg Union is essential for a full understanding not only of its child *Rerum Novarum* but also of the directions Catholic social thought has taken since. The Fribourg Union laid down certain parameters for commitment to social reform that have survived more or less intact through much of this century. They include: (1) no absolute rejection of private property; (2) no support for class struggle; (3) no formal endorsement of capitalism, a system which in many ways undercuts the organic model of society inherited from medieval thought; (4) a preferential option for the rights of workers; and (5) firm support of unionization based on a fresh interpretation of the classical organic model.

Rerum Novarum
On the Condition of Workers

POPE LEO XIII

May 15, 1891

To Our Venerable Brethren the Patriarchs, Primates, Archbishops, Bishops and Other Ordinaries of Places Having Peace and Communion with the Apostolic See

Venerable Brethren
Health and Apostolic Benediction

1. Once the passion for revolutionary change was aroused—a passion long disturbing governments—it was bound to follow sooner or later that eagerness for change would pass from the political sphere over into the related field of economics. In fact, new developments in industry, new techniques striking out on new paths, changed relations of employer and employee, abounding wealth among a very small number and destitution among the masses, increased self-reliance on the part of workers as well as a closer bond of union with one another, and, in addition to all this, a decline in morals have caused conflict to break forth.

2. The momentous nature of the questions involved in this conflict is evident from the fact that it keeps men's minds in anxious expectation, occupying the talents of the learned, the discussions of the wise and experienced, the assemblies of the people, the judgment of lawmakers, and the deliberations of rulers, so that now no topic more strongly holds men's interests.

3. Therefore, venerable brethren, with the cause of the Church and the common welfare before us, we have thought it advisable, following our custom on other occasions when we issued to you the encyclicals *On Political Power, On Human Liberty, On the Christian Constitution of States*, and others of similar nature, which seemed opportune to refute erroneous opinions, that we ought to do the same now, and for the same reasons, *On the Condition of Workers*. We have on occasion touched more than once upon this subject. In this encyclical, however, consciousness of our apostolic office admonishes us to treat the entire question thoroughly, in order that the principles may stand out in clear light, and the conflict may thereby be brought to an end as required by truth and equity.

4. The problem is difficult to resolve and is not free from dangers. It is hard indeed to fix the boundaries of the rights and duties within which the rich and the proletariat—those who furnish material things and those who furnish work—ought to be restricted in relation to each other. The controversy is truly dangerous, for in various places it is being twisted by turbulent and crafty men to pervert judgment as to truth and seditiously to incite the masses.

5. In any event, we see clearly, and all are agreed that the poor must be speedily and fittingly cared for, since the great majority of them live undeservedly in miserable and wretched conditions.

6. After the old trade guilds had been destroyed in the last century, and no protection was substituted in their place, and when public institutions and legislation had cast off traditional religious teaching, it gradually came about that the present age handed over the workers, each alone and defenseless, to the inhumanity of employers and the unbridled greed of competitors. A devouring usury, although often condemned by the Church, but practiced nevertheless under another form by avaricious and grasping men, has increased the evil; and in addition the whole process of production as well as trade in every kind of goods has been brought almost entirely under the power of a few, so that a very few rich and exceedingly rich men have laid a yoke almost of slavery on the unnumbered masses of nonowning workers.

7. To cure this evil, the Socialists, exciting the envy of the poor toward the rich, contend that it is necessary to do away with private possession of goods and in its place to make the goods of individuals common to all, and that the men who preside over a municipality or who direct the entire state should act as administrators of these goods. They hold that, by such a transfer of private goods from private individuals to the community, they can cure the present evil through dividing wealth and benefits equally among the citizens.

8. But their program is so unsuited for terminating the conflict that it actually injures the workers themselves. Moreover, it is highly unjust, because it violates the rights of lawful owners, perverts the functions of the state, and throws governments into utter confusion.

9. Clearly the essential reason why those who engage in any gainful occupation undertake labor, and at the same time the end to which workers immediately look, is to procure property for themselves and to retain it by individual right as theirs and as their very own. When the worker places his energy and his labor at the disposal of another, he does so for the purpose of getting the means necessary for livelihood. He seeks in return for the work done, accordingly, a true and full right not only to demand his wage but to dispose of it as he sees fit. Therefore, if he saves something by restricting expenditures and invests his savings in a piece of land in order to keep the fruit of his thrift more safe, a holding of this kind is certainly nothing else than his wage under a different form; and on this account land which the worker thus buys is necessarily under his full control as much as the wage which he earned by his labor. But, as is obvious, it is clearly in this that the ownership of movable and immovable goods consists. Therefore, inasmuch as the Socialists seek to transfer the goods of private persons to the community at large, they make the lot of all wage earners worse, because in abolishing the freedom to dispose of wages they take away from them by this very act the hope and the opportunity of increasing their property and of securing advantages for themselves.

10. But, what is of more vital concern, they propose a remedy openly in conflict with justice, inasmuch as nature confers on man the right to possess things privately as his own.

11. In this respect also there is the widest difference between man and other living things. For brute beasts are not self-ruling, but are ruled and governed by a two-fold innate instinct, which not only keeps their faculty of action alert and develops their powers properly but also impels and determines their individual movements. By one instinct they are induced to protect themselves and their lives; by the other, to preserve their species. In truth, they attain both ends readily by using what is before them and within immediate range; and they cannot, of course, go further because they are moved to action by the senses alone and by the separate things perceived by the senses. Man's nature is quite different. In man there is likewise the entire and full perfection of animal nature, and consequently on this ground there is given to man, certainly no less than to every kind of living thing, to enjoy the benefits of corporeal goods. Yet animal nature, however perfectly possessed, is far from embracing human nature, but rather is much lower than human nature, having been created to serve and obey it. What stands out and excels in us, what makes man man and distinguishes him generically from the brute, is the mind or reason. And owing to the fact that this animal alone has reason, it is necessary that man have goods not only to be used, which is common to all living things, but also to be possessed by stable and perpetual right; and this applies not merely to those goods which are consumed by use, but to those also which endure after being used.

12. This is even more clearly evident, if the essential nature of human beings is examined more closely. Since man by his reason understands innumerable things, linking and combining the future with the present, and since he is master of his own actions, therefore, under the eternal law, and under the power of God most wisely ruling all things, he rules himself by the foresight of his own counsel. Wherefore it is in his power to choose the things which he considers best adapted to benefit him not only in the present but also in the future. Whence it follows that dominion not only over the fruits of the earth but also over the earth itself ought to rest in man, since he sees that things necessary for the future are furnished him out of the produce of the earth. The needs of every man are subject, as it were, to constant recurrences, so that, satisfied today, they make new demands tomorrow. Therefore, nature necessarily gave man something stable and perpetually lasting on which he can count for continuous support. But nothing can give continuous support of this kind save the earth with its great abundance.

13. There is no reason to interpose provision by the state, for man is older than the state. Wherefore he had to possess by nature his own right to protect his life and body before any polity had been formed.

14. The fact that God gave the whole human race the earth to use and enjoy cannot indeed in any manner serve as an objection against private possessions. For God is said to have given the earth to mankind in common, not because he intended indiscriminate ownership of it by all, but because he assigned no part to anyone in ownership, leaving the limits of private possessions to be fixed by the industry of men and the institutions of peoples. Yet, however the earth may be apportioned among private owners, it does not cease to serve the common interest of all, inasmuch as no living being is sustained except by what the fields bring forth. Those who lack resources supply labor, so that it can be truly affirmed that the entire scheme of securing a livelihood consists in the labor which a person expends either on his own land or in some working occupation, the compensation for which is drawn ultimately from no other source than from the varied products of the earth and is exchanged for them.

15. For this reason it also follows that private possessions are clearly in accord with nature. The earth indeed produces in great abundance the things to preserve and, especially, to perfect life, but of itself it could not produce them without human cultivation and care. Moreover, since man expends his mental energy and his bodily strength in procuring the goods of nature, by this very act he appropriates that part of physical nature to himself which he has cultivated. On it he leaves impressed, as it were, a kind of image of his person, so that it must be altogether just that he should possess that part as his very own and that no one in any way should be permitted to violate his right.

16. The force of these arguments is so evident that it seems amazing that certain revivers of obsolete theories dissent from them. These men grant the individual the use of the soil and the varied fruits of the farm, but absolutely deny him the right to hold as owner either the ground on which he has built or the farm he has cultivated. When they deny this right they fail to see that a man will be defrauded of the things his labor has produced. The land, surely, that has been worked by the hand and the art of the tiller greatly changes in aspect. The wilderness is made fruitful; the barren field, fertile. But those things through which the soil has been improved so inhere in the soil and are so thoroughly intermingled with it, that they are for the most part quite inseparable from it. And, after all, would justice permit anyone to own and enjoy that upon which another has toiled? As effects follow the cause producing them, so it is just that the fruit of labor belongs precisely to those who have performed the labor.

17. Rightly therefore, the human race as a whole, moved in no wise by the dissenting opinions of a few, and observing nature carefully, has found in the law of nature itself the basis of the distribution of goods, and, by the practice of all ages, has consecrated private possession as something best adapted to man's nature and to peaceful and tranquil living together. Now civil laws, which, when just, derive their power from the natural law itself, confirm and, even by the use of force, protect this right of which we speak.—And this same right has been sanctioned by the authority of the divine law, which forbids us most strictly even to desire what belongs to another. "Thou shalt not covet thy neighbor's wife, nor his house, nor his field, nor his maid-servant, nor his ox, nor his ass, nor anything that is his."[1]

18. Rights of this kind which reside in individuals are seen to have much greater validity when viewed as fitted into and connected with the obligations of human beings in family life.

19. There is no question that in choosing a state of life it is within the power and discretion of individuals to prefer the one or the other state, either to follow the counsel of Jesus Christ regarding virginity or to bind oneself in marriage. No law of man can abolish the natural and primeval right of marriage, or in any way set aside the chief purpose of matrimony established in the beginning by the authority of God: "Increase and multiply."[2] Behold, therefore, the family, or rather the society of the household, a very small society indeed, but a true one, and older than any polity! For that reason it must have certain rights and duties of its own entirely independent of the state. Thus, right of ownership, which we have shown to be bestowed on individual persons by nature, must be assigned to man in his capacity as head of a family. Nay rather, this right is all the stronger, since the human person in family life embraces much more.

20. It is a most sacred law of nature that the father of a family see that his offspring are provided with the necessities of life, and nature even prompts him to desire to provide and to furnish his children, who, in fact reflect and in a sense continue his person, with the means of decently protecting themselves against harsh fortune in the uncertainties of life. He can do this surely in no other way than by owning fruitful goods to transmit by inheritance to his children. As already noted, the family like the state is by the same token a society in the strictest sense of the term, and it is governed by its own proper authority, namely, by that of the father. Wherefore, assuming, of

---

[1]Dt 5:21.
[2]Gn 1:28.

course, that those limits be observed which are fixed by its immediate purpose, the family assuredly possesses rights, at least equal with those of civil society, in respect to choosing and employing the things necessary for its protection and its just liberty. We say "at least equal" because, inasmuch as domestic living together is prior both in thought and in fact to uniting into a polity, it follows that its rights and duties are also prior and more in conformity with nature. But if citizens, if families, after becoming participants in common life and society, were to experience injury in a commonwealth instead of help, impairment of their rights instead of protection, society would be something to be repudiated rather than to be sought for.

21. To desire, therefore, that the civil power should enter arbitrarily into the privacy of homes is a great and pernicious error. If a family perchance is in such extreme difficulty and is so completely without plans that it is entirely unable to help itself, it is right that the distress be remedied by public aid, for each individual family is a part of the community. Similarly, if anywhere there is a grave violation of mutual rights within the family walls, public authority shall restore to each his right: for this is not usurping the rights of citizens, but protecting and confirming them with just and due care. Those in charge of public affairs, however, must stop here: nature does not permit them to go beyond these limits. Paternal authority is such that it can be neither abolished nor absorbed by the state, because it has the same origin in common with that of man's own life. "Children are a part of their father," and, as it were, a kind of extension of the father's person; and, strictly speaking, not through themselves, but through the medium of the family society in which they are begotten, they enter into and participate in civil society. And for the very reason that children "are by nature part of their father . . . before they have the use of free will, they are kept under the care of their parents."[3] Inasmuch as the Socialists, therefore, disregard care by parents and in its place introduce care by the state, they act *against natural justice* and dissolve the structure of the home.

22. And apart from the injustice involved, it is also only too evident what turmoil and disorder would obtain among all classes; and what a harsh and odious enslavement of citizens would result! The door would be open to mutual envy, detraction, and dissension. If incentives to ingenuity and skill in individual persons were to be abolished, the very fountains of wealth would necessarily dry up; and the equality conjured up by the Socialist imagination would, in reality, be nothing but uniform wretchedness and meanness for one and all, without distinction.

---

[3]St. Thomas, *Summa theologica* II-II, Q. 10, Art. 12.

23. From all these conversations, it is perceived that the fundamental principle of Socialism which would make all possessions public property is to be utterly rejected because it injures the very ones whom it seeks to help, contravenes the natural rights of individual persons, and throws the functions of the state and public peace into confusion. Let it be regarded, therefore, as established that in seeking help for the masses this principle before all is to be considered as basic, namely, that private ownership must be preserved inviolate. With this understood, we shall explain whence the desired remedy is to be sought.
24. We approach the subject with confidence and surely by our right, for the question under consideration is certainly one for which no satisfactory solution will be found unless religion and the Church have been called upon to aid. Moreover, since the safeguarding of religion and of all things within the jurisdiction of the Church is primarily our stewardship, silence on our part might be regarded as failure in our duty.
25. Assuredly, a question as formidable as this requires the attention and effort of others as well, namely, the heads of the state, employers and the rich, and, finally, those in whose behalf efforts are being made, the workers themselves. Yet without hesitation we affirm that if the Church is disregarded, human striving will be in vain. Manifestly, it is the Church which draws from the Gospel the teachings through which the struggle can be composed entirely or, after its bitterness is removed, can certainly become more tempered. It is the Church, again, that strives not only to instruct the mind but to regulate by her precepts the life and morals of individuals, that ameliorates the condition of the workers through her numerous and beneficient institutions, and that wishes and aims to have the thought and energy of all classes of society united to this end, that the interests of the workers be protected as fully as possible. And to accomplish this purpose she holds that the laws and the authority of the state, within reasonable limits, ought to be employed.
26. Therefore, let it be laid down in the first place that a condition of human existence must be borne with, namely, that in civil society the lowest cannot be made equal with the highest. Socialists, of course, agitate the contrary, but all struggling against nature is vain. There are truly very great and very many natural differences among men. Neither the talents, nor the skill, nor the health, nor the capacities of all are the same, and unequal fortune follows of itself upon necessary inequality in respect to these endowments. And clearly this condition of things is adapted to benefit both individuals and the community; for to carry on its affairs community life requires varied aptitudes and diverse services, and to perform these diverse services men are impelled most by differences in individual property holdings.
27. So far as bodily labor is concerned, man even before the Fall was not destined to be wholly idle; but certainly what his will at that time

would have freely embraced to his soul's delight, necessity afterwards forced him to accept, with a feeling of irksomeness, for the expiation of his guilt. "Cursed be the earth in thy work: in thy labor thou shalt eat of it all the days of thy life."[4] Likewise there is to be no end on earth of other hardships, for the evil consequences of sin are hard, trying, and bitter to bear, and will necessarily accompany men even to the end of life. Therefore, to suffer and endure is human, and although men may strive in all possible ways, they will never be able by any power or art wholly to banish such tribulations from human life. If any claim they can do this, if they promise the poor in their misery a life free from all sorrow and vexation and filled with repose and perpetual pleasures, they actually impose upon these people and perpetuate a fraud which will ultimately lead to evils greater than the present. The best course is to view human affairs as they are and, as we have stated, at the same time to seek appropriate relief for these troubles elsewhere.

28. It is a capital evil with respect to the question we are discussing to take for granted that the one class of society is of itself hostile to the other, as if nature had set rich and poor against each other to fight fiercely in implacable war. This is so abhorrent to reason and truth that the exact opposite is true; for just as in the human body the different members harmonize with one another, whence arises that disposition of parts and proportion in the human figure rightly called symmetry, so likewise nature has commanded in the case of the state that the two classes mentioned should agree harmoniously and should properly form equally balanced counterparts to each other. Each needs the other completely: neither capital can do without labor, nor labor without capital. Concord begets beauty and order in things. Conversely, from perpetual strife there must arise disorder accompanied by bestial cruelty. But for putting an end to conflict and for cutting away its very roots, there is wondrous and multiple power in Christian institutions.

29. And first and foremost, the entire body of religious teaching and practice, of which the Church is the interpreter and guardian, can preeminently bring together and unite the rich and the poor by recalling the two classes of society to their mutual duties, and in particular to those duties which derive from justice.

30. Among these duties the following concern the poor and the workers: To perform entirely and conscientiously whatever work has been voluntarily and equitably agreed upon; not in any way to injure the property or to harm the person of employers; in protecting their own interests, to refrain from violence and never to engage in rioting; not to associate with vicious men who craftily hold out exaggerated hopes

[4]Gn 3:17.

and make huge promises, a course usually ending in vain regrets and in the destruction of wealth.

31. The following duties, on the other hand, concern rich men and employers: Workers are not to be treated as slaves; justice demands that the dignity of human personality be respected in them, ennobled as it has been through what we call the Christian character. If we hearken to natural reason and to Christian philosophy, gainful occupations are not a mark of shame to man, but rather of respect, as they provide him with an honorable means of supporting life. It is shameful and inhuman, however, to use men as things for gain and to put no more value on them than what they are worth in muscle and energy. Likewise it is enjoined that the religious interests and the spiritual well-being of the workers receive proper consideration. Wherefore, it is the duty of employers to see that the worker is free for adequate periods to attend to his religious obligations; not to expose anyone to corrupting influences or the enticements of sin, and in no way to alienate him from care for his family and the practice of thrift. Likewise, more work is not to be imposed than strength can endure, nor that kind of work which is unsuited to a worker's age or sex.

32. Among the most important duties of employers the principal one is to give every worker what is justly due him. Assuredly, to establish a rule of pay in accord with justice, many factors must be taken into account. But, in general, the rich and employers should remember that no laws, either human or divine, permit them for their own profit to oppress the needy and the wretched or to seek gain from another's want. To defraud anyone of the wage due him is a great crime that calls down avenging wrath from Heaven. "Behold, the wages of the laborers . . . which have been kept back by you unjustly, cry out: and their cry has entered into the ears of the Lord of Hosts."[5] Finally, the rich must religiously avoid harming in any way the savings of the workers either by coercion, or by fraud, or by the arts of usury; and the more for this reason, that the workers are not sufficiently protected against injustices and violence, and their property, being so meager, ought to be regarded as all the more sacred. Could not the observance alone of the foregoing laws remove the bitterness and the causes of conflict?

33. But the Church, with Jesus Christ as her teacher and leader, seeks greater things than this; namely, by commanding something more perfect, she aims at joining the two social classes to each other in closest neighborliness and friendship. We cannot understand and evaluate mortal things rightly unless the mind reflects upon the other life, the life which is immortal. If this other life indeed were taken

---

[5]Jas 5:4.

away, the form and true notion of the right would immediately perish; nay, this entire world would become an enigma insoluble to man. Therefore, what we learn from nature itself as our teacher is also a Christian dogma and on it the whole system and structure of religion rests, as it were, on its main foundation; namely, that, when we have left this life, only then shall we truly begin to live. God has not created man for the fragile and transitory things of this world, but for Heaven and eternity, and he has ordained the earth as a place of exile, not as our permanent home. Whether you abound in, or whether you lack, riches, and all the other things which are called good, is of no importance in relation to eternal happiness. But how you use them, that is truly of utmost importance. Jesus Christ by his "plentiful redemption" has by no means taken away the various tribulations with which mortal life is interwoven, but has so clearly transformed them into incentives to virtue and sources of merit that no mortal can attain eternal reward unless he follows the bloodstained footsteps of Jesus Christ. "If we endure, we shall also reign with him."[6] By the labors and suffering which he voluntarily accepted, he has wondrously lightened the burden of suffering and labor, and not only by his example but also by his grace and by holding before us the hope of eternal reward. He has made endurance of sorrows easier: "for our present light affliction, which is for the moment, prepares for us an eternal weight of glory that is beyond all measure."[7]

34. Therefore, the well-to-do are admonished that wealth does not give surcease of sorrow, and that wealth is of no avail unto the happiness of eternal life but is rather a hindrance;[8] that the threats[9] pronounced by Jesus Christ, so unusual coming from him, ought to cause the rich to fear; and that on one day the strictest account for the use of wealth must be rendered to God as Judge.

35. On the use of wealth we have the excellent and extremely weighty teaching, which, although found in a rudimentary stage in pagan philosophy, the Church has handed down in a completely developed form and causes to be observed not only in theory but in everyday life. The foundation of this teaching rests on this, that the just ownership of money is distinct from the just use of money.

36. To own goods privately, as we saw above, is a right natural to man, and to exercise this right, especially in life in society, is not only lawful, but clearly necessary. "It is lawful for man to own his own things. It is even necessary for human life."[10] But if the question be asked: How ought man use his possessions? the Church replies with-

---

[6] 2 Tm 2:12.
[7] 2 Cor 4:17.
[8] Mt 19:23-24.
[9] Lk 6:24-25.
[10] St. Thomas, *Summa theologica*, II-II, Q. 66, Art. 2.

out hesitation: "As to this point, man ought not regard external goods as his own, but as common so that, in fact, a person should readily share them when he sees others in need. Wherefore the apostle says: 'Charge the rich of this world . . . to give readily, to share with others.'"[11] No one, certainly, is obliged to assist others out of what is required for his own necessary use or for that of his family, or even to give to others what he himself needs to maintain his station in life becomingly and decently: "No one is obliged to live unbecomingly."[12] But when the demands of necessity and propriety have been sufficiently met, it is a duty to give to the poor out of that which remains. "Give that which remains as alms."[13] These are duties not of justice, except in cases of extreme need, but of Christian charity, which obviously cannot be enforced by legal action. But the laws and judgments of men yield precedence to the law and judgment of Christ the Lord, who in many ways urges the practice of alms-giving: "It is more blessed to give than to receive,"[14] and who will judge a kindness done or denied to the poor as done or denied to himself. "As long as you did it for one of these, the least of my brethren you did it for me."[15] The substance of all this is the following: whoever has received from the bounty of God a greater share of goods, whether corporeal and external, or of the soul, has received them for this purpose, namely, that he employ them for his own perfection and, likewise, as a servant of Divine Providence, for the benefit of others.

> Therefore, he that hath talent, let him constantly see to it that he be not silent; he that hath an abundance of goods, let him be on the watch that he grow not slothful in the generosity of mercy; he that hath a trade whereby he supports himself, let him be especially eager to share with his neighbor the use and benefit thereof.[16]

37. Those who lack fortune's goods are taught by the Church that, before God as Judge, poverty is no disgrace, and that no one should be ashamed because he makes his living by toil. And Jesus Christ has confirmed this by act and by deed, who for the salvation of men, "being rich, became poor";[17] and although he was the Son of God and God himself, yet he willed to seem and to be thought the son of a carpenter; nay, he even did not disdain to spend a great part of his life at the work of a carpenter. "Is not this the carpenter, the Son of

[11]Ibid. Q. 65, Art. 2.
[12]St. Thomas, *Summa theologica*, Q. 32, Art. 6.
[13]Lk 11:41.
[14]Acts 20:35.
[15]Mt 25:40.
[16]St. Gregory the Great, *In Evang. Hom.* IX, 7.
[17]2 Cor 8:9.

Mary?"[18] Those who contemplate this divine example will more easily understand these truths: True dignity and excellence in men resides in moral living, that is, in virtue; virtue is the common inheritance of man, attainable equally by the humblest and the mightiest, by the rich and the poor; and the reward of eternal happiness will follow upon virtue and merit alone, regardless of the person in whom they may be found. Nay, rather the favor of God himself seems to incline more toward the unfortunate as a class; for Jesus Christ calls the poor[19] blessed, and he invites most lovingly all who are in labor or sorrow[20] to come to him for solace, embracing with special love the lowly and those harassed by injustice. At the realization of these things the proud spirit of the rich is easily brought down, and the downcast heart of the afflicted is lifted up; the former are moved toward kindness, the latter, toward reasonableness in their demands. Thus the distance between the classes which pride seeks is reduced, and it will easily be brought to pass that the two classes, with hands clasped in friendship, will be united in heart.

38. Yet, if they obey Christian teachings, not merely friendship but brotherly love also will bind them to each other. They will feel and understand that all men indeed have been created by God, their common Father; that all strive for the same object of good, which is God himself, who alone can communicate to both men and angels perfect and absolute happiness; that all equally have been redeemed by the grace of Jesus Christ and restored to the dignity of the sons of God, so that they are clearly united by the bonds of brotherhood not only with one another but also with Christ the Lord, "the firstborn among many brethren,"[21] and further, that the goods of nature and the gifts of Divine Grace belong in common and without distinction to all human kind, and that no one, unless he is unworthy, will be deprived of the inheritance of Heaven. "But if we are sons, we are also heirs: heirs indeed of God and joint heirs with Christ."[22]

39. Such is the economy of duties and rights according to Christian philosophy. Would it not seem that all conflict would soon cease wherever this economy were to prevail in civil society?

40. Finally, the Church does not consider it enough to point out the way of finding the cure, but she administers the remedy herself. For she occupies herself fully in training and forming men according to discipline and doctrine; and through the agency of bishops and clergy, she causes the health-giving streams of this doctrine to be diffused as widely as possible. Furthermore, she strives to enter into men's

---

[18]Mk 6:3.
[19]Mt 5:3.
[20]Mt 11:28.
[21]Rom 8:29.
[22]Rom 8:17.

minds and to bend their wills so that they may suffer themselves to be ruled and governed by the discipline of the divine precepts. And in this field, which is of first and greatest importance because in it the whole substance and matter of benefits consists, the Church indeed has a power that is especially unique. For the instruments which she uses to move souls were given her for this very purpose by Jesus Christ, and they have an efficacy implanted in them by God. Such instruments alone can properly penetrate the inner recesses of the heart and lead man to obedience to duty, to govern the activities of his self-seeking mind, to love God and his neighbors with a special and sovereign love, and to overcome courageously all things that impede the path of virtue.

41. In this connection it is sufficient briefly to recall to mind examples from history. We shall mention events and facts that admit of no doubt, namely, that human society in its civil aspects was renewed fundamentally by Christian institutions; that, by virtue of this renewal, mankind was raised to a higher level, nay, was called back from death to life, and enriched with such a degree of perfection as had never existed before and was not destined to be greater in any succeeding age; and that, finally, the same Jesus Christ is the beginning and the end of these benefits; for as all things have proceeded from him, so they must be referred back to him. When, with the acceptance of the light of the Gospel, the world had learned the great mystery of the Incarnation of the Word and the redemption of man, the life of Jesus Christ, God and man, spread through the nations and imbued them wholly with his doctrine, with his precepts, and with his laws. Wherefore, if human society is to be healed, only a return to Christian life and institutions will heal it. In the case of decaying societies it is most correctly prescribed that, if they wish to be regenerated, they must be recalled to their origins. For the perfection of all associations is this, namely, to work for and to attain the purpose for which they were formed, so that all social actions should be inspired by the same principle which brought the society itself into being. Wherefore, turning away from the original purpose is corruption, while going back to this purpose is recovery, and just as we affirm this as unquestionably true of the entire body of the commonwealth, in like manner we affirm it of that order of citizens who sustain life by labor and who constitute the vast majority of society.

42. But it must not be supposed that the Church so concentrates her energies on caring for souls as to overlook things which pertain to mortal and earthly life. As regards the nonowning workers specifically, she desires and strives that they rise from their most wretched state and enjoy better conditions. And to achieve this result she makes no small contribution by the very fact that she calls men to and trains them in virtue. For when Christian morals are completely observed, they yield of themselves a certain measure of prosperity to material existence, because they win the favor of God, the source and fountain of all goods; because they restrain the twin plagues of life—excessive desire for wealth and thirst[23] for pleasure—which too often make man wretched amidst the very abundance of riches; and because finally, Christian morals make men content with a moderate livelihood and make them supplement income by thrift, removing them far from the vices which swallow up both modest sums and huge fortunes, and dissipate splendid inheritances.

43. But, in addition, the Church provides directly for the well-being of the nonowning workers by instituting and promoting activities which she knows to be suitable to relieve their distress. Nay, even in the field of works of mercy, she has always so excelled that she is highly praised by her very enemies. The force of mutual charity among the first Christians was such that the wealthier very often divested themselves of their riches to aid others; wherefore: "Nor was there anyone among them in want."[24] To the deacons, an order founded expressly for this purpose, the apostles assigned the duty of dispensing alms daily; and the apostle Paul, although burdened with the care of all the churches, did not hesitate to spend himself on toilsome journeys in order to bring alms personally to the poorer Christians. Monies of this kind, contributed voluntarily by the Christians in every assembly, Tertullian calls "piety's deposit fund," because they were expended to "support and bury poor people, to supply the wants of orphan boys and girls without means of support, of aged household servants, and of such, too, as had suffered shipwreck."[25]

44. Thence, gradually there came into existence that patrimony which the Church has guarded with religious care as the property of the poor. Nay, even disregarding the feeling of shame associated with begging, she provided aid for the wretched poor. For, as the common parent of rich and poor, with charity everywhere stimulated to the highest degree, she founded religious societies and numerous other useful bodies, so that, with the aid which these furnished, there was scarcely any form of human misery that went uncared for.

45. And yet many today go so far as to condemn the Church as the ancient pagans once did, for such outstanding charity, and would substitute in lieu thereof a system of benevolence established by the laws of the state. But no human devices can ever be found to supplant Christian charity, which gives itself entirely for the benefit of others. This virtue belongs to the Church alone, for, unless it is derived from the Most Sacred Heart of Jesus, it is in no wise a virtue; and whosoever departs from the Church wanders far from Christ.

---

[23]Cf. 1 Tm 6:10.
[24]Acts 4:34.
[25]*Apol. II*, 39.

46. But there can be no question that, to attain our purpose, those helps also which are within the power of men are necessary. Absolutely all who are concerned with the matter must, according to their capacity, bend their efforts to this same end and work for it. And this activity has a certain likeness to Divine Providence governing the world; for generally we see effects flow from the concert of all the elements upon which as causes these effects depend.

47. But it is now in order to inquire what portion of the remedy should be expected from the state. By state here we understand not the form of government which this or that people has, but rather that form which right reason in accordance with nature requires and the teachings of divine wisdom approve, matters that we have explained specifically in our encyclical *On the Christian Constitution of States*.

48. Therefore those governing the state ought primarily to devote themselves to the service of individual groups and of the whole commonwealth, and through the entire scheme of laws and institutions to cause both public and individual well-being to develop spontaneously out of the very structure and administration of the state. For this is the duty of wise statesmanship and the essential office of those in charge of the state. Now, states are made prosperous especially by wholesome morality, properly ordered family life, protection of religion and justice, moderate imposition and equitable distribution of public burdens, progressive development of industry and trade, thriving agriculture, and by all other things of this nature, which the more actively they are promoted, the better and happier the life of the citizens is destined to be. Therefore, by virtue of these things, it is within the competence of the rulers of the state that, as they benefit other groups, they also improve in particular the condition of the workers. Furthermore, they do this with full right and without laying themselves open to any charge of unwarranted interference. For the state is bound by the very law of its office to serve the common interest. And the richer the benefits which come from this general providence on the part of the state, the less necessary it will be to experiment with other measures for the well-being of workers.

49. This ought to be considered, as it touches the question more deeply, namely, that the state has one basic purpose for existence, which embraces in common the highest and the lowest of its members. Nonowning workers are unquestionably citizens by nature in virtue of the same right as the rich, that is, true and vital parts whence, through the medium of families, the body of the state is constituted; and it hardly need be added that they are by far the greatest number in every urban area. Since it would be quite absurd to look out for one portion of the citizens and to neglect another, it follows that public authority ought to exercise due care in safeguarding the well-being and the interests of nonowning workers. Unless this is done, justice, which commands that everyone be given his own, will be violated. Wherefore St. Thomas says wisely: "Even as part and whole are in a certain way the same, so too that which pertains to the whole pertains in a certain way to the part also."[26] Consequently, among the numerous and weighty duties of rulers who would serve their people well, this is first and foremost, namely, that they protect equitably each and every class of citizens, maintaining inviolate that justice especially which is called *distributive*.

50. Although all citizens, without exception, are obliged to contribute something to the sum total common goods, some share of which naturally goes back to each individual, yet all can by no means contribute the same amount and in equal degree. Whatever the vicissitudes that occur in the forms of government, there will always be those differences in the condition of citizens without which society could neither exist nor be conceived. It is altogether necessary that there be some who dedicate themselves to the service of the state, who make laws, who dispense justice, and finally, by whose counsel and authority civil and military affairs are administered. These men, as is clear, play the chief role in the state, and among every people are to be regarded as occupying first place, because they work for the common good most directly and preeminently. On the other hand, those engaged in some calling benefit the state, but not in the same way as the men just mentioned, nor by performing the same duties; yet they, too, in a high degree, although less directly, serve the public weal. Assuredly, since social good must be of such a character that men through its acquisition are made better, it must necessarily be founded chiefly on virtue.

51. Nevertheless, an abundance of corporeal and external goods is likewise a characteristic of a well constituted state, "the use of which goods is necessary for the practice of virtue."[27] To produce these goods the labor of the workers, whether they expend their skill and strength on farms or in factories, is most efficacious and necessary. Nay, in this respect, their energy and effectiveness are so important that it is incontestable that the wealth of nations originates from no other source than from the labor of workers. Equity therefore commands that public authority show proper concern for the worker so that from what he contributes to the common good he may receive what will enable him, housed, clothed, and secure, to live his life without hardship. Whence, it follows that all those measures ought to be favored which seem in any way capable of benefiting the condition of workers. Such solicitude is so far from injuring anyone, that it is destined rather to benefit all, because it is of absolute interest to

---

[26] *Summa theologica*, II-II, Q. 61, Art. 1 and 2.
[27] St. Thomas, *De regimine principum*, I, 15.

the state that those citizens should not be miserable in every respect from whom such necessary goods proceed.

52. It is not right, as we have said, for either the citizen or the family to be absorbed by the state; it is proper that the individual and the family should be permitted to retain their freedom of action, so far as this is possible without jeopardizing the common good and without injuring anyone. Nevertheless, those who govern must see to it that they protect the community and its constituent parts: the community, because nature has entrusted its safeguarding to the sovereign power in the state to such an extent that the protection of the public welfare is not only the supreme law, but is the entire cause and reason for sovereignty; and the constituent parts, because philosophy and Christian faith agree that the administration of the state has from nature as its purpose, not the benefit of those to whom it has been entrusted, but the benefit of those who have been entrusted to it. And since the power of governing comes from God and is a participation, as it were, in his supreme sovereignty, it ought to be administered according to the example of the divine power, which looks with paternal care to the welfare of individual creatures as well as to that of all creation. If, therefore, any injury has been done to or threatens either the common good or the interests of individual groups, which injury cannot in any other way be repaired or prevented, it is necessary for public authority to intervene.

53. It is vitally important to public as well as to private welfare that there be peace and good order; likewise, that the whole regime of family life be directed according to the ordinances of God and the principles of nature, that religion be observed and cultivated, that sound morals flourish in private and public life, that justice be kept sacred and that no one be wronged with impunity by another, and that strong citizens grow up, capable of supporting, and, if necessary, of protecting the state. Wherefore, if at any time disorder should threaten because of strikes or concerted stoppages of work, if the natural bonds of family life should be relaxed among the poor, if religion among the workers should be outraged by failure to provide sufficient opportunity for performing religious duties, if in factories danger should assail the integrity of morals through the mixing of the sexes or other pernicious incitements to sin, or if the employer class should oppress the working class with unjust burdens or should degrade them with conditions inimical to human personality or to human dignity, if health should be injured by immoderate work and such as is not suited to sex or age—in all these cases, the power and authority of the law, but of course within certain limits, manifestly ought to be employed. And these limits are determined by the same reason which demands the aid of the law, that is, the law ought not undertake more, nor it go farther, than the remedy of evils or the removal of danger requires.

54. Rights indeed, by whomsoever possessed, must be religiously protected; and public authority, in warding off injuries and punishing wrongs, ought to see to it that individuals may have and hold what belongs to them. In protecting the rights of private individuals, however, special consideration must be given to the weak and the poor. For the nation, as it were, of the rich, is guarded by its own defenses and is in less need of governmental protection, whereas the suffering multitude, without the means to protect itself, relies especially on the protection of the state. Wherefore, since wage workers are numbered among the great mass of the needy, the state must include them under its special care and foresight.

55. But it will be well to touch here expressly on certain matters of special importance. The capital point is this, that private property ought to be safeguarded by the sovereign power of the state and through the bulwark of its laws. And especially, in view of such a great flaming up of passion at the present time, the masses ought to be kept within the bounds of their moral obligations. For while justice does not oppose our striving for better things, on the other hand, it does forbid anyone to take from another what is his and, in the name of a certain absurd equality, to seize forcibly the property of others; nor does the interest of the common good itself permit this. Certainly, the great majority of working people prefer to secure better conditions by honest toil, without doing wrong to anyone. Nevertheless, not a few individuals are found who, imbued with evil ideas and eager for revolution, use every means to stir up disorder and incite to violence. The authority of the state, therefore, should intervene and, by putting restraint upon such disturbers, protect the morals of workers from their corrupting arts and lawful owners from the danger of spoliation.

56. Labor which is too long and too hard and the belief that pay is inadequate not infrequently give workers cause to strike and become voluntarily idle. This evil, which is frequent and serious, ought to be remedied by public authority, because such interruption of work inflicts damage not only upon employers and upon the workers themselves, but also injures trade and commerce and the general interests of the state; and, since it is usually not far removed from violence and rioting, it very frequently jeopardizes public peace. In this matter it is more effective and salutary that the authority of the law anticipate and completely prevent the evil from breaking out by removing early the causes from which it would seem that conflict between employers and workers is bound to arise.

57. And in like manner, in the case of the worker, there are many things which the power of the state should protect; and, first of all, the goods of his soul. For however good and desirable mortal life be, yet it is not the ultimate goal for which we are born, but a road only and a means for perfecting, through knowledge of truth and love of good, the life of the soul. The soul bears the express image and likeness of God, and there resides in it that sovereignty through the medium of which man has been bidden to rule all created nature below him and to make all lands and all seas serve his interests. "Fill the earth and subdue it, and rule over the fishes of the sea and the fowls of the air and all living creatures that move upon the earth."[28] In this respect all men are equal, and there is no difference between rich and poor, between masters and servants, between rulers and subjects: "For there is the same Lord of all."[29] No one may with impunity outrage the dignity of man, which God himself treats with great reverence, nor impede his course to that level of perfection which accords with eternal life in heaven. Nay, more, in this connection a man cannot even by his own free choice allow himself to be treated in a way inconsistent with his nature, and suffer his soul to be enslaved; for there is no question here of rights belonging to man, but of duties owed to God, which are to be religiously observed.

58. Hence follows necessary cessation from toil and work on Sundays and Holy Days of Obligation. Let no one, however, understand this in the sense of greater indulgence of idle leisure, and much less in the sense of that kind of cessation from work, such as many desire, which encourages vice and promotes wasteful spending of money, but solely in the sense of a repose from labor made sacred by religion. Rest combined with religion calls man away from toil and the business of daily life to admonish him to ponder on heavenly goods and to pay his just and due homage to the Eternal Diety. This is especially the nature, and this the cause, of the rest to be taken on Sundays and Holy Days of Obligation, and God has sanctioned the same in the Old Testament by a special law: "Remember thou keep holy the Sabbath Day,"[30] and he himself taught it by his own action: namely the mystical rest taken immediately after he had created man: "He rested on the seventh day from all his work which he had done."[31]

59. Now as concerns the protection of corporeal and physical goods, the oppressed workers, above all, ought to be liberated from the savagery of greedy men, who inordinately use human beings as things for gain. Assuredly, neither justice nor humanity can countenance the exaction of so much work that the spirit is dulled from excessive toil and that along with it the body sinks crushed from exhaustion. The working energy of a man, like his entire nature, is circumscribed by definite limits beyond which it cannot go. It is developed indeed by exercise and use, but only on condition that a man cease from work at regular intervals and rest. With respect to daily work, there-

---

[28]Gn 1:28.
[29]Rom 10:12.
[30]Ex 20:8.
[31]Gn 2:2.

fore, care ought to be taken not to extend it beyond the hours that human strength warrants. The length of rest intervals ought to be decided on the basis of the varying nature of the work, of the circumstances of time and place, and of the physical condition of the workers themselves. Since the labor of those who quarry stone from the earth, or who mine iron, copper, and other underground materials, is much more severe and harmful to health, the working period for such men ought to be correspondingly shortened. The seasons of the year also must be taken into account; for often a given kind of work is easy to endure in one season but cannot be endured at all in another, or not without the greatest difficulty.

60. Finally, it is not right to demand of a woman or a child what a strong adult man is capable of doing or would be willing to do. Nay, as regards children, special care ought to be taken that the factory does not get hold of them before age has sufficiently matured their physical, intellectual, and moral powers. For budding strength in childhood, like greening verdure in spring, is crushed by premature harsh treatment; and under such circumstances all education of the child must needs be foregone. Certain occupations likewise are less fitted for women, who are intended by nature for work of the home—work indeed which especially protects modesty in women and accords by nature with the education of children and the well-being of the family. Let it be the rule everywhere that workers be given as much leisure as will compensate for the energy consumed by toil, for rest from work is necessary to restore strength consumed by use. In every obligation which is mutually contracted between employers and workers, this condition, either written or tacit, is always present, that both kinds of rest be provided for; nor would it be equitable to make an agreement otherwise, because no one has the right to demand of, or to make an agreement with anyone to neglect those duties which bind a man to God or to himself.

61. We shall now touch upon a matter of very great importance, and one which must be correctly understood in order to avoid falling into error on one side or the other. We are told that free consent fixes the amount of a wage; that therefore the employer, after paying the wage agreed to would seem to have discharged his obligation and not to owe anything more; that only then would injustice be done if either the employer should refuse to pay the whole amount of the wage, or the worker should refuse to perform all the work to which he had committed himself; and that in these cases, but in no others, is it proper for the public authority to intervene to safeguard the rights of each party.

62. An impartial judge would not assent readily or without reservation to this reasoning, because it is not complete in all respects; one factor to be considered, and one of the greatest importance, is missing. To work is to expend one's energy for the purpose of securing the things necessary for the various needs of life and especially for its preservation. "In the sweat of thy face shalt thou eat bread."[32] Accordingly, in man labor has two marks, as it were, implanted by nature, so that it is truly *personal*, because work energy inheres in the person and belongs completely to him by whom it is expended and for whose use it is destined by nature; and, secondly, that it is *necessary,* because man has need of the fruit of his labors to preserve his life, and nature itself, which must be most strictly obeyed, commands him to preserve it. If labor should be considered only under the aspect that it is personal, there is no doubt that it would be entirely in the worker's power to set the amount of the agreed wage at too low a figure. For inasmuch as he performs work by his own free will, he can also by his own free will be satisfied with either a paltry wage for his work or even with none at all. But this matter must be judged far differently, if with the factor of *personality* we combine the factor of *necessity,* from which indeed the former is separable in thought but not in reality. In fact, to preserve one's life is a duty common to all individuals, and to neglect this duty is a crime. Hence arises necessarily the right of securing things to sustain life, and only a wage earned by his labor gives a poor man the means to acquire these things.

63. Let it be granted then that worker and employer may enter freely into agreements and, in particular, concerning the amount of the wage; yet there is always underlying such agreements an element of natural justice, and one greater and more ancient than the free consent of contracting parties, namely, that the wage shall not be less than enough to support a worker who is thrifty and upright. If, compelled by necessity or moved by fear of a worse evil, a worker accepts a harder condition, which although against his will he must accept because the employer or contractor imposes it, he certainly submits to force, against which justice cries out in protest.

64. But in these and similar questions, such as the number of hours of work in each kind of occupation and the health safeguards to be provided, particularly in factories, it will be better, in order to avoid unwarranted governmental intervention, especially since circumstances of business, season, and place are so varied, that decision be reserved to the organizations of which we are about to speak below, or else to pursue another course whereby the interests of the workers may be adequately safeguarded—the state, if the occasion demands, to furnish help and protection.

65. If a worker receives a wage sufficiently large to enable him to provide comfortably for himself, his wife and his children, he will, if prudent, gladly strive to practice thrift; and the result will be, as

---

[32]Gn 3:19.

nature itself seems to counsel, that after expenditures are deducted there will remain something over and above through which he can come into the possession of a little wealth. We have seen, in fact, that the whole question under consideration cannot be settled effectually unless it is assumed and established as a principle, that the right of private property must be regarded as sacred. Wherefore, the law ought to favor this right and, so far as it can, see that the largest possible number among the masses of the population prefer to own property.

66. If this is done, excellent benefits will follow, foremost among which will surely be a more equitable division of goods. For the violence of public disorder has divided cities into two classes of citizens, with an immense gulf lying between them. On the one side is a faction exceedingly powerful because exceedingly rich. Since it alone has under its control every kind of work and business, it diverts to its own advantage and interest all production sources of wealth and exerts no little power in the administration itself of the state. On the other side are the needy and helpless masses, with minds inflamed and always ready for disorder. But if the productive activity of the multitude can be stimulated by the hope of acquiring some property in land, it will gradually come to pass that, with the difference between extreme wealth and extreme penury removed, one class will become neighbor to the other. Moreover, there will surely be a greater abundance of the things which the earth produces. For when men know they are working on what belongs to them, they work with far greater eagerness and diligence. Nay, in a word, they learn to love the land cultivated by their own hands, whence they look not only for food but for some measure of abundance for themselves and their dependents. All can see how much this willing eagerness contributes to an abundance of produce and the wealth of a nation. Hence, in the third place, will flow the benefit that men can easily be kept from leaving the country in which they have been born and bred; for they would not exchange their native country for a foreign land if their native country furnished them sufficient means of living.

67. But these advantages can be attained only if private wealth is not drained away by crushing taxes of every kind. For since the right of possessing goods privately has been conferred not by man's law, but by nature, public authority cannot abolish it, but can only control its exercise and bring it into conformity with the commonweal. Public authority therefore would act unjustly and inhumanly, if in the name of taxes it should appropriate from the property of private individuals more than is equitable.

68. Finally, employers and workers themselves can accomplish much in this matter, manifestly through those institutions by the help of which the poor are opportunely assisted and the two classes of society are brought closer to each other. Under this category come associations for giving mutual aid; various agencies established by the foresight of private persons to care for the worker and likewise for his dependent wife and children in the event that an accident, sickness, or death befalls him; and foundations to care for boys and girls, for adolescents, and for the aged.

69. But associations of workers occupy first place, and they include within their circle nearly all the rest. The beneficent achievements of the guilds of artisans among our ancestors have long been well known. Truly, they yielded noteworthy advantages not only to artisans, but, as many monuments bear witness, brought glory and progress to the arts themselves. In our present age of greater culture, with its new customs and ways of living, and with the increased number of things required by daily life, it is most clearly necessary that workers' associations be adapted to meet the present need. It is gratifying that societies of this kind composed either of workers alone or of workers and employers together are being formed everywhere, and it is truly to be desired that they grow in number and in active vigor. Although we have spoken of them more than once, it seems well to show in this place that they are highly opportune and are formed by their own right, and, likewise to show how they should be organized and what they should do.

70. Inadequacy of his own strength, learned from experience, impels and urges a man to enlist the help of others. Such is the teaching of Holy Scripture: "It is better therefore that two should be together, than one: for they have the advantage of their society. If one fall he shall be supported by the other; woe to him that is alone, for when he falleth he hath none to life him up."[33] And this also: "A brother that is helped by his brother, is like a strong city."[34] Just as man is drawn by this natural propensity into civil union and association, so also he seeks with his fellow citizens to form other societies, admittedly small and not perfect, but societies nonetheless.

71. Between these latter and the large society of the state, there is, because of their different immediate purposes, a very great distinction. The end of civil society concerns absolutely all members of this society, since the end of civil society is centered in the common good, in which latter, one and all in due proportion have a right to participate. Wherefore, this society is called *public*, because through it "men share with one another in establishing a commonwealth."[35] On the other hand, societies which are formed, so to speak, within its bosom are considered *private* and are such because their immediate object is private advantage, appertaining to those alone who are thus associ-

---

[33]Eccl 4:9-10.
[34]Prv 18:19.
[35]St.Thomas, *Contra impugnantes Dei cultum et religionem* II, 8.

ated together. "Now a private society is one which is formed to carry out some private business, as when two or three enter into association for the purpose of engaging together in trade."[36]

72. Although private societies exist within the state and are, as it were, so many parts of it, still it is not within the authority of the state universally and *per se* to forbid them to exist as such. For man is permitted by a right of nature to form private societies; the state, on the other hand, has been instituted to protect and not to destroy natural right, and if it should forbid its citizens to enter into associations, it would clearly do something contradictory to itself because both the state itself and private associations are begotten of one and the same principle, namely, that men are by nature inclined to associate. Occasionally there are times when it is proper for the laws to oppose associations of this kind, that is, if they professedly seek after any objective which is clearly at variance with good morals, with justice or with the welfare of the state. Indeed, in these cases the public power shall justly prevent such associations from forming and shall also justly dissolve those already formed. Nevertheless, it must use the greatest precaution lest it appear to infringe on the rights of its citizens, and lest, under the pretext of public benefit it enact any measure that sound reason would not support. For laws are to be obeyed only insofar as they conform with right reason and thus with the external law of God.[37]

73. Here come to our mind for consideration the various confraternities, societies, and religious orders which the authority of the Church and the piety of Christians have brought into being; and history down to our own times speaks of the wonderful benefit they have been to the human race. Since societies of this character, even if judged in the light of reason alone, have been formed for an honest purpose, it is clear that they have been formed in accordance with natural right. But in whatever respect they concern religion, they are properly subject to the Church alone. Therefore those in charge of the state cannot in justice arrogate to themselves any right over them or assume their administration to themselves. Rather it is the office of the state to respect, to conserve, and as occasion may require, to protect them from injustice. Yet we have seen something entirely different being done, especially at the present time. In many places the state has violated associations of this kind, and in fact with manifold injury, since it has put them in the bonds of the civil law, has divested them

---

[36]Ibid.

[37]"Human law has the essential nature of law only insofar as it is in accordance with right reason, and thus manifestly it derives from the eternal law. But insofar as it deviates from reason, it is called unjust law, and so it does not have the essential nature of law, but rather of a kind of violence." (St. Thomas, *Summa theologica*, I-II, Q. 93, Art. 3 ad 2.)

of their lawful right to be considered legal persons, and has robbed them of their property. In this property the Church possessed her rights, and individual association members possessed theirs, as did also the persons who donated this property for a designated purpose as well as those for whose benefit and relief it had been donated. Consequently, we cannot refrain from deploring such vicious and unjust acts of robbery, and so much the more because we see the road being closed to Catholic associations, which are law-abiding and in every respect useful, at the very time when it is being decreed that most assuredly men are permitted by law to form associations, and at the very time when this freedom is being lavishly granted in actual fact to men urging courses of conduct pernicious at once to religion and to the state.

74. Certainly, the number of associations of almost every possible kind, especially of associations of workers, is now far greater than ever before. This is not the place to inquire whence many of them originate, what object they have, or how they proceed. But the opinion is, and it is one confirmed by a good deal of evidence, that they are largely under the control of secret leaders and that these leaders apply principles which are in harmony with neither Christianity nor the welfare of states, and that, after having possession of all available work, they contrive that those who refuse to join with them will be forced by want to pay the penalty. Under these circumstances, workers who are Christians must choose one of two things; either to join associations in which it is greatly to be feared that there is danger to religion, or to form their own associations and unite their forces in such a way that they may be able manfully to free themselves from such unjust and intolerable oppression. Can they who refuse to place man's highest good in imminent jeopardy hesitate to affirm that the second course is by all means to be followed?

75. Many of our Faith are indeed to be highly commended, who, having rightly perceived what the times require of them, are experimenting and striving to discover how by honest means they can raise the nonowning working class to higher living levels. They have championed their cause and are endeavoring to increase the prosperity of both families and individuals, and at the same time to regulate justly the mutual obligations which rest upon workers and employers and to foster and strengthen in both consciousness of duty and observance of the precepts of the Gospel—precepts, in truth, which hold man back from excess and prevent him from overstepping the bounds of moderation and, in the midst of the widest divergences among persons and things, maintain harmony in the state. For this reason, we see eminent men meeting together frequently to exchange ideas, to combine their forces, and to deliberate on the most expedient programs of action. Others are endeavoring to unite the various kinds of workers in suitable associations, are assisting them with advice and money, and making plans to prevent a lack of honest and profitable work. The bishops are giving encouragement and bestowing support; and under their authority and auspices many from the ranks of the clergy, both regular and diocesan, are showing zealous care for all that pertains to the spiritual improvement of the members of these associations. Finally, there are not wanting Catholics of great wealth, yet voluntary sharers, as it were, in the lot of the wage workers, who by their own generous contributions are striving to found and extend associations through which the worker is readily enabled to obtain from his toil not only immediate benefits, but also assurance of honorable retirement in the future. How much good such manifold and enthusiastic activity has contributed to the benefit of all is too well known to make discussion necessary. From all this, we have taken auguries of good hope for the future, provided that societies of this kind continually grow and that they are founded with wise organization. Let the state protect these lawfully associated bodies of citizens; let it not, however, interfere with their private concerns and order of life; for vital activity is set in motion by an inner principle, and it is very easily destroyed, as we know, by intrusion from without.

76. Unquestionably, wise direction and organization are essential to these associations in order that in their activities there be unity of purpose and concord of wills. Furthermore, if citizens have free right to associate, as in fact they do, they also must have the right freely to adopt the organization and the rules which they judge most appropriate to achieve their purpose. We do not feel that the precise character in all details which the aforementioned direction and organization of associations ought to have can be determined by fast and fixed rules, since this is a matter to be decided rather in the light of the temperament of each people, of experiment and practice, of the nature and character of the work, of the extent of trade and commerce, and of other circumstances of a material and temporal kind, all of which must be carefully considered. In summary, let this be laid down as a general and constant law: Workers' associations ought to be so constituted and so governed as to furnish the most suitable and most convenient means to attain the object proposed, which consists in this, that the individual members of the association secure, so far as possible, an increase in the goods of body, of soul, and of prosperity.

77. It is clear, however, that moral and religious perfection ought to be regarded as their principal goal, and that their social organization as such ought above all to be directed completely by this goal. For otherwise they would degenerate in nature and would be little better than those associations in which no account is ordinarily taken of religion. Besides, what would it profit a worker to secure through an association an abundance of goods, if his soul through lack of its proper food should run the risk of perishing? "What doth it profit a man, if he gain the whole world, but suffer the loss of his own soul?"[38] Christ Our Lord teaches that this in fact must be considered the mark whereby a Christian is distinguished from a pagan: "After all these things the Gentiles seek—seek ye first the kingdom of God and his justice, and all these things shall be given you besides."[39] Therefore, having taken their principles from God, let those associations provide ample opportunity for religious instruction so that individual members may understand their duties to God, that they may well know what to believe, what to hope for, and what to do for eternal salvation, and that with special care they may be fortified against erroneous opinions and various forms of corruption. Let the worker be exhorted to the worship of God and the pursuit of piety, especially to religious observance of Sundays and Holy Days. Let him learn to reverence and love the Church, the common Mother of all, and likewise to observe her precepts and to frequent her Sacraments, which are the divine means for purifying the soul from the stains of sin and for attaining sanctity.

78. When the regulations of associations are founded upon religion, the way is easy toward establishing the mutual relations of the members so that peaceful living together and prosperity will result. Offices in the associations are to be distributed properly in accordance with the common interest, and in such a way, moreover, that wide difference in these offices may not create discord. It is of special importance that obligations be apportioned wisely and be clearly defined, to the end that no one is done an injustice. Let the funds be disbursed equitably in such way that the amount of benefit to be paid out to members is fixed beforehand in accordance with individual needs, and let the rights and duties of employers be properly adjusted to the rights and duties of workers. If any one in these two groups feels that he has been injured in any way, nothing is more to be desired than that prudent and upright men of the same body be available, and that the association regulations themselves prescribe that the dispute be settled according to the decision of these men.

79. It must also be specially provided that the worker at no time be without sufficient work, and that the monies paid into the treasury of the association furnish the means of assisting individual members in need, not only during sudden and unforeseen changes in industry, but also whenever anyone is stricken by sickness, by old age, or by misfortune.

80. Through these regulations, provided they are readily accepted, the interests and welfare of the poor will be adequately cared for.

---

[38]Mt 16:26.
[39]Mt 6:32-33.

Associations of Catholics, moreover, will undoubtedly be of great importance in promoting prosperity in the state. Through past events we can, without temerity, foresee the future. Age presses hard upon age, but there are wondrous similarities in history, governed as it is by the Providence of God, who guides and directs the continuity and the chain of events in accordance with that purpose which he set before himself in creating the human race. In the early ages, when the Church was in her youth, we know that the reproach was hurled at the Christians that the great majority of them lived by precarious alms or by toil. Yet, although destitute of wealth and power, they succeeded in winning the good will of the rich and the protection of the mighty. All could see that they were energetic, industrious, peace-loving, and exemplarily devoted to the practice of justice and especially of charity. In the presence of life and conduct such as this, all prejudice vanished, the taunting voices of the malevolent were silenced, and the falsehoods of inveterate superstition yielded little by little to Christian truth.

81. The condition of workers is a subject of bitter controversy at the present time; and whether this controversy is resolved in accordance with reason or otherwise, is in either event of utmost importance to the state. But Christian workers will readily resolve it in accordance with reason, if, united in associations and under wise leaders, they enter upon the path which their fathers and their ancestors followed to their own best welfare as well as to that of the state. For, no matter how strong the power of prejudice and passion in man, yet, unless perversity of will has deadened the sense of the right and just, the good will of citizens is certain to be more freely inclined toward those whom they learn to know as industrious and temperate, and who clearly place justice before profit and conscientious observance of duty before all else. Under these circumstances there will follow also this great advantage, that no little hope and opportunity for developing a sound attitude will be afforded those workers who live in complete disdain of the Christian Faith or in a manner foreign to its profession. These men indeed, for the most part, know that they have been deceived by illusory hopes and by false appearances. They are conscious of being most inhumanly treated by greedy employers, that almost no greater value is being placed on them than the amount of gain they yield by their toil, and that in the associations, moreover, in whose meshes they are caught, there exist in place of charity and love, internal dissensions which are the inseparable companions of aggravating and irreligious poverty. Broken in spirit, and worn out in body, how gladly many would free themselves from a servitude so degrading! Yet they dare not because either human shame or the fear of want prevents them. It is remarkable how much associations of Catholics can contribute to the welfare of all such men if they invite those wavering in uncertainty to their bosom in order to remedy their difficulties, and if they receive the penitents into their trust and protection.

82. These, venerable brethren, are the persons, and this is the procedure to be employed in dealing with this most difficult question. Everyone according to his position ought to gird himself for the task, and indeed as speedily as possible, lest, by delaying the remedy, the evil, which is already of vast dimensions, become incurable. Let those in charge of states make use of the provision afforded by laws and institutions; let the rich and employers be mindful of their duties; let the workers, whose cause is at stake, press their claims with reason. And since religion alone, as we said in the beginning, can remove the evil, root and branch, let all reflect upon this: First and foremost Christian morals must be reestablished, without which even the weapons of prudence, which are considered especially effective, will be of no avail to secure well-being.

83. So far as the Church is concerned, at no time and in no manner will she permit her efforts to be wanting, and she will contribute all the more help in proportion as she has more freedom of action. Let this be understood in particular by those whose duty it is to promote the public welfare. Let the members of the Sacred Ministry exert all their strength of mind and all their diligence, and venerable brethren, under the guidance of your authority and example, let them not cease to impress upon men of all ranks the principles of Christian living as found in the Gospel; by all means in their power let them strive for the well-being of peoples; and especially let them aim both to preserve in themselves and to arouse in others, in the highest equally as well as in the lowest, the mistress and queen of the virtues, charity. Certainly, the well-being which is so longed for is chiefly to be expected from an abundant outpouring of charity; of Christian charity, we mean, which is in epitome the law of the Gospel, and which, always ready to sacrifice itself for the benefit of others, is man's surest antidote against the insolence of the world and immoderate love of self; the divine office and features of this virtue being described by the apostle Paul in these words: "Charity is patient, is kind . . . is not self-seeking . . . bears with all things . . . endures all things."[40]

84. As a pledge of divine favor and as a token of our affection, most lovingly in the Lord we bestow on each of you, venerable brethren, on your clergy and on your people, the Apostolic Blessing.

85. Given in Rome, at St. Peter's, the 15th day of May, in the year 1891, the fourteenth of our pontificate.

Leo XIII

---

[40] 1 Cor 13:4-7.

Introduction to Quadragesimo Anno

On the fortieth anniversary of *Rerum Novarum,* Pope Pius XI issued the second major social encyclical. *Quadragesimo Anno* repeats many of the themes of Leo XIII: the dignity of labor; the rights of workers to organize and even to participate to some degree in ownership, management and profit; the incompatibility of Christian social teaching with communist or socialist economic philosophies.

Though staying more or less within the lines established by *Rerum Novarum,* the encyclical breaks some new ground. Economic concentration had become far more threatening in 1931 than it was in 1891, and Pius XI addresses it squarely. Too few people are entrusted with making basic economic decisions in our society, he says. This results in policies that favor an increasingly small group. The desire for absolute dominance in the economic sphere has totally corrupted the legitimate desire to turn a profit. The whole economy is ruled by harshness and cruelty, especially toward the poor. The Pope demands that this oppression cease.

Quadragesimo Anno's deep concern about economic concentration led to the introduction of an idea destined to become a centerpiece of subsequent Catholic social thought—the principle of subsidiarity. (Though it has roots in *Rerum Novarum,* Pius XI gave subsidiarity its classic formulation.) The principle holds that it is a serious violation of just social order to allow larger political entities to absorb functions that smaller and lower communities can ably carry out. Subsidiarity assigns to the state the responsibility of assisting in the empowerment of smaller groups. The state must not attempt to destroy these groups nor interfere with their operations. The Pope describes the principle as fixed and unchangeable, permitting no compromise.

The principle was not the product of theological reflection alone. There is little doubt that socialism's championing of state centralization was responsible for the importance subsidiarity assumed in Catholic teaching. Today the principle has become somewhat of an ideological football in discussions of Catholic perspectives on economics.

Some would prefer to replace subsidiarity with the principle of participation. The Church could remain neutral regarding the degree of government intervention, as long as a given political system guarantees a real voice to all its citizens. Pope Paul VI's *Populorum Progressio* seems to lean in this direction. Other commentators strongly assert the principle of subsidiarity in defense of an unrestrained form of capitalism, using it as justification for keeping the state from controlling basic economic dynamics. Still others take the middle ground, emphasizing the central place of subsidiarity but rejecting any interpretation of it that glorifies voluntary associations over state institutions or implies unconditionally that "that government governs best which governs least."

Those who adopt this last perspective believe that the term "subsidiarity" must be more precisely defined. As used by Pius XI and his followers, they say, subsidiarity was never intended as a description of the state itself, but rather as a description of how the state ought to relate to freely associated groups devoted to human welfare. The proper Catholic view, according to this line of interpretation, understands social function as a cooperative effort of the governmental and private sectors. Neither should be deemed more important in the overall workings of a society.

This internal Catholic discussion of subsidiarity seems to be far from resolved. Without question it will continue unabated in the future.

Quadragesimo Anno

On Reconstructing the Social Order

POPE PIUS XI

May 15, 1931

To Our Venerable Brethren, the Patriarchs, Primates, Archbishops, Bishops and Other Ordinaries, in Peace and Communion with the Holy See, and Likewise to All the Faithful of the Catholic World: On Reconstructing Social Order and on Perfecting It in Conformity with the Law of the Gospel, in Honor of the Fortieth Anniversary of the Encyclical of Leo XIII, On the Condition of Workers

Venerable Brethren and Beloved Children
Health and Apostolic Benediction

1. Forty years have passed since Leo XIII's peerless encyclical, *On the Condition of Workers,* first saw the light, and the whole Catholic world, filled with grateful recollection, is undertaking to commemorate it with befitting solemnity.

2. Other encyclicals of our predecessor had in a way prepared the path for that outstanding document and proof of pastoral care: namely, those on the family and the Holy Sacrament of Matrimony as the source of human society,[1] on the origin of civil authority[2] and its proper relations with the Church,[3] on the chief duties of Christian citizens,[4] against the tenets of Socialism,[5] against false teachings on human liberty,[6] and others of the same nature fully expressing the mind of Leo XIII. Yet the encyclical, *On the Condition of Workers,* compared with the rest had this special distinction that at a time when it was most opportune and actually necessary to do so, it laid down for all mankind the surest rules to solve aright that difficult problem of human relations called "the social question."

---

[1]Encyclical, *Arcanum,* Feb. 10, 1880.
[2]Encyclical, *Diuturnum,* June 20, 1881.
[3]Encyclical, *Immortale Dei,* Nov. 1, 1885.
[4]Encyclical, *Sapientiae Christianae,* Jan. 10, 1890.
[5]Encyclical, *Quod Apostolici Muneris,* Dec. 28, 1878.
[6]Encyclical, *Libertas,* June 20, 1888.

The Occasion

3. For toward the close of the nineteenth century, the new kind of economic life that had arisen and the new developments of industry had gone to the point in most countries that human society was clearly becoming divided more and more into two classes. One class, very small in number, was enjoying almost all the advantages which modern inventions so abundantly provided; the other, embracing the huge multitude of working people, oppressed by wretched poverty, was vainly seeking escape from the straits wherein it stood.

4. Quite agreeable, of course, was this state of things to those who thought it in their abundant riches the result of inevitable economic laws and accordingly, as if it were for charity to veil the violation of justice which lawmakers not only tolerated but at times sanctioned, wanted the whole care of supporting the poor committed to charity alone. The workers, on the other hand, crushed by their hard lot, were barely enduring it and were refusing longer to bend their necks beneath so galling a yoke; and some of them, carried away by the heat of evil counsel, were seeking the overturn of everything, while others, whom Christian training restrained from such evil designs, stood firm in the judgment that much in this had to be wholly and speedily changed.

5. The same feeling those many Catholics, both priests and laymen, shared, whom a truly wonderful charity had long spurred on to relieve the unmerited poverty of the nonowning workers, and who could in no way convince themselves that so enormous and unjust an inequality in the distribution of this world's goods truly conforms to the designs of the all-wise Creator.

6. Those men were without question sincerely seeking an immediate remedy for this lamentable disorganization of states and a secure safeguard against worse dangers. Yet such is the weakness of even the best of human minds that, now rejected as dangerous innovators, now hindered in the good work by their very associates advocating other courses of action, and, uncertain in the face of various opinions, they were at a loss which way to turn.

7. In such a sharp conflict of minds, therefore, while the question at issue was being argued this way and that, nor always with calmness, all eyes as often before turned to the Chair of Peter, to that sacred depository of all truth whence words of salvation pour forth to all the world. And to the feet of Christ's Vicar on earth were flocking in unaccustomed numbers, men well versed in social questions, employers, and workers themselves, begging him with one voice to point out, finally, the safe road to them.

8. The wise Pontiff long weighed all this in his mind before God; he summoned the most experienced and learned to counsel; he pondered the issues carefully and from every angle. At last, admonished "by the consciousness of His Apostolic Office"[7] lest silence on his part might be regarded as failure in his duty[8] he decided, in virtue of the Divine Teaching Office entrusted to him, to address not only the whole Church of Christ but all mankind.

9. Therefore on the fifteenth day of May, 1891, that long awaited voice thundered forth; neither daunted by the arduousness of the problem nor weakened by age with vigorous energy, it taught the whole human family to strike out in the social question upon new paths.

Chief Headings

10. You know, venerable brethren and beloved children, and understand full well the wonderful teaching which has made the encyclical, *On the Condition of Workers,* illustrious forever. The Supreme Pastor in this letter, grieving that so large a portion of mankind should "live undeservedly in miserable and wretched conditions,"[9] took it upon himself with great courage to defend "the cause of the workers whom the present age had handed over, each alone and defenseless, to the inhumanity of employers and the unbridled greed of competitors."[10] He sought no help from either Liberalism or Socialism, for the one had proved that it was utterly unable to solve the social problem aright, and the other, proposing a remedy far worse than the evil itself, would have plunged human society into greater dangers.

11. Since a problem was being treated "for which no satisfactory solution" is found "unless religion and the Church have been called upon to aid,"[11] the pope, clearly exercising his right and correctly holding that the guardianship of religion and the stewardship over those things that are closely bound up with it had been entrusted especially to him and relying solely upon the unchangeable principles drawn from the treasury of right reason and Divine Revelation, confidently and *as one having authority,*[12] declared and proclaimed "the rights and duties within which the rich and proletariat—those who furnish material things and those who furnish work—ought to be restricted in relation to each other,"[13] and what the Church, heads of states and the people themselves directly concerned ought to do.

---

[7]Encyclical, *On the Condition of Workers,* May 15, 1891, § 3.
[8]Ibid. cf. § 24.
[9]Ibid. cf. § 5.
[10]Ibid. cf. § 6.
[11]Ibid. cf. § 24.
[12]Cf. Mt 7:29.
[13]Encyclical, *On the Condition of Workers,* § 4.

12. The apostolic voice did not thunder forth in vain. On the contrary, not only did the obedient children of the Church hearken to it with marvelling admiration and hail it with the greatest applause, but many also who were wandering far from the truth, from the unity of the faith, and nearly all who since then either in private study or in enacting legislation have concerned themselves with the social and economic question.

13. Feeling themselves vindicated and defended by the Supreme Authority on earth, Christian workers received this encyclical with special joy. So, too, did all those noble-hearted men who, long solicitous for the improvement of the condition of the workers, had up to that time encountered almost nothing but indifference from many, and even rankling suspicion, if not open hostility, from some. Rightly, therefore, have all these groups constantly held the apostolic encyclical from that time in such high honor that to signify their gratitude they are wont, in various places and in various ways, to commemorate it every year.

14. However, in spite of such great agreement, there were some who were not a little disturbed; and so it happened that the teaching of Leo XIII, so noble and lofty and so utterly new to worldly ears, was held suspect by some, even among Catholics, and to certain ones it even gave offense. For it boldly attacked and overturned the idols of Liberalism, ignored longstanding prejudices, and was in advance of its time beyond all expectation, so that the slow of heart disdained to study this new social philosophy and the timid feared to scale so lofty a height. There were some also who stood, indeed, in awe at its splendor, but regarded it as a kind of imaginary ideal of perfection more desirable than attainable.

Scope of the Present Encyclical

15. Venerable brethren and beloved children, as all everywhere and especially Catholic workers who are pouring from all sides into this Holy City, are celebrating with such enthusiasm the solemn commemoration of the fortieth anniversary of the encyclical *On the Condition of Workers,* we deem it fitting on this occasion to recall the great benefits this encyclical has brought to the Catholic Church and to all human society; to defend the illustrious Master's doctrine on the social and economic question against certain doubts and to develop it more fully as to some points; and lastly, summoning to court the contemporary economic regime and passing judgment on Socialism, to lay bare the root of the existing social confusion and at the same time point the only way to sound restoration; namely, the Christian reform of morals. All these matters which we undertake to treat will fall under three main headings, and this entire encyclical will be devoted to their development.

I. Benefits Which Have Come from *On the Condition of Workers*

16. To begin with the topic which we have proposed first to discuss, we cannot refrain, following the counsel of St. Ambrose[14] who says that "no duty is more important than that of returning thanks," from offering our fullest gratitude to Almighty God for the immense benefits that have come through Leo's encyclical to the Church and to human society. If indeed we should wish to review these benefits even cursorily, almost the whole history of the social question during the last forty years would have to be recalled to mind. These benefits can be reduced conveniently, however, to three main points, corresponding to the three kinds of help which our predecessor ardently desired for the accomplishment of his great work of restoration.

1. What the Church Has Done

17. In the first place Leo himself clearly stated what ought to be expected from the Church:

> Manifestly it is the Church which draws from the Gospel the teachings through which the struggle can be composed entirely, or, after its bitterness is removed, can certainly become more tempered. It is the Church, again, that strives not only to instruct the mind, but to regulate by her precepts the life and morals of individuals, and that ameliorates the condition of the workers through her numerous and beneficent institutions.[15]

In Teachings

18. The Church did not let these rich fountains lie quiescent in her bosom, but from them drew copiously for the common good of the longed-for peace. Leo himself and his successors, showing paternal charity and pastoral constancy always, in defense especially of the poor and the weak,[16] proclaimed and urged without ceasing again

---

[14]St. Ambrose, *De excessu fratris sui Satyri* I. 44.
[15]Encyclical, *On the Condition of Workers*, § 25.
[16]Let it be sufficient to mention some of these only: Leo XIII's apostolic letter *Praeclara*, June 20, 1894, and encyclical *Graves de Communi*, Jan. 18, 1901; Pius X's motu proprio *De Actione Populari Christiana*, Dec. 8, 1903; Benedict XV's encyclical *Ad Beatissimi*, Nov. 1, 1914; Pius IX's encyclical *Ubi Arcano*, Dec. 23, 1922, and encyclical *Rite Expiatis*, Apr. 30, 1926.

and again by voice and pen the teaching on the social and economic question which *On the Condition of Workers* presented, and adapted it fittingly to the needs of time and of circumstance. And many bishops have done the same, who in their continual and able interpretation of this same teaching have illustrated it with commentaries and in accordance with the mind and instructions of the Holy See provided for its application to the conditions and institutions of diverse regions.[17]

19. It is not surprising, therefore, that many scholars, both priests and laymen, led especially by the desire that the unchanged and unchangeable teaching of the Church should meet new demands and needs more effectively, have zealously undertaken to develop, with the Church as their guide and teacher, a social and economic science in accord with the conditions of our time.

20. And so, with Leo's encyclical pointing the way and furnishing the light, a true Catholic social science has arisen, which is daily fostered and enriched by the tireless efforts of those chosen men whom we have termed auxiliaries of the Church. They do not, indeed, allow their science to lie hidden behind learned walls. As the useful and well attended courses instituted in Catholic universities, colleges, and seminaries, the social congresses and "weeks" that are held at frequent intervals with most successful results, the study groups that are promoted, and finally the timely and sound publications that are disseminated everywhere and in every possible way, clearly show, these men bring their science out into the full light and stress of life.

21. Nor is the benefit that has poured forth from Leo's encyclical confined within these bounds; for the teaching which *On the Condition of Workers* contains has gradually and imperceptibly worked its way into the minds of those outside Catholic unity who do not recognize the authority of the Church. Catholic principles on the social question have as a result, passed little by little into the patrimony of all human society, and we rejoice that the eternal truths which our predecessor of glorious memory proclaimed so impressively have been frequently invoked and defended not only in non-Catholic books and journals but in legislative halls also and courts of justice.

22. Furthermore, after the terrible war, when the statesmen of the leading nations were attempting to restore peace on the basis of a thorough reform of social conditions, did not they, among the norms agreed upon to regulate in accordance with justice and equity the labor of the workers, give sanction to many points that so remarkably coincide with Leo's principles and instructions as to seem consciously

---

[17] Cf. *La Hiérarchie catholique et le problème social depuis l'Encyclique "Rerum Novarum,"* 1891-1931, pp. XVI-335; ed. "Union internationale d'Etudes sociales fondée à Malines, en 1920, sous la présidence du Card. Mercier." Paris, Éditions "Spes," 1931.

taken therefrom? The encyclical *On the Condition of Workers*, without question, has become a memorable document and rightly to it may be applied the words of Isaiah: "He shall set up a standard to the nations."[18]

In Applying the Teachings

23. Meanwhile, as Leo's teachings were being widely diffused in the minds of men, with learned investigations leading the way, they have come to be put into practice. In the first place, zealous efforts have been made, with active good will, to lift up that class which on account of the modern expansion of industry had increased to enormous numbers but not yet had obtained its rightful place or rank in human society and was, for that reason, all but neglected and despised—the workers, we mean—to whose improvement, to the great advantage of souls, the diocesan and regular clergy, though burdened with other pastoral duties, have under the leadership of the bishops devoted themselves. This constant work, undertaken to fill the workers' souls with the Christian spirit, helped much also to make them conscious of their true dignity and render them capable, by placing clearly before them the rights and duties of their class, of legitimately and happily advancing and even of becoming leaders of their fellows.

24. From that time on, fuller means of livelihood have been more securely obtained; for not only did works of beneficence and charity begin to multiply at the urging of the Pontiff, but there have also been established everywhere new and continuously expanding organizations in which workers, craftsmen, farmers, and employees of every kind, with the counsel of the Church and frequently under the leadership of her priests, give and receive mutual help and support.

2. *What Civil Authority Has Done*

25. With regard to civil authority, Leo XIII, boldly breaking through the confines imposed by Liberalism, fearlessly taught that government must not be thought a mere guardian of law and of good order, but rather must put forth every effort so that "through the entire scheme of laws and institutions. . . . both public and individual well-being may develop spontaneously out of the very structure and administration of the state."[19] Just freedom of action must, of course, be left both to individual citizens and to families, yet only on condition that the common good be preserved and wrong to any individual be

[18]Is 11:12.
[19]Encyclical, *On the Condition of Workers*, § 48.

abolished. The function of the rulers of the state, moreover, is to watch over the community and its parts; but in protecting private individuals in their rights, chief consideration ought to be given to the weak and the poor. "For the nation, as it were, of the rich is guarded by its own defenses and is in less need of governmental protection, whereas the suffering multitude, without the means to protect itself relies especially on the protection of the state. Wherefore, since wage-workers are numbered among the great mass of the needy, the state must include them under its special care and foresight."[20]

26. We, of course, do not deny that even before the encyclical of Leo, some rulers of peoples had provided for certain of the more urgent needs of the workers and curbed more flagrant acts of injustice inflicted upon them. But after the apostolic voice had sounded from the Chair of Peter throughout the world, rulers of nations, more fully alive at last to their duty, devoted their minds and attention to the task of promoting a more comprehensive and fruitful social policy.

27. And while the principles of Liberalism were tottering, which had long prevented effective action by those governing the state, the encyclical *On the Condition of Workers* in truth impelled peoples themselves to promote a social policy on truer grounds and with greater intensity, and so strongly encouraged good Catholics to furnish valuable help to heads of states in this field that they often stood forth as illustrious champions of this new policy even in legislatures. Sacred ministers of the Church, thoroughly imbued with Leo's teaching, have, in fact, often proposed to the votes of the peoples' representatives the very social legislation that has been enacted in recent years and have resolutely demanded and promoted its enforcement.

28. A new branch of law, wholly unknown to the earlier time, has arisen from this continuous and unwearied labor to protect vigorously the sacred rights of the workers that flow from their dignity as men and as Christians. These laws undertake the protection of life, health, strength, family, homes, workshops, wages and labor hazards, in fine, everything which pertains to the conditions of wage workers, with special concern for women and children. Even though these laws do not conform exactly everywhere and in all respects to Leo's recommendations, still it is undeniable that much in them savors of the encyclical, *On the Condition of Workers,* to which great credit must be given for whatever improvement has been achieved in the workers' condition.

---

[20]Ibid. § 54.

3. What the Parties Directly Concerned Have Done

29. Finally, the wise Pontiff showed that "employers and workers themselves can accomplish much in this matter, manifestly through those institutions by the help of which the poor are opportunely assisted and the two classes of society are brought closer to each other."[21] First place among these institutions, he declares, must be assigned to associations that embrace either workers alone or workers and employers together. He goes into considerable detail in explaining and commending these associations and expounds with a truly wonderful wisdom their nature, purpose, timeliness, rights, duties, and regulations.

30. These teachings were issued indeed most opportunely. For at that time in many nations those at the helm of state, plainly imbued with Liberalism, were showing little favor to workers' associations of this type; nay, rather they openly opposed them, and while going out of their way to recognize similar organizations of other classes and show favor to them, they were with criminal injustice denying the natural right to form associations to those who needed it most to defend themselves from ill treatment at the hands of the powerful. There were even some Catholics who looked askance at the efforts of workers to form associations of this type as if they smacked of a socialistic or revolutionary spirit.

Workers' Associations

31. The rules, therefore, which Leo XIII issued in virtue of his authority, deserve the greatest praise in that they have been able to break down this hostility and dispel these suspicions; but they have even a higher claim to distinction in that they encouraged Christian workers to found mutual associations according to their various occupations, taught them how to do so, and resolutely confirmed in the path of duty a goodly number of those to whom socialist organizations strongly attracted by claiming to be the sole defenders and champions of the lowly and oppressed.

32. With respect to the founding of these societies, the encyclical *On the Condition of Workers* most fittingly declared that

> workers' associations ought to be so constituted and so governed as to furnish the most suitable and most convenient means to attain the object proposed, which consists in this, that the individual mem-

---

[21]Ibid. § 68.

> bers of the association secure, so far as possible, an increase in the goods of body, of soul, and of prosperity.

Yet it is clear that "moral and religious perfection ought to be regarded as their principal goal, and that their social organization as such ought above all to be directed completely by this goal.[22] For "when the regulations of associations are founded upon religion, the way is easy toward establishing the mutual relations of the members, so that peaceful living together and prosperity will result."[23]

33. To the founding of these associations the clergy and many of the laity devoted themselves everywhere with truly praiseworthy zeal, eager to bring Leo's program to full realization. Thus associations of this kind have molded truly Christian workers who, in combining harmoniously the diligent practice of their occupation with the salutary precepts of religion, protect effectively and resolutely their own temporal interests and rights, keeping a due respect for justice and a genuine desire to work together with other classes of society for the Christian renewal of all social life.

34. These counsels and instructions of Leo XIII were put into effect differently in different places according to varied local conditions. In some places one and the same association undertook to attain all the ends laid down by the Pontiff; in others, because circumstances suggested or required it, a division of work developed and separate associations were formed. Of these, some devoted themselves to the defense of the rights and legitimate interests of their members in the labor market; others took over the work of providing mutual economic aid; finally, still others gave all their attention to the fulfillment of religious and moral duties and other obligations of like nature.

35. This second method has especially been adopted where either the laws of a country, of certain special economic institutions, or that deplorable dissension of minds and hearts so widespread in contemporary society and an urgent necessity of combating with united purpose and strength the massed ranks of revolutionarists, have prevented Catholics from founding purely Catholic labor unions. Under these conditions, Catholics seem almost forced to join secular labor unions. These unions, however, should always profess justice and equity and give Catholic members full freedom to care for their own conscience and obey the laws of the Church. It is clearly the office of bishops, when they know that these associations are on account of circumstances necessary and are not dangerous to religion, to approve of Catholic workers joining them, keeping before their eyes, however, the principles and precautions laid down by our predecessor, Pius X

---

[22]Ibid. § 77.
[23]Ibid. § 78.

of holy memory.[24] Among these precautions the first and chief is this: Side by side with these unions there should always be associations zealously engaged in imbuing and forming their members in the teaching of religion and morality so that they in turn may be able to permeate the unions with that good spirit which should direct them in all their activity. As a result, the religious associations will bear good fruit even beyond the circle of their own membership.

36. To the encyclical of Leo, therefore, must be given this credit, that these associations of workers have so flourished everywhere that while, alas, still surpassed in numbers by socialist and communist organizations, they already embrace a vast multitude of workers and are able, within the confines of each nation as well as in wider assemblies, to maintain vigorously the rights and legitimate demands of Catholic workers and insist also on the salutary Christian principles of society.

Associations in Other Classes

37. Leo's learned treatment and vigorous defense of the natural right to form associations began, furthermore, to find ready application to other associations also and not alone to those of the workers. Hence no small part of the credit must, it seems, be given to this same encyclical of Leo for the fact that among farmers and others of the middle class most useful associations of this kind are seen flourishing to a notable degree and increasing day by day, as well as other institutions of a similar nature in which spiritual development and economic benefit are happily combined.

Associations of Employers

38. But if this cannot be said of organizations which our same predecessor intensely desired established among employers and managers of industry—and we certainly regret that they are so few—the condition is not wholly due to the will of men but to far graver difficulties that hinder associations of this kind which we know well and estimate at their full value. There is, however, strong hope that these obstacles also will be removed soon, and even now we greet with the deepest joy of our soul, certain by no means insignificant attempts in this direction, the rich fruits of which promise a still richer harvest in the future.[25]

---

[24] Pius X, encyclical, *Singulari Quadam*, Sept. 24, 1912.
[25] Cf. the Letter of the Sacred Congregation of the Council to the Bishop of Lille, June 5, 1929.

Conclusion: On the Condition of Workers, the Magna Charta of the Social Order

39. All these benefits of Leo's encyclical, venerable brethren and beloved children, which we have outlined rather than fully described, are so numerous and of such import as to show plainly that this immortal document does not exhibit a merely fanciful, even if beautiful, ideal of human society. Rather did our predecessor draw from the Gospel and, therefore, from an everliving and life-giving fountain, teachings capable of greatly mitigating, if not immediately terminating that deadly internal struggle which is rending the family of mankind. The rich fruits which the Church of Christ and the whole human race have, by God's favor, reaped therefrom unto salvation prove that some of this good seed, so lavishly sown 40 years ago, fell on good ground. On the basis of the long period of experience, it cannot be rash to say that Leo's encyclical has proved itself the *Magna Charta* upon which all Christian activity in the social field ought to be based, as on a foundation. And those who would seem to hold in little esteem this papal encyclical and its commemoration either blaspheme what they know not, or understand nothing of what they are only superficially acquainted with, or if they do understand convict themselves formally of injustice and ingratitude.

40. Yet since in the course of these same years, certain doubts have arisen concerning either the correct meaning of some parts of Leo's encyclical or conclusions to be deduced therefrom, which doubts in turn have even among Catholics given rise to controversies that are not always peaceful; and since, furthermore, new needs and changed conditions of our age have made necessary a more precise application of Leo's teaching or even certain additions thereto, we most gladly seize this fitting occasion, in accord with our apostolic office through which we are debtors to all,[26] to answer, so far as in us lies, these doubts and these demands of the present day.

II. The Authority of the Church in Social and Economic Matters

41. Yet before proceeding to explain these matters, that principle which Leo XIII so clearly established must be laid down at the outset here, namely, that there resides in us the right and duty to pronounce with supreme authority upon social and economic matters.[27] Certainly

[26]Cf. Rom 1:14.
[27]Cf. Encyclical, *On the Condition of Workers*, §§ 24-25.

the Church was not given the commission to guide men to an only fleeting and perishable happiness but to that which is eternal. Indeed "the Church holds that it is unlawful for her to mix without cause in these temporal concerns"[28]; however, she can in no wise renounce the duty God entrusted to her to interpose her authority, not of course in matters of technique for which she is neither suitably equipped nor endowed by office, but in all things that are connected with the moral law. For as to these, the deposit of truth that God committed to us and the grave duty of disseminating and interpreting the whole moral law, and of urging it in season and out of season, bring under and subject to our supreme jurisdiction not only social order but economic activities themselves.

42. Even though economics and moral science employs each its own principles in its own sphere, it is, nevertheless, an error to say that the economic and moral orders are so distinct from and alien to each other that the former depends in no way on the latter. Certainly the laws of economics, as they are termed, being based on the very nature of material things and on the capacities of the human body and mind, determine the limits of what productive human effort cannot, and of what it can attain in the economic field and by what means. Yet it is reason itself that clearly shows, on the basis of the individual and social nature of things and of men, the purpose which God ordained for all economic life.

43. But it is only the moral law which, just as it commands us to seek our supreme and last end in the whole scheme of our activity, so likewise commands us to seek directly in each kind of activity those purposes which we know that nature, or rather God the Author of nature, established for that kind of action, and in orderly relationship to subordinate such immediate purposes to our supreme and last end. If we faithfully observe this law, then it will follow that the particular purposes, both individual and social, that are sought in the economic field will fall in their proper place in the universal order of purposes, and we, in ascending through them, as it were by steps, shall attain the final end of all things, that is God, to himself and to us, the supreme and inexhaustible Good.

1. *On Ownership or the Right of Property*

44. But to come down to particular points, we shall begin with ownership or the right of property. Venerable brethren and beloved children, you know that our predecessor of happy memory strongly defended the right of property against the tenets of the Socialists of his time by showing that its abolition would result, not to the advan-

[28] Pius XI, encyclical, *Ubi Arcano*, Dec. 23, 1922.

tage of the working class, but to their extreme harm. Yet since there are some who calumniate the Supreme Pontiff, and the Church herself, as if she had taken and were still taking the part of the rich against the nonowning workers—certainly no accusation is more unjust than that—and since Catholics are at variance with one another concerning the true and exact mind of Leo, it has seemed best to vindicate this, that is, the Catholic teaching on this matter from calumnies and safeguard it from false interpretations.

Its Individual and Social Character

45. First, then, let it be considered as certain and established that neither Leo nor those theologians who have taught under the guidance and authority of the Church have ever denied or questioned the twofold character of ownership, called usually individual or social according as it regards either separate persons or the common good. For they have always unanimously maintained that nature, rather the Creator himself, has given man the right of private ownership not only that individuals may be able to provide for themselves and their families but also that the goods which the Creator destined for the entire family of mankind may through this institution truly serve this purpose. All this can be achieved in no wise except through the maintenance of a certain and definite order.

46. Accordingly, twin rocks of shipwreck must be carefully avoided. For, as one is wrecked upon, or comes close to, what is known as *individualism* by denying or minimizing the social and public character of the right of property, so by rejecting or minimizing the private and individual character of this same right, one inevitably runs into *collectivism* or at least closely approaches its tenets. Unless this is kept in mind, one is swept from his course upon the shoals of that moral, juridical, and social modernism which we denounced in the encyclical issued at the beginning of our pontificate.[29] And, in particular, let those realize this who, in their desire for innovation, do not scruple to reproach the Church with infamous calumnies, as if she had allowed to creep into the teachings of her theologians a pagan concept of ownership which must be completely replaced by another that they with amazing ignorance call Christian.

Obligations Inherent in Ownership

47. In order to place definite limits on the controversies that have arisen over ownership and its inherent duties there must be first laid down as a foundation a principle established by Leo XIII: The right

---

[29] Ibid.

of property is distinct from its use.[30] That justice called commutative commands sacred respect for the division of possessions and forbids invasion of others' rights through the exceeding of the limits of one's own property; but the duty of owners to use their property only in a right way does not come under this type of justice, but under other virtues, obligations of which "cannot be enforced by legal action."[31] Therefore, they are in error who assert that ownership and its right use are limited by the same boundaries; and it is much farther still from the truth to hold that a right to property is destroyed or lost by reason of abuse or nonuse.

48. Those, therefore, are doing a work that is truly salutary and worthy of all praise who, while preserving harmony among themselves and the integrity of the traditional teaching of the Church, seek to define the inner nature of these duties and their limits whereby either the right of property itself or its use, that is, the exercise of ownership, is circumscribed by the necessities of social living. On the other hand, those who seek to restrict the individual character of ownership to such a degree that in fact they destroy it are mistaken and in error.

What the State Can Do

49. It follows from what we have termed the individual and at the same time social character of ownership, that men must consider in this matter not only their own advantage but also the common good. To define these duties in detail when necessity requires and the natural law has not done so, is the function of those in charge of the state. Therefore, public authority, under the guiding light always of the natural and divine law, can determine more accurately upon consideration of the true requirements of the common good, what is permitted and what is not permitted to owners in the use of their property. Moreover, Leo XIII wisely taught "that God has left the limits of private possessions to be fixed by the industry of men and institutions of peoples."[32] That history proves ownership, like other elements of social life, to be not absolutely unchanging, we once declared as follows:

> What divers forms has property had, from that primitive form among rude and savage peoples, which may be observed in some places even in our time, to the form of possession in the patriarchal age; and so further to the various forms under tyranny (we are using the word tyranny in its classical sense); and then through the feudal

---

[30] Encyclical, *On the Condition of Workers, § 35.*
[31] Ibid. § 36.
[32] Ibid. § 14.

and monarchial forms down to the various types which are to be found in more recent times.[33]

That the state is not permitted to discharge its duty arbitrarily is, however, clear. The natural right itself both of owning goods privately and of passing them on by inheritance ought always to remain intact and inviolate, since this indeed is a right that the state cannot take away: "For man is older than the state,"[34] and also, "domestic living together is prior both in thought and in fact to uniting into a polity."[35] Wherefore the wise Pontiff declared that it is grossly unjust for a state to exhaust private wealth through the weight of imposts and taxes. "For since the right of possessing goods privately has been conferred not by man's law, but by nature, public authority cannot abolish it, but can only control its exercise and bring it into conformity with the commonweal."[36] Yet when the state brings private ownership into harmony with the needs of the common good, it does not commit a hostile act against private owners but rather does them a friendly service; for it thereby effectively prevents the private possession of goods, which the Author of nature in his most wise providence ordained for the support of human life, from causing intolerable evils and thus rushing to its own destruction; it does not destroy private possessions, but safeguards them; and it does not weaken private property rights, but strengthens them.

Obligations with Respect to Superfluous Income

50. Furthermore, a person's superfluous income, that is, income which he does not need to sustain life fittingly and with dignity, is not left wholly to his own free determination. Rather the Sacred Scriptures and the Fathers of the Church constantly declare in the most explicit language that the rich are bound by a very grave precept to practice almsgiving, beneficence, and munificence.

51. Expending larger incomes so that opportunity for gainful work may be abundant, provided, however, that this work is applied to producing really useful goods, ought to be considered, as we deduce from the principles of the Angelic Doctor,[37] an outstanding exemplification of the virtue of munificence and one particularly suited to the needs of the times.

---

[33] Allocation to the Convention of Italian Catholic Action, May 16, 1926.
[34] Encyclical, *On the Condition of Workers*, § 12.
[35] Ibid. § 20.
[36] Ibid. § 67.
[37] Cf. St. Thomas, *Summa theologica*, II-II, Q. 134.

Titles of Acquiring Ownership

52. That ownership is originally acquired both by occupancy of a thing not owned by any one and by labor, or, as is said, by specification, the tradition of all ages as well as the teaching of our predecessor Leo clearly testifies. For, whatever some idly say to the contrary, no injury is done to any person when a thing is occupied that is available to all but belongs to no one; however, only that labor which a man performs in his own name and by virtue of which a new form or increase has been given to a thing grants him title to these fruits.

2. *Property (Capital) and Labor*

53. Far different is the nature of work that is hired out to others and expended on the property of others. To this indeed especially applies what Leo XIII says is "incontestable," namely, that "the wealth of nations originates from no other source than from the labor of workers."[38] For is it not plain that the enormous volume of goods that makes up human wealth is produced by and issues from the hands of the workers that either toil unaided or have their efficiency marvelously increased by being equipped with tools or machines? Every one knows, too, that no nation has ever risen out of want and poverty to a better and nobler condition save by the enormous and combined toil of all the people, both those who manage work and those who carry out directions. But it is no less evident that, had not God the Creator of all things, in keeping with his goodness, first generously bestowed natural riches and resources—the wealth and forces of nature—such supreme efforts would have been idle and vain, indeed could never even have begun. For what else is work but to use or exercise the energies of mind and body on or through these very things? And in the application of natural resources to human use the law of nature, or rather God's will promulgated by it, demands that right order be observed. This order consists in this: that each thing have its proper owner. Hence it follows that unless a man is expending labor on his own property, the labor of one person and the property of another must be associated, for neither can produce anything without the other. Leo XIII certainly had this in mind when he wrote: "Neither capital can do without labor, nor labor without capital."[39] Wherefore it is wholly false to ascribe to property alone or to labor alone whatever has been obtained through the combined effort of

---

[38] Encyclical, *On the Condition of Workers*, § 51.
[39] Ibid. § 28.

both, and it is wholly unjust for either, denying the efficacy of the other, to arrogate to itself whatever has been produced.

Unjust Claims of Capital

54. Property, that is, capital, has undoubtedly long been able to appropriate too much to itself. Whatever was produced, whatever returns accrued, capital claimed, for itself, hardly leaving to the worker enough to restore and renew his strength. For the doctrine was preached that all accumulation of capital falls by an absolutely insuperable economic law to the rich, and that by the same law the workers are given over and bound to perpetual want, to the scantiest of livelihoods. It is true, indeed, that things have not always and everywhere corresponded with this sort of teaching of the so-called Manchesterian Liberals; yet it cannot be denied that economic-social institutions have moved steadily in that direction. That these false ideas, these erroneous suppositions, have been vigorously assailed, and not by those alone who through them were being deprived of their innate right to obtain better conditions, will surprise no one.

Unjust Claims of Labor

55. And therefore, to the harassed workers there have come intellectuals, as they are called, setting up in opposition to a fictitious law the equally fictitious moral principle that all products and profits, save only enough to repair and renew capital, belong by very right to the workers. This error, much more specious than that of certain of the Socialists who hold that whatever serves to produce goods ought to be transferred to the state, or, as they say socialized, is consequently all the more dangerous and the more apt to deceive the unwary. It is an alluring poison which many have eagerly drunk whom open Socialism had not been able to deceive.

The Guiding Principle of Just Distribution

56. Unquestionably, so as not to close against themselves the road to justice and peace through these false tenets, both parties ought to have been forewarned by the wise words of our predecessor: "However the earth may be apportioned among private owners, it does not cease to serve the common interests of all."[40] This same doctrine we ourselves also taught above in declaring that the division of goods which results from private ownership was established by nature itself in order that created things may serve the needs of mankind in fixed

---

[40]Ibid. § 14.

and stable order. Lest one wander from the straight path of truth, this is something that must be continually kept in mind.

57. But not every distribution among human beings of property and wealth is of a character to attain either completely or to a satisfactory degree of perfection the end which God intends. Therefore, the riches that economic-social developments constantly increase ought to be so distributed among individual persons and classes that the common advantage of all, which Leo XIII had praised, will be safeguarded; in other words, that the common good of all society will be kept inviolate. By this law of social justice, one class is forbidden to exclude the other from sharing in the benefits. Hence the class of the wealthy violates this law no less, when, as if free from care on account of its wealth, it thinks it the right order of things for it to get everything and the worker nothing, than does the nonowning working class when, angered deeply at outraged justice and too ready to assert wrongly the one right it is conscious of, it demands for itself everything as if produced by its own hands, and attacks and seeks to abolish, therefore, all property and returns or incomes, of whatever kind they are or whatever the function they perform in human society, that have not been obtained by labor, and for no other reason save that they are of such a nature. And in this connection we must not pass over the unwarranted and unmerited appeal made by some to the apostle when he said: "If any man will not work neither let him eat."[41] For the apostle is passing judgment on those who are unwilling to work, although they can and ought to, and he admonishes us that we ought diligently to use our time and energies of body and mind and not be a burden to others when we can provide for ourselves. But the apostle in no wise teaches that labor is the sole title to a living or an income.[42]

58. To each, therefore, must be given his own share of goods, and the distribution of created goods, which, as every discerning person knows, is laboring today under the gravest evils due to the huge disparity between the few exceedingly rich and the unnumbered propertyless, must be effectively called back to and brought into conformity with the norms of the common good, that is, social justice.

3. Redemption of the Nonowning Workers

59. The redemption of the nonowning workers—this is the goal that our predecessor declared must necessarily be sought. And the point is the more emphatically to be asserted and more insistently repeated because the commands of the Pontiff, salutary as they are, have not

[41] 2 Thes 3:10.
[42] Cf. 2 Thes 3:8-10.

infrequently been consigned to oblivion either because they were deliberately suppressed by silence or thought impracticable although they both can and ought to be put into effect. And these commands have not lost their force and wisdom for our time because that *pauperism* which Leo XIII beheld in all its horror is less widespread. Certainly the condition of the workers has been improved and made more equitable especially in the more civilized and wealthy countries where the workers can no longer be considered universally overwhelmed with misery and lacking the necessities of life. But since manufacturing and industry have so rapidly pervaded and occupied countless regions, not only in the countries called new, but also in the realms of the Far East that have been civilized from antiquity, the number of the nonowning working poor has increased enormously and their groans cry to God from the earth. Added to them is the huge army of rural wage workers, pushed to the lowest level of existence and deprived of all hope of ever acquiring "some property in land,"[43] and, therefore, permanently bound to the status of nonowning worker unless suitable and effective remedies are applied.

Nonowning Status to Be Overcome through the Nonowning Workers Obtaining Property

60. Yet while it is true that the status of nonowning worker is to be carefully distinguished from pauperism, nevertheless the immense multitude of the nonowning workers on the one hand and the enormous riches of certain very wealthy men on the other establish an unanswerable argument that the riches which are so abundantly produced in our age of *industrialism*, as it is called, are not rightly distributed and equitably made available to the various classes of the people.

61. Therefore, with all our strength and effort we must strive that at least in the future the abundant fruits of production will accrue equitably to those who are rich and will be distributed in ample sufficiency among the workers—not that these may become remiss in work, for man is born to labor as the bird to fly—but that they may increase their property by thrift, that they may bear, by wise management of this increase in property, the burdens of family life with greater ease and security, and that, emerging from that insecure lot in life in whose uncertainties nonowning workers are cast, they may be able not only to endure the vicissitudes of earthly existence but have also assurance that when their lives are ended they will provide in some measure for those they leave after them.

[43]Encyclical, *On the Condition of Workers*, § 66.

62. All these things which our predecessor has not only suggested but clearly and openly proclaimed, we emphasize with renewed insistence in our present encyclical; and unless utmost efforts are made without delay to put them into effect, let no one persuade himself that public order, peace, and the tranquillity of human society can be effectively defended against agitators of revolution.

4. *Just Wages and Salaries*

63. As we have already indicated, following in the footsteps of our predecessor, it will be impossible to put these principles into practice unless the nonowning workers through industry and thrift advance to the state of possessing some little property. But except from pay for work, from what source can a man who has nothing else but work from which to obtain food and the necessaries of life set anything aside for himself through practicing frugality? Let us, therefore, explaining and developing wherever necessary Leo XIII's teachings and precepts, take up this question of wages and salaries which he called one "of very great importance."[44]

Working for Wages Not Essentially Wrong

64. First of all, those who declare that a contract of hiring and being hired is unjust of its own nature, and hence a partnership-contract must take its place, are certainly in error and gravely misrepresent our predecessor whose encyclical not only accepts working for wages or salaries but deals at some length with its regulation in accordance with the rules of justice.

65. We consider it more advisable, however, in the present condition of human society that, so far as is possible, the work-contract be somewhat modified by a partnership-contract, as is already being done in various ways and with no small advantage to workers and owners. Workers and other employees thus become sharers in ownership or management or participate in some fashion in the profits received.

66. The just amount of pay, however, must be calculated not on a single basis but on several, as Leo XIII already wisely declared in these words: "To establish a rule of pay in accord with justice, many factors must be taken into account."[45]

67. By this statement he plainly condemned the shallowness of those who think that this most difficult matter is easily solved by the application of a single rule or measure—and one quite false.

---

[44]Ibid. § 61.
[45]Ibid. § 31.

68. For they are greatly in error who do not hesitate to spread the principle that labor is worth and must be paid as much as its products are worth, and that consequently the one who hires out his labor has the right to demand all that is produced through his labor. How far this is from the truth is evident from what we have already explained in treating of property and labor.

The Individual and Social Character of Work

69. It is obvious that, as in the case of ownership, so in the case of work, especially work hired out to others, there is a social aspect also to be considered in addition to the personal or individual aspect. For man's productive effort cannot yield its fruits unless a truly social and organic body exists, unless a social and juridical order watches over the exercise of work, unless the various occupations, being interdependent, cooperate with and mutually complete one another, and, what is still more important, unless mind, material things, and work combine and form as it were a single whole. Therefore, where the social and individual nature of work is neglected, it will be impossible to evaluate work justly and pay it according to justice.

Three Points to Be Considered

70. Conclusions of the greatest importance follow from this two-fold character which nature has impressed on human work, and it is in accordance with these that wages ought to be regulated and established.

a) Support of the Worker and His Family
71. In the first place, the worker must be paid a wage sufficient to support him and his family.[46] That the rest of the family should also contribute to the common support, according to the capacity of each, is certainly right, as can be observed especially in the families of farmers, but also in the families of many craftsmen and small shopkeepers. But to abuse the years of childhood and the limited strength of women is grossly wrong. Mothers, concentrating on household duties, should work primarily in the home or in its immediate vicinity. It is an intolerable abuse, and to be abolished at all cost, for mothers on account of the father's low wage to be forced to engage in gainful occupations outside the home to the neglect of their proper cares and duties, especially the training of children. Every effort must therefore be made that fathers of families receive a wage large enough to meet ordinary family needs adequately. But if this cannot always be done

[46]Cf. Encyclical, *Casti Connubii*, Dec. 31, 1930.

under existing circumstances, social justice demands that changes be introduced as soon as possible whereby such a wage will be assured to every adult workingman. It will not be out of place here to render merited praise to all, who with a wise and useful purpose, have tried and tested various ways of adjusting the pay for work to family burdens in such a way that, as these increase, the former may be raised and indeed, if the contingency arises, there may be enough to meet extraordinary needs.

b) Condition of the Business

72. In determining the amount of the wage, the condition of a business and of the one carrying it on must also be taken into account; for it would be unjust to demand excessive wages which a business cannot stand without its ruin and consequent calamity to the workers. If, however, a business makes too little money, because of lack of energy or lack of initiative or because of indifference to technical and economic progress, that must not be regarded a just reason for reducing the compensation of the workers. But if the business in question is not making enough money to pay the workers an equitable wage because it is being crushed by unjust burdens or forced to sell its product at less than a just price, those who are thus the cause of the injury are guilty of grave wrong, for they deprive workers of their just wage and force them under the pinch of necessity to accept a wage less than fair.

73. Let, then, both workers and employers strive with united strength and counsel to overcome the difficulties and obstacles and let a wise provision on the part of public authority aid them in so salutary a work. If, however, matters come to an extreme crisis, it must be finally considered whether the business can continue or the workers are to be cared for in some other way. In such a situation, certainly most serious, a feeling of close relationship and a Christian concord of minds ought to prevail and function effectively among employers and workers.

c) Requirements of the Common Good

74. Lastly, the amount of the pay must be adjusted to the public economic good. We have shown above how much it helps the common good for workers and other employees, by setting aside some part of their income which remains after necessary expenditures, to attain gradually to the possession of a moderate amount of wealth. But another point, scarcely less important, and especially vital in our times, must not be overlooked: namely, that the opportunity to work be provided to those who are able and willing to work. This opportunity depends largely on the wage and salary rate, which can help as long as it is kept within proper limits, but which on the other hand can be an obstacle if it exceeds these limits. For everyone knows that an excessive lowering of wages, or their increase beyond due measure, causes unemployment. This evil, indeed, especially as we see it prolonged and injuring so many during the years of our pontificate, has plunged workers into misery and temptations, ruined the prosperity of nations, and put in jeopardy the public order, peace, and tranquillity of the whole world. Hence it is contrary to social justice when, for the sake of personal gain and without regard for the common good, wages and salaries are excessively lowered or raised; and this same social justice demands that wages and salaries be so managed, through agreement of plans and wills, in so far as can be done, as to offer to the greatest possible number the opportunity of getting work and obtaining suitable means of livelihood.

75. A right proportion among wages and salaries also contributes directly to the same result; and with this is closely connected a right proportion in the prices at which the goods are sold that are produced by the various occupations, such as agriculture, manufacturing, and others. If all these relations are properly maintained, the various occupations will combine and coalesce into, as it were, a single body and like members of the body mutually aid and complete one another. For then only will the social economy be rightly established and attain its purposes when all and each are supplied with all the goods that the wealth and resources of nature, technical achievement, and the social organization of economic life can furnish. And these goods ought indeed to be enough both to meet the demands of necessity and decent comfort and to advance people to that happier and fuller condition of life which, when it is wisely cared for, is not only no hindrance to virtue but helps it greatly.[47]

5. Social Order to Be Restored

76. What we have thus far stated regarding an equitable distribution of property and regarding just wages concerns individual persons and only indirectly touches social order, to the restoration of which according to the principles of sound philosophy and to its perfection according to the sublime precepts of the law of the Gospel, our predecessor, Leo XIII, devoted all his thoughts and care.

77. Still, in order that what he so happily initiated may be solidly established, that what remains to be done may be accomplished, and that even more copious and richer benefits may accrue to the family of mankind, two things are especially necessary: reform of institutions and correction of morals.

---

[47]Cf. St. Thomas, *De regimine principum* I, 15; encyclical, *On the Condition of Workers*, §§ 49-51.

78. When we speak of the reform of institutions, the state comes chiefly to mind, not as if universal well-being were to be expected from its activity, but because things have come to such a pass through the evil of what we have termed *individualism*, that, following upon the overthrow and near extinction of that rich social life which was once highly developed through associations of various kinds, there remain virtually only individuals and the state. This is to the great harm of the state itself; for, with a structure of social governance lost, and with the taking over of all the burdens which the wrecked associations once bore, the state has been overwhelmed and crushed by almost infinite tasks and duties.
79. As history abundantly proves, it is true that on account of changed conditions many things which were done by small associations in former times cannot be done now save by large associations. Still, that most weighty principle, which cannot be set aside or changed, remains fixed and unshaken in social philosophy: Just as it is gravely wrong to take from individuals what they can accomplish by their own initiative and industry and give it to the community, so also it is an injustice and at the same time a grave evil and disturbance of right order to assign to a greater and higher association what lesser and subordinate organizations can do. For every social activity ought of its very nature to furnish help to the members of the body social, and never destroy and absorb them.
80. The supreme authority of the state ought, therefore, to let subordinate groups handle matters and concerns of lesser importance, which would otherwise dissipate its efforts greatly. Thereby the state will more freely, powerfully, and effectively do all those things that belong to it alone because it alone can do them: directing, watching, urging, restraining, as occasion requires and necessity demands. Therefore, those in power should be sure that the more perfectly a graduated order is kept among the various associations, in observance of the principle of *subsidiary function*, the stronger social authority and effectiveness will be and the happier and more prosperous the condition of the state.

Mutual Cooperation of Industries and Professions

81. First and foremost, the state and every good citizen ought to look to and strive toward this end: that the conflict between the hostile classes be abolished and harmonious cooperation of the industries and professions be encouraged and promoted.
82. The social policy of the state, therefore, must devote itself to the reestablishment of the industries and professions. In actual fact, human society now, for the reason that it is founded on classes with divergent aims and hence opposed to one another and therefore inclined to

enmity and strife, continues to be in a violent condition and is unstable and uncertain.

83. Labor, as our predecessor explained well in his encyclical,[48] is not a mere commodity. On the contrary, the worker's human dignity in it must be recognized. It therefore cannot be bought and sold like a commodity. Nevertheless, as the situation now stands, hiring and offering for hire in the so-called labor market separate men into two divisions, as into battle lines, and the contest between these divisions turns the labor market itself almost into a battlefield where, face to face, the opposing lines struggle bitterly. Everyone understands that this grave evil which is plunging all human society to destruction must be remedied as soon as possible. But complete cure will not come until this opposition has been abolished and well-ordered members of the social body—industries and professions—are constituted in which men may have their place, not according to the position each has in the labor market but according to the respective social functions which each performs. For under nature's guidance it comes to pass that just as those who are joined together by nearness of habitation establish towns, so those who follow the same industry or profession—whether in the economic or other field—form guilds or associations, so that many are wont to consider these self-governing organizations, if not essential, at least natural to civil society.

84. Because order, as St. Thomas well explains,[49] is unity arising from the harmonious arrangement of many objects, a true, genuine social order demands that the various members of a society be united together by some strong bond. This unifying force is present not only in the producing of goods or the rendering of services—in which the employers and employees of an identical industry or profession collaborate jointly—but also in that common good, to achieve which all industries and professions together ought, each to the best of its ability, to cooperate amicably. And this unity will be the stronger and more effective, the more faithfully individuals and the industries and professions themselves strive to do their work and excel in it.

85. It is easily deduced from what has been said that the interests common to the whole industry or profession should hold first place in these guilds. The most important among these interests is to promote the cooperation in the highest degree of each industry and profession for the sake of the common good of the country. Concerning matters, however, in which particular points, involving advantage or detriment to employers or workers, may require special care and protection, the two parties, when these cases arise, can

---

[48]Cf. Encyclical, *On the Condition of Workers*, § 31.
[49]St. Thomas, *Contra Gentiles*, III, 71; cf. *Summa theologica*, I, Q. 65, Art. 2.

deliberate separately or as the situation requires reach a decision separately.

86. The teaching of Leo XIII on the form of political government, namely, that men are free to choose whatever form they please, provided that proper regard is had for the requirements of justice and of the common good, is equally applicable in due proportion, it is hardly necessary to say, to the guilds of the various industries and professions.[50]

87. Moreover, just as inhabitants of a town are wont to found associations with the widest diversity of purposes, which each is quite free to join or not, so those engaged in the same industry or profession will combine with one another into associations equally free for purposes connected in some manner with the pursuit of the calling itself. Since these free associations are clearly and lucidly explained by our predecessor of illustrious memory, we consider it enough to emphasize this one point: People are quite free not only to found such associations, which are a matter of private order and private right, but also in respect to them "freely to adopt the organization and the rules which they judge most appropriate to achieve their purpose."[51] The same freedom must be asserted for founding associations that go beyond the boundaries of individual callings. And may these free organizations, now flourishing and rejoicing in their salutary fruits, set before themselves the task of preparing the way, in conformity with the mind of Christian social teaching, for those larger and more important guilds, industries and professions, which we mentioned before, and make every possible effort to bring them to realization.

The Directing Principle of Economic Life to Be Restored

88. Attention must be given also to another matter that is closely connected with the foregoing. Just as the unity of human society cannot be founded on an opposition of classes, so also the right ordering of economic life cannot be left to a free competition of forces. For from this source, as from a poisoned spring, have originated and spread all the errors of individualist economic teaching. Destroying through forgetfulness or ignorance the social and moral character of economic life, it held that economic life must be considered and treated as altogether free from and independent of public authority, because in the market, i.e., in the free struggle of competitors, it would have a principle of self-direction which governs it much more perfectly than would the intervention of any created intellect. But free com-

[50]Encyclical, *Immortale Dei*, Nov. 1, 1885.
[51]Cf. encyclical, *On the Condition of Workers*, § 76.

petition, while justified and certainly useful provided it is kept within certain limits, clearly cannot direct economic life—a truth which the outcome of the application in practice of the tenets of this evil individualistic spirit has more than sufficiently demonstrated. Therefore, it is most necessary that economic life be again subjected to and governed by a true and effective directing principle. This function is one that the economic dictatorship which has recently displaced free competition can still less perform, since it is a headstrong power and a violent energy that, to benefit people, needs to be strongly curbed and wisely ruled. But it cannot curb and rule itself. Loftier and nobler principles—social justice and social charity—must, therefore, be sought whereby this dictatorship may be governed firmly and fully. Hence, the institutions themselves of peoples and, particularly those of all social life, ought to be penetrated with this justice, and it is most necessary that it be truly effective, that is, establish a juridical and social order which will, as it were, give form and shape to all economic life. Social charity, moreover, ought to be as the soul of this order, an order which public authority ought to be ever ready effectively to protect and defend. It will be able to do this the more easily as it rids itself of those burdens which, as we have stated above, are not properly its own.

89. Furthermore, since the various nations largely depend on one another in economic matters and need one another's help, they should strive with a united purpose and effort to promote by wisely conceived pacts and institutions a prosperous and happy international cooperation in economic life.

90. If the members of the body social are, as was said, reconstituted, and if the directing principle of economic-social life is restored, it will be possible to say in a certain sense even of this body what the apostle says of the mystical body of Christ: "The whole body (being closely joined and knit together through every joint of the system according to the functioning in due measure of each single part) derives its increase to the building up of itself in love."[52]

91. Recently, as all know, there has been inaugurated a special system of syndicates and corporations of the various callings which in view of the theme of this encyclical it would seem necessary to describe here briefly and comment upon appropriately.

92. The civil authority itself constitutes the syndicate as a juridical personality in such a manner as to confer on it simultaneously a certain monopoly-privilege, since only such a syndicate, when thus approved, can maintain the rights (according to the type of syndicate) of workers or employers, and since it alone can arrange for the placement of labor and conclude so-termed labor agreements. Anyone is

---

[52]Eph 4:16.

free to join a syndicate or not, and only within these limits can this kind of syndicate be called free; for syndical dues and special assessments are exacted of absolutely all members of every specified calling or profession, whether they are workers or employers; likewise all are bound by the labor agreements made by the legally recognized syndicate. Nevertheless, it has been officially stated that this legally recognized syndicate does not prevent the existence, without legal status however, of other associations made up of persons following the same calling.

93. The associations, or corporations, are composed of delegates from the two syndicates (that is, of workers and employers) respectively of the same industry or profession and, as true and proper organs and institutions of the state, they direct the syndicates and coordinate their activities in matters of common interest toward one and the same end.

94. Strikes and lockouts are forbidden; if the parties cannot settle their dispute, public authority intervenes.

95. Anyone who gives even slight attention to the matter will easily see what are the obvious advantages in the system we have thus summarily described: The various classes work together peacefully, socialist organizations and their activities are repressed, and a special magistracy exercises a governing authority. Yet lest we neglect anything in a matter of such great importance and that all points treated may be properly connected with the more general principles which we mentioned above and with those which we intend shortly to add, we are compelled to say that to our certain knowledge there are not wanting some who fear that the state, instead of confining itself as it ought to the furnishing of necessary and adequate assistance, is substituting itself for free activity; that the new syndical and corporative order savors too much of an involved and political system of administration; and that (in spite of those more general advantages mentioned above, which are of course fully admitted) it rather serves particular political ends than leads to the reconstruction and promotion of a better social order.

96. To achieve this latter lofty aim, and in particular to promote the common good truly and permanently, we hold it is first and above everything wholly necessary that God bless it and, secondly, that all men of good will work with united effort toward that end. We are further convinced, as a necessary consequence, that this end will be attained the more certainly the larger the number of those ready to contribute toward it their technical, occupational, and social knowledge and experience; and also, what is more important, the greater the contribution made thereto of Catholic principles and their application, not indeed by Catholic Action (which excludes strictly syndical or political activities from its scope) but by those sons of ours whom Catholic Action imbues with Catholic principles and trains for carrying on an apostolate under the leadership and teaching guidance of the Church—of that Church which in this field also that we have described, as in every other field where moral questions are involved and discussed, can never forget or neglect through indifference its divinely imposed mandate to be vigilant and to teach.

97. What we have taught about the reconstruction and perfection of social order can surely in no wise be brought to realization without reform of morality, the very record of history clearly shows. For there was a social order once which, although indeed not perfect or in all respects ideal, nevertheless, met in a certain measure the requirements of right reason, considering the conditions and needs of the time. If that order has long since perished, that surely did not happen because the order could not have accommodated itself to changed conditions and needs by development and by a certain expansion, but rather because men, hardened by too much love of self, refused to open the order to the increasing masses as they should have done, or because, deceived by allurements of a false freedom and other errors, they became impatient of every authority and sought to reject every form of control.

98. There remains to us, after again calling to judgment the economic system now in force and its most bitter accuser, Socialism, and passing explicit and just sentence upon them, to search out more thoroughly the root of these many evils and to point out that the first and most necessary remedy is a reform of morals.

III. The Great Changes since Leo's Time

99. important indeed have the changes been which both the economic system and Socialism have undergone since Leo XIII's time.

100. That, in the first place, the whole aspect of economic life is vastly altered, is plain to all. You know, venerable brethren and beloved children, that the encyclical of our predecessor of happy memory had in view chiefly that economic system, wherein, generally, some provide capital while others provide labor for a joint economic activity. And in a happy phrase he described it thus: "Neither capital can do without labor, nor labor without capital."[53]

1. The Changed Aspect of Economic Life

101. With all his energy Leo XIII sought to adjust this economic system according to the norms of right order; hence, it is evident that

[53]Encyclical, *On the Condition of Workers,* § 28.

this system is not to be condemned in itself. And surely it is not of its own nature vicious. But it does violate right order when capital hires workers, that is, the nonowning working class, with a view to and under such terms that it directs business and even the whole economic system according to its own will and advantage, scorning the human dignity of the workers, the social character of economic activity and social justice itself, and the common good.

102. Even today this is not, it is true, the only economic system in force everywhere; for there is another system also, which still embraces a huge mass of humanity, significant in numbers and importance, as for example, agriculture, wherein the greater portion of mankind honorably and honestly procures its livelihood. This group, too, is being crushed with hardships and with difficulties, to which our predecessor devotes attention in several places in his encyclical and which we ourselves have touched upon more than once in our present letter.

103. But, with the diffusion of modern industry throughout the whole world, the capitalist economic regime has spread everywhere to such a degree, particularly since the publication of Leo XIII's encyclical, that it has invaded and pervaded the economic and social life of even those outside its orbit and is unquestionably impressing on it its advantages, disadvantages and vices, and, in a sense, is giving it its own shape and form.

104. Accordingly, when directing our special attention to the changes which the capitalist economic system has undergone since Leo's time, we have in mind the good not only of those who dwell in regions given over to capital and industry, but of all mankind.

Dictatorship Has Succeeded Free Competition

105. In the first place, it is obvious that not only is wealth concentrated in our times but an immense power and despotic economic dictatorship is consolidated in the hands of a few, who often are not owners but only the trustees and managing directors of invested funds which they administer according to their own arbitrary will and pleasure.

106. This dictatorship is being most forcibly exercised by those who, since they hold the money and completely control it, control credit also and rule the lending of money. Hence they regulate the flow, so to speak, of the lifeblood whereby the entire economic system lives, and have so firmly in their grasp the soul, as it were, of economic life that no one can breathe against their will.

107. This concentration of power and might, the characteristic mark, as it were, of contemporary economic life, is the fruit that the unlimited freedom of struggle among competitors has of its own nature produced, and which lets only the strongest survive; and this is often the same as saying, those who fight the most violently, those who give least heed to their conscience.

108. This accumulation of might and of power generates in turn three kinds of conflict. First, there is the struggle for economic supremacy itself; then there is the bitter fight to gain supremacy over the state in order to use in economic struggles its resources and authority; finally there is conflict between states themselves, not only because countries employ their power and shape their policies to promote every economic advantage of their citizens, but also because they seek to decide political controversies that arise among nations through the use of their economic supremacy and strength.

The Tragic Consequences

109. The ultimate consequences of the individualist spirit in economic life are those which you yourselves, venerable brethren and beloved children, see and deplore: Free competition has destroyed itself; economic dictatorship has supplanted the free market; unbridled ambition for power has likewise succeeded greed for gain; all economic life has become tragically hard, inexorable, and cruel. To these are to be added the grave evils that have resulted from an intermingling and shameful confusion of the functions and duties of public authority with those of the economic sphere—such as, one of the worst, the virtual degradation of the majesty of the state, which although it ought to sit on high like a queen and supreme arbitress, free from all partiality and intent upon the one common good and justice, is become a slave, surrendered and delivered to the passions and greed of men. And as to international relations, two different streams have issued from the one fountainhead: On the one hand, economic nationalism or even economic imperialism; on the other, a no less deadly and accursed internationalism of finance or international imperialism whose country is where profit is.

Remedies

110. In the second part of this encyclical where we have presented our teaching, we have described the remedies for these great evils so explicitly that we consider it sufficient at this point to recall them briefly. Since the present system of economy is founded chiefly upon ownership and labor, the principles of right reason, that is, of Christian social philosophy, must be kept in mind regarding ownership and labor and their association together, and must be put into actual practice. First, so as to avoid the reefs of individualism and collectivism, the two-fold character, that is individual and social, both of capital or ownership and of work or labor must be given due and rightful weight. Relations of one to the other must be made to conform to the laws of strictest justice—commutative justice, as it is called—with the support, however, of Christian charity. Free competition, kept within definite and due limits, and still more economic dictatorship, must be effectively brought under public authority in these matters which pertain to the latter's function. The public institutions themselves, of peoples, moreover, ought to make all human society conform to the needs of the common good; that is, to the norm of social justice. If this is done, that most important division of social life, namely, economic activity, cannot fail likewise to return to right and sound order.

2. *The Changes of Socialism*

111. Socialism, against which our predecessor, Leo XIII, had especially to inveigh, has since his time changed no less profoundly than the form of economic life. For Socialism, which could then be termed almost a single system and which maintained definite teachings reduced into one body of doctrine, has since then split chiefly into two sections, often opposing each other and even bitterly hostile, without either one however abandoning a position fundamentally contrary to Christian truth that was characteristic of Socialism.

a) The More Violent Section, or Communism

112. One section of Socialism has undergone almost the same change that the capitalistic economic system, as we have explained above, has undergone. It has sunk into Communism. Communism teaches and seeks two objectives: Unrelenting class warfare and absolute extermination of private ownership. Not secretly or by hidden methods does it do this, but publicly, openly and by employing every and all means, even the most violent. To achieve these objectives there is nothing which it does not dare, nothing for which it has respect or reverence; and when it has come to power, it is incredible and portent-like in its cruelty and inhumanity. The horrible slaughter and destruction through which it has laid waste vast regions of eastern Europe and Asia are the evidence; how much an enemy and how openly hostile it is to Holy Church and to God himself is, alas, too well proved by facts and fully known to all. Although we, therefore, deem it superfluous to warn upright and faithful children of the Church regarding the impious and iniquitous character of Communism, yet we cannot without deep sorrow contemplate the heedlessness of those who apparently make light of these impending dangers, and with sluggish inertia allow the widespread propagation of doctrine which seeks by violence and slaughter to destroy society altogether. All the more gravely to be condemned is the folly of those who neglect to remove or change the conditions that inflame the minds of peoples, and pave the way for the overthrow and destruction of society.

b) The More Moderate Section Which Has Retained the Name Socialism

113. The other section, which has kept the name Socialism, is surely more moderate. It not only professes the rejection of violence but modifies and tempers to some degree, if it does not reject entirely, the class struggle and the abolition of private ownership. One might say that, terrified by its own principles and by the conclusions drawn therefrom by Communism, Socialism inclines toward and in a certain measure approaches the truths which Christian tradition has always held sacred; for it cannot be denied that its demands at times come very near those that Christian reformers of society justly insist upon.

It Departs Somewhat from the Class Struggle and from the Abolition of Private Ownership

114. For if the class struggle abstains from enmities and mutual hatred, it gradually changes into an honest discussion of differences founded on a desire for justice, and if this is not that blessed social peace which we all seek, it can and ought to be the point of departure from which to move forward to the mutual cooperation of the industries and professions. So also the war declared on private ownership, more and more abated, is being so restricted that now, finally, not the possession itself of the means of production is attacked but rather a kind of sovereignty over society which ownership has, contrary to all right, seized and usurped. For such sovereignty belongs in reality not to owners but to the public authority. If the foregoing happens, it can come even to the point that imperceptibly these ideas of the more moderate Socialism will no longer differ from the desires and demands of those who are striving to remold human society on the basis of Christian principles. For certain kinds of property, it is rightly contended, ought to be reserved to the state since they carry with them a dominating power so great that it cannot without danger to the general welfare be entrusted to private individuals.
115. Such just demands and desires have nothing in them now which is inconsistent with Christian truth, and much less are they special to Socialism. Those who work solely toward such ends have, therefore, no reason to become socialists.

Can a Middle Course Be Followed?

116. Yet let no one think that all the socialist groups or factions that are not communist have, without exception, recovered their senses to this extent either in fact or in name. For the most part they do not reject the class struggle or the abolition of ownership, but only in some degree modify them. Now if these false principles are modified and to some extent erased from the program, the question arises, or rather is raised without warrant by some, whether the principles of Christian truth cannot perhaps be also modified to some degree and be tempered so as to meet Socialism halfway and, as it were, by a middle course, come to agreement with it. There are some allured by the foolish hope that socialists in this way will be drawn to us. A vain hope! Those who want to be apostles among socialists ought to profess Christian truth whole and entire, openly and sincerely, and not connive at error in any way. If they truly wish to be heralds of the Gospel, let them above all strive to show to socialists that socialist claims, so far as they are just, are far more strongly supported by the principles of Christian faith and much more effectively promoted through the power of Christian charity.

117. But what if Socialism has really been so tempered and modified as to the class struggle and private ownership that there is in it no longer anything to be censured on these points? Has it thereby renounced its contradictory nature to the Christian religion? This is the question that holds many minds in suspense. And numerous are the Catholics who, although they clearly understand that Christian principles can never be abandoned or diminished seem to turn their eyes to the Holy See and earnestly beseech us to decide whether this form of Socialism has so far recovered from false doctrines that it can be accepted without the sacrifice of any Christian principle and in a certain sense be baptized. That we, in keeping with our fatherly solicitude, may answer their petitions, we make this pronouncement: Whether considered as a doctrine, or an historical fact, or a movement, Socialism, if it remains truly Socialism, even after it has yielded to truth and justice on the points which we have mentioned, cannot be reconciled with the teachings of the Catholic Church because its concept of society itself is utterly foreign to Christian truth.

Its Concept of Society and Man's Social Character Is Utterly Foreign to Christian Truth

118. For, according to Christian teaching, man, endowed with a social nature, is placed on this earth so that by leading a life in society and under an authority ordained of God[54] he may fully cultivate and develop all his faculties unto the praise and glory of his Creator; and that by faithfully fulfilling the duties of his craft or other calling he may obtain for himself temporal and at the same time eternal happiness. Socialism, on the other hand, wholly ignoring and indifferent to this sublime end of both man and society, affirms that human association has been instituted for the sake of material advantage alone.

---

[54]Cf. Rom 13:1.

119. Because of the fact that goods are produced more efficiently by a suitable division of labor than by the scattered efforts of individuals, socialists infer that economic activity, only the material ends of which enter into their thinking, ought of necessity to be carried on socially. Because of this necessity, they hold that men are obliged, with respect to the producing of goods, to surrender and subject themselves entirely to society. Indeed, possession of the greatest possible supply of things that serve the advantages of this life is considered of such great importance that the higher goods of man, liberty not excepted, must take a secondary place and even be sacrificed to the demands of the most efficient production of goods. This damage to human dignity, undergone in the "socialized" process of production, will be easily offset, they say, by the abundance of socially produced goods which will pour out in profusion to individuals to be used freely at their pleasure for comforts and cultural development. Society, therefore, as Socialism conceives it, can on the one hand neither exist nor be thought of without an obviously excessive use of force; on the other hand, it fosters a liberty no less false, since there is no place in it for true social authority, which rests not on temporal and material advantages but descends from God alone, the Creator and last end of all things.[55]

Catholic and Socialist Are Contradictory Terms

120. If Socialism, like all errors, contains some truth (which, moreover, the Supreme Pontiffs have never denied), it is based nevertheless on a theory of human society peculiar to itself and irreconcilable with true Christianity. Religious socialism, Christian socialism, are contradictory terms; no one can be at the same time a good Catholic and a true socialist.

Socialism Pervading Morality and Culture

121. All these admonitions which have been renewed and confirmed by our solemn authority must likewise be applied to a certain new kind of socialist activity, hitherto little known but now carried on among many socialist groups. It devotes itself above all to the training of the mind and character. Under the guise of affection it tries in particular to attract children of tender age and win them to itself, although it also embraces the whole population in its scope in order finally to produce true socialists who would shape human society to the tenets of Socialism.

122. Since in our encyclical, *The Christian Education of Youth*,[56] we have fully taught the principles that Christian education insists on and the

---

[55] Cf. Encyclical, *Diuturnum illud*, June 29, 1881.
[56] Encyclical, *Divini illius Magistri*, Dec. 31, 1929.

ends it pursues, the contradiction between these principles and ends and the activities and aims of this Socialism that is pervading morality and culture is so clear and evident that no demonstration is required here. But they seem to ignore or underestimate the grave dangers that it carries with it who think it of no importance courageously and zealously to resist them according to the gravity of the situation. It belongs to our pastoral office to warn these persons of the grave and imminent evil: let all remember that Liberalism is the father of this Socialism that is pervading morality and culture and that Bolshevism will be its heir.

Catholic Deserters to the Socialist Camp

123. Accordingly, venerable brethren, you can well understand with what great sorrow we observe that not a few of our sons, in certain regions especially, although we cannot be convinced that they have given up the true faith and right will, have deserted the camp of the Church and gone over to the ranks of Socialism, some to glory openly in the name of socialist and to profess socialist doctrines, others through thoughtlessness or even, almost against their wills to join associations which are socialist by profession or in fact.

124. In the anxiety of our paternal solicitude, we give ourselves to reflection and try to discover how it could happen that they should go so far astray and we seem to hear what many of them answer and plead in excuse: The Church and those proclaiming attachment to the Church favor the rich, neglect the workers and have no concern for them; therefore, to look after themselves they had to join the ranks of Socialism.

125. It is certainly most lamentable, venerable brethren, that there have been, nay, that even now there are men who, although professing to be Catholics, are almost completely unmindful of that sublime law of justice and charity that binds us not only to render to everyone what is his but to succor brothers in need as Christ the Lord himself,[57] and—what is worse—out of greed for gain do not scruple to exploit the workers. Even more, there are men who abuse religion itself, and under its name try to hide their unjust exactions in order to protect themselves from the manifestly just demands of the workers. The conduct of such we shall never cease to censure gravely. For they are the reason why the Church could, even though undeservedly, have the appearance of and be charged with taking the part of the rich and with being quite unmoved by the necessities and hardships of those who have been deprived, as it were, of their natural inheritance. The whole history of the Church plainly demon-

[57]Cf. Jas 2.

strates that such appearances are unfounded and such charges unjust. The encyclical itself, whose anniversary we are celebrating, is clearest proof that it is the height of injustice to hurl these calumnies and reproaches at the Church and her teaching.

They Are Invited to Return

126. Although pained by the injustice and downcast in fatherly sorrow, it is so far from our thought to repulse or to disown children who have been miserably deceived and have strayed so far from the truth and salvation that we cannot but invite them with all possible solicitude to return to the maternal bosom of the Church. May they lend ready ears to our voice, may they return whence they have left, to the home that is truly their Father's, and may they stand firm there where their own place is, in the ranks of those who, zealously following the admonitions which Leo promulgated and we have solemnly repeated, are striving to restore society according to the mind of the Church on the firmly established basis of social justice and social charity. And let them be convinced that nowhere, even on earth, can they find full happiness save with him who, being rich, became poor for our sakes that through his poverty we might become rich,[58] who was poor and in labors from his youth, who invited to himself all that labor and are heavily burdened that he might refresh them fully in the love of his heart,[59] and who, lastly, without any respect for persons will require more of them to whom more has been given[60] and "will render to everyone according to his conduct."[61]

3. *A Renewal of Morals*

127. Yet, if we look into the matter more carefully and more thoroughly, we shall clearly perceive that, preceding this ardently desired social restoration, there must be a renewal of the Christian spirit, from which so many immersed in economic life have, far and wide, unhappily fallen away, lest all our efforts be wasted and our house be builded not on a rock but on shifting sand.[62]

128. And so, venerable brethren and beloved sons, having surveyed the present economic system, we have found it laboring under the gravest of evils. We have also summoned Communism and Socialism again to judgment and have found all their forms, even the most modified, to wander far from the precepts of the Gospel.

---

[58] 2 Cor 8:9.
[59] Mt 11:28.
[60] Cf Lk 12:48.
[61] Mt 16:27.
[62] Mt 7:24ff.

129. "Wherefore," to use the words of our predecessor, "if human society is to be healed, only a return to Christian life and institutions will heal it."[63] For this alone can provide effective remedy for that excessive care for passing things that is the origin of all vices; and this alone can draw away men's eyes, fascinated by and wholly fixed on the changing things of the world, and raise them toward Heaven. Who would deny that human society is in most urgent need of this cure now?

The Chief Form of Disorder in the Contemporary Regime: Loss of Souls

130. Minds of all, it is true, are affected almost solely by temporal upheavals, disasters, and calamities. But if we examine things critically with Christian eyes, as we should, what are all these compared with the loss of souls? Yet it is not rash by any means to say that the whole scheme of social and economic life is now such as to put in the way of vast numbers of mankind most serious obstacles which prevent them from caring for the one thing necessary; namely, their eternal salvation.

131. We, made shepherd and protector by the Prince of Shepherds, who redeemed them by his blood, of a truly innumerable flock, cannot hold back our tears when contemplating this greatest of their dangers. Nay rather, fully mindful of our pastoral office and with paternal solicitude, we are continually meditating on how we can help them; and we have summoned to our aid the untiring zeal also of others who are concerned on grounds of justice or charity. For what will it profit men to become expert in more wisely using their wealth, even to gaining the whole world, if thereby they suffer the loss of their souls?[64] What will it profit to teach them sound principles of economic life if in unbridled and sordid greed they let themselves be swept away by their passion for property, so that "hearing the commandments of the Lord they do all things contrary."[65]

Causes of This Loss

132. The root and font of this defection in economic and social life from the Christian law, and of the consequent apostasy of great numbers of workers from the Catholic faith, are the disordered passions of the soul, the sad result of original sin which has so destroyed the wonderful harmony of man's faculties that, easily led astray by his

[63]Encyclical, *On the Condition of Workers*, § 41.
[64]Cf. Mt 16:26.
[65]Cf. Jgs 2:17.

evil desires, he is strongly incited to prefer the passing goods of this world to the lasting goods of Heaven. Hence arises that unquenchable thirst for riches and temporal goods, which has at all times impelled men to break God's laws and trample upon the rights of their neighbors, but which, on account of the present system of economic life, is laying far more numerous snares for human frailty. Since the instability of economic life, and especially of its structure, exacts of those engaged in it most intense and unceasing effort, some have become so hardened to the stings of conscience as to hold that they are allowed, in any manner whatsoever, to increase their profits and use means, fair or foul, to protect their hard-won wealth against sudden changes of fortune. The easy gains that a market unrestricted by any law opens to everybody attracts large numbers to buying and selling goods, and they, their one aim being to make quick profits with the least expenditure of work, raise or lower prices by their uncontrolled business dealings so rapidly according to their own caprice and greed that they nullify the wisest forecasts of producers. The laws passed to promote corporate business, while dividing and limiting the risk of business, have given occasion to the most sordid license. For we observe that consciences are little affected by this reduced obligation of accountability; that furthermore, by hiding under the shelter of a joint name, the worst of injustices and frauds are perpetrated; and that, too, directors of business companies, forgetful of their trust, betray the rights of those whose savings they have undertaken to administer. Lastly, we must not omit to mention those crafty men who, wholly unconcerned about any honest usefulness of their work, do not scruple to stimulate the baser human desires and, when they are aroused, use them for their own profit.

133. Strict and watchful moral restraint enforced vigorously by governmental authority could have banished these enormous evils and even forestalled them; this restraint, however, has too often been sadly lacking. For since the seeds of a new form of economy were bursting forth just when the principles of rationalism had been implanted and rooted in many minds, there quickly developed a body of economic teaching far removed from the true moral law, and, as a result, completely free rein was given to human passions.

134. Thus it came to pass that many, much more than ever before, were solely concerned with increasing their wealth by any means whatsoever, and that in seeking their own selfish interests before everything else they had no conscience about committing even the gravest of crimes against others. Those first entering upon this broad way that leads to destruction[66] easily found numerous imitators of their iniquity by the example of their manifest success, by their inso-

[66]Cf. Mt 7:13.

lent display of wealth, by their ridiculing the conscience of others, who, as they said, were troubled by silly scruples, or lastly by crushing more conscientious competitors.

135. With the rulers of economic life abandoning the right road, it was easy for the rank and file of workers everywhere to rush headlong also into the same chasm; and all the more so, because very many managements treated their workers like mere tools, with no concern at all for their souls, without indeed even the least thought of spiritual things. Truly the mind shudders at the thought of the grave dangers to which the morals of workers (particularly young workers) and the modesty of girls and women are exposed in modern factories; when we recall how often the present economic scheme, and particularly the shameful housing conditions, create obstacles to the family bond and normal family life; when we remember how many obstacles are put in the way of the proper observance of Sundays and Holy Days; and when we reflect upon the universal weakening of that truly Christian sense through which even rude and unlettered men were wont to value higher things, and upon its substitution by the single preoccupation of getting in any way whatsoever one's daily bread. And thus bodily labor, which Divine Providence decreed to be performed, even after original sin, for the good at once of man's body and soul, is being everywhere changed into an instrument of perversion; for dead matter comes forth from the factory ennobled, while men there are corrupted and degraded.

Remedies

a) *Economic Life Should Be Given Form and Shape in Accordance with Christian Principles*

136. No genuine cure can be furnished for this lamentable ruin of souls, which, so long as it continues, will frustrate all efforts to regenerate society, unless men return openly and sincerely to the teaching of the Gospel, to the precepts of him who alone has the words of everlasting life,[67] words which will never pass away, even if Heaven and earth will pass away.[68] All experts in social problems are seeking eagerly a structure so fashioned in accordance with the norms of reason that it can lead economic life back to sound and right order. But this order, which we ourselves ardently long for and with all our efforts promote, will be wholly defective and incomplete unless all the activities of men harmoniously unite to imitate and attain, insofar as it lies within human strength, the marvelous unity of the divine plan. We mean that perfect order which the Church with great force

[67]Cf. Jn 6:69.
[68]Cf. Mt 24:35.

and power preaches and which right human reason itself demands, that all things be directed to God as the first and supreme end of all created activity, and that all created good under God be considered as mere instruments to be used only insofar as they conduce to the attainment of the supreme end. Nor is it to be thought that gainful occupations are thereby belittled or judged less consonant with human dignity; on the contrary, we are taught to recognize in them with reverence the manifest will of the Divine Creator who placed man upon the earth to work it and use it in a multitude of ways for his needs. Those who are engaged in producing goods, therefore, are not forbidden to increase their fortune in a just and lawful manner; for it is only fair that he who renders service to the community and makes it richer should also, through the increased wealth of the community, be made richer himself according to his position, provided that all these things be sought with due respect for the laws of God and without impairing the rights of others and that they be employed in accordance with faith and right reason. If these principles are observed by everyone, everywhere, and always, not only the production and acquisition of goods but also the use of wealth, which now is seen to be so often contrary to right order, will be brought back soon within the bounds of equity and just distribution. The sordid love of wealth, which is the shame and great sin of our age, will be opposed in actual fact by the gentle yet effective law of Christian moderation which commands man to seek first the Kingdom of God and his justice, with the assurance that, by virtue of God's kindness and unfailing promise, temporal goods also, insofar as he has need of them, shall be given him besides.[69]

b) The Role of Charity

137. But in effecting all this, the law of charity, "which is the bond of perfection,"[70] must always take a leading role. How completely deceived, therefore, are those rash reformers who concern themselves with the enforcement of justice alone—and this, commutative justice—and in their pride reject the assistance of charity! Admittedly, no vicarious charity can substitute for justice which is due as an obligation and is wrongfully denied. Yet even supposing that everyone should finally receive all that is due him, the widest field for charity will always remain open. For justice alone can, if faithfully observed, remove the causes of social conflict but can never bring about union of minds and hearts. Indeed all the institutions for the establishment of peace and the promotion of mutual help among men, however perfect these may seem, have the principal foundation

[69]Cf. Mt 6:33.
[70]Col 3:14.

of their stability in the mutual bond of minds and hearts whereby the members are united with one another. If this bond is lacking, the best of regulations come to naught, as we have learned by too frequent experience. And so, then only will true cooperation be possible for a single common good when the constituent parts of society deeply feel themselves members of one great family and children of the same Heavenly Father; nay, that they are one body in Christ, "but severally members one of another,"[71] so that "if one member suffers anything, all the members suffer with it."[72] For then the rich and others in positions of power will change their former indifference toward their poorer brothers into a solicitous and active love, listen with kindliness to their just demands, and freely forgive their possible mistakes and faults. And the workers, sincerely putting aside every feeling of hatred or envy which the promoters of social conflict so cunningly exploit, will not only accept without rancor the place in human society assigned them by Divine Providence, but rather will hold it in esteem, knowing well that everyone according to his function and duty is toiling usefully and honorably for the common good and is following closely in the footsteps of him who, being in the form of God, willed to be a carpenter among men and be known as the son of a carpenter.

An Arduous Task

138. Therefore, out of this new diffusion throughout the world of the spirit of the Gospel, which is the spirit of Christian moderation and universal charity, we are confident there will come that longed for and full restoration of human society in Christ, and that "Peace of Christ in the Kingdom of Christ," to accomplish which, from the very beginning of our pontificate, we firmly determined and resolved within our heart to devote all our care and all our pastoral solicitude,[73] and toward this same highly important and most necessary end now, you also, venerable brethren who with us rule the Church of God under the mandate of the Holy Ghost,[74] are earnestly toiling with wholly praiseworthy zeal in all parts of the world, even in the regions of the holy missions to the infidels. Let well-merited acclamations of praise be bestowed upon you and at the same time upon all those, both clergy and laity, who we rejoice to see, are daily participating and valiantly helping in this same great work, our beloved sons engaged in Catholic Action, who with a singular zeal are undertaking with us the solution of the social problems insofar as by virtue of her divine

---

[71]Rom 12:5.
[72]1 Cor 12:26.
[73]Encyclical, *Ubi Arcano*, Dec. 23, 1922.
[74]Cf. Acts 20:28.

institution this is proper to and devolves upon the Church. All these we urge in the Lord, again and again, to spare no labors and let no difficulties conquer them, but rather to become day by day more courageous and more valiant.[75] Arduous indeed is the task which we propose to them, for we know well that on both sides, both among the upper and the lower classes of society, there are many obstacles and barriers to be overcome. Let them not, however, lose heart; to face bitter combats is a mark of Christians, and to endure grave labors to the end is a mark of them who, as good soldiers of Christ,[76] follow him closely.

139. Relying therefore solely on the all-powerful aid of him "who wishes all men to be saved,"[77] let us strive with all our strength to help those unhappy souls who have turned from God and, drawing them away from the temporal cares in which they are too deeply immersed, let us teach them to aspire with confidence to the things that are eternal. Sometimes this will be achieved much more easily than seems possible at first sight to expect. For if wonderful spiritual forces lie hidden, like sparks beneath ashes, within the secret recesses of even the most abandoned man—certain proof that his soul is naturally Christian—how much the more in the hearts of those many upon many who have been led into error rather through ignorance or environment.

140. Moreover, the ranks of the workers themselves are already giving happy and promising signs of a social reconstruction. To our soul's great joy, we see in these ranks also the massed companies of young workers, who are receiving the counsel of Divine Grace with willing ears and striving with marvelous zeal to gain their comrades for Christ. No less praise must be accorded to the leaders of workers' organizations who, disregarding their own personal advantage and concerned solely about the good of their fellow members, are striving prudently to harmonize the just demands of their members with the prosperity of their whole occupation and also to promote these demands, and who do not let themselves be deterred from so noble a service by any obstacle or suspicion. Also, as anyone may see, many young men, who by reason of their talent or wealth will soon occupy high places among the leaders of society, are studying social problems with deeper interest, and they arouse the joyful hope that they will dedicate themselves wholly to the restoration of society.

---

[75]Cf. Dt 31:7.
[76]Cf. 2 Tm 2:3.
[77]1 Tm 2:4.

The Way to Proceed

141. The present state of affairs, venerable brethren, clearly indicates the way in which we ought to proceed. For we are now confronted, as more than once before in the history of the Church, with a world that in large part has almost fallen back into paganism. That these whole classes of men may be brought back to Christ whom they have denied, we must recruit and train from among them, themselves, auxiliary soldiers of the Church who know them well and their minds and wishes, and can reach their hearts with a tender brotherly love. The first and immediate apostle to the workers ought to be workers; the apostles to those who follow industry and trade ought to be from among them themselves.

142. It is chiefly your duty, venerable brethren, and of your clergy, to search diligently for these lay apostles both of workers and of employers, to select them with prudence, and to train and instruct them properly. A difficult task, certainly, is thus imposed on priests, and to meet it, all who are growing up as the hope of the Church, must be duly prepared by an intensive study of the social question. Especially is it necessary that those whom you intend to assign in particular to this work should demonstrate that they are men possessed of the keenest sense of justice, who will resist with true manly courage the dishonest demands or the unjust acts of anyone, who will excel in the prudence and judgment which avoids every extreme, and, above all, who will be deeply permeated by the charity of Christ, which alone has the power to subdue firmly but gently the hearts and wills of men to the laws of justice and equity. Upon this road so often tried by happy experience, there is no reason why we should hesitate to go forward with all speed.

143. These our beloved sons who are chosen for so great a work, we earnestly exhort in the Lord to give themselves wholly to the training of the men committed to their care, and in the discharge of this eminently priestly and apostolic duty to make proper use of the resources of Christian education by teaching youth, forming Christian organizations, and founding study groups guided by principles in harmony with the Faith. But above all, let them hold in high esteem and assiduously employ for the good of their disciples that most valuable means of both personal and social restoration which, as we taught in our encyclical, *Mens Nostra*,[78] is to be found in the Spiritual Exercises. In that letter we expressly mentioned and warmly recommended not only the Spiritual Exercises for all the laity, but also the highly beneficial workers' retreats. For in that school of the spirit, not only are the best of Christians developed but true apostles also

[78]Encyclical, *Mens Nostra*, Dec. 20, 1929.

are trained for every condition of life and are enkindled with the fire of the heart of Christ. From this school they will go forth as did the apostles from the upper room of Jerusalem, strong in faith, endowed with an invincible steadfastness in persecution, burning with zeal, interested solely in spreading everywhere the Kingdom of Christ.

144. Certainly there is the greatest need now of such valiant soldiers of Christ who will work with all their strength to keep the human family safe from the dire ruin into which it would be plunged were the teachings of the Gospel to be flouted, and that order of things permitted to prevail which tramples underfoot no less the laws of nature than those of God. The Church of Christ, built upon an unshakable rock, has nothing to fear for herself, as she knows for a certainty that the gates of hell shall never prevail against her.[79] Rather, she knows full well, through the experience of many centuries, that she is wont to come forth from the most violent storms stronger than ever and adorned with new triumphs. Yet her maternal heart cannot but be moved by the countless evils with which so many thousands would be afflicted during storms of this kind, and above all by the consequent enormous injury to spiritual life which would work eternal ruin to so many souls redeemed by the Blood of Jesus Christ.

145. To ward off such great evils from human society nothing, therefore, is to be left untried; to this end may all our labors turn, to this all our energies, to this our fervent and unremitting prayers to God! For with the assistance of Divine Grace the fate of the human family rests in our hands.

146. Venerable brethren and beloved sons, let us not permit the children of this world to appear wiser in their generation than we who by the Divine Goodness are the children of the light.[80] We find them, indeed, selecting and training with the greatest shrewdness alert and resolute devotees who spread their errors ever wider day by day through all classes of men and in every part of the world. And whenever they undertake to attack the Church of Christ more violently, we see them put aside their internal quarrels, assembling in full harmony in a single battle line with a completely united effort, and work to achieve their common purpose.

Close Union and Cooperation Are Urged

147. Surely there is not one that does not know how many and how great are the works that the tireless zeal of Catholics is striving everywhere to carry out, both for social and economic welfare as well as in the fields of education and religion. But this admirable and un-

---

[79]Cf. Mt 16:18.
[80]Cf. Lk 16:8.

remitting activity not infrequently shows less effectiveness because of the dispersion of its energies in too many different directions. Therefore, let all men of good will stand united, all who under the shepherds of the Church wish to fight this good and peaceful battle of Christ; and under the leadership and teaching guidance of the Church let all strive according to the talent, powers, and position of each to contribute something to the Christian reconstruction of human society which Leo XIII inaugurated through his immortal encyclical, *On the Condition of Workers*, seeking not themselves and their own interests, but those of Jesus Christ,[81] not trying to press at all costs their own counsels, but ready to sacrifice them, however excellent, if the greater common good should seem to require it, so that in all and above all Christ may reign, Christ may command, to whom be "honor and glory and dominion forever and ever."[82]

148. That this may happily come to pass, to all of you, venerable brethren and beloved children, who are members of the vast Catholic family entrusted to us, but with the especial affection of our heart to workers and to all others engaged in manual occupations, committed to us more urgently by Divine Providence, and to Christian employers and managements, with paternal love we impart the Apostolic Benediction.

149. Given at Rome, at Saint Peter's, the fifteenth day of May, in the year 1931, the tenth year of our pontificate.

Pope Pius XI

[81]Cf. Phil 2:21.
[82]Rv 5:13.

Introduction to Christmas Messages

Although he is a major figure in twentieth century Catholicism, Pope Pius XII never issued formal, comprehensive social encyclicals like many of his predecessors and successors. Nevertheless, Pius made a significant contribution to the growth of Catholic social doctrine through a series of Christmas addresses from 1939 to 1957. Those for 1940, 1941 and 1942 are the most significant. They form a bridge between the prewar documents *Rerum Novarum* and *Quadragesimo Anno* and later statements from the II Vatican Council, the 1971 Synod of Bishops, and Popes John XXIII and Paul VI. Both John and Paul publicly acknowledged indebtedness to these Christmas messages, and recent interpreters of Catholic social teaching have underlined their importance as well.

Several points deserve emphasis regarding the outlook expressed in these addresses. Pius XII introduced some significant shifts in orientation. His concern is no longer only the faith and dignity of European workers. The grim realities of a world war beyond any previous experience have jarred everyone, including the Pope and Catholic leadership in general, into a broader vision. Unlike many of Europe's philosophers, the Pope does not convey a sense of dread and despair about what humanity might become after the war. His message is fundamentally one of hope, hope for a major reconstruction of the social order, not only in Europe but throughout the world.

We must fully appreciate the significance of this papal call for a new social order. The traditional social barriers, the aristocratic privileges that the Fribourg Union and the earlier social encyclicals tried in some measure to preserve, were cast aside in the Christmas addresses. Pius XII's mind-set is profoundly different from that of Leo XIII. It is subtly revolutionary as regards official Catholicism's attitudes toward society. Only a worldwide rethinking and reconstitution of the economic order can secure the human dignity to which all people have a claim, a dignity whose ultimate source is God.

Henceforth, Catholic teaching on economic issues will be animated by a concern for human dignity pure and simple, not by a fear of social upheaval or a fear that the working classes will drift away from the Church. This sense of human dignity as a touchstone for all teaching on economics will be picked up by subsequent popes.

Several other economic themes also draw our attention in the Christmas messages. First, the Pope places squarely on the shoulders of the economically powerful states the responsibility to work for a new economic order free of the disequilibrium that marked prewar conditions. He clearly spells this out in the 1941 address: "A new economic order was to be gradually evolved which gives all nations the means to secure for their citizens an appropriate standard of life." While Pius XII repeats earlier papal condemnations of Marxist and socialist economic programs, he recognizes that it is not enough to condemn. The problems that gave rise to these unacceptable economic models are real. Christian leaders must use the political power at their disposal to guarantee participation and dignity for all men and women. His words of prophetic challenge are not directed primarily at the Church's opponents. They are meant for the Catholic faithful, especially those with some influence on economic decision-making in the capitalist nations.

Second, we detect in these addresses a much greater awareness of the importance of economics for human self-definition. In no way does the Pope endorse economics as the principal shaper of personhood. Granting economics primacy in human self-understanding is the fundamental problem the Pope sees in Marxism and most forms of socialism. However, Pius XII suggests that one cannot comprehend fully the religious dimensions of human existence without appreciating how profoundly economics affects life for good or ill. The economic and the religious realms are deeply intertwined. A piety that totally ignores economic injustice is a false piety. A religious outlook that fails to recognize the deep connections between egoism and its sinful impact on society does not stand in full accord with the Christian Gospel.

While the Pope never directly connects such egoism with capitalism, the implications are present: "This egoism has to be replaced by a genuine Christian solidarity of a legal and economic character . . . (1940)." The Christmas messages continue the papal tradition of questioning prevailing capitalist practices while condemning Marxist social analysis outright.

Third, the Pope, more clearly than his predecessors, speaks of definite links between war and economic injustice. While it would be wrong to say that Pius XII sees war as exclusively rooted in economics, the ties in his mind are strong and pervasive. No analysis of war, including the great war then raging in Europe, can be complete without understanding its economic causes. In the same way, any genuine proposals for peace must include plans for economic reconstruction resulting in greater justice for all. Real peace without economic justice is impossible; on this point the Pope is unequivocal.

Finally, although Pius XII does not engage in the detailed discussion of subsidiarity found in *Quadragesimo Anno,* his commitment to the principle on several levels can be seen throughout the three addresses. Smaller economic units within a society must be given adequate room to function, richer nations must not excessively impose on poorer ones, and the individual person must have the freedom to engage in economic activity without undue interference from the state.

This last point, which calls to mind the economics-religion relationship just mentioned, represents a new appreciation of economics in papal statements. "Economics," says the Pope, "represents a universal and most exalted center of activity . . . (1942)." Pius XII here sows the seeds for a theology of co-creational responsibility, exercised especially in creative human labor, that will receive fuller expression in Pope John Paul II's *Laborem Exercens* and in the Canadian bishops' statement on economics. It is also a theme that has acquired increasing prominence in the reflections of the American bishops on economic matters. This theme in turn lays the foundation for an allied assertion—namely, that labor takes priority over capital—which John Paul has strongly emphasized.

Christmas Message

POPE PIUS XII

December 1940

Selections*

* * *

It is now one year since we made some fundamental declarations on the basic conditions of a peace built on justice, equity and honor, which could, therefore, be lasting. Although their realization has been put off to a later date by events, these principles have lost nothing of their truth and reality. We have to face today a fact of fundamental importance. Out of the passionate strife of the parties concerning peace and war aims, a common opinion emerges. It is that all Europe, as well as the separate nations, are in such a process of transformation that the beginning of a new period is clearly recognizable. Europe and the political order of its nations—it is emphasized—will cease to be what they have been heretofore. There will be something newer, something better, something more developed, organically sounder, freer, and stronger than in the past. All the weaknesses revealed by the light of recent events are to be avoided. It is true that the different opinions and aims diverge; yet they agree in their wish to establish a new order and in their conviction that a return to the old order is neither possible nor desirable.

The desire for renewal is not only dictated by the *rerum novarum cupido* but by the realization of deficiencies prevailing today, and by the firm determination to establish a new and just national and international order giving security. No one can be surprised that this desire should be especially strong in those strata of society which live by the work of their hands, and which are doomed to experience the hardships of national or international disturbances more than anybody else. Still less could it be ignored by the Church, which, as the common mother of all, is bound to hear and to understand the outcries of suffering mankind.

In such a strife of opinions the Church cannot be invoked to listen to one side more than to another. Within the divine laws given not only to the individual, but also the nations, there is a wide sphere in which the most varied forms of political life have ample freedom of expression. The effects of one or other political system, however,

*Editor's Note: Deleted material in this document is indicated in the text by the symbol * * *.

depend on circumstances and reasons which, considered in themselves, are beyond the scope of the Church's activity. As protector and prophet of faith and morality the Church has only one interest and one desire, namely, to fulfill her educational mission and to carry religious teaching to all peoples without exception so that every nation may be enabled to avail itself of the principles laid down by Christianity in order to establish a dignified and spiritually ennobled life which is the source of real happiness. More than once the Church has had to preach to deaf ears. Times of adversity are more frequent than times of happiness; pain is sometimes better than cheap success. Let us hope that mankind and each single nation may grow more mature out of its present tribulations, with eyes able to distinguish between the genuine and the fallacious, with an ear alert for the voice of reason, be it pleasant or unpleasant, with a mind which, open to reality, is really determined to fulfill the demands of life and justice, not only when its own demands are met, but also when the equitable demands of others are heard.

Only in such a state of mind does the tempting slogan of a new order acquire a beautiful, dignified and lasting conception based on moral principles. Only then can the danger be avoided that this slogan should come to be interpreted as a liberty-destroying mechanism enforced by violence, without sincerity, consent, joy, dignity or honor, oppressing souls. Only then can mankind be given a new hope, an aim which corresponds to the noble effort.

The necessary premises for such a new order are as follows:

(1) Victory over the hatred which divides the nations today and the disappearance of systems and actions which breed this hatred. As a matter of fact, in some countries an unbridled propaganda is to be seen: it does not recoil from methodical distortion of the truth in order to show the enemy nations in a falsified and vilifying light. He, however, who really wants the good of the people and wants to contribute to the future cooperation of nations and to preserve this cooperation from incalculable damage, will consider it as his sacred duty to uphold the natural ideals of truth, justice and charity.

(2) Victory over distrust which exerts a paralyzing pressure on international law and makes all honest understanding impossible. Therefore, return to the principle of mutual trust. Return to the loyalty for treaties without which the secure cooperation of nations and especially, the living side by side of strong and weak nations, are inconceivable. The foundation of justice is loyalty, reliability and truth of the pledged word, and of the understanding which has been reached.

(3) Victory over the dismal principle that utility is the foundation and aim of law, and that might can create right. This principle is bound to upset all international relations and is unacceptable to all

weaker nations. Therefore, return to honest, serious and moral international relations. This conception does not exclude the desire for the honorable improvement of conditions or the right to defend oneself if peaceful life has been attacked, or to repair the damage sustained thereby.

(4) Victory over those potential conflicts arising out of the disequilibrium of world economy. Therefore, a new economic order has to be gradually evolved which gives all nations the means to secure for their citizens an appropriate standard of life.

(5) Victory over the kind of egoism which, relying on its own power, aims at impairing the honor and liberty of individuals. This egoism has to be replaced by a genuine Christian solidarity of a legal and economic character, and by a brotherly cooperation of the nations, the sovereignty of which has been duly secured.

Revered brothers and beloved sons, we have a great longing for the moment when arms will be laid down and peace treaties signed, a deep desire that mankind should then have enough wisdom to prepare the foundations of a lasting and equitable order. We pray to God that it may be soon and we admonish you to unite your prayers with ours that the Almighty may preserve the world from the fate which would befall it if the mistakes and misunderstandings of the past were renewed in another form and the future of the nations were ruled not by genuine freedom, but by new and increased unhappiness. We pray that those on whom the realization of the future order will depend may realize that the real victor is only he who conquers himself. With infinite faith, we put our desires and our hopes into the tiny hands of the newborn Savior; we pray with you, with all priests and laymen of the Holy Church, that mankind may be freed from discord. With this prayer on our lips and with this thought in our hearts, we give to you and to all our sons throughout the world, and especially the war victims of all nations, our apostolic blessing.

Christmas Message

POPE PIUS XII

December 1941

Selections*

* * *

Cooperation for Peace

Now the destruction brought about by the present war is on so vast a scale that it is imperative that there be not added to it also the further ruin of a frustrated and deluded peace. In order to avoid so great a calamity it is fitting that in the formulation of that peace there should be assured the cooperation, with sincerity of will and energy, with the purpose of a generous participation not only of this or that party, not only of this or that people, but of all people, yea, rather of all humanity. It is a universal undertaking for the common good which requires the collaboration of all Christendom in the religious and moral aspects of the new edifice that is to be constructed.

We are, therefore, making use of our right or better, we are fulfilling our duty as today, on this eve of the holy feast of Christmas, the divine dawn of hope and of peace for the world, with all the authority of our apostolic ministry, and with the fervent impulse of our heart, we direct the attention and the consideration of the entire world to the dangers which lie in wait to threaten a peace which is to be the well-prepared basis for a truly new order and which is to fulfill the expectation and desires of all peoples for a more tranquil future.

New Order of Moral Law

Such a new order, which all peoples desire to see brought into being after the trials and the ruins of this war, must be founded on that immovable and unshakable rock, the moral law which he has engraved with indelible characters in the hearts of men: that moral law whose observance must be inculcated and fostered by the public

*Editor's Note: Deleted material in this document is indicated in the text by the symbol * * *.

opinion of all nations and of all states with such a unanimity of voice and energy that no one may dare to call into doubt or weaken its binding force.

Like a shining beacon, this moral law must direct by the light of its principles the course of action of men and of states, and they must all follow its admonishing, salutary and profitable precepts if they do not wish to abandon to the tempest and to ultimate shipwreck every labor and every effort for the establishment of a new order.

Consequently, recapitulating and integrating what we have expounded on other occasions, we insist once again on certain fundamental conditions essential for an international order which will guarantee for all peoples a just and lasting peace and which will be a bountiful source of well-being and prosperity.

Within the limits of a new order founded on moral principles there is no room for the violation of the freedom, integrity and security of other states, no matter what may be their territorial extension of their capacity for defense.

Duty of the Powerful States

It is inevitable that the powerful states should, by reason of their greater potentialities and their power, play leading roles in the formation of economic groups comprising not only themselves but also smaller and weaker states as well, it is, nevertheless, indispensable that in the interests of the common good they, as all others, respect the rights of those smaller states to political freedom, to economic development and to the adequate protection, in the case of conflicts between nations, of that neutrality which is theirs according to the natural, as well as international, law.

In this way, and in this way only, shall they be able to obtain a fitting share of the common good and assure the material and spiritual welfare of the peoples concerned.

Within the limits of a new order founded on moral principles, there is no place for open or occult oppression of the cultural and linguistic characteristics of national minorities, for the hindrance or restriction of their economic resources, for the limitation or abolition of their natural fertility. The more conscientiously the government of the state respects the rights of minorities, the more confidently and the more effectively can it demand from its subjects a loyal fulfillment of those civil obligations which are common to all citizens.

Resources Must Be Shared

Within the limits of a new order founded on moral principles, there is no place for that cold and calculating egoism which tends to hoard the economic resources and materials destined for the use of all to such an extent that the nations less favored by nature are not permitted access to them.

In this regard, it is for us a source of great consolation to see admitted the necessity of a participation of all in the natural riches of the earth, even on the part of those nations which in the fulfillment of this principle belong to the category of *givers* and not to that of *receivers*.

It is, however, a conformity which the principles of equity that the solution of a question so vital to the world economy should be arrived at methodically and in easy stages, with the necessary guarantees, drawing useful lessons from the omissions and mistakes of the past.

If, in the future peace, this point were not to be courageously dealt with, there would remain in the relations between peoples a deep and far-reaching root, blossoming forth into bitter dissensions and burning jealousies, and which would lead eventually to new conflicts. It must, however, be noted how closely the satisfactory solution to this problem is connected with another fundamental point which we shall treat next.

Christmas Message

POPE PIUS XII

December 1942

Selections*

* * *

International Relations and Order within the Nations

In our last Christmas message, we expounded the principles which Christian thought suggest, for the establishment of an international order of friendly relations and collaboration such as to conform to the demands of God's Law. Today we shall, with the consent, we feel, and the interested attention of all upright men, pause to consider very carefully and with equal impartiality, the fundamental laws of the internal order of the states and peoples.

International relations and internal order are intimately related. International equilibrium and harmony depend on the internal equilibrium and development of the individual states in the material, social and intellectual spheres. A firm and steady peace policy towards other nations is, in fact, impossible without a spirit of peace within the nation which inspires trust. It is only, then, by striving for an integral peace, a peace in both fields, that people will be freed from the cruel nightmare of war, and the material and psychological causes of further discord and disorder will be diminished and gradually eliminated. Every society, worthy of the name, has originated in a desire for peace, and hence aims at attaining peace, that "tranquil living together in order" in which St. Thomas finds the essence of peace. Two primary elements, then, regulate social life, a living together in order, and a living together in tranquillity.

Living Together in Order

Order, which is fundamental in an association of men (of beings, that is, who strive to attain an end appropriate to their nature), is

*Editor's Note: Deleted material in this document is indicated in the text by the symbol * * *.

not merely external linking up of parts which are numerically distinct. It is rather, and must be, a tendency and an ever more perfect approach to an internal union; and this does not exclude differences founded in fact and sanctioned by the will of God or by supernatural standard.

A clear understanding of the genuine fundamentals of all social life has a capital importance today as never before, when mankind, impregnated by the poison of error and social aberrations, tormented by the fever of discordant desires, doctrines, and aims, is excitedly tossing about in the disorder which it has itself created, and is experiencing the destructive force of false ideas, that disregard the law of God or are opposed to it. And since disorder can only be overcome by an order which is not merely superimposed and fictitious (just as darkness with its fearful and depressing effects can only be driven away by light and not by will-o'-the-wisps); so security, reorganizations, progressive improvement cannot be expected and cannot be brought about unless by a return of large and influential sections to correct notions about society.

It is a return which calls for the grace of God in large measure, and for a resolute will, ready and prepared for sacrifice on the part of good farseeing men. From these influential circles who are more capable of penetrating and appreciating the beauty of just social norms, there will pass on and infiltrate into the masses the clear knowledge of the true, divine, spiritual origin of social life. Thus the way will be cleared for the reawakening, the growth and the fixing of those moral principles without which even the proudest achievements create but a babel in which the citizens, though they live inside the same walls, speak different and incoherent languages.

God, the First Cause and Ultimate Foundation of Individual and Social Life

From individual and social life we should rise to God, the First Cause and Ultimate Foundation, as he is the Creator of the first conjugal society, from which we have the society which is the family, and the society, of peoples and of nations. As an image, albeit imperfect, of its exemplar, the one and triune God, who through the mystery of the Incarnation, redeemed and raised human nature, life in society, in its ideals and in its end, possesses by the light of reason and of revelation a moral authority and an absoluteness which transcend every temporal change.

It has a power of attraction that, far from being weakened or lessened by delusions, errors, failures, draws irresistibly the noblest and most faithful souls to the Lord, to take up with renewed energy, with added knowledge, with new studies, methods and means, the enterprises which in other times and circumstances were tried in vain.

Development and Perfection of the Human Person

The origin and the primary scope of social life is the conservation, development and perfection of the human person, helping him to realize accurately the demands and values of religion and culture set by the Creater for every man and for all mankind, both as a whole and in its natural ramifications.

A social teaching or a social reconstruction program which denies or prescinds from this internal essential relation to God of everything that regards men, is on a false course; and while it builds up with one hand, it prepares with the other the materials which sooner or later will undermine and destroy the whole fabric. And when it disregards the respect due to the human person and to the life which is proper to that person, and gives no thought to it in its organization, in legislative and executive activity, then instead of serving society, it harms it; instead of encouraging and stimulating social thought, instead of realizing its hopes and expectations, it strips it of all real value and reduces it to a utilitarian formula which is openly rejected by constantly increasing groups.

If social life implies intrinsic unity, it does not, at the same time, exclude differences which are founded in fact and nature. When we hold fast to God, the Supreme Controller of all that relates to man, then the similarities no less than the differences of men find their allotted place in the fixed order of being, of values, and hence also of morality. When, however, this foundation is removed, there is a dangerous lack of cohesion in the various spheres of culture; the frontier of true value becomes uncertain and shifting, even to the point where mere external factors, and often blind instincts, come to determine, according to the prevalent fashion of the day, who is to have control of this or that direction.

After the fateful economy of the past decades, during which the lives of all citizens were subordinated to the stimulus of gain, there now succeeds another and no less fateful policy which, while it considers everybody with reference to the state, excludes all thought of ethics or religion. This is a fatal travesty, a fatal error. It is calculated to bring about far-reaching consequences for social life, which is never nearer to losing its noblest prerogatives than when it thinks it can deny or forget with impunity the external source of its own dignity: God.

Reason, enlightened by faith, assigns to individuals and to particular societies in the social organization a definite and exalted place. It knows, to mention only the most important, that the whole political and economic activity of the state is directed to the permanent realization of the common good.

In a conception of society which is pervaded and sanctioned by religious thought, the influence of economics and of every other sphere of cultural activity represents a universal and most exalted center of activity, very rich in its variety and coherent in its harmony, in which men's intellectual equality and diversity of occupation come into their own and secure adequate expression. When this is not so, work is depreciated and the worker is belittled.

* * *

The World of Labor

In one field of social life, where for a whole century there was agitation and bitter conflict, there is today a calm, at least on the surface. We speak of the vast and evergrowing world of labor, of the immense army of workers, of breadwinners and dependents. If we consider the present with its wartime exigencies, as an admitted fact, then this calm may be called a necessary and reasonable demand; but if we look at the present situation in the light of justice, and with reference to a legitimately regulated labor movement, then the tranquillity will remain only apparent, until the scope of such a movement be attained.

Always moved by religious motives, the Church has condemned the various forms of Marxist Socialism; and she condemns them today, because it is her permanent right and duty to safeguard men from currents of thought and influences that jeopardize their external salvation. But the Church cannot ignore or overlook the fact that the worker, in his efforts to better his lot, is opposed by a machinery which is not only not in accordance with nature, but is a variance with God's plan and with the purpose he had in creating the goods of earth.

In spite of the fact that the ways they followed were and are false and to be condemned, what man, and especially what priest or Christian, could remain deaf to the cries that rise from the depths and call for justice and a spirit of brotherly collaboration in a world ruled by a just God? Such silence would be culpable and unjustifiable before God, and contrary to the inspired teaching of the apostle, who, while he inculcates the need of resolution in the fight against error, also knows that we must be full of sympathy for those who err, and openminded in our understanding of their aspirations, hopes and motives.

When he blessed our first parents, God said: "Increase and multiply and fill the earth and subdue it." And to the first father of a family, he said later: "In the sweat of thy face shalt thou eat bread." The dignity of the human person, then, requires normally as a natural foundation of life the right to the use of the goods of the earth. To this right corresponds the fundamental obligation to grant private ownership of property, if possible, to all. Positive legislation regulating private ownership may change and more or less restrict its use. But if legislation is to play its part in the pacification of the community, it must prevent the worker, who is or will be a father of a family, from being condemned to an economic dependence and slavery which is irreconcilable with his rights as a person. Whether this slavery arises from the exploitation of private capital or from the power of the state, the result is the same. Indeed, under the pressure of a state which dominates all and controls the whole field of public and private life, even going into the realm of ideas and beliefs and of conscience, this lack of liberty can have the more serious consequences, as experience shows and proves.

Five Fundamental Points for the Order and Pacification of Human Society

* * *

The essential aim of this necessary and holy crusade is that the Star of Peace, the Star of Bethlehem, may shine out again over the whole mankind in all its brilliant splendor and reassuring consolation as a pledge and augury of a future better, more fruitful and happier. It is true that the road from night to full day will be long; but of decisive importance are the first steps on the path, the first five milestones of which bear chiselled on them the following maxims:

1. Dignity and Rights of the Human Person

He who would have the star of peace shine out and stand over society should cooperate, for his part, in giving back to the human person the dignity given to it by God from the very beginning; should oppose the excessive herding of men, as if they were a mass without a soul; their economic, social, political, intellectual and moral inconsistency; their dearth of solid principles and strong convictions, their surfeit of instinctive sensible excitement and their fickleness.

He should favor, by every lawful means, in every sphere of life, social institutions in which a full personal responsibility is assured and guaranteed both in the early and the eternal order of things. He should uphold respect for and the practical realization of the following fundamental personal rights; the right to maintain and develop one's corporal, intellectual and moral life and especially the right to religious formation and education; the right to worship God in private and public and to carry on religious works of charity; the right to marry and to achieve the aim of married life; the right to conjugal and domestic society; the right to work, as the indispensable means towards the maintenance of family life; the right to free choice of state of life, and hence, too, of the priesthood or religious life; the right to the use of material goods; in keeping with his duties and social limitations.

2. *Defense of Social Unity and Especially of the Family in Principle*

He who would have the star of peace shine out and stand over society should reject every form of materialism which sees in the people only a herd of individuals who, divided and without any internal cohesion, are considered as a mass to be lorded over and treated arbitrarily; he should strive to understand society as an intrinsic unity, which has grown up and matured under the guidance of providence, a unity which within the bounds assigned to it and according to its own peculiar gifts—tends, with the collaboration of the various classes and professions, towards the eternal and every new aim of culture and religion.

He should defend the indissolubility of matrimony; he should give to the family—that unique cell of the people—space, light and air so that it may attend to its mission of perpetuating new life, and of educating children in a spirit corresponding to its own true religious convictions, and that it may preserve, fortify and reconstitute, according to its powers, its proper economic, spiritual, moral and juridic unity. He should take care that the material and spiritual advantages of the family be shared by the domestic servants; he should strive to secure for every family a dwelling where a materially and morally healthy family life may be seen in all its vigor and worth; he should take care that the place of work be not so separated from the home as to make the head of the family and educator of the children a virtual stranger to his own household; he should take care above all that the bond of trust and mutual help should be reestablished between the family and the public school, that bond which in other times gave such happy results, but which now has been replaced by mistrust where the school, influenced and controlled by the spirit of materialism, corrupts and destroys what the parents have instilled into the minds of the children.

3. *Dignity and Prerogative of Labor*

He who have the star of peace shine out and stand over society should give to work the place assigned to it by God from the beginning. As an indispensable means towards gaining over the world that mastery which God wishes, for his glory, all work has an inherent dignity and at the same time a close connection with the perfection of the person; this is the noble dignity and privilege of work which is not in any way cheapened by the fatigue and the burden, which have to be borne as the effect of original sin, in obedience and submission to the will of God.

Those who are familiar with the great encyclicals of our predecessors and our own previous messages know well that the Church does not hesitate to draw the practical conclusions which are derived from the moral nobility of work, and to give them all the support of her authority. These exigencies include, besides a just wage which covers the needs of the worker and his family, the conservation and perfection of a social order which will make possible an assured, even if modest, private property for all classes of society, which will promote higher education for the children of the working class who are especially endowed with intelligence and good will, will promote the care and the practice of the social spirit in one's immediate neighborhood, in the district, the province, the people and the nation, a spirit which, by smoothing over friction arising from privileges or class interests, removes from the workers the sense of isolation through the assuring experience of a genuinely human, and fraternally Christian, solidarity.

The progress and the extent of urgent social reforms depend on the economic possibilities of single nations. It is only through an intelligent and generous sharing of forces between the strong and the weak that it will be possible to effect a universal pacification in such wise as not to leave behind centers of conflagration and infection from which new disasters may come. There are evident signs which go to show that, in the ferment of all the prejudices and feelings of hate, those inevitable but lamentable offspring of the war psychosis, there is still aflame in the people the consciousness of their intimate mutual dependence for good or for evil, nay, that this consciousness is more alive and active. It is not true that deep thinkers see ever more clearly in the renunciation of egoism and national isolation, the way to general salvation, ready as they are to demand of their peoples a heavy participation in the sacrifices necessary for social well-being in other peoples?

May this Christmas message of ours, addressed to all those who are animated by a good and generous heart, encourage and increase the legions of these social crusades in every nation. And may God deign to give to their peaceful cause the victory of which their noble enterprise is worthy.

4. The Rehabilitation of Juridic Order

He who would have the star of peace shine out and stand over social life should collaborate towards a complete rehabilitation of the juridical order. The juridic sense of today is often altered and overturned by the profession and the practice of positivism and a utilitarianism which are subjected and bound to the service of determined groups, classes and movements, whose programs direct and determine the course of legislation and the practices of the courts. The cure of this situation becomes feasible when we awaken again the consciousness of a juridical order resting on the supreme dominion of God, and safeguarded from all human whims; a consciousness of an order which stretches forth its arm, in protection or punishment, over the unforgettable rights of man and protects them against the attacks of every human power.

From the juridic order, as willed by God, flows man's inalienable right to juridical security, and by this very fact to a definite sphere of rights, immune from all arbitrary attack. The relations of man to man, of the individual to society, to authority, to civil duties; the relations of society and of authority to the individual, should be placed on a firm juridic footing and be guarded, when the need arises, by the authority of the courts. This supposes:

(a) A tribunal and a judge who take their directions from a clearly formulated and defined right.

(b) Clear juridical norms which may not be overturned by unwarranted appeals to a supposed popular sentiment or by merely utilitarian considerations.

(c) The recognition of the principle that even the state and the functionaries and organizations depend on it are obliged to repair and to withdraw measures which are harmful to the liberty, property, honor, progress of health of the individuals.

5. *The Conception of the State According to the Christian Spirit*

He who would have the star of peace shine out and stand over human society should cooperate towards the setting up of a state conception and practice founded on reasonable discipline, exalted kindliness and a responsible Christian spirit. He should help to restore the state and its power to the service of human society, to the full recognition of the respect due to the human person and his efforts to attain his eternal destiny. He should apply and devote himself to dispelling the errors which aim at causing the state and its authority to deviate from the path of morality, at severing them from the eminently ethical bond which links them to individual and social life, and at making them deny or in practice ignore their essential dependence on the will of the Creator. He should work for the recognition and diffusion of the truth which teaches, even in matters of this world, that the deepest meaning, the ultimate moral basis and the universal validity of "reigning" lies in "serving."

Consideration on the World War and the Renovation of Society

Beloved children, may God grant that while you listen to our voice your heart may be profoundly stirred and moved by the deeply felt seriousness, the loving solicitude, the unremitting insistence, with which we drive home these thoughts, which are meant as an appeal to the conscience of the world, and a rallying cry to all those who are ready to ponder and weigh the grandeur of their mission and responsibility by the vastness of this universal disaster.

A great part of mankind, and, let us not shirk from saying it, not a few who call themselves Christians, have to some extent their share in the collective responsibility for the growth of error and for the harm and the lack of moral fiber in the society of today.

What is this world war, with all its attendant circumstances, whether they be remote or proximate causes, its progress and material, legal and moral effects? What is it but the crumbling process, not expected, perhaps, by the thoughtless but seen and depreciated by those whose gaze penetrated into the realities of a social order which—hid its mortal weakness and its unbridled lust for gain and power? That which in peacetime lay coiled up, broke loose at the outbreak of war in a sad succession of acts at variance with the human and Christian sense. International agreements to make war less inhuman by confining it to the combatants to regulate the procedure of occupation and imprisonment of the conquered remained in various places a dead letter. And who can see the end of this progressive demoralization of the people, who can wish to watch helplessly this disastrous progress? Should they not rather, over the ruins of a social order which has given such tragic proof of its ineptitude as a factor for the good of the people, gather together the hearts of all those who are magnanimous and upright, in the solemn vow not to rest until in all peoples and all nations of the earth a vast legion shall be formed of those handfuls of men who, bent on bringing back society to its center of gravity, which is the law of God, aspire to the service of the human person and of his common life ennobled in God.

Mankind owes that vow to the countless dead who lie buried on the field of battle: The sacrifice of their lives in the fulfillment of their duty is a holocaust offered for a new and better social order. Mankind owes that vow to the innumerable sorrowing host of mothers, widows and orphans who have seen the light, the solace and the support of their lives wrenched from them. Mankind owes that vow to those numberless exiles whom the hurricane of war has torn from their native land and scattered in the land of the stranger; who can make their own the lament of the prophet: "Our inheritance is turned to aliens; our house to strangers." Mankind owes that vow to the hundreds of thousands of persons who, without any fault on their part, sometimes only because of their nationality or race, have been consigned to death or to a slow decline. Mankind owes that vow to the many thousands of noncombatants, women, children, sick and aged, from whom aerial warfare—whose horrors we have from the beginning frequently denounced—has without discrimination or through inadequate precautions, taken life, goods, health, home, charitable refuge, or house of prayer. Mankind owes that vow to the flood of tears and bitterness, to the accumulation of sorrow and suffering, emanating from the murderous ruin of the dreadful conflict and crying to Heaven to send down the Holy Spirit to liberate the world from the inundation of violence and terror.

And where could you with greater assurance and trust and with more efficacious faith place this vow for the renewal of society than at the foot of the "Desired of all Nations" who lies before us in the crib with all the charm of his sweet humanity as a babe, but also in the dynamic attraction of his incipient mission as Redeemer? Where could this noble and holy crusade for the cleaning and renewal of society have a more significant consecration or find a more potent inspiration than at Bethlehem, where the new Adam appears in the adorable mystery of the Incarnation? For it is at his fountains of truth and grace that mankind should find the water of life if it is not to perish in the desert of this life; "Of his fullness we all have received." His fullness of grace and truth flows as freely today as it has for twenty centuries on the world.

His light can overcome the darkness, the rays of his love can conquer the icy egoism which holds, so many back from becoming great and conspicuous in their higher life. To you, crusader-volunteers of a distinguished new society, lift up the new call for moral and Christian rebirth, declare war on the darkness which comes from deserting God, on the coldness that comes from strife between brothers. It is a fight for the human race, which is gravely ill and must be healed in the name of conscience ennobled by Christianity.

* * *

Introduction to Mater et Magistra and Pacem in Terris

As far as economic teaching is concerned, the election of Pope John XXIII put the war years behind for the Church. It was time to expand on the vision laid out by Pius XII in the Christmas messages; the new order for which he called must be brought into reality. John XXIII set about this task by calling the II Vatican Council and issuing two social encyclicals, *Mater et Magistra* and *Pacem in Terris*. Neither is confined to a discussion of economic questions, but both have sections which are crucial for the development of Catholic thought in this field. Four issues stand out: (1) private property, (2) the role of government, (3) the international perspective, and (4) pluralism.

In *Mater et Magistra,* John gives an updated interpretation of the classical theme of private property. The encyclical opens with an analysis of the course of Catholic thinking on the issue since *Rerum Novarum*. Catholic thought, the Pope says, has treated the use of property more and more in a socialized context over the course of the past 70 years. John attributes this shift in large part to generally increased interdependence among the peoples of the world. This new "multiplication of social relationships," resulting in "a daily more complex interdependence of citizens," has become a major feature of modern life. The Church must give central place to this emerging reality in any reflections it offers on economic affairs.

The Pope believes that private property remains a pillar of Catholic social thought, but he clothes the concept in somewhat different garb than his predecessors did. He speaks of "private initiative" rather than "private property," and asserts that public authorities have the obligation to ensure an effective output of goods for the benefit of all citizens. *Mater et Magistra* seems to elevate government intervention in the use of property to a moral plane equal to that of private initiative, and this on a continuing—not a last resort—basis. For the foreseeable future, if not permanently, government must play a major role if economic policies are to meet the goal of basic human subsistence on a global scale.

It is important to add that John XXIII rejects rigid government control of private initiative. Such an approach, he feels, will cause deep economic stagnation. Nevertheless, the Pope holds out little hope of reducing economic inequalities throughout the world without a partnership between government and the private sector. On this point *Mater et Magistra* is unbending. *Rerum Novarum* and *Quadragesimo Anno* both placed limits on the use of private property, but left the decision on observing these limits primarily to the judgment of the individual believer. To a great degree, *Mater et Magistra* transfers responsibility for that decision to the state, in a development that has great significance for the Catholic approach to private property. *Pacem in Terris* repeats the claim that social duty is inherent in any legitimate notion of private property and that government has an ongoing, direct role in economic affairs.

Let us turn now from the relationship between government and private property to the relationship between government and nongovernmental groups in society. In *Rerum Novarum* Pope Leo XIII was extremely cautious in positing any significant role for government in the economic sphere, faced as he was with a very doctrinaire form of European socialism. Pius XI took a somewhat more relaxed attitude. He allowed for some governmental action as one means whereby society might come to grips with the social and economic problems plaguing the world of the 1930s. Nevertheless, *Quadragesimo Anno* offers at most a small opening for a direct government role. Reserve with respect to governmental intervention in the work of voluntary associations remains clearly dominant in the first two social encyclicals.

John XXIII introduced a significant reorientation of Catholic thought on the question of state intervention. In his judgment, contemporary economic realities no longer permit reserve. While voluntary groups need to operate as important mediating structures in society, they cannot make the necessary economic reforms on their own. The Pope urged a new partnership between voluntary groups and the government and even argued that on certain occasions government is duty bound to take the initiative if economic justice is to be achieved.

A third feature of John's writings is the internationalization of Catholicism's focus on economic questions. Though, as we have seen earlier, Pius XII introduced this shift in his Christmas addresses, his views never gained the same worldwide hearing as Pope John's. After John, Catholic attention was no longer fixed on the condition of the working classes of Europe and North America. The concern was now global and more closely directed toward the inherent injustice in some existing international economic structures. Catholicism became aware of a reality most clearly articulated in the 1971 synodal document on justice in the world—social structural sin.

The concept of structural sin added a new dimension. For Pope John the ultimate cause of economic exploitation remains human sinfulness, but the embodiment of such sinfulness in societal institutions extends and intensifies its effects beyond the immediate context of the actual human act. It is insufficient for the Church to call for individual conversion regarding economic justice. Catholicism must also challenge economic decision-makers to revamp the basic structures of world finance and trade if the plight of so many in the Third World is to be substantially and permanently relieved.

The papacy of John XXIII brought First World Catholics into dialogue with Third World Catholicism for the first time. The primary impetus and focus for this dialogue was the II Vatican Council. The years immediately following the Council saw less stress on maintaining the dignity of the worker (though that concern was not lost altogether) and more on suggesting ways to transform the economic structures of world society to guarantee basic subsistence for all people. We should emphasize that John XXIII never suggested the total abandonment of the prevailing capitalist system. On this point the Pope, despite his harsh critiques of current economic realities, echoes his predecessors: capitalism must be significantly revamped, not scrapped in favor of socialism. The Pope's pleas for justice, however, definitely go beyond the mere concern for unionization and workers' rights that dominated earlier encyclicals.

Pluralism is the final characteristic of the new era of social teaching ushered in by *Mater et Magistra* and *Pacem in Terris*. Though John rejects socialism as the answer to international economic problems, his rejection is not as all-inclusive and harsh as in earlier official Catholic statements. The Pope does not see economics as so powerful a threat to Catholic faith as previous popes did. He seems far more open to tolerating socialist economic schemes in regions where local conditions seem to warrant them. While he certainly is not ready to move to the more neutral stance on socioeconomic models found in Paul VI, he is willing to recognize that the Church cannot endorse one scheme for all nations. The push for adoption of the so-called organic model developed by the Fribourg Union and canonized by *Rerum Novarum* has ended.

A feature peculiar to *Pacem in Terris* should be highlighted in any discussion of John XXIII's contributions to Catholic teaching on economic issues. (This encyclical's subject is the attainment of peace. It is very interesting that the Pope even includes sections dealing with economics. Without doubt he shared Pius XII's opinion that the roots of war are profoundly economic in nature.) While it does not abandon the traditional notion of economic duties, *Pacem in Terris* emphasizes that each individual possesses economic rights. These rights include the opportunity to work without coercion, to enjoy safe working conditions (the special problems of women are noted in this regard), to participate in the economic process to the full extent of one's abilities, to receive just recompense for work and to own private property.

The rights enumerated in *Pacem in Terris* were all asserted previously, but the Pope's mode of argumentation represents a significant change. This document relies far more on natural law arguments than *Mater et Magistra, Gaudium et Spes* or any subsequent official Catholic declaration. While references to natural law are buttressed with appeals to previous Catholic teaching, the encyclical's principal assertion is that through human reason we can discover a natural order. Once understood, this order can serve as the basis for a renewed spirit of international harmony. At the heart of the natural order lies individual human dignity, which becomes the source of all economic rights for the Pope. This approach represents a fundamental reversal of the old medieval model. The individual person can now legitimately make economic claims against society.

Many have applauded the introduction of rights language into the Catholic discussion of economic justice. This language has been used any number of times in subsequent statements, even though later argumentation tends to be grounded far more in biblical tradition than in natural law. Some commentators, however, remain uneasy with this rights approach. They feel it makes an almost impossible demand on society: that is, achieving equality of result in the economic sphere rather than just equality of access. This demand tends to generate unrealistic expectations which, when unmet, may cause upheaval and the adoption of social schemes that make matters even worse. These same commentators tax the Pope with leaving us an unresolved tension between economic rights and economic duties. How is it possible to integrate rights and duties in economic life when the two concepts derive from different philosophic traditions?

Mater et Magistra

On Christianity and Social Progress

POPE JOHN XXIII

May 15, 1961

Selections*

* * *

Part II
Explanation and Development of the Teachings of *Rerum Novarum*

Private Initiative and State Intervention in Economic Life

51. At the outset it should be affirmed that in economic affairs first place is to be given to the private initiative of individual men who, either working by themselves, or with others in one fashion or another, pursue their common interests.

52. But in this matter, for reasons pointed out by our predecessors, it is necessary that public authorities take active interest, the better to increase output of goods and to further social progress for the benefit of all citizens.

53. This intervention of public authorities that encourages, stimulates, regulates, supplements, and complements, is based on the *principle of subsidiarity*[24] as set forth by Pius XI in his encyclical *Quadragesimo Anno:*

> It is a fundamental principle of social philosophy, fixed and unchangeable, that one should not withdraw from individuals and commit to the community what they can accomplish by their own enterprise and industry. So, too, it is an injustice and at the same time a grave evil and a disturbance of right order, to transfer to the larger and higher collectivity functions which can be performed and provided for by lesser and subordinate bodies. Inasmuch as every social activity should, by its very nature, prove a help to members of the body social, it should never destroy or absorb them.[25]

---

*Editor's Note: Deleted material in this document is indicated in the text by the symbol * * *.

[24] *Acta Apostolicae Sedis*, XXIII (1931), p. 203.

[25] Ibid., p. 203.

54. Indeed, as is easily perceived, recent developments of science and technology provide additional reasons why, to a greater extent than heretofore, it is within the power of public authorities to reduce imbalances, whether these be between various sectors of economic life, or between different regions of the same nation, or even between different peoples of the world as a whole. These same developments make it possible to keep fluctuations in the economy within bounds, and to provide effective measures for avoiding mass unemployment. Consequently, it is requested again and again of public authorities responsible for the common good, that they intervene in a wide variety of economic affairs, and that, in a more extensive and organized way than heretofore, they adapt institutions, tasks, means, and procedures to this end.

55. Nevertheless, it remains true that precautionary activities of public authorities in the economic field, although widespread and penetrating, should be such that they not only avoid restricting the freedom of private citizens, but also increase it, so long as the basic rights of each individual person are preserved inviolate. Included among these is the right and duty of each individual normally to provide the necessities of life for himself and his dependents. This implies that whatever be the economic system, it allow and facilitate for every individual the opportunity to engage in productive activity.

56. Furthermore, the course of events thus far makes it clear that there cannot be a prosperous and well-ordered society unless both private citizens and public authorities work together in economic affairs. Their activity should be characterized by mutual and amicable efforts, so that the roles assigned to each fit in with requirements of the common good, as changing times and customs suggest.

57. Experience, in fact, shows that where private initiative of individuals is lacking, political tyranny prevails. Moreover, much stagnation occurs in various sectors of the economy, and hence all sorts of consumer goods and services, closely connected with needs of the body and more especially of the spirit, are in short supply. Beyond doubt, the attainment of such goods and services provides remarkable opportunity and stimulus for individuals to exercise initiative and industry.

58. Where, on the other hand, appropriate activity of the state is lacking or defective, commonwealths are apt to experience incurable disorders, and there occurs exploitation of the weak by the unscrupulous strong, who flourish, unfortunately, like cockle among the wheat, in all times and places.

Complexity of Social Structure

Direction of the Trend

59. One of the principal characteristics of our time is the multiplication of social relationships, that is, a daily more complex interdependence of citizens, introducing into their lives and activities many and varied forms of association, recognized for the most part in private and even in public law. This tendency seemingly stems from a number of factors operative in the present era, among which are technical and scientific progress, greater productive efficiency, and a higher standard of living among citizens.

60. These developments in social living are at once both a symptom and a cause of the growing intervention of public authorities in matters which, since they pertain to the more intimate aspects of personal life, are of serious moment and not without danger. Such, for example, are the care of health, the instruction and education of youth, the choice of a personal career, the ways and means of rehabilitating or assisting those handicapped mentally or physically. But this trend also indicates and in part follows from that human and natural inclination, scarcely resistible, whereby men are impelled voluntarily to enter into association in order to attain objectives which each one desires, but which exceed the capacity of single individuals. This tendency has given rise, especially in recent years, to organizations and institutes on both national and international levels, which relate to economic and social goals, to cultural and recreational activities, to athletics, to various professions, and to political affairs.

Evaluation

61. Such an advance in social relationships definitely brings numerous services and advantages. It makes possible, in fact, the satisfaction of many personal rights, especially those of economic and social life; these relate, for example, to the minimum necessities of human life, to health services, to the broadening and deepening of elementary education, to a more fitting training in skills, to housing, to labor, to suitable leisure and recreation. In addition, through the ever more perfect organization of modern means for the diffusion of thought—press, cinema, radio, television—individuals are enabled to take part in human events on a worldwide scale.

62. But as these various forms of association are multiplied and daily extended, it also happens that in many areas of activity, rules and laws controlling and determining relationships of citizens are multiplied. As a consequence, opportunity for free action by individuals is restricted within narrower limits. Methods are often used, procedures are adopted, and such an atmosphere develops wherein it becomes difficult for one to make decisions independently of outside influences, to do anything on his own initiative, to carry out in a fitting way his rights and duties, and to fully develop and perfect his personality. Will men perhaps, then become automatons, and cease to be personally responsible, as these social relationships multiply more and more? It is a question which must be answered negatively.

63. Actually, increased complexity of social life by no means results from a blind drive of natural forces. Indeed, as stated above, it is the creation of free men who are so disposed to act by nature as to be responsible for what they do. They must, of course, recognize the laws of human progress and the development of economic life and take these into account. Furthermore, men are not altogether free of their milieu.

64. Accordingly, advances in social organization can and should be so brought about that maximum advantages accrue to citizens while at the same time disadvantages are averted or at least minimized.

65. That these desired objectives be more readily obtained, it is necessary that public authorities have a correct understanding of the common good. This embraces the sum total of those conditions of social living, whereby men are enabled more fully and more readily to achieve their own perfection. Hence, we regard it as necessary that the various intermediary bodies and the numerous social undertakings wherein an expanded social structure primarily finds expression, be ruled by their own laws, and as the common good itself progresses, pursue this objective in a spirit of sincere concord among themselves. Nor is it less necessary that the above mentioned groups present the form and substance of a true community. This they will do, only if individual members are considered and treated as persons, and are encouraged to participate in the affairs of the group.

66. Accordingly, as relationships multiply between men, binding them more closely together, commonwealths will more readily and appropriately order their affairs to the extent these two factors are kept in balance: (1) the freedom of individual citizens and groups of citizens to act autonomously, while cooperating one with the other; (2) the activity of the state whereby the undertakings of private individuals and groups are suitably regulated and fostered.

67. Now if social systems are organized in accordance with the above norms and moral laws, their extension does not necessarily mean that individual citizens will be gravely discriminated against or excessively burdened. Rather, we can hope that this will enable man not only to develop and perfect his natural talents, but also will lead to an appropriate structuring of the human community. Such a structure, as our predecessor of happy memory, Pius XI, warned in his encyclical letter

Quadragesimo Anno,[26] is absolutely necessary for the adequate fulfillment of the rights and duties of social life.

Remuneration for Work

Standards of Justice and Equity

68. Our heart is filled with profound sadness when we observe, as it were, with our own eyes a wretched spectacle indeed—great masses of workers who, in not a few nations, and even in whole continents, receive too small a return from their labor. Hence, they and their families must live in conditions completely out of accord with human dignity. This can be traced, for example, to the fact that in these regions, modern industrial techniques either have only recently been introduced or have made less than satisfactory progress.
69. It happens in some of these nations that, as compared with the extreme need of the majority, the wealth and conspicuous consumption of a few stand out, and are in open and bold contrast with the lot of the needy. It happens in other places that excessive burdens are placed upon men in order that the commonwealth may achieve within a brief span, an increase of wealth such as can by no means be achieved without violating the laws of justice and equity. Finally, it happens elsewhere that a disproportionate share of the revenue goes toward the building up of national prestige, and that large sums of money are devoted to armaments.
70. Moreover, in the economically developed countries, it frequently happens that great, or sometimes very great, remuneration is had for the performance of some task of lesser importance or doubtful utility. Meanwhile, the diligent and profitable work that whole classes of decent and hard-working citizens perform, receives too low a payment and one insufficient for the necessities of life, or else, one that does not correspond to the contribution made to the community, or to the revenues of the undertakings in which they are engaged, or to the national income.
71. Wherefore, we judge it to be our duty to reaffirm once again that just as remuneration for work cannot be left entirely to unregulated competition, neither may it be decided arbitrarily at the will of the more powerful. Rather, in this matter, the norms of justice and equity should be strictly observed. This requires that workers receive a wage sufficient to lead a life worthy of man and to fulfill family responsibilities properly. But in determining what constitutes an appropriate wage, the following must necessarily be taken into account: first of all, the contribution of individuals to the economic effort; the eco-

---

[26]Cf., Ibid., p. 222f.

nomic state of the enterprises within which they work; the requirements of each community, especially as regards overall employment; finally, what concerns the common good of all peoples, namely, of the various states associated among themselves, but differing in character and extent.

72. It is clear that the standards of judgment set forth above are binding always and everywhere. However, the measure in which they are to be applied in concrete cases cannot be established unless account is taken of the resources at hand. These resources can and in fact do vary in quantity and quality among different peoples, and may even change within the same country with the passing of time.

Balancing Economic Development and Social Progress

73. Whereas in our era the economies of various countries are evolving very rapidly, more especially since the last great war, we take this opportunity to draw the attention of all to a strict demand of social justice, which explicitly requires that, with the growth of the economy, there occur a corresponding social development. Thus, all classes of citizens will benefit equitably from an increase in national wealth. Toward this end vigilance should be exercised and effective steps taken that class differences arising from disparity of wealth not be increased, but lessened so far as possible.

74. "National wealth"—as our predecessor of happy memory, Pius XII, rightfully observed

> inasmuch as it is produced by the common efforts of the citizenry, has no other purpose than to secure without interruption those material conditions in which individuals are enabled to lead a full and perfect life. Where this is consistently the case, then such a people is to be judged truly rich. For the system where both the common prosperity is achieved and individuals exercise their right to use material goods, conforms fully to norms laid down by God the Creator.[27]

From this it follows that the economic prosperity of any people is to be assessed not so much from the sum total of goods and wealth possessed as from the distribution of goods according to norms of justice, so that everyone in the community can develop and perfect himself. For this, after all, is the end toward which all economic activity of a community is by nature ordered.

75. We must here call attention to the fact that in many countries today, the economic system is such that large and medium size productive enterprises achieve rapid growth precisely because they finance

---

[27]Cf. *Acta Apostolicae Sedis*, XXXIII (1941), p. 200.

replacement and plant expansion from their own revenues. Where this is the case, we believe that such companies should grant to workers some share in the enterprise, especially where they are paid no more than the minimum wage.

76. In this matter, the principle laid down by our predecessor of happy memory, Pius XI, in the encyclical letter *Quadragesimo Anno*, should be borne in mind: "It is totally false to ascribe to a single factor of production what is in fact produced by joint activity; and it is completely unjust for one factor to arrogate to itself what is produced, ignoring what has been contributed by other factors."[28]

77. The demands of justice referred to, can be met in various ways, as experience shows. Not to mention other ways, it is very desirable that workers gradually acquire some share in the enterprise by such methods as seem more appropriate. For today, more than in the times of our predecessor, "every effort should be made that at least in the future, only an equitable share of the fruits of production accumulate in the hands of the wealthy, and a sufficient and ample portion go to the workingmen."[29]

78. But we should remember that adjustments between remuneration for work and revenues are to be brought about in conformity with the requirements of the common good, both of one's own community and of the entire human family.

79. Considering the common good on the national level, the following points are relevant and should not be overlooked: to provide employment for as many workers as possible; to take care lest privileged groups arise even among the workers themselves; to maintain a balance between wages and prices; to make accessible the goods and services for a better life to as many persons as possible; either to eliminate or to keep within bounds the inequalities that exist between different sectors of the economy—that is, between agriculture, industry and services; to balance properly any increases in output with advances in services provided to citizens, especially by public authority; to adjust, as far as possible, the means of production to the progress of science and technology; finally, to ensure that the advantages of a more humane way of existence not merely subserve the present generation but have regard for future generations as well.

80. As regards the common good of human society as a whole, the following conditions should be fulfilled: that the competitive striving of peoples to increase output be free of bad faith; that harmony in economic affairs and a friendly and beneficial cooperation be fostered; and, finally, that effective aid be given in developing the economically underdeveloped nations.

---

[28] *Acta Apostolicae Sedis*, XXIII (1931), p. 195.
[29] Ibid., p. 198.

81. It is evident from what has been said that these demands of the common good, on both the national and world levels, should be borne in mind, when there is question of determining the share of earnings assigned to those responsible for directing the productive enterprise, or as interest and dividends to those who have invested capital.

Demands of Justice as Regards Productive Institutions

Institutions Conforming to the Dignity of Man

82. Justice is to be observed not merely in the distribution of wealth, but also in regard to the conditions under which men engage in productive activity. There is, in fact, an innate need of human nature requiring that men engaged in productive activity have an opportunity to assume responsibility and to perfect themselves by their efforts.
83. Consequently, if the organization and structure of economic life be such that the human dignity of workers is compromised, or their sense of responsibility is weakened, or their freedom of action is removed, then we judge such an economic order to be unjust, even though it produces a vast amount of goods, whose distribution conforms to the norms of justice and equity.

Reaffirmation of a Directive

84. Nor is it possible in economic affairs to determine in one formula all the measures that are more conformable to the dignity of man, or are more suitable in developing in him a sense of responsibility. Nevertheless, our predecessor of happy memory, Pius XII, appropriately laid down certain norms of action:

> Small and medium-sized holdings in agriculture, in the arts and crafts, in commerce and industry, should be safeguarded and fostered. Such enterprises should join together in mutual-aid societies in order that the services and benefits of large-scale enterprises will be available to them. So far as these larger enterprises are concerned, work agreements should in some way be modified by partnership arrangements.[30]

Artisan Enterprises and Cooperative Associations

85. Wherefore, conformably to requirements of the common good and the state of technology, artisan and farm enterprises of family type should be safeguarded and fostered, as should also cooperatives

---

[30]Radio Broadcast, September 1, 1944; cf. *A.A.S.*, XXXVI (1944), p. 254.

that aim to complement and perfect such enterprises.

86. We shall return shortly to the subject of farm enterprises. Here, we think it appropriate to say something about artisan enterprises and cooperative associations.

87. Above all, it must be emphasized that enterprises and bodies of this sort, in order that they may survive and flourish, should be continuously adapted—both in their productive structure and in their operating methods—to new conditions of the times. These new conditions constantly arise from advances in science and technology, or from changing consumer needs and preferences. It is especially appropriate that all this be done by the craftsmen themselves and by the associates in the cooperatives.

88. Hence, it is most fitting not only that both these groups be suitably formed in technical and in spiritual and intellectual matters, but also that they be joined together professionally. Nor is it less fitting that the state make special provision for them in regard to instruction, taxes, credit facilities, social security and insurance.

89. Moreover, the measures taken by the state on behalf of the craftsmen and members of cooperatives are also justified by the fact that these two categories of citizens are producers of genuine wealth, and contribute to the advance of civilization.

90. Accordingly, we paternally exhort our beloved sons, craftsmen and members of cooperatives throughout the world, that they fully realize the dignity of their role in society, since, by their work, the sense of responsibility and spirit of mutual aid can be daily more intensified among the citizenry, and the desire to work with dedication and originality be kept alive.

Participation of Workers in Medium-size and Large Enterprises

91. Furthermore, as did our predecessors, we regard as justifiable the desire of employees to be partners in enterprises with which they are associated and wherein they work. We do not think it possible, however, to decide with certain and explicit norms the manner and degree of such partnership, since this must be determined according to the state of the individual productive enterprises. For the situation is not everywhere the same, and, in fact, it can change suddenly within one and the same enterprise. Nevertheless, we do not doubt that employees should have an active part in the affairs of the enterprise wherein they work, whether these be private or public. But it is of the utmost importance that productive enterprises assume the character of a true human fellowship whose spirit suffuses the dealings, activities, and standing of all its members.

92. This requires that mutual relations between employers and directors on the one hand and the employees of the enterprise on the other, be marked by mutual respect, esteem, and good will. It also demands that all collaborate sincerely and harmoniously in their joint undertaking, and that they perform their work not merely with the objective of deriving an income, but also of carrying out the role assigned them and of performing a service that results in benefit to others. This means that the workers may have a say in, and may make a contribution toward, the efficient running and development of the enterprise. Thus, our predecessor of happy memory, Pius XII, clearly indicated: "The economic and social functions which everyone aspires to fulfill, require that efforts of individuals be not wholly subjected to the will of others."[31] Beyond doubt, an enterprise truly in accord with human dignity should safeguard the necessary and efficient unity of administration. But it by no means follows that those who work daily in such an enterprise are to be considered merely as servants, whose sole function is to execute orders silently, and who are not allowed to interject their desires and interests, but must conduct themselves as idle standbys when it comes to assignment and direction of their tasks.

93. Finally, attention is drawn to the fact that the greater amount of responsibility desired today by workers in productive enterprises, not merely accords with the nature of man, but also is in conformity with historical developments in the economic, social, and political fields.

94. Unfortunately, in our day, there occur in economic and social affairs many imbalances that militate against justice and humanity. Meanwhile, throughout all of economic life, errors are spread that seriously impair its operation, purposes, organization, and the fulfillment of responsibilities. Nevertheless, it is an undeniable fact that the more recent productive systems, thanks to the impulse deriving from advances in technology and science, are becoming more modern and efficient, and are expanding at a faster rate than in the past. This demands of workers greater abilities and professional qualifications. Accordingly, workers should be provided with additional aids and time to achieve a suitable and more rounded formation, and to carry out more fittingly their duties as regards studies, morals, and religion.

95. Thus it happens that in our day youths can be allotted additional years to acquire a basic education and necessary skills.

96. Now if these things be done, a situation will emerge wherein workers are enabled to assume greater responsibilities even within their own enterprises. As regards the commonwealth as such, it is of great importance that all ranks of citizens feel themselves daily more obligated to safeguard the common good.

---

[31] Allocution, October 8, 1956; cf. *A.A.S.*, XLVIII (1956), pp. 799-800.

Participation of Workers at All Levels

97. Now, as is evident to all, in our day associations of workers have become widespread, and for the most part have been given legal status within individual countries and even across national boundaries. These bodies no longer recruit workers for purposes of strife, but rather for pursuing a common aim. And this is achieved especially by collective bargaining between associations of workers and those of management. But it should be emphasized how necessary, or at least very appropriate, it is to give workers an opportunity to exert influence outside the limits of the individual productive unit, and indeed within all ranks of the commonwealth.
98. The reason is that individual productive units, whatever their size, efficiency, or importance within the commonwealth, are closely connected with the overall economic and social situations in each country, whereon their own prosperity ultimately depends.
99. Nevertheless, to decide what is more helpful to the overall economic situation is not the prerogative of individual productive enterprises, but pertains to the public authorities and to those institutions which, established either nationally or among a number of countries, function in various sectors of economic life. From this is evident the propriety or necessity of ensuring that not only managers or agents of management are represented before such authorities and institutions, but also workers or those who have the responsibility of safeguarding the rights, needs, and aspirations of workers.
100. It is fitting, therefore, that our thoughts and paternal affection be directed toward the various professional groups and associations of workers which, in accord with principles of Christian teaching, carry on their activities on several continents. We are aware of the many and great difficulties experienced by these beloved sons of ours, as they effectively worked in the past and continue to strive, both within their national boundaries and throughout the world, to vindicate the rights of workingmen and to improve their lot and conduct.
101. Furthermore, we wish to give deserved praise to the work of these our sons. Their accomplishments are not always immediately evident, but nevertheless permeate practically the entire field of labor, spreading correct norms of action and thought, and the beneficial influence of the Christian religion.
102. And we wish also to praise paternally those dear sons of ours who, imbued with Christian principles, give their special attention to other labor associations and those groups of workingmen that follow the laws of nature and respect the religious and moral liberty of individuals.
103. Nor can we at this point neglect to congratulate and to express our esteem for the International Labor Organization—variously signified popularly by the letters OIL or ILO or OIT—which, for many

years, has done effective and valuable work in adapting the economic and social order everywhere to the norms of justice and humanity. In such an order, the legitimate rights of workers are recognized and preserved.

Private Property

Changed Conditions

104. In recent years, as we are well aware, the role played by the owners of capital in very large productive enterprises has been separated more and more from the role of management. This has occasioned great difficulties for governments, whose duty it is to make certain that directors of the principal enterprises, especially those of greatest influence in the economic life of the entire country, do not depart from the requirements of the common good. These difficulties, as we know from experience, are by no means less, whether it be private citizens or public bodies that make the capital investments requisite for large-scale enterprises.

105. It is also quite clear that today the number of persons is increasing who, because of recent advances in insurance programs and various systems of social security, are able to look to the future with tranquillity. This sort of tranquillity once was rooted in the ownership of property, albeit modest.

106. It sometimes happens in our day that men are more inclined to seek some professional skill than possession of goods. Moreover, such men have greater esteem for income from labor or rights arising from labor, than for that deriving from capital investment or rights associated therewith.

107. This clearly accords with the inherent characteristics of labor, inasmuch as this proceeds directly from the human person, and hence is to be thought more of than wealth in external goods. These latter, by their very nature, must be regarded as instruments. This trend indicates an advance in civilization.

108. Economic conditions of this kind have occasioned popular doubt as to whether, under present circumstances, a principle of economic and social life, firmly enunciated and defended by our predecessors, has lost its force or is to be regarded as of lesser moment; namely, the principle whereby it is established that men have from nature a right of privately owning goods, including those of a productive kind.

Confirmation of the Right of Private Property

109. Such a doubt has no foundation. For the right of private property, including that pertaining to goods devoted to productive enterprises, is permanently valid. Indeed, it is rooted in the very nature of things, whereby we learn that individual men are prior to civil society, and hence, that civil society is to be directed toward man as its end. Indeed, the right of private individuals to act freely in economic affairs is recognized in vain, unless they are at the same time given an opportunity of freely selecting and using things necessary for the exercise of this right. Moreover, experience and history testify that where political regimes do not allow to private individuals the possession also of productive goods, the exercise of human liberty is violated or completely destroyed in matters of primary importance. Thus it becomes clear that in the right of property, the exercise of liberty finds both a safeguard and a stimulus.

110. This explains the fact that sociopolitical groups and associations which endeavor to reconcile freedom with justice within society, and which until recently did not uphold the right of private property in productive goods, have now, enlightened by the course of social events, modified their views and are disposed actually to approve this right.

111. Accordingly, we make our own the insistence of our predecessor of happy memory, Pius XII:

> In defending the right of private property, the Church has in mind a very important ethical aim in social matters. She does not, of course, strive to uphold the present state of affairs as if it were an expression of the divine will. And even less does she accept the patronage of the affluent and wealthy, while neglecting the rights of the poor and needy. . . . The Church rather does intend that the institution of private property be such as is required by the plan of divine wisdom and the law of nature.[32]

Private ownership should safeguard the rights of the human person, and at the same time make its necessary contribution to the establishment of right order in society.

112. While recent developments in economic life progress rapidly in a number of countries, as we have noted, and produce goods ever more efficiently, justice and equity require that remuneration for work also be increased within limits allowed by the common good. This enables workers to save more readily and hence to achieve some property status of their own. Wherefore, it is indeed surprising that some reject the natural role of private ownership. For it is a right which continually draws its force and vigor from the fruitfulness of labor, and which, accordingly, is an effective aid in safeguarding the dignity of the human person and the free exercise of responsibility in all fields of endeavor. Finally, it strengthens the stability and tran-

---

[32]Radio Broadcast, September 1, 1944; cf. *A.A.S.*, XXXVI (1944), p. 253.

quillity of family life, thus contributing to the peace and prosperity of the commonwealth.

Effective Distribution

113. It is not enough, then, to assert that man has from nature the right of privately possessing goods as his own, including those of productive character, unless, at the same time, a continuing effort is made to spread the use of this right through all ranks of the citizenry.
114. Our predecessor of happy memory, Pius XII, clearly reminded us that on the one hand the dignity of the human person necessarily "requires the right of using external goods in order to live according to the right norm of nature. And to this right corresponds a most serious obligation, which requires that, so far as possible, there be given to all an opportunity of possessing private property."[33] On the other hand, the nobility inherent in work, besides other requirements, demands "the conservation and perfection of a social order that makes possible a secure, although modest, property to all classes of the people."[34]
115. It is especially appropriate that today, more than heretofore, widespread private ownership should prevail, since, as noted above, the number of nations increases wherein the economic systems experience daily growth. Therefore, by prudent use of various devices already proven effective, it will not be difficult for the body politic to modify economic and social life so that the way is made easier for widespread private possession of such things as durable goods, homes, gardens, tools requisite for artisan enterprises and family-type farms, investments in enterprises of medium or large size. All of this has occurred satisfactorily in some nations with developed social and economic systems.

Public Property

116. Obviously, what we have said above does not preclude ownership of goods pertaining to production of wealth by states and public agencies, especially "if these carry with them power too great to be left in private hands, without injury to the community at large."[35]
117. It seems characteristic of our times to vest more and more ownership of goods in the state and in other public bodies. This is partially explained by the fact that the common good requires public authorities to exercise ever greater responsibilities. However, in this matter,

---

[33]Radio Broadcast, December 24, 1942; cf. *A.A.S.*, XXXV (1943), p. 17.
[34]Cf. Ibid., p. 20.
[35]Encyclical letter *Quadragesimo Anno; A.A.S.*, XXIII (1931), p. 214.

the *principle of subsidiarity*, already mentioned above, is to be strictly observed. For it is lawful for states and public corporations to expand their domain of ownership only when manifest and genuine requirements of the common good so require, and then with safeguards, lest the possession of private citizens be diminished beyond measure, or, what is worse, destroyed.

118. Finally, we cannot pass over in silence the fact that economic enterprises undertaken by the state or by public corporations should be entrusted to citizens outstanding in skill and integrity, who will carry out their responsiblities to the commonwealth with a deep sense of devotion. Moreover, the activity of these men should be subjected to careful and continuing supervision, lest, in the administration of the state itself, there develop an economic imperialism in the hands of a few. For such a development is in conflict with the highest good of the commonwealth.

Social Function of Property

119. Our predecessors have always taught that in the right of private property there is rooted a social responsibility. Indeed, in the wisdom of God the Creator, the overall supply of goods is assigned, first of all, that all men may lead a decent life. As our predecessor of happy memory, Leo XIII, clearly reminded us in the encyclical letter *Rerum Novarum*,

> This is the heart of the matter: whoever has received from the divine bounty a larger share of blessings, whether these be corporal or external or gifts of the mind, has received them to use for his own perfection, and, at the same time, as the minister of God's providence, for the benefit of others. "He who has a talent" (says St. Gregory the Great), "let him take care that he hides it not; he who has abundance, let him arouse himself to mercy and generosity; he who has skill in managing affairs, let him make special effort to share the use and utility thereof with his neighbor."[36]

120. Although in our day, the role assigned the state and public bodies has increased more and more, it by no means follows that the social function of private ownership is obsolescent, as some seem to think. For social responsibility in this matter derives its force from the very right of private property. Furthermore, it is quite clear that there always will be a wide range of difficult situations, as well as hidden and grave needs, which the manifold providence of the state leaves untouched, and of which it can in no way take account. Wherefore, there is always wide scope for humane action by private citizens

[36] *Acta Leonis* XIII, XI (1891), p. 114.

and for Christian charity. Finally, it is evident that in stimulating efforts relating to spiritual welfare, the work done by individual men or by private civic groups has more value than what is done by public authorities.

121. Moreover, it is well to recall here that the right of private ownership is clearly evident in the Gospels, which reveal Jesus Christ ordering the rich to share their goods with the poor so as to turn them into spiritual possessions: "Do not lay up for yourselves treasures on earth, where rust and moth consume, and where thieves break in and steal; but lay up for yourselves treasures in heaven, where neither rust nor moth consumes nor thieves break in and steal."[37] And the divine Master states that whatever is done for the poor is done for him: "Amen I say to you, as long as you did it for one of these, the least of my brethren, you did it for me."[38]

Part III
New Aspects of the Social Question

122. The progress of events and of time have made it increasingly evident that the relationships between workers and management in productive enterprises must be readjusted according to norms of justice and charity. But the same is also true of the systems whereby various types of economic activity and the differently endowed regions within a country ought to be linked together. Meanwhile, within the overall human community, many nations with varied endowments have not made identical progress in their economic and social affairs.

Just Requirements in the Matter of Interrelated Productive Sectors

Agriculture: A Depressed Sector

123. First of all, to lay down some norms in regard to agriculture, we would note that the overall number of rural dwellers seemingly has not diminished. Beyond doubt, however, many farmers have abandoned their rural birthplace, and seek out either the more populous centers or the cities themselves. Now since this is the case in almost all countries, and since it affects large numbers of human beings, problems concerning life and dignity of citizens arise, which are indeed difficult to overcome.

---

[37]Mt 6: 19-20.
[38]Mt 25: 40.

124. Thus, as economic life progresses and expands, the percentage of rural dwellers diminishes, while the great number of industrial and service workers increases. Yet, we feel that those who transfer from rural activities to other productive enterprises often are motivated by reasons arising from the very evolution of economic affairs. Very often, however, they are caught up by various enticements of which the following are noteworthy: a desire to escape from a confined environment offering no prospect of a more comfortable life; the wish, so common in our age, to undertake new activities and to acquire new experiences; the attraction of quickly acquired goods and fortunes; a longing after a freer life, with the advantages that larger towns and cities usually provide. But there is no doubt about this point: rural dwellers leave the fields because nearly everywhere they see their affairs in a state of depression, both as regards labor productivity and the level of living of farm populations.

125. Accordingly, in this grave matter, about which enquiries are made in nearly all countries, we should first of all ask what is to be done to prevent so great imbalances between agriculture, industry, and the services in the matter of productive efficiency? Likewise, what can be done to minimize differences between the rural standard of living and that of city dwellers whose money income is derived from industry or some service or other? Finally, how can it be brought about that those engaged in agricultural pursuits no longer regard themselves as inferior to others? Indeed, rural dwellers should be convinced not only that they can strengthen and develop their personalities by their toil, but also that they can look forward to the future vicissitudes with confidence.

126. Accordingly, we judge it opportune in this connection to lay down some norms of permanent validity; although, as is evident, these must be adapted as various circumstances of time and place permit, or suggest, or absolutely require.

Provision for Essential Public Services

127. First, it is necessary that everyone, and especially public authorities, strive to effect improvements in rural areas as regards the principal services needed by all. Such are, for example: highway construction; transport services; marketing facilities; pure drinking water; housing; medical services; elementary, trade, and professional schools; things requisite for religion and for recreation; finally, furnishings and equipment needed in the modern farm home. Where these requirements for a dignified farm life are lacking to rural dwellers, economic and social progress does not occur at all, or else very slowly. Under such conditions, nothing can be done to keep men from deserting the fields, nor can anyone readily estimate their number.

Gradual and Orderly Development of the Economic System

128. It is desirable, moreover, that economic development of commonwealths proceed in orderly fashion, meanwhile preserving appropriate balance between the various sectors of the economy. In particular, care must be had that within the agricultural sector innovations are introduced as regards productive technology, whether these relate to productive methods, or to cultivation of the fields, or to equipment for the rural enterprise, as far as the overall economy allows or requires. And all this should be done as far as possible, in accordance with technical advances in industry and in the various services.

129. In this way, agriculture not only absorbs a larger share of industrial output, but also demands a higher quality of services. In its turn, agriculture offers to the industrial and service sectors of the economy, as well as to the community as a whole, those products which in kind and in quantity better meet consumer needs. Thus, agriculture contributes to stability of the purchasing power of money, a very positive factor for the orderly development of the entire economic system.

130. By proceeding in this manner, the following advantages, among others, arise: first of all, it is easier to know the origins and destinations of rural dwellers displaced by modernization of agriculture. Thereupon, they can be instructed in skills needed for other types of work. Finally, economic aids and helps will not be lacking for their intellectual and cultural development, so that they can fit into new social groups.

Appropriate Economic Policy

131. To achieve orderly progress in various sectors of economic life, it is absolutely necessary that as regards agriculture, public authorities give heed and take action in the following matters: taxes and duties, credit, insurance, prices, the fostering of requisite skills, and, finally, improved equipment for rural enterprises.

Taxation

132. As regards taxation, assessment according to ability to pay is fundamental to a just and equitable system.

133. But in determining taxes for rural dwellers, the general welfare requires public authorities to bear in mind that income in a rural economy is both delayed and subject to greater risk. Moreover, there is difficulty in finding capital so as to increase returns.

Capital at Suitable Interest

134. Accordingly, those with money to invest are more inclined to invest it in enterprises other than in the rural economy. And for the same reason, rural dwellers cannot pay high rates of interest. Nor are they generally able to pay prevailing market rates for capital wherewith to carry on and expand their operations. Wherefore, the general welfare requires that public authorities not merely make special provision for agricultural financing, but also for establishment of banks that provide capital to farmers at reasonable rates of interest.

Social Insurance and Social Security

135. It also seems necessary to make provision for a twofold insurance, one covering agricultural output, the other covering farmers and their families. Because, as experience shows, the income of individual farmers is, on the average, less than that of workers in industry and the services, it does not seem to be fully in accord with the norms of social justice and equity to provide farmers with insurance or social security benefits that are inferior to those of other classes of citizens. For those insurance plans or provisions that are established generally should not differ markedly one from the other, whatever be the economic sector wherein the citizens work, or from which they derive their income.

136. Moreover, since social security and insurance can help appreciably in distributing national income among the citizens according to justice and equity, these systems can be regarded as means whereby imbalances among various classes of citizens are reduced.

Price Protection

137. Since agricultural products have special characteristics, it is fitting that their price be protected by methods worked out by economic experts. In this matter, although it is quite helpful that those whose interests are involved take steps to safeguard themselves, setting up, as it were, appropriate goals, public authorities cannot stand entirely aloof from the stabilization procedure.

138. Nor should this be overlooked, that, generally speaking, the price of rural products is more a recompense for farmers' labor than for capital investment.

139. Thus, our predecessor of happy memory, Pius XI, touching on the welfare of the human community, appropriately notes in his encyclical letter *Quadragesimo Anno*, that "a reasonable relationship between different wages here enters into consideration." But he immediately adds, "Intimately connected with this is a reasonable relationship between the prices obtained for the products of the various economic groups: agrarian, industrial, and so forth."[39]

140. Inasmuch as agricultural products are destined especially to satisfy the basic needs of men, it is necessary that their price be such that all can afford to buy them. Nevertheless, there is manifest injustice in placing a whole group of citizens, namely, the farmers, in an inferior economic and social status, with less purchasing power than required for a decent livelihood. This, indeed, is clearly contrary to the common good of the country.

Strengthening Farm Income

141. In rural areas it is fitting that industries be fostered and common services be developed that are useful in preserving, processing, and finally, in transporting farm products. There is need, moreover, to establish councils and activities relating to various sectors of economic and professional affairs. By such means, suitable opportunity is given farm families to supplement their incomes, and that within the milieu wherein they live and work.

Appropriate Organization of Farming Enterprises

142. Finally, no one person can lay down a universal rule regarding the way in which rural affairs should be definitely organized, since in these matters there exists considerable variation within each country, and the difference is even greater when we consider the various regions of the world. However, those who hold man and the family in proper esteem, whether this be based upon nature alone, or also upon Christian principles, surely look toward some form of agricultural enterprise, and particularly of the family type, which is modeled upon the community of men wherein mutual relationships of members and the organization of the enterprise itself are conformed to norms of justice and Christian teaching. And these men strive mightily that such organization of rural life be realized as far as circumstances permit.

143. The family farm will be firm and stable only when it yields money income sufficient for decent and humane family living. To bring this about, it is very necessary that farmers generally receive instruction, be kept informed of new developments, and be technically assisted by trained men. It is also necessary that farmers form among themselves mutual-aid societies; that they establish professional associations; that they function efficiently in public life, that is, in various administrative bodies and in political affairs.

---

[39]Cf. *Acta Apostolicae Sedis*, XXIII (1931), p. 202.

Rural Workers: Participants in Improving Conditions

144. We are of the opinion that in rural affairs, the principal agents and protagonists of economic improvement, of cultural betterment, or of social advance, should be the men personally involved, namely, the farmers themselves. To them it should be quite evident that their work is most noble, because it is undertaken, as it were, in the majestic temple of creation; because it often concerns the life of plants and animals, a life inexhaustible in its expression, inflexible in its laws, rich in allusions to God, Creator and Provider. Moreover, labor in the fields not only produces various foodstuffs wherewith humankind is nourished, but also furnishes an increasing supply of raw materials for industry.

145. Furthermore, this is a work endowed with a dignity of its own, for it bears a manifold relationship to the mechanical arts, chemistry, and biology: these must be continually adapted to the requirements of emerging situations because scientific and technological advance is of great importance in rural life. Work of this kind, moreover, possesses a special nobility because it requires farmers to understand well the course of the seasons and to adapt themselves to the same; that they await patiently what the future will bring; that they appreciate the importance and seriousness of their duties; that they constantly remain alert and ready for new developments.

Solidarity and Cooperation

146. Nor may it be overlooked that in rural areas, as indeed in every productive sector, farmers should join together in fellowships, especially when the family itself works the farm. Indeed, it is proper for rural workers to have a sense of solidarity. They should strive jointly to set up mutual-aid societies and professional associations. All these are very necessary either to keep rural dwellers abreast of scientific and technical progress, or to protect the prices of goods produced by their labor. Besides, acting in this manner, farmers are put on the same footing as other classes of workers who, for the most part, join together in such fellowships. Finally, by acting thus, farmers will achieve an importance and influence in public affairs proportionate to their own role. For today it is unquestionably true that the solitary voice speaks, as they say, to the winds.

Recognizing Demands of the Common Good

147. But when rural dwellers, just as other classes of workers, wish to make their influence and importance felt, they should never disregard moral duties or civil law. Rather they should strive to bring their rights and interests into line with the rights and needs of other classes, and to refer the same to the common good. In this connection, farmers who strive vigorously to improve the yield of their farm may rightly demand that their efforts be aided and complemented by public authorities, provided they themselves keep in mind the common needs of all and also relate their own efforts to the fulfillment of these needs.

148. Wherefore, we wish to honor appropriately those sons of ours who everywhere in the world, either by founding and fostering mutual-aid societies or some other type of association, watchfully strive that in all civic affairs farmers enjoy not merely economic prosperity but also a status in keeping with justice.

Vocation and Mission

149. Since everything that makes for man's dignity, perfection, and development seems to be invoked in agricultural labor, it is proper that man regard such work as an assignment from God with a sublime purpose. It is fitting, therefore, that man dedicate work of this kind to the most provident God who directs all events for the salvation of men. Finally, the farmer should take upon himself, in some measure, the task of educating himself and others for the advancement of civilization.

Aid to Less Developed Areas

150. It often happens that in one and the same country citizens enjoy different degrees of wealth and social advancement. This especially happens because they dwell in areas which, economically speaking, have grown at different rates. Where such is the case, justice and equity demand that the government make efforts either to remove or to minimize imbalances of this sort. Toward this end, efforts should be made, in areas where there has been less economic progress, to supply the principal public services, as indicated by circumstances of time and place and in accord with the general level of living. But in bringing this about, it is necessary to have very competent administration and organization to take careful account of the following: labor supply, internal migration, wages, taxes, interest rates, and investments in industries that foster other skills and developments—all of which will further not merely the useful employment of workers and the stimulation of initiative, but also the exploitation of resources locally available.

151. But it is precisely the measures for advancement of the general welfare which civil authorities must undertake. Hence, they should take steps, having regard for the needs of the whole community, that progress in agriculture, industry, and services be made at the same time and in a balanced manner so far as possible. They should have this goal in mind, that citizens in less developed countries—in giving attention to economic and social affairs, as well as to cultural matters—feel themselves to be the ones chiefly responsible for their own progress. For a citizen has a sense of his own dignity when he contributes the major share to progress in his own affairs.

152. Hence, those also who rely on their resources and initiative should contribute as best they can to the equitable adjustment of economic life in their own community. Nay, more, those in authority should favor and help private enterprise in accordance with the *principle of subsidiarity*, in order to allow private citizens themselves to accomplish as much as is feasible.

Imbalances between Land and Population

153. It is appropriate to recall at this point that in a number of nations there exists a discrepancy between available agricultural land and the number of rural dwellers. Some nations experience a shortage of citizens, but have rich land resources; others may have many citizens but an insufficiency of agricultural land.

154. Nor are there lacking nations wherein, despite their great resource potential, farmers use such primitive and obsolete methods of cultivation that they are unable to produce what is needed for the entire population. On the other hand, in certain countries, agriculture has so adapted itself to recent advances that farmers produce surpluses which to some extent harm the economy of the entire nation.

155. It is evident that both the solidarity of the human race and the sense of brotherhood which accords with Christian principles, require that some peoples lend others energetic help in many ways. Not merely would this result in a freer movement of goods, of capital, and of men, but it also would lessen imbalances between nations. We shall treat of this point in more detail below.

156. Here, however, we cannot fail to express our approval of the efforts of the institute known as FAO, which concerns itself with the feeding of peoples and the improvement of agriculture. This institute has the special goal of promoting mutual accord among peoples, of bringing it about that rural life is modernized in less developed nations, and finally, that help is brought to people experiencing food shortages.

Requirements of Justice as between Nations Differing in Economic Development

Problem of the Modern World

157. Perhaps the most pressing question of our day concerns the relationship between economically advanced commonwealths and those that are in process of development. The former enjoy the conveniences of life; the latter experience dire poverty. Yet, today men are so intimately associated in all parts of the world that they feel, as it were, as if they are members of one and the same household. Therefore, the nations that enjoy a sufficiency and abundance of everything may not overlook the plight of other nations whose citizens experience such domestic problems that they are all but overcome by poverty and hunger, and are not able to enjoy basic human rights. This is all the more so, inasmuch as countries each day seem to become more dependent on each other. Consequently, it is not easy for them to keep the peace advantageously if excessive imbalances exist in their economic and social conditions.

158. Mindful of our role of universal father, we think it opportune to stress here what we have stated in another connection: "We all share responsibility for the fact that populations are undernourished.[40] [Therefore], it is necessary to arouse a sense of responsibility in individuals and generally, especially among those more blessed with this world's goods."[41]

159. As can be readily deduced, and as the Church has always seriously warned, it is proper that the duty of helping the poor and unfortunate should especially stir Catholics, since they are members of the Mystical Body of Christ. "In this we have come to know the love of God," said John the apostle, "that he laid down his life for us; and we likewise ought to lay down our life for the brethren. He who has the goods of this world and sees his brother in need and closes his heart to him, how does the love of God abide in him?"[42]

160. Wherefore, we note with pleasure that countries with advanced productive systems are lending aid to less privileged countries, so that these latter may the more readily improve their condition.

Emergency Assistance

161. It is clear to everyone that some nations have surpluses in foodstuffs, particularly of farm products, while elsewhere large masses of people experience want and hunger. Now justice and humanity require that these richer countries come to the aid of those in need. Accordingly, to destroy entirely or to waste goods necessary for the lives of men, runs counter to our obligations in justice and humanity.

162. We are quite well aware that to produce surpluses, especially of farm products, in excess of the needs of a country, can occasion harm to various classes of citizens. Nevertheless, it does not therefore

---

[40] Allocution, May 3, 1960; cf. *A.A.S.*, LII (1960), p. 465.
[41] Cf. Ibid.
[42] 1 Jn 3:16-17.

follow that nations with surpluses have no obligation to aid the poor and hungry where some particular emergency arises. Rather, diligent efforts should be made that inconveniences arising from surplus goods be minimized and borne by every citizen on a fair basis.

Scientific, Technical, and Financial Cooperation

163. However, the underlying causes of poverty and hunger will not be removed in a number of countries by these means alone. For the most part, the causes are to be found in the primitive state of the economy. To effect a remedy, all available avenues should be explored with a view, on the one hand, to instruct citizens fully in necessary skills and in carrying out their responsibilities, and, on the other hand, to enable them to acquire the capital wherewith to promote economic growth by ways and means adapted to our times.
164. It has not escaped our attention that in recent years there has grown in many minds a deep awareness of their duty to aid poorer countries still lacking suitable economic development, in order that these may more readily make economic and social progress.
165. Toward this end, we look to councils, either of a number of nations, or within individual nations; we look to private enterprises and societies to exert daily more generous efforts on behalf of such countries, transmitting to them requisite productive skills. For the same reason help is given to as many youths as possible that they may study in the great universities of more developed countries, thus acquiring a knowledge of the arts and sciences in line with the standards of our time. Moreover, international banks, single nations, or private citizens often make loans to these countries that they may initiate various programs calculated to increase production. We gladly take this opportunity to give due praise to such generous activity. It is hoped that in the future the richer countries will make greater and greater efforts to provide developing countries with aid designed to promote sciences, technology, and economic life.

Avoidance of Past Errors

166. In this matter we consider it our duty to offer some warnings.
167. First of all, it seems only prudent for nations which thus far have made little or no progress, to weigh well the principal factor in the advance of nations that enjoy abundance.
168. Prudent foresight and common need demand that not only more goods be produced, but that this be done more efficiently. Likewise, necessity and justice require that wealth produced be distributed equitably among all citizens of the commonwealth. Accordingly, efforts should be made to ensure that improved social conditions accompany economic advancement. And it is very important that such advances

occur simultaneously in the agricultural, industrial, and various service sectors.

Respect for Individual Characteristics of Countries

169. It is indeed clear to all that countries in process of development often have their own individual characteristics, and that these arise from the nature of the locale, or from cultural tradition, or from some special trait of the citizens.
170. Now when economically developed countries assist the poorer ones, they not only should have regard for these characteristics and respect them, but also should take special care lest, in aiding these nations, they seek to impose their own way of life upon them.

Disinterested Aid

171. Moreover, economically developed countries should take particular care lest, in giving aid to poorer countries, they endeavor to turn the prevailing political situation to their own advantage, and seek to dominate them.
172. Should perchance such attempts be made, this clearly would be but another form of colonialism, which, although disguised in name, merely reflects their earlier but outdated dominion, now abandoned by many countries. When international relations are thus obstructed, the orderly progress of all peoples is endangered.
173. Genuine necessity, as well as justice, require that whenever countries give attention to the fostering of skills or commerce, they should aid the less developed nations without thought of domination, so that these latter eventually will be in a position to progress economically and socially on their own initiative.
174. If this be done, it will help much toward shaping a community of all nations, wherein each one, aware of its rights and duties, will have regard for the prosperity of all.

Respect for a Hierarchy of Values

175. There is no doubt that when a nation makes progress in science, technology, economic life, and the prosperity of its citizens, a great contribution is made to civilization. But all should realize that these things are not the highest goods, but only instruments for pursuing such goods.
176. Accordingly, we note with sorrow that in some nations economic life indeed progresses, but that not a few men are there to be found, who have no concern at all for the just ordering of goods. No doubt, these men either completely ignore spiritual values, or put these out of their minds, or else deny they exist. Nevertheless, while

they pursue progress in science, technology, and economic life, they make so much of external benefits that for the most part they regard these as the highest goods of life. Accordingly, there are not lacking grave dangers in the help provided by more affluent nations for development of the poorer ones. For among the citizens of these latter nations, there is operative a general awareness of the higher values on which moral teaching rests—an awareness derived from ancient traditional custom which provides them with motivation.

177. Thus, those who seek to undermine in some measure the right instincts of these peoples, assuredly do something immoral. Rather, those attitudes, besides being held in honor, should be perfected and refined, since upon them true civilization depends.

Contribution of the Church

178. Moreover, the Church by divine right pertains to all nations. This is confirmed by the fact that she already is everywhere on earth and strives to embrace all peoples.

179. Now, those peoples whom the Church has joined to Christ have always reaped some benefits, whether in economic affairs or in social organization, as history and contemporary events clearly record. For everyone who professes Christianity promises and gives assurance that he will contribute as far as he can to the advancement of civil institutions. He must also strive with all his might not only that human dignity suffer no dishonor, but also, by the removal of every kind of obstacle, that all those forces be promoted which are conducive to moral living and contribute to it.

180. Moreover, when the Church infuses her energy into the life of a people, she neither is, nor feels herself to be, an alien institution imposed upon that people from without. This follows from the fact that wherever the Church is present, there individual men are reborn or resurrected in Christ. Those who are thus reborn or who have risen again in Christ feel themselves oppressed by no external force. Rather, realizing they have achieved perfect liberty, they freely move toward God. Hence, whatever is seen by them as good and morally right, that they approve and put into effect.

181. "The Church of Jesus Christ," as our predecessor Pius XII clearly stated

> is the faithful guardian of God's gracious wisdom. Hence, she makes no effort to discourage or belittle those characteristics and traits which are proper to particular nations, and which peoples religiously and tenaciously guard, quite justly, as a sacred heritage. She aims indeed at a unity which is profound and in conformity with that heavenly love whereby all are moved in their innermost being. She does not seek a uniformity which is merely external in its effects and calculated to weaken the fiber of the peoples concerned. And

all careful rules that contribute to the wise development and growth within bounds of these capacities and forces, which indeed have their deeply rooted ethnic traits, have the Church's approval and maternal prayers, provided they are not in opposition to those duties which spring from the common origin and destiny of all mortal men.[43]

182. We note with deep satisfaction that Catholic men, citizens of the less developed nations, are for the most part second to no other citizens in furthering efforts of their countries to make progress economically and socially according to their capacity.

183. Furthermore, we note that Catholic citizens of the richer nations are making extensive efforts to ensure that aid given by their own countries to needy countries is directed increasingly toward economic and social progress. In this connection, it seems specially praiseworthy that appreciable aid in various forms is provided increasingly each year to young people from Africa and Asia, so that they may pursue literary and professional studies in the great universities of Europe and America. The same applies to the great care that has been taken in training for every responsibility of their office men prepared to go to less developed areas, there to carry out their profession and duties.

184. To those sons of ours who, by promoting solicitously the progress of peoples and by spreading, as it were, a wholesome civilizing influence, everywhere demonstrate the perennial vitality of Holy Church and her effectiveness, we wish to express our paternal praise and gratitude.

* * *

International Cooperation

World Dimensions of Important Human Problems

200. Since the relationships between countries today are closer in every region of the world, by reason of science and technology, it is proper that peoples become more and more interdependent.

201. Accordingly, contemporary problems of moment—whether in the fields of science and technology, or of economic and social affairs, or of public administration, or of cultural advancement—these, because they may exceed the capacities of individual states, very often affect a number of nations and at times all the nations of the earth.

---

[43]Encyclical letter *Summi Pontificatus; A.A.S.*, XXXI (1939), pp. 428-29.

202. As a result, individual countries, although advanced in culture and civilization, in number and industry of citizens, in wealth, in geographical extent, are not able by themselves to resolve satisfactorily their basic problems. Accordingly, because states must on occasion complement or perfect one another, they really consult their own interests only when they take into account at the same time the interests of others. Hence, dire necessity warns commonwealths to cooperate among themselves and provide mutual assistance.

Mutual Distrust

203. Although this becomes more and more evident each day to individuals and even to all peoples, men, and especially those with high responsibility in public life, for the most part seem unable to accomplish the two things toward which peoples aspire. This does not happen because peoples lack scientific, technical, or economic means, but rather because they distrust one another. Indeed, men and hence states, stand in fear of one another. One country fears lest another is contemplating aggression and lest the other seize an opportunity to put such plans into effect. Accordingly, countries customarily prepare defenses for their cities and homeland, namely, armaments designed to deter other countries from aggression.

204. Consequently, the energies of man and the resources of nature are very widely directed by peoples to destruction rather than to the advantage of the human family, and both individual men and entire peoples become so deeply solicitous that they are prevented from undertaking more important works.

Failure to Acknowledge the Moral Order

205. The cause of this state of affairs seems to be that men, more especially leaders of states, have differing philosophies of life. Some even dare to assert that there exists no law of truth and right which transcends external affairs and man himself, which of necessity pertains to everyone, and, finally, which is equitable for all men. Hence, men can agree fully and surely about nothing, since one and the same law of justice is not accepted by all.

206. Although the word *justice* and the related term *demands of justice* are on everyone's lips, such verbalizations do not have the same meaning for all. Indeed, the opposite frequently is the case. Hence, when leaders invoke *justice* or the *demands of justice,* not only do they disagree as to the meaning of the words, but frequently find in them an occasion of serious contention. And so they conclude that there is no way of achieving their rights or advantages, unless they resort to force, the root of very serious evils.

God, the Foundation of the Moral Order

207. That mutual faith may develop among rulers and nations and may abide more deeply in their minds, the laws of truth and justice first must be acknowledged and preserved on all sides.
208. However, the guiding principles of morality and virtue can be based only on God; apart from him, they necessarily collapse. For man is composed not merely of body, but of soul as well, and is endowed with reason and freedom. Now such a composite being absolutely requires a moral law rooted in religion, which, far better than any external force or advantage, can contribute to the resolution of problems affecting the lives of individual citizens or groups of citizens, or with a bearing upon single states or all states together.
209. Yet, there are today those who assert that, in view of the flourishing state of science and technology, men can achieve the highest civilization even apart from God and by their own unaided powers. Nevertheless, it is because of this very progress in science and technology that men often find themselves involved in difficulties which affect all peoples, and which can be overcome only if they duly recognize the authority of God, author and ruler of man and of all nature.
210. That this is true, the advances of science seem to indicate, opening up, as they do, almost limitless horizons. Thus, an opinion is implanted in many minds that inasmuch as mathematical sciences are unable to discern the innermost nature of things and their changes, or express them in suitable terms, they can scarcely draw inferences about them. And when terrified men see with their own eyes that the vast forces deriving from technology and machines can be used for destruction as well as for the advantage of peoples, they rightly conclude that things pertaining to the spirit and to moral life are to be preferred to all else, so that progress in science and technology do not result in destruction of the human race, but prove useful as instruments of civilization.
211. Meanwhile it comes to pass that in more affluent countries men, less and less satisfied with external goods, put out of their minds the deceptive image of a happy life to be lived here forever. Likewise, not only do men grow daily more conscious that they are fully endowed with all the rights of the human person, but they also strive mightily that relations among themselves become more equitable and more conformed to human dignity. Consequently, men are beginning to recognize that their own capacities are limited, and they seek spiritual things more intensively than heretofore. All of which seems to give some promise that not only individuals, but even peoples may come to an understanding for extensive and extremely useful collaboration.

Part IV
Reconstruction of Social Relationships in Truth, Justice and Love

Incomplete and Erroneous Philosophies of Life

212. As in the past, so too in our day, advances in science and technology have greatly multiplied relationships between citizens; it seems necessary, therefore, that the relationships themselves, whether within a single country or between all countries, be brought into more humane balance.

213. In this connection many systems of thought have been developed and committed to writing; some of these already have been dissipated as mist by the sun; others remain basically unchanged today; still others now elicit less and less response from men. The reason for this is that these popularized fancies neither encompass man, whole and entire, nor do they affect his inner being. Moreover, they fail to take into account the weaknesses of human nature, such as sickness and suffering: weaknesses that no economic or social system, no matter how advanced, can completely eliminate. Besides, men everywhere are moved by a profound and unconquerable sense of religion, which no force can ever destroy nor shrewdness suppress.

214. In our day, a very false opinion is popularized which holds that the sense of religion implanted in men by nature is to be regarded as something adventitious or imaginary, and hence, is to be rooted completely from the mind as altogether inconsistent with the spirit of our age and the progress of civilization. Yet, this inward proclivity of man to religion confirms the fact that man himself was created by God, and irrevocably tends to him. Thus we read in Augustine: "Thou hast made us for Thyself, O Lord, and our hearts are restless until they rest in Thee."[46]

215. Wherefore, whatever the progress in technology and economic life, there can be neither justice nor peace in the world, so long as men fail to realize how great is their dignity; for they have been created by God and are his children. We speak of God, who must be regarded as the first and final cause of all things he has created. Separated from God, man becomes monstrous to himself and others. Consequently, mutual relationships between men absolutely require a right ordering of the human conscience in relation to God, the source of all truth, justice, and love.

[46] *Confessions*, I, 1.

216. It is well known and recognized by everyone that in a number of countries, some of ancient Christian culture, many of our very dear brothers and sons have been savagely persecuted for a number of years. How this situation, since it reveals the great dignity of the persecuted, and the refined cruelty of their persecutors, leads many to reflect on the matter, though it has not yet healed the wounds of the persecuted.

217. However, no folly seems more characteristic of our time than the desire to establish a firm and meaningful temporal order, but without God, its necessary foundation. Likewise, some wish to proclaim the greatness of man, but with the source dried up from which such greatness flows and receives nourishment: that is, by impeding and, if it were possible, stopping the yearning of souls for God. But the turn of events in our times, whereby the hopes of many are shattered and not a few have come to grief, unquestionably confirm the words of Scripture: "Unless the Lord build the house, they labor in vain who build it."[47]

The Church's Traditional Teaching Regarding Man's Social Life

218. What the Catholic Church teaches and declares regarding the social life and relationships of men is beyond question for all time valid.

219. The cardinal point of this teaching is that individual men are necessarily the foundation, cause, and end of all social institutions. We are referring to human beings, insofar as they are social by nature, and raised to an order of existence that transcends and subdues nature.

220. Beginning with this very basic principle whereby the dignity of the human person is affirmed and defended, Holy Church—especially during the last century and with the assistance of learned priests and laymen, specialists in the field—has arrived at clear social teachings whereby the mutual relationships of men are ordered. Taking general norms into account, these principles are in accord with the nature of things and the changed conditions of man's social life, or with the special genius of our day. Moreover, these norms can be approved by all.

221. But today, more than ever, principles of this kind must not only be known and understood, but also applied to those systems and methods, which the various situations of time or place either suggest or require. This is indeed a difficult, though lofty, task. Toward its fulfillment we exhort not only our brothers and sons everywhere, but all men of good will.

---

[47] Ps 126:1.

Study of Social Matters

222. Above all, we affirm that the social teaching proclaimed by the Catholic Church cannot be separated from her traditional teaching regarding man's life.

223. Wherefore, it is our earnest wish that more and more attention be given to this branch of learning. First of all, we urge that attention be given to such studies in Catholic schools on all levels, and especially in seminaries, although we are not unaware that in some of these latter institutions this is already being done admirably. Moreover, we desire that social study of this sort be included among the religious materials used to instruct and inspire the lay apostolate, either in parishes or in associations. Let this diffusion of knowledge be accomplished by every modern means: that is, in journals, whether daily or periodical; in doctrinal books, both for the learned and the general reader; and finally, by means of radio and television.

224. We judge that our sons among the laity have much to contribute through their work and effort, that this teaching of the Catholic Church regarding the social question be more and more widely diffused. This they can do, not merely by learning it themselves and governing their actions accordingly, but also by taking special care that others also come to know its relevance.

225. Let them be fully persuaded that in no better way can they show this teaching to be correct and effective, than by demonstrating that present day social difficulties will yield to its application. In this way they will win minds today antagonistic to the teaching because they do not know it. Perhaps it will also happen that such men will find some enlightenment in the teaching.

Application of Social Teaching

226. But social norms of whatever kind are not only to be explained but also applied. This is especially true of the Church's teaching on social matters, which has truth as its guide, justice as its end, and love as its driving force.

227. We consider it, therefore, of the greatest importance that our sons, in addition to knowing these social norms, be reared according to them.

228. To be complete, the education of Christians must relate to the duties of every class. It is therefore necessary that Christians thus inspired, conform their behavior in economic and social affairs to the teachings of the Church.

229. If it is indeed difficult to apply teaching of any sort to concrete situations, it is even more so when one tries to put into practice the teaching of the Catholic Church regarding social affairs. This is especially true for the following reasons: there is deeply rooted in each man an instinctive and immoderate love of his own interests; today there is widely diffused in society a materialistic philosophy of life; it is difficult at times to discern the demands of justice in a given situation.

230. Consequently, it is not enough for men to be instructed, according to the teachings of the Church, on their obligation to act in a Christian manner in economic and social affairs. They must also be shown ways in which they can properly fulfill their duty in this regard.

231. We do not regard such instructions as sufficient, unless there be added to the work of instruction that of the formation of man, and unless some action follow upon the teaching, by way of experience.

232. Just as, proverbially, no one really enjoys liberty unless he uses it, so no one really knows how to act according to Catholic teaching in the economic and social fields, unless he acts according to this teaching in the same area.

A Task for Lay Apostolate

233. Accordingly, in popular instruction of this kind, it seems proper that considerable attention be paid to groups promoting the lay apostolate, especially those whose aim is to ensure that efforts in our present concern draw their inspiration wholly from Christian law. Seeing that members of such groups can first train themselves by daily practice in these matters, they subsequently will be able the better to instruct young people in fulfilling obligations of this kind.

234. It is not inappropriate in this connection to remind all, the great no less than the lowly, that the will to preserve moderation and to bear difficulties, by God's grace, can in no wise be separated from the meaning of life handed down to us by Christian wisdom.

235. But today, unfortunately, very many souls are preoccupied with an inordinate desire for pleasure. Such persons see nothing more important in the whole of life than to seek pleasure, to quench the thirst for pleasure. Beyond doubt, grave ills to both soul and body proceed therefrom. Now in this matter, it must be admitted that one who judges even with the aid of human nature alone, concludes that it is the part of the wise and prudent man to preserve balance and moderation in everything, and to restrain the lower appetites. He who judges matters in the light of Divine Revelation, assuredly will not overlook the fact that the Gospel of Christ and the Catholic Church, as well as the ascetical tradition handed down to us, all demand that Christians steadfastly mortify themselves and bear the inconveniences of life with singular patience. These virtues, in addition to fostering a firm and moderate rule of mind over body, also present an opportunity of satisfying the punishment due to sin, from which, except for Jesus Christ and his Immaculate Mother, no one is exempt.

Practical Suggestions

236. The teachings in regard to social matters for the most part are put into effect in the following three stages: first, the actual situation is examined; then, the situation is evaluated carefully in relation to these teachings; then only is it decided what can and should be done in order that the traditional norms may be adapted to circumstances of time and place. These three steps are at times expressed by the three words: *observe, judge, act.*

237. Hence, it seems particularly fitting that youth not merely reflect upon this order of procedure, but also, in the present connection, follow it to the extent feasible, lest what they have learned be regarded merely as something to be thought about but not acted upon.

238. However, when it comes to reducing these teachings to action, it sometimes happens that even sincere Catholic men have differing views. When this occurs they should take care to have and to show mutual esteem and regard, and to explore the extent to which they can work in cooperation among themselves. Thus they can in good time accomplish what necessity requires. Let them also take great care not to weaken their efforts in constant controversies. Nor should they, under pretext of seeking what they think best, meanwhile, fail to do what they can and hence should do.

239. But in the exercise of economic and social functions, Catholics often come in contact with men who do not share their view of life. On such occasions, those who profess Catholicism must take special care to be consistent and not compromise in matters wherein the integrity of religion or morals would suffer harm. Likewise, in their conduct they should weigh the opinions of others with fitting courtesy and not measure everything in the light of their own interests. They should be prepared to join sincerely in doing whatever is naturally good or conducive to good. If, indeed, it happens that in these matters sacred authorities have prescribed or decreed anything, it is evident that this judgment is to be obeyed promptly by Catholics. For it is the Church's right and duty not only to safeguard principles relating to the integrity of religion and morals, but also to pronounce authoritatively when it is a matter of putting these principles into effect.

Manifold Action and Responsibility

240. But what we have said about the norms of instruction should indeed be put into practice. This has special relevance for those beloved sons of ours who are in the ranks of the laity inasmuch as their activity ordinarily centers around temporal affairs and making plans for the same.

241. To carry out this noble task, it is necessary that laymen not only should be qualified, each in his own profession, and direct their energies in accordance with rules suited to the objective aimed at, but also should conform their activity to the teaching and norms of the Church in social matters. Let them put sincere trust in her wisdom; let them accept her admonitions as sons. Let them reflect that, when in the conduct of life they do not carefully observe principles and norms laid down by the Church in social matters, and which we ourselves reaffirm, then they are negligent in their duty and often injure the rights of others. At times, matters can come to a point where confidence in this teaching is diminished, as if it were indeed excellent but really lacks the force which the conduct of life requires.

* * *

Pacem in Terris
On Establishing Universal Peace in Truth, Justice, Charity and Liberty

POPE JOHN XXIII

April 11, 1963

To Our Venerable Brothers the Patriarchs, Primates, Archbishops, Bishops and Other Local Ordinaries in Peace and Communion with the Apostolic See to the Clergy and Faithful of the Whole World and to All Men of Good Will

Selections*

Introduction

Order in the Universe

Venerable Brothers and Beloved Children,
Health and Apostolic Benediction

1. Peace on earth, which all men of every era have most eagerly yearned for, can be firmly established only if the order laid down by God be dutifully observed.

2. The progress of learning and the inventions of technology clearly show that, both in living things and in the forces of nature, an astonishing order reigns, and they also bear witness to the greatness of man, who can understand that order and create suitable instruments to harness those forces of nature and use them to his benefit.

3. But the progress of science and the inventions of technology show above all the infinite greatness of God who created the universe and man himself. He created all things out of nothing, pouring into them the abundance of his wisdom and goodness, so that the holy psalmist praises God in these words: "O Lord our master, the majesty of thy name fills all the earth."[1] Elsewhere he says: "What diversity, Lord, in thy creatures! What wisdom has designed them all!"[2] God also

---

*Editor's Note: Deleted material in this document is indicated in the text by the symbol * * *.
[1]Ps 8:1.
[2]Ps 103:24.

created man in his own "image and likeness,"[3] endowed him with intelligence and freedom, and made him lord of creation, as the same psalmist declares in the words: "Thou hast placed him only a little below the angels, crowning him with glory and honor and bidding him rule over the works of thy hands. Thou hast put all under his dominion."[4]

Order in Human Beings

4. How strongly does the turmoil of individual men and peoples contrast with the perfect order of the universe! It is as if the relationships which bind them together could be controlled only by force.

5. But the Creator of the world has imprinted in man's heart an order which his conscience reveals to him and enjoins him to obey: "This shows that the obligations of the law are written in their hearts; their conscience utters its own testimony."[5] And how could it be otherwise? For whatever God has made shows forth his infinite wisdom, and it is manifested more clearly in the things which have greater perfection.[6]

6. But fickleness of opinion often produces this error, that many think that the relationships between men and states can be governed by the same laws as the forces and irrational elements of the universe, whereas the laws governing them are of quite a different kind and are to be sought elsewhere, namely, where the Father of all things wrote them, that is, in the nature of man.

7. By these laws men are most admirably taught, first of all how they should conduct their mutual dealings among themselves, then how the relationships between the citizens and the public authorities of each state should be regulated, then how states should deal with one another, and finally how, on the one hand individual men and states, and on the other hand the community of all peoples, should act towards each other, the establishment of such a community being urgently demanded today by the requirements of universal common good.

---

[3]Cf. Gn 1:26.
[4]Ps 8:6-8.
[5]Rom 2:15.
[6]Cf. Ps 18:8-11.

Part I
Order between Men

Every Man Is a Person with Rights and Duties

8. First of all, it is necessary to speak of the order which should exist between men.
9. Any human society, if it is to be well-ordered and productive, must lay down as a foundation this principle, namely, that every human being is a person, that is, his nature is endowed with intelligence and free will. Indeed, precisely because he is a person he has rights and obligations flowing directly and simultaneously from his very nature.[7] And as these rights and obligations are universal and inviolable so they cannot in any way be surrendered.
10. If we look upon the dignity of the human person in the light of divinely revealed truth, we cannot help but esteem it far more highly; for men are redeemed by the blood of Jesus Christ, they are by grace the children and friends of God and heirs of eternal glory.

Rights

The Right to Life and a Worthy Standard of Living
11. Beginning our discussion of the rights of man, we see that every man has the right to life, to bodily integrity, and to the means which are suitable for the proper development of life; these are primarily food, clothing, shelter, rest, medical care, and finally the necessary social services. Therefore a human being also has the right to security in cases of sickness, inability to work, widowhood, old age, unemployment, or in any other case in which he is deprived of the means of subsistence through no fault of his own.[8]

Rights Pertaining to Moral and Cultural Values
12. By the natural law every human being has the right to respect for his person, to his good reputation; the right to freedom in searching for truth and in expressing and communicating his opinions, and in pursuit of art, within the limits laid down by the moral order and the common good; and he has the right to be informed truthfully about public events.

---

[7]Cf. Radio Message of Pius XII, Christmas Eve, 1942, A.A.S. XXXV, 1943, pp. 9-24. Discourse of John XXIII, Jan. 4, 1963, A.A.S. LV, 1963, pp. 89-91.
[8]Cf. encyclical, *Divini Redemptoris*, Pius XI, A.A.S. XXIX, 1937, p. 78; Radio Message of Pius XII, Pentecost, June 1, 1941, A.A.S. XXXIII, 1941, pp. 195-205.

13. The natural law also gives man the right to share in the benefits of culture, and therefore the right to a basic education and to technical and professional training in keeping with the stage of educational development in the country to which he belongs. Every effort should be made to ensure that persons be enabled, on the basis of merit, to go on to higher studies, so that, as far as possible, they may occupy posts and take on responsibilities in human society in accordance with their natural gifts and the skills they have acquired.[9]

The Right to Worship God according to One's Conscience

14. This too must be listed among the rights of a human being, to honor God according to the sincere dictates of his own conscience, and therefore the right to practice his religion privately and publicly. For as Lactantius so clearly taught: "We were created for the purpose of showing to the God who bore us the submission we owe him, of recognizing him alone, and of serving him. We are obliged and bound by this duty to God; from this religion itself receives its name."[10] And on this point our predecessor of immortal memory, Leo XIII, declared:

> This genuine, this honorable freedom of the sons of God, which most nobly protects the dignity of the human person, is greater than any violence or injustice; it has always been sought by the Church, and always most dear to her. This was the freedom which the apostles claimed with intrepid constancy, which the apologists defended with their writings, and which the martyrs in such numbers consecrated with their blood.[11]

The Right to Choose Freely One's State of Life

15. Human beings have the right to choose freely the state of life which they prefer, and therefore the right to set up a family, with equal rights and duties for man and woman, and also the right to follow a vocation to the priesthood or the religious life.[12]

16. The family, grounded on marriage freely contracted, monogamous and indissoluble, is and must be considered the first and essential cell of human society. From this it follows that most careful provision must be made for the family both in economic and social matters as well as those which are of a cultural and moral nature, all of which look to the strengthening of the family and helping it carry out its function.

---

[9]Cf. Radio Message of Pius XII, Christmas Eve, 1942, A.A.S. XXXV, 1943, pp. 9-24.
[10]*Divinae Institutiones*, Book IV, Chapter 28, 2, Patrologia Latina, 6, 535.
[11]Encyclical, *Libertas Praestantissimum, Acta Leonis XIII*, VIII, 1888, pp. 237-238.
[12]Cf. Radio Message of Pius XII, Christmas Eve, 1942, A.A.S. XXXV, 1943, pp. 9-24.

17. Parents, however, have a prior right in the support and education of their children.[13]

Economic Rights

18. If we turn our attention to the economic sphere it is clear that man has a right by the natural law not only to an opportunity to work, but also to go about his work without coercion.[14]

19. To these rights is certainly joined the right to demand working conditions in which physical health is not endangered, morals are safeguarded, and young people's normal development is not impaired. Women have the right to working conditions in accordance with their requirements and their duties as wives and mothers.[15]

20. From the dignity of the human person, there also arises the right to carry on economic activities according to the degree of responsibility of which one is capable.[16] Furthermore—and this must be specially emphasized—the worker has a right to a wage determined according to criterions of justice, and sufficient, therefore, in proportion to the available resources, to give the worker and his family a standard of living in keeping with the dignity of the human person. In this regard, our predecessor Pius XII said:

> To the personal duty to work imposed by nature, there corresponds and follows the natural right of each individual to make of his work the means to provide for his own life and the lives of his children; so fundamental is the law of nature which commands man to preserve his life.[17]

21. The right to private property, even of productive goods, also derives from the nature of man. This right, as we have elsewhere declared, "is an effective means for safeguarding the dignity of the human person and for the exercise of responsibility in all fields; it strengthens and gives serenity to family life, thereby increasing the peace and prosperity of the state."[18]

22. However, it is opportune to point out that there is a social duty essentially inherent in the right of private property.[19]

---

[13]Cf. encyclical, *Casti Connubii,* Pius XI, A.A.S. XXII, 1930, pp. 539-592, Radio Message of Pius XII, Christmas Eve, 1942, A.A.S. XXXV, 1943, pp. 9-24.

[14]Cf. Radio Message of Pius XII, Pentecost, June 1, 1941, A.A.S. XXXIII, 1941, p. 201.

[15]Cf. encyclical, *Rerum Novarum,* Leo XIII, *Acta Leonis XIII,* XI, 1891, pp. 128-129.

[16]Cf. encyclical, *Mater et Magistra,* John XXIII, A.A.S. LIII, 1961, p. 422.

[17]Cf. Radio Message, Pentecost, June 1, 1941, A.A.S. XXXIII, 1941, p. 201.

[18]Encyclical, *Mater et Magistra,* A.A.S. LIII, 1961, p. 428.

[19]Cf. Ibid., p. 430.

The Right of Meeting and Association

23. From the fact that human beings are by nature social, there arises the right of assembly and association. They have also the right to give the societies of which they are members the form they consider most suitable for the aim they have in view, and to act within such societies on their own initiative and on their own responsibility in order to achieve their desired objectives.[20]

24. And, as we ourselves in the encyclical *Mater et Magistra* have strongly urged, it is by all means necessary that a great variety of organizations and intermediate groups be established which are capable of achieving a goal which an individual cannot effectively attain by himself. These societies and organizations must be considered the indispensable means to safeguard the dignity of the human person and freedom while leaving intact a sense of responsibility.[21]

The Right to Emigrate and Immigrate

25. Every human being has the right to freedom of movement and of residence within the confines of his own country; and, when there are just reasons for it, the right to emigrate to other countries and take up residence there.[22] The fact that one is a citizen of a particular state does not detract in any way from his membership in the human family as a whole, nor from his citizenship in the world community.

Political Rights

26. The dignity of the human person involves the right to take an active part in public affairs and to contribute one's part to the common good of the citizens. For, as our predecessor of happy memory, Pius XII, pointed out: "The human individual, far from being an object and, as it were, a merely passive element in the social order, is in fact, must be and must continue to be, its subject, its foundation and its end."[23]

27. The human person is also entitled to a juridical protection of his rights, a protection that should be efficacious, impartial and inspired by the true norms of justice. As our predecessor Pius XII teaches:

> That perpetual privilege proper to man, by which every individual has a claim to the protection of his rights, and by which there is assigned to each a definite and particular sphere of rights, immune

---

[20]Cf. encyclical, *Rerum Novarum*, Leo XIII, *Acta Leonis XIII*, XI, 1891, pp. 134-142; encyclical, *Quadragesimo Anno*, Pius XI, A.A.S. XXIII, 1931, pp. 199-200; encyclical, *Sertum Laetitiae*, Pius XII, A.A.S. XXXI, 1939, pp. 635-644.

[21]Cf. A.A.S. LIII, 1961, p. 430.

[22]Cf. Radio Message of Pius XII, Christmas Eve, 1952, A.A.S. XLV, 1953, pp. 33-46.

[23]Cf. Radio Message, Christmas Eve, 1944, A.A.S. XXXVII, 1945, p. 12.

from all arbitrary attacks, is the logical consequence of the order of justice willed by God.[24]

Duties

Rights and Duties Necessarily Linked in the One Person

28. The natural rights with which we have been dealing are, however, inseparably connected, in the very person who is their subject, with just as many respective duties; and rights as well as duties find their source, their sustenance and their inviolability in the natural law which grants or enjoins them.

29. Therefore, to cite a few examples, the right of every man to life is correlative with the duty to preserve it; his right to a decent standard of living with the duty of living it becomingly; and his right to investigate the truth freely, with the duty of seeking it ever more completely and profoundly.

Reciprocity of Rights and Duties between Persons

30. Once this is admitted, it also follows that in human society to one man's right there corresponds a duty in all other persons: the duty, namely, of acknowledging and respecting the right in question. For every fundamental human right draws its indestructible moral force from the natural law, which in granting it imposes a corresponding obligation. Those, therefore, who claim their own rights, yet altogether forget or neglect to carry out their respective duties, are people who build with one hand and destroy with the other.

Mutual Collaboration

31. Since men are social by nature they are meant to live with others and to work for one another's welfare. A well-ordered human society requires that men recognize and observe their mutual rights and duties. It also demands that each contribute generously to the establishment of a civic order in which rights and duties are more sincerely and effectively acknowledged and fulfilled.

32. It is not enough, for example, to acknowledge and respect every man's right to the means of subsistence if we do not strive to the best of our ability for a sufficient supply of what is necessary for his sustenance.

33. The society of men must not only be organized but must also provide them with abundant resources. This certainly requires that they observe and recognize their mutual rights and duties; it also requires that they collaborate in the many enterprises that modern civilization either allows or encourages or even demands.

---

[24]Cf. Radio Message, Christmas Eve, 1942, A.A.S. XXXV, 1943, p. 21.

An Attitude of Responsibility

34. The dignity of the human person also requires that every man enjoy the right to act freely and responsibly. For this reason, therefore, in social relations man should exercise his rights, fulfill his obligations and, in the countless forms of collaboration with others, act chiefly on his own responsibility and initiative. This is to be done in such a way that each one acts on his own decision, of set purpose and from a consciousness of his obligation, without being moved by force or pressure brought to bear on him externally. For any human society that is established on relations of force must be regarded as inhuman, inasmuch as the personality of its members is repressed or restricted, when in fact they should be provided with appropriate incentives and means for developing and perfecting themselves.

Social Life in Truth, Justice, Charity and Freedom

35. A civic society is to be considered well-ordered, beneficial and in keeping with human dignity if it is grounded on truth. As the apostle Paul exhorts us: "Away with falsehood then; let everyone speak out the truth to his neighbor; membership of the body binds us to one another."[25] This will be accomplished when each one duly recognizes both his rights and his obligations towards others. Furthermore, human society will be such as we have just described it, if the citizens, guided by justice, apply themselves seriously to respecting the rights of others and discharging their own duties; if they are moved by such fervor of charity as to make their own the needs of others and share with others their own goods: if finally, they work for a closer fellowship in the world of spiritual values. Yet this is not sufficient; for human society is bound together by freedom, that is to say, in ways and means in keeping with the dignity of its citizens, who accept the responsibility of their actions, precisely because they are by nature rational beings.

36. Therefore, venerable brothers and beloved children, human society must primarily be considered something pertaining to the spiritual. Through it, in the bright light of truth men should share their knowledge, be able to exercise their rights and fulfill their obligations, be inspired to seek spiritual values, mutually derive genuine pleasure from the beautiful of whatever order it be, always be readily disposed to pass on to others the best of their own cultural heritage and eagerly strive to make their own the spiritual achievements of others. These benefits not only influence, but at the same time give aim and scope to all that has bearing on cultural expressions, economic and social institutions, political movements and forms, laws, and all other struc-

---

[25]Eph 4: 25.

tures by which society is outwardly established and constantly developed.

God and the Moral Order

37. The order which prevails in society is by nature moral. Grounded as it is in truth, it must function according to the norms of justice, it should be inspired and perfected by mutual love, and finally it should be brought to an ever more refined and human balance in freedom.

38. Now an order of this kind, whose principles are universal, absolute and unchangeable, has its ultimate source in the one true God, who is personal and transcends human nature. Inasmuch as God is the first Truth and the highest Good, he alone is that deepest source from which human society can draw its vitality, if that society is to be well-ordered, beneficial, and in keeping with human dignity.[26] As St. Thomas Aquinas says:

> Human reason is the norm of the human will, according to which its goodness is measured, because reason derives from the eternal law which is the divine reason itself. It is evident then that the goodness of the human will depends much more on the eternal law than on human reason.[27]

Characteristics of the Present Day

39. Our age has three distinctive characteristics.

40. First of all, the working classes have gradually gained ground in economic and public affairs. They began by claiming their rights in the socioeconomic sphere; they extended their action then to claims on the political level, and finally applied themselves to the acquisition of the benefits of a more refined culture. Today, therefore, workers all over the world refuse to be treated as if they were irrational objects without freedom, to be used at the arbitrary disposition of others. They insist that they be always regarded as men with a share in every sector of human society: in the social and economic sphere, in the fields of learning and culture, and in public life.

41. Secondly, it is obvious to everyone that women are now taking a part in public life. This is happening more rapidly perhaps in nations of Christian civilization, and, more slowly but broadly, among peoples who have inherited other traditions or cultures. Since women are becoming ever more conscious of their human dignity, they will not tolerate being treated as mere material instruments, but demand rights befitting a human person both in domestic and public life.

42. Finally, in the modern world human society has taken on an entirely new appearance in the field of social and political life. For

---

[26]Radio Message of Pius XII, Christmas Eve, 1942, A.A.S. XXXV, 1943, p. 14.

[27]*Summa Theologica*, Ia-IIae, q. 19, a. 4; cf. a. 9.

since all nations have either achieved or are on the way to achieving independence, there will soon no longer exist a world divided into nations that rule others and nations that are subject to others.

43. Men all over the world have today—or will soon have—the rank of citizens in independent nations. No one wants to feel subject to political powers located outside his own country or ethnical group. Thus in very many human beings the inferiority complex which endured for hundreds and thousands of years is disappearing, while in others there is an attenuation and gradual fading of the corresponding superiority complex which had its roots in social-economic privileges, sex or political standing.

44. On the contrary, the conviction that all men are equal by reason of their natural dignity has been generally accepted. Hence racial discrimination can in no way be justified, at least doctrinally or in theory. And this is of fundamental importance and significance for the formation of human society according to those principles which we have outlined above. For, if a man becomes conscious of his rights, he must become equally aware of his duties. Thus he who possesses certain rights has likewise the duty to claim those rights as marks of his dignity, while all others have the obligation to acknowledge those rights and respect them.

45. When the relations of human society are expressed in terms of rights and duties, men become conscious of spiritual values, understand the meaning and significance of truth, justice, charity and freedom, and become deeply aware that they belong to this world of values. Moreover, when moved by such concerns, they are brought to a better knowledge of the true God who is personal and transcendent, and thus they make the ties that bind them to God the solid foundation and supreme criterion of their lives, both of that life which they live interiorly in the depths of their own souls and of that in which they are united to other men in society.

Part II
Relations between Individuals and the Public Authority within a Single State

* * *

Attainment of the Common Good Is the Purpose of the Public Authority

53. Individual citizens and intermediate groups are obliged to make their specific contributions to the common welfare. One of the chief consequences of this is that they must bring their own interests into harmony with the needs of the community, and must contribute their goods and their services as civil authorities have prescribed, in accord with the norms of justice and within the limits of their competence. Clearly then those who wield power in the state must do this by such acts which not only have been justly carried out, but which also either have the common welfare primarily in view or which can lead to it.

54. Indeed since the whole reason for the existence of civil authorities is the realization of the common good, it is clearly necessary that, in pursuing this objective, they should respect its essential elements, and at the same time conform their laws to the circumstances of the day.[37]

Essentials of the Common Good

55. Assuredly, the ethnic characteristics of the various human groups are to be respected as constituent elements of the common good,[38] but these values and characteristics by no means exhaust the content of the common good. For the common good since it is intimately bound up with human nature cannot therefore exist fully and completely unless the human person is taken into consideration and the essential nature and realization of the common good be kept in mind.[39]

56. In the second place, the very nature of the common good requires that all members of the state be entitled to share in it, although in different ways according to each one's tasks, merits and circumstances. For this reason, every civil authority must take pains to promote the common good of all, without preference for any single citizen or civic group. As our predecessor of immortal memory, Leo XIII, has said: "The civil power must not serve the advantage of any one individual, or of some few persons, inasmuch as it was established for the common good of all."[40] Considerations of justice and equity, however, can at times demand that those involved in civil government give more attention to the less fortunate members of the community, since they are less able to defend their rights and to assert their legitimate claims.[41]

57. In this context, we judge that attention should be called to the fact that the common good touches the whole man, the needs both of his body and of his soul. Hence it follows that the civil authorities

---

[37] Cf. Radio Message of Pius XII, Christmas Eve, 1942, A.A.S. XXXV, 1943, p. 13; encyclical, *Immortale Dei*, Leo XIII, *Acta Leonis XIII*, V, 1885, p. 120.
[38] Cf. encyclical, *Summi Pontificatus*, Pius XII, A.A.S. XXXI, 1939, pp. 412-453.
[39] Cf. encyclical, *Mit brennender Sorge*, Pius XI, A.A.S. XXIX, 1937, p. 159; encyclical, *Divini Redemptoris*, A.A.S. XXIX, 1937, pp. 65-106.
[40] Encyclical, *Immortale Dei, Acta Leonis XIII*, V, 1885, p. 121.
[41] Cf. encyclical, *Rerum Novarum*, Leo XIII, *Acta Leonis XIII*, XI, 1891, pp. 133-134.

must undertake to effect the common good by ways and means that are proper to them; that is, while respecting the hierarchy of values, they should promote simultaneously both the material and the spiritual welfare of the citizens.[42]

58. These principles are clearly contained in the doctrine stated in our encyclical, *Mater et Magistra*, where we emphasized that the common good of all "embraces the sum total of those conditions of social living whereby men are enabled to achieve their own integral perfection more fully and more easily."[43]

59. Men, however, composed as they are of bodies and immortal souls, can never in this mortal life succeed in satisfying all their needs or in attaining perfect happiness. Therefore the common good is to be procured by such ways and means which not only are not detrimental to man's eternal salvation but which positively contribute to it.[44]

Responsibilities of the Public Authority, and Rights and Duties of Individuals

60. It is agreed that in our time the common good is chiefly guaranteed when personal rights and duties are maintained. The chief concern of civil authorities must therefore be to ensure that these rights are acknowledged, respected, coordinated with other rights, defended and promoted, so that in this way each one may more easily carry out his duties. For "to safeguard the inviolable rights of the human person, and to facilitate the fulfillment of his duties, should be the chief duty of every public authority."[45]

61. This means that, if any government does not acknowledge the rights of man or violates them, it not only fails in its duty, but its orders completely lack juridical force.[46]

Reconciliation and Protection of Rights and Duties of Individuals

62. One of the fundamental duties of civil authorities, therefore, is to coordinate social relations in such fashion that the exercise of one man's rights does not threaten others in the exercise of their own

---

[42]Cf. encyclical, *Summi Pontificatus*, Pius XII, A.A.S. XXXI, 1939, p. 433.
[43]A.A.S. LIII, 1961, p. 19.
[44]Cf. encyclical, *Quadragesimo Anno*, Pius XI, A.A.S. XXIII, 1931, p. 215.
[45]Cf. Radio Message of Pius XII, Pentecost, June 1, 1941, A.A.S. XXXIII, 1941, p. 200.
[46]Cf. encyclical, *Mit brennender Sorge*, Pius XI, A.A.S. XXIX, 1937, p. 159; encyclical, *Divini Redemptoris*, A.A.S. XXIX, 1937, p. 79; Radio Message of Pius XII, Christmas Eve, 1942, A.A.S. XXXV, 1943, pp. 9-24.

rights nor hinder them in the fulfillment of their duties. Finally, the rights of all should be effectively safeguarded and, if they have been violated, completely restored.[47]

Duty of Promoting the Rights of Individuals

63. It is also demanded by the common good that civil authorities should make earnest efforts to bring about a situation in which individual citizens can easily exercise their rights and fulfill their duties as well. For experience has taught us that, unless these authorities take suitable action with regard to economic, political and cultural matters, inequalities between the citizens tend to become more and more widespread, especially in the modern world, and as a result human rights are rendered totally ineffective and the fulfillment of duties is compromised.

64. It is therefore necessary that the administration give wholehearted and careful attention to the social as well as to the economic progress of the citizens, and to the development, in keeping with the development of the productive system, of such essential services as the building of roads, transportation, communications, water supply, housing, public health, education, facilitation of the practice of religion, and recreational facilities. It is necessary also that governments make efforts to see that insurance systems are made available to the citizens, so that, in case of misfortune or increased family responsibilities, no person will be without the necessary means to maintain a decent standard of living. The government should make similarly effective efforts to see that those who are able to work can find employment in keeping with their aptitudes, and that each worker receives a wage in keeping with the laws of justice and equity. It should be equally the concern of civil authorities to ensure that workers be allowed their proper responsibility in the work undertaken in industrial organization, and to facilitate the establishment of intermediate groups which will make social life richer and more effective. Finally, it should be possible for all the citizens to share as far as they are able in their country's cultural advantages.

Harmonious Relation between Public Authority's Two Forms of Intervention

65. The common good requires that civil authorities maintain a careful balance between coordinating and protecting the rights of the citizens, on the one hand, and promoting them, on the other. It

[47]Cf. encyclical, *Divini Redemptoris*, Pius XI, A.A.S. XXIX, 1937, p. 81; Radio Message of Pius XII, Christmas Eve, 1942, A.A.S. XXXV, 1943, pp. 9-24.

should not happen that certain individuals or social groups derive special advantage from the fact that their rights have received preferential protection. Nor should it happen that governments in seeking to protect these rights, become obstacles to their full expression and free use.

> For this principle must always be retained: that state activity in the economic field, no matter what its breadth or depth may be, ought not to be exercised in such a way as to curtail an individual's freedom of personal initiative. Rather it should work to expand that freedom as much as possible by the effective protection of the essential personal rights of each and every individual.[48]

66. The same principle should inspire the various steps which governments take in order to make it possible for the citizens more easily to exercise their rights and fulfill their duties in every sector of social life.

* * *

Part III
Relations between States

Subjects of Rights and Duties

80. Our predecessors have constantly maintained, and we join them in reasserting, that nations are reciprocally subjects of rights and duties. This means that their relationships also must be harmonized in truth, in justice, in a working solidarity, in liberty. The same natural law, which governs relations between individual human beings, serves also to regulate the relations of nations with one another.
81. This is readily clear to anyone if he would consider that the heads of states can in no way put aside their natural dignity while they represent their country and provide for its welfare, and that they are never allowed to depart from the natural law by which they are bound and which is the norm of their conduct.
82. Moreover, it is inconceivable that men because they are heads of government are forced to put aside their human endowments. On the contrary, they occupy this place of eminence for the very reason that they have earned a reputation as outstanding members of the

[48]Encyclical, *Mater et Magistra*, John XXIII, A.A.S. LIII, 1961, p. 415.

body politic in view of their excellent intellectual endowments and accomplishments.

83. Indeed it follows from the moral order itself that authority is necessary for civil society, for civil society is ruled by authority; and that authority cannot be used to thwart the moral order without instantly collapsing because its foundation has been destroyed. This is the warning of God himself:

> A word, then, for the kings' ears to hear, kings' hearts to heed: a message for you, rulers, wherever you be! Listen well, all you that have multitudes at your command, foreign hordes to do your bidding. Power is none but comes to you from the Lord, nor any royalty but from One who is above all. He it is that will call you to account for your doings with a scrutiny that reads your inmost thoughts.[53]

84. Lastly it is to be borne in mind that also in the regulating of relations between states, authority is to be exercised for the achievement of the common good, which constitutes the reason for its existence.

85. But a fundamental factor of the common good is acknowledgment of the moral order and exact observance of its commands.

> A well established order among nations must be built upon the unshakable and unchangeable rock of the moral law, made manifest in the order of nature by the Creator himself and by him engraved on the hearts of men with letters that can never be effaced. . . . Like the rays of a gleaming beacon, its principles must guide the plans and policies of men and nations. From its signals, which give warning and point out the safe and sure course, they must get their norms and guidance if they would not see all their laborious efforts to establish a new order condemned to tempest and shipwreck.[54]

In Truth

86. First among the rules governing the relations between states is that of truth. This calls, above all, for the elimination of every trace of racism, and the consequent recognition of the principle that all states are by nature equal in dignity. Each of them accordingly is vested with the right to existence, to self-development, to the means fitting to its attainment, and to be the one primarily responsible for this self-development. Add to that the right of each to its good name, and to the respect which is its due.

---

[53]Wis 6:1-4.

[54]Cf. Radio Message of Pius XII, Christmas Eve, 1941, A.A.S. XXIV, 1942, p. 16.

87. Very often, experience has taught us, individuals will be found to differ enormously, in knowledge, power, talent and wealth. From this, however, no justification is ever found for those who surpass the rest to subject others to their control in any way. Rather they have a more serious obligation which binds each and everyone to lend mutual assistance to others in their efforts for improvement.
88. Likewise it can happen that one country surpasses another in scientific progress, culture and economic development. But this superiority, far from permitting it to rule others unjustly, imposes the obligation to make a greater contribution to the general development of the people.
89. In fact, men cannot by nature be superior to others since all enjoy an equal natural dignity. From this it follows that countries too do not differ at all from one another in the dignity which they derive from nature. Individual states are like a body whose members are human beings. Furthermore, we know from experience that nations are wont to be very sensitive in all matters which in any way concern their dignity and honor, and rightly so.
90. Truth further demands that the various media of social communications made available by modern progress, which enable the nations to know each other better, be used with serene objectivity. That need not, of course, rule out any legitimate emphasis on the positive aspects of their way of life. But methods of information which fall short of the truth, and by the same token impair the reputation of this people or that, must be discarded.[55]

In Justice

91. Relations between nations are to be further regulated by justice. This implies, over and above recognition of their mutual rights, the fulfillment of their respective duties.
92. Since nations have a right to exist, to develop themselves, to acquire a supply of the resources necessary for their development, to defend their good name and the honor due to them, it follows that they are likewise bound by the obligation of effectively guarding each of these rights and of avoiding those actions by which these rights can be jeopardized. As men in their private enterprises cannot pursue their own interests to the detriment of others, so too states cannot lawfully seek that development of their own resources which brings harm to other states and unjustly oppresses them. This statement of St. Augustine seems to be very apt in this regard: "What are king-

[55]Cf. Radio Message of Pius XII, Christmas Eve, 1940, A.A.S. XXXIII, 1941, pp. 5-14.

doms without justice but large bands of robbers?"[56]

93. Not only can it happen, but it actually does happen that the advantages and conveniences which nations strive to acquire for themselves become objects of contention; nevertheless, the resulting disagreements must be settled, not by force, nor by deceit or trickery, but rather in the only manner which is worthy of the dignity of man, i.e., by a mutual assessment of the reasons on both sides of the dispute, by a mature and objective investigation of the situation, and by an equitable reconciliation of differences of opinion.

The Treatment of Minorities

94. Closely related to this point is the political trend which since the nineteenth century has gathered momentum and gained ground everywhere, namely, the striving of people of the same ethnic group to become independent and to form one nation. Since this cannot always be accomplished for various reasons, the result is that minorities often dwell within the territory of a people of another ethnic group, and this is the source of serious problems.

95. In the first place, it must be made clear that justice is seriously violated by whatever is done to limit the strength and numerical increase of these lesser peoples; the injustice is even more serious if vicious attempts of this kind are aimed at the very extinction of these groups.

96. It is especially in keeping with the principles of justice that effective measures be taken by the civil authorities to improve the lot of the citizens of an ethnic minority, particularly when that betterment concerns their language, the development of their natural gifts, their ancestral customs, and their accomplishments and endeavors in the economic order.[57]

97. It should be noted, however, that these minority groups, either because of their present situation which they are forced to endure, or because of past experiences, are often inclined to exalt beyond due measure anything proper to their own people, and to such a degree as to look down on things common to all mankind as if the welfare of the human family must yield to the good of their own ethnic group. Reason rather demands that these very people recognize also the advantages that accrue to them from their peculiar circumstances; for instance, no small contribution is made toward the development of their particular talents and spirit by their daily dealings with people

---

[56]*De civitate Dei*, Book IV, Chapter 4; Patrologia Latina, 41, 115; cf. Radio Message of Pius XII, Christmas Eve, 1939, A.A.S. XXXII, 1940, pp. 5-13.

[57]Cf. Radio Message of Pius XII, Christmas Eve, 1941, A.A.S. XXXIV, 1942, pp. 10-21.

who have grown up in a different culture since from this association they can gradually make their own the excellence which belongs to the other ethnic group. But this will happen only if the minorities through association with the people who live around them make an effort to share in their customs and institutions. Such, however, will not be the case if they sow discord which causes great damage and hinders progress.

Active Solidarity

98. Since the mutual relations among nations must be regulated by the norm of truth and justice, they must also derive great advantage from an energetic union of mind, heart and resources. This can be effected at various levels by mutual cooperation in many ways, as is happening in our own time with beneficial results in the economic, social, political, educational, public health and sports spheres. We must remember that, of its very nature, civil authority exists, not to confine its people within the boundaries of their nation, but rather to protect, above all else, the common good of that particular civil society, which certainly cannot be divorced from the common good of the entire human family.

99. So it happens that civil societies in pursuing their interests not only must not harm others, but must join their plans and forces whenever the efforts of an individual government cannot achieve its desired goals; but in the execution of such common efforts, great care must be taken lest what helps some nations should injure others.

100. Furthermore, the universal common good requires that in every nation friendly relations be fostered in all fields between the citizens and their intermediate societies. Since in many parts of the world there are groups of people of varying ethnic backgrounds, we must be on our guard against isolating one ethnic group from its fellow men. This is clearly inconsistent with modern conditions since distances which separate people from each other have been almost wiped out. Neither are we to overlook the fact that men of every ethnic group, in addition to their own characteristic endowments by which they are distinguished from the rest of men, have other important gifts of nature in common with their fellow men by which they can make more and more progress and perfect themselves, particularly in matters that pertain to the spirit. They have the right and duty therefore to live in communion with one another.

The Proper Balance between Population, Land and Capital

101. Everyone certainly knows that in some parts of the world there is an imbalance between the amount of arable land and the size of

the population, and in other parts between the fertility of the soil and available farm implements. Consequently, necessity demands a cooperative effort on the part of the people to bring about a quicker exchange of goods, or of capital, or the migration of people themselves.
102. In this case we think it is most opportune that as far as possible employment should seek the worker, not vice versa. For then most citizens have an opportunity to increase their holdings without being forced to leave their native environment and seek a new home with many a heartache, and adopt a new state of affairs and make new social contacts with other citizens.

* * *

In Liberty

120. It has also to be borne in mind that relations between states should be based on freedom, that is to say, that no country may unjustly oppress others or unduly meddle in their affairs. On the contrary, all should help to develop in others a sense of responsibility, a spirit of enterprise, and an earnest desire to be the first to promote their own advancement in every field.

The Evolution of Economically Underdeveloped Countries

121. Because all men are joined together by reason of their common origin, their redemption by Christ, and their supernatural destiny, and are called to form one Christian family, we appealed in the encyclical *Mater et Magistra* to economically developed nations to come to the aid of those which were in the process of development.[61]
122. We are greatly consoled to see how widely that appeal has been favorably received; and we are confident that even more so in the future it will contribute to the end that the poorer countries, in as short a time as possible, will arrive at that degree of economic development which will enable every citizen to live in conditions more in keeping with his human dignity.
123. But it is never sufficiently repeated that the cooperation, to which reference has been made, should be effected with the greatest respect for the liberty of the countries being developed, for these must realize that they are primarily responsible, and that they are the principal artisans in the promotion of their own economic development and social progress.
124. Our predecessor Pius XII already proclaimed that

---

[61]A.A.S. LIII, 1961, pp. 440-441.

> in the field of a new order founded on moral principles, there is no room for violation of freedom, integrity and security of other nations, no matter what may be their territorial extension or their capacity for defense. It is inevitable that the powerful states, by reason of their greater potential and their power, should pave the way in the establishment of economic groups comprising not only themselves but also smaller and weaker states as well. It is nevertheless indispensable that in the interests of the common good they, as all others, should respect the rights of those smaller states to political freedom, to economic development and to the adequate protection, in the case of conflicts between nations, of that neutrality which is theirs according to the natural, as well as international, law. In this way, and in this way only, will they be able to obtain a fitting share of the common good, and assure the material and spiritual welfare of their people.[62]

125. It is vitally important, therefore, that the wealthier states, in providing varied forms of assistance to the poorer, should respect the moral values and ethnic characteristics peculiar to each, and also that they should avoid any intention of political domination. If this is done, "a precious contribution will be made towards the formation of a world community, a community in which each member, whilst conscious of its own individual rights and duties, will work in a relationship of equality towards the attainment of the universal common good."[63]

Signs of the Times

126. Men are becoming more and more convinced that disputes which arise between states should not be resolved by recourse to arms, but rather by negotiation.

127. We grant indeed that this conviction is chiefly based on the terrible destructive force of modern weapons and a fear of the calamities and frightful destruction which such weapons would cause. Therefore, in an age such as ours which prides itself on its atomic energy it is contrary to reason to hold that war is now a suitable way to restore rights which have been violated.

128. Nevertheless, unfortunately, the law of fear still reigns among peoples, and it forces them to spend fabulous sums for armaments, not for aggression they affirm—and there is no reason for not believing them—but to dissuade others from aggression.

129. There is reason to hope, however, that by meeting and negotiating, men may come to discover better the bonds that unite them

---

[62]Cf. Radio Message, Christmas Eve, 1941, A.A.S. XXXIV, 1942, pp. 16-17.
[63]Encyclical, *Mater et Magistra*, John XXIII, A.A.S. LIII, 1961, p. 443.

together, deriving from the human nature which they have in common; and that they may also come to discover that one of the most profound requirements of their common nature is this: that between them and their respective peoples it is not fear which should reign but love, a love which tends to express itself in a collaboration that is loyal, manifold in form and productive of many benefits.

* * *

Introduction to Gaudium et Spes

Gaudium et Spes, II Vatican Council's *Pastoral Constitution on the Church in the Modern World,* epitomizes in many ways the spirit and breadth of vision present at the Council. The Council Fathers completely discarded the original draft of the document and mandated a new commission to produce a draft reflecting the Church's growing pastoral engagement with victims of injustice. Indeed, economic injustice is a major concern of the document that the commission eventually formulated and the Council approved. The tone of *Gaudium et Spes* and its principles of morality in economic life echo closely the teachings of the two popes who guided the Council's work, John XXIII and Paul VI.

It is important to notice what *Gaudium et Spes* does not say. The Council Fathers deliberately refrained from speaking about *a* Catholic social doctrine because it was necessary to maintain a certain flexibility. If the Catholic social teaching is to apply to the diverse social situations throughout the world, the Church can have no monolithic doctrine on economics or any comprehensive, rigid program for securing economic justice. The Council clearly heard the voices of non-Western Catholics uneasy with much of the individualism in Western capitalist economies and who likewise saw little relevance for *Rerum Novarum*'s organic model in their lands. The message of *Gaudium et Spes* is loud and clear: the Church must remain open in terms of basic economic models.

The issue of private property represents another important aspect of *Gaudium et Spes'* perspective on economics. The Council did not posit any direct link between private property and natural law. In other words, no Catholic may argue, according to II Vatican, that private property is an inherent right of every individual. This is significant because it opens the door for Catholic participation in more socialist models of government. On this point *Gaudium et Spes* stands somewhat closer to Paul VI than to John XXIII. Although John said that the right of private property carries with it a corresponding social duty, he did include private property in his charter of economic rights in *Pacem in Terris. Gaudium et Spes* has a different emphasis. The Fathers assign great importance to the access "of both individuals and communities to some control over material goods," but add: "The right of private control, however, is not opposed to the right inherent in various forms of public ownership. . . . By its very nature, private property has a social quality deriving from the law of the communal purpose of earthly goods."

The communitarian ideal is a strong motif in *Gaudium et Spes*. The human person is to be respected in his or her own right; the Council sees personal dignity as an outgrowth of the reality of the Incarnation. We cannot stop there in our understanding of humanity, however. Full human dignity can be attained only in a communitarian setting. Community is integral to the authentic self-definition of every person. This communitarian emphasis is not mere theological speculation. It has central implications for the organization of international economic life. It is the basis for the sense of interdependence that must pervade economic relations among nations. It is the motivating force for the Council's challenge to rich countries to find ways of helping less developed ones.

Several other elements of *Gaudium et Spes'* economic teaching deserve mention. The principle of subsidiarity is reaffirmed in the call for more coordinated and effective international economic structures; economic injustice is credited as a cause of war; and notice is taken of economic problems in the realm of agriculture. This last point is of particular interest. Although several social encyclicals, including *Mater et Magistra,* allude to the increasing economic difficulties farmers face in both developed and developing nations, many church people believe that rural life has received insufficient attention. Catholic social teaching has focused almost exclusively on the urban poor.

Gaudium et Spes

Pastoral Constitution on the Church in the Modern World

Paul, Bishop,
Servant of the Servants of God
Together with the Fathers
of the Sacred Council

December 7, 1965

Selections*

* * *

Part I
The Church and Man's Calling

* * *

Chapter II
The Community of Mankind

23. One of the salient features of the modern world is the growing interdependence of men one on the other, a development promoted chiefly by modern technical advances. Nevertheless brotherly dialogue among men does not reach its perfection on the level of technical progress, but on the deeper level of interpersonal relationships. These demand a mutual respect for the full spiritual dignity of the person. Christian revelation contributes greatly to the promotion of this communion between persons, and at the same time leads us to a deeper understanding of the laws of social life which the Creator has written into man's moral and spiritual nature.

Since rather recent documents of the Church's teaching authority have dealt at considerable length with Christian doctrine about human society,[1] this council is merely going to call to mind some of the more

*Editor's Note: Deleted material in this document is indicated in the text by the symbol * * *.

[1]Cf. John XXIII, encyclical letter, *Mater et Magistra*, May 15, 1961; A.A.S. 53 (1961), pp. 401-464; John XXIII, encyclical letter *Pacem in Terris*, April 11, 1963: A.A.S. 55 (1963), pp. 257-304; Paul VI, encyclical letter, *Ecclesiam Suam*, Aug. 6, 1964: A.A.S. 54 (1964), pp. 609-659.

basic truths, treating their foundations under the light of revelation. Then it will dwell more at length on certain of their implications having special significance for our day.

24. God, who has fatherly concern for everyone, has willed that all men should constitute one family and treat one another in a spirit of brotherhood. For having been created in the image of God, who "from one man has created the whole human race and made them live all over the face of the earth" (Acts 17:26), all men are called to one and the same goal, namely God himself.

For this reason, love for God and neighbor is the first and greatest commandment. Sacred Scripture, however, teaches us that the love of God cannot be separated from love of neighbor: "If there is any other commandment, it is summed up in this saying: Thou shalt love thy neighbor as thyself. . . . Love therefore is the fulfillment of the Law" (Rom 13:9, 10; cf. 1 Jn 4:20). To men growing daily more dependent on one another, and to a world becoming more unified every day, this truth proves to be of paramount importance.

Indeed, the Lord Jesus, when he prayed to the Father, "that all may be one . . . as we are one" (Jn 17:21, 22) opened up vistas closed to human reason, for he implied a certain likeness between the union of the divine Persons, and the unity of God's sons in truth and charity. This likeness reveals that man, who is the only creature on earth which God willed for itself, cannot fully find himself except through a sincere gift of himself.[2]

25. Man's social nature makes it evident that the progress of the human person and the advance of society itself hinge on one another. For the beginning, the subject and the goal of all social institutions is and must be the human person, which for its part and by its very nature stands completely in need of social life.[3] Since this social life is not something added on to man, through his dealings with others, through reciprocal duties, and through fraternal dialogue he develops all his gifts and is able to rise to his destiny.

Among those social ties which man needs for his development some, like the family and political community, relate with greater immediacy to his innermost nature; others originate rather from his free decision. In our era, for various reasons, reciprocal ties and mutual dependencies increase day by day and give rise to a variety of associations and organizations, both public and private. This development, which is called socialization, while certainly not without its dangers, brings with it many advantages with respect to consolidating

---

[2]Cf. Lk 17:33.
[3]Cf. St. Thomas, 1 *Ethica Lect.* 1.

and increasing the qualities of the human person, and safeguarding his rights.[4]

But if by this social life the human person is greatly aided in responding to his destiny, even in its religious dimensions, it cannot be denied that men are often diverted from doing good and spurred toward evil by the social circumstances in which they live and are immersed from their birth. To be sure the disturbances which so frequently occur in the social order result in part from the natural tensions of economic, political and social forms. But at a deeper level they flow from man's pride and selfishness, which contaminate even the social sphere. When the structure of affairs is flawed by the consequences of sin, man, already born with a bent toward evil, finds there new inducements to sin, which cannot be overcome without strenuous efforts and the assistance of grace.

26. Every day human interdependence tightens and spreads by degrees over the whole world. As a result the common good, that is, the sum of those conditions of social life which allow social groups and their individual members relatively thorough and ready access to their own fulfillment, today takes on an increasingly universal complexion and consequently involves rights and duties with respect to the whole human race. Every social group must take account of the needs and legitimate aspirations of other groups, and even of the general welfare of the entire human family.[5]

At the same time, however, there is a growing awareness of the exalted dignity proper to the human person, since he stands above all things, and his rights and duties are universal and inviolable. Therefore, there must be made available to all men everything necessary for leading a life truly human, such as food, clothing, and shelter; the right to choose a state of life freely and to found a family, the right to education, to employment, to a good reputation, to respect, to appropriate information, to activity in accord with the upright norm of one's own conscience, to protection of privacy and to rightful freedom, even in matters religious.

Hence, the social order and its development must always work to the benefit of the human person if the disposition of affairs is to be subordinate to the personal realm and not contrariwise, as the Lord indicated when he said that the Sabbath was made for man, and not man for the Sabbath.[6]

This social order requires constant improvement. It must be founded on truth, built on justice and animated by love; in freedom it should

[4]Cf. John XXIII, encyclical letter, *Mater et Magistra:* A.A.S. 53 (1961), p. 418. Cf. Pius XI, encyclical letter, *Quadragesimo Anno:* A.A.S. 23 (1931), p. 222 ff.
[5]Cf. John XXIII, encyclical letter, *Mater et Magistra:* A.A.S. 53 (1961).
[6]Cf. Mk 2:27.

grow every day toward a more human balance.[7] An improvement in attitudes and numerous changes in society will have to take place if these objectives are to be gained.

God's Spirit, who with a marvelous providence directs the unfolding of time and renews the face of the earth, is not absent from this development. The ferment of the Gospel too has aroused and continues to arouse in man's heart the irresistible requirements of his dignity.

27. Coming down to practical and particularly urgent consequences, this council lays stress on reverence for man; everyone must consider his every neighbor without exception as another self, taking into account first of all his life and the means necessary to living it with dignity,[8] so as not to imitate the rich man who had no concern for the poor man Lazarus.[9]

In our times a special obligation binds us to make ourselves the neighbor of every person without exception, and of actively helping him when he comes across our path, whether he be an old person abandoned by all, a foreign laborer unjustly looked down upon, a refugee, a child born of an unlawful union and wrongly suffering for a sin he did not commit, or a hungry person who disturbs our conscience by recalling the voice of the Lord, "As long as you did it for one of these the least of my brethren, you did it for me" (Mt 25:40).

Furthermore, whatever is opposed to life itself, such as any type of murder, genocide, abortion, euthanasia, or wilful self-destruction, whatever violates the integrity of the human person, such as mutilation, torments inflicted on body or mind, attempts to coerce the will itself; whatever insults human dignity, such as subhuman living conditions, arbitrary imprisonment, deportation, slavery, prostitution, the selling of women and children; as well as disgraceful working conditions, where men are treated as mere tools for profit, rather than as free and responsible persons; all these things and others of their like are infamies indeed. They poison human society, but they do more harm to those who practice them than those who suffer from the injury. Moreover, they are a supreme dishonor to the Creator.

28. Respect and love ought to be extended also to those who think or act differently than we do in social, political and even religious matters. In fact, the more deeply we come to understand their ways of thinking through such courtesy and love, the more easily will we be able to enter into dialogue with them.

This love and good will, to be sure, must in no way render us indifferent to truth and goodness. Indeed love itself impels the dis-

---

[7]Cf. John XXIII, encyclical letter, *Pacem in Terris:* A.A.S. 55 (1963), p. 266.
[8]Cf. Jas 2:15-16.
[9]Cf. Lk 16:19-31.

ciples of Christ to speak the saving truth to all men. But it is necessary to distinguish between error, which always merits repudiation, and the person in error, who never loses the dignity of being a person even when he is flawed by false or inadequate religious notions.[10] God alone is the judge and searcher of hearts; for that reason he forbids us to make judgments about the internal guilt of anyone.[11]

The teaching of Christ even requires that we forgive injuries,[12] and extends the law of love to include every enemy, according to the command of the New Law: "You have heard that it was said: Thou shalt love thy neighbor and hate thy enemy. But I say to you: love your enemies, do good to those who hate you, and pray for those who persecute and calumniate you" (Mt 5:43, 44).

29. Since all men possess a rational soul and are created in God's likeness, since they have the same nature and origin, have been redeemed by Christ and enjoy the same divine calling and destiny, the basic equality of all must receive increasingly greater recognition.

True, all men are not alike from the point of view of varying physical power and the diversity of intellectual and moral resources. Nevertheless, with respect to the fundamental rights of the person, every type of discrimination, whether social or cultural, whether based on sex, race, color, social condition, language or religion, is to be overcome and eradicated as contrary to God's intent. For in truth it must still be regretted that fundamental personal rights are not yet being universally honored. Such is the case of a woman who is denied the right to choose a husband freely, to embrace a state of life or to acquire an education or cultural benefits equal to those recognized for men.

Therefore, although rightful differences exist between men, the equal dignity of persons demands that a more humane and a just condition of life be brought about. For excessive economic and social differences between the members of the one human family or population groups cause scandal, and militate against social justice, equity, the dignity of the human person, as well as social and international peace.

Human institutions, both private and public, must labor to minister to the dignity and purpose of man. At the same time let them put up a stubborn fight against any kind of slavery, whether social or political, and safeguard the basic rights of man under every political system. Indeed human institutions themselves must be accommodated by degrees to the highest of all realities, spiritual ones, even

---

[10]Cf. John XXIII, encyclical letter, *Pacem in Terris:* A.A.S. 55 (1963), pp. 299-300.
[11]Cf. Lk 6:37-38; Mt 7:1-2; Rom 2:1-11; 14:10-12.
[12]Cf. Mt 5:43-47.

though meanwhile, a long enough time will be required before they arrive at the desired goal.

30. Profound and rapid changes make it more necessary that no one ignoring the trend of events or drugged by laziness, content himself with a merely individualistic morality. It becomes increasingly true that the obligations of justice and love are fulfilled only if each person, contributing to the common good, according to his own abilities and the needs of others, also promotes and assists the public and private institutions dedicated to bettering the conditions of human life. Yet there are those who, while professing grand and rather noble sentiments, nevertheless in reality live always as if they cared nothing for the needs of society. Many in various places even make light of social laws and precepts, and do not hesitate to resort to various frauds and deceptions in avoiding just taxes or other debts due to society. Others think little of certain norms of social life, for example those designed for the protection of health, or laws establishing speed limits; they do not even avert to the fact that by such indifference they imperil their own life and that of others.

Let everyone consider it his sacred obligation to esteem and observe social necessities as being among the primary duties of modern man. For the more unified the world becomes, the more plainly do the offices of men extend beyond particular groups and spread by degrees to the whole world. But this development cannot occur unless individual men and their associations cultivate in themselves the moral and social virtues, and promote them in society; thus, with the needed help of Divine Grace men who are truly new and artisans of a new humanity can be forthcoming.

31. Individual men, in order to discharge with greater exactness the obligations of their conscience toward themselves and the various groups to which they belong, must be carefully educated to a higher degree of culture through the use of the immense resources available today to the human race. Above all the education of youth from every social background has to be undertaken, so that there can be produced not only men and women of refined talents, but those great-souled persons who are so desperately required by our times.

Now a man can scarcely arrive at the needed sense of responsibility, unless his living conditions allow him to become conscious of his dignity, and to rise to his destiny by spending himself for God and for others. But human freedom is often crippled when a man encounters extreme poverty, just as it withers when he indulges in too many of life's comforts and imprisons himself in a kind of splendid isolation. Freedom acquires new strength, by contrast, when a man consents to the unavoidable requirements of social life, takes on the manifold demands of human partnership, and commits himself to the service of the human community.

Hence, the will to play one's role in common endeavors should be everywhere encouraged. Praise is due to those national processes which allow the largest possible number of citizens to participate in public affairs with genuine freedom. Account must be taken, to be sure, of the actual conditions of each people and the firmness required by public authority. If every citizen is to feel inclined to take part in the activities of the various groups which make up the social body, these must offer advantages which will attract members and dispose them to serve others. We can justly consider that the future of humanity lies in the hands of those who are strong enough to provide coming generations with reasons for living and hoping.

32. As God did not create man for life in isolation, but for the formation of social unity, so also "it has pleased God to make men holy and save them not merely as individuals, without bond or link between them, but by making them into a single people, a people which acknowledges him in truth and serves him in holiness."[13] So from the beginning of salvation history he has chosen men not just as individuals but as members of a certain community. Revealing his mind to them, God called these chosen ones "his people" (Ex 3:7, 12), and even made a covenant with them on Sinai.[14]

This communitarian character is developed and consummated in the work of Jesus Christ. For the very Word made flesh willed to share in the human fellowship. He was present at the wedding of Cana, visited the house of Zachaeus, ate with publicans and sinners. He revealed the love of the Father and the sublime vocation of man in terms of the most common of social realities and by making use of the speech and imagery of plain everyday life. Willingly obeying the laws of his country, he sanctified those human ties, especially family ones, which are the foundation of social structures. He chose to lead the life proper to an artisan of his time and place.

In his preaching he clearly taught the sons of God to treat one another as brothers. In his prayers he pleaded that all his disciples might be "one." Indeed as the Redeemer of all, he offered himself for all even to the point of death. "Greater love than this no one has, that one lay down his life for his friends" (Jn 15:13). He commanded his apostles to preach to all peoples the Gospel's message that the human race was to become the Family of God, in which the fullness of the Law would be love.

As the firstborn of many brethren and by the giving of his Spirit, he founded after his death and resurrection a new brotherly community composed of all those who receive him in faith and in love.

---

[13]Cf. *Dogmatic Constitution on the Church*, Chapter II, n. 9: A.A.S. 57 (1965), pp. 12-13.
[14]Cf. Ex 24:1-8.

This he did through his Body, which is the Church. There everyone, as members one of the other, would render mutual service according to the different gifts bestowed on each.

This solidarity must be constantly increased until that day on which it will be brought to perfection. Then, saved by grace, men will offer flawless glory to God as a family beloved of God and of Christ their brother.

Chapter III
Man's Activity throughout the World

33. Through his labors and his native endowments man has ceaselessly striven to better his life. Today, however, especially with the help of science and technology, he has extended his mastery over nearly the whole of nature and continues to do so. Thanks to increased opportunities for many kinds of social contact among nations, the human family is gradually recognizing that it comprises a single world community and is making itself so. Hence many benefits once looked for, especially from heavenly powers, man has now enterprisingly procured for himself.

In the face of these immense efforts which already preoccupy the whole human race, men raise numerous questions among themselves. What is the meaning and value of this feverish activity? How should all these things be used? To the achievement of what goal are the strivings of individuals and societies heading? The Church guards the heritage of God's Word and draws from it moral and religious principles without always having at hand the solution to particular problems. As such she desires to add the light of revealed truth to mankind's store of experience, so that the path which humanity has taken in recent times will not be a dark one.

34. Throughout the course of the centuries, men have labored to better the circumstances of their lives through a monumental amount of individual and collective effort. To believers, this point is settled: considered in itself, this human activity accords with God's will. For man, created to God's image, received a mandate to subject to himself the earth and all it contains, and to govern the world with justice and holiness;[1] a mandate to relate himself and the totality of things to him who was to be acknowledged as the Lord and Creator of all. Thus, by the subjection of all things to man, the name of God would be wonderful in all the earth.[2]

This mandate concerns the whole range of everyday activity as well. For while providing the substance of life for themselves and

---

[1]Cf. Gn 1:26-27; 9:2-3; Wis 9:3.
[2]Cf. Ps 8: 7, 10.

their families, men and women are performing their activities in a way which appropriately benefits society. They can justly consider that by their labor they are unfolding the Creator's work, consulting the advantages of their brother men, and are contributing by their personal industry to the realization in history of the divine plan.[3]

Thus, far from thinking that works produced by man's own talent and energy are in opposition to God's power, and that the rational creature exists as a kind of rival to the Creator, Christians are convinced that the triumphs of the human race are a sign of God's grace and the flowering of his own mysterious design. For the greater man's power becomes, the further his individual and community responsibility extends. Hence it is clear that men are not deterred by the Christian message from building up the world, or impelled to neglect the welfare of their fellows, but that they are rather more stringently bound to do these very things.[4]

35. Human activity, to be sure, takes its significance from its relationship to man. Just as it proceeds from man, so it is ordered toward man. For when a man works he not only alters things and society, he develops himself as well. He learns much, he cultivates his resources, he goes outside of himself and beyond himself. Rightly understood, this kind of growth is of greater value than any external riches which can be garnered. A man is more precious for what he is than for what he has.[5] Similarly, all that men do to obtain greater justice, wider brotherhood, a more humane ordering of social relationships has greater worth than technical advances. For these advances can supply the material for human progress, but of themselves alone they can never actually bring it about.

Hence, the norm of human activity is this: that in accord with the divine plan and will, it harmonize with the genuine good of the human race, and that it allow men as individuals and as members of society to pursue their total vocation and fulfill it.

36. Now many of our contemporaries seem to fear that a closer bond between human activity and religion will work against the independence of men, of societies, or of the sciences.

If by the autonomy of earthly affairs we mean that created things and societies themselves enjoy their own laws and values which must be gradually deciphered, put to use, and regulated by men, then it is entirely right to demand that autonomy. This is not merely required by modern man, but harmonizes also with the will of the Creator. For by the very circumstance of their having been created, all things

---

[3]Cf. John XXIII, encyclical letter, *Pacem in Terris:* A.A.S. 55 (1963), p. 297.
[4]Cf. Message to all mankind sent by the Fathers at the beginning of the Second Vatican Council, Oct. 20, 1962: A.A.S. 54 (1962), p. 823.
[5]Cf. Paul VI, Address to the Diplomatic Corps, Jan. 7, 1965: A.A.S. 57 (1965), p. 232.

are endowed with their own stability, truth, goodness, proper laws and order. Man must respect these as he isolates them by the appropriate methods of the individual sciences or arts. Therefore if methodical investigation within every branch of learning is carried out in a genuinely scientific manner and in accord with moral norms, it never truly conflicts with faith, for earthly matters and the concerns of faith derive from the same God.[6] Indeed whoever labors to penetrate the secrets of reality with a humble and steady mind, even though he is unaware of the fact, is nevertheless being led by the hand of God, who holds all things in existence, and gives them their identity. Consequently, we cannot but deplore certain habits of mind, which are sometimes found too among Christians, which do not sufficiently attend to the rightful independence of science and which, from the arguments and controversies they spark, lead many minds to conclude that faith and science are mutually opposed.[7]

But if the expression, the autonomy of temporal affairs, is taken to mean that created things do not depend on God, and that man can use them without any reference to their Creator, anyone who acknowledges God will see how false such a meaning is. For without the Creator the creature would disappear. For their part, however, all believers of whatever religion always hear his revealing voice in the discourse of creatures. When God is forgotten, however, the creature itself grows unintelligible.

37. Sacred Scripture teaches the human family what the experience of the ages confirms: that while human progress is a great advantage to man, it brings with it a strong temptation. For when the order of values is jumbled and bad is mixed with the good, individuals and groups pay heed solely to their own interests, and not to those of others. Thus it happens that the world ceases to be a place of true brotherhood. In our own day, the magnified power of humanity threatens to destroy the race itself.

For a monumental struggle against the powers of darkness pervades the whole history of man. The battle was joined from the very origins of the world and will continue until the last day, as the Lord has attested.[8] Caught in this conflict, man is obliged to wrestle constantly if he is to cling to what is good, nor can he achieve his own integrity without great efforts and the help of God's grace.

That is why Christ's church, trusting in the design of the Creator, acknowledges that human progress can serve man's true happiness, yet she cannot help echoing the apostle's warning: "Be not conformed

---

[6]Cf. First Vatican Council, *Dogmatic Constitution on the Catholic Faith,* Chapter III: Denz. 1785-1786 (3004-3005).
[7]Cf. Msgr. Pio Paschini, Vita e Opere di Galileo Galilei, 2 volumes, Vatican Press (1964).
[8]Cf. Mt 24:13; 13:24-30, 36-43.

to this world" (Rom 12:2). Here by the world is meant that spirit of vanity and malice which transforms into an instrument of sin those human energies intended for the service of God and man.

Hence if anyone wants to know how this unhappy situation can be overcome, Christians will tell him that all human activity, constantly imperiled by man's pride and deranged self-love, must be purified and perfected by the power of Christ's cross and resurrection. For redeemed by Christ and made a new creature in the Holy Spirit, man is able to love the things themselves created by God, and ought to do so. He can receive them from God and respect and reverence them as flowing constantly from the hand of God. Grateful to his benefactor for these creatures, using and enjoying them in detachment and liberty of spirit, man is led forward into a true possession of them, as having nothing, yet possessing all things.[9] "All are yours, and you are Christ's and Christ is God's" (1 Cor 3:22-23).

38. For God's Word, through whom all things were made was himself made flesh and dwelt on man's earth.[10] Thus he entered the world's history as a perfect man, taking that history up into himself and summarizing it.[11] He himself revealed to us that "God is love" (1 Jn 4:8) and at the same time taught us that the new command of love was the basic law of human perfection and hence of the world's transformation.

To those, therefore, who believe in divine love, he gives assurance that the way of love lies open to men and that the effort to establish a universal brotherhood is not a hopeless one. He cautions them at the same time that this love is not something to be reserved for important matters, but must be pursued chiefly in the ordinary circumstances of life. Undergoing death itself for all of us sinners,[12] he taught us by example that we too must shoulder that cross which the world and the flesh inflict upon those who search after peace and justice. Appointed Lord by his resurrection and given all power in heaven and on earth,[13] Christ is now at work in the hearts of men through the energy of his Spirit, arousing not only a desire for the age to come, but by that very fact animating, purifying and strengthening those noble longings too by which the human family makes its life more human and strives to render the whole earth submissive to this goal.

Now, the gifts of the Spirit are diverse: while he calls some to give clear witness to the desire for a heavenly home and to keep that desire fresh among the human famiy, he summons others to dedicate

---

[9]Cf. 2 Cor 6:10.
[10]Cf. Jn 1:3, 14.
[11]Cf. Eph 1:10.
[12]Cf. Jn 3:6; Rom 5: 8-10.
[13]Cf. Acts 2:36; Mt 28:18.

themselves to the earthly service of men and to make ready the material of the celestial realm by this ministry of theirs. Yet he frees all of them so that by putting aside love of self and bringing all earthly resources into the service of human life they can devote themselves to that future when humanity itself will become an offering accepted by God.[14]

The Lord left behind a pledge of this hope and strength for life's journey in that sacrament of faith where natural elements refined by man are gloriously changed into his Body and Blood, providing a meal of brotherly solidarity and a foretaste of the heavenly banquet.

39. We do not know the time for the consummation of the earth and of humanity,[15] nor do we know how all things will be transformed. As deformed by sin, the shape of this world will pass away;[16] but we are taught that God is preparing a new dwelling place and a new earth where justice will abide,[17] and whose blessedness will answer and surpass all the longings for peace which spring up in the human heart.[18] Then, with death overcome, the sons of God will be raised up in Christ, and what was sown in weakness and corruption will be clothed with incorruptibility.[19] Enduring with charity and its fruits,[20] all that creation[21] which God made on man's account will be unchained from the bondage of vanity.

Therefore, while we are warned that it profits a man nothing if he gain the whole world and lose himself,[22] the expectation of a new earth must not weaken but rather stimulate our concern for cultivating this one. For here grows the body of a new human family, a body which even now is able to give some kind of foreshadowing of the new age.

Hence, while earthly progress must be carefully distinguished from the growth of Christ's Kingdom, to the extent that the former can contribute to the better ordering of human society, it is of vital concern to the Kingdom of God.[23]

For after we have obeyed the Lord, and in his Spirit nurtured on earth the values of human dignity, brotherhood and freedom, and indeed all the good fruits of our nature and enterprise, we will find them again, but freed of stain, burnished and transfigured, when Christ hands over to the Father: "a kingdom eternal and universal,

---

[14]Cf. Rom 15:16.
[15]Cf. Acts 1:7.
[16]Cf. 1 Cor 7:31; St. Irenaeus, *Adversus haereses*, V, 36, PG, VIII, 1221.
[17]Cf. 2 Cor 5:2; 2 Pt 3:13.
[18]Cf. 1 Cor 2:9; Rv 21:4-5.
[19]Cf. 1 Cor 15:42, 53.
[20]Cf. 1 Cor 13:8; 3:14.
[21]Cf. Rom 8:19-21.
[22]Cf. Lk 9:25.
[23]Cf. Pius XI, encyclical letter, *Quadragesimo Anno:* A.A.S. 23 (1931).

a kingdom of truth and life, of holiness and grace, of justice, love and peace."[24] On this earth that Kingdom is already present in mystery. When the Lord returns it will be brought into full flower.

* * *

Part II
Some Problems of Special Urgency

* * *

Chapter III
Economic and Social Life

63. In the economic and social realms, too, the dignity and complete vocation of the human person and the welfare of society as a whole are to be respected and promoted. For man is the source, the center, and the purpose of all economic and social life.

Like other areas of social life, the economy of today is marked by man's increasing domination over nature, by closer and more intense relationships between citizens, groups, and countries and their mutual dependence, and by the increased intervention of the state. At the same time progress in the methods of production and in the exchange of goods and services has made the economy an instrument capable of better meeting the intensified needs of the human family.

Reasons for anxiety, however, are not lacking. Many people, especially in economically advanced areas, seem, as it were, to be ruled by economics, so that almost their entire personal and social life is permeated with a certain economic way of thinking. Such is true both of nations that favor a collective economy and of others. At the very time when the development of economic life could mitigate social inequalities (provided that it be guided and coordinated in a reasonable and human way), it is often made to embitter them; or, in some places, it even results in a decline of the social status of the underprivileged and in contempt for the poor. While an immense number of people still lack the absolute necessities of life, some, even in less advanced areas, live in luxury or squander wealth. Extravagance and wretchedness exist side by side. While a few enjoy very great power of choice, the majority are deprived of almost all possibility of acting on their own initiative and responsibility, and often subsist in living and working conditions unworthy of the human person.

---

[24]Preface of the Feast of Christ the King.

A similar lack of economic and social balance is to be noticed between agriculture, industry, and the services, and also between different parts of one and the same country. The contrast between the economically more advanced countries and other countries is becoming more serious day by day, and the very peace of the world can be jeopardized thereby.

Our contemporaries are coming to feel these inequalities with an ever sharper awareness, since they are thoroughly convinced that the ampler technical and economic possibilities which the world of today enjoys can and should correct this unhappy state of affairs. Hence, many reforms in the socioeconomic realm and a change of mentality and attitude are required of all. For this reason the Church down through the centuries and in the light of the Gospel has worked out the principles of justice and equity demanded by right reason both for individual and social life and for international life, and she has proclaimed them especially in recent times. This Sacred Council intends to strengthen these principles according to the circumstances of this age and to set forth certain guidelines, especially with regard to the requirements of economic development.[1]

Section I Economic Development

64. Today more than ever before attention is rightly given to the increase of the production of agricultural and industrial goods and of the rendering of services, for the purpose of making provision for the growth of population and of satisfying the increasing desires of the human race. Therefore, technical progress, an inventive spirit, an eagerness to create and to expand enterprises, the application of methods of production, and the strenuous efforts of all who engage in production—in a word, all the elements making for such development—must be promoted. The fundamental purpose of this production is not the mere increase of products nor profit or control but rather the service of man, and indeed of the whole man with regard for the full range of his material needs and the demands of his intellectual, moral, spiritual, and religious life; this applies to every man whatsoever and to every group of men, of every race and of every part of the world. Consequently, economic activity is to be carried on according to its own methods and laws within the limits of the

[1]Cf. Pius XII, address on March 23, 1952: AAS 44 (1953), p. 273; John XXIII, Allocution to the Catholic Association of Italian Workers, May 1, 1959: AAS 51 (1959), p. 358.

moral order,[2] so that God's plan for mankind may be realized.[3]

65. Economic development must remain under man's determination and must not be left to the judgment of a few men or groups possessing too much economic power or of the political community alone or of certain more powerful nations. It is necessary, on the contrary, that at every level the largest possible number of people and, when it is a question of international relations, all nations have an active share in directing that development. There is need as well of the coordination and fitting and harmonious combination of the spontaneous efforts of individuals and of free groups with the undertakings of public authorities.

Growth is not to be left solely to a kind of mechanical course of economic activity of individuals, nor to the authority of government. For this reason, doctrines which obstruct the necessary reforms under the guise of a false liberty, and those which subordinate the basic rights of individual persons and groups to the collective organization of production must be shown to be erroneous.[4]

Citizens, on the other hand, should remember that it is their right and duty, which is also to be recognized by the civil authority, to contribute to the true progress of their own community according to their ability. Especially in underdeveloped areas, where all resources must urgently be employed, those who hold back their unproductive resources or who deprive their community of the material or spiritual aid that it needs—saving the personal right of migration—gravely endanger the common good.

66. To satisfy the demands of justice and equity, strenuous efforts must be made, without disregarding the rights of persons or the natural qualities of each country, to remove as quickly as possible the immense economic inequalities, which now exist and in many cases are growing and which are connected with individual and social discrimination. Likewise, in many areas, in view of the special difficulties of agriculture relative to the raising and selling of produce, country people must be helped both to increase and to market what they produce, and to introduce the necessary development and renewal and also obtain a fair income. Otherwise, as too often happens, they

---

[2]Cf. Pius XI, encyclical letter, *Quadragesimo Anno:* AAS 23 (1931), p. 190 ff. Pius XII, address of March 23, 1952: AAS 44 (1952), p. 276 ff; John XXIII, encyclical letter, *Mater et Magistra:* AAS 53 (1961), p. 450; Vatican Council II, *Decree on the Media of Social Communication*, chapter I, n. 6: AAS 56 (1964), p. 147.

[3]Cf. Mt 16:26; Lk 16:1-31; Col 3:17.

[4]Cf. Leo XIII, encyclical letter, *Libertas*, in *Acta Leonis XIII*, t. VIII, p. 220 ff; Pius XI, encyclical letter, *Quadragesimo Anno:* AAS 23 (1931), p. 191 ff; Pius XI, encyclical letter, *Divini Redemptoris:* AAS 39 (1937), p. 65 ff; Pius XII, *Nuntius natalicius 1941:* AAS 34 (1942), p. 10 ff; John XXIII, encyclical letter, *Mater et Magistra:* AAS 53 (1961), pp. 401-464.

will remain in the condition of lower-class citizens. Let farmers themselves, especially young ones, apply themselves to perfecting their professional skill, for without it, there can be no agricultural advance.[5]

Justice and equity likewise require that the mobility, which is necessary in a developing economy, be regulated in such a way as to keep the life of individuals and their families from becoming insecure and precarious. When workers come from another country or district and contribute to the economic advancement of a nation or region by their labor, all discrimination as regards wages and working conditions must be carefully avoided. All the people, moreover, above all the public authorities, must treat them not as mere tools of production but as persons, and must help them to bring their families to live with them and to provide themselves with a decent dwelling; they must also see to it that these workers are incorporated into the social life of the country or region that receives them. Employment opportunities, however, should be created in their own areas as far as possible.

In economic affairs which today are subject to change, as in the new forms of industrial society in which automation, for example, is advancing, care must be taken that sufficient and suitable work and the possibility of the appropriate technical and professional formation are furnished. The livelihood and the human dignity especially of those who are in very difficult conditions because of illness or old age must be guaranteed.

Section II Certain Principles Governing Socioeconomic Life as a Whole

67. Human labor which is expended in the production and exchange of goods or in the performance of economic services is superior to the other elements of economic life, for the latter have only the nature of tools.

This labor, whether it is engaged in independently or hired by someone else, comes immediately from the person, who as it were stamps the things of nature with his seal and subdues them to his will. By his labor a man ordinarily supports himself and his family, is joined to his fellow men and serves them, and can exercise genuine charity and be a partner in the work of bringing divine creation to perfection. Indeed, we hold that through labor offered to God man is associated with the redemptive work of Jesus Christ, who conferred an eminent dignity on labor when at Nazareth he worked with his own hands. From this there follows for every man the duty of work-

---

[5]In reference to agricultural problems cf. especially John XXIII, encyclical letter, *Mater et Magistra:* AAS 53 (1961), p. 341 ff.

ing faithfully and also the right to work. It is the duty of society, moreover, according to the circumstances prevailing in it, and in keeping with its role, to help the citizens to find sufficient employment. Finally, remuneration for labor is to be such that man may be furnished the means to cultivate worthily his own material, social, cultural, and spiritual life and that of his dependents, in view of the function and productiveness of each one, the conditions of the factory or workshop, and the common good.[6]

Since economic activity for the most part implies the associated work of human beings, any way of organizing and directing it which might be detrimental to any working men and women would be wrong and inhuman. It happens too often, however, even in our days, that workers are reduced to the level of being slaves to their own work. This is by no means justified by the so-called economic laws. The entire process of productive work, therefore, must be adapted to the needs of the person and to his way of life, above all to his domestic life, especially in respect to mothers of families, always with due regard for sex and age. The opportunity, moreover, should be granted to workers to unfold their own abilities and personality through the performance of their work. Applying their time and strength to their employment with a due sense of responsibility, they should also all enjoy sufficient rest and leisure to cultivate their familial, cultural, social and religious life. They should also have the opportunity freely to develop the energies and potentialities which perhaps they cannot bring to much fruition in their professional work.

68. In economic enterprises it is persons who are joined together, that is, free and independent human beings created to the image of God. Therefore, taking account of the prerogatives of each—owners or employers, management or labor—and without doing harm to the necessary unity of management, the active sharing of all in the administration and profits of these enterprises in ways to be properly determined should be promoted.[7] Since more often, however, decisions concerning economic and social conditions, on which the future lot of the workers and of their children depends, are made not within

---

[6]Cf. Leo XIII, encyclical letter, *Rerum Novarum:* AAS 23 (1890-91), p. 649, p. 662; Pius XI, encyclical letter, *Quadragesimo Anno:* AAS 23 (1931), pp. 200-201; Pius XI, encyclical letter, *Divini Redemptoris:* AAS 29 (1937), p. 92; Pius XII, Radio Address on Christmas Eve, 1942: AAS 35 (1943), p. 20; Pius XII, allocution of June 13, 1943: AAS 35 (1943), p. 172; Pius XII, Radio Address to the Workers of Spain, March 11, 1951: AAS 43 (1951), p. 215; John XXIII, encyclical letter, *Mater et Magistra:* AAS 53 (1961), p. 419.

[7]Cf. John XXIII, encyclical letter, *Mater et Magistra:* AAS 53 (1961), pp. 408, 424, 427; however, the word *curatione* has been taken from the Latin text of the encyclical letter, *Quadragesimo Anno:* AAS 23 (1931), p. 199. Under the aspect of the evolution of the question cf. also: Pius XII, allocution of June 3, 1950: AAS 42 (1950), pp. 485-488; Paul VI, allocution of June 8, 1964: AAS 56 (1964), pp. 574-579.

the business itself but by institutions on a higher level, the workers themselves should have a share also in determining these conditions—in person or through freely elected delegates.

Among the basic rights of the human person is to be numbered the right of freely founding unions for working people. These should be able truly to represent them and to contribute to the organizing of economic life in the right way. Included is the right of freely taking part in the activity of these unions without risk of reprisal. Through this orderly participation joined to progressive economic and social formation, all will grow day by day in the awareness of their own function and responsibility, and thus they will be brought to feel that they are comrades in the whole task of economic development and in the attainment of the universal common good according to their capacities and aptitudes.

When, however, socioeconomic disputes arise, efforts must be made to come to a peaceful settlement. Although recourse must always be had first to a sincere dialogue between the parties, the strike, nevertheless, can remain even in present-day circumstances a necessary, though ultimate, means for the defense of the workers' own rights and the fulfillment of their just desires. As soon as possible, however, ways should be sought to resume negotiations and discussions leading toward reconciliation.

69. God intended the earth with everything contained in it for the use of all human beings and peoples. Thus, under the guidance of justice together with charity, created goods should be in abundance for all in an equitable manner.[8] Whatever the forms of property may be, as adapted to the legitimate institutions of peoples, according to diverse and changeable circumstances, attention must always be paid to this universal goal of earthly goods. In using them, therefore, man should regard the external things that he legitimately possesses not only as his own but also as common in the sense that they should be able to benefit not only him but also others as well.[9] On the other hand, the right of having a share of earthly goods sufficient for oneself and one's family belongs to everyone. The Fathers and Doctors of the Church held this opinion, teaching that men are obliged to come to the relief of the poor and to do so not merely out of their super-

---

[8]Cf. Pius XII, encyclical, *Sertum Laetitiae:* AAS 31 (1939), p. 642; John XXIII, consistorial allocution: AAS 52 (1960), pp. 5-11; John XXIII, encyclical letter, *Mater et Magistra:* AAS 53 (1961), p. 411.

[9]Cf. St. Thomas, *Summa Theologica:* II-II, q. 32, a. 5 ad 2; Ibid. q. 66, a. 2: cf. explanation in Leo XIII, encyclical letter, *Rerum Novarum:* AAS 23 (1890-91) p. 651; cf. also Pius XII, allocution of June 1, 1941: AAS 33 (1941), p. 199; Pius XII, birthday radio address 1954: AAS 47 (1955), p. 27.

fluous goods.[10] If one is in extreme necessity, he has the right to procure for himself what he needs out of the riches of others.[11] Since there are so many people prostrate with hunger in the world, this Sacred Council urges all, both individuals and governments, to remember the aphorism of the Fathers, "Feed the man dying of hunger, because if you have not fed him, you have killed him,"[12] and really to share and use their earthly goods, according to the ability of each, especially by supporting individuals or peoples with the aid by which they may be able to help and develop themselves.

In economically less advanced societies the common destination of earthly goods is partly satisfied by means of the customs and traditions proper to the community, by which the absolute essentials are furnished to each member. An effort must be made, however, to avoid regarding certain customs as altogether unchangeable, if they no longer answer the new needs of this age. On the other hand, imprudent action should not be taken against respectable customs which, provided they are suitably adapted to present-day circumstances, do not cease to be very useful. Similarly in highly developed nations a body of social institutions dealing with protection and security can, for its own part, bring to reality the common destination of earthly goods. Family and social services, especially those that provide for culture and education, should be further promoted. When all these things are being organized, vigilance is necessary to prevent the citizens from being led into a certain inertia vis-à-vis society or from rejecting the burden of taking up office or from refusing to serve.

---

[10] Cf. St. Basil, *Hom. in illud Lucae "Destruam horrea mea,"* n. 2 (PG 31, 263); Lactantius, *Divinarum institutionum*, lib. V. on justice (PL 6, 565 B); St. Augustine, *In Ioann. Ev.* tr. 50, n. 6 (PL 35, 1760); St. Augustine, *Enarratio in Ps.* CXLVII, 12 (PL 37, 192); St. Gregory the Great, *Homiliae in Ev.*, hom. 20 (PL 76, 1165); St. Gregory the Great, *Regulae Pastoralis liber*, pars III, c. 21 (PL 77, 87); St. Bonaventure, *In III Sent.* d. 33, dub. 1 (ed Quaracchi, III, 728); St. Bonaventure, *In IV Sent.* d. 15, p. II, a.2 q.1 (ed. cit. IV, 371 b); q. *de superfluo* (ms. Assisi, Bibl. Comun. 186, ff. 112ª-113ª); St. Albert the Great, *In III Sent.*, d. 33, a.3, sol. 1 (ed. Borgnet XXVIII, 611); Id. *In IV Sent.* d. 15, a. 16 (ed. cit. XXIX, 494-497). As for the determination of what is superfluous in our day and age, cf. John XXIII, radio-television message of Sept. 11, 1962: AAS 54 (1962) p. 682: "The obligation of every man, the urgent obligation of the Christian man, is to reckon what is superfluous by the measure of the needs of others, and to see to it that the administration and the distribution of created goods serve the common good."

[11] In that case, the old principle holds true: "In extreme necessity all goods are common, that is, all goods are to be shared." On the other hand, for the order, extension, and manner by which the principle is applied in the proposed text, besides the modern authors: cf. St. Thomas, *Summa Theologica* II-II, q. 66, a. 7. Obviously, for the correct application of the principle, all the conditions that are morally required must be met.

[12] Cf. Gratian, *Decretum*, C. 21, dist. LXXXVI (ed. Friedberg I, 302). This axiom is also found already in PL 54, 591 A (cf. in Antonianum 27 (1952) 349-366).

70. Investments, for their part, must be directed toward providing employment and sufficient income for the people both now and in the future. Whoever make decisions concerning these investments and the planning of the economy—whether they be individuals or groups or public authorities—are bound to keep these objectives in mind and to recognize their serious obligation of making sure, on the one hand, that provision be made for the necessities required for a decent life both of individuals and of the whole community and, on the other, of looking out for the future and of establishing a proper balance between the needs of present-day consumption, both individual and collective, and the demands of investing for the generation to come. They should also always bear in mind the urgent needs of underdeveloped countries or regions. In monetary matters they should beware of hurting the welfare of their own country or of other countries. Care should also be taken lest the economically weak countries unjustly suffer any loss from a change in the value of money.

71. Since property and other forms of private ownership of external goods contribute to the expression of the personality, and since, moreover, they furnish one an occasion to exercise his function in society and in the economy, it is very important that the access of both individuals and communities to some ownership of external goods be fostered.

Private property or some ownership of external goods confers on everyone a sphere wholly necessary for the autonomy of the person and the family, and it should be regarded as an extension of human freedom. Lastly, since it adds incentives for carrying on one's function and duty, it constitutes one of the conditions for civil liberties.[13]

The forms of such ownership of property are varied today and are becoming increasingly diversified. They all remain, however, a cause of security not to be underestimated, in spite of social funds, rights, and services provided by society. This is true not only of material goods but also of intangible goods such as professional skills.

The right of private ownership, however, is not opposed to the right inherent in various forms of public property. Goods can be transferred to the public domain only by the competent authority, according to the demands and within the limits of the common good, and with fair compensation. Furthermore, it is the right of public

---

[13]Cf. Leo XIII, encyclical letter, *Rerum Novarum:* AAS 23 (1890-91), pp. 643-646; Pius XI, encyclical letter, *Quadragesimo Anno:* AAS 23 (1931), p. 191; Pius XII, Radio Message of June 1, 1941: AAS 33 (1941), p. 199; Pius XII, Radio Message on Christmas Eve 1942: AAS 35 (1943), p. 17; Pius XII, Radio Message of Sept. 1, 1944: AAS 36 (1944), p. 253; John XXIII, encyclical letter, *Mater et Magistra:* AAS 53 (1961), pp. 428-429.

authority to prevent anyone from misusing his private property to the detriment of the common good.[14]

By its very nature private property has a social quality which is based on the law of the common destination of earthly goods.[15] If this social quality is overlooked, property often becomes an occasion of a passionate desire for wealth and serious disturbances, so that a pretext is given to those who attack private property for calling the right itself into question.

In many underdeveloped regions there are large or even extensive rural estates which are only slightly cultivated or lie completely idle for the sake of profit, while the majority of the people either are without land or have only very small fields, and, on the other hand, it is evidently urgent to increase the productivity of the fields. Not infrequently those who are hired to work for the landowners or who till a portion of the land as tenants receive a wage or income unworthy of a human being, lack decent housing and are exploited by middlemen. Deprived of all security, they live under such personal servitude that almost every opportunity of acting on their own initiative and responsibility is denied to them and all advancement in human culture and all sharing in social and political life is forbidden to them. According to different circumstances, therefore, reforms are necessary: that income may grow, working conditions should be improved, security in employment increased, and an incentive to working on one's own initiative given. Indeed, insufficiently cultivated estates should be distributed to those who can make these lands fruitful; in this case, the necessary ways and means, especially educational aids and the right facilities for cooperative organization, must be supplied. Whenever, nevertheless, the common good requires expropriation, compensation must be reckoned in equity after all the circumstances have been weighed.

72. Christians who take an active part in present-day socioeconomic development and fight for justice and charity should be convinced that they can make a great contribution to the prosperity of mankind and to the peace of the world. In these activities let them, either as individuals or as members of groups, give a shining example. Having acquired the skills and experience which are absolutely necessary, they should observe the right order in their earthly activities in faithfulness to Christ and his Gospel. Thus their whole life, both individual and social, will be permeated with the spirit of the beatitudes, notably with a spirit of poverty.

---

[14]Cf. Pius XI, encyclical letter, *Quadragesimo Anno:* AAS 23 (1931), p. 214; John XXIII, encyclical letter, *Mater et Magistra:* AAS 53 (1961), p. 429.
[15]Cf. Pius XII, Radio Message of Pentecost 1941: AAS 44 (1941), p. 199; John XXIII, encyclical letter, *Mater et Magistra:* AAS 53 (1961), p. 430.

Whoever in obedience to Christ seeks first the Kingdom of God, takes therefrom a stronger and purer love for helping all his brethren and for perfecting the work of justice under the inspiration of charity.[16]

* * *

Chapter V
The Fostering of Peace and the Promotion of a Community of Nations

Section II Setting up an International Community

83. In order to build up peace the causes of discord among men, especially injustice, which foment wars must above all be rooted out. Not a few of these causes come from excessive economic inequalities and from putting off the steps needed to remedy them. Other causes of discord, however, have their source in the desire to dominate and in a contempt for persons. And, if we look for deeper causes, we find them in human envy, distrust, pride, and other egotistical passions. Man cannot bear so many ruptures in the harmony of things. Consequently, the world is constantly beset by strife and violence between men, even when no war is being waged. Besides, since these same evils are present in the relations between various nations as well, in order to overcome or forestall them and to keep violence once unleashed within limits, it is absolutely necessary for countries to cooperate to better advantage, to work together more closely, and jointly to organize international bodies and to work tirelessly for the creation of organizations which will foster peace.

84. In view of the increasingly close ties of mutual dependence today between all the inhabitants and peoples of the earth, the fitting pursuit and effective realization of the universal common good now require of the community of nations that it organize itself in a manner suited to its present responsibilities, especially toward the many parts of the world which are still suffering from unbearable want.

To reach this goal, organizations of the international community, for their part, must make provision for men's different needs, both in the fields of social life—such as food supplies, health, education, labor and also in certain special circumstances which can crop up here and there; e.g., the need to promote the general improvement of

---

[16]For the right use of goods according to the doctrine of the New Testament, cf. Lk 3:11; 10: 30 ff; 11:41; 1 Pt 5:3; Mk 8:36; 12:39-41; Jas 5:1-6; 1 Tm 6:8; Eph 4:28; 2 Cor 8:13; 1 Jn 3:17 ff.

developing countries, or to alleviate the distressing conditions in which refugees dispersed throughout the world find themselves, or also to assist migrants and their families.

International and regional organizations which are already in existence are certainly well-deserving of the human race. These are the first efforts at laying the foundations on an international level for a community of all men to work for the solution to the serious problems of our times, to encourage progress everywhere, and to obviate wars of whatever kind. In all of these activities the Church rejoices in the spirit of true brotherhood flourishing between Christians and non-Christians as it strives to make ever more strenuous efforts to relieve widespread misery.

85. The present solidarity of mankind also calls for a revival of greater international cooperation in the economic field. Although nearly all peoples have become autonomous, they are far from being free of every form of undue dependence, and far from escaping all danger of serious internal difficulties.

The development of a nation depends on human and financial aids. The citizens of each country must be prepared by education and professional training to discharge the various tasks of economic and social life. But this in turn requires the aid of foreign specialists who, when they give aid, will not act as overlords, but as helpers and fellow workers. Developing nations will not be able to procure material assistance unless radical changes are made in the established procedures of modern world commerce. Other aid should be provided as well by advanced nations in the form of gifts, loans or financial investments. Such help should be accorded with generosity and without greed on the one side, and received with complete honesty on the other side.

If an authentic economic order is to be established on a worldwide basis, an end will have to be put to profiteering, to national ambition, to the appetite for political supremacy, to militaristic calculations, and to machinations for the purpose of spreading and imposing ideologies.

86. The following norms seem useful for such cooperation:

a) Developing nations should take great pains to seek as the object of progress to express and secure the total human fulfillment of their citizens. They should bear in mind that progress arises and grows above all out of the labor and genius of the nations themselves because it has to be based, not only on foreign aid, but especially on the full utilization of their own resources, and on the development of their own culture and traditions. Those who exert the greatest influence on others should be outstanding in this respect.

b) On the other hand, it is a very important duty of the advanced nations to help the developing nations in discharging their above-mentioned responsibilities. They should therefore gladly carry out on their own home front those spiritual and material readjustments that are required for the realization of this universal cooperation.

Consequently, in business dealings with weaker and poorer nations, they should be careful to respect their welfare, for these countries need the income they receive on the sale of their home-made products to support themselves.

c) It is the role of the international community to coordinate and promote development, but in such a way that the resources ear-marked for this purpose will be allocated as effectively as possible, and with complete equity. It is likewise this community's duty, with due regard for the principle of subsidiarity, so to regulate economic relations throughout the world that these will be carried out in accordance with the norms of justice.

Suitable organizations should be set up to foster and regulate international business affairs, particularly with the underdeveloped countries, and to compensate for losses resulting from an excessive inequality of power among the various nations. This type of organization, in unison with technical, cultural, and financial aid, should provide the help which developing nations need so that they can advantageously pursue their own economic advancement.

d) In many cases there is an urgent need to revamp economic and social structures. But one must guard against proposed technical solutions that are untimely. This is particularly true of those solutions providing man with material conveniences, which are nevertheless contrary to man's spiritual nature and advancement. For "not by bread alone does man live, but by every word which proceeds from the mouth of God" (Mt 4:4). Every sector of the family of man carries within itself and in its best traditions some portion of the spiritual treasure entrusted by God to humanity, even though many may not be aware of the source from which it comes.

87. International cooperation is needed today especially for those peoples who, besides facing so many other difficulties, likewise undergo pressures due to a rapid increase in population. There is an urgent need to explore, with the full and intense cooperation of all, and especially of the wealthier nations, ways whereby the human necessities of food and a suitable education can be furnished and shared with the entire human community. But some peoples could greatly improve upon the conditions of their life if they would change over from antiquated methods of farming to the new technical methods, applying them with needed prudence according to their own circumstances. Their life would likewise be improved by the establishment of a better social order and by a fairer system for the distribution of land ownership.

Governments undoubtedly have rights and duties, within the limits of their proper competency, regarding the population problem in their respective countries, for instance, with regard to social and family life legislation, or with regard to the migration of country-dwellers to the cities, or with respect to information concerning the condition and needs of the country. Since men today are giving thought to this problem and are so greatly disturbed over it, it is desirable in addition that Catholic specialists, especially in the universities, skillfully pursue and develop studies and projects on all these matters.

But there are many today who maintain that the increase in world population, or at least the population increase in some countries, must be radically curbed by every means possible and by any kind of intervention on the part of public authority. In view of this contention, the council urges everyone to guard against solutions, whether publicly or privately supported, or at times even imposed, which are contrary to the moral law. For in keeping with man's inalienable right to marry and generate children, the decision concerning the number of children they will have depends on the correct judgment of the parents and it cannot in any way be left to the judgment of public authority. But since the judgment of the parents presupposes a rightly formed conscience, it is of the utmost importance that the way be open for everyone to develop a correct and genuinely human responsibility which respects the divine law and takes into consideration the circumstances of the place and the time. But sometimes this requires an improvement in educational and social conditions, and, above all, formation in religion or at least a complete moral training. Men should judiciously be informed, furthermore, of scientific advances in exploring methods whereby spouses can be helped in regulating the number of their children and whose safeness has been well proven and whose harmony with the moral order has been ascertained.

88. Christians should cooperate willingly and wholeheartedly in establishing an international order that includes a genuine respect for all freedoms and amicable brotherhood between all. This is all the more pressing since the greater part of the world is still suffering from so much poverty that it is as if Christ himself were crying out in these poor to beg the charity of the disciples. Do not let men, then, be scandalized because some countries with a majority of citizens who are counted as Christians have an abundance of wealth, whereas others are deprived of the necessities of life and are tormented with hunger, disease,and every kind of misery. The spirit of poverty and charity are the glory and witness of the Church of Christ.

Those Christians are to be praised and supported, therefore, who volunteer their services to help other men and nations. Indeed, it is the duty of the whole People of God, following the word and example of the bishops, to alleviate as far as they are able the sufferings of the modern age. They should do this too, as was the ancient custom in the Church, out of the substance of their goods, and not only out of what is superfluous.

The procedure of collecting and distributing aid, without being inflexible and completely uniform, should nevertheless be carried on in an orderly fashion in dioceses, nations, and throughout the entire world. Wherever it seems fitting, this activity of Catholics should be carried on in unison with other Christian brothers. For the spirit of charity does not forbid, but on the contrary commands that charitable activity be carried out in a careful and orderly manner. Therefore, it is essential for those who intend to dedicate themselves to the service of the developing nations to be properly trained in appropriate institutes.

89. Since, in virtue of her mission received from God, the Church preaches the Gospel to all men and dispenses the treasures of grace, she contributes to the ensuring of peace everywhere on earth and to the placing of the fraternal exchange between men on solid ground by imparting knowledge of the divine and natural law. Therefore, to encourage and stimulate cooperation among men, the Church must be clearly present in the midst of the community of nations, both through her official channels and through the full and sincere collaboration of all Christians—a collaboration motivated solely by the desire to be of service to all.

This will come about more effectively if the faithful themselves, conscious of their responsibility as men and as Christians, will exert their influence in their own milieu to arouse a ready willingness to cooperate with the international community. Special care must be given, in both religious and civic education, to the formation of youth in this regard.

90. An outstanding form of international activity on the part of Christians is found in the joint efforts which, both as individuals and in groups, they contribute to institutes already established or to be established for the encouragement of cooperation among nations. There are also various Catholic associations on the international level which can contribute in many ways to the building up of a peaceful and fraternal community of nations. These should be strengthened by augmenting in them the number of well qualified collaborators, by increasing needed resources, and by a suitable coordination of their forces. For today both effective action and the need for dialogue demand joint projects. Moreover, such associations contribute much to the development of a universal outlook—something certainly appropriate for Catholics. They also help to form an awareness of genuine universal solidarity and responsibility.

Finally, it is very much to be desired that Catholics, in order to fulfill their role properly in the international community, should seek to cooperate actively and in a positive manner both with their separated brothers, who together with them profess the Gospel of charity, and with all men thirsting for true peace.

The council, considering the immensity of the hardships which still afflict the greater part of mankind today, regards it as most opportune that an organism of the universal Church be set up in order that both the justice and love of Christ toward the poor might be developed everywhere. The role of such an organism would be to stimulate the Catholic community to promote progress in needy regions and international social justice.

* * *

Introduction to Populorum Progressio and Octogesima Adveniens

The papacy of Paul VI brought with it a vigorous endorsement of the themes set forth in *Mater et Magistra* and *Gaudium et Spes.* Some commentators argue, however, that Pope Paul overturned the methodology which dominated earlier Roman statements on social questions. Paul's approach seems to them far more inductive than deductive in its rationale for social commitment and far more open to pluralism with regard to social models. Catholicism is no longer seen as tied to a social system based on natural law. There is considerable difference between Paul VI and the perspective of John XXIII in *Pacem in Terris,* where the natural law argument predominated.

The encyclical *Populorum Progressio* and the apostolic letter *Octogesima Adveniens,* which Pope Paul sent to the president of the Pontifical Commission on Justice and Peace to mark the eightieth anniversary of *Rerum Novarum,* introduce a language change. We can no longer speak of Catholic social *doctrine,* only of Catholic social teaching or the social teaching inherent in the Gospel. *Octogesima Adveniens* illustrates well this spirit in the writings of Paul VI:

> If it [i.e., the social teaching of the Church] does not intervene to authenticate a given structure or to propose a ready-made model, it does not thereby limit itself to recalling general principles. It develops through reflection applied to the changing situations of this world, under the driving force of the Gospel as the source of renewal when its message is accepted in its totality and with all its demands.

This pluralistic, decentralized approach to economic problems flows quite directly from the change in ecclesiological vision wrought by the II Vatican Council. As the Pope notes in *Octogesima Adveniens,* the Council gives the local church a much greater role than heretofore in forming moral judgments on local economic and political conditions.

The Pope's pluralism also raises the question whether Christian commitment to bluntly socialist or even Marxist options is possible. Paul squarely faces this issue in *Octogesima Adveniens,* perhaps because some in the Church were interpreting *Populorum Progressio* as providing such an opening. He strongly criticizes the ideologies behind many socialist movements and warns Christians against the tendency to idealize socialism while ignoring the real restrictive and oppressive features of existing socialist societies. In so doing he shows himself, at least in this latter stage of his papacy, less receptive than John XXIII to Marxist economics. He feels it would prove "illusory and dangerous" for Christians to use Marxist analysis in economic affairs, and especially to endorse class struggle as indispensable for achieving economic justice. Having issued a rather sober warning, however, he stops short of condemning all cooperation by Catholics and socialists in promoting economic justice.

Another prominent feature of Paul VI's thought is the significant restriction he places on the notion of private property. He goes well beyond the positions of Leo XIII, Pius XI, and even John XXIII. In one of its best-known and most controversial sections, *Populorum Progressio* speaks of the right of the state to expropriate certain pieces of private property which are ill-used or underused, or whose use causes hardship for the people or is detrimental to the interests of the nation. He likewise labels unacceptable the practice of the rich who transfer their wealth to foreign lands "without care for the manifest wrong they inflict on their country by doing this."

Related to *Populorum Progressio*'s critique of private property is its comprehensive review of international economic structures. In this review, the Pope raises serious questions about the justice of most of our present governmental and private economic structures. Explicit reference is made to the harmful effects of multinational corporations' growing control of capital resources. Increasing concentration of wealth in the world has become a major concern for the Pope. Somehow this concentration must be broken and a new spirit of global solidarity developed. Then redesigned economic structures must be put in place to reflect this spirit. However, new structures will not come about through the internal dynamics of the economic system alone. Writing four years later in *Octogesima Adveniens*, Paul VI calls for concerted political action to achieve this renewal through meaningful political change and broader participation in political decision-making.

Paul also brings to maturity a theme that appeared in several previous statements from Rome. "Development is the new name for peace," he tells us in *Populorum Progressio*. The link between economic justice and any authentic definition of peace has now been fused beyond rupture. In an oft-quoted statement, the Pope says: "Peace cannot be limited to a mere absence of war, the result of an ever-precarious balance of forces. No, peace is something that is built up day after day, in the pursuit of the order intended by God, which implies a more perfect form of justice among men." Though the peace-justice linkage remains a source of tension between Western peace activists and persons struggling for justice in the Third World, Paul

VI has definitely placed Catholic social teaching on the side of those who maintain that heightened economic justice is an indispensable barometer of progress in peacemaking.

Finally, notice should be taken of *Octogesima Adveniens'* language regarding a special concern for the poor: "In teaching us charity, the Gospel instructs us in the preferential respect due the poor and the special situation they have in society: the more fortunate should renounce some of their rights so as to place their goods more generously at the service of others." This statement marks the first stage in what the Latin American bishops at Puebla and the Canadian bishops in their statement on economics will later develop as "the preferential option for the poor."

Populorum Progressio
On Promoting the Development of Peoples

POPE PAUL VI

March 26, 1967

To Bishops, Priests, Religious, The Faithful of the Whole Catholic World and Likewise to All Men of Good Will

Selections*

* * *

I

6. While today we see that men are seeking to find a more secure food supply, cure for diseases, steady employment, increasing personal responsibility with security from oppression and freedom from degradation endangering the dignity of man, better education, in a word while men seek to be more active, to learn more, to possess more and consequently to enhance their value, we see at the same time that great numbers are living in conditions which frustrate their just desires. Moreover, nations which have recently become independent, almost of necessity seek the addition of social and economic progress, worthy of man and gained by his own power, to their political independence so that their citizens may first gain their legitimate advancement as men, and then take the place due to them in the community of nations.

7. Although the resources inherited from the past are not sufficient to accomplish this difficult and very important task, nevertheless they are not to be considered entirely lacking. It must, however, be admitted that colonizing countries at times sought nothing but their own advantage, aggrandizement, and glory, and when they relinquished their rule, left those countries in an ill-balanced economy, based, for example, on the production of one kind of crop, the market price of which is subject to very great and sudden changes. Though

*Editor's Note: Deleted material in this document is indicated in the text by the symbol * * *.

it must be acknowledged that some harm has stemmed from *colonialism* from which other evils arose later, it is nevertheless necessary to give grateful recognition to the merits of colonizers who have conferred real benefits on not a few undeveloped lands by employing the skill of their scientists and technicians whose benefits still endure. Although the framework of the structures which these nations left are not to be considered complete and perfect they nevertheless made it possible to decrease ignorance and disease and opened to these peoples convenient communications and finally improved living conditions.

8. Moreover while what we have just said must indeed be admitted, it is nevertheless clear that these structures are not entirely suited to cope with the grave economic condition of our time. For unless modern technological civilization is somehow regulated it necessarily follows that inequalities among peoples in respect to increased production far from being removed will rather grow worse, and that the richer nations will have rapid growth and the more needy peoples will only develop slowly. These inequalities among nations are daily increasing since some produce food in greater supply than their population needs, while others are cruelly either in want of food, or are uncertain about their ability to export to other countries what little they have produced.

9. At the same time, however, social conflicts have crept over almost the whole world. And the disquiet which beset the poorer classes of citizens in industrialized regions has also passed to those regions whose economy is based almost exclusively on agriculture so that the farmers themselves are today aware of their "wretched and miserable lot."[9] In the same frame of reference is the fact that the unbecoming and invidious inequalities, of which we speak, extend not only to the possession of goods, but even more to the exercise of power. For it happens in certain regions that while a small and select number enjoys a most refined culture, the needy meanwhile and the scattered inhabitants "lack almost every possibility of acting on their own initiative and responsibility, spending their lives in living and working conditions unworthy of human beings."[10]

* * *

17. But each man is a member of society and therefore belongs to the entire community of men. Consequently not merely this or that man, but all without exception are called to promote the full development

---

[9]Encyclical letter, *Rerum Novarum*, May 15, 1891: Acta Leonis XIII, t. XI (1892) p. 98.

[10]Vatican Council II, *Pastoral Constitution on the Church in the Modern World, Gaudium et Spes*, n. 63, AAS 58 (1966) p. 1085.

of the whole human society. All forms of civilization rise, flourish, and decline. But like the waves of the ocean, when the tide swells one wave reaches further inland than the other, so too does the human race proceed in the course of history. We who have succeeded as heirs to generations gone by and who have reaped the fruits of the toil of our contemporaries are under obligations to all men. For this reason we have no right to put aside all concern for those through whom the human family will be enlarged after we have filled the span of our own life. The mutual bond of all mankind, which is a reality, not only confers benefits upon us but also imposes obligations.

18. This development of individuals and of the whole human race could be jeopardized if the true hierarchy of values were to be falsely assessed. Since man's desire to provide himself with necessities is legitimate beyond doubt, it follows that work itself by which we acquire these goods becomes a duty: "If any man will not work, neither let him eat."[16] But the acquisition of earthly possessions can lead man to inordinate desire, to seeking ever more plentiful resources, to the will to increase his own power. The avarice of individuals, of families, and of nations can affect the poorer no less than the richer, and can drive both to *materialism* which stifles their souls.

19. An evergrowing supply of possessions is not to be so highly valued either by nations or by individuals as to be considered the ultimate goal. For all development has a twofold effect; on the one hand it is necessary for man so that he develop himself as a human being more and more, on the other it imprisons him as it were if it is sought as the highest good beyond which one is not to look. When this takes place hearts are hardened, minds are closed, men unite not to foster friendship but to gain advantage and as a consequence easily fall into opposition and disunity. Consequently the exclusive quest for economic possessions not only impedes man's development as a human being but also opposes his true greatness. For both nations and men who are infected with the vice of avarice give clearest evidence of moral underdevelopment.

20. If a greater number of technicians is necessary for the further progress of development, there is far greater need of wise men with keen minds to investigate a new *humanism* by which modern man accepting the far-surpassing blessings of love, friendship, prayer, and contemplation[17] will be able, so to say, to find himself. When this has been accomplished it will be possible to achieve true development

---

[16]2 Thes 3:10.

[17]Cf., for example, J. Maritain, *Les Conditions spirituelles du progrès et de la paix*, in *Rencontre des cultures à l'UNESCO sous le signe du Concile Decuménique Vatican II*, Paris: Mame, 1966, p. 66.

fully and completely which consists in each and everyone's passing from less human to more human living conditions.

21. These must be said to be dwelling in less human living conditions: first, those who are hard pressed by such destitution as to lack either the minimum subsistence necessary for life or who are almost crushed by moral deficiency which they have brought upon themselves by excessive self-love; second, those who are oppressed by social structures which abuses of ownership or power, exploitation of workers or unjust transactions have created. Contrariwise the following indicate with sufficient clarity that more human living conditions have been achieved: first, the passing from destitution to the possession of necessities, winning the struggle against social ills, broader knowledge, acquisition of culture; second, increased esteem for the dignity of others, an inclination for the spirit of poverty,[18] cooperation for the common good, the will for peace; then acknowledgement by man of the highest good, the recognition of God himself, the author and end of these blessings; finally, and especially faith, the gift of God, accepted by men of good will, and unity in the love of Christ who has called us to share as sons the life of the living God the Father of all men.

22. Already on the first page of Sacred Scripture we read these words: "Fill the earth and subdue it."[19] By these words we are taught that all things of the world have been created for man, and that this task has been entrusted to him to enhance their value by the resources of his intellect, and by his toil to complete and perfect them for his own use. Now if the earth has been created for the purpose of furnishing individuals either with the necessities of a livelihood or the means for progress, it follows that each man has the right to get from it what is necessary for him. The Second Ecumenical Vatican Council has reminded us of this in these words: "God destined the earth with all that it contains for the use of all men and nations, in such a way that created things in fair share should accrue to all men under the leadership of justice with charity as a companion."[20] All other rights, whatever they are, including property rights and the right of free trade must be subordinated to this norm; they must not hinder it, but must rather expedite its application. It must be considered a serious and urgent social obligation to refer these rights to their original purpose.

23. "He who has the goods of this world and sees his brother in need and closes his heart to him, how does the love of God abide in him?"[21]

---

[18]Cf. Mt 5:3.
[19]Gn 1:28.
[20]*Gaudium et Spes*, n. 69, #1.
[21]1 Jn 3:17.

It is well known to all how seriously the Fathers of the Church described the obligation of the affluent to those in need: "You are not making a gift to the poor man from your possessions," says St. Ambrose, "but you are returning what is his. For what is common has been given for the use of all, you make exclusive use of it. The earth belongs to all, not to the rich."[22] These words declare that private ownership confers on no one a supreme and unconditional right. No one is allowed to set aside solely for his own advantage possessions which exceed his needs when others lack the necessities of life. Briefly, "according to the traditional teaching of the Fathers of the Church and of outstanding theologians the right of ownership is never to be used to the detriment of the common good." If perchance there be a conflict between acquired private rights and the primary needs of the community it pertains to the public authorities "to seek a solution to these questions with the active participation of individuals and social groups."[23]

24. The common good, therefore, at times demands the expropriation of an estate if it happens that some estates impede the common prosperity either on account of their vast size, or because of their small or negligible cultivation, or cause extreme poverty to the population or bring serious harm to the country. While the Second Vatican Council declares this without ambiguity,[24] it teaches no less clearly that the revenues derived from this source are not to be left to men's good pleasure and that plans for excessive profit made only for one's own advantage should be prohibited. It is by no means lawful therefore that citizens with abundant income derived from the resources and work of their native land transfer a large part of their income to foreign countries looking solely to their own private advantage, giving no consideration to their own country on which they inflict obvious harm by this conduct.[25]

25. The introduction of industry which is necessary both for economic growth and human progress, indicates and promotes development. By using the powers of his intellect and with great toil man gradually discovers the hidden laws of nature and puts its resources to more profitable use. Consequently as he controls his way of life he is also spurred on more and more to new investigations and discoveries, to taking a calculated risk, to set about tasks with courage, to initiate generous projects, to sharpen his sense of responsibility.

---

[22] *De Nabuthe*, c. 12, n. 53; (P.L. 14, 747). Cf. J. R. Palanque, *Saint Ambroise et l'empire romain*, Paris: de Boccard, 1933, pp. 336f.
[23] Cf. Letter of the Cardinal Secretary of State to Catholic men attending social life studies in Brest published in *L'homme et la révolution urbaine*, Lyons, Chronique sociale, 1965, pp. 8-9.
[24] *Gaudium et Spes*, n. 71, #6.
[25] Cf. ibid., n. 65, #3.

26. But out of these new conditions opinions have somehow crept into human society according to which profit was considered the chief incentive to foster economic development, competition the supreme law of economics, private ownership of the means of production an absolute right which recognizes neither limits nor concomitant social duty. This type of unbridled *liberalism* paved the way for a type of tyranny rightly condemned by our predecessor Pius XI as the source of the *internationalism of finance* or *international imperialism*.[26] Such economic abuses will never be rejected as completely as they ought to be because the economy must only serve man,[27] a point about which it is fitting once more to give a serious admonition. But if it must be admitted that so many hardships, so many injustices and fratricidal conflicts whose effects we feel even now, trace their origin to a form of *capitalism*, one would falsely attribute those evils to industrial growth which more correctly are to be blamed on the pernicious opinions about economics which accompanied that growth. On the contrary, justice demands that we admit that not only the organization of labor but also industrial progress made a necessary contribution to promote development.

27. Likewise, even though a kind of mystical teaching about work has at times been given exaggerated praise, it is no less certain that God ordered work and gave it his blessing. Created according to the image of God, "man must cooperate with the Creator to perfect the work of creation and must in turn place upon the earth the spiritual image stamped upon himself."[28] When God endowed man with intellect, power to reason, and sensitivity he gave him the means with which to complete and perfect, as it were, the work begun by himself; for whoever engages in work, be he artist, artisan, manager, laborer, farmer, in a certain sense creates. As he struggles with materials which resist his efforts man as it were leaves some imprint of himself upon them while at the same time refining his persistency, skill, and power to think. Furthermore since work which men share together causes them to have common hopes, sorrows, desires, and joys it unites their wills, their minds, and hearts. For when men work they recognize one another as brothers.[29]

28. Work, however, has a twofold effect: because it holds out the promise of money, pleasure and power, it incites some to excessive

---

[26]Encyclical letter, *Quadragesimo Anno*, May 15, 1931, AAS 23 (1931), p. 212.
[27]Cf., for example, Colin Clark, *The Conditions of Economic Progress*, 3rd ed., London: Macmillan and Co., and New York: St. Martin's Press, 1960, pp. 3-6.
[28]Cf. Letter of the Cardinal Secretary of State to Catholic men attending social life studies at Lyons published in *Le travail et travailleurs dans la société contemporaire*, Lyons, Chronique sociale, 1965, p. 6.
[29]Cf., for example, M.D. Chenu, OP, *Pour une théologie du travail*, Paris: Editions du Seuil, 1955.

self-love and others to civil discord; but it also causes the development of professional awareness, a sense of duty and love of neighbor. Although work today has been rendered more scientific and is better organized, it can, however, jeopardize the very dignity of man who becomes its slave, so to say, for only then is work to be called human when it is based on intelligence and freedom. Our predecessor of happy memory, John XXIII, gave a stern warning that it was absolutely necessary that workers be restored to their dignity and that they actually be made sharers in the work they do together "and that productive enterprises must assume the character of a partnership of human beings by the spirit of which individual relationships and various functions and obligations are profoundly influenced."[30] Men's work has a far higher significance if it is considered in the light of Christianity because it also has as its purpose to promote the establishing of a supernatural world here on earth[31] which will indeed not be perfect and complete until we reach the stage of forming that man who in St. Paul's words is "in the mature measure of the fullness of Christ."[32]

29. We must make haste since too many are suffering, and the gap, as it were, is widening between the development of some and the stagnating, even deteriorating condition of others. The task to be completed, therefore, must go forward properly and consistently, lest moderation, which is so necessary, be lost. For agrarian reform made in haste will perhaps not accomplish its objective; too rapid industrialization can throw institutions still needed into disorder and prepare the way for social ills and indeed retard men's progress.

30. There are without doubt situations which, because of their injustice, cry out bitterly for God's punishment. For when entire populations, deprived of the necessities of life, are so subjected to the domination of others that they are denied any self-initiated activity, responsibility, attainment of higher culture, and participation in social and public life, men are easily tempted to remove by force the injustice done to human dignity.

31. It is indeed a well-known fact that insurrection and rebellion—barring the case of a clear and longstanding tyranny which violates the basic rights of the human person and which is bound up with serious harm to the common good—beget new injustices, inflict new inequalities, and goad men on to new destruction. It is not lawful to ward off a real existing evil in such a way as to bring on a greater misfortune.

---

[30] *Mater et Magistra*, AAS 53 (1961), n. 423.
[31] Cf., for example, O. von Nell-Breuning, SJ, *Wirtschaft und Gesellschaft*, volume 1: Grundfragen, Freiburg, Herder, 1956, pp. 183-184.
[32] Eph 4:13.

32. We want our position clearly understood. The present situation must be met with courage and the injustices which follow in its train must be fought and overcome. Development demands a bold approach to changes by which things will be thoroughly renovated. We must strive without delay that urgent situations be remedied. Everyone should generously and eagerly share in it especially those who by reason of their education, position and power have the greatest influence. Setting the example let them give some of their possessions to this cause as some of our fellow bishops have done.[33] In this way they will live up to men's expectation and faithfully follow the Holy Spirit since "the ferment of the Gospel has stirred up in man's heart, and continues to do so, an irresistible demand for his dignity."[34]

33. The initiatives of individuals and the fluctuations of competition will not assure the success of development. For it is not lawful to go to such lengths that the resources and power of the rich become even greater, and the distress of the needy be increased and the enslavement of the oppressed aggravated. Programs, therefore, are necessary "to encourage, stimulate, coordinate, supplement and supply for the deficiencies"[35] of the activity of individuals and intermediary agencies. It is the function of public authorities to establish and enjoin the objectives to be attained, the plans to be followed, and the means to achieve them; also to stimulate the energies of all involved in this common activity. But they must be careful to associate the projects of individuals and intermediary agencies with this kind of work. For in this way complete collectivization and arbitrary economic management are avoided which are contrary to freedom and take away the exercise of the basic rights of the human person.

34. For every program geared to increased production must have no other end in view than to serve the human person, namely: to lessen inequalities, to remove discrimination, to free men from the bonds of servitude and to enable them to improve their condition in the temporal order, achieve moral development, and perfect their spiritual endowments. When we speak of development care must be given both to social progress and economic growth. The increase of national wealth is not sufficient for its equitable distribution; the progress of technology is not enough to make the earth a more suitable place to live in as if it had been made more humane. Those who are striving for development should be warned by the mistakes of their predecessors to avoid the dangers in this area. The predominance of technologists, or *technocracy*, as it is called, if it gains the upperhand

---

[33]Cf., for example, *Pastorales Litterae de civili progressu et de pace*, Paris, Pax Christi, 1965 of Emmanuel Larrain Errazuriz, Bishop of Talca, Chile, president of the Episcopal Conference of Latin America.
[34]*Gaudium et Spes*, n. 26, #4.
[35]*Mater et Magistra*, AAS 53 (1961), p. 414.

in the next generation will be able to bring on evils no less deplorable than those which *liberalism,* as it is called, brought in the previous generation. Economics and technology lack all meaning if they are not turned to the good of man whom they must serve. But man is a man only insofar as being the master of his own actions and the judge of their importance, he himself is the architect of his progress and this must be in keeping with his nature which the Creator gave him and the possibilities and demands of which he freely assumes.

* * *

II

43. The complete development of the individual must be joined with that of the human race and must be accomplished by mutual effort. In the city of Bombay we said: "Man must meet man, nation meet nation as brothers and sisters, as children of God. With this mutual good will and friendship, with this sacred harmony of minds we must in like manner undertake the task of providing the future common prosperity of the human race."[47] We also urged that definite and effective ways be sought through which to form duly organized institutions and unite projects to share available resources with others and that true friendship between nations be established.

44. In the first place the more affluent are bound by these obligations which are based on a natural and supernatural brotherhood presenting a threefold aspect: first, a duty of mutual relationship, that is a duty on the part of richer nations to give assistance to nations still developing; then, the duty of social justice which consists in improving trade relations between the more prosperous and weaker nations; finally, the duty of charity to all men by which more human relationship for all is promoted in which all must give and receive, and in which the progress of some should not impede the development of others. This is truly a serious matter since the future of civilization depends upon it.

45. "And if a brother or sister"—as St. James says—"be naked and in want of daily food, and one of you says: 'Go in peace, be warmed and filled' yet you do not give them what is necessary for the body, what does it profit?"[48] Today no one can be ignorant of the fact that on some continents countless men and women are tormented by

---

[47] Address to the representatives of various non-Christian communities, Dec. 3, 1964, AAS 57 (1965), p. 132.
[48] Jas 2:15-16.

hunger, countless boys and girls are wasting away from malnutrition so that not a few are snatched away by death in the prime of life and that in many other regions physical growth and mental development are impeded by the same cause and that as a consequence the population of whole regions weighed down with distress is despondent.

46. There have already been anxious appeals for help. The appeal of our predecessor of happy memory, John XXIII, was promptly heeded;[49] we repeated it in our Christmas message of 1963[50] and again in 1966 in our appeal for aid to India.[51] The international project of the Food and Agriculture Organization (FAO) which the Apostolic See warmly encouraged, has met with generous response. Our institute *Caritas Internationalis* is at work everywhere, and many Catholics at the urging of our brother bishops without sparing themselves are striving to help the needy and gradually to widen the circle of those they cherish as their neighbors.

47. But these appeals and projects, just as funds privately and publicly allocated, gifts, and loans are not sufficient. For it is not simply a question of eliminating hunger and reducing poverty. It is not enough to combat destitution, urgent and necessary as this is. The point at issue is the establishment of a human society in which everyone, regardless of race, religion or nationality, can live a truly human life free from bondage imposed by men and the forces of nature not sufficiently mastered, a society in which freedom is not an empty word, and where Lazarus the poor man can sit at the same table as the rich man.[52] This demands no little generosity, many inconveniences willingly endured, and constant effort on the part of the rich man himself. Let each one examine his conscience which speaks in a new tone of voice, so to say, to our age. Is each one ready to help with his own money projects and missions duly organized for poor relief? Is he ready to pay more taxes so that the public authorities can more vigorously promote development? Is he ready to pay a higher price for imported goods so that the producers get a fairer return? Is he ready, if it is necessary and he be in the prime of life, to quit his native land to help emerging countries?

48. Since the duty of solidarity among individuals holds good also for nations, "advanced . . . nations have a very serious duty of helping developing nations."[53] This teaching of the council must be implemented. If it is in keeping with reason that a nation be the first to enjoy the gifts bestowed upon it by Divine Providence as the fruit of

---

[49]Cf. *Mater et Magistra*, AAS 53 (1961), pp. 440f.
[50]Radio Message of Christmas Eve, 1963, AAS 56 (1964), pp. 57-58.
[51]Cf. *Encicliche e Discorsi di Paolo VI*, volume IX, Rome, ed. Paoline, 1966, pp. 132-36.
[52]Cf. Lk 16: 19-31.
[53]*Gaudium et Spes*, n. 86, #3.

its own labor, no nation, however, should venture to put aside its wealth for its own use only. Individual nations must raise the level of the quantity and quality of production to give the life of all their citizens truly human dignity and give assistance to the common development of the human race. Since privation in underdeveloped regions is increasing it is fitting that an affluent country give a part of its production to alleviate the distress of these regions; it is also fitting that an affluent country train teachers, engineers, technicians, and scholars to serve these areas with their knowledge and skill.

49. This moreover must be repeated: what is superfluous in richer regions must serve the needs of the regions in want. The rule according to which in the past those were to be helped who are more closely bound to us now applies to all who are in need throughout the world; the first to benefit from this will be the rich. Their avarice if continued will call down the punishment of God and arouse the anger of the poor and the consequences cannot be foreseen. Countries now flourishing but intent only on their own advantage, bring disaster upon their most treasured possessions if they sacrifice the will for greater and truer excellence to the desire for greater possessions. The parable of the rich man whose fields yielded such an abundant harvest that he did not know where to store it, is rightly applied to them: "But God said to him: 'Thou fool, this night do they demand thy soul of thee.' "[54]

50. To be fully effective these efforts cannot be haphazard and isolated, neither should they be in opposition to one another because of some persons' desire for prestige and power; for our times demand concerted planning which is more effective and better than that aid which is left to individual good will as the occasion suggests. As we said above there must be accurate studies, objectives must be defined, ways and means must be indicated and efforts must be made simultaneously by selected persons to satisfy the needs of the present and meet foreseeable demands. Indeed such planning transcends the limits of economic growth and social development since it gives meaning and importance to the work to be accomplished, and while it gives proper organization to human endeavor it confers on the individual more dignity and strength.

51. But we must go further. When we were at Bombay to attend the international Eucharistic Congress we asked the heads of states to use a part of the expenditure for military equipment to establish a world fund for the purpose of giving aid to destitute peoples.[55] Though this fund is primarily intended to combat want, it also serves to pro-

---

[54]Lk 12:20.

[55]Message to the world, delivered to journalists on Dec. 4, 1964. Cf. AAS 57 (1965), p. 135.

mote development. For only harmonious international cooperation, of which the fund would be both a symbol and an instrumentality, could succeed in putting an end to senseless rivalries on the one hand, and on the other serve as the beginning of mutual, peaceful, and beneficial dialogues between nations.

52. There surely is no doubt that bilateral and multilateral agreements must be observed, for they make it possible for beneficial ties of friendship based on juridical and political equality to follow happily upon relationships of dependence and the animosities which the era of colonialism brought with it. These agreements, if joined with a general plan of mutual international assistance, leave absolutely no room for suspicion. Those who enjoy the advantages of these agreements have less cause for distrust and fear, that under the guise of financial aid or technical assistance to be given, they are submitting to a neocolonialism by which their civil liberty is diminished and heavy financial burdens are imposed while at the same time the dominance of a few is either strengthened or established.

53. Who does not see that in consequence of the world fund which we have mentioned an opportunity will be given to make some deduction in expenditures suggested either by fear or by arrogance? While so many people are going hungry, while so many families are suffering destitution, while so many people spend their lives submerged in the darkness of ignorance, while so many schools, hospitals, homes worthy of the name, are needed, every public or private squandering, every expenditure either of nations or individuals made for the sake of pretentious parade, finally every financially depleting arms race—all these we say become a scandalous and intolerable crime. The most serious obligation enjoined on us demands that we openly denounce it. Would that those in authority listened to us before it is too late.

54. For this reason it is absolutely necessary that all peoples take part in that dialogue which we ardently sought in the first encyclical we issued, *Ecclesiam Suam*.[56] Were this dialogue to take place between those who provide aid and those who are its beneficiaries, the result could easily be achieved that the aid to be given would be equitably apportioned not only according to the generosity and wealth of the donors, but also according to the real need for assistance and the ability of using the aid on the part of the recipients. There will consequently then be no danger that developing nations be overwhelmed with a debt in the payment of which they spend their chief gains. Both parties will be able to reach an agreement on the interest and the time for repaying the loan under conditions however which are satisfactory to both sides, namely, by balancing free gifts, interest-

---

[56]Cf. AAS 56 (1964), pp. 639f.

free or low-interest loans, and the years for gradually repaying the loan. Beyond doubt, to those who give aid guarantees will have to be given about the use of money loaned that the transaction be carried out according to the agreement and with reasonable results, for idlers and parasites are not to be encouraged. Those, however, who make use of the aid will be able rightly and deservedly to demand that no one interfere in the conduct of their government or disturb their social order. Since sovereign states are involved, it is their exclusive right to conduct their own affairs, to determine their policy, and to choose the form of government they prefer. This, then, is indispensable that nations collaborate with each other without constraint and with equal dignity, that they at the same time work at creating a civil society truly worthy of man.

55. But it seems that a plan of this kind cannot be carried out in regions where families are preoccupied with the sole worry about their daily sustenance who consequently are unable to plan work with which to make the rest of their life less wretched. These men and women therefore must be encouraged with every assistance, and urged to follow willingly a course leading to their own development, and at the same time acquire the means necessary for progress. This common task without doubt demands constant, prompt, concerted action. All, however, should be convinced that this must be done without delay, for the life of the poorer nations, civil peace in developing countries, in fact the peace of the world, are at stake.

56. But all efforts, and they are not insignificant, which are made to help gradually developing countries either by financial or technical assistance could prove to be disappointing and useless, if the relief derived from them were to be in great measure nullified as a result of variable trade relations which exist between richer and poorer countries. For the latter would be robbed of all hope and confidence when they feared that the former would take back what they had already given.

57. Goods manufactured in their own lands are the principal export of industrialized countries; less developed countries, however, have nothing else to sell but raw material and what the land produces. On account of technical progress the value of the products of the former rapidly increases and the products themselves are very easily sold. But the raw materials supplied by less developed countries are subject to very great and sudden price changes and are consequently far outclassed by the increasing value of the industrial products. As a result serious difficulties are caused for countries with slight progress in industrialization since their hope in great measure has to be placed in exports to balance the economy and to carry out their plans for economic development. For this reason nations struggling against poverty become still poorer, but those endowed with all resources are enriched with even greater wealth.

58. It is therefore clear that the rule of free trade is no longer satisfactory if it is used as the sole norm in regulating international relations. On the other hand it is advantageous as often as the parties involved do not differ too much in resources; in fact it stimulates them to greater progress and gives a deserved reward to their efforts. For this reason highly industrialized countries come to the conclusion that there is a law of justice in the rule of free trade. The verdict, however, must be different when very unequal situations obtain between countries, for prices which have been agreed upon *freely* in the market can have completely unfair consequences. It must be admitted that in this matter the fundamental principle of *liberalism* as the norm of commercial transactions is called into question.

59. Now the teaching which our predecessor of immortal memory, Leo XIII, propounded in the encyclical *Rerum Novarum* is also valid today according to which the consent of contracting parties in positions too unequal is by no means a sufficient guarantee of the equity of the agreement, and the rule of free agreement must be governed by the natural law.[57] The encyclical's teaching on the just wage for individual workers must deservedly be applied also to international agreements, for commercial transactions can no longer depend solely on the law of free competition since it all too frequently creates economic dictatorship. Consequently freedom of trade can only then be called fair when it is in accord with the demands of social justice.

60. For the rest, the economically developed countries themselves have understood this since they are striving by adopting appropriate plans to establish in their own economy a balance which competition when carried on at each one's whim frequently disturbs. It happens therefore that these countries frequently care for the needs of their own agriculture by shifting the burden to other economic enterprises which show greater growth. It likewise happens that the same countries to promote commercial relations particularly within a common market direct their financial, fiscal, and social progress policies in such a way that opportunities for buying and selling favorable to their condition be afforded industries competing with unequal resources.

61. In this matter completely equal standards are necessary. What is observed in the economy in individual countries, and what is allowed to economically developed countries, the same must be observed in trade relations between richer and poorer nations. Competition to be sure is not to be excluded from commerce, but it must be kept within those limits which make it just and fair and therefore worthy of man. In the trade carried on between richer and poorer economies conditions are too dissimilar and opportunities for action too unequal. The concept of justice to be worthy of man and correct demands that in

---

[57] *Cf. Acta Leonis XIII*, t.XI (1892), p. 131.

international trade at least some equitable and equal opportunity of buying and selling be given to competitors. Though this equality cannot be speedily attained, nevertheless, to hasten its attainment there must already now be some genuine equality in discussions and in determining prices. And again in this area international agreements on a sufficiently broad basis can be very useful, for by these agreements general norms can be set up to regulate price, promote production, and speed up the growth of certain new industries. Everyone sees the efficacy of the help which is given by this common striving for greater justice in regulating international commercial relations and for developing nations; its effects are not merely for the moment but endure for a long time.

62. But there are also other obstacles and hindrances keeping human society as it now exists from becoming more equitable and from being more firmly and fully based on the solidarity of the human race, they are: nationalism and racism. For it is evident to all that peoples who have only recently become politically independent are very jealous of the national unity they have gained but not yet consolidated, and guard it with all their strength; and likewise that nations distinguished for their ancient culture glory in their institutions as an ancestral heritage. However, these feelings, by no means blameworthy to be sure, must be sublimated by charity which embraces all mankind. Nationalism is divisive and stands in the way of a people's genuine advantages, but it causes most serious harm particularly in those areas where the needs of the national economy demand on the contrary the pooling of efforts, or of knowledge, or of financial resources to carry out the plans for economic development and to increase and strengthen commercial and cultural ties.

63. Now racism is not exclusively characteristic of countries which have recently become autonomous where it hides itself behind rivalries of tribes or political factions not only very detrimental to justice but also endangering civil peace and welfare. When colonial domination flourished this rivalry frequently stirred up discord between the colonists and the native population while at the same time standing in the way of mutual and profitable understanding and stirring up rancor on account of injustices actually inflicted. It continues to be an obstacle to collaboration among poverty-stricken people and sows the seeds of discord and enmity within countries as often as either individuals or families see themselves unjustly deprived of the basic rights of the rest of the citizens on account of race or color with contempt for man's inalienable rights.

64. These conditions, since they portend many dangers fill our soul with anguish and sorrow. Nevertheless we cherish the fond hope that mutual suspicions of nations, and selfishness will someday be overcome by a stronger desire for collaboration and a more profound awareness of human solidarity. Nor are we without hope that economically less developed countries will be encouraged and benefited by their proximity to others in the same condition, and that together they will join their large territories into a unit where by united efforts they may promote the development of each one's own region. We also hope that these peoples will adopt common plans of action, coordinate their investments, distribute proportionately to each the means of production, and organize the sale of the products. We also hope that either multilateral or international organizations, making the necessary arrangements, will adopt plans to help the more needy nations to free themselves from the barriers by which they still seem to be held back and to find, without detriment to their own native character, the means of human and social development.

65. This is the objective which must be achieved. Since world unity seems daily more operative it must allow all peoples, to use the phrase, to be the architects of their own fortune. International relations, far more than is right, have thus far been based on force and this, alas, has been as it were the chief characteristic of the past. May the joyous era be reached when international relations will bear only this hallmark, that is, regard and friendship to be expressed in assistance with mutual respect and collaboration based on it, that individual nations accepting with full conviction their obligation and duty promote the improvement of all. Nations now emerging and with fewer resources demand that they be allowed to play a specific role for the construction of a more fitting world, one namely in which the rights and duties belonging to each person are most conscientiously protected. Because their request is obviously a fair one it must consequently be heeded and granted by all.

66. Human society is suffering from a serious illness. Its cause is more correctly found in the severed bonds of brotherhood both between man and nations, than in the diminished or monopolized resources of nature.

67. Consequently we shall always insist upon giving a generous welcome to others which is at once a duty of human solidarity and Christian charity, a duty which is incumbent on households and also cultural institutions of host countries. The number of homes and hostels especially for the young must be increased. This must be done first to protect the young against loneliness, despair, and fear which sap their energies; secondly to keep them from unhealthy influences in which they find themselves while a certain fatal necessity forces a comparison between the dire poverty of their native land and the luxury and waste with which we may say they are surrounded; likewise to guard them against subversive opinions and violent movements as they reflect on their wretched and unhappy lot;[58] and finally

[58]Cf. ibid., p. 98.

to give to these persons, welcomed with brotherly love, examples of upright living, in which genuine and effective Christian charity and the highest spiritual values are esteemed.

68. As we reflect on this we must deplore the fact that very many young people who go to more affluent countries to study those disciplines, gain a knowledge of those arts and that culture whereby they could in time render distinguished service to their native land, if they there receive an excellent training, nevertheless very frequently lose their esteem for the spiritual values which are commonly found as a precious heritage in the culture of the land where they grew to maturity.

69. Emigrant workers too must be welcomed. Frequently they put up with living conditions unworthy of a human being and are forced to live most economically on the wages paid them in order to support the family which still remains in their native land and is hard pressed by poverty.

70. We direct our appeal moreover to all those who in the interests of their business go to recently industrialized countries, namely industrialists, merchants, the leaders, and representatives of these large organizations. It can happen that these men are imbued with social sensitivity in their own country, why then do they now turn to harsh methods of serving only their own interests when they go to less developed countries to operate their industries? Indeed the greater opportunity they enjoy ought to give them incentives to be the leaders of social development and human progress in the place where they carry on their lucrative business. Even more, the very shrewdness in organizing ability which they have in full measure, should show them ways of using the labor of the natives beneficially, to train skilled workers, to teach engineers, and other superintendents, to encourage their ingenuity and initiative, to give them more important positions so as to make them capable in the near future for a share in the management. Meanwhile, however, let justice always rule the relations between employer and employee. And contracts lawfully drawn up, with all obligations properly arranged, should govern the same relations. Finally, no one, whatever his status, should unjustly be subject to the arbitrariness of others.

71. Still we have cause for great joy for from day to day the number of experts is growing who are being sent abroad either by international organizations, or by mutual agreements, or under private auspices to stimulate the development of these countries. These emissaries to be sure must "conduct themselves not as domineering persons, but as helpers and collaborators."[59] For every people quickly finds out whether those who have come to help are motivated by good

---

[59]*Gaudium et Spes*, n. 85, #2.

will, or whether they merely want to introduce new techniques, or also wish to enhance man's true dignity. Nor need there be any doubt that the people will reject their message unless it is filled with fraternal charity.

72. If then technical skill is necessary the signs and proofs too of genuine love must be joined with it. The experts, free from inordinate love of their country and shrinking from every appearance of unjust discrimination, should grow accustomed to share their work and skill with every man clearly convinced that because of the knowledge and experience in which they excel, absolutely no preeminence is to be given them in all areas. Although the civilization which shaped their character contains elements as it were of a universal humanism, it must not, however, be considered the only one, nor must it look with disdain on other cultures, and consequently if it should be introduced into foreign countries it must be thoroughly adapted to their nature. Therefore those who undertake a mission of this kind must see to it that they carefully investigate the history, the special characteristics, and the store of knowledge of the country in which they live as guests. From this will follow a contact of one culture with the other by which both will be enriched.

73. When genuine dialogue between different national cultures is established as in the case between individual men, a fraternal meeting of minds readily has its beginnings. Programs initiated for human development to be implemented by common effort bring nations together if all, the chief government officials and the lowest artisan, are enkindled with brotherly love and ardently desire the establishment of a civilization of world solidarity. Then a dialogue will begin based on man but not on the produce of the land or products of technology. This will be very advantageous if it shows the nations engaged in dialogue the way to achieve economic progress and greater spiritual growth; if technicians will act as educators, and finally if education will be characterized by a loftier spiritual and moral tone to promote not only economic but also human growth. Then the bonds of the relationships which have been formed will retain their strength even when the assistance has come to an end. Who fails to see how much such closer bonds contribute to preserving peace on earth?

74. We know that very many young people have already willingly and eagerly answered the invitation of our predecessor of happy memory, Pius XII, encouraging the laity to missionary work.[60] We also know that other young people have of their own accord put themselves at the disposal of organizations which either publicly or privately give aid to developing nations. Consequently we have learned

---

[60]Cf. encyclical letter, *Fidei Donum*, Apr. 21, 1957, AAS 49 (1957), p. 246.

with no little joy that in some countries *military service* can at least to some degree be replaced by *social service* or by *service* pure and simple. We give these projects and the men of good will who are engaged in them our loving blessing. Would that all who declare themselves Christ's disciples heeded his appeal: "I was hungry and you gave me to eat; I was thirsty and you gave me to drink; I was a stranger and you took me in; naked and you covered me; sick and you visited me; I was in prison and you came to me."[61] No one may look with indifference on the lot of his brothers who are still weighed down by such poverty and afflicted with ignorance and pining away with insecurity. The soul of every Christian must be moved by these miseries as Christ was when he said: "I have compassion on the multitude."[62]

75. Let all therefore in humble supplication pray to God the Father Almighty that the human race not unaware of such misfortunes apply itself with intelligence and determination to abolish them. But the devotion of everyone's prayer must be matched by each one's firm determination to combat underdevelopment to the extent of his strength and resources. Would that individuals, social groups, and whole nations joined hands in brotherly manner, and that the strong, setting aside their own advantage, would help the weak to make progress devoting all their wisdom, enthusiasm, and charity to the task. For he who is animated with genuine love is the one who in particular applies his mental acumen to discover the causes of misery and find ways to combat them and boldly overcome them. Since he is a peacemaker "he will continue on his course bearing the lamp of joy and shedding its light and charm on the hearts of men throughout the whole world helping them to recognize across all frontiers the faces of brothers and friends."[63]

76. Excessive social, economic, and cultural inequalities among nations stir up strife and contention and frequently imperil the peace. Therefore upon our return from our peace journey to the United Nations we declared before the Fathers of the Ecumenical Council: "We must give our attention to nations still in the process of developing, that is to state the matter more clearly, our charity to the poor in the world, and their number is beyond counting, must become more solicitous, more effective, and more generous."[64] Therefore, when we combat misery, and struggle against injustice we are providing not only for man's prosperity but also for his spiritual and moral development and are therefore promoting the welfare of the whole human race. Indeed peace is not simply to be reduced to the elimination of

---

[61] Mt 25:35-36.
[62] Mk 8:2.
[63] Cf. Allocution, John XXIII, May 10, 1963, AAS 55 (1963), p. 455.
[64] AAS 57 (1965), p. 896.

all war, as if it consisted in a precarious balance of power. Peace is achieved by constant effort day after day, provided that order is kept in sight which was established by God and which demands a more perfect form of justice among men.[65]

77. Since nations are each the architects of their own development they assume a task and responsibility of such magnitude that they will never be able to accomplish it if they live in isolation. Therefore agreements between poorer nations of the same region on mutual assistance, common programs of broader scope to help them, likewise other agreements of greater importance made to coordinate plans of action with other nations are, so to speak, so many milestones of this road which leads to peace while it promotes progress.

78. This international cooperation which embraces the whole world demands institutions which prepare the way for it, coordinate, and direct it until a new juridical order is established which all recognize as fixed and firm. Most willingly indeed do we give our support to public organizations which are already undertaking this work to promote the development of nations and we earnestly desire that they gain greater influence. On this point while in New York when we addressed the ambassadors of the United Nations we said: "It is your function to unite in the bonds of brotherhood not one or the other nation, but all . . . Who does not see the necessity of progressively reaching the establishment of a world authority capable of acting effectively in the juridical and political sphere?"[66]

79. Some perhaps consider such hopes empty dreams. It is possible that their outlook is not fully realistic, that they have not yet sensed the dynamics of this age in which men wish to live in closer bonds of brotherhood, and even though they be held back by their ignorance, mistakes, and sins, and though they often relapse into barbarism or stray far from the path of salvation, they nevertheless slowly and even imperceptibly draw near to their Creator. Now this striving for a more human way of life does indeed demand effort and entails inconveniences but these very sufferings endured out of love for our brothers and for their benefit can be most conducive to the development of the human race. For the faithful clearly know that union with the expiatory sacrifice of the Divine Redeemer contributes most to "building up the body of Christ,"[67] that it attains its full measure in the gathering together of the People of God.

80. But since we must proceed on this journey united in mind and will we consider it our duty to warn all of the gravity and scope of

---

[65]Cf. encyclical letter, John XXIII, *Pacem in Terris*, AAS 55 (1963), p. 301.
[66]AAS 57 (1965), p. 880.
[67]Eph 4:12. Cf. Vatican Council II, *Dogmatic Constitution on the Church, Lumen Gentium*, n. 13; AAS 57 (1965), p. 17.

this project and the urgent necessity of completing the task. The time for action is here since the following are at stake: the survival of so many innocent children, the possibility of so many families weighed down by poverty to find living conditions fit for a human being, finally the peace of the world and the very survival of civilization. It is the duty of all men and nations to assume their responsibility in a matter of such importance.

*   *   *

Octogesima Adveniens

On the Occasion of the Eightieth Anniversary of the Encyclical Rerum Novarum

POPE PAUL VI

May 14, 1971

To Cardinal Maurice Roy, President of the Council of the Laity and of the Pontifical Commission Justice and Peace

Selections*

Venerable Brother,

1. The eightieth anniversary of the publication of the encyclical *Rerum Novarum,* the message of which continues to inspire action for social justice, prompts us to take up again and to extend the teaching of our predecessors, in response to the new needs of a changing world. The Church, in fact, travels forward with humanity and shares its lot in the setting of history. At the same time that she announces to men the Good News of God's love and of salvation in Christ, she clarifies their activity in the light of the Gospel and in this way helps them to correspond to God's plan of love and to realize the fullness of their aspirations.

Universal Appeal for More Justice

2. It is with confidence that we see the Spirit of the Lord pursuing his work in the hearts of men and in every place gathering together Christian communities conscious of their responsibilities in society. On all the continents, among all races, nations and cultures, and under all conditions the Lord continues to raise up authentic apostles of the Gospel.

We have had the opportunity to meet these people, to admire them and to give them our encouragement in the course of our recent journeys. We have gone into the crowds and have heard their appeals, cries of distress and at the same time cries of hope. Under these circumstances we have seen in a new perspective the grave problems of our time. These problems of course are particular to each part of

*Editor's Note: Deleted material in this document is indicated in the text by the symbol * * *.

the world, but at the same time they are common to all mankind, which is questioning itself about its future and about the tendency and the meaning of the changes taking place. Flagrant inequalities exist in the economic, cultural and political development of the nations: while some regions are heavily industrialized, others are still at the agricultural stage; while some countries enjoy prosperity, others are struggling against starvation; while some peoples have a high standard of culture, others are still engaged in eliminating illiteracy. From all sides there rises a yearning for more justice and a desire for a better guaranteed peace in mutual respect among individuals and peoples.

Diversity of Situations

3. There is of course a wide diversity among the situations in which Christians—willingly or unwillingly—find themselves according to regions, sociopolitical systems and cultures. In some places they are reduced to silence, regarded with suspicion and as it were kept on the fringe of society, enclosed without freedom in a totalitarian system. In other places they are a weak minority whose voice makes itself heard with difficulty. In some other nations, where the Church sees her place recognized, sometimes officially so, she too finds herself subjected to the repercussions of the crisis which is unsettling society; some of her members are tempted by radical and violent solutions from which they believe that they can expect a happier outcome. While some people, unaware of present injustices, strive to prolong the existing situation, others allow themselves to be beguiled by revolutionary ideologies which promise them, not without delusion, a definitively better world.

4. In the face of such widely varying situations it is difficult for us to utter a unified message and to put forward a solution which has universal validity. Such is not our ambition, nor is it our mission. It is up to the Christian communities to analyze with objectivity the situation which is proper to their own country, to shed on it the light of the Gospel's unalterable words and to draw principles of reflection, norms of judgment and directives for action from the social teaching of the Church. This social teaching has been worked out in the course of history and notably, in this industrial era, since the historic date of the message of Pope Leo XIII on "the condition of the workers," and it is an honor and joy for us to celebrate today the anniversary of that message. It is up to these Christian communities, with the help of the Holy Spirit, in communion with the bishops who hold responsibility and in dialogue with other Christian brethren and all men of good will, to discern the options and commitments which are called for in order to bring about the social, political and economic changes seen in many cases to be urgently needed. In this search for the changes which should be promoted, Christians must first of all renew their confidence in the forcefulness and special character of the demands made by the Gospel. The Gospel is not out-of-date because it was proclaimed, written and lived in a different sociocultural context. Its inspiration, enriched by the living experience of Christian tradition over the centuries, remains ever new for converting men and for advancing the life of society. It is not however to be utilized for the profit of particular temporal options, to the neglect of its universal and eternal message.[1]

Specific Message of the Church

5. Amid the disturbances and uncertainties of the present hour, the Church has a specific message to proclaim and a support to give to men in their efforts to take in hand and give direction to their future. Since the period in which the encyclical *Rerum Novarum* denounced in a forceful and imperative manner the scandal of the condition of the workers in the nascent industrial society, historical evolution has led to an awareness of other dimensions and other applications of social justice. The encyclicals *Quadragesimo Anno*[2] and *Mater et Magistra*[3] already noted this fact. The recent council for its part took care to point them out, in particular in the Pastoral Constitution *Gaudium et Spes*. We ourself have already continued these lines of thought in our encyclical *Populorum Progressio*. "Today," we said, "the principal fact that we must all recognize is that the social question has become worldwide."[4] "A renewed consciousness of the demands of the Gospel makes it the Church's duty to put herself at the service of all, to help them grasp their serious problem in all its dimensions, and to convince them that solidarity in action at this turning point in human history is a matter of urgency."[5]

6. It will moreover be for the forthcoming Synod of Bishops itself to study more closely and to examine in greater detail the Church's mission in the face of grave issues raised today by the question of justice in the world. But the anniversary of *Rerum Novarum*, venerable brother, gives us the opportunity today to confide our preoccupations and thoughts in the face of this problem to you as President of the Pontifical Commission Justice and Peace and of the Council of Laity. In this way it is also our wish to offer these bodies of the Holy See

[1] *Gaudium et Spes*, 10:AAS 58 (1966), p. 1033.
[2] AAS 23 (1931), p. 209ff.
[3] AAS 53 (1961), p. 429.
[4] 3:AAS 59 (1967), p. 258.
[5] Ibid., 1:p. 257.

our encouragement in their ecclesial activity in the service of men.

Extent of Present-day Changes

7. In so doing, our purpose—without however forgetting the permanent problems already dealt with by our predecessors—is to draw attention to a number of questions. These are questions which because of their urgency, extent and complexity must in the years to come take first place among the preoccupations of Christians, so that with other men the latter may dedicate themselves to solving the new difficulties which put the very future of man in jeopardy. It is necessary to situate the problems created by the modern economy in the wider context of a new civilization. These problems include human conditions of production, fairness in the exchange of goods and in the division of wealth, the significance of the increased needs of consumption and the sharing of responsibility. In the present changes, which are so profound and so rapid, each day man discovers himself anew, and he questions himself about the meaning of his own being and of his collective survival. Reluctant to gather the lessons of a past that he considers over and done with and too different from the present, man nevertheless needs to have light shed upon his future—a future which he perceives to be as uncertain as it is changing—by permanent eternal truths. These are truths which are certainly greater than man but, if he so wills, he can himself find their traces.[6]

New Social Problems

Urbanization

8. A major phenomenon draws our attention, as much in the industrialized countries as in those which are developing: urbanization.

After long centuries, agrarian civilization is weakening. Is sufficient attention being devoted to the arrangement and improvement of the life of the country people, whose inferior and at times miserable economic situation provokes the flight to the unhappy crowded conditions of the city outskirts, where neither employment nor housing awaits them?

This unceasing flight from the land, industrial growth, continual demographic expansion and the attraction of urban centers bring about concentrations of population, the extent of which is difficult to imagine, for people are already speaking in terms of a "megalopolis"

[6]Cf. 2 Cor 4:17.

grouping together tens of millions of persons. Of course there exist medium-sized towns, the dimension of which ensures a better balance in the population. While being able to offer employment to those that progress in agriculture makes available, they permit an adjustment of the human environment which better avoids the proletarianism and crowding of the great built-up areas.

9. The inordinate growth of these centers accompanies industrial expansion, without being identified with it. Based on technological research and the transformation of nature, industrialization constantly goes forward, giving proof of incessant creativity. While certain enterprises develop and are concentrated, others die or change their location. Thus new social problems are created: professional or regional unemployment, redeployment and mobility of persons, permanent adaptation of workers and disparity of conditions in the different branches of industry. Unlimited competition utilizing the modern means of publicity incessantly launches new products and tries to attract the consumer, while earlier industrial installations which are still capable of functioning become useless. While very large areas of the population are unable to satisfy their primary needs, superfluous needs are ingeniously created. It can thus rightly be asked if, in spite of all his conquests, man is not turning back against himself the results of his activity. Having rationally endeavored to control nature,[7] is he not now becoming the slave of the objects which he makes?

Christians in the City

10. Is not the rise of an urban civilization which accompanies the advance of industrial civilization a true challenge to the wisdom of man, to his capacity for organization and to his farseeing imagination? Within industrial society urbanization upsets both the ways of life and the habitual structures of existence: the family, the neighborhood, and the very framework of the Christian community. Man is experiencing a new loneliness; it is not in the face of a hostile nature which it has taken him centuries to subdue, but in an anonymous crowd which surrounds him and in which he feels himself a stranger. Urbanization, undoubtedly an irreversible stage in the development of human societies, confronts man with difficult problems. How is he to master its growth, regulate its organization, and successfully accomplish its animation for the good of all?

In this disordered growth, new proletariats are born. They install themselves in the heart of the cities sometimes abandoned by the rich; they dwell on the outskirts, which become a belt of misery besieging in a still silent protest the luxury which blatantly cries out

[7] *Populorum Progressio*, 25:AAS 59 (1967), pp. 269-270.

from centers of consumption and waste. Instead of favoring fraternal encounter and mutual aid, the city fosters discrimination and also indifference. It lends itself to new forms of exploitation and of domination whereby some people in speculating on the needs of others derive inadmissible profits. Behind the facades, much misery is hidden, unsuspected even by the closest neighbors; other forms of misery spread where human dignity founders: delinquency, criminality, abuse of drugs and eroticism.

11. It is in fact the weakest who are the victims of dehumanizing living conditions, degrading for conscience and harmful for the family institution. The promiscuity of working people's housing makes a minimum of intimacy impossible; young couples waiting in vain for a decent dwelling at a price they can afford are demoralized and their union can thereby even be endangered; youth escape from a home which is too confined and seek in the streets compensations and companionships which cannot be supervised. It is the grave duty of those responsible to strive to control this process and to give it direction.

There is an urgent need to remake at the level of the street, of the neighborhood or of the great agglomerative dwellings the social fabric whereby man may be able to develop the needs of his personality. Centers of special interest and of culture must be created or developed at the community and parish levels with different forms of associations, recreational centers, and spiritual and community gatherings where the individual can escape from isolation and form anew fraternal relationships.

12. To build up the city, the place where men and their expanded communities exist, to create new modes of neighborliness and relationships, to perceive an original application of social justice and to undertake responsibility for this collective future, which is foreseen as difficult, is a task in which Christians must share. To those who are heaped up in an urban promiscuity which becomes intolerable it is necessary to bring a message of hope. This can be done by brotherhood which is lived and by concrete justice. Let Christians, conscious of this new responsibility, not lose heart in view of the vast and faceless society; let them recall Jonah who traversed Niniveh, the great city, to proclaim therein the good news of God's mercy and was upheld in his weakness by the sole strength of the word of Almighty God. In the Bible, the city is in fact often the place of sin and pride, the pride of man who feels secure enough to be able to build his life without God and even to affirm that he is powerful against God. But there is also the example of Jerusalem, the Holy City, the place where

God is encountered, the promise of the city which comes from on high.[8]

Youth

13. Urban life and industrial change bring strongly to light questions which until now were poorly grasped. What place, for example, in this world being brought to birth, should be given to youth? Everywhere dialogue is proving to be difficult between youth, with its aspirations, renewal and also insecurity for the future, and the adult generations. It is obvious to all that here we have a source of serious conflicts, division and opting out, even within the family, and a questioning of modes of authority, education for freedom and the handing on of values and beliefs, which strikes at the deep roots of society.

The Role of Women

Similarly, in many countries a charter for women which would put an end to an actual discrimination and would establish relationships of equality in rights and of respect for their dignity is the object of study and at times of lively demands. We do not have in mind that false equality which would deny the distinctions laid down by the Creator himself and which would be in contradiction with woman's proper role, which is of such capital importance, at the heart of the family as well as within society. Developments in legislation should on the contrary be directed to protecting her proper vocation and at the same time recognizing her independence as a person, and her equal rights to participate in cultural, economic, social and political life.

Workers

14. As the Church solemnly reaffirmed in the recent council, "the beginning, the subject and the goal of all social institutions is and must be the human person."[9] Every man has the right to work, to a chance to develop his qualities and his personality in the exercise of his profession, to equitable remuneration which will enable him and his family "to lead a worthy life on the material, social, cultural and spiritual level"[10] and to assistance in case of need arising from sickness or age.

---

[8]Cf. Rv 3:12; 21:2.
[9]*Gaudium et Spes*, 25:AAS 58 (1966), p. 1045.
[10]Ibid., 67: p. 1089.

Although for the defense of these rights democratic societies accept today the principle of labor union rights, they are not always open to their exercise. The important role of union organizations must be admitted: their object is the representation of the various categories of workers, their lawful collaboration in the economic advance of society, and the development of the sense of their responsibility for the realization of the common good. Their activity, however, is not without its difficulties. Here and there the temptation can arise of profiting from a position of force to impose, particularly by strikes—the right to which as a final means of defense remains certainly recognized—conditions which are too burdensome for the overall economy and for the social body, or to desire to obtain in this way demands of a directly political nature. When it is a question of public services, required for the life of an entire nation, it is necessary to be able to assess the limit beyond which the harm caused to society becomes inadmissible.

Victims of Changes

15. In short, progress has already been made in introducing, in the area of human relationships, greater justice and greater sharing of responsibilities. But in this immense field much remains to be done. Further reflection, research and experimentation must be actively pursued, unless one is to be late in meeting the legitimate aspirations of the workers—aspirations which are being increasingly asserted accordingly as their education, their consciousness of their dignity and the strength of their organizations increase.

Egoism and domination are permanent temptations for men. Likewise an ever finer discernment is needed, in order to strike at the roots of newly arising situations of injustice and to establish progressively a justice which will be less and less imperfect. In industrial change, which demands speedy and constant adaptation, those who will find themselves injured will be more numerous and at a greater disadvantage from the point of view of making their voices heard. The Church directs her attention to these new *poor*—the handicapped and the maladjusted, the old, different groups of those on the fringe of society, and so on—in order to recognize them, help them, defend their place and dignity in a society hardened by competition and the attraction of success.

Discrimination

16. Among the victims of situations of injustice, unfortunately no new phenomenon, must be placed those who are discriminated against, in law or in fact, on account of their race, origin, color, culture, sex or religion.

Racial discrimination possesses at the moment a character of very great relevance by reason of the tension which it stirs up both within certain countries and on the international level. Men rightly consider unjustifiable and reject as inadmissible the tendency to maintain or introduce legislation or behavior systematically inspired by racialist prejudice. The members of mankind share the same basic rights and duties, as well as the same supernatural destiny. Within a country which belongs to each one, all should be equal before the law, find equal admittance to economic, cultural, civic and social life and benefit from a fair sharing of the nation's riches.

Right to Emigrate

17. We are thinking also of the precarious situation of a great number of emigrant workers whose condition as foreigners makes it all the more difficult for them to make any sort of social vindication, in spite of their real participation in the economic effort of the country that receives them. It is urgently necessary for people to go beyond a narrowly nationalist attitude in their regard and to give them a charter which will assure them a right to emigrate, favor their integration, facilitate their professional advancement and give them access to decent housing where, if such is the case, their families can join them.[11]

Linked to this category are the people who, to find work, or to escape a disaster or a hostile climate, leave their regions and find themselves without roots among other people.

It is everyone's duty, but especially that of Christians,[12] to work with energy for the establishment of universal brotherhood, the indispensable basis for authentic justice and the condition for enduring peace:

> We cannot in truthfulness call upon that God who is the Father of all if we refuse to act in a brotherly way toward certain men, created to God's image. A man's relationship with God the Father and his relationship with his brother men are so linked together that Scripture says: 'He who does not love does not know God' (1 Jn 4:8).[13]

Creating Employment

18. With demographic growth, which is particularly pronounced in the young nations, the number of those failing to find work and driven to misery or parasitism will grow in the coming years unless the conscience of man rouses itself and gives rise to a general move-

---

[11] *Populorum Progressio*, 69:AAS 59 (1967), pp. 290-291.
[12] Cf. Mt 25:35.
[13] *Nostra Aetate*, 5:AAS 58 (1966), p. 743.

ment of solidarity through an effective policy of investment and of organization of production and trade, as well as of education. We know the attention given to these problems within international organizations, and it is our lively wish that their members will not delay bringing their actions into line with their declarations.

It is disquieting in this regard to note a kind of fatalism which is gaining a hold even on people in positions of responsibility. This feeling sometimes leads to Malthusian solutions inculcated by active propaganda for contraception and abortion. In this critical situation, it must on the contrary be affirmed that the family, without which no society can stand, has a right to the assistance which will assure it of the conditions for a healthy development. "It is certain," we said in our encyclical *Populorum Progressio,*

> that public authorities can intervene, within the limit of their competence, by favoring the availability of appropriate information and by adopting suitable measures, provided that these be in conformity with the moral law and that they respect the rightful freedom of married couples. Where the inalienable right to marriage and procreation is lacking, human dignity has ceased to exist.[14]

19. In no other age has the appeal to the imagination of society been so explicit. To this should be devoted enterprises of invention and capital as important as those invested for armaments or technological achievements. If man lets himself rush ahead without foreseeing in good time the emergence of new social problems, they will become too grave for a peaceful solution to be hoped for.

Media of Social Communication

20. Among the major changes of our times, we do not wish to forget to emphasize the growing role being assumed by the media of social communication and their influence on the transformation of mentalities, of knowledge, of organizations and of society itself. Certainly they have many positive aspects. Thanks to them news from the entire world reaches us practically in an instant, establishing contacts which supersede distances and creating elements of unity among all men. A greater spread of education and culture is becoming possible. Nevertheless, by their very action the media of social communication are reaching the point of representing as it were a new power. One cannot but ask about those who really hold this power, the aims that they pursue and the means they use, and finally, about the effect of their activity on the exercise of individual liberty, both in the political and ideological spheres and in social, economic and cultural life. The

[14] 37: AAS 59 (1967), p. 276.

men who hold this power have a grave moral responsibility with respect to the truth of the information that they spread, the needs and the reactions that they generate and the values which they put forward. In the case of television, moreover, what is coming into being is an original mode of knowledge and a new civilization: that of the image.

Naturally, the public authorities cannot ignore the growing power and influence of the media of social communication and the advantages and risks which their use involves for the civic community and for its development and real perfecting.

Consequently they are called upon to perform their own positive function for the common good by encouraging every constructive expression, by supporting individual citizens and groups in defending the fundamental values of the person and of human society, and also by taking suitable steps to prevent the spread of what would harm the common heritage of values on which orderly civil progress is based.[15]

The Environment

21. While the horizon of man is thus modified being according to the images that are chosen for him, another transformation is making itself felt, one which is the dramatic and unexpected consequence of human activity. Man is suddenly becoming aware that by an ill-considered exploitation of nature he risks destroying it and becoming in his turn the victim of this degradation. Not only is the material environment becoming a permanent menace—pollution and refuse, new illnesses and absolute destructive capacity—but the human framework is no longer under man's control, thus creating an environment for tomorrow which may well be intolerable. This is a wide-ranging social problem which concerns the entire human family.

The Christian must turn to these new perceptions in order to take on responsibility, together with the rest of men, for a destiny which from now on is shared by all.

Fundamental Aspirations and Currents of Ideas

22. While scientific and technological progress continues to overturn man's surroundings, his patterns of knowledge, work, consumption and relationships, two aspirations persistently make themselves felt in these new contexts, and they grow stronger to the extent that he becomes better informed and better educated: the aspiration to equal-

---

[15] *Inter Mirifica*, 12: AAS 56 (1964), p. 149.

ity and the aspiration to participation, two forms of man's dignity and freedom.

Advantages and Limitations of Juridical Recognition

23. Through this statement of the rights of man and the seeking for international agreements for the application of these rights, progress has been made towards inscribing these two aspirations in deeds and structures.[16] Nevertheless various forms of discrimination continually reappear—ethnic, cultural, religious, political and so on. In fact, human rights are still too often disregarded, if not scoffed at, or else they receive only formal recognition. In many cases legislation does not keep up with real situations. Legislation is necessary, but it is not sufficient for setting up true relationships of justice and equality. In teaching us charity, the Gospel instructs us in the preferential respect due to the poor and the special situation they have in society: the more fortunate should renounce some of their rights so as to place their goods more generously at the service of others. If, beyond legal rules, there is really no deeper feeling of respect for and service to others, then even equality before the law can serve as an alibi for flagrant discrimination, continued exploitation and actual contempt. Without a renewed education in solidarity, an overemphasis of equality can give rise to an individualism in which each one claims his own rights without wishing to be answerable for the common good.

In this field, everyone sees the highly important contribution of the Christian spirit, which moreover answers man's yearning to be loved. "Love for man, the prime value of the earthly order," ensures the conditions for peace, both social peace and international peace, by affirming our universal brotherhood.[17]

* * *

Ideologies and Human Liberty

26. Therefore the Christian who wishes to live his faith in a political activity which he thinks of as service cannot without contradicting himself adhere to ideological systems which radically or substantially go against his faith and his concept of man. He cannot adhere to the Marxist ideology, to its atheistic materialism, to its dialectic of violence and to the way it absorbs individual freedom in the collectivity, at the same time denying all transcendence to man and his personal

[16]Cf. *Pacem in Terris*: AAS 55 (1963), p. 261ff.
[17]Cf. Message for the World Day of Peace, 1971: AAS 63 (1971), pp. 5-9.

and collective history; nor can he adhere to the liberal ideology which believes it exalts individual freedom by withdrawing it from every limitation, by stimulating it through exclusive seeking of interest and power, and by considering social solidarities as more or less automatic consequences of individual initiatives, not as an aim and a major criterion of the value of the social organization.

27. Is there need to stress the possible ambiguity of every social ideology? Sometimes it leads political or social activity to be simply the application of an abstract, purely theoretical idea; at other times it is thought which becomes a mere instrument at the service of activity as a simple means of a strategy. In both cases is it not man that risks finding himself alienated? The Christian faith is above and is sometimes opposed to the ideologies, in that it recognizes God, who is transcendent and the Creator, and who, through all the levels of creation, calls on man as endowed with responsibility and freedom.

28. There would also be the danger of giving adherence to an ideology which does not rest on a true and organic doctrine, to take refuge in it as a final and sufficient explanation of everything, and thus to build a new idol, accepting, at times without being aware of doing so, its totalitarian and coercive character. And people imagine they find in it a justification for their activity, even violent activity, and an adequate response to a generous desire to serve. The desire remains but it allows itself to be consumed by an ideology which, even if it suggests certain paths to man's liberation, ends up by making him a slave.

29. It has been possible today to speak of a retreat of ideologies. In this respect the present time may be favorable for an openness to the concrete transcendence of Christianity. It may also be a more accentuated sliding towards a new positivism: universalized technology as the dominant form of activity, as the overwhelming pattern of existence, even as a language, without the question of its meaning being really asked.

Historical Movements

30. But outside of this positivism which reduces man to a single dimension even if it be an important one today and by so doing mutilates him, the Christian encounters in his activity concrete historical movements sprung from ideologies and in part distinct from them. Our venerated predecessor Pope John XXIII in *Pacem in Terris* already showed that it is possible to make a distinction:

> Neither can false philosophical teachings regarding the nature, origin and destiny of the universe and of man be identified with historical movements that have economic, social, cultural or political ends, not even when these movements have originated from those teachings and have drawn and still draw inspiration therefrom.

> Because the teachings, once they are drawn up and defined, remain always the same, while the movements, being concerned with historical situations in constant evolution, cannot but be influenced by these latter and cannot avoid, therefore, being subject to changes, even of a profound nature. Besides, who can deny that those movements, insofar as they conform to the dictates of right reason and are interpreters of the lawful aspirations of the human person, contain elements that are positive and deserving of approval?[20]

Attraction of Socialist Currents

31. Some Christians are today attracted by socialist currents and their various developments. They try to recognize therein a certain number of aspirations which they carry within themselves in the name of their faith. They feel that they are part of that historical current and wish to play a part within it. Now this historical current takes on, under the same name, different forms according to different continents and cultures, even if it drew its inspiration, and still does in many cases, from ideologies incompatible with faith. Careful judgment is called for. Too often Christians attracted by socialism tend to idealize it in terms which, apart from anything else, are very general: a will for justice, solidarity and equality. They refuse to recognize the limitations of the historical socialist movements, which remain conditioned by the ideologies from which they originated. Distinctions must be made to guide concrete choices between the various levels of expression of socialism: a generous aspiration and a seeking for a more just society, historical movements with a political organization and aim, and an ideology which claims to give a complete and self-sufficient picture of man. Nevertheless, these distinctions must not lead one to consider such levels as completely separate and independent. The concrete link which, according to circumstances, exists between them must be clearly marked out. This insight will enable Christians to see the degree of commitment possible along these lines, while safeguarding the values, especially those of liberty, responsibility and openness to the spiritual, which guarantee the integral development of man.

Historical Evolution of Marxism

32. Other Christians even ask whether an historical development of Marxism might not authorize certain concrete rapprochements. They note in fact that a certain splintering of Marxism, which until now showed itself to be a unitary ideology which explained in atheistic

---

[20] AAS 55 (1963), p. 300.

terms the whole of man and the world since it did not go outside their development process. Apart from the ideological confrontation officially separating the various champions of Marxism-Leninism in their individual interpretations of the thought of its founders, and apart from the open opposition between the political systems which make use of its name today, some people lay down distinctions between Marxism's various levels of expression.

33. For some, Marxism remains essentially the active practice of class struggle. Experiencing the ever present and continually renewed force of the relationships of domination and exploitation among men, they reduce Marxism to no more than a struggle—at times with no other purpose—to be pursued and even stirred up in permanent fashion. For others, it is first and foremost the collective exercise of political and economic power under the direction of a single party, which would be the sole expression and guarantee of the welfare of all, and would deprive individuals and other groups of any possibility of initiative and choice. At a third level, Marxism, whether in power or not, is viewed as a socialist ideology based on historical materialism and the denial of everything transcendent. At other times, finally, it presents itself in a more attenuated form, one also more attractive to the modern mind: as a scientific activity, as a rigorous method of examining social and political reality, and as the rational link, tested by history, between theoretical knowledge and the practice of revolutionary transformation. Although this type of analysis gives a privileged position to certain aspects of reality to the detriment of the rest, and interprets them in the light of its ideology, it nevertheless furnishes some people not only with a working tool but also a certitude preliminary to action: the claim to decipher in a scientific manner the mainsprings of the evolution of society.

34. While, through the concrete existing form of Marxism, one can distinguish these various aspects and the questions they pose for the reflection and activity of Christians, it would be illusory and dangerous to reach a point of forgetting the intimate link which radically binds them together, to accept the elements of Marxist analysis without recognizing their relationships with ideology, and to enter into the practice of class struggle and its Marxist interpretations, while failing to note the kind of totalitarian and violent society to which this process leads.

The Liberal Ideology

35. On another side, we are witnessing a renewal of the liberal ideology. This current asserts itself both in the name of economic efficiency, and for the defense of the individual against the increasingly overwhelming hold of organizations, and as a reaction against the totalitarian tendencies of political powers. Certainly, personal initiative must be maintained and developed. But do not Christians who take this path tend to idealize liberalism in their turn, making it a proclamation in favor of freedom? They would like a new model, more adapted to present-day conditions, while easily forgetting that at the very root of philosophical liberalism is an erroneous affirmation of the autonomy of the individual in his activity, his motivation and the exercise of his liberty. Hence, the liberal ideology likewise calls for careful discernment on their part.

Christian Discernment

36. In this renewed encounter of the various ideologies, the Christian will draw from the sources of his faith and the Church's teaching the necessary principles and suitable criteria to avoid permitting himself to be first attracted by and then imprisoned within a system whose limitations and totalitarianism may well become evident to him too late, if he does not perceive them in their roots. Going beyond every system, without however failing to commit himself concretely to serving his brothers, he will assert, in the very midst of his options, the specific character of the Christian contribution for a positive transformation of society.[21]

Rebirth of Utopias

37. Today, moreover, the weaknesses of the ideologies are better perceived through the concrete systems in which they are trying to affirm themselves. Bureaucratic socialism, technocratic capitalism and authoritarian democracy are showing how difficult it is to solve the great human problem of living together in justice and equality. How in fact could they escape the materialism, egoism or constraint which inevitably go with them? This is the source of a protest which is springing up more or less everywhere, as a sign of a deep-seated sickness, while at the same time we are witnessing the rebirth of what it is agreed to call *utopias*. These claim to resolve the political problem of modern societies better than the ideologies. It would be dangerous to disregard this. The appeal to a utopia is often a convenient excuse for those who wish to escape from concrete tasks in order to take refuge in an imaginary world. To live in a hypothetical future is a facile alibi for rejecting immediate responsibilities. But it must clearly be recognized that this kind of criticism of existing society often provokes the forward-looking imagination both to perceive in the present the disregarded possibility hidden within it, and to direct itself towards a fresh future; it thus sustains social dynamism by the confidence

[21]Cf. *Gaudium et Spes*, 11:AAS 58 (1966), p. 1033.

that it gives to the inventive powers of the human mind and heart; and, if it refuses no overture, it can also meet the Christian appeal. The Spirit of the Lord, who animates man renewed in Christ, continually breaks down the horizons within which his understanding likes to find security and the limits to which his activity would willingly restrict itself; there dwells within him a power which urges him to go beyond every system and every ideology. At the heart of the world there dwells the mystery of man discovering himself to be God's son in the course of a historical and psychological process in which constraint and freedom as well as the weight of sin and the breath of the Spirit alternate and struggle for the upper hand.

The dynamism of Christian faith here triumphs over the narrow calculations of egoism. Animated by the power of the Spirit of Jesus Christ, the Savior of mankind, and upheld by hope, the Christian involves himself in the building up of the human city, one that is to be peaceful, just and fraternal and acceptable as an offering to God.[22] In fact, "the expectation of a new earth must not weaken but rather stimulate our concern for cultivating this one. For here grows the body of a new human family, a body which even now is able to give some kind of foreshadowing of the new age."[23]

The Questioning of the Human Sciences

38. In this world dominated by scientific and technological change, which threatens to drag it towards a new positivism, another more fundamental doubt is raised. Having subdued nature by using his reason, man now finds that he himself is as it were imprisoned within his own rationality; he in turn becomes the object of science. The *human sciences* are today enjoying a significant flowering. On the one hand they are subjecting to critical and radical examination the hitherto accepted knowledge about man, on the grounds that this knowledge seems either too empirical or too theoretical. On the other hand, methodological necessity and ideological presuppositions too often lead the human sciences to isolate, in the various situations, certain aspects of man, and yet to give these an explanation which claims to be complete or at least an interpretation which is meant to be all-embracing from a purely quantitative or phenomenological point of view. This scientific reduction betrays a dangerous presumption. To give a privileged position in this way to such an aspect of analysis is to mutilate man and, under the pretext of a scientific procedure, to make it impossible to understand man in his totality.

---

[22] Cf. Rom 15:16.
[23] *Gaudium et Spes*, 39:AAS 58 (1966), p. 1057.

39. One must be no less attentive to the action which the human sciences can instigate, giving rise to the elaboration of models of society to be subsequently imposed on men as scientifically tested types of behavior. Man can then become the object of manipulations directing his desires and needs and modifying his behavior and even his system of values. There is no doubt that there exists here a grave danger for the societies of tomorrow and for man himself. For even if all agree to build a new society at the service of men, it is still essential to know what sort of man is in question.

* * *

Ambiguous Nature of Progress

41. This better knowledge of man makes it possible to pass a better critical judgment upon and to elucidate a fundamental notion that remains at the basis of modern societies as their motive, their measure and their goal: namely, progress. Since the nineteenth century, western societies and, as a result, many others have put their hopes in ceaselessly renewed and indefinite progress. They saw this progress as man's effort to free himself in face of the demands of nature and of social constraints; progress was the condition for and the yardstick of human freedom. Progress, spread by the modern media of information and by the demand for wider knowledge and greater consumption, has become an omnipresent ideology. Yet a doubt arises today regarding both its value and its result. What is the meaning of this never-ending, breathless pursuit of a progress that always eludes one just when one believes one has conquered it sufficiently in order to enjoy it in peace? If it is not attained, it leaves one dissatisfied. Without doubt, there has been just condemnation of the limits and even the misdeeds of a merely quantitative economic growth; there is a desire to attain objectives of a qualitative order also. The quality and the truth of human relations, the degree of participation and of responsibility, are no less significant and important for the future of society than the quantity and variety of the goods produced and consumed.

Overcoming the temptation to wish to measure everything in terms of efficiency and of trade, and in terms of the interplay of forces and interests, man today wishes to replace these quantitative criteria with the intensity of communication, the spread of knowledge and culture, mutual service and a combining of efforts for a common task. Is not genuine progress to be found in the development of moral consciousness, which will lead man to exercise a wider solidarity and to open himself freely to others and to God? For a Christian, progress necessarily comes up against the eschatological mystery of death. The death of Christ and his resurrection and the outpouring of the Spirit of the Lord help man to place his freedom, in creativity and gratitude, within the context of the truth of all progress and the only hope which does not deceive.[26]

Christians Face to Face with These New Problems

Dynamism of the Church's Social Teaching

42. In the face of so many new questions the Church makes an effort to reflect in order to give an answer, in its own sphere, to men's expectations. If today the problems seem original in their breadth and their urgency, is man without the means of solving them? It is with all its dynamism that the social teaching of the Church accompanies men in their search. If it does not intervene to authenticate a given structure or to propose a ready-made model, it does not thereby limit itself to recalling general principles. It develops through reflection applied to the changing situations of this world, under the driving force of the Gospel as the source of renewal when its message is accepted in its totality and with all its demands. It also develops with the sensitivity proper to the Church which is characterized by a disinterested will to serve and by attention to the poorest.

Finally, it draws upon its rich experience of many centuries which enables it, while continuing its permanent preoccupations, to undertake the daring and creative innovations which the present state of the world requires.

For Greater Justice

43. There is a need to establish a greater justice in the sharing of goods, both within national communities and on the international level. In international exchanges there is a need to go beyond relationships based on force, in order to arrive at agreements reached with the good of all in mind. Relationships based on force have never in fact established justice in a true and lasting manner, even if at certain times the alternation of positions can often make it possible to find easier conditions for dialogue. The use of force moreover leads to the setting in motion of opposing forces, and from this springs a climate of struggle which opens the way to situations of extreme violence and to abuses.[27]

---

[26] Cf. Rom 5:5.
[27] *Populorum Progressio*, 56ff.: AAS 59 (1967), pp. 285ff.

But, as we have often stated, the most important duty in the realm of justice is to allow each country to promote its own development, within the framework of a cooperation free from any spirit of domination, whether economic or political. The complexity of the problems raised is certainly great, in the present intertwining of mutual dependences. Thus it is necessary to have the courage to undertake a revision of the relationships between nations, whether it is a question of the international division of production, the structure of exchanges, the control of profits, the monetary system—without forgetting the actions of human solidarity—to question the models of growth of the rich nations and change people's outlooks, so that they may realize the prior call of international duty, and to renew international organizations so that they may increase in effectiveness.

44. Under the driving force of new systems of production, national frontiers are breaking down, and we can see new economic powers emerging, the multinational enterprises, which by the concentration and flexibility of their means can conduct autonomous strategies which are largely independent of the national political powers and therefore not subject to control from the point of view of the common good. By extending their activities, these private organizations can lead to a new and abusive form of economic domination on the social, cultural and even political level. The excessive concentration of means and powers that Pope Pius XI already condemned on the fortieth anniversary of *Rerum Novarum* is taking on a new and very real image.

Change of Attitudes and Structures

45. Today men yearn to free themselves from need and dependence. But this liberation starts with the interior freedom that men must find again with regard to their goods and their powers; they will never reach it except through a transcendent love for man, and, in consequence, through a genuine readiness to serve. Otherwise, as one can see only too clearly, the most revolutionary ideologies lead only to a change of masters; once installed in power in their turn, these new masters surround themselves with privileges, limit freedoms and allow other forms of injustice to become established.

Thus many people are reaching the point of questioning the very model of society. The ambition of many nations, in the competition that sets them in opposition and which carries them along, is to attain technological, economic and military power. This ambition then stands in the way of setting up structures in which the rhythm of progress would be regulated with a view to greater justice, instead of accentuating inequalities and living in a climate of distrust and struggle which would unceasingly compromise peace.

* * *

Call to Action

Need to Become Involved in Action

48. In the social sphere, the Church has always wished to assume a double function: first, to enlighten minds in order to assist them to discover the truth and to find the right path to follow amid the different teachings that call for their attention; and second, to take part in action and to spread, with a real care for service and effectiveness, the energies of the Gospel. Is it not in order to be faithful to this desire that the Church has sent on an apostolic mission among the workers priests who, by sharing fully the condition of the worker, are at that level the witnesses to the Church's solicitude and seeking?

It is to all Christians that we address a fresh and insistent call to action. In our encyclical on the development of peoples we urged that all should set themselves to the task:

> Laymen should take up as their own proper task the renewal of the temporal order. If the role of the hierarchy is to teach and to interpret authentically the norms of morality to be followed in this matter, it belongs to the laity, without waiting passively for orders and directives, to take the initiative freely and to infuse a Christian spirit into the mentality, customs, laws and structures of the community in which they live.[33]

Let each one examine himself, to see what he has done up to now, and what he ought to do. It is not enough to recall principles, state intentions, point to crying injustices and utter prophetic denunciations; these words will lack real weight unless they are accompanied for each individual by a livelier awareness of personal responsibility and by effective action. It is too easy to throw back on others responsibility for injustices, if at the same time one does not realize how each one shares in it personally, and how personal conversion is needed first. This basic humility will rid action of all inflexibility and sectarianism; it will also avoid discouragement in the face of a task which seems limitless in size. The Christian's hope comes primarily from the fact that he knows that the Lord is working with us in the world, continuing in his Body which is the Church—and, through the Church, in the whole of mankind—the Redemption which was accomplished on the cross and which burst forth in victory on the morning of the Resurrection.[34] This hope springs also from the fact that the Christian knows that other men are at work, to undertake

[33]81: AAS 59 (1967), pp. 296-297.
[34]Cf. Mt 28:30; Phil 2:8-11.

actions of justice and peace working for the same ends. For beneath an outward appearance of indifference, in the heart of every man there is a will to live in brotherhood and a thirst for justice and peace, which is to be expanded.

49. Thus, amid the diversity of situations, functions and organizations, each one must determine, in his conscience, the actions which he is called to share in. Surrounded by various currents into which, beside legitimate aspirations, there insinuate themselves more ambiguous tendencies, the Christian must make a wise and vigilant choice and avoid involving himself in collaboration without conditions and contrary to the principles of a true humanism, even in the name of a genuinely felt solidarity. If in fact he wishes to play a specific part as a Christian in accordance with his faith—a part that unbelievers themselves expect of him—he must take care in the midst of his active commitment to clarify his motives and to rise above the objectives aimed at, by taking a more all-embracing view which will avoid the danger of selfish particularism and oppressive totalitarianism.

Pluralism of Options

50. In concrete situations, and taking account of solidarity in each person's life, one must recognize a legitimate variety of possible options. The same Christian faith can lead to different commitments.[35] The Church invites all Christians to take up a double task of inspiring and of innovating, in order to make structures evolve, so as to adapt them to the real needs of today. From Christians who at first sight seem to be in opposition, as a result of starting from differing options, she asks an effort at mutual understanding of the other's positions and motives; a loyal examination of one's behavior and its correctness will suggest to each one an attitude of more profound charity which, while recognizing the differences, believes nonetheless in the possibility of convergence and unity. "The bonds which unite the faithful are mightier than anything which divides them."[36]

It is true that many people, in the midst of modern structures and conditioning circumstances, are determined by their habits of thought and their functions, even apart from the safeguarding of material interests. Others feel so deeply the solidarity of classes and cultures that they reach the point of sharing without reserve all the judgments and options of their surroundings.[37] Each one will take great care to examine himself and to bring about that true freedom according to

[35] *Gaudium et Spes*, 43:AAS 58 (1966), p. 1061.
[36] Ibid., 93:p. 1113.
[37] Cf. 1 Thes 5:21.

Christ which makes one receptive to the universal in the very midst of the most particular conditions.

51. It is in this regard too that Christian organizations, under their different forms, have a responsibility for collective action. Without putting themselves in the place of the institutions of civil society, they have to express, in their own way and rising above their particular nature, the concrete demands of the Christian faith for a just, and consequently necessary, transformation of society.[38]

Today more than ever the Word of God will be unable to be proclaimed and heard unless it is accompanied by the witness of the power of the Holy Spirit, working within the action of Christians in the service of their brothers, at the points in which their existence and their future are at stake.

52. In expressing these reflections to you, venerable brother, we are of course aware that we have not dealt with all the social problems that today face the man of faith and men of good will. Our recent declarations—to which has been added your message of a short time ago on the occasion of the launching of the Second Development Decade—particularly concerning the duties of the community of nations in the serious question of the integral and concerted development of man, are still fresh in people's minds. We address these present reflections to you with the aim of offering to the Council of the Laity and the Pontifical Commission Justice and Peace some fresh contributions, as well as an encouragement, for the pursuit of their task of "awakening the People of God to a full understanding of its role at the present time" and of "promoting the apostolate on the international level."[39]

It is with these sentiments, venerable brother, that we impart to you our apostolic blessing.

From the Vatican, May 14, 1971.

Paulus PP. VI

---

[38] *Lumen Gentium*, 31:AAS 57 (1965), pp. 37-38; *Apostolicam Actuositatem*, 5:AAS 58 (1966), p. 842.

[39] *Catholicam Christi Ecclesiam*, AAS 59 (1967), pp. 26 and 27.

Introduction to Justice in the World

The spirit of Paul VI's teachings on economic issues strongly influenced the bishops who gathered in Rome for the 1971 Synod to discuss justice in the world. In addition, many of the bishops from Latin America had participated in the historic assembly at Medellin, Colombia in 1968, where a new course was charted for the Church in the region, a course that centered around a commitment to the poor.

Even more firmly than the conciliar documents, *Justice in the World* shows the internationalization of Catholic experience and Catholic concern. While lacking the same authority as an encyclical or a conciliar decree, it nonetheless serves to reaffirm the direction Paul VI took in *Populorum Progressio* and the Latin American bishops endorsed at Medellin. Representative bishops from around the world chose to follow the Pope's lead in spite of considerable criticism of *Populorum Progressio* from conservative Catholic circles.

Though we are chiefly interested in the Synod's views on economic matters, it is necessary to mention the particular spirituality with which its economic teaching is interwoven. This spirituality has a distinctly Incarnational thrust, which in turn implies a second characteristic: commitment to the liberation of oppressed humanity around the globe. In what has become a classic element in contemporary Catholic spirituality, the bishops remind us that "Action on behalf of justice and participation in the transformation of the world fully appear . . . as a constitutive dimension of the preaching of the Gospel or, in other words, of the Church's redemption of the human race and its liberation from every oppressive situation." All Catholics who wish to possess a Gospel-inspired spirituality are called to join in the struggle for economic betterment. The bishops will accept no compromise in this regard. The Synod has brought to a climax various tendencies present in official Catholicism since the issuance of *Mater et Magistra.*

Turning to its perspective on economic questions, we find *Justice in the World* strongly committed to the right of *have-not* nations to self-development "in the face of international systems of domination." This right to development is viewed as "a dynamic interpenetration of all those fundamental human rights upon which the aspirations of individuals and nations are based." The bishops insist on the need to alter basic social structures that inhibit realization of the right to development.

This is a crucial point. The Synod has recognized that Catholic spirituality must go beyond mere personal conversion, as important as that is. We must confront social structural sin, especially insofar as such sin permeates the international economic structures of our time. While this notion of social structural sin had been developing for some years, the 1971 Synod brought it to the attention of the Catholic world in a bolder way than ever before. The bishops remain convinced that only if substantive adjustments are made in the world economy will the just aspirations of the underdeveloped nations be satisfied. These adjustments involve enabling the developing nations to acquire a greater degree of self-determination in economic affairs and a stronger voice in setting international economic policy.

Justice in the World clearly opts for an international resolution of current economic injustices. Only in an international context, the bishops believe, can the developed and developing nations work out new economic relationships that assure the latter more equitable prices for their raw materials and open up new markets to them in the industrialized world. The Synod document comes quite close to calling for a new international economic order, as subsequently propounded by the organization of developing countries through United Nations channels.

Like *Populorum Progressio, Justice in the World* has elicited sharply different reactions within Catholicism. Many hail it as an historic attempt to reorient the Church worldwide just as the Medellin conference placed the Church in Latin America squarely behind the people's quest for justice. Others feel the document too closely echoes Third World rhetoric and is unfair to the developed countries. These critics also remain unconvinced that much economic development will be accomplished in an international context. In their judgment, bilateral negotiations and restricted forms of cooperation will ultimately prove far more effective.

The debate continues today.

Justice in the World

SYNOD OF BISHOPS

Rome, 1971

Introduction

Gathered from the whole world, in communion with all who believe in Christ and with the entire human family, and opening our hearts to the Spirit who is making the whole of creation new, we have questioned ourselves about the mission of the People of God to further justice in the world.

Scrutinizing the *signs of the times* and seeking to detect the meaning of emerging history, while at the same time sharing the aspirations and questionings of all those who want to build a more human world, we have listened to the Word of God that we might be converted to the fulfilling of the divine plan for the salvation of the world.

Even though it is not for us to elaborate a very profound analysis of the situation of the world, we have nevertheless been able to perceive the serious injustices which are building around the world of men a network of domination, oppression and abuses which stifle freedom and which keep the greater part of humanity from sharing in the building up and enjoyment of a more just and more fraternal world.

At the same time we have noted the inmost stirring moving the world in its depths. There are facts constituting a contribution to the furthering of justice. In associations of men and among peoples themselves there is arising a new awareness which shakes them out of any fatalistic resignation and which spurs them on to liberate themselves and to be responsible for their own destiny. Movements among men are seen which express hope in a better world and a will to change whatever has become intolerable.

Listening to the cry of those who suffer violence and are oppressed by unjust systems and structures, and hearing the appeal of a world that by its perversity contradicts the plan of its Creator, we have shared our awareness of the Church's vocation to be present in the heart of the world by proclaiming the Good News to the poor, freedom to the oppressed, and joy to the afflicted. The hopes and forces which are moving the world in its very foundations are not foreign to the dynamism of the Gospel, which through the power of the Holy Spirit frees men from personal sin and from its consequences in social life.

The uncertainty of history and the painful convergences in the ascending path of the human community direct us to sacred history; there God has revealed himself to us, and made known to us, as it is brought progressively to realization, his plan of liberation and salvation which is once and for all fulfilled in the Paschal Mystery of Christ. Action on behalf of justice and participation in the transformation of the world fully appear to us as a constitutive dimension of the preaching of the Gospel, or, in other words, of the Church's mission for the redemption of the human race and its liberation from every oppressive situation.

I
Justice and World Society

Crisis of Universal Solidarity

The world in which the Church lives and acts is held captive by a tremendous paradox. Never before have the forces working for bringing about a unified world society appeared so powerful and dynamic; they are rooted in the awareness of the full basic equality as well as of the human dignity of all. Since men are members of the same human family, they are indissolubly linked with one another in the one destiny of the whole world, in the responsibility for which they all share.

The new technological possibilities are based upon the unity of science, on the global and simultaneous character of communications and on the birth of an absolutely interdependent economic world. Moreover, men are beginning to grasp a new and more radical dimension of unity; for they perceive that their resources, as well as the precious treasures of air and water—without which there cannot be life—and the small delicate biosphere of the whole complex of all life on earth, are not infinite, but on the contrary must be saved and preserved as a unique patrimony belonging to all mankind.

The paradox lies in the fact that within this perspective of unity the forces of division and antagonism seem today to be increasing in strength. Ancient divisions between nations and empires, between races and classes, today possess new technological instruments of destruction. The arms race is a threat to man's highest good, which is life; it makes poor peoples and individuals yet more miserable, while making richer those already powerful; it creates a continuous danger of conflagration, and in the case of nuclear arms, it threatens to destroy all life from the face of the earth. At the same time new divisions are being born to separate man from his neighbor. Unless combatted and overcome by social and political action, the influence of the new industrial and technological order favors the concentration of wealth, power and decision-making in the hands of a small public or private controlling group. Economic injustice and lack of social participation keep a man from attaining his basic human and civil rights.

In the last 25 years a hope has spread through the human race that economic growth would bring about such a quantity of goods that it would be possible to feed the hungry at least with the crumbs falling from the table, but this has proved a vain hope in underdeveloped areas and in pockets of poverty in wealthier areas, because of the rapid growth of population and of the labor force, because of rural stagnation and the lack of agrarian reform, and because of the massive migratory flow to the cities, where the industries, even though endowed with huge sums of money, nevertheless provide so few jobs that not infrequently one worker in four is left unemployed. These stifling oppressions constantly give rise to great numbers of *marginal* persons, ill-fed, inhumanly housed, illiterate and deprived of political power as well as of the suitable means of acquiring responsibility and moral dignity.

Furthermore, such is the demand for resources and energy by the richer nations, whether capitalist or socialist, and such are the effects of dumping by them in the atmosphere and the sea that irreparable damage would be done to the essential elements of life on earth, such as air and water, if their high rates of consumption and pollution, which are constantly on the increase, were extended to the whole of mankind.

The strong drive towards global unity, the unequal distribution which places decisions concerning three quarters of income, investment and trade in the hands of one third of the human race, namely the more highly developed part, the insufficiency of a merely economic progress, and the new recognition of the material limits of the biosphere—all this makes us aware of the fact that in today's world new modes of understanding human dignity are arising.

The Right to Development

In the face of international systems of domination, the bringing about of justice depends more and more on the determined will for development.

In the developing nations and in the so-called socialist world, that determined will asserts itself especially in a struggle for forms of claiming one's rights and self-expression, a struggle caused by the evolution of the economic system itself.

This aspiring to justice asserts itself in advancing beyond the threshold at which begins a consciousness of enhancement of personal worth (cf. *Populorum Progressio* 15; A.A.S. 59, 1967, p. 265) with regard both to the whole man and the whole of mankind. This is expressed in an awareness of the right to development. The right to development must be seen as a dynamic interpenetration of all those fundamental human rights upon which the aspirations of individuals and nations are based.

This desire however will not satisfy the expectations of our time if it ignores the objective obstacles which social structures place in the way of conversion of hearts, or even of the realization of the ideal of charity. It demands on the contrary that the general condition of being marginal in society be overcome, so that an end will be put to the systematic barriers and vicious circles which oppose the collective advance towards enjoyment of adequate remuneration of the factors of production, and which strengthen the situation of discrimination with regard to access to opportunities and collective services from which a great part of the people are now excluded. If the developing nations and regions do not attain liberation through development, there is a real danger that the conditions of life created especially by colonial domination may evolve into a new form of colonialism in which the developing nations will be the victims of the interplay of international economic forces. That right to development is above all a right to hope according to the concrete measure of contemporary humanity. To respond to such a hope, the concept of evolution must be purified of those myths and false convictions which have up to now gone with a thought pattern subject to a kind of deterministic and automatic notion of progress.

By taking their future into their own hands through a determined will for progress, the developing peoples—even if they do not achieve the final goal—will authentically manifest their own personalization. And in order that they may cope with the unequal relationships within the present world complex, a certain responsible nationalism gives them the impetus needed to acquire an identity of their own. From this basic self-determination can come attempts at putting together new political groupings allowing full development to these peoples; there can also come measures necessary for overcoming the inertia which could render fruitless such an effort—as in some cases population pressure; there can also come new sacrifices which the growth of planning demands of a generation which wants to build its own future.

On the other hand, it is impossible to conceive true progress without recognizing the necessity—within the political system chosen—of a development composed both of economic growth and participation; and the necessity too of an increase in wealth implying as well social progress by the entire community as it overcomes regional imbalance and islands of prosperity. Participation constitutes a right which is to be applied both in the economic and in the social and political field.

While we again affirm the right of people to keep their own identity, we see ever more clearly that the fight against a modernization destructive of the proper characteristics of nations remains quite ineffective as long as it appeals only to sacred historical customs and venerable ways of life. If modernization is accepted with the intention that it serve the good of the nation, men will be able to create a culture which will constitute a true heritage of their own in the manner of a true social memory, one which is active and formative of authentic creative personality in the assembly of nations.

Voiceless Injustices

We see in the world a set of injustices which constitute the nucleus of today's problems and whose solution requires the undertaking of tasks and functions in every sector of society, and even on the level of the global society towards which we are speeding in this last quarter of the twentieth century. Therefore we must be prepared to take on new functions and new duties in every sector of human activity and especially in the sector of world society, if justice is really to be put into practice. Our action is to be directed above all at those men and nations which because of various forms of oppression and because of the present character of our society are silent, indeed voiceless, victims of injustice.

Take, for example, the case of migrants. They are often forced to leave their own country to find work, but frequently find the doors closed in their faces because of discriminatory attitudes, or, if they can enter, they are often obliged to lead an insecure life or are treated in an inhuman manner. The same is true of groups that are less well off on the social ladder such as workers and especially farm workers who play a very great part in the process of development.

To be especially lamented is the condition of so many millions of refugees, and of every group or people suffering persecution—sometimes in institutionalized form—for racial or ethnic origin or on tribal grounds. This persecution on tribal grounds can at times take on the characteristics of genocide.

In many areas justice is seriously injured with regard to people who are suffering persecution for their faith, or who are in many ways being ceaselessly subjected by political parties and public authorities, to an action of oppressive atheization, or who are deprived of religious liberty either by being kept from honoring God in public worship, or by being prevented from publicly teaching and spreading their faith, or by being prohibited from conducting their temporal affairs according to the principles of their religion.

Justice is also being violated by forms of oppression, both old and new, springing from restriction of the rights of individuals. This is occurring both in the form of repression by the political power and of violence on the part of private reaction, and can reach the extreme of affecting the basic conditions of personal integrity. There are well known cases of torture, especially of political prisoners, who besides are frequently denied due process or who are subjected to arbitrary procedures in their trial. Nor can we pass over the prisoners of war who even after the Geneva Convention are being treated in an inhuman manner.

The fight against legalized abortion and against the imposition of contraceptives and the pressures exerted against war are significant forms of defending the right to life.

Furthermore, contemporary consciousness demands truth in the communications systems, including the right to the image offered by the media and the opportunity to correct its manipulation. It must be stressed that the right, especially that of children and the young, to education and to morally correct conditions of life and communications media is once again being threatened in our days. The activity of families in social life is rarely and insufficiently recognized by state institutions. Nor should we forget the growing number of persons who are often abandoned by their families and by the community: the old, orphans, the sick and all kinds of people who are rejected.

The Need for Dialogue

To obtain true unity of purpose, as is demanded by the world society of men, a mediatory role is essential to overcome day by day the opposition, obstacles and ingrained privileges which are to be met with in the advance towards a more human society.

But effective mediation involves the creation of a lasting atmosphere of dialogue. A contribution to the progressive realization of this can be made by men unhampered by geopolitical, ideological or socioeconomic conditions or by the generation gap. To restore the meaning of life by adherence to authentic values, the participation and witness of the rising generation of youth is as necessary as communication among peoples.

II
The Gospel Message and the Mission of the Church

In the face of the present-day situation of the world, marked as it is by the grave sin of injustice, we recognize both our responsibility and our inability to overcome it by our own strength. Such a situation urges us to listen with a humble and open heart to the word of God, as he shows us new paths towards action in the cause of justice in the world.

The Saving Justice of God through Christ

In the Old Testament God reveals himself to us as the liberator of the oppressed and the defender of the poor, demanding from man faith in him and justice towards man's neighbor. It is only in the observance of the duties of justice that God is truly recognized as the liberator of the oppressed.

By his action and teaching Christ united in an indivisible way the relationship of man to God and the relationship of man to other men. Christ lived his life in the world as a total giving of himself to God for the salvation and liberation of men. In his preaching he proclaimed the fatherhood of God towards all men and the intervention of God's justice on behalf of the needy and the oppressed (Lk 6:21-23). In this way he identified himself with his "least brethren," as he stated: "As you did it to one of the least of these my brethren, you did it to me" (Mt 25:40).

From the beginning the Church has lived and understood the death and resurrection of Christ as a call by God to conversion in the faith of Christ and in fraternal love, perfected in mutual help even to the point of a voluntary sharing of material goods.

Faith in Christ, the Son of God and the Redeemer, and love of neighbor constitute a fundamental theme of the writers of the New Testament. According to St. Paul, the whole of the Christian life is summed up in faith effecting that love and service of neighbor which involve the fulfillment of the demands of justice. The Christian lives under the interior law of liberty, which is a permanent call to man to turn away from self-sufficiency to confidence in God and from concern for self to a sincere love of neighbor. Thus takes place his genuine liberation and the gift of himself for the freedom of others.

According to the Christian message, therefore, man's relationship to his neighbor is bound up with his relationship to God; his response to the love of God, saving us through Christ, is shown to be effective in his love and service of men. Christian love of neighbor and justice cannot be separated. For love implies an absolute demand for justice, namely a recognition of the dignity and rights of one's neighbor. Justice attains its inner fullness only in love. Because every man is truly a visible image of the invisible God and a brother of Christ, the Christian finds in every man God himself and God's absolute demand for justice and love.

The present situation of the world, seen in the light of faith, calls us back to the very essence of the Christian message, creating in us a deep awareness of its true meaning and of its urgent demands. The mission of preaching the Gospel dictates at the present time that we should dedicate ourselves to the liberation of man even in his present existence in this world. For unless the Christian message of love and justice shows its effectiveness through action in the cause of justice in the world, it will only with difficulty gain credibility with the men of our times.

The Mission of the Church, Hierarchy and Christians

The Church has received from Christ the mission of preaching the gospel message, which contains a call to man to turn away from sin to the love of the Father, universal brotherhood and a consequent demand for justice in the world. This is the reason why the Church has the right, indeed the duty, to proclaim justice on the social, national and international level, and to denounce instances of injustice, when the fundamental rights of man and his very salvation demand it. The Church, indeed, is not alone responsible for justice in the world; however, she has a proper and specific responsibility which is identified with her mission of giving witness before the world of the need for love and justice contained in the gospel message, a witness to be carried out in Church institutions themselves and in the lives of Christians.

Of itself it does not belong to the Church, insofar as she is a religious and hierarchical community, to offer concrete solutions in the social, economic and political spheres for justice in the world. Her mission involves defending and promoting the dignity and fundamental rights of the human person.

The members of the Church, as members of society, have the same right and duty to promote the common good as do other citizens. Christians ought to fulfill their temporal obligations with fidelity and competence. They should act as a leaven in the world, in their family, professional, social, cultural and political life. They must accept their responsibilities in this entire area under the influence of the Gospel and the teaching of the Church. In this way they testify to the power of the Holy Spirit through their action in the service of men in those things which are decisive for the existence and the future of humanity. While in such activities they generally act on their own initiative without involving the responsibility of the ecclesiastical hierarchy, in a sense they do involve the responsibility of the Church whose members they are.

III
The Practice of Justice

The Church's Witness

Many Christians are drawn to give authentic witness on behalf of justice by various modes of action for justice, action inspired by love in accordance with the grace which they have received from God. For some of them, this action finds its place in the sphere of social and political conflicts in which Christians bear witness to the Gospel by pointing out that in history there are sources of progress other than conflict, namely love and right. This priority of love in history draws other Christians to prefer the way of nonviolent action and work in the area of public opinion.

While the Church is bound to give witness to justice, she recognizes that anyone who ventures to speak to people about justice must first be just in their eyes. Hence we must undertake an examination of the modes of acting and of the possessions and life style found within the Church herself.

Within the Church rights must be preserved. No one should be deprived of his ordinary rights because he is associated with the Church in one way or another. Those who serve the Church by their labor, including priests and religious, should receive a sufficient livelihood and enjoy the social security which is customary in their region. Lay people should be given fair wages and a system for promotion. We reiterate the recommendations that lay people should exercise more important functions with regard to Church property and should share in its administration.

We also urge that women should have their own share of responsibility and participation in the community life of society and likewise of the Church.

We propose that this matter be subjected to a serious study employing adequate means: for instance, a mixed commission of men and women, religious and lay people, of differing situations and competence.

The Church recognizes everyone's right to suitable freedom of expression and thought. This includes the right of everyone to be heard in a spirit of dialogue which preserves a legitimate diversity within the Church.

The form of judicial procedure should give the accused the right to know his accusers and also the right to a proper defense. To be complete, justice should include speed in its procedure. This is especially necessary in marriage cases.

Finally, the members of the Church should have some share in the drawing up of decisions, in accordance with the rules given by the Second Vatican Ecumenical Council and the Holy See, for instance with regard to the setting up of councils at all levels.

In regard to temporal possessions, whatever be their use, it must never happen that the evangelical witness which the Church is required to give becomes ambiguous. The preservation of certain positions of privilege must constantly be submitted to the test of this principle. Although in general it is difficult to draw a line between what is needed for right use and what is demanded by prophetic witness, we must certainly keep firmly to this principle: our faith demands of us a certain sparingness in use, and the Church is obliged to live and administer its own goods in such a way that the Gospel is proclaimed to the poor. If instead the Church appears to be among the rich and the powerful of this world its credibility is diminished.

Our examination of conscience now comes to the life style of all: bishops, priests, religious and lay people. In the case of needy peoples it must be asked whether belonging to the Church places people on a rich island within an ambient of poverty. In societies enjoying a higher level of consumer spending, it must be asked whether our life style exemplifies that sparingness with regard to consumption which we preach to others as necessary in order that so many millions of hungry people throughout the world may be fed.

Educating to Justice

Christians' specific contribution to justice is the day-to-day life of the individual believer acting like the leaven of the Gospel in his family, his school, his work and his social and civic life. Included with this are the perspectives and meaning which the faithful can give to human effort. Accordingly, educational method must be such as to teach men to live their lives in its entire reality and in accord with the evangelical principles of personal and social morality which are expressed in the vital Christian witness of one's life.

The obstacles to the progress which we wish for ourselves and for mankind are obvious. The method of education very frequently still in use today encourages narrow individualism. Part of the human family lives immersed in a mentality which exalts possessions. The school and the communications media, which are often obstructed by the established order, allow the formation only of the man desired by that order, that is to say, man in its image, not a new man but a copy of man as he is.

But education demands a renewal of heart, a renewal based on the recognition of sin in its individual and social manifestations. It will also inculcate a truly and entirely human way of life in justice, love and simplicity. It will likewise awaken a critical sense, which will lead us to reflect on the society in which we live and on its values; it will make men ready to renounce these values when they cease to promote justice for all men. In the developing countries, the principal aim of this education for justice consists in an attempt to awaken consciences to a knowledge of the concrete situation and in a call to secure a total improvement; by these means the transformation of the world has already begun.

Since this education makes men decidedly more human, it will help them to be no longer the object of manipulation by communications media or political forces. It will instead enable them to take in hand their own destinies and bring about communities which are truly human.

Accordingly, this education is deservedly called a continuing education, for it concerns every person and every age. It is also a practical education: it comes through action, participation and vital contact with the reality of injustice.

Education for justice is imparted first in the family. We are well aware that not only Church institutions but also other schools, trade unions and political parties are collaborating in this.

The content of this education necessarily involves respect for the person and for his dignity. Since it is world justice which is in question here, the unity of the human family within which, according to God's plan, a human being is born must first of all be seriously affirmed. Christians find a sign of this solidarity in the fact that all human beings are destined to become in Christ sharers in the divine nature.

The basic principles whereby the influence of the Gospel has made itself felt in contemporary social life are to be found in the body of teaching set out in a gradual and timely way from the encyclical *Rerum Novarum* to the letter *Octogesima Adveniens*. As never before, the Church has, through the Second Vatican Council's constitution *Gaudium et Spes*, better understood the situation in the modern world, in which the Christian works out his salvation by deeds of justice. *Pacem in Terris* gave us an authentic charter of human rights. In *Mater et Magistra* international justice begins to take first place; it finds more elaborate expression in *Populorum Progressio*, in the form of a true and suitable treatise on the right to development, and in *Octogesima Adveniens* is found a summary of guidelines for political action.

Like the apostle Paul, we insist, welcome or unwelcome, that the Word of God should be present in the center of human situations. Our interventions are intended to be an expression of that faith which is today binding on our lives and on the lives of the faithful. We all desire that these interventions should always be in conformity with circumstances of place and time. Our mission demands that we should courageously denounce injustice, with charity, prudence and firmness, in sincere dialogue with all parties concerned. We know that our denunciations can secure assent to the extent that they are an expression of our lives and are manifested in continuous action.

The liturgy, which we preside over and which is the heart of the Church's life, can greatly serve education for justice. For it is a thanksgiving to the Father in Christ, which through its communitarian form places before our eyes the bonds of our brotherhood and again and again reminds us of the Church's mission. The liturgy of the word, catechesis and the celebration of the sacraments have the power to help us to discover the teaching of the prophets, the Lord and the apostles on the subject of justice. The preparation for baptism is the beginning of the formation of the Christian conscience. The practice of penance should emphasize the social dimension of sin and of the sacrament. Finally, the Eucharist forms the community and places it at the service of men.

Cooperation between Local Churches

That the Church may really be the sign of that solidarity which the family of nations desires, it should show in its own life greater cooperation between the churches of rich and poor regions through spiritual communion and division of human and material resources. The present generous arrangements for assistance between churches could be made more effective by real coordination (Sacred Congregation for the Evangelization of Peoples and the Pontifical Council *Cor Unum*), through their overall view in regard to the common administration of the gifts of God, and through fraternal solidarity, which would always encourage autonomy and responsibility on the part of the beneficiaries in the determination of criteria and the choice of concrete programs and their realization.

This planning must in no way be restricted to economic programs; it should instead stimulate activities capable of developing that human and spiritual formation which will serve as the leaven needed for the integral development of the human being.

Ecumenical Collaboration

Well aware of what has already been done in this field, together with the Second Vatican Ecumenical Council we very highly commend cooperation with our separated Christian brethren for the promotion of justice in the world, for bringing about development of peoples and for establishing peace. This cooperation concerns first and foremost activities for securing human dignity and man's fundamental rights, especially the right to religious liberty. This is the source of our common efforts against discrimination on the grounds of differences of religion, race and color, culture and the like. Collaboration extends also to the study of the teaching of the Gospel insofar as it is the source of inspiration for all Christian activity. Let the Secretariat for Promoting Christian Unity and the Pontifical Commission Justice and Peace devote themselves in common counsel to developing effectively this ecumenical collaboration.

In the same spirit we likewise commend collaboration with all believers in God in the fostering of social justice, peace and freedom; indeed we commend collaboration also with those who, even though they do not recognize the Author of the world, nevertheless, in their esteem for human values, seek justice sincerely and by honorable means.

International Action

Since the Synod is of a universal character, it is dealing with those questions of justice which directly concern the entire human family. Hence, recognizing the importance of international cooperation for social and economic development, we praise above all else the inestimable work which has been done among the poorer peoples by the local churches, the missionaries and the organizations supporting them; and we intend to foster those initiatives and institutions which are working for peace, international justice and the development of man. We therefore urge Catholics to consider well the following propositions:

1. Let recognition be given to the fact that international order is rooted in the inalienable rights and dignity of the human being. Let the United Nations Declaration of Human Rights be ratified by all governments who have not yet adhered to it, and let it be fully observed by all.
2. Let the United Nations—which because of its unique purpose should promote participation by all nations—and international organizations be supported insofar as they are the beginning of a system capable of restraining the armaments race, discouraging trade in weapons, securing disarmament and settling conflicts by peaceful methods of legal action, arbitration and international police action. It is absolutely necessary that international conflicts should not be settled by war, but that other methods better befitting human nature should be found. Let a strategy of nonviolence be fostered also, and let conscientious objection be recognized and regulated by law in each nation.
3. Let the aims of the Second Development Decade be fostered. These include the transfer of a precise percentage of the annual income of the richer countries to the developing nations, fairer prices for raw materials, the opening of the markets of the richer nations and, in some fields, preferential treatment for exports of manufactured goods from the developing nations. These aims represent first guidelines for a graduated taxation of income as well as for an economic and social plan for the entire world. We grieve whenever richer nations turn their backs on this ideal goal of worldwide sharing and responsibility. We hope that no such weakening of international solidarity will take away their force from the trade discussions being prepared by the United Nations Conference on Trade and Development (UNCTAD).
4. The concentration of power which consists in almost total domination of economics, research, investment, freight charges, sea transport and securities should be progressively balanced by institutional arrangements for strengthening power and opportunities with regard to responsible decision by the developing nations and by full and

equal participation in international organizations concerned with development. Their recent *de facto* exclusion from discussions on world trade and also the monetary arrangements which vitally affect their destiny are an example of lack of power which is inadmissible in a just and responsible world order.

5. Although we recognize that international agencies can be perfected and strengthened, as can any human instrument, we stress also the importance of the specialized agencies of the United Nations, in particular those directly concerned with the immediate and more acute questions of world poverty in the field of agrarian reform and agricultural development, health, education, employment, housing, and rapidly increasing urbanization. We feel we must point out in a special way the need for some fund to provide sufficient food and protein for the real mental and physical development of children. In the face of the population explosion we repeat the words by which Pope Paul VI defined the functions of public authority in his encyclical *Populorum Progressio*:

> There is no doubt that public authorities can intervene, within the limit of their competence, by favoring the availability of appropriate information and by adopting suitable measures, provided that these be in conformity with the moral law and that they absolutely respect the rightful freedom of married couples (37; A.A.S. 59, 1967, p. 276).

6. Let governments continue with their individual contributions to a development fund, but let them also look for a way whereby most of their endeavors may follow multilateral channels, fully preserving the responsibility of the developing nations, which must be associated in decision-making concerning priorities and investments.

7. We consider that we must also stress the new worldwide preoccupation which will be dealt with for the first time in the conference on the human environment to be held in Stockholm in June 1972. It is impossible to see what right the richer nations have to keep up their claim to increase their own material demands, if the consequence is either that others remain in misery or that the danger of destroying the very physical foundations of life on earth is precipitated. Those who are already rich are bound to accept a less material way of life, with less waste, in order to avoid the destruction of the heritage which they are obliged by absolute justice to share with all other members of the human race.

8. In order that the right to development may be fulfilled by action:

a) people should not be hindered from attaining development in accordance with their own culture;

b) through mutual cooperation, all peoples should be able to become the principal architects of their own economic and social development;

c) every people, as active and responsible members of human society, should be able to cooperate for the attainment of the common good on an equal footing with other peoples.

Recommendations of the Synod

The examination of conscience which we have made together, regarding the Church's involvement in action for justice, will remain ineffective if it is not given flesh in the life of our local churches at all their levels. We also ask the episcopal conferences to continue to pursue the perspectives which we have had in view during the days of this meeting and to put our recommendations into practice, for instance by setting up centers of social and theological research.

We also ask that there be recommended to the Pontifical Commission Justice and Peace, the Council of the Secretariat of the Synod and to competent authorities, the description, consideration and deeper study of the wishes and desires of our assembly, and that these bodies should bring to a successful conclusion what we have begun.

IV
A Word of Hope

The power of the Spirit, who raised Christ from the dead, is continuously at work in the world. Through the generous sons and daughters of the Church likewise, the People of God is present in the midst of the poor and of those who suffer oppression and persecution; it lives in its own flesh and its own heart the Passion of Christ and bears witness to his resurrection.

The entire creation has been groaning till now in an act of giving birth, as it waits for the glory of the children of God to be revealed (cf. Rom 8:22). Let Christians therefore be convinced that they will yet find the fruits of their own nature and effort cleansed of all impurities in the new earth which God is now preparing for them, and in which there will be the kingdom of justice and love, a kingdom which will be fully perfected when the Lord will come himself.

Hope in the coming kingdom is already beginning to take root in the hearts of men. The radical transformation of the world in the Paschal Mystery of the Lord gives full meaning to the efforts of men, and in particular of the young, to lessen injustice, violence and hatred and to advance all together in justice, freedom, brotherhood and love.

At the same time as it proclaims the Gospel of the Lord, its Redeemer and Savior, the Church calls on all, especially the poor, the oppressed and the afflicted, to cooperate with God to bring about liberation from every sin and to build a world which will reach the fullness of creation only when it becomes the work of man for man.

Introduction to Evangelii Nuntiandi

The 1974 Synod of Bishops concentrated on working out a contemporary theology of evangelization. Hence the document that Pope Paul VI issued in the wake of the Synod's deliberations, *Evangelii Nuntiandi,* is not central to the development of Catholic thought on economic issues. It does make several relevant points, however.

First, the Pope reaffirms the intimate tie between gospel proclamation and the struggle for social justice. Evangelization must address the total liberation of humanity, which includes liberation from economic deprivation: "Prompted by the love of Christ and illumined by the light of the Gospel, let us nurture the hope that the Church, in more faithfully fulfilling the work of evangelization, will announce the total salvation of man or rather his complete liberation, and from now on will start to bring this about."

Second, Paul unreservedly endorses the notion of structural sin as he calls upon the faithful "to eliminate the social consequences of sin which are translated into unjust social and political structures." Third, *Octogesima Adveniens'* emphasis on having a special concern for the poor is repeated. Finally, the Pope introduces the notion of solidarity with the economically oppressed, a theme that has become a rallying cry for many Catholics ministering in the developing world.

Pope Paul VI and the 1974 Synod faced up to the criticisms leveled against *Justice in the World* and *Octogesima Adveniens* and stood its ground. The basic themes of 1971 were underscored with a new vigor.

Evangelii Nuntiandi
On Evangelization in the Modern World

POPE PAUL VI

December 8, 1975

To the Episcopate, to the Clergy and to All the Faithful of the Entire World

Selections*

* * *

I
From Christ the Evangelizer to the Evangelizing Church

Witness and Mission of Jesus

6. The witness that the Lord gives of himself and that Saint Luke gathered together in his Gospel—"I must proclaim the Good News of the kingdom of God"[12]—without doubt has enormous consequences, for it sums up the whole mission of Jesus: "That is what I was sent to do."[13] These words take on their full significance if one links them with the previous verses, in which Christ has just applied to himself the words of the Prophet Isaiah: "The Spirit of the Lord has been given to me, for he has anointed me. He has sent me to bring the Goods News to the poor."[14]

Going from town to town, preaching to the poorest—and frequently the most receptive—the joyful news of the fulfillment of the promises and of the Covenant offered by God is the mission for which Jesus declares that he is sent by the Father. And all the aspects of his mystery—the Incarnation itself, his miracles, his teaching, the gathering together of the disciples, the sending out of the Twelve, the

*Editor's Note: Deleted material in this document is indicated in the text by the symbol * * *.
[12]Lk 4:43.
[13]Ibid.
[14]Lk 4:18; cf. Is 61:1.

Cross and the Resurrection, the permanence of his presence in the midst of his own—were components of his evangelizing activity.

Jesus, the First Evangelizer

7. During the Synod, the bishops very frequently referred to this truth: Jesus himself, the Good News of God,[15] was the very first and the greatest evangelizer; he was so through and through: to perfection and to the point of the sacrifice of his earthly life.

To evangelize: what meaning did this imperative have for Christ? It is certainly not easy to express in a complete synthesis the meaning, the content and the modes of evangelization as Jesus conceived it and put it into practice. In any case the attempt to make such a synthesis will never end. Let it suffice for us to recall a few essential aspects.

Proclamation of the Kingdom of God

8. As an evangelizer, Christ first of all proclaims a kingdom, the Kingdom of God; and this is so important that, by comparison, everything else becomes "the rest," which is "given in addition."[16] Only the Kingdom therefore is absolute, and it makes everything else relative. The Lord will delight in describing in many ways the happiness of belonging to this Kingdom (a paradoxical happiness which is made up of things that the world rejects),[17] the demands of the Kingdom and its Magna Charta,[18] the heralds of the Kingdom,[19] its mysteries,[20] its children,[21] the vigilance and fidelity demanded of whoever awaits its definitive coming.[22]

Proclamation of Liberating Salvation

9. As the kernel and center of his Good News, Christ proclaims salvation, this great gift of God which is liberation from everything that oppresses man but which is above all liberation from sin and the Evil One, in the joy of knowing God and being known by him, of seeing him, and of being given over to him. All of this is begun during the life of Christ and definitively accomplished by his death and

---

[15]Cf. Mk 1:1; Rom 1:1-3.
[16]Cf. Mt 6:33.
[17]Cf. Mt 5:3-12.
[18]Cf. Mt 5,7.
[19]Cf. Mt 10.
[20]Cf. Mt 13.
[21]Cf. Mt 18.
[22]Cf. Mt 24, 25.

resurrection. But it must be patiently carried on during the course of history, in order to be realized fully on the day of the final coming of Christ, whose date is known to no one except the Father.[23]

At the Price of Crucifying Effort

10. This Kingdom and this salvation, which are the key words of Jesus Christ's evangelization, are available to every human being as grace and mercy, and yet at the same time each individual must gain them by force—they belong to the violent, says the Lord,[24] through toil and suffering, through a life lived according to the Gospel, through abnegation and the cross, through the spirit of the beatitudes. But above all each individual gains them through a total interior renewal which the Gospel calls *metanoia;* it is a radical conversion, a profound change of mind and heart.[25]

Tireless Preaching

11. Christ accomplished this proclamation of the Kingdom of God through the untiring preaching of a word which, it will be said, has no equal elsewhere: "Here is a teaching that is new, and with authority behind it."[26] "And he won the approval of all, and they were astonished by the gracious words that came from his lips."[27] "There has never been anybody who has spoken like him."[28] His words reveal the secret of God, his plan and his promise, and thereby change the heart of man and his destiny.

With Evangelical Signs

12. But Christ also carries out this proclamation by innumerable signs, which amaze the crowds and at the same time draw them to him in order to see him, listen to him and allow themselves to be transformed by him: the sick are cured, water is changed into wine, bread is multiplied, the dead come back to life. And among all these signs there is the one to which he attaches great importance: the humble and the poor are evangelized, become his disciples and gather together "in his name" in the great community of those who believe in him. For this Jesus who declared, "I must preach the Good News of the

---

[23]Cf. Mt 24:36; Acts 1:7; 1 Thes 5:1-2.
[24]Cf. Mt 11:12; Lk 16:16.
[25]Cf. Mt 4:17.
[26]Mk 1:27.
[27]Lk 4:22.
[28]Jn 7:46.

Kingdom of God,"[29] is the same Jesus of whom John the evangelist said that he had come and was to die "to gather together in unity the scattered children of God."[30] Thus he accomplishes his revelation, completing it and confirming it by the entire revelation that he makes of himself, by words and deeds, by signs and miracles, and more especially by his death, by his resurrection and by the sending of the Spirit of Truth.[31]

For an Evangelized and Evangelizing Community

13. Those who sincerely accept the Good News, through the power of this acceptance and of shared faith, therefore gather together in Jesus' name in order to seek together the Kingdom, build it up and live it. They make up a community which is in its turn evangelizing. The command to the Twelve to go out and proclaim the Good News is also valid for all Christians, though in a different way. It is precisely for this reason that Peter calls Christians "a people set apart to sing the praises of God,"[32] those marvelous things that each one was able to hear in his own language.[33] Moreover, the Good News of the Kingdom which is coming and which has begun is meant for all people of all times. Those who have received the Good News and who have been gathered by it into the community of salvation can and must communicate and spread it.

Evangelization: Vocation Proper to the Church

14. The Church knows this. She has a vivid awareness of the fact that the Savior's words, "I must proclaim the Good News of the Kingdom of God,"[34] apply in all truth to herself. She willingly adds with Saint Paul: "Not that I boast of preaching the Gospel, since it is a duty that has been laid on me; I should be punished if I did not preach it!"[35] It is with joy and consolation that at the end of the great Assembly of 1974 we heard these illuminating words: "We wish to confirm once more that the task of evangelizing all people constitutes the essential mission of the Church."[36] It is a task and mission which the vast and profound changes of present-day society make all the

---

[29]Lk 4:43.
[30]Jn 11:52.
[31]Cf. Second Vatican Ecumenical Council, *Dogmatic Constitution on Divine Revelation, Dei Verbum*, 4:AAS 58 (1966), pp. 818-819.
[32]1 Pt 2:9.
[33]Cf. Acts 2:11.
[34]Lk 4:43.
[35]1 Cor 9:16.
[36]"Declaration of the Synod Fathers," 4: *L'Osservatore Romano* (October 27, 1974), p.6.

more urgent. Evangelizing is in fact the grace and vocation proper to the Church, her deepest identity. She exists in order to evangelize, that is to say in order to preach and teach, to be the channel of the gift of grace, to reconcile sinners with God, and to perpetuate Christ's sacrifice in the Mass, which is the memorial of his death and glorious resurrection.

* * *

III
The Content of Evangelization

Essential Content and Secondary Elements

25. In the message which the Church proclaims there are certainly many secondary elements. Their presentation depends greatly on changing circumstances. They themselves also change. But there is the essential content, the living substance, which cannot be modified or ignored without seriously diluting the nature of evangelization itself.

Witness Given to the Father's Love

26. It is not superfluous to recall the following points: to evangelize is first of all to bear witness, in a simple and direct way, to God revealed by Jesus Christ, in the Holy Spirit; to bear witness that in his Son God has loved the world—that in his Incarnate Word he has given being to all things and has called men to eternal life. Perhaps this attestation of God will be for many people the unknown God[55] whom they adore without giving him a name, or whom they seek by a secret call of the heart when they experience the emptiness of all idols. But it is fully evangelizing in manifesting the fact that for man the Creator is not an anonymous and remote power; he is the Father: ". . . that we should be called children of God; and so we are."[56] And thus we are one another's brothers and sisters in God.

At the Center of the Message: Salvation in Jesus Christ

27. Evangelization will also always contain—as the foundation, center and at the same time summit of its dynamism—a clear proclamation that, in Jesus Christ, the Son of God made man, who died

[55]Cf. Acts 17:22-23.
[56]1 Jn 3:1; cf. Rom 8:14-17.

and rose from the dead, salvation is offered to all men, as a gift of God's grace and mercy.[57] And not an immanent salvation, meeting material or even spiritual needs, restricted to the framework of temporal existence and completely identified with temporal desires, hopes, affairs and struggles, but a salvation which exceeds all these limits in order to reach fulfillment in a communion with the one and only divine Absolute: a transcendent and eschatological salvation, which indeed has its beginning in this life but which is fulfilled in eternity.

Under the Sign of Hope

28. Consequently evangelization cannot but include the prophetic proclamation of a hereafter, man's profound and definitive calling, in both continuity and discontinuity with the present situation: beyond time and history, beyond the transient reality of this world, and beyond the things of this world, of which a hidden dimension will one day be revealed—beyond man himself, whose true destiny is not restricted to his temporal aspect but will be revealed in the future life.[58] Evangelization therefore also includes the preaching of hope in the promises made by God in the new Covenant in Jesus Christ, the preaching of God's love for us and of our love for God; the preaching of brotherly love for all men—the capacity of giving and forgiving, of self-denial, of helping one's brother and sister—which, springing from the love of God, is the kernel of the Gospel; the preaching of the mystery of evil and of the active search for good. The preaching likewise—and this is always urgent—of the search for God himself through prayer which is principally that of adoration and thanksgiving, but also through communion with the visible sign of the encounter with God which is the Church of Jesus Christ; and this communion in its turn is expressed by the application of those other signs of Christ living and acting in the Church which are the sacraments. To live the sacraments in this way, bringing their celebration to a true fullness, is not, as some would claim, to impede or to accept a distortion of evangelization: it is rather to complete it. For in its totality, evangelization—over and above the preaching of a message—consists in the implantation of the Church, which does not exist without the driving force

---

[57]Cf. Eph 2:8; Rom 1:16. Cf. Sacred Congregation for the Doctrine of the Faith, *Declaratio ad fidem tuendam in mysteria Incarnationis et SS. Trinitatis e quibusdam recentibus erroribus* (February 21, 1972): AAS 64 (1972), pp. 237-241.

[58]Cf. 1 Jn 3:2; Rom 8:29; Phil 3:20-21. Cf. Second Vatican Ecumenical Council, *Dogmatic Constitution on the Church, Lumen Gentium*, 48-51: AAS 57 (1965), pp. 53-58.

which is the sacramental life culminating in the Eucharist.[59]

Message Touching Life as a Whole

29. But evangelization would not be complete if it did not take account of the unceasing interplay of the Gospel and of man's concrete life, both personal and social. This is why evangelization involves an explicit message, adapted to the different situations constantly being realized, about the rights and duties of every human being, about family life without which personal growth and development is hardly possible,[60] about life in society, about international life, peace, justice and development—a message especially energetic today about liberation.

A Message of Liberation

30. It is well known in what terms numerous bishops from all the continents spoke of this at the last Synod, especially the bishops from the Third World, with a pastoral accent resonant with the voice of the millions of sons and daughters of the Church who make up those peoples. Peoples, as we know, engaged with all their energy in the effort and struggle to overcome everything which condemns them to remain on the margin of life: famine, chronic disease, illiteracy, poverty, injustices in international relations and especially in commercial exchanges, situations of economic and cultural neocolonialism sometimes as cruel as the old political colonialism. The Church, as the bishops repeated, has the duty to proclaim the liberation of millions of human beings, many of whom are her own children—the duty of assisting the birth of this liberation, of giving witness to it, of ensuring that it is complete. This is not foreign to evangelization.

Necessarily Linked to Human Advancement

31. Between evangelization and human advancement—development and liberation—there are in fact profound links. These include links of an anthropological order, because the man who is to be evangelized is not an abstract being but is subject to social and economic questions. They also include links in the theological order, since one cannot dissociate the plan of creation from the plan of Redemption. The latter plan touches the very concrete situations of injustice to be com-

---

[59] Cf. Sacred Congregation for the Doctrine of Faith, *Declaratio circa Catholicam Doctrinam de Ecclesia contra non-nullos errores hodiernos tuendam* (June 24, 1973): AAS 65 (1973), pp. 396-408.

[60] Cf. Second Vatican Ecumenical Council, *Pastoral Constitution on the Church in the Modern World, Gaudium et Spes*, 47-52: AAS 58 (1966), pp. 1067-1074; Paul VI, encyclical letter, *Humanae vitae*: AAS 60 (1968), pp. 481-503.

batted and of justice to be restored. They include links of the eminently evangelical order, which is that of charity: how in fact can one proclaim the new commandment without promoting in justice and in peace the true, authentic advancement of man? We ourself have taken care to point this out by recalling that it is impossible to accept

> that in evangelization one could or should ignore the importance of the problems so much discussed today, concerning justice, liberation, development and peace in the world. This would be to forget the lesson which comes to us from the Gospel concerning love of our neighbor who is suffering and in need.[61]

The same voices which during the Synod touched on this burning theme with zeal, intelligence and courage have, to our great joy, furnished the enlightening principles for a proper understanding of the importance and profound meaning of liberation, such as it was proclaimed and achieved by Jesus of Nazareth and such as it is preached by the Church.

Without Reduction or Ambiguity

32. We must not ignore the fact that many, even generous Christians who are sensitive to the dramatic questions involved in the problem of liberation, in their wish to commit the Church to the liberation effort are frequently tempted to reduce her mission to the dimensions of a simply temporal project. They would reduce her aims to a man-centered goal; the salvation of which she is the messenger would be reduced to material well-being. Her activity, forgetful of all spiritual and religious preoccupation, would become initiatives of the political or social order. But if this were so, the Church would lose her fundamental meaning. Her message of liberation would no longer have any originality and would easily be open to monopolization and manipulation by ideological systems and political parties. She would have no more authority to proclaim freedom as in the name of God. This is why we have wished to emphasize, in the same address at the opening of the Synod, "the need to restate clearly the specifically religious finality of evangelization. This latter would lose its reason for existence if it were to diverge from the religious axis that guides it: the Kingdom of God, before anything else, in its fully theological meaning. . . ."[62]

---

[61] Paul VI, Address for the Opening of the Third General Assembly of the Synod of Bishops (September 27, 1974): AAS 66 (1974), p. 562.
[62] Ibid.

Evangelical Liberation

33. With regard to the liberation which evangelization proclaims and strives to put into practice one should rather say this:

—it cannot be contained in the simple and restricted dimension of economics, politics, social or cultural life; it must envisage the whole man, in all his aspects, right up to and including his openness to the absolute, even the Divine Absolute;

—it is therefore attached to a certain concept of man, to a view of man which it can never sacrifice to the needs of any strategy, practice or short-term efficiency.

Centered on the Kingdom of God

34. Hence, when preaching liberation and associating herself with those who are working and suffering for it, the Church is certainly not willing to restrict her mission only to the religious field and dissociate herself from man's temporal problems. Nevertheless she reaffirms the primacy of her spiritual vocation and refuses to replace the proclamation of the Kingdom by the proclamation of forms of human liberation; she even states that her contribution to liberation is incomplete if she neglects to proclaim salvation in Jesus Christ.

On an Evangelical Concept of Man

35. The Church links human liberation and salvation in Jesus Christ, but she never identifies them, because she knows through revelation, historical experience and the reflection of faith that not every notion of liberation is necessarily consistent and compatible with an evangelical vision of man, of things and of events; she knows too that in order that God's Kingdom should come it is not enough to establish liberation and to create well-being and development.

And what is more, the Church has the firm conviction that all temporal liberation, all political liberation—even if it endeavors to find its justification in such or such a page of the Old or New Testament, even if it claims for its ideological postulates and its norms of action theological data and conclusions, even if it pretends to be today's theology—carries within itself the germ of its own negation and fails to reach the ideal that it proposes for itself, whenever its profound motives are not those of justice in charity, whenever its zeal lacks a truly spiritual dimension and whenever its final goal is not salvation and happiness in God.

Involving a Necessary Conversion

36. The Church considers it to be undoubtedly important to build up structures which are more human, more just, more respectful of the rights of the person and less oppressive and less enslaving, but she is conscious that the best structures and the most idealized systems soon become inhuman if the inhuman inclinations of the human heart are not made wholesome, if those who live in these structures or who rule them do not undergo a conversion of heart and of outlook.

Excluding Violence

37. The Church cannot accept violence, especially the force of arms—which is uncontrollable once it is let loose—and indiscriminate death as the path to liberation, because she knows that violence always provokes violence and irresistibly engenders new forms of oppression and enslavement which are often harder to bear than those from which they claimed to bring freedom. We said this clearly during our journey in Colombia: "We exhort you not to place your trust in violence and revolution: that is contrary to the Christian spirit, and it can also delay instead of advancing that social uplifting to which you lawfully aspire."[63] "We must say and reaffirm that violence is not in accord with the Gospel, that it is not Christian; and that sudden or violent changes of structures would be deceitful, ineffective of themselves, and certainly not in conformity with the dignity of the people."[64]

Specific Contribution of the Church

38. Having said this, we rejoice that the Church is becoming ever more conscious of the proper manner and strictly evangelical means that she possesses in order to collaborate in the liberation of many. And what is she doing? She is trying more and more to encourage large numbers of Christians to devote themselves to the liberation of men. She is providing these Christian *liberators* with the inspiration of faith, the motivation of fraternal love, a social teaching which the true Christian cannot ignore and which he must make the foundation of his wisdom and of his experience in order to translate it concretely into forms of action, participation and commitment. All this must characterize the spirit of a committed Christian, without confusion with tactical attitudes or with the service of a political system. The Church strives always to insert the Christian struggle for liberation into the universal plan of salvation which she herself proclaims.

What we have just recalled comes out more than once in the Synod debates. In fact we devoted to this theme a few clarifying words in

---

[63]Paul VI, Address to the Campesinos of Colombia (August 23, 1968): AAS 60 (1968), p. 623.

[64]Paul VI, Address for the Day of Development at Bogotá (August 23, 1968): AAS 60 (1968), p. 627; cf. St. Augustine *Epistola* 229, 2: PL 33, 102b.

our address to the Fathers at the end of the Assembly.[65]

It is to be hoped that all these considerations will help to remove the ambiguity which the word *liberation* very often takes on in ideologies, political systems or groups. The liberation which evangelization proclaims and prepares is the one which Christ himself announced and gave to man by his sacrifice.

Religious Liberty

39. The necessity of ensuring fundamental human rights cannot be separated from this just liberation which is bound up with evangelization and which endeavors to secure structures safeguarding human freedoms. Among these fundamental human rights, religious liberty occupies a place of primary importance. We recently spoke of the relevance of this matter, emphasizing

> how many Christians still today, because they are Christians, because they are Catholics, live oppressed by systematic persecution! The drama of fidelity to Christ and of the freedom of religion continues, even if it is disguised by categorical declarations in favor of the rights of the person and of life in society![66]

* * *

[65]Paul VI, Address for the Closing of the Third General Assembly of the Synod of Bishops (October 26, 1974): AAS 66 (1974), p. 637.
[66]Address given on October 15, 1975: *L'Osservatore Romano* (October 17, 1975).

Introduction to Redemptor Hominis and Laborem Exercens

Although Pope John Paul II has taken the Church's discussion of economic questions in some new directions, by and large, he repeats the basic affirmations of John XXIII and the II Vatican Council.

Human society was not the primary focus of John Paul's first encyclical, *Redemptor Hominis,* but it does include some reflections on economics. The tone is very similar to what we find in Paul VI and *Justice in the World*. The Pope calls for an end to a consumer mentality and to unjust social situations that increasingly threaten humanity and the environment. He castigates rich countries for their greed at the expense of poorer ones. In John Paul's mind the present world economy needs a major overhaul: "This difficult road of indispensable transformation of the structures of economic life is one on which it will not be easy to go forward without the intervention of a true conversion of mind, will and heart. The task requires resolute commitment by individuals and peoples that are free and linked in solidarity." This sense of solidarity must generate a search for economic mechanisms that promote the dignity of people in the developing world.

The principal contribution of *Redemptor Hominis* to Catholic social thought is the foundation it lays for John Paul II's detailed reflections on economics in the subsequent *Laborem Exercens*. In his first encyclical, the Pope seems to say that all social commitment derives from the Church's Christological vision. God's act in Jesus Christ, the Incarnation, is the root of concern for human dignity. Thus the Church's participation in the struggle for human rights, is based on something more than natural law or simple humanitarian impulse. Moreover, its participation in this struggle is not secondary to its supernatural mission. On the contrary, a proper appreciation of the Christological vision reveals that the struggle for human rights is an integral part of that mission.

The Pope has added further theological validation for the spirituality articulated by the Synods of 1971 and 1974. John Paul discerns an historical dimension to the notion of divine grace. This grace is not merely the source of personal unity between creature and Creator. It becomes an enabling force that allows men and women to act as *divine agents* for the transformation of life on earth. Put another way, in *Redemptor Hominis* the spiritual is unquestionably historical.

For John Paul, change in the economic sphere has more to do with the human dignity of workers than with their faith. Even more, working for economic justice, as for any other form of justice, is a way of manifesting Christological reality to the world, of making visible the human dignity inherent in the *Word-made-flesh.* In a way we have come full circle from Leo XIII's concern that continuing economic injustice might erode the faith of the European working classes. The link between faith and economic justice, which was not so strongly stressed by John XXIII and Paul VI, has been reasserted, but it is integral rather than consequential.

John Paul follows much the same track in *Laborem Exercens.* However, he makes some direct applications of principle to the economic realm. Some have described this encyclical as an ongoing philosophical meditation on human work in all its variety.

Two themes in particular emerge as central to the vision laid out in *Laborem Exercens.* The first is the centrality of work to the whole social question. The Pope makes the traditional point that exploitative working conditions are immoral. Their sinfulness becomes even more invidious, however, when we consider the dignity of the human person as a result of the Incarnation. John Paul harshly criticizes any economic system, capitalist or collectivist, that reduces work to a mere instrument. His comments also imply the priority of labor over capital. The Pope's way of stating this reality may be unique, but it is in line with the balance that has prevailed in Catholic social thought from the beginning.

The second major theme in *Laborem Exercens* strikes a somewhat new chord. Work is analyzed not only in its potential to dehumanize, but also as a means whereby the human person cooperates directly in the sanctification of all creation. While Pius XII put forth related ideas in the Christmas addresses, John Paul has developed them far more extensively and systematically. *Redemptor Hominis'* teaching that "the spiritual is the historical" is clearly applied to the realm of economic activity. Work becomes a vehicle for exercising co-creatorship.

The creation theology found in *Laborem Exercens* has caused considerable discussion in Catholic circles. Some believe it firmly supports democratic capitalism. In this interpretation, the Pope has restored the individual person graced by God as the central point of reference in any authentic economic system. He has destroyed the basis for class struggle and shifted the measure of a system's success from liberation to the presence of creativity. Further, he firmly supports capital as the material embodiment of labor and elevates private ownership above national or collectivized ownership on the grounds that the former gives more play to the creative aspects of individual work.

Others, equally in support of the encyclical, take a considerably different view. They see it as a fundamental challenge to Western capitalism, including its American version. The Pope's strong endorsement of unionization, as well as his call for new forms of profit-sharing and of comanagement and co-ownership of productive property, challenge many of capitalism's most sacred tenets.

There is little question that *Laborem Exercens* focuses on the individual in a way more reminiscent of the early encyclicals than the writings of Paul VI and the 1971 Synod. However, it is a distortion to herald the Pope as a champion of capitalism. The following passage clarifies the papal viewpoint: "We can speak of socializing only when the subject character of society is ensured, that is to say, when on the basis of his work each person is fully entitled to consider himself a part owner of the great workbench at which he is working with everyone else."

Here John Paul seems to be endorsing democratic socialism far more than democratic capitalism. The key to understanding his words may lie in the economic models for Polish society that the Solidarity movement suggested. The encyclical is very much a product of the theory and experience of that movement. When we examine Solidarity's proposals, we find a moderate form of socialism with many of the features of comanagement and co-ownership advocated in *Laborem Exercens*.

As we have noted, social analysis in *Laborem Exercens* revolves around an understanding of the human person. Far less is said about sinful social structures, and the Pope does not endorse the limited nationalization and state expropriation of private goods to which Paul VI gave qualified support. Moreover, he does not repeat Paul's direct critique of international economic institutions. Neither of John Paul's encyclicals reflect the experience of economic injustice in the Third World in the same way as *Populorum Progressio, Octogesima Adveniens,* and *Justice in the World* do.

John Paul II may believe that the Church was starting to take its cue on economic policy too much from outsiders. He appears to be attempting, like the Fribourg Union and the early encyclicals, to create a specifically Catholic social model. This model may be intended to reform both Western and Eastern economies in the direction of greater justice and participation. However, while John Paul may feel a need to qualify what some took as official Catholic preference for Third World forms of socialism after the II Vatican Council, he certainly maintains the prophetic critique of capitalism that is a consistent element in Catholic reflections on economics since Leo XIII.

Redemptor Hominis

Redeemer of Man

POPE JOHN PAUL II

March 4, 1979

To His Venerable Brothers in the Episcopate, the Priests, the Religious Families, the Sons and Daughters of the Church and to All Men and Women of Good Will at the Beginning of His Papal Ministry

Selections*

* * *

III
Redeemed Man and His Situation in the Modern World

13. Christ United Himself with Each Man

When we penetrate by means of the continually and rapidly increasing experience of the human family into the mystery of Jesus Christ, we understand with greater clarity that there is at the basis of all these ways that the Church of our time must follow, in accordance with the wisdom of Pope Paul VI,[86] one single way: it is the way that has stood the test of centuries and it is also the way of the future. Christ the Lord indicated this way especially, when, as the council teaches, "by his Incarnation, he, the Son of God, in a certain way *united himself with each man*."[87] The Church therefore sees its fundamental task in enabling that union to be brought about and renewed continually. The Church wishes to serve this single end: that each person may be able to find Christ, in order that Christ may walk with each person the path of life, with the power of the truth about man

*Editor's Note: Deleted material in this document is indicated in the text by the symbol * * *.

[86]Cf. Pope Paul VI: encyclical, *Ecclesiam suam*: AAS 56 (1964) 609-659.

[87]Vatican Council II: *Pastoral Constitution on the Church in the Modern World, Gaudium et Spes*, 22: AAS 58 (1966) 1042.

and the world that is contained in the mystery of the Incarnation and the Redemption and with the power of the love that is radiated by that truth. Against a background of the ever increasing historical processes, which seem at the present time to have results especially within the spheres of various systems, ideological concepts of the world and regimes, Jesus Christ becomes, in a way, newly present, in spite of all his apparent absences, in spite of all the limitations of the presence and of the institutional activity of the Church. Jesus Christ becomes present with the power of the truth and the love that are expressed in him with unique unrepeatable fullness in spite of the shortness of his life on earth and the even greater shortness of his public activity.

Jesus Christ is the chief way for the Church. He himself is our way "to the Father's house"[88] and is the way to each man. On this way leading from Christ to man, on this way on which Christ unites himself with each man, nobody can halt the Church. This is an exigency of man's temporal welfare and of his eternal welfare. Out of regard for Christ and in view of the mystery that constitutes the Church's own life, the Church cannot remain insensible to whatever serves man's true welfare, any more than she can remain indifferent to what threatens it. In various passages in its documents the Second Vatican Council has expressed the Church's fundamental solicitude that life in "the world should conform more to man's surpassing dignity"[89] in all its aspects, so as to make that life "ever more human."[90] This is the solicitude of Christ himself, the good Shepherd of all men. In the name of this solicitude, as we read in the council's pastoral constitution, "the Church must in no way be confused with the political community, nor bound to any political system. She is at once a sign and a safeguard of the transcendence of the human person."[91]

Accordingly, what is in question here is man in all his truth, in his full magnitude. We are not dealing with the *abstract* man, but the real, *concrete, historical* man. We are dealing with *each* man, for each one is included in the mystery of the Redemption and with each one Christ has united himself for ever through this mystery. Every man comes into the world through being conceived in his mother's womb and being born of his mother, and precisely on account of the mystery of the Redemption is entrusted to the solicitude of the Church. Her solicitude is about the whole man and is focussed on him in an altogether special manner. The object of her care is man in his unique unrepeatable human reality, which keeps intact the image and like-

[88]Cf. Jn 14:1 ff.
[89]Vatican Council II: *Pastoral Constitution on the Church in the Modern World, Gaudium et Spes,* 91: AAS 58 (1966) 1113.
[90]Ibid., 38: l. c., p. 1056.
[91]Ibid., 76: l. c., p. 1099.

ness of God himself.[92] The council points out this very fact when, speaking of that likeness, it recalls that "man is the only creature on earth that God willed for itself."[93] Man as "willed" by God, as "chosen" by him from eternity and called, destined for grace and glory—this is "each" man, "the most concrete" man, "the most real"; this is man in all the fullness of the mystery in which he has become a sharer in Jesus Christ, the mystery in which each one of the four thousand million human beings living on our planet has become a sharer from the moment he is conceived beneath the heart of his mother.

14. For the Church All Ways Lead to Man

The Church cannot abandon man, for his "destiny," that is to say his election, calling, birth and death, salvation or perdition, is so closely and unbreakably linked with Christ. We are speaking precisely of each man on this planet, this earth that the Creator gave to the first man, saying to the man and the woman: "subdue it and have dominion."[94] Each man in all the unrepeatable reality of what he is and what he does, of his intellect and will, of his conscience and heart. Man who in his reality has, because he is a "person," a history of his life that is his own and, most important, a history of his soul that is his own. Man who, in keeping with the openness of his spirit within and also with the many diverse needs of his body and his existence in time, writes this personal history of his through numerous bonds, contacts, situations, and social structures linking him with other men, beginning to do so from the first moment of his existence on earth, from the moment of his conception and birth. Man in the full truth of his existence, of his personal being and also of his community and social being—in the sphere of his own family, in the sphere of society and very diverse contexts, in the sphere of his own nation or people (perhaps still only that of his clan or tribe), and in the sphere of the whole of mankind—this man is the primary route that the Church must travel in fulfilling her mission: *he is the primary and fundamental way for the Church,* the way traced out by Christ himself, the way that leads invariably through the mystery of the Incarnation and the Redemption.

It was precisely this man in all the truth of his life, in his conscience, in his continual inclination to sin and at the same time in his continual aspiration to truth, the good, the beautiful, justice and love that the

[92]Cf. Gn 1:26.
[93]Vatican Council II: *Pastoral Constitution on the Church in the Modern World, Gaudium et Spes,* 24: AAS 58 (1966) 1045.
[94]Gn 1:28.

Second Vatican Council had before its eyes when, in outlining his situation in the modern world, it always passed from the external elements of this situation to the truth within humanity:

> In man himself many elements wrestle with one another. Thus, on the one hand, as a creature he experiences his limitations in a multitude of ways. On the other, he feels himself to be boundless in his desires and summoned to a higher life. Pulled by manifold attractions, he is constantly forced to choose among them and to renounce some. Indeed, as a weak and sinful being, he often does what he would not, and fails to do what he would. Hence he suffers from internal divisions, and from these flow so many and such great discords in society.[95]

This man is the way for the Church—a way that, in a sense, is the basis of all the other ways that the Church must walk—because man—every man without any exception whatever—has been redeemed by Christ, and because with man—with each man without any exception whatever—Christ is in a way united, even when man is unaware of it: "Christ who died and was raised up for all, provides man"—each man and every man—"with the light and the strength to measure up to his supreme calling."[96]

Since this man is the way for the Church, the way for her daily life and experience, for her mission and toil, the Church of today must be aware in an always new manner of man's "situation." That means that she must be aware of his possibilities, which keep returning to their proper bearings and thus revealing themselves. She must likewise be aware of the threats to man and of all that seems to oppose the endeavor "to make human life ever more human"[97] and make every element of this life correspond to man's true dignity—in a word, she must be aware of *all that is opposed* to that process.

15. *What Modern Man Is Afraid of*

Accordingly, while keeping alive in our memory the picture that was so perspicaciously and authoritatively traced by the Second Vatican Council, we shall try once more to adapt it to the *signs of the times* and to the demands of the situation, which is continually changing and evolving in certain directions.

The man of today seems ever to be under threat from what he produces, that is to say from the result of the work of his hands and,

---

[95]Vatican Council II: *Pastoral Constitution on the Church in the Modern World, Gaudium et Spes*, 10: AAS 58 (1966) 1032.
[96]Ibid., 10: l. c., p. 1033.
[97]Ibid., 38: l. c., p. 1056; Pope Paul VI: encyclical, *Populorum Progressio*, 21: AAS 59 (1967) 267-268.

even more so, of the work of his intellect and the tendencies of his will. All too soon, and often in an unforeseeable way, what this manifold activity of man yields is not only subjected to *alienation*, in the sense that it is simply taken away from the person who produces it, but rather it turns against man himself, at least in part, through the indirect consequences of its effects returning on himself. It is or can be directed against him. This seems to make up the main chapter of the drama of present-day human existence in its broadest and universal dimension. Man therefore lives increasingly in fear. He is afraid that what he produces—not all of it, of course, or even most of it, but part of it and precisely that part that contains a special share of his genius and initiative—can radically turn against himself; he is afraid that it can become the means and instrument for an unimaginable self-destruction, compared with which all the cataclysms and catastrophes of history known to us seem to fade away. This gives rise to a question: Why is it that the power given to man from the beginning by which he was to subdue the earth[98] turns against himself, producing an understandable state of disquiet, of conscious or unconscious fear and of menace, which in various ways is being communicated to the whole of the present-day human family and is manifesting itself under various aspects?

This state of menace for man from what he produces shows itself in various directions and various degrees of intensity. We seem to be increasingly aware of the fact that the exploitation of the earth, the planet on which we are living, demands rational and honest planning. At the same time, exploitation of the earth not only for industrial but also for military purposes and the uncontrolled development of technology outside the framework of a long-range authentically humanistic plan often bring with them a threat to man's natural environment, alienate him in his relations with nature and remove him from nature. Man often seems to see no other meaning in his natural environment than what serves for immediate use and consumption. Yet it was the Creator's will that man should communicate with nature as an intelligent and noble *master* and *guardian*, and not as a heedless *exploiter* and *destroyer*.

The development of technology and the development of contemporary civilization, which is marked by the ascendancy of technology, demand a proportional development of morals and ethics. For the present, this last development seems unfortunately to be always left behind. Accordingly, in spite of the marvel of this progress, in which it is difficult not to see also authentic signs of man's greatness, signs that in their creative seeds were revealed to us in the pages of the

---

[98]Cf. Gn 1:28.

Book of Genesis, as early as where it describes man's creation,[99] this progress cannot fail to give rise to disquiet on many counts. The first reason for disquiet concerns the essential and fundamental question: Does this progress, which has man for its author and promoter, make human life on earth *more human* in every aspect of that life? Does it make it more *worthy of man*? There can be no doubt that in various aspects it does. But the question keeps coming back with regard to what is most essential—whether in the context of this progress man, as man, is becoming truly better, that is to say more mature spiritually, more aware of the dignity of his humanity, more responsible, more open to others, especially the neediest and the weakest, and readier to give and to aid all.

This question must be put by Christians, precisely because Jesus Christ has made them so universally sensitive about the problem of man. The same question must be asked by all men, especially those belonging to the social groups that are dedicating themselves actively to development and progress today. As we observe and take part in these processes we cannot let ourselves be taken over merely by euphoria or be carried away by one-sided enthusiasm for our conquests, but we must all ask ourselves, with absolute honesty, objectivity and a sense of moral responsibility, the essential questions concerning man's situation today and in the future. Do all the conquests attained until now and those projected for the future for technology accord with man's moral and spiritual progress? In this context is man, as man, developing and progressing or is he regressing and being degraded in his humanity? In men and *in man's world*, which in itself is a world of moral good and evil, does good prevail over evil? In men and among men is there a growth of social love, of respect for the rights of others—for every man, nation and people—or on the contrary is there an increase of various degrees of selfishness, exaggerated nationalism instead of authentic love of country, and also the propensity to dominate others beyond the limits of one's legitimate rights and merits and the propensity to exploit the whole of material progress and that in the technology of production for the exclusive purpose of dominating others or of favoring this or that imperialism?

These are the essential questions that the Church is bound to ask herself, since they are being asked with greater or less explicitness by the thousands of millions of people now living in the world. The subject of development and progress is on everybody's lips and appears in the columns of all the newspapers and other publications in all the languages of the modern world. Let us not forget however that this subject contains not only affirmations and certainties but also ques-

[99]Cf. Gn 1, 2.

tions and points of anguished disquiet. The latter are no less important than the former. They fit in with the dialectical nature of human knowledge and even more with the fundamental need for solicitude by man for man, for his humanity, and for the future of people on earth. Inspired by eschatological faith, the Church considers an essential, unbreakably united element of her mission this solicitude for man, for his humanity, for the future of men on earth and therefore also for the course set for the whole of development and progress. She finds the principle of this solicitude in Jesus Christ himself, as the Gospels witness. This is why she wishes to make it grow continually through her relationship with Christ, reading man's situation in the modern world in accordance with the most important signs of our time.

16. Progress or Threat

If therefore our time, the time of our generation, the time that is approaching the end of the second millennium of the Christian era, shows itself a time of great progress, it is also seen as a time of threat in many forms for man. The Church must speak of this threat to all people of good will and must always carry on a dialogue with them about it. Man's situation in the modern world seems indeed to be far removed from the objective demands of the moral order, from the requirements of justice, and even more of social love. We are dealing here only with that which found expression in the Creator's first message to man at the moment in which he was giving him the earth, to "subdue" it.[100] This first message was confirmed by Christ the Lord in the mystery of the Redemption. This is expressed by the Second Vatican Council in these beautiful chapters of its teaching that concern man's "kingship," that is to say his call to share in the kingly function—the *munus regale*—of Christ himself.[101] The essential meaning of this "kingship" and "dominion" of man over the visible world, which the Creator himself gave man for his task, consists in the priority of ethics over technology, in the primacy of the person over things, and in the superiority of spirit over matter.

This is why all phases of present-day progress must be followed attentively. Each stage of that progress must, so to speak, be x-rayed from this point of view. What is in question is the advancement of persons, not just the multiplying of things that people can use. It is a matter—as a contemporary philosopher has said and as the council

---

[100]Gn 1:28; cf. Vatican Council II: *Decree on the Social Communications Media, Inter Mirifica*, 6: AAS 56 (1964) 147; *Pastoral Constitution on the Church in the Modern World, Gaudium et Spes*, 74, 78: AAS 58 (1966) 1095-1096, 1101-1102.
[101]Cf. Vatican Council II: *Dogmatic Constitution on the Church, Lumen Gentium*, 10, 36: AAS 57 (1965) 14-15, 41-42.

has stated—not so much of "having more" as of "being more."[102] Indeed there is already a real perceptible danger that, while man's dominion over the world of things is making enormous advances, he should lose the essential threads of his dominion and in various ways let his humanity be subjected to the world and become himself something subject to manipulation in many ways—even if the manipulation is often not perceptible directly—through the whole of the organization of community life, through the production system and through pressure from the means of social communication. Man cannot relinquish himself or the place in the visible world that belongs to him; he cannot become the slave of things, the slave of economic systems, the slave of production, the slave of his own products. A civilization purely materialistic in outline condemns man to such slavery, even if at times, no doubt, this occurs contrary to the intentions and the very premises of its pioneers. The present solicitude for man certainly has at its root this problem. It is not a matter here merely of giving an abstract answer to the question: Who is man? It is a matter of the whole of the dynamism of life and civilization. It is a matter of the meaningfulness of the various initiatives of everyday life and also of the premises for many civilization programs, political programs, economic ones, social ones, state ones, and many others.

If we make bold to describe man's situation in the modern world as far removed from the objective demands of the moral order, from the exigencies of justice, and still more from social love, we do so because this is confirmed by the well-known facts and comparisons that have already on various occasions found an echo in the pages of statements by the popes, the council and the synod.[103] Man's situation today is certainly not uniform but marked with numerous differences. These differences have causes in history, but they also

---

[102]Cf. Vatican Council II: *Pastoral Constitution on the Church in the Modern World, Gaudium et Spes*, 35: AAS 58 (1966) 1053; Pope Paul VI: *Address to Diplomatic Corps*, 7 January 1965: AAS 57 (1965) 232; encyclical, *Populorum Progressio*, 14: AAS 59 (1967) 264.

[103]Cf. Pope Pius XII: *Radio Message on the Fiftieth Anniversary of Leo XIII's* encyclical, *Rerum Novarum*, 1 June 1941: AAS 33 (1941) 195-205; *Christmas Radio Message*, 24 December 1941: AAS 34 (1942) 10-21; *Christmas Radio Message*, 24 December 1942: AAS 35 (1943) 9-24; *Christmas Radio Message*, 24 December 1943: AAS 36 (1944) 11-24; *Christmas Radio Message*, 24 December 1944: AAS 37 (1945) 10-23; *Address to the Cardinals*, 24 December 1945: AAS 38 (1946) 15-25; *Address to the Cardinals*, 24 December 1946: AAS 39 (1947) 7-17; *Christmas Radio Message*, 24 December 1947: AAS 40 (1948) 8-16; Pope John XXIII: encyclical, *Mater et Magistra*: AAS 53 (1961) 401-464; encyclical, *Pacem in Terris*: AAS 55 (1963) 257-304; Pope Paul VI: encyclical, *Ecclesiam Suam*: AAS 56 (1964) 609-659; *Address to the General Assembly of the United Nations*, 4 October 1965: AAS 57 (1965) 877-885; encyclical, *Populorum Progressio*: AAS 59 (1967) 257-299; *Address to the Campesinos of Colombia*, 23 August 1968: RRS 60 (1968) 619-623; *Speech to the General Assembly of the Latin-American Episcopate*, 24 August 1968: AAS 60 (1968) 639-649; *Speech to*

have strong ethical effects. Indeed everyone is familiar with the picture of the consumer civilization, which consists in a certain surplus of goods necessary for man and for entire societies—and we are dealing precisely with the rich highly developed societies—while the remaining societies—at least broad sectors of them—are suffering from hunger, with many people dying each day of starvation and malnutrition. Hand in hand go a certain abuse of freedom by one group—an abuse linked precisely with a consumer attitude uncontrolled by ethics—and a limitation by it of the freedom of the others, that is to say those suffering marked shortages and being driven to conditions of even worse misery and destitution.

This pattern, which is familiar to all, and the contrast referred to in the documents giving their teaching, by the popes of this century, most recently by John XXIII and by Paul VI,[104] represent, as it were, the gigantic development of the parable in the Bible of the rich banqueter and the poor man Lazarus.[105] So widespread is the phenomenon that it brings into question the financial, monetary, production and commercial mechanisms that, resting on various political pressures, support the world economy. These are proving incapable either of remedying the unjust social situations inherited from the past or of dealing with the urgent challenges and ethical demands of the present. By submitting man to tensions created by himself, dilapidating at an accelerated pace material and energy resources, and compromising the geophysical environment, these structures unceasingly make the areas of misery spread, accompanied by anguish, frustration and bitterness.[106]

We have before us here a great drama that can leave nobody indifferent. The person who, on the one hand, is trying to draw the maximum profit and, on the other hand, is paying the price in damage

---

the Conference of FAO, 16 November 1970: AAS 62 (1970) 830-838; apostolic letter, *Octogesima adveniens*: AAS 63 (1971) 401-441; *Address to the Cardinals*, 23 June 1972: AAS 64 (1972) 496-505; Pope Paul VI: *Address to the Third General Conference of the Latin-American Episcopate*, 28 January 1979: AAS 71 (1979) 187 ff.; *Address to the Indians at Cuilipan*, 29 January 1979: l.c., pp. 207 ff.; *Address to the Guadalajara Workers*, 30 January 1979: l. c., pp. 221 ff.; *Address to the Monterrey Workers*, 31 January 1979: l. c., pp. 240-242; Vatican Council II: *Declaration on Religious Freedom, Dignitatis humanae*: AAS 58 (1966) 929-941; *Pastoral Constitution on the Church in the Modern World, Gaudium et Spes*: AAS 58 (1966) 1025-1115; Documenta Synodi Episcoporum: *De iustitia in mundo*: AAS 63 (1971) 923-941.

[104] Cf. Pope John XXIII: encyclical, *Mater et Magistra*: AAS 53 (1961) 418 ff.; encyclical, *Pacem in Terris*: AAS 55 (1963) 289 ff.; Pope Paul VI, encyclical, *Populorum Progressio*: AAS 59 (1967) 257-299.

[105] Cf. Lk 16: 19-31.

[106] Cf. Pope John Paul II: *Homily at Santo Domingo*, 25 January 1979, 3: AAS 71 (1979) 157 ff.; *Address to Indians and Campesinos at Oaxaca*, 30 January 1979, 2: l.c., pp. 207 ff.; *Address to Monterrey Workers*, 31 January 1979, 4: l. c., p. 242.

and injury is always man. The drama is made still worse by the presence close at hand of the privileged social classes and of the rich countries, which accumulate goods to an excessive degree and the misuse of whose riches very often becomes the cause of various ills. Add to this the fever of inflation and the plague of unemployment—these are further symptoms of the moral disorder that is being noticed in the world situation and therefore requires daring creative resolves in keeping with man's authentic dignity.[107]

Such a task is not an impossible one. The principle of solidarity, in a wide sense, must inspire the effective search for appropriate institutions and mechanisms, whether in the sector of trade, where the laws of healthy competition must be allowed to lead the way, or on the level of a wider and more immediate redistribution of riches and of control over them, in order that the economically developing peoples may be able not only to satisfy their essential needs but also to advance gradually and effectively.

This difficult road of indispensable transformation of the structures of economic life is one on which it will not be easy to go forward without the intervention of a true conversion of mind, will and heart. The task requires resolute commitment by individuals and peoples that are free and linked in solidarity. All too often freedom is confused with the instinct for individual or collective interest or with the instinct for combat and domination, whatever be the ideological colors with which they are covered. Obviously these instincts exist and are operative, but no truly human economy will be possible unless they are taken up, directed and dominated by the deepest powers in man, which decide the true culture of peoples. These are the very sources for the effort which will express man's true freedom and which will be capable of ensuring it in the economic field also. Economic development, with every factor in its adequate functioning, must be constantly programed and realized within a perspective of universal joint development of each individual and people, as was convincingly recalled by my predecessor Paul VI in *Populorum Progressio*. Otherwise, the category of "economic progress" becomes in isolation a superior category subordinating the whole of human existence to its partial demands, suffocating man, breaking up society, and ending by entangling itself in its own tensions and excesses.

It is possible to undertake this duty. This is testified by the certain facts and the results, which it would be difficult to mention more analytically here. However, one thing is certain: at the basis of this gigantic sector it is necessary to establish, accept and deepen the sense

---

[107] Cf. Pope Paul VI, apostolic letter, *Octogesima Adveniens*, 42: AAS 63 (1971) 431.

of moral responsibility, which man must undertake. Again and always man.

This responsibility becomes especially evident for us Christians when we recall—and we should always recall it—the scene of the last judgment according to the words of Christ related in Matthew's Gospel.[108]

This eschatological scene must always be "applied" to man's history; it must always be made the "measure" for human acts as an essential outline for an examination of conscience by each and every one: "I was hungry and you gave me no food . . . naked and you did not clothe me . . . in prison and you did not visit me."[109] These words become charged with even stronger warning, when we think that, instead of bread and cultural aid, the new states and nations awakening to independent life are being offered, sometimes in abundance, modern weapons and means of destruction placed at the service of armed conflicts and wars that are not so much a requirement for defending their just rights and their sovereignty but rather a form of chauvinism, imperialism, and neocolonialism of one kind or another. We all know well that the areas of misery and hunger on our globe could have been made fertile in a short time, if the gigantic investments for armaments at the service of war and destruction had been changed into investments for food at the service of life.

This consideration will perhaps remain in part an "abstract" one. It will perhaps offer both "sides" an occasion for mutual accusation, each forgetting its own faults. It will perhaps provoke new accusations against the Church. The Church, however, which has no weapons at her disposal apart from those of the spirit, of the word and of love, cannot renounce her proclamation of "the word . . . in season and out of season."[110] For this reason she does not cease to implore each side of the two and to beg everybody in the name of God and in the name of man: Do not kill! Do not prepare destruction and extermination for men! Think of your brothers and sisters who are suffering hunger and misery! Respect each one's dignity and freedom!

* * *

[108]Cf. Mt 25:31-46.
[109]Mt 25:42, 43.
[110]2 Tm 4:2.

Laborem Exercens

On Human Work
On the Ninetieth Anniversary of *Rerum Novarum*

POPE JOHN PAUL II

September 14, 1981

To His Venerable Brothers in the Episcopate, to the Priests, to the Religious Families, to the Sons and Daughters of the Church and to All Men and Women of Good Will

Venerable Brothers and Dear Sons and Daughters
Greetings and the Apostolic Blessing

Through work man must earn his daily bread[1] and contribute to the continual advance of science and technology and, above all, to elevating unceasingly the cultural and moral level of the society within which he lives in community with those who belong to the same family. And work means any activity by man, whether manual or intellectual, whatever its nature or circumstances; it means any human activity that can and must be recognized as work, in the midst of all the many activities of which man is capable and to which he is predisposed by his very nature, by virtue of humanity itself. Man is made to be in the visible universe an image and likeness of God himself[2] and he is placed in it in order to subdue the earth.[3] From the beginning therefore he is called to work. Work is one of the characteristics that distinguish man from the rest of creatures, whose activity for sustaining their lives cannot be called work. Only man is capable of work, and only man works, at the same time by work occupying his existence on earth. Thus work bears a particular mark of man and of humanity, the mark of a person operating within a community of persons. And this mark decides its interior characteristics, in a sense it constitutes its very nature.

[1]Cf. Ps 127 (128):2; cf. also Gn 3:17-19; Prv 10:22; Ex 1:8-14; Jer 22:13.
[2]Cf. Gn 1:26.
[3]Cf. Gn 1:28.

I. Introduction

1. Human Work on the Ninetieth Anniversary of Rerum Novarum

Since May 15 of the present year was the ninetieth anniversary of the publication by the great pope of the "social question," Leo XIII, of the decisively important encyclical which begins with the words "*rerum novarum*," I wish to devote this document to human work and, even more, to man in the vast context of the reality of work. As I said in the encyclical *Redemptor Hominis*, published at the beginning of my service in the See of St. Peter in Rome, man "is the primary and fundamental way for the Church,"[4] precisely because of the inscrutable mystery of redemption in Christ; and so it is necessary to return constantly to this way and to follow it ever anew in the various aspects in which it shows us all the wealth and at the same time all the toil of human existence on earth.

Work is one of these aspects, a perennial and fundamental one, one that is always relevant and constantly demands renewed attention and decisive witness. Because fresh questions and problems are always arising, there are always fresh hopes, but also fresh fears and threats connected with this basic dimension of human existence: Man's life is built up every day from work, from work it derives its specific dignity, but at the same time work contains the unceasing measure of human toil and suffering and also of the harm and injustice which penetrate deeply into social life within individual nations and on the international level. While it is true that man eats the bread produced by the work of his hands[5]—and this means not only the daily bread by which his body keeps alive but also the bread of science and progress, civilization and culture—it is also a perennial truth that he eats this bread by "the sweat of his face,"[6] that is to say, not only by personal effort and toil, but also in the midst of many tensions, conflicts and crises, which in relationship with the reality of work disturb the life of individual societies and also of all humanity.

We are celebrating the ninetieth anniversary of the encyclical *Rerum Novarum* on the eve of new developments in technological, economic and political conditions which, according to many experts, will influence the world of work and production no less than the industrial revolution of the last century. There are many factors of a general nature: the widespread introduction of automation into many spheres

[4]Encyclical, *Redemptor Hominis*, 14: AAS 71 (1979), p. 284.
[5]Cf. Ps 127 (128):2.
[6]Gn 3:19.

of production, the increase in the cost of energy and raw materials, the growing realization that the heritage of nature is limited and that it is being intolerably polluted, and the emergence on the political scene of peoples who, after centuries of subjection, are demanding their rightful place among the nations and in international decision-making. These new conditions and demands will require a reordering and adjustment of the structures of the modern economy and of the distribution of work. Unfortunately, for millions of skilled workers these changes may perhaps mean unemployment, at least for a time, or the need for retraining. They will very probably involve a reduction or a less rapid increase in material well-being for the more developed countries. But they can also bring relief and hope to the millions who today live in conditions of shameful and unworthy poverty.

It is not for the Church to analyze scientifically the consequences that these changes may have on human society. But the Church considers it her task always to call attention to the dignity and rights of those who work, to condemn situations in which that dignity and those rights are violated, and to help to guide the above-mentioned changes so as to ensure authentic progress by man and society.

2. *In the Organic Development of the Church's Social Action and Teaching*

It is certainly true that work as a human issue is at the very center of the "social question" to which, for almost a 100 years since the publication of the above-mentioned encyclical, the Church's teaching and the many undertakings connected with her apostolic mission have been especially directed. The present reflections on work are not intended to follow a different line, but rather to be in organic connection with the whole tradition of this teaching and activity. At the same time, however, I am making them, according to the indication in the Gospel, in order to bring out from the heritage of the Gospel "what is new and what is old."[7] Certainly work is part of "what is old"—as old as man and his life on earth. Nevertheless, the general situation of man in the modern world, studied and analyzed in its various aspects of geography, culture and civilization, calls for the discovery of the new meanings of human work. It likewise calls for the formulation of the new tasks that in this sector face each individual, the family, each country, the whole human race and finally the Church herself.

During the years that separate us from the publication of the encyclical *Rerum Novarum*, the social question has not ceased to engage the Church's attention. Evidence of this are the many documents of the

[7]Cf. Mt 13:52.

magisterium issued by the popes and by the Second Vatican Council, pronouncements by individual episcopates, and the activity of the various centers of thought and of practical apostolic initiatives, both on the international level and at the level of the local churches. It is difficult to list here in detail all the manifestations of the commitment of the Church and of Christians in the social question for they are too numerous. As a result of the council, the main coordinating center in this field is the Pontifical Commission for Justice and Peace, which has corresponding bodies within the individual bishops' conferences. The name of this institution is very significant. It indicates that the social question must be dealt with in its whole complex dimension. Commitment to justice must be closely linked with commitment to peace in the modern world. This twofold commitment is certainly supported by the painful experience of the two great world wars which in the course of the last 90 years have convulsed many European countries and, at least partially, countries in other continents. It is supported, especially since World War II, by the permanent threat of a nuclear war and the prospect of the terrible self-destruction that emerges from it.

If we follow the main line of development of the documents of the supreme magisterium of the Church, we find in them an explicit confirmation of precisely such a statement of the question. The key position, as regards the question of world peace, is that of John XXIII's encyclical *Pacem in Terris*. However, if one studies the development of the question of social justice, one cannot fail to note that, whereas during the period between *Rerum Novarum* and Pius XI's *Quadragesimo Anno* the Church's teaching concentrates mainly on the just solution of the "labor question" within individual nations, in the next period the Church's teaching widens its horizon to take in the whole world. The disproportionate distribution of wealth and poverty and the existence of some countries and continents that are developed and of others that are not call for a leveling out and for a search for ways to ensure just development for all. This is the direction of the teaching in John XXIII's encyclical *Mater et Magistra*, in the pastoral constitution *Gaudium et Spes* of the Second Vatican Council and in Paul VI's encyclical *Populorum Progressio*.

This trend of development of the Church's teaching and commitment in the social question exactly corresponds to the objective recognition of the state of affairs. While in the past the *class* question was especially highlighted as the center of this issue, in more recent times it is the *world* question that is emphasized. Thus, not only the sphere of class is taken into consideration, but also the world sphere of inequality and injustice and, as a consequence, not only the class dimension, but also the world dimension of the tasks involved in the path toward the achievement of justice in the modern world. A complete analysis of the situation of the world today shows in an even deeper and fuller way the meaning of the previous analysis of social injustices; and it is the meaning that must be given today to efforts to build justice on earth, not concealing thereby unjust structures, but demanding that they be examined and transformed on a more universal scale.

3. The Question of Work, the Key to the Social Question

In the midst of all these processes—those of the diagnosis of objective social reality and also those of the Church's teaching in the sphere of the complex and many-sided social question—the question of human work naturally appears many times. This issue is, in a way, a constant factor both of social life and of the Church's teaching. Furthermore, in this teaching attention to the question goes back much further than the last 90 years. In fact the Church's social teaching finds its source in Sacred Scripture, beginning with the Book of Genesis and especially in the Gospel and the writings of the apostles. From the beginning it was part of the Church's teaching, her concept of man and life in society, and especially the social morality which she worked out according to the needs of the different ages. This traditional patrimony was then inherited and developed by the teaching of the popes on the modern "social question," beginning with the encyclical *Rerum Novarum*. In this context, study of the question of work, as we have seen, has continually been brought up to date while maintaining that Christian basis of truth which can be called ageless.

While in the present document we return to this question once more—without however any intention of touching on all the topics that concern it—this is not merely in order to gather together and repeat what is already contained in the Church's teaching. It is rather in order to highlight—perhaps more than has been done before—the fact that human work is a key, probably the essential key, to the whole social question, if we try to see that question really from the point of view of man's good. And if the solution—or rather the gradual solution—of the social question, which keeps coming up and becomes ever more complex, must be sought in the direction of "making life more human,"[8] then the key, namely human work, acquires fundamental and decisive importance.

---

[8]Second Vatican Ecumenical Council, *Pastoral Constitution on the Church in the Modern World, Gaudium et Spes*, 38: AAS 58 (1966), p. 1055.

II. Work and Man

4. *In the Book of Genesis*

The Church is convinced that work is a fundamental dimension of man's existence on earth. She is confirmed in this conviction by considering the whole heritage of the many sciences devoted to man: anthropology, paleontology, history, sociology, psychology, and so on; they all seem to bear witness to this reality in an irrefutable way. But the source of the Church's conviction is above all the revealed word of God, and therefore what is a conviction of the intellect is also a conviction of faith. The reason is that the Church—and it is worthwhile stating it at this point—believes in man: she thinks of man and addresses herself to him not only in the light of historical experience, not only with the aid of the many methods of scientific knowledge, but in the first place in the light of the revealed word of the living God. Relating herself to man, she seeks to express the eternal designs and transcendent destiny which the living God, the creator and redeemer, has linked with him.

The Church finds in the very first pages of the Book of Genesis the source of her conviction that work is a fundamental dimension of human existence on earth. An analysis of these texts makes us aware that they express—sometimes in an archaic way of manifesting thought—the fundamental truths about man, in the context of the mystery of creation itself. These truths are decisive for man from the very beginning, and at the same time they trace out the main lines of his earthly existence, both in the state of original justice and also after the breaking, caused by sin, of the creator's original covenant with creation in man. When man, who had been created "in the image of God . . . male and female,"[9] hears the words: "Be fruitful and multiply, and fill the earth and subdue it,"[10] even though these words do not refer directly and explicitly to work, beyond any doubt they indirectly indicate it as an activity for man to carry out in the world. Indeed, they show its very deepest essence. Man is the image of God partly through the mandate received from his creator to subdue, to dominate, the earth. In carrying out this mandate, man, every human being, reflects the very action of the creator of the universe.

Work understood as a *transitive* activity, that is to say, an activity beginning in the human subject and directed toward an external object, presupposes a specific dominion by man over "the earth," and in its turn it confirms and develops this dominion. It is clear that the term

[9] Gn 1:27.
[10] Gn 1:28.

the earth of which the biblical text speaks is to be understood in the first place as that fragment of the visible universe that man inhabits. By extension, however, it can be understood as the whole of the visible world insofar as it comes within the range of man's influence and of his striving to satisfy his needs. The expression "subdue the earth" has an immense range. It means all the resources that the earth (and indirectly the visible world) contains and which, through the conscious activity of man, can be discovered and used for his ends. And so these words, placed at the beginning of the Bible, never cease to be relevant. They embrace equally the past ages of civilization and economy, as also the whole of modern reality and future phases of development, which are perhaps already to some extent beginning to take shape, though for the most part they are still almost unknown to man and hidden from him.

While people sometimes speak of periods of *acceleration* in the economic life and civilization of humanity or of individual nations, linking these periods to the progress of science and technology and especially to discoveries which are decisive for social and economic life, at the same time it can be said that none of these phenomena of acceleration exceeds the essential content of what was said in that most ancient of biblical texts. As man, through his work, becomes more and more the master of the earth, and as he confirms his dominion over the visible world, again through his work, he nevertheless remains in every case and at every phase of this process within the creator's original ordering. And this ordering remains necessarily and indissolubly linked with the fact that man was created, as male and female, "in the image of God." This process is, at the same time, universal: It embraces all human beings, every generation, every phase of economic and cultural development, and at the same time it is a process that takes place within each human being, in each conscious human subject. Each and every individual is at the same time embraced by it. Each and every individual, to the proper extent and in an incalculable number of ways, takes part in the giant process whereby man "subdues the earth" through his work.

5. *Work in the Objective Sense: Technology*

This universality and, at the same time, this multiplicity of the process of "subduing the earth" throw light upon human work, because man's dominion over the earth is achieved in and by means of work. There thus emerges the meaning of work in an objective sense, which finds expression in the various epochs of culture and civilization. Man dominates the earth by the very fact of domesticating animals, rearing them and obtaining from them the food and clothing he needs, and by the fact of being able to extract various natural resources from the earth and the seas. But man "subdues the earth" much more when he begins to cultivate it and then to transform its products, adapting them to his own use. Thus agriculture constitutes through human work a primary field of economic activity and an indispensable factor of production. Industry in its turn will always consist in linking the earth's riches—whether nature's living resources, or the products of agriculture, or the mineral or chemical resources—with man's work, whether physical or intellectual. This is also in a sense true in the sphere of what are called service industries and also in the sphere of research, pure or applied.

In industry and agriculture man's work has today in many cases ceased to be mainly manual, for the toil of human hands and muscles is aided by more and more highly perfected machinery. Not only in industry but also in agriculture we are witnessing the transformations made possible by the gradual development of science and technology. Historically speaking this, taken as a whole, has caused great changes in civilization, from the beginning of the *industrial era* to the successive phases of development through new technologies, such as the electronics and the microprocessor technology in recent years.

While it may seem that in the industrial process it is the machine that works and man merely supervises it, making it function and keeping it going in various ways, it is also true that for this very reason industrial development provides grounds for reproposing in new ways the question of human work. Both the original industrialization that gave rise to what is called the worker question and the subsequent industrial and postindustrial changes show in an eloquent manner that, even in the age of ever more mechanized work, the proper subject of work continues to be man.

The development of industry and of the various sectors connected with it, even the most modern electronics technology, especially in the fields of miniaturization, communications and telecommunications and so forth, shows how vast is the role of technology, that ally of work that human thought has produced in the interaction between the subject and object of work (in the widest sense of the word). Understood in this case not as a capacity or aptitude for work, but rather as a whole set of instruments which man uses in his work, technology is undoubtedly man's ally. It facilitates his work, perfects, accelerates and augments it. It leads to an increase in the quantity of things produced by work and in many cases improves their quality. However it is also a fact that in some instances technology can cease to be man's ally and become almost his enemy, as when the mechanization of work supplants him, taking away all personal satisfaction and the incentive to creativity and responsibility, when it deprives many workers of their previous employment or when, through exalting the machine, it reduces man to the status of its slave.

If the biblical words "subdue the earth" addressed to man from the very beginning are understood in the context of the whole modern age, industrial and postindustrial, then they undoubtedly include also a relationship with technology, with the world of machinery which is the fruit of the work of the human intellect and a historical confirmation of man's dominion over nature.

The recent stage of human history, especially that of certain societies, brings a correct affirmation of technology as a basic coefficient of economic progress; but at the same time this affirmation has been accompanied by and continues to be accompanied by essential questions concerning human work in relationship to its subject, which is man. These questions are particularly charged with content and tension of an ethical and social character. They therefore constitute a continual challenge for institutions of many kinds, for states and governments, for systems and international organizations; they also constitute a challenge for the Church.

6. Work in the Subjective Sense: Man as the Subject of Work

In order to continue our analysis of work, an analysis linked with the word of the Bible telling man that he is to subdue the earth, we must concentrate our attention on work in the subjective sense, much more than we did on the objective significance, barely touching upon the vast range of problems known intimately and in detail to scholars in various fields and also, according to their specializations, to those who work. If the words of the Book of Genesis to which we refer in this analysis of ours speak of work in the objective sense in an indirect way, they also speak only indirectly of the subject of work; but what they say is very eloquent and is full of great significance.

Man has to subdue the earth and dominate it, because as the "image of God" he is a person, that is to say, a subjective being capable of acting in a planned and rational way, capable of deciding about himself and with a tendency to self-realization. As a person, man is therefore the subject of work. As a person he works, he performs various actions belonging to the work process; independently of their objective content, these actions must all serve to realize his humanity, to fulfill the calling to be a person that is his by reason of his very humanity. The principal truths concerning this theme were recently recalled by the Second Vatican Council in the constitution *Gaudium et Spes*, especially in chapter 1, which is devoted to man's calling.

And so this "dominion" spoken of in the biblical text being meditated upon here refers not only to the objective dimension of work, but at the same time introduces us to an understanding of its subjective dimension. Understood as a process whereby man and the human race subdue the earth, work corresponds to this basic biblical concept only when throughout the process man manifests himself and confirms himself as the one who "dominates." This dominion, in a certain sense, refers to the subjective dimension even more than to the objective one: This dimension conditions the very ethical nature of work. In fact there is no doubt that human work has an ethical value of its own, which clearly and directly remains linked to the fact that the one who carries it out is a person, a conscious and free subject, that is to say, a subject that decides about himself.

This truth, which in a sense constitutes the fundamental and perennial heart of Christian teaching on human work, has had and continues to have primary significance for the formulation of the important social problems characterizing whole ages.

The ancient world introduced its own typical differentiation of people into classes according to the type of work done. Work which demanded from the worker the exercise of physical strength, the work of muscles and hands, was considered unworthy of free men and was therefore given to slaves. By broadening certain aspects that already belonged to the Old Testament, Christianity brought about a fundamental change of ideas in this field, taking the whole content of the gospel message as its point of departure, especially the fact that the one who, while being God, became like us in all things[11] devoted most of the years of his life on earth to manual work at the carpenter's bench. This circumstance constitutes in itself the most eloquent *gospel of work*, showing that the basis for determining the value of human work is not primarily the kind of work being done, but the fact that the one who is doing it is a person. The sources of the dignity of work are to be sought primarily in the subjective dimension, not in the objective one.

Such a concept practically does away with the very basis of the ancient differentiation of people into classes according to the kind of work done. This does not mean that from the objective point of view human work cannot and must not be rated and qualified in any way. It only means that the primary basis of the value of work is man himself, who is its subject. This leads immediately to a very important conclusion of an ethical nature: However true it may be that man is destined for work and called to it, in the first place work is "for man" and not man "for work." Through this conclusion one rightly comes to recognize the preeminence of the subjective meaning of work over the objective one. Given this way of understanding things and presupposing that different sorts of work that people do can have greater or lesser objective value, let us try nevertheless to show that each sort is judged above all by the measure of the dignity of the subject of work, that is to say, the person, the individual who carries it out. On the other hand, independent of the work that every man does, and presupposing that this work constitutes a purpose—at times a

[11] Cf. Heb 2:17; Phil 2:5-8.

very demanding one—of his activity, this purpose does not possess a definitive meaning in itself. In fact, in the final analysis it is always man who is the purpose of the work, whatever work it is that is done by man—even if the common scale of values rates it as the merest service, as the most monotonous, even the most alienating work.

7. A Threat to the Right Order of Values

It is precisely these fundamental affirmations about work that always emerged from the wealth of Christian truth, especially from the very message of the *gospel of work*, thus creating the basis for a new way of thinking, judging and acting. In the modern period, from the beginning of the industrial age, the Christian truth about work had to oppose the various trends of materialistic and economistic thought.

For certain supporters of such ideas, work was understood and treated as a sort of merchandise that the worker—especially the industrial worker—sells to the employer, who at the same time is the possessor of the capital, that is to say, of all the working tools and means that make production possible. This way of looking at work was widespread especially in the first half of the nineteenth century. Since then explicit expressions of this sort have almost disappeared and have given way to more human ways of thinking about work and evaluating it. The interaction between the worker and the tools and means of production has given rise to the development of various forms of capitalism—parallel with various forms of collectivism—into which other socioeconomic elements have entered as a consequence of new concrete circumstances, of the activity of workers' associations and public authorities, and of the emergence of large transnational enterprises. Nevertheless, the danger of treating work as a special kind of merchandise or as an impersonal force needed for production (the expression *work force* is in fact in common use) always exists, especially when the whole way of looking at the question of economics is marked by the premises of materialistic economism.

A systematic opportunity for thinking and evaluating in this way, and in a certain sense a stimulus for doing so, is provided by the quickening process of the development of a one-sidedly materialistic civilization, which gives prime importance to the objective dimension of work, while the subjective dimension—everything in direct or indirect relationship with the subject of work—remains on a secondary level. In all cases of this sort, in every social situation of this type, there is a confusion or even a reversal of the order laid down from the beginning by the words of the Book of Genesis: Man is treated as an instrument of production,[12] whereas he—he alone, independent

[12]Cf. Pope Pius XI, encyclical, *Quadragesimo Anno*: AAS 23 (1931), p. 221.

of the work he does—ought to be treated as the effective subject of work and its true maker and creator. Precisely this reversal of order, whatever the program or name under which it occurs, should rightly be called *Capitalism*—in the sense more fully explained below. Everybody knows that Capitalism has a definite historical meaning as a system, an economic and social system, opposed to *Socialism* or *Communism*. But in the light of the analysis of the fundamental reality of the whole economic process—first and foremost of the production structure that work is—it should be recognized that the error of early Capitalism can be repeated wherever man is in a way treated on the same level as the whole complex of the material means of production, as an instrument and not in accordance with the true dignity of his work—that is to say, where he is not treated as subject and maker, and for this very reason as the true purpose of the whole process of production.

This explains why the analysis of human work in the light of the words concerning man's "dominion" over the earth goes to the very heart of the ethical and social question. This concept should also find a central place in the whole sphere of social and economic policy, both within individual countries and in the wider field of international and intercontinental relationships, particularly with reference to the tensions making themselves felt in the world not only between East and West but also between North and South. Both John XXIII in the encyclical *Mater et Magistra* and Paul VI in the encyclical *Populorum Progressio* gave special attention to these dimensions of the modern ethical and social question.

8. Worker Solidarity

When dealing with human work in the fundamental dimension of its subject, that is to say, the human person doing the work, one must make at least a summary evaluation of developments during the 90 years since *Rerum Novarum* in relation to the subjective dimension of work. Although the subject of work is always the same, that is to say man, nevertheless wide-ranging changes take place in the objective aspect. While one can say that, by reason of its subject, work is one single thing (one and unrepeatable every time), yet when one takes into consideration its objective directions, one is forced to admit that there exist many works, many different sorts of work. The development of human civilization brings continual enrichment in this field. But at the same time, one cannot fail to note that in the process of this development not only do new forms of work appear but also others disappear. Even if one accepts that on the whole this is a normal phenomenon, it must still be seen whether certain ethically and socially dangerous irregularities creep in and to what extent.

It was precisely one such wide-ranging anomaly that gave rise in the last century to what has been called *the worker question,* sometimes described as *the proletariat question.* This question and the problems connected with it gave rise to a just social reaction and caused the impetuous emergence of a great burst of solidarity between workers, first and foremost industrial workers. The call to solidarity and common action addressed to the workers—especially to those engaged in narrowly specialized, monotonous and depersonalized work in industrial plants, where the machine tends to dominate man—was important and eloquent from the point of view of social ethics. It was the reaction against the degradation of man as the subject of work and against the unheard-of accompanying exploitation in the field of wages, working conditions and social security for the worker. This reaction united the working world in a community marked by great solidarity.

Following the lines laid down by the encyclical *Rerum Novarum* and many later documents of the Church's magisterium, it must be frankly recognized that the reaction against the system of injustice and harm that cried to heaven for vengeance[13] and that weighed heavily upon workers in that period of rapid industrialization was justified from the point of view of social morality. This state of affairs was favored by the liberal sociopolitical system, which in accordance with its "economistic" premises, strengthened and safeguarded economic initiative by the possessors of capital alone, but did not pay sufficient attention to the rights of the workers, on the grounds that human work is solely an instrument of production, and that capital is the basis, efficient factor and purpose of production.

From that time, worker solidarity, together with a clearer and more committed realization by others of workers' rights, has in many cases brought about profound changes. Various forms of neocapitalism or collectivism have developed. Various new systems have been thought out. Workers can often share in running businesses and in controlling their productivity, and in fact do so. Through appropriate associations they exercise influence over conditions of work and pay, and also over social legislation. But at the same time various ideological or power systems and new relationships which have arisen at various levels of society have allowed flagrant injustices to persist or have created new ones. On the world level, the development of civilization and of communications has made possible a more complete diagnosis of the living and working conditions of man globally, but it has also revealed other forms of injustice much more extensive than those which in the last century stimulated unity between workers for particular solidarity in the working world. This is true in countries which

---

[13]Dt 24:15; Jas 5:4; and also Gn 4:10.

have completed a certain process of industrial revolution. It is also true in countries where the main working milieu continues to be agriculture or other similar occupations.

Movements of solidarity in the sphere of work—a solidarity that must never mean being closed to dialogue and collaboration with others—can be necessary also with reference to the condition of social groups that were not previously included in such movements, but which in changing social systems and conditions of living are undergoing what is in effect *proletarianization* or which actually already find themselves in a proletariat situation, one which, even if not yet given that name, in fact deserves it. This can be true of certain categories or groups of the working *intelligentsia,* especially when ever wider access to education and an ever increasing number of people with degrees or diplomas in the fields of their cultural preparation are accompanied by a drop in demand for their labor. This unemployment of intellectuals occurs or increases when the education available is not oriented toward the types of employment or service required by the true needs of society, or when there is less demand for work which requires education, at least professional education, than for manual labor, or when it is less well paid. Of course, education in itself is always valuable and an important enrichment of the human person; but in spite of that, proletarianization processes remain possible.

For this reason there must be continued study of the subject of work and of the subject's living conditions. In order to achieve social justice in the various parts of the world, in the various countries and in the relationships between them, there is a need for ever new movements of solidarity of the workers and with the workers. This solidarity must be present whenever it is called for by the social degrading of the subject of work, by exploitation of the workers and by the growing areas of poverty and even hunger. The Church is firmly committed to this cause for she considers it her mission, her service, a proof of her fidelity to Christ, so that she can truly be the *Church of the poor*. And the poor appear under various forms; they appear in various places and at various times; in many cases they appear as a result of the violation of the dignity of human work: either because the opportunities for human work are limited as a result of the scourge of unemployment or because a low value is put on work and the rights that flow from it, especially the right to a just wage and to the personal security of the worker and his or her family.

9. Work and Personal Dignity

Remaining within the context of man as the subject of work, it is now appropriate to touch upon, at least in a summary way, certain problems that more closely define the dignity of human work in that they make it possible to characterize more fully its specific moral value. In doing this we must always keep in mind the biblical calling to "subdue the earth,"[14] in which is expressed the will of the creator that work should enable man to achieve that "dominion" in the visible world that is proper to him.

God's fundamental and original intention with regard to man, whom he created in his image and after his likeness,[15] was not withdrawn or canceled out even when man, having broken the original covenant with God, heard the words: "In the sweat of your face you shall eat bread."[16] These words refer to the sometimes heavy toil that from then onward has accompanied human work; but they do not alter the fact that work is the means whereby man achieves that "dominion" which is proper to him over the visible world, by "subjecting" the earth. Toil is something that is universally known, for it is universally experienced. It is familiar to those doing physical work under sometimes exceptionally laborious conditions. It is familiar not only to agricultural workers, who spend long days working the land, which sometimes "bears thorns and thistles,"[17] but also to those who work in mines and quarries, to steelworkers at their blast furnaces, to those who work in builders' yards and in construction work, often in danger of injury or death. It is also familiar to those at an intellectual workbench; to scientists; to those who bear the burden of grave responsibility for decisions that will have a vast impact on society. It is familiar to doctors and nurses, who spend days and nights at their patients' bedside. It is familiar to women, who sometimes without proper recognition on the part of society and even of their own families bear the daily burden and responsibility for their homes and the upbringing of their children. It is familiar to all workers and, since work is a universal calling, it is familiar to everyone.

And yet in spite of all this toil—perhaps, in a sense, because of it—work is a good thing for man. Even though it bears the mark of a *bonum arduum*, in the terminology of St. Thomas,[18] this does not take away the fact that, as such, it is a good thing for man. It is not only good in the sense that it is useful or something to enjoy; it is also good as being something worthy, that is to say, something that corresponds to man's dignity, that expresses this dignity and increases it. If one wishes to define more clearly the ethical meaning of work, it is this truth that one must particularly keep in mind. Work is a good thing for man—a good thing for his humanity—because through work man not only transforms nature, adapting it to his own needs,

[14]Cf. Gn 1:28.
[15]Cf. Gn 1:26-27.
[16]Gn 3:19.
[17]Heb 6:8; cf. Gn 3:18.
[18]Cf. *Summa Th.*, I-II, q. 40, a. 1, c.; I-II, q. 34, a. 2, ad 1.

but he also achieves fulfillment as a human being and indeed in a sense becomes "more a human being."

Without this consideration it is impossible to understand the meaning of the virtue of industriousness, and more particularly it is impossible to understand why industriousness should be a virtue: For virtue, as a moral habit, is something whereby man becomes good as man.[19] This fact in no way alters our justifiable anxiety that in work, whereby matter gains in nobility, man himself should not experience a lowering of his own dignity.[20] Again, it is well known that it is possible to use work in various ways against man, that it is possible to punish man with the system of forced labor in concentration camps, that work can be made into a means for oppressing man, and that in various ways it is possible to exploit human labor, that is to say, the workers. All this pleads in favor of the moral obligation to link industriousness as a virtue with the social order of work, which will enable man to become in work "more a human being" and not be degraded by it not only because of the wearing out of his physical strength (which, at least up to a certain point, is inevitable), but especially through damage to the dignity and subjectivity that are proper to him.

10. Work and Society: Family and Nation

Having thus confirmed the personal dimension of human work, we must go on to the second sphere of values which is necessarily linked to work. Work constitutes a foundation for the formation of family life, which is a natural right and something that man is called to. These two spheres of values—one linked to work and the other consequent on the family nature of human life—must be properly united and must properly permeate each other. In a way, work is a condition for making it possible to found a family, since the family requires the means of subsistence which man normally gains through work. Work and industriousness also influence the whole process of education in the family, for the very reason that everyone "becomes a human being" through, among other things, work, and becoming a human being is precisely the main purpose of the whole process of education. Obviously, two aspects of work in a sense come into play here: the one making family life and its upkeep possible, and the other making possible the achievement of the purposes of the family, especially education. Nevertheless, these two aspects of work are linked to one another and are mutually complementary in various points.

---

[19]Ibid.
[20]Cf. Pope Pius XI, encyclical, *Quadragesimo Anno*: AAS 23 (1931), pp. 221-222.

It must be remembered and affirmed that the family constitutes one of the most important terms of reference for shaping the social and ethical order of human work. The teaching of the Church has always devoted special attention to this question, and in the present document we shall have to return to it. In fact, the family is simultaneously a community made possible by work and the first school of work, within the home, for every person.

The third sphere of values that emerges from this point of view—that of the subject of work—concerns the great society to which man belongs on the basis of particular cultural and historical links. This society—even when it has not yet taken on the mature form of a nation—is not only the great educator of every man, even though an indirect one (because each individual absorbs within the family the contents and values that go to make up the culture of a given nation); it is also a great historical and social incarnation of the work of all generations. All of this brings it about that man combines his deepest human identity with membership of a nation, and intends his work also to increase the common good developed together with his compatriots, thus realizing that in this way work serves to add to the heritage of the whole human family, of all the people living in the world.

These three spheres are always important for human work in its subjective dimension. And this dimension, that is to say, the concrete reality of the worker, takes precedence over the objective dimension. In the subjective dimension there is realized, first of all, that "dominion" over the world of nature to which man is called from the beginning according to the words of the Book of Genesis. The very process of "subduing the earth," that is to say work, is marked in the course of history and especially in recent centuries by an immense development of technological means. This is an advantageous and positive phenomenon, on condition that the objective dimension of work does not gain the upper hand over the subjective dimension, depriving man of his dignity and inalienable rights or reducing them.

III. Conflict between Labor and Capital in the Present Phase of History

11. Dimensions of the Conflict

The sketch of the basic problems of work outlined above draws inspiration from the texts at the beginning of the Bible and in a sense forms the very framework of the Church's teaching, which has remained unchanged throughout the centuries within the context of different historical experiences. However, the experiences preceding and following the publication of the encyclical *Rerum Novarum* form a background that endows that teaching with particular expressiveness and the eloquence of living relevance. In this analysis, work is seen as a great reality with a fundamental influence on the shaping in a human way of the world that the creator has entrusted to man; it is a reality closely linked with man as the subject of work and with man's rational activity. In the normal course of events this reality fills human life and strongly affects its value and meaning. Even when it is accompanied by toil and effort, work is still something good, and so man develops through love for work. This entirely positive and creative, educational and meritorious character of man's work must be the basis for the judgments and decisions being made today in its regard in spheres that include human rights, as is evidenced by the international declarations on work and the many labor codes prepared either by the competent legislative institutions in the various countries or by organizations devoting their social, or scientific and social, activity to the problems of work. One organization fostering such initiatives on the international level is the International Labor Organization, the oldest specialized agency of the United Nations.

In the following part of these considerations I intend to return in greater detail to these important questions, recalling at least the basic elements of the Church's teaching on the matter. I must however first touch on a very important field of questions in which her teaching has taken shape in this latest period, the one marked and in a sense symbolized by the publication of the encyclical *Rerum Novarum*.

Throughout this period, which is by no means yet over, the issue of work has of course been posed on the basis of the great conflict that in the age of and together with industrial development emerged between *capital* and *labor*, that is to say between the small but highly influential group of entrepreneurs, owners or holders of the means of production, and the broader multitude of people who lacked these means and who shared in the process of production solely by their labor. The conflict originated in the fact that the workers put their powers at the disposal of the entrepreneurs and these, following the principle of maximum profit, tried to establish the lowest possible wages for the work done by the employees. In addition there were other elements of exploitation connected with the lack of safety at work and of safeguards regarding the health and living conditions of the workers and their families.

This conflict, interpreted by some as a socioeconomic class conflict, found expression in the ideological conflict between liberalism, understood as the ideology of Capitalism, and Marxism, understood as the ideology of scientific Socialism and Communism, which professes to act as the spokesman for the working class and the worldwide proletariat. Thus the real conflict between labor and capital was transformed into a systematic class struggle conducted not only by ideological means, but also and chiefly by political means. We are familiar with the history of this conflict and with the demands of both sides. The Marxist program, based on the philosophy of Marx and Engels, sees in class struggle the only way to eliminate class injustices in society and to eliminate the classes themselves. Putting this program into practice presupposes the collectivization of the means of production so that through the transfer of these means from private hands to the collectivity, human labor will be preserved from exploitation.

This is the goal of the struggle carried on by political as well as ideological means. In accordance with the principle of "the dictatorship of the proletariat," the groups that as political parties follow the guidance of Marxist ideology aim by the use of various kinds of influence, including revolutionary pressure, to win a monopoly of power in each society in order to introduce the collectivist system into it by eliminating private ownership of the means of production. According to the principal ideologists and leaders of this broad international movement, the purpose of this program of action is to achieve the social revolution and to introduce Socialism and finally the communist system throughout the world.

As we touch on this extremely important field of issues, which constitute not only a theory but a whole fabric of socioeconomic, political and international life in our age, we cannot go into the details, nor is this necessary, for they are known both from the vast literature on the subject and by experience. Instead we must leave the context of these issues and go back to the fundamental issue of human work, which is the main subject of the considerations in this document. It is clear indeed that this issue, which is of such importance for man—it constitutes one of the fundamental dimensions of his earthly existence and of his vocation—can also be explained only by taking into account the full context of the contemporary situation.

12. The Priority of Labor

The structure of the present-day situation is deeply marked by many conflicts caused by man, and the technological means produced by human work play a primary role in it. We should also consider here the prospect of worldwide catastrophe in the case of a nuclear war, which would have almost unimaginable possibilities of destruction. In view of this situation we must first of all recall a principle that has always been taught by the Church: the principle of the priority of labor over capital. This principle directly concerns the process of production: In this process labor is always a primary efficient cause, while capital, the whole collection of means of production, remains a mere instrument or instrumental cause. This principle is an evident truth that emerges from the whole of man's historical experience.

When we read in the first chapter of the Bible that man is to subdue the earth, we know that these words refer to all the resources contained in the visible world and placed at man's disposal. However, these resources can serve man only through work. From the beginning there is also linked with work the question of ownership, for the only means that man has for causing the resources hidden in nature to serve himself and others is his work. And to be able through his work to make these resources bear fruit, man takes over ownership of small parts of the various riches of nature: those beneath the ground, those in the sea, on land or in space. He takes over all these things by making them his workbench. He takes them over through work and for work.

The same principle applies in the successive phases of this process, in which the first phase always remains the relationship of man with the resources and riches of nature. The whole of the effort to acquire knowledge with the aim of discovering these riches and specifying the various ways in which they can be used by man and for man teaches us that everything that comes from man throughout the whole process of economic production, whether labor or the whole collection of means of production and the technology connected with these means (meaning the capability to use them in work), presupposes these riches and resources of the visible world, riches and resources that man finds and does not create. In a sense man finds them already prepared, ready for him to discover them and to use them correctly in the productive process. In every phase of the development of his work, man comes up against the leading role of the gift made by nature, that is to say, in the final analysis, by the creator. At the beginning of man's work is the mystery of creation. This affirmation, already indicated as my starting point, is the guiding thread of this document and will be further developed in the last part of these reflections.

Further consideration of this question should confirm our conviction of the priority of human labor over what in the course of time we have grown accustomed to calling capital. Since the concept of capital includes not only the natural resources placed at man's disposal, but also the whole collection of means by which man appropriates natural resources and transforms them in accordance with his needs (and thus in a sense humanizes them), it must immediately be noted that all these means are the result of the historical heritage of human labor. All the means of production, from the most primitive to the ultramodern ones—it is man that has gradually developed them: man's experience and intellect. In this way there have appeared not only the simplest instruments for cultivating the earth, but also through adequate progress in science and technology, the more modern and complex ones: machines, factories, laboratories and computers. Thus everything that is at the service of work, everything that in the present state of technology constitutes its ever more highly perfected instrument, is the result of work.

This gigantic and powerful instrument—the whole collection of means of production that in a sense are considered synonymous with capital—is the result of work and bears the signs of human labor. At the present stage of technological advance, when man, who is the subject of work, wishes to make use of this collection of modern instruments, the means of production, he must first assimilate cognitively the result of the work of the people who invented those instruments, who planned them, built them and perfected them, and who continue to do so. Capacity for work—that is to say, for sharing efficiently in the modern production process—demands greater and greater preparation and, before all else, proper training. Obviously it remains clear that every human being sharing in the production process, even if he or she is only doing the kind of work for which no special training or qualifications are required, is the real efficient subject in this production process, while the whole collection of instruments, no matter how perfect they may be in themselves, are only a mere instrument subordinate to human labor.

This truth, which is part of the abiding heritage of the Church's teaching, must always be emphasized with reference to the question of the labor system and with regard to the whole socioeconomic system. We must emphasize and give prominence to the primacy of man in the production process, the primacy of man over things. Everything contained in the concept of capital in the strict sense is only a collection of things. Man, as the subject of work and independent of the work he does—man alone is a person. This truth has important and decisive consequences.

13. Economism and Materialism

In the light of the above truth we see clearly, first of all, that capital cannot be separated from labor; in no way can labor be opposed to capital or capital to labor, and still less can the actual people behind these concepts be opposed to each other, as will be explained later. A labor system can be right, in the sense of being in conformity with the very essence of the issue and in the sense of being intrinsically true and also morally legitimate, if in its very basis it overcomes the opposition between labor and capital through an effort at being shaped in accordance with the principle put forward above: the principle of the substantial and real priority of labor, of the subjectivity of human labor and its effective participation in the whole production process, independent of the nature of the services provided by the worker.

Opposition between labor and capital does not spring from the structure of the production process or from the structure of the economic process. In general the latter process demonstrates that labor and what we are accustomed to call capital are intermingled; it shows that they are inseparably linked. Working at any workbench, whether a relatively primitive or an ultramodern one, a man can easily see that through his work he enters into two inheritances: the inheritance of what is given to the whole of humanity in the resources of nature and the inheritance of what others have already developed on the basis of those resources, primarily by developing technology, that is to say, by producing a whole collection of increasingly perfect instruments for work. In working, man also "enters into the labor of others."[21] Guided both by our intelligence and by the faith that draws light from the word of God, we have no difficulty in accepting this image of the sphere and process of man's labor. It is a consistent image, one that is humanistic as well as theological. In it man is the master of the creatures placed at his disposal in the visible world. If some dependence is discovered in the work process, it is dependence on the giver of all the resources of creation and also on other human beings, those to whose work and initiative we owe the perfected and increased possibilities of our own work. All that we can say of everything in the production process which constitutes a whole collection of things, the instruments, the capital, is that it conditions man's work; we cannot assert that it constitutes as it were an impersonal subject putting man and man's work into a position of dependence.

This consistent image, in which the principle of the primacy of person over things is strictly preserved, was broken up in human thought, sometimes after a long period of incubation in practical living. The break occurred in such a way that labor was separated from capital and set in opposition to it, and capital was set in opposition to labor, as though they were two impersonal forces, two production factors juxtaposed in the same "economistic" perspective. This way of stating the issue contained a fundamental error, what we can call the error of economism, that of considering human labor solely according to its economic purpose. This fundamental error of thought can and must be called an error of materialism, in that economism directly or indirectly includes a conviction of the primacy and superiority of the material, and directly or indirectly places the spiritual and the personal (man's activity, moral values and such matters) in a position of subordination to material reality. This is still not theoretical materialism in the full sense of the term, but it is certainly practical materialism, a materialism judged capable of satisfying man's needs not so much on the grounds of premises derived from materialist theory as on the grounds of a particular way of evaluating things and so on the grounds of a certain hierarchy of goods based on the greater immediate attractiveness of what is material.

---

[21] Cf. Jn 4:38.

The error of thinking in the categories of economism went hand in hand with the formation of a materialist philosophy, as this philosophy developed from the most elementary and common phase (also called common materialism, because it professes to reduce spiritual reality to a superfluous phenomenon) to the phase of what is called dialectical materialism. However, within the framework of the present consideration, it seems that economism had a decisive importance for the fundamental issue of human work, in particular for the separation of labor and capital and for setting them up in opposition as two production factors viewed in the above-mentioned economistic perspective; and it seems that economism influenced this nonhumanistic way of stating the issue before the materialist philosophical system did. Nevertheless it is obvious that materialism, including its dialectical form, is incapable of providing sufficient and definitive bases for thinking about human work, in order that the primacy of man over the capital instrument, the primacy of the person over things, may find in it adequate and irrefutable confirmation and support. In dialectical materialism too man is not first and foremost the subject of work and the efficient cause of the production process, but continues to be understood and treated, in dependence on what is material, as a kind of resultant of the economic or production relations prevailing at a given period.

Obviously the antinomy between labor and capital under consideration here—the antinomy in which labor was separated from capital and set up in opposition to it, in a certain sense on the ontic level as if it were just an element like any other in the economic process—did not originate merely in the philosophy and economic theories of the eighteenth century; rather it originated in the whole of the economic and social practice of that time, the time of the birth and rapid development of industrialization, in which what was mainly seen was the possibility of vastly increasing material wealth, means, while the end, that is to say man, who should be served by the means, was ignored. It was this practical error that struck a blow first and foremost against human labor, against the working man, and caused the ethically just social reaction already spoken of above. The same error, which is now part of history and which was connected with the period of primitive Capitalism and Liberalism, can nevertheless be repeated in other circumstances of time and place if people's thinking starts from the same theoretical or practical premises. The only chance there seems to be for radically overcoming this error is through adequate changes both in theory and in practice, changes in line with the definite conviction of the primacy of the person over things and of human labor over capital as a whole collection of means of production.

14. Work and Ownership

The historical process briefly presented here has certainly gone beyond its initial phase, but it is still taking place and indeed is spreading in the relationships between nations and continents. It needs to be specified further from another point of view. It is obvious that when we speak of opposition between labor and capital, we are not dealing only with abstract concepts or impersonal forces operating in economic production. Behind both concepts there are people, living, actual people: On the one side are those who do the work without being the owners of the means of production, and on the other side those who act as entrepreneurs and who own these means or represent the owners. Thus the issue of ownership or property enters from the beginning into the whole of this difficult historical process. The encyclical *Rerum Novarum*, which has the social question as its theme, stresses this issue also, recalling and confirming the Church's teaching on ownership, on the right to private property even when it is a question of the means of production. The encyclical *Mater et Magistra* did the same.

The above principle, as it was then stated and as it is still taught by the Church, diverges radically from the program of collectivism as proclaimed by Marxism and put into practice in various countries in the decades following the time of Leo XIII's encyclical. At the same time it differs from the program of Capitalism practiced by Liberalism and by the political systems inspired by it. In the latter case, the difference consists in the way the right to ownership or property is understood. Christian tradition has never upheld this right as absolute and untouchable. On the contrary, it has always understood this right within the broader context of the right common to all to use the goods of the whole of creation: The right to private property is subordinated to the right to common use, to the fact that goods are meant for everyone.

Furthermore, in the Church's teaching, ownership has never been understood in a way that could constitute grounds for social conflict in labor. As mentioned above, property is acquired first of all through work in order that it may serve work. This concerns in a special way ownership of the means of production. Isolating these means as a separate property in order to set it up in the form of capital in opposition to labor—and even to practice exploitation of labor—is contrary to the very nature of these means and their possession. They cannot be possessed against labor, they cannot even be possessed for possession's sake, because the only legitimate title to their possession—whether in the form of private ownership or in the form of public or collective ownership—is that they should serve labor and thus by serving labor that they should make possible the achievement of the first principle of this order, namely the universal destination of goods and the right to common use of them. From this point of view, therefore, in consideration of human labor and of common access to the goods meant for man, one cannot exclude the socialization, in suitable conditions, of certain means of production. In the course of the decades since the publication of the encyclical *Rerum Novarum*, the Church's teaching has always recalled all these principles, going back to the arguments formulated in a much older tradition, for example, the well-known arguments of the *Summa Theologiae* of St. Thomas Aquinas.[22]

In the present document, which has human work as its main theme, it is right to confirm all the effort with which the Church's teaching has striven and continues to strive always to ensure the priority of work and thereby man's character as a subject in social life and especially in the dynamic structure of the whole economic process. From this point of view the position of rigid *Capitalism* continues to remain unacceptable, namely the position that defends the exclusive right to private ownership of the means of production as an untouchable dogma of economic life. The principle of respect for work demands that this right should undergo a constructive revision both in theory and in practice. If it is true that capital, as the whole of the means of production, is at the same time the product of the work of generations, it is equally true that capital is being unceasingly created through the work done with the help of all these means of production, and these means can be seen as a great workbench at which the present generation of workers is working day after day. Obviously we are dealing here with different kinds of work, not only so-called manual labor, but also the many forms of intellectual work, including white-collar work and management.

In the light of the above, the many proposals put forward by experts in Catholic social teaching and by the highest magisterium of the Church take on special significance:[23] proposals for joint ownership of the means of work, sharing by the workers in the management and/or profits of businesses, so-called shareholding by labor, etc. Whether these various proposals can or cannot be applied concretely, it is clear that recognition of the proper position of labor and the worker in the production process demands various adaptations in the sphere of the right to ownership of the means of production. This is so not only in view of older situations but also, first and foremost, in view of the whole of the situation and the problems in the second

---

[22]On the right to property see *Summa Th.*, II-II, q. 66, arts. 2 and 6; *De Regimine Principum*, book 1, chapters 15 and 17. On the social function of property see *Summa Th.*, II-II, q. 134, art. 1, ad 3.
[23]Cf. Pope Pius XI, encyclical, *Quadragesimo Anno*: AAS 23 (1931), p. 199; Second Vatican Council, *Pastoral Constitution on the Church in the Modern World, Gaudium et Spes*, 68: AAS 58 (1966), pp. 1089-1090.

half of the present century with regard to the so-called Third World and the various new independent countries that have arisen, especially in Africa but elsewhere as well, in place of the colonial territories of the past.

Therefore, while the position of rigid Capitalism must undergo continual revision in order to be reformed from the point of view of human rights, both human rights in the widest sense and those linked with man's work, it must be stated that from the same point of view these many deeply desired reforms cannot be achieved by an a priori elimination of private ownership of the means of production. For it must be noted that merely taking these means of production (capital) out of the hands of their private owners is not enough to ensure their satisfactory socialization. They cease to be the property of a certain social group, namely the private owners, and become the property of organized society, coming under the administration and direct control of another group of people, namely those who, though not owning them, from the fact of exercising power in society manage them on the level of the whole national or the local economy.

This group in authority may carry out its task satisfactorily from the point of view of the priority of labor, but it may also carry it out badly by claiming for itself a monopoly of the administration and disposal of the means of production and not refraining even from offending basic human rights. Thus, merely converting the means of production into state property in the collectivist systems is by no means equivalent to socializing that property. We can speak of socializing only when the subject character of society is ensured, that is to say, when on the basis of his work each person is fully entitled to consider himself a part-owner of the great workbench at which he is working with everyone else. A way toward that goal could be found by associating labor with the ownership of capital, as far as possible, and by producing a wide range of intermediate bodies with economic, social and cultural purposes; they would be bodies enjoying real autonomy with regard to the public powers, pursuing their specific aims in honest collaboration with each other and in subordination to the demands of the common good, and they would be living communities both in form and in substance in the sense that the members of each body would be looked upon and treated as persons and encouraged to take an active part in the life of the body.[24]

15. The Personalist *Argument*

Thus the principle of the priority of labor over capital is a postulate of the order of social morality. It has key importance both in the

[24]Cf. Pope John XXIII, encyclical, *Mater et Magistra*: AAS 53 (1961), p. 419.

system built on the principle of private ownership of the means of production and also in the systems in which private ownership of these means has been limited even in a radical way. Labor is in a sense inseparable from capital; in no way does it accept the antinomy, that is to say, the separation and opposition with regard to the means of production that has weighed upon human life in recent centuries as a result of merely economic premises. When man works, using all the means of production, he also wishes the fruit of his work to be used by himself and others, and he wishes to be able to take part in the very work process as a sharer in responsibility and creativity at the workbench to which he applies himself.

From this spring certain specific rights of workers, corresponding to the obligation of work. They will be discussed later. But here it must be emphasized in general terms that the person who works desires not only due remuneration for his work; he also wishes that within the production process provision be made for him to be able to know that in his work, even on something that is owned in common, he is working *for himself*. This awareness is extinguished within him in a system of excessive bureaucratic centralization, which makes the worker feel that he is just a cog in a huge machine moved from above, that he is for more reasons than one a mere production instrument rather than a true subject of work with an initiative of his own. The Church's teaching has always expressed the strong and deep conviction that man's work concerns not only the economy but also, and especially, personal values. The economic system itself and the production process benefit precisely when these personal values are fully respected. In the mind of St. Thomas Aquinas,[25] this is the principal reason in favor of private ownership of the means of production. While we accept that for certain well-founded reasons exceptions can be made to the principle of private ownership—in our own time we even see that the system of socialized ownership has been introduced—nevertheless the personalist argument still holds good both on the level of principles and on the practical level. If it is to be rational and fruitful, any socialization of the means of production must take this argument into consideration. Every effort must be made to ensure that in this kind of system also the human person can preserve his awareness of working *for himself*. If this is not done, incalculable damage is inevitably done throughout the economic process, not only economic damage but first and foremost damage to man.

[25]Cf. *Summa Th.*, II-II, q. 65, a. 2.

IV. Rights of Workers

16. Within the Broad Context of Human Rights

While work, in all its many senses, is an obligation, that is to say a duty, it is also a source of rights on the part of the worker. These rights must be examined in the broad context of human rights as a whole, which are connatural with man and many of which are proclaimed by various international organizations and increasingly guaranteed by the individual states for their citizens. Respect for this broad range of human rights constitutes the fundamental condition for peace in the modern world: peace both within individual countries and societies and in international relations, as the Church's magisterium has several times noted, especially since the encyclical *Pacem in Terris*. The human rights that flow from work are part of the broader context of those fundamental rights of the person.

However, within this context they have a specific character corresponding to the specific nature of human work as outlined above. It is in keeping with this character that we must view them. Work is, as has been said, an obligation, that is to say, a duty, on the part of man. This is true in all the many meanings of the word. Man must work both because the creator has commanded it and because of his own humanity, which requires work in order to be maintained and developed. Man must work out of regard for others, especially his own family, but also for the society he belongs to, the country of which he is a child and the whole human family of which he is a member, since he is the heir to the work of generations and at the same time a sharer in building the future of those who will come after him in the succession of history. All this constitutes the moral obligation of work, understood in its wide sense. When we have to consider the moral rights corresponding to this obligation of every person with regard to work, we must always keep before our eyes the whole vast range of points of reference in which the labor of every working subject is manifested.

For when we speak of the obligation of work and of the rights of the worker that correspond to this obligation, we think in the first place of the relationship between the employer, direct or indirect, and the worker.

The distinction between the direct and the indirect employer is seen to be very important when one considers both the way in which labor is actually organized and the possibility of the formation of just or unjust relationships in the field of labor.

Since the direct employer is the person or institution with whom the worker enters directly into a work contract in accordance with definite conditions, we must understand as the indirect employer many different factors, other than the direct employer, that exercise a determining influence on the shaping both of the work contract and, consequently, of just or unjust relationships in the field of human labor.

17. Direct and Indirect Employer

The concept of indirect employer includes both persons and institutions of various kinds and also collective labor contracts and the principles of conduct which are laid down by these persons and institutions and which determine the whole socioeconomic system or are its result. The concept of *indirect employer* thus refers to many different elements. The responsibility of the indirect employer differs from that of the direct employer—the term itself indicates that the responsibility is less direct—but it remains a true responsibility: The indirect employer substantially determines one or another facet of the labor relationship, thus conditioning the conduct of the direct employer when the latter determines in concrete terms the actual work contract and labor relations. This is not to absolve the direct employer from his own responsibility, but only to draw attention to the whole network of influences that condition his conduct. When it is a question of establishing an ethically correct labor policy, all these influences must be kept in mind. A policy is correct when the objective rights of the worker are fully respected.

The concept of indirect employer is applicable to every society and in the first place to the state. For it is the state that must conduct a just labor policy. However, it is common knowledge that in the present system of economic relations in the world there are numerous links between individual states, links that find expression, for instance, in the import and export process, that is to say, in the mutual exchange of economic goods, whether raw materials, semimanufactured goods or finished industrial products. These links also create mutual dependence, and as a result it would be difficult to speak in the case of any state, even the economically most powerful, of complete self-sufficiency or autarky.

Such a system of mutual dependence is in itself normal. However it can easily become an occasion for various forms of exploitation or injustice and as a result influence the labor policy of individual states; and finally it can influence the individual worker who is the proper subject of labor. For instance the highly industrialized countries, and even more the businesses that direct on a large scale the means of industrial production (the companies referred to as multinational or transnational), fix the highest possible prices for their products, while trying at the same time to fix the lowest possible prices for raw materials or semimanufactured goods. This is one of the causes of an ever increasing disproportion between national incomes. The gap between most of the richest countries and the poorest ones is not diminishing or being stabilized, but is increasing more and more to the detriment, obviously, of the poor countries. Evidently this must have an effect on local labor policy and on the worker's situation in the economically disadvantaged societies. Finding himself in a system thus conditioned, the direct employer fixes working conditions below the objective requirements of the workers, especially if he himself wishes to obtain the highest possible profits from the business which he runs (or from the businesses which he runs, in the case of a situation of socialized ownership of the means of production).

It is easy to see that this framework of forms of dependence linked with the concept of the indirect employer is enormously extensive and complicated. It is determined, in a sense, by all the elements that are decisive for economic life within a given society and state, but also by much wider links and forms of dependence. The attainment of the worker's rights cannot however be doomed to be merely a result of economic systems which on a larger or smaller scale are guided chiefly by the criterion of maximum profit. On the contrary, it is respect for the objective rights of the worker—every kind of worker: manual or intellectual, industrial or agricultural, etc.—that must constitute the adequate and fundamental criterion for shaping the whole economy, both on the level of the individual society and state and within the whole of the world economic policy and of the systems of international relationships that derive from it.

Influence in this direction should be exercised by all the international organizations whose concern it is, beginning with the United Nations. It appears that the International Labor Organization and the Food and Agriculture Organization of the United Nations and other bodies too have fresh contributions to offer on this point in particular. Within the individual states there are ministries or public departments and also various social institutions set up for this purpose. All of this effectively indicates the importance of the indirect employer—as has been said above—in achieving full respect for the worker's rights, since the rights of the human person are the key element in the whole of the social moral order.

18. The Employment Issue

When we consider the rights of workers in relation to the indirect employer, that is to say, all the agents at the national and international level that are responsible for the whole orientation of labor policy, we must first direct our attention to a fundamental issue: the question of finding work or, in other words, the issue of suitable employment for all who are capable of it. The opposite of a just and right situation in this field is unemployment, that is to say, the lack of work for those who are capable of it. It can be a question of general unemployment or of unemployment in certain sectors of work. The role of the agents included under the title of indirect employer is to act against unemployment, which in all cases is an evil and which, when it reaches a certain level, can become a real social disaster. It is particularly painful when it especially affects young people, who after appropriate cultural, technical and professional preparation fail to find work and see their sincere wish to work and their readiness to take on their own responsibility for the economic and social development of the community sadly frustrated. The obligation to provide unemployment benefits, that is to say, the duty to make suitable grants indispensable for the subsistence of unemployed workers and their families, is a duty springing from the fundamental principle of the moral order in this sphere, namely the principle of the common use of goods or, to put it in another and still simpler way, the right to life and subsistence.

In order to meet the danger of unemployment and to ensure employment for all, the agents defined here as *indirect employer* must make provision for overall planning with regard to the different kinds of work by which not only the economic life, but also the cultural life of a given society is shaped; they must also give attention to organizing that work in a correct and rational way. In the final analysis this overall concern weighs on the shoulders of the state, but it cannot mean one-sided centralization by the public authorities. Instead, what is in question is a just and rational coordination, within the framework of which the initiative of individuals, free groups and local work centers and complexes must be safeguarded, keeping in mind what has been said above with regard to the subject character of human labor.

The fact of the mutual dependence of societies and states and the need to collaborate in various areas mean that, while preserving the sovereign rights of each society and state in the field of planning and organizing labor in its own society, action in this important area must also be taken in the dimension of international collaboration by means of the necessary treaties and agreements. Here too the criterion for these pacts and agreements must more and more be the criterion of human work considered as a fundamental right of all human beings, work which gives similar rights to all those who work in such a way that the living standard of the workers in the different societies will less and less show those disturbing differences which are unjust and are apt to provoke even violent reactions. The international organizations have an enormous part to play in this area. They must let themselves be guided by an exact diagnosis of the complex situations and of the influence exercised by natural, historical, civil and other such circumstances. They must also be more highly operative with regard to plans for action jointly decided on, that is to say, they must be more effective in carrying them out.

In this direction, it is possible to actuate a plan for universal and proportionate progress by all in accordance with the guidelines of Paul VI's encyclical *Populorum Progressio*. It must be stressed that the constitutive element in this progress and also the most adequate way to verify it in a spirit of justice and peace, which the Church proclaims and for which she does not cease to pray to the Father of all individuals and of all peoples, is the continual reappraisal of man's work, both in the aspect of its objective finality and in the aspect of the dignity of the subject of all work, that is to say, man. The progress in question must be made through man and for man and it must produce its fruit in man. A test of this progress will be the increasingly mature recognition of the purpose of work and increasingly universal respect for the rights inherent in work in conformity with the dignity of man, the subject of work.

Rational planning and the proper organization of human labor in keeping with individual societies and states should also facilitate the discovery of the right proportions between the different kinds of employment: work on the land, in industry, in the various services, white-collar work and scientific or artistic work, in accordance with the capacities of individuals and for the common good of each society and of the whole of mankind. The organization of human life in accordance with the many possibilities of labor should be matched by a suitable system of instruction and education aimed first of all at developing mature human beings, but also aimed at preparing people specifically for assuming to good advantage an appropriate place in the vast and socially differentiated world of work.

As we view the whole human family throughout the world, we cannot fail to be struck by a disconcerting fact of immense proportions: the fact that while conspicuous natural resources remain unused there are huge numbers of people who are unemployed or underemployed and countless multitudes of people suffering from hunger. This is a fact that without any doubt demonstrates that both within the individual political communities and in their relationships on the continental and world levels there is something wrong with the organization of work and employment, precisely at the most critical and socially most important points.

19. Wages and Other Social Benefits

After outlining the important role that concern for providing employment for all workers plays in safeguarding respect for the inalienable rights of man in view of his work, it is worthwhile to take a closer look at these rights, which in the final analysis are formed within the relationship between worker and direct employer. All that has been said above on the subject of the indirect employer is aimed at defining these relationships more exactly, by showing the many forms of conditioning within which these relationships are indirectly formed. This consideration does not however have a purely descriptive purpose; it is not a brief treatise on economics or politics. It is a matter of highlighting the deontological and moral aspect. The key problem of social ethics in this case is that of just remuneration for work done. In the context of the present there is no more important way for securing a just relationship between the worker and the employer than that constituted by remuneration for work. Whether the work is done in a system of private ownership of the means of production or in a system where ownership has undergone a certain socialization, the relationship between the employer (first and foremost the direct employer) and the worker is resolved on the basis of the wage, that is, through just remuneration of the work done.

It should also be noted that the justice of a socioeconomic system and, in each case, its just functioning, deserve in the final analysis to be evaluated by the way in which man's work is properly remunerated in the system. Here we return once more to the first principle of the whole ethical and social order, namely the principle of the common use of goods. In every system, regardless of the fundamental relationships within it between capital and labor, wages, that is to say remuneration for work, are still a practical means whereby the vast majority of people can have access to those goods which are intended for common use: both the goods of nature and manufactured goods. Both kinds of goods become accessible to the worker through the wage which he receives as remuneration for his work. Hence in every case a just wage is the concrete means of verifying the justice of the whole socioeconomic system and, in any case, of checking that it is functioning justly. It is not the only means of checking, but it is a particularly important one and in a sense the key means.

This means of checking concerns above all the family. Just remuneration for the work of an adult who is responsible for a family means remuneration which will suffice for establishing and properly maintaining a family and for providing security for its future. Such remuneration can be given either through what is called a family wage—that is, a single salary given to the head of the family for his work, sufficient for the needs of the family without the spouse having to take up gainful employment outside the home—or through other social measures such as family allowances or grants to mothers devoting themselves exclusively to their families. These grants should correspond to the actual needs, that is, to the number of dependents for as long as they are not in a position to assume proper responsibility for their own lives.

Experience confirms that there must be a social reevaluation of the mother's role, of the toil connected with it and of the need that children have for care, love and affection in order that they may develop into responsible, morally and religiously mature and psychologically stable persons. It will redound to the credit of society to make it possible for a mother—without inhibiting her freedom, without psychological or practical discrimination, and without penalizing her as compared with other women—to devote herself to taking care of her children and educating them in accordance with their needs, which vary with age. Having to abandon these tasks in order to take up paid work outside the home is wrong from the point of view of the good of society and of the family when it contradicts or hinders these primary goals of the mission of a mother.[26]

In this context it should be emphasized that on a more general level the whole labor process must be organized and adapted in such a way as to respect the requirements of the person and his or her forms of life, above all life in the home, taking into account the individual's age and sex. It is a fact that in many societies women work in nearly every sector of life. But it is fitting that they should be able to fulfill their tasks in accordance with their own nature, without being discriminated against and without being excluded from jobs for which they are capable, but also without lack of respect for their family aspirations and for their specific role in contributing, together with men, to the good of society. The true advancement of women requires that labor should be structured in such a way that women do not have to pay for their advancement by abandoning what is specific to them and at the expense of the family, in which women as mothers have an irreplaceable role.

Besides wages, various social benefits intended to ensure the life and health of workers and their families play a part here. The expenses involved in health care, especially in the case of accidents at work, demand that medical assistance should be easily available for workers and that as far as possible it should be cheap or even free of charge. Another sector regarding benefits is the sector associated with the right to rest. In the first place this involves a regular weekly rest comprising at least Sunday and also a longer period of rest, namely the holiday or vacation taken once a year or possibly in several shorter periods during the year. A third sector concerns the right to a pension and to insurance for old age and in case of accidents at work. Within the sphere of these principal rights there develops a whole system of particular rights which, together with remuneration for work, determine the correct relationship between worker and employer. Among these rights there should never be overlooked the right to a working environment and to manufacturing processes which are not harmful to the workers' physical health or to their moral integrity.

---

[26]Second Vatican Ecumenical Council, *Pastoral Constitution on the Church in the Modern World, Gaudium et Spes*, 67: AAS 58 (1966), p. 1089.

20. Importance of Unions

All these rights, together with the need for the workers themselves to secure them, give rise to yet another right: the right of association, that is, to form associations for the purpose of defending the vital interests of those employed in the various professions. These associations are called labor or trade unions. The vital interests of the workers are to a certain extent common for all of them; at the same time, however, each type of work, each profession, has its own specific character which should find a particular reflection in these organizations.

In a sense, unions go back to the medieval guilds of artisans, insofar as those organizations brought together people belonging to the same craft and thus on the basis of their work. However, unions differ from the guilds on this essential point: The modern unions grew up from the struggle of the workers—workers in general but especially the industrial workers—to protect their just rights vis-à-vis the entrepreneurs and the owners of the means of production. Their task is to defend the existential interests of workers in all sectors in which their rights are concerned. The experience of history teaches that organizations of this type are an indispensable element of social life, especially in modern industrialized societies. Obviously this does not mean that only industrial workers can set up associations of this type. Representatives of every profession can use them to ensure their own rights. Thus there are unions of agricultural workers and of white-collar workers; there are also employers' associations. All, as has been said above, are further divided into groups or subgroups according to particular professional specializations.

Catholic social teaching does not hold that unions are no more than a reflection of the class structure of society and that they are a mouthpiece for a class struggle which inevitably governs social life. They are indeed a mouthpiece for the struggle for social justice, for the just rights of working people in accordance with their individual professions. However, this struggle should be seen as a normal endeavor *for* the just good: In the present case, for the good which corresponds to the needs and merits of working people associated by profession; but it is not a struggle *against* others. Even if in controversial questions the struggle takes on a character of opposition toward others, this is because it aims at the good of social justice, not for the sake of struggle or in order to eliminate the opponent. It is characteristic of work that it first and foremost unites people. In this consists its social power: the power to build a community. In the final analysis, both those who work and those who manage the means of production or who own them must in some way be united in this community. In the light of this fundamental structure of all work—in the light of the fact that, in the final analysis, labor and capital are indispensable components of the process of production in any social system—it is clear that even if it is because of their work needs that people unite to secure their rights, their union remains a constructive factor of social order and solidarity, and it is impossible to ignore it.

Just efforts to secure the rights of workers who are united by the same profession should always take into account the limitations imposed by the general economic situation of the country. Union demands cannot be turned into a kind of group or class egoism, although they can and should also aim at correcting—with a view to the common good of the whole of society—everything defective in the system of ownership of the means of production or in the way these are managed. Social and socioeconomic life is certainly like a system of *connected vessels*, and every social activity directed toward safeguarding the rights of particular groups should adapt itself to this system.

In this sense, union activity undoubtedly enters the field of politics, understood as prudent concern for the common good. However, the role of unions is not to *play politics* in the sense that the expression is commonly understood today. Unions do not have the character of political parties struggling for power; they should not be subjected to the decision of political parties or have too close links with them. In fact, in such a situation they easily lose contact with their specific role, which is to secure the just rights of workers within the framework of the common good of the whole of society; instead they become an instrument used for other purposes.

Speaking of the protection of the just rights of workers according to their individual professions, we must of course always keep in mind that which determines the subjective character of work in each profession, but at the same time, indeed before all else, we must keep in mind that which conditions the specific dignity of the subject of the work. The activity of union organizations opens up many possibilities in this respect, including their efforts to instruct and educate the workers and to foster their self-education. Praise is due to the work of the schools, what are known as workers' or people's universities and the training programs and courses which have developed and are still developing this field of activity. It is always to be hoped that, thanks to the work of their unions, workers will not only have more, but above all be more: in other words that they will realize their humanity more fully in every respect.

One method used by unions in pursuing the just rights of their members is the strike or work stoppage, as a kind of ultimatum to the competent bodies, especially the employers. This method is recognized by Catholic social teaching as legitimate in the proper conditions and within just limits.

In this connection workers should be assured the right to strike, without being subjected to personal penal sanctions for taking part in a strike. While admitting that it is a legitimate means, we must at the same time emphasize that a strike remains, in a sense, an extreme means. It must not be abused; it must not be abused especially for "political" purposes.

Furthermore, it must never be forgotten that, when essential community services are in question, they must in every case be ensured, if necessary by means of appropriate legislation. Abuse of the strike weapon can lead to the paralysis of the whole of socioeconomic life, and this is contrary to the requirements of the common good of society, which also corresponds to the properly understood nature of work itself.

21. Dignity of Agricultural Work

All that has been said thus far on the dignity of work, on the objective and subjective dimensions of human work, can be directly applied to the question of agricultural work and to the situation of the person who cultivates the earth by toiling in the fields.

This is a vast sector of work on our planet, a sector not restricted to one or other continent, nor limited to the societies which have already attained a certain level of development and progress. The world of agriculture, which provides society with the goods it needs for its daily sustenance, is of fundamental importance.

The conditions of the rural population and of agricultural work vary from place to place, and the social position of agricultural workers differs from country to country. This depends not only on the level of development of agricultural technology but also, and perhaps more, on the recognition of the just rights of agricultural workers and, finally, on the level of awareness regarding the social ethics of work.

Agricultural work involves considerable difficulties, including unremitting and sometimes exhausting physical effort and a lack of appreciation on the part of society, to the point of making agricultural people feel that they are social outcasts and of speeding up the phenomenon of their mass exodus from the countryside to the cities and unfortunately to still more dehumanizing living conditions. Added to this are the lack of adequate professional training and of proper equipment, the spread of a certain individualism, and also objectively unjust situations. In certain developing countries, millions of people are forced to cultivate the land belonging to others and are exploited by the big landowners, without any hope of ever being able to gain possession of even a small piece of land of their own. There is a lack of forms of legal protection for the agricultural workers themselves and for their families in case of old age, sickness or unemployment. Long days of hard physical work are paid miserably. Land which could be cultivated is left abandoned by the owners. Legal titles to possession of a small portion of land that someone has personally cultivated for years are disregarded or left defenseless against the *land hunger* of more powerful individuals or groups. But even in the economically developed countries, where scientific research, technological achievements and state policy have brought agriculture to a very advanced level, the right to work can be infringed when the farmworkers are denied the possibility of sharing in decisions concerning their services, or when they are denied the right to free association with a view to their just advancement socially, culturally and economically.

In many situations radical and urgent changes are therefore needed in order to restore to agriculture—and to rural people—their just value as the basis for a healthy economy, within the social community's development as a whole. Thus it is necessary to proclaim and promote the dignity of work, of all work but especially of agricultural work, in which man so eloquently "subdues" the earth he has received as a gift from God and affirms his "dominion" in the visible world.

22. *The Disabled Person and Work*

Recently, national communities and international organizations have turned their attention to another question connected with work, one full of implications: the question of disabled people. They too are fully human subjects with corresponding innate, sacred and inviolable rights, and, in spite of the limitations and sufferings affecting their bodies and faculties, they point up more clearly the dignity and greatness of man. Since disabled people are subjects with all their rights, they should be helped to participate in the life of society in all its aspects and at all the levels accessible to their capacities. The disabled person is one of us and participates fully in the same humanity that we possess. It would be radically unworthy of man, and a denial of our common humanity, to admit to the life of the community, and thus admit to work, only those who are fully functional. To do so would be to practice a serious form of discrimination, that of the strong and healthy aginst the weak and sick. Work in the objective sense should be subordinated, in this circumstance too, to the dignity of man, to the subject of work and not to economic advantage.

The various bodies involved in the world of labor, both the direct and the indirect employer, should therefore, by means of effective and appropriate measures, foster the right of disabled people to professional training and work, so that they can be given a productive activity suited to them. Many practical problems arise at this point, as well as legal and economic ones; but the community, that is to say, the public authorities, associations and intermediate groups, business enterprises and the disabled themselves should pool their ideas and resources so as to attain this goal that must not be shirked: that disabled people may be offered work according to their capabilities, for this is demanded by their dignity as persons and as subjects of work. Each community will be able to set up suitable structures for finding or creating jobs for such people both in the usual public or private enterprises, by offering them ordinary or suitably adapted jobs, and in what are called *protected* enterprises and surroundings.

Careful attention must be devoted to the physical and psychological working conditions of disabled people—as for all workers—to their just remuneration, to the possibility of their promotion, and to the elimination of various obstacles. Without hiding the fact that this is a complex and difficult task, it is to be hoped that a correct concept of labor in the subjective sense will produce a situation which will make it possible for disabled people to feel that they are not cut off from the working world or dependent upon society, but that they are full-scale subjects of work, useful, respected for their human dignity and called to contribute to the progress and welfare of their families and of the community according to their particular capacities.

23. Work and the Emigration Question

Finally, we must say at least a few words on the subject of emigration in search of work. This is an age-old phenomenon which nevertheless continues to be repeated and is still today very widespread as a result of the complexities of modern life.

Man has the right to leave his native land for various motives—and also the right to return—in order to seek better conditions of life in another country. This fact is certainly not without difficulties of various kinds. Above all it generally constitutes a loss for the country which is left behind. It is the departure of a person who is also a member of a great community united by history, tradition and culture; and that person must begin life in the midst of another society united by a different culture and very often by a different language. In this case, it is the loss of a subject of work, whose efforts of mind and body could contribute to the common good of his own country, but these efforts, this contribution, are instead offered to another society which in a sense has less right to them than the person's country of origin.

Nevertheless, even if emigration is in some aspects an evil, in certain circumstances it is, as the phrase goes, a necessary evil. Everything should be done—and certainly much is being done to this end—to prevent this material evil from causing greater moral harm; indeed every possible effort should be made to ensure that it may bring benefit to the emigrant's personal, family and social life, both for the country to which he goes and the country which he leaves. In this area much depends on just legislation, in particular with regard to the rights of workers. It is obvious that the question of just legislation enters into the context of the present considerations, especially from the point of view of these rights.

The most important thing is that the person working away from his native land, whether as a permanent emigrant or as a seasonal worker, should not be placed at a disadvantage in comparison with the other workers in that society in the matter of working rights. Emigration in search of work must in no way become an opportunity for financial or social exploitation. As regards the work relationship, the same criteria should be applied to immigrant workers as to all other workers in the society concerned. The value of work should be measured by the same standard and not according to the difference in nationality, religion or race. For even greater reason the situation of constraint in which the emigrant may find himself should not be exploited. All these circumstances should categorically give way, after special qualifications have of course been taken into consideration, to the fundamental value of work, which is bound up with the dignity of the human person. Once more the fundamental principle must be repeated: the hierarchy of values and the profound meaning of work itself require that capital should be at the service of labor and not labor at the service of capital.

V. Elements for a Spirituality of Work

24. A Particular Task for the Church

It is right to devote the last part of these reflections about human work, on the occasion of the ninetieth anniversary of the encyclical *Rerum Novarum,* to the spirituality of work in the Christian sense. Since work in its subjective aspect is always a personal action, an *actus personae,* it follows that the whole person, body and spirit, participates in it, whether it is manual or intellectual work. It is also to the whole person that the word of the living God is directed, the evangelical message of salvation, in which we find many points which concern human work and which throw particular light on it.

These points need to be properly assimilated: an inner effort on the part of the human spirit, guided by faith, hope and charity, is needed in order that through these points the work of the individual human being may be given the meaning which it has in the eyes of God and by means of which work enters into the salvation process on a par with the other ordinary yet particularly important components of its texture.

The Church considers it her duty to speak out on work from the viewpoint of its human value and of the moral order to which it belongs, and she sees this as one of her important tasks within the service that she renders to the evangelical message as a whole.

At the same time she sees it as her particular duty to form a spirituality of work which will help all people to come closer, through work, to God, the creator and redeemer, to participate in his salvific plan for man and the world and to deepen their friendship with Christ in their lives by accepting, through faith, a living participation in his threefold mission as priest, prophet and king, as the Second Vatican Council so eloquently teaches.

25. *Work as a Sharing in the Activity of the Creator*

As the Second Vatican Council says,

> throughout the course of the centuries, men have labored to better the circumstances of their lives through a monumental amount of individual and collective effort. To believers, this point is settled: Considered in itself, such human activity accords with God's will. For man, created to God's image, received a mandate to subject to himself the earth and all that it contains, and to govern the world with justice and holiness; a mandate to relate himself and the totality of things to him who was to be acknowledged as the Lord and creator of all. Thus, by the subjection of all things to man, the name of God would be wonderful in all the earth.[27]

The word of God's revelation is profoundly marked by the fundamental truth that man, created in the image of God, shares by his work in the activity of the creator and that, within the limits of his own human capabilities, man in a sense continues to develop that activity, and perfects it as he advances further and further in the discovery of the resources and values contained in the whole of creation. We find this truth at the very beginning of Sacred Scripture, in the Book of Genesis, where the creation activity itself is presented in the form of "work" done by God during "six days,"[28] "resting" on the seventh day.[29] Besides, the last book of Sacred Scripture echoes the same respect for what God has done through his creative "work" when it proclaims: "Great and wonderful are your deeds, O Lord God the Almighty";[30] this is similar to the Book of Genesis, which concludes the description of each day of creation with the statement: "And God saw that it was good."[31]

This description of creation, which we find in the very first chapter of the Book of Genesis, is also in a sense the first *gospel of work*. For

---

[27] Second Vatican Ecumenical Council, *Pastoral Constitution on the Church in the Modern World, Gaudium et Spes,* 34: AAS 58 (1966), pp. 1052-1053.
[28] Cf. Gn 2:2; Ex 20:8, 11; Dt 5:12-14.
[29] Cf. Gn 2:3.
[30] Rv 15:3.
[31] Gn 1:4, 10, 12, 18, 21, 25, 31.

it shows what the dignity of work consists of: It teaches that man ought to imitate God, his creator, in working, because man alone has the unique characteristic of likeness to God. Man ought to imitate God both in working and also in resting, since God himself wished to present his own creative activity under the form of work and rest.

This activity by God in the world always continues, as the words of Christ attest: "My father is working still . . .";[32] he works with creative power by sustaining in existence the world that he called into being from nothing, and he works with salvific power in the hearts of those whom from the beginning he has destined for "rest"[33] in union with himself in his "father's house."[34]

Therefore man's work too not only requires a rest every "seventh day,"[35] but also cannot consist in the mere exercise of human strength in external action; it must leave room for man to prepare himself, by becoming more and more what in the will of God he ought to be, for the "rest" that the Lord reserves for his servants and friends.[36]

Awareness that man's work is a participation in God's activity ought to permeate, as the council teaches, even

> the most ordinary everyday activities. For, while providing the substance of life for themselves and their families, men and women are performing their activities in a way which appropriately benefits society. They can justly consider that by their labor they are unfolding the creator's work, consulting the advantages of their brothers and sisters, and contributing by their personal industry to the realization in history of the divine plan.[37]

This Christian spirituality of work should be a heritage shared by all. Especially in the modern age, the spirituality of work should show the maturity called for by the tensions and restlessness of mind and heart.

> Far from thinking that works produced by man's own talent and energy are in opposition to God's power, and that the rational creature exists as a kind of rival to the creator, Christians are convinced that the triumphs of the human race are a sign of God's greatness and the flowering of his own mysterious design. For the greater man's power becomes, the farther his individual and community responsibility extends. . . . People are not deterred by the Christian message from building up the world, or impelled to neglect the

---

[32] Jn 5:17.
[33] Cf. Heb 4:1, 9-10.
[34] Jn 14:2.
[35] Cf. Dt 5:12-14; Ex 20:8-12.
[36] Cf. Mt 25:21.
[37] Second Vatican Ecumenical Council, *Pastoral Constitution on the Church in the Modern World, Gaudium et Spes*, 34: AAS 58 (1966), pp. 1052-1053.

> welfare of their fellows. They are, rather, more stringently bound to do these very things.[38]

The knowledge that by means of work man shares in the work of creation constitutes the most profound motive for undertaking it in various sectors. "The faithful, therefore," we read in the constitution *Lumen Gentium*,

> must learn the deepest meaning and the value of all creation, and its orientation to the praise of God. Even by their secular activity they must assist one another to live holier lives.
>
> In this way the world will be permeated by the spirit of Christ and more effectively achieve its purpose in justice, charity and peace. . . . Therefore, by their competence in secular fields and by their personal activity, elevated from within by the grace of Christ, let them work vigorously so that by human labor, technical skill, and civil culture, created goods may be perfected according to the design of the creator and the light of his word.[39]

26. Christ, the Man of Work

The truth that by means of work man participates in the activity of God himself, his creator, was given particular prominence by Jesus Christ—the Jesus at whom many of his first listeners in Nazareth "were astonished, saying, 'Where did this man get all this? What is the wisdom given to him? . . . Is not this the carpenter?'"[40]

For Jesus not only proclaimed but first and foremost fulfilled by his deeds the Gospel, the word of eternal wisdom, that had been entrusted to him. Therefore, this was also *the gospel of work*, because he who proclaimed it was himself a man of work, a craftsman like Joseph of Nazareth.[41] And if we do not find in his words a special command to work—but rather on one occasion a prohibition against too much anxiety about work and life[42]—at the same time the eloquence of the life of Christ is unequivocal.

He belongs to the *working world*, he has appreciation and respect for human work. It can indeed be said that he looks with love upon human work and the different forms that it takes, seeing in each one of these forms a particular facet of man's likeness with God, the creator and father. Is it not he who says: "My father is the vinedresser,"[43] and in various ways puts into his teaching the fundamen-

---

[38] Ibid.
[39] Second Vatican Ecumenical Council, *Dogmatic Constitution on the Church, Lumen Gentium*, 36: AAS 57 (1965), p. 41.
[40] Mk 6:1-3.
[41] Cf. Mt 13:55.
[42] Cf. Mt 6:25-34.
[43] Jn 15:1.

tal truth about work which is already expressed in the whole tradition of the Old Testament, beginning with the Book of Genesis?

The books of the Old Testament contain many references to human work and to the individual professions exercised by man: for example, the doctor,[44] the pharmacist,[45] the craftsman or artist,[46] the blacksmith[47]—we could apply these words to today's foundry workers—the potter,[48] the farmer,[49] the scholar,[50] the sailor,[51] the builder,[52] the musician,[53] the shepherd,[54] and the fisherman.[55]

The words of praise for the work of women are well known.[56] In his parables on the kingdom of God, Jesus Christ constantly refers to human work: that of the shepherd,[57] the farmer,[58] the doctor,[59] the sower,[60] the householder,[61] the servant,[62] the steward,[63] the fisherman,[64] the merchant,[65] the laborer.[66] He also speaks of the various forms of women's work.[67] He compares the apostolate to the manual work of harvesters[68] or fishermen.[69] He refers to the work of scholars too.[70]

This teaching of Christ on work, based on the example of his life during his years in Nazareth, finds a particularly lively echo in the teaching of the apostle Paul. Paul boasts of working at his trade (he was probably a tentmaker),[71] and thanks to that work he was able even as an apostle to earn his own bread.[72]

---

[44]Cf. Sir 38:1-3.
[45]Cf. Sir 38:4-8.
[46]Cf. Ex 31:1-5; Sir 38:29-30.
[47]Cf. Gn 4:22; Is 44:12.
[48]Cf. Jer 18:3-4; Sir 38:29-30.
[49]Cf. Gn 9:20; Is 5:1-2.
[50]Cf. Eccl 12:9-12; Sir 39:1-8.
[51]Cf. Ps 107(108):23-30; Wis 14:2-3a.
[52]Cf. Gn 11:3; 2 Kgs 12:12-13; 22:5-6.
[53]Cf. Gn 4:21.
[54]Cf. Gn 4:2; 37:3; Ex 3:1; I Sm 16:11; et passim.
[55]Cf. Ez 47:10.
[56]Cf. Prv 31:15-27.
[57]E.g. Jn 10:1-16.
[58]Cf. Mk 12:1-12.
[59]Cf. Lk 4:23.
[60]Cf. Mk 4:1-9.
[61]Cf. Mt 13:52.
[62]Cf. Mt 24:45; Lk 12:42-48.
[63]Cf. Lk 16:1-8.
[64]Cf. Mt 13:47-50.
[65]Cf. Mt 13:45-46.
[66]Cf. Mt 20:1-6.
[67]Cf. Mt 13:33; Lk 15:8-9.
[68]Cf. Mt 9:37; Jn 4:35-38.
[69]Cf. Mt 4:19.
[70]Cf. Mt 13:52.
[71]Cf. Acts 18:3.
[72]Cf. Acts 20:34-35.

"With toil and labor we worked night and day, that we might not burden any of you."[73] Hence his instructions, in the form of exhortation and command, on the subject of work: "Now such persons we command and exhort in the Lord Jesus Christ to do their work in quietness and to earn their own living," he writes to the Thessalonians.[74] In fact, noting that some "are living in idleness . . . not doing any work,"[75] the apostle does not hesitate to say in the same context: "If any one will not work, let him not eat."[76] In another passage he encourages his readers: "Whatever your task, work heartily, as serving the Lord and not men, knowing that from the Lord you will receive the inheritance as your reward."[77]

The teachings of the apostle of the gentiles obviously have key importance for the morality and spirituality of human work. They are an important complement to the great though discreet gospel of work that we find in the life and parables of Christ, in what Jesus "did and taught."[78]

On the basis of these illuminations emanating from the source himself, the Church has always proclaimed what we find expressed in modern terms in the teaching of the Second Vatican Council:

> Just as human activity proceeds from man, so it is ordered toward man. For when a man works he not only alters things and society, he develops himself as well. He learns much, he cultivates his resources, he goes outside of himself and beyond himself. Rightly understood, this kind of growth is of greater value than any external riches which can be garnered . . . . Hence, the norm of human activity is this: that in accord with the divine plan and will, it should harmonize with the genuine good of the human race, and allow people as individuals and as members of society to pursue their total vocation and fulfill it.[79]

Such a vision of the values of human work, or in other words such a spirituality of work, fully explains what we read in the same section of the council's pastoral constitution with regard to the right meaning of progress:

> A person is more precious for what he is than for what he has. Similarly, all that people do to obtain greater justice, wider brotherhood, and a more humane ordering of social relationships has

---

[73] 2 Thes 3:8. Saint Paul recognizes that missionaries have a right to their keep: 1 Cor 9:6-14; Gal 6:6; 2 Thes 3:9; cf. Lk 10:7.
[74] 2 Thes 3:12.
[75] 2 Thes 3:11.
[76] 2 Thes 3:10.
[77] Col 3:23-24.
[78] Cf. Acts 1:1.
[79] Second Vatican Ecumenical Council, *Pastoral Constitution on the Church in the Modern World, Gaudium et Spes,* 35: AAS 58 (1966), p. 1053.

> greater worth than technical advances. For these advances can supply the material for human progress, but of themselves alone they can never actually bring it about.[80]

This teaching on the question of progress and development—a subject that dominates present-day thought—can be understood only as the fruit of a tested spirituality of human work; and it is only on the basis of such a spirituality that it can be realized and put into practice. This is the teaching, and also the program, that has its roots in *the gospel of work.*

27. Human Work in the Light of the Cross and the Resurrection of Christ

There is yet another aspect of human work, an essential dimension of it, that is profoundly imbued with the spirituality based on the Gospel. All work, whether manual or intellectual, is inevitably linked with toil. The Book of Genesis expresses it in a truly penetrating manner: The original blessing of work contained in the very mystery of creation and connected with man's elevation as the image of God is contrasted with the curse that sin brought with it: "Cursed is the ground because of you; in toil you shall eat of it all the days of your life."[81] This toil connected with work marks the way of human life on earth and constitutes an announcement of death: "In the sweat of your face you shall eat bread till you return to the ground, for out of it you were taken."[82] Almost as an echo of these words, the author of one of the wisdom books says: "Then I considered all that my hands had done and the toil I had spent in doing it."[83] There is no one on earth who could not apply these words to himself.

In a sense, the final word of the Gospel on this matter as on others is found in the paschal mystery of Jesus Christ. It is here that we must seek an answer to these problems so important for the spirituality of human work. The paschal mystery contains the cross of Christ and his obedience unto death, which the apostle contrasts with the disobedience which from the beginning has burdened man's history on earth.[84] It also contains the elevation of Christ, who by means of death on a cross returns to his disciples in the resurrection with the power of the Holy Spirit.

Sweat and toil, which work necessarily involves in the present condition of the human race, present the Christian and everyone who

[80] Ibid.
[81] Gn 3:17.
[82] Gn 3:19.
[83] Eccl 2:11.
[84] Cf. Rom 5:19.

is called to follow Christ with the possibility of sharing lovingly in the work that Christ came to do.[85] This work of salvation came about through suffering and death on a cross. By enduring the toil of work in union with Christ crucified for us, man in a way collaborates with the son of God for the redemption of humanity. He shows himself a true disciple of Christ by carrying the cross in his turn every day[86] in the activity that he is called upon to perform.

Christ, "undergoing death itself for all of us sinners, taught us by example that we too must shoulder that cross which the world and the flesh inflict upon those who pursue peace and justice"; but also, at the same time,

> appointed Lord by his resurrection and given all authority in heaven and on earth, Christ is now at work in people's hearts through the power of his Spirit. . . . He animates, purifies and strengthens those noble longings too by which the human family strives to make its life more human and to render the whole earth submissive to this goal.[87]

The Christian finds in human work a small part of the cross of Christ and accepts it in the same spirit of redemption in which Christ accepted his cross for us. In work, thanks to the light that penetrates us from the resurrection of Christ, we always find a glimmer of new life, of the new good, as if it were an announcement of "the new heavens and the new earth"[88] in which man and the world participate precisely through the toil that goes with work. Through toil—and never without it. On the one hand, this confirms the indispensability of the cross in the spirituality of human work; on the other hand, the cross which this toil constitutes reveals a new good springing from work itself, from work understood in depth and in all its aspects and never apart from work.

Is this new good—the fruit of human work—already a small part of that "new earth" where justice dwells?[89] If it is true that the many forms of toil that go with man's work are a small part of the cross of Christ, what is the relationship of this new good to the resurrection of Christ? The council seeks to reply to this question also, drawing light from the very sources of the revealed word:

> Therefore, while we are warned that it profits a man nothing if he gains the whole world and loses himself (cf. Lk 9:25), the expectation of a new earth must not weaken but rather stimulate our concern

---

[85] Cf. Jn 17:4.
[86] Cf. Lk 9:23.
[87] Second Vatican Ecumenical Council, *Pastoral Constitution on the Church in the Modern World, Gaudium et Spes*, 38: AAS 58 (1966), pp. 1055-1056.
[88] Cf. 2 Pt 3:13; Rv 21:1.
[89] Cf. 2 Pt 3:13.

> for cultivating this one. For here grows the body of a new human family, a body which even now is able to give some kind of foreshadowing of the new age. Earthly progress must be carefully distinguished from the growth of Christ's kingdom. Nevertheless, to the extent that the former can contribute to the better ordering of human society, it is of vital concern to the kingdom of God.[90]

In these present reflections devoted to human work we have tried to emphasize everything that seemed essential to it, since it is through man's labor that not only "the fruits of our activity" but also "human dignity, brotherhood and freedom" must increase on earth.[91] Let the Christian who listens to the word of the living God, uniting work with prayer, know the place that his work has not only in earthly progress but also in the development of the kingdom of God, to which we are all called through the power of the Holy Spirit and through the word of the Gospel.

In concluding these reflections, I gladly impart the apostolic blessing to all of you, venerable brothers and beloved sons and daughters.

I prepared this document for publication on last May 15, on the ninetieth anniversary of the encyclical *Rerum Novarum,* but it is only after my stay in the hospital that I have been able to revise it definitively.

Given at Castelgandolfo, on the 14th day of September, the feast of the triumph of the cross, in the year 1981, the third of the pontificate.

John Paul II

[90]Second Vatican Ecumenical Council, *Pastoral Constitution on the Church in the Modern World, Gaudium et Spes,* 39: AAS 58 (1966), p. 1057.
[91]Ibid.

Introduction to the Addresses in the United States and Canada

Four of the talks Pope John Paul II gave during his travels to the United States and Canada are very significant for his teaching on economic matters. This is true not only because of their content but also because they offer clues to the proper interpretation of his encyclicals, particularly *Laborem Exercens*.

The 1979 addresses at the United Nations and at Yankee Stadium are rooted in the same theological premise—human dignity flowing from the reality of the Incarnation—that anchors the two encyclicals. The Pope avoided formal theological language in his United Nations address, but the Incarnation clearly lies behind the sense of human dignity so fundamental to the papal remarks. (His theology is more explicit in the opening lines of the talk at Yankee Stadium.) One notes the absence of an appeal to natural law as a basis for economic justice in the manner of *Pacem in Terris*. The Pope grounds his social theory in a theological/philosophical analysis of which human dignity and human creativity are the cornerstones: "Every analysis must necessarily start from the premise that—although each person lives in a particular concrete social and historical context—every human being is endowed with a dignity that must never be lessened, impaired or destroyed but must instead be respected and safeguarded if peace is really to be built up."

The United Nations address does have one direct link with *Pacem in Terris*. It asserts without qualification that there exist fundamental economic rights of which no one may be deprived. These include the right to property, to work, to adequate working conditions and to a just wage, as well as related rights to food, clothing, housing and health care. The Pope has reasserted the propriety of using rights language in speaking about economically related areas of human life. This is important because many question whether the designation of so many rights does not place too great an economic burden on society. John Paul seems to be saying *no*. Every individual can legitimately make claims in these economic areas. While society may not be able to meet fully all these claims at any given moment, it can never rest easy while economic rights remain unsatisfied. The Pope also seems to consider these rights crucial to any proper notion of human dignity from a religious perspective.

John Paul associates himself with Paul VI's central notion that development is the new name for peace. War is ultimately rooted in exploitation, including economic exploitation. These words epitomize John Paul's perspective: "This is a new and deeply relevant vision of the cause of peace, one that goes deeper and is more radical. It is a vision that sees the genesis, and in a sense the substance, of war in the more complex forms emanating from injustice viewed in all its various aspects. . . ." The Pope recognizes both in the United Nations address and in his talk at Yankee Stadium that the development that leads to peace will not come about without major structural changes within nations and among nations. The Yankee Stadium address clearly charges American Catholics to work for such changes in domestic and international policy.

As we have noted, while John Paul II may be less explicit in his analysis of structural economic injustice than Paul VI, he is not shifting the focus of Catholic social thought as much as some claim. When he speaks of solidarity as a basis for world peace, when he warns against rich countries draining off reserves of energy and raw materials at the expense of poorer nations, he is certainly on the same wavelength as Pope Paul and the 1971 Synod. His address before the United Nations undercuts the proposition that *Laborem Exercens* represents a fundamental change of direction: "People must become aware that economic tensions within countries and in the relationship between states and even between entire continents contain within themselves substantial elements that restrict or violate human rights."

The United Nations address also challenges those who think it improper to gauge the performance of an economic system by other than narrowly defined economic criteria:

> the fundamental criterion for comparing social, economic and political systems . . . must be *the humanistic criterion*, namely the measure in which each system is really capable of reducing, restraining and eliminating as far as possible the various forms of exploitation of man and of ensuring for him, through work, not only the just distribution of the indispensable material goods, but also a participation, in keeping with his dignity, in the whole process of production and in the social life that grows up around that process.

The 1984 addresses of John Paul II in Edmonton and Newfoundland, Canada serve to clarify further how we should interpret the theological vision presented in *Redemptor Hominis* and *Laborem Exercens*. They confirm even more forcefully than the United Nations and Yankee Stadium statements that this vision owes much to Paul VI and the 1971 Synod.

In Newfoundland, John Paul had the opportunity to speak about economic issues in a region where many people have been directly hurt by economic failures. Though he dwells on the primary local issue—the depression in the fishing industry—his principles have far broader application. It quickly becomes apparent from reading this brief talk that the Pope is deeply aware of the need for major structural changes in the world economy if fishermen or any other laborers are to achieve greater dignity.

John Paul offers a critique of unrestrained capitalism on two counts. First, he expresses grave reservations about the growing concentration of capital in ever larger corporations, which leaves control of markets in a few hands. Such concentration destroys the organization of production by small units, a system the Pope believes can better provide humane working conditions for laborers. Second, John Paul argues that free enterprise alone cannot guarantee adequate production and distribution of food (and, by implication, of other necessities). There is a definite need for governmental intervention and planning: "The responsible stewardship of all the earth's resources, and especially food, requires long-range planning at the different levels of government, in cooperation with industries and workers."

The Pope goes on to apply his economic model from *Laborem Exercens* to the Newfoundland fishing situation. He recommends the promotion of fishing cooperatives, collective agreements between fishermen and management, and even partnerships or forms of joint ownership. (These recommendations may not have seemed so bold in Canada as they would in the United States. Over the years, Canada has experimented more widely with socialist-leaning models than we have in this country.) He also supported a basic principle of the Canadian bishops' economic statement: "the value and dignity of labor." Preserving this dignity requires the creation of economic models that allow for worker participation in decisions regarding the work process and the use of capital produced.

The Pope's address in Edmonton is his most specific statement on the international economic order, as viewed in the light of the Incarnationally-based theology of human dignity he detailed in his two major encyclicals. Speaking with clear moral indignation and sometimes departing from his prepared text, John Paul told Canada and other wealthy nations of the North that they will be ultimately judged by their actions toward the poor peoples of the South. "Poor people and poor nations—poor in different ways, not only lacking food, but also deprived of freedom and other human rights—will sit in judgment on those people who take these goods away from them, amassing to themselves the imperialistic monopoly of economic and political supremacy at the expense of others."

John Paul here speaks words of prophetic warning to those who control international economic decision-making. Invoking the New

Testament parable of Lazarus and the rich man, a persistent theme in his writings, he cautions the world's economic elite that to remain comfortable amid global poverty is to place their eternal salvation at risk. John Paul II's remarks here and in his other North American talks match, and perhaps even go beyond, the criticisms of *Populorum Progressio* and *Justice in the World*. No interpretation of *Laborem Exercens* can be legitimate that fails to take into account the forthright assertions in these addresses.

On Pilgrimage
The Address at the United Nations

POPE JOHN PAUL II

October 2, 1979

Selections*

* * *

11. It is therefore necessary to make a continuing and even more energetic effort to do away with the very possibility of provoking war, and to make such catastrophes impossible by influencing the attitudes and convictions, the very intentions and aspirations of governments and peoples. This duty, kept constantly in mind by the United Nations organization and each of its institutions, must also be a duty for every society, every regime, every government. This task is certainly served by initiatives aimed at international cooperation for the fostering of development. As Paul VI said at the end of his encyclical *Populorum Progressio*: "If the new name for peace is development, who would not wish to labor for it with all his powers?" However, this task must also be served by constant reflection and activity aimed at discovering the very roots of hatred, destructiveness and contempt—the roots of everything that produces the temptation to war, not so much in the hearts of the nations as in the inner determination of the systems that decide the history of whole societies. In this titanic labor of building up the peaceful future of our planet the United Nations organization has undoubtedly a key function and guiding role, for which it must refer to the just ideals contained in the Universal Declaration of Human Rights. For this declaration has struck a real blow against the many deep roots of war, since the spirit of war, in its basic primordial meaning, springs up and grows to maturity where the inalienable rights of man are violated.

This is a new and deeply relevant vision of the cause of peace, one that goes deeper and is more radical. It is a vision that sees the genesis, and in a sense the substance, of war in the more complex forms emanating from injustice viewed in all its various aspects; this injustice first attacks human rights and thereby destroys the organic unity of the social order and it then affects the whole system of

*Editor's Note: Deleted material in this document is indicated in the text by the symbol * * *.

international relations. Within the Church's doctrine, the encyclical *Pacem in Terris* by John XXIII provides in synthetic form a view of this matter that is very close to the ideological foundation of the United Nations organization. This must therefore form the basis to which one must loyally and perseveringly adhere in order to establish true peace on earth.

12. By applying this criterion we must diligently examine which principal tensions in connection with the inalienable rights of man can weaken the construction of this peace which we all desire so ardently and which is the essential goal of the efforts of the United Nations organization. It is not easy, but it must be done. Anyone who undertakes it must take up a totally objective position and be guided by sincerity, readiness to acknowledge one's prejudices and mistakes and readiness even to renounce one's own particular interests, including any of these interests. It is by sacrificing these interests for the sake of peace that we serve them best. After all, in whose political interest can it ever be to have another war?

Every analysis must necessarily start from the premise that—although each person lives in a particular concrete social and historical context—every human being is endowed with a dignity that must never be lessened, impaired or destroyed but must instead be respected and safeguarded, if peace is really to be built up.

13. In a movement that one hopes will be progressive and continuous, the Universal Declaration of Human Rights and the other international and national juridical instruments are endeavoring to create general awareness of the dignity of the human being, and to define at least some of the inalienable rights of man. Permit me to enumerate some of the most important human rights that are universally recognized: the right to life, liberty and security of person; the right to food, clothing, housing, sufficient health care, rest and leisure; the right to freedom of expression, education and culture; the right to freedom of thought, conscience and religion; and the right to manifest one's religion either individually or in community, in public or in private; the right to choose a state of life, to found a family and to enjoy all conditions necessary for family life; the right to property and work, to adequate working conditions and a just wage; the right of assembly and association; the right to freedom of movement, to internal and external migration; the right to nationality and residence; the right to political participation and the right to participate in the free choice of the political system of the people to which one belongs. All these human rights taken together are in keeping with the substance of the dignity of the human being, understood in his entirety, not as reduced to one dimension only. These rights concern the satisfaction of man's essential needs, the exercise of his freedoms and his relationships with others; but always and everywhere they concern man, they concern man's full human dimension.

14. Man lives at the same time both in the world of material values and in that of spiritual values. For the individual living and hoping man, his needs, freedoms and relationships with others never concern one sphere of values alone, but belong to both. Material and spiritual realities may be viewed separately in order to understand better that in the concrete human being they are inseparable, and to see that any threat to human rights, whether in the field of material realities or in that of spiritual realities, is equally dangerous for peace, since in every instance it concerns man in his entirety. Permit me, distinguished ladies and gentlemen, to recall a constant rule of the history of humanity, a rule that is implicitly contained in all that I have already stated with regard to integral development and human rights. The rule is based on the relationship between spiritual values and material or economic values. In this relationship, it is the spiritual values that are preeminent, both on account of the nature of these values and also for reasons concerning the good of man. The preeminence of the values of the spirit defines the proper sense of earthly material goods and the way to use them. This preeminence is therefore at the basis of a just peace. It is also a contributing factor to ensuring that material development, technical development and the development of civilization are at the service of what constitutes man. This means enabling man to have full access to truth, to moral development, and to the complete possibility of enjoying the goods of culture which he has inherited, and of increasing them by his own creativity. It is easy to see that material goods do not have unlimited capacity for satisfying the needs of man. They are not in themselves easily distributed and, in the relationship between those who possess and enjoy them and those who are without them, they give rise to tension, dissension and division that will often even turn into open conflict. Spiritual goods, on the other hand, are open to unlimited enjoyment by many at the same time, without diminution of the goods themselves. Indeed, the more people share in such goods, the more they are enjoyed and drawn upon, the more then do these goods show their indestructible and immortal worth. This truth is confirmed, for example, by the works of creativity—I mean by the works of thought, poetry, music, and the figurative arts, fruits of man's spirit.

15. A critical analysis of our modern civilization shows that in the last hundred years it has contributed as never before to the development of material goods, but that it has also given rise, both in theory and still more in practice, to a series of attitudes in which sensitivity to the spiritual dimension of human existence is diminished to a greater or less extent, as a result of certain premises which reduce the meaning of human life chiefly to the many different material and economic factors—I mean to the demands of production, the market, consumption, the accumulation of riches or of the growing bureaucracy with which an attempt is made to regulate these very processes. Is this not the result of having subordinated man to one single conception and sphere of values?

16. What is the link between these reflections and the cause of peace and war? Since, as I have already stated, material goods by their very nature provoke conditionings and divisions, the struggle to obtain these goods becomes inevitable in the history of humanity. If we cultivate this one-sided subordination of man to material goods alone, we shall be incapable of overcoming this state of need. We shall be able to attenuate it and avoid it in particular cases, but we shall not succeed in eliminating it systematically and radically, unless we emphasize more and pay greater honor, before everyone's eyes, in the sight of every society, to the second dimension of the goods of man: the dimension that does not divide people but puts them into communication with each other, associates them and unites them.

I consider that the famous opening words of the Charter of the United Nations, in which the peoples of the United Nations, determined to save succeeding generations from the scourge of war, solemnly reaffirmed "faith in fundamental human rights, in the dignity and worth of the human person, in the equal rights of men and women and of nations large and small," are meant to stress this dimension.

Indeed, the fight against incipient wars cannot be carried out on a merely superficial level, by treating the symptoms. It must be done in a radical way, by attacking the causes. The reason I have called attention to the dimension constituted by spiritual realities is my concern for the cause of peace, peace which is built up by men and women uniting around what is most fully and profoundly human, around what raises them above the world about them and determines their indestructible grandeur—indestructible in spite of the death to which everyone on earth is subject. I would like to add that the Catholic Church and, I think I can say, the whole of Christianity sees in this very domain its own particular task. The Second Vatican Council helped to establish what the Christian faith has in common with the various non-Christian religions in this aspiration. The Church is therefore grateful to all who show respect and good will with regard to this mission of hers and do not impede it or make it difficult. An analysis of the history of mankind, especially at its recent stage, shows how important is the duty of revealing more fully the range of the goods that are linked with the spiritual dimension of human existence. It shows how important this task is for building peace and how serious is any threat to human rights. Any violation of them, even in a peace situation, is a form of warfare against humanity.

It seems that in the modern world there are two main threats. Both concern human rights in the field of international relations and human rights within the individual states or societies.

17. The first of these systematic threats against human rights is linked in an overall sense with the distribution of material goods. This distribution is frequently unjust both within individual societies and on the planet as a whole. Everyone knows that these goods are given to man not only as nature's bounty; they are enjoyed by him chiefly as the fruit of his many activities, ranging from the simplest manual and physical labor to the most complicated forms of industrial production and highly qualified and specialized research and study. Various forms of inequality in the possession of material goods, and in the enjoyment of them, can often be explained by different historical and cultural causes and circumstances. But, while these circumstances can diminish the moral responsibility of people today, they do not prevent the situations of inequality from being marked by injustice and social injury.

People must become aware that economic tensions within countries and in the relationship between states and even between entire continents contain within themselves substantial elements that restrict or violate human rights. Such elements are the exploitation of labor and many other abuses that affect the dignity of the human person. It follows that the fundamental criterion for comparing social, economic and political systems is not, and cannot be, the criterion of hegemony and imperialism; it can be, and indeed it must be, the humanistic criterion, namely the measure in which each system is really capable of reducing, restraining and eliminating as far as possible the various forms of exploitation of man and of ensuring for him through work, not only the just distribution of the indispensable material goods, but also a participation, in keeping with his dignity, in the whole process of production and in the social life that grows up around that process. Let us not forget that, although man depends on the resources of the material world for his life, he cannot be their slave, but he must be their master. The words of the Book of Genesis, "Fill the earth and subdue it" (Gn 1:28), are in a sense a primary and essential directive in the field of economy and of labor policy.

18. Humanity as a whole, and the individual nations, have certainly made remarkable progress in this field during the last 100 years. But it is a field in which there is never any lack of systematic threats and violations of human rights. Disturbing factors are frequently present in the form of the frightful disparities between excessively rich individuals and groups on the one hand, and on the other hand the majority made up of the poor or indeed of the destitute, who lack food and opportunities for work and education and are in great numbers condemned to hunger and disease. And concern is also caused at times by the radical separation of work from property, by man's indifference to the production enterprise to which he is linked only by a work obligation, without feeling that he is working for a good that will be his or for himself. It is no secret that the abyss separating the minority of the excessively rich from the multitude of the destitute is a very grave symptom in the life of any society. This must also be said with even greater insistence with regard to the abyss separating countries and regions of the earth. Surely the only way to overcome this serious disparity between areas of satiety and areas of hunger and depression is through coordinated cooperation by all countries. This requires above all else a unity inspired by an authentic perspective of peace. Everything will depend on whether these differences and contrasts in the sphere of the possession of goods will be systematically reduced through truly effective means, on whether the belts of hunger, malnutrition, destitution, underdevelopment, disease and illiteracy will disappear from the economic map of the earth, and on whether peaceful cooperation will avoid imposing conditions of exploitation and economic or political dependence, which would only be a form of neocolonialism.

* * *

Special Sensitivity toward Those in Distress

The Address at Yankee Stadium

POPE JOHN PAUL II

October 2, 1979

1. "Peace be with you!"

These were the first words that Jesus spoke to his apostles after his resurrection. With these words the risen Christ restored peace to their hearts, at a time when they were still in a state of shock after the first terrible experience of Good Friday. Tonight in the name of the Lord Jesus Christ, in the power of his spirit, in the midst of a world that is anxious about its own existence, I repeat these words to you, for they are words of life: "Peace be with you!"

Jesus does not merely give us peace. He gives us his peace accompanied by his justice. He is peace and justice. He becomes our peace and our justice.

What does this mean? It means that Jesus Christ—the Son of God made man, the perfect man—perfects, restores and manifests in himself the unsurpassable dignity that God wishes to give to man from the beginning. He is the one who realizes in himself what man has the vocation to be: the one who is fully reconciled with the Father, fully one in himself, fully devoted to others. Jesus Christ is living peace and living justice.

Jesus Christ makes us sharers in what he is. Through his incarnation, the Son of God in a certain manner united himself with every human being. In our inmost being he has recreated us; in our inmost being he has reconciled us with God, reconciled us with ourselves, reconciled us with our brothers and sisters: He is our peace.

2. What unfathomable riches we bear within us, and in our Christian communities! We are bearers of the justice and peace of God! We are not primarily painstaking builders of a justice and peace that are merely human, always wearing out and always fragile. We are primarily the humble beneficiaries of the very life of God, who is justice and peace in the bond of charity. During Mass, when the priest greets us with these words: "The peace of the Lord be with you always," let us think primarily of this peace which is God's gift: Jesus Christ our peace. And when, before Communion, the priest invites us to give one another a sign of peace, let us think primarily of the fact that we are invited to exchange with one another the peace of Christ who dwells within us, who invites us to share in his body and blood, for our joy and for the service of all humanity.

For God's justice and peace cry out to bear fruit in human works of justice and peace, in all the spheres of actual life. When we Christians make Jesus Christ the center of our feelings and thoughts, we do not turn away from people and their needs. On the contrary, we are caught up in the eternal movement of God's love that comes to meet us; we are caught up in the movement of the Son, who came among us, who became one of us; we are caught in the movement of the Holy Spirit, who visits the poor, calms fevered hearts, binds up wounded hearts, warms cold hearts, and gives us the fullness of his gifts. The reason why man is the primary and fundamental way for the Church is that the Church walks in the footsteps of Jesus: It is Jesus who has shown her this road. This road passes in an unchangeable way through the mystery of the incarnation and redemption; it leads from Christ to man. The Church looks at the world through the very eyes of Christ. Jesus is the principle of her solicitude for man (cf. *Redemptor Hominis,* 13-18).

3. The task is immense. And it is an enthralling one. I have just emphasized various aspects of it before the General Assembly of the United Nations, and I shall touch upon others during my apostolic journey across your country. Today, let me just dwell on the spirit and nature of the Church's contribution to the cause of justice and peace, and let me also mention certain urgent priorities which your service to humanity ought to concentrate upon today.

Social thinking and social practice inspired by the Gospel must always be marked by a special sensitivity toward those who are most in distress, those who are extremely poor, those suffering from all the physical, mental and moral ills that afflict humanity including hunger, neglect, unemployment and despair. There are many poor people of this sort around the world. There are many in your own midst. On many occasions, your nation has gained a well-deserved reputation for generosity, both public and private.

Be faithful to that tradition, in keeping with your vast possibilities and present responsibilities. The network of charitable works of each kind that the Church has succeeded in creating here is a valuable means for effectively mobilizing generous undertakings aimed at relieving the situations of distress that continually arise both at home and elsewhere in the world. Make an effort to ensure that this form of aid keeps its irreplaceable character as a fraternal and personal encounter with those who are in distress; if necessary, reestablish this very character against all the elements that work in the opposite direction. Let this sort of aid be respectful of the freedom and dignity of those being helped, and let it be a means of forming the conscience of the givers.

4. But this is not enough. Within the framework of your national institutions and in cooperation with all your compatriots, you will also want to seek out the structural reasons which foster or cause the different forms of poverty in the world and in your own country, so that you can apply the proper remedies. You will not allow yourselves to be intimidated or discouraged by oversimplified explanations, which are more ideological than scientific—explanations which try to account for a complex evil by some single cause. But neither will you recoil before the reforms—even profound ones—of attitudes and structures that may prove necessary in order to recreate over and over again the conditions needed by the disadvantaged if they are to have a fresh chance in the hard struggle of life. The poor of the United States and of the world are your brothers and sisters in Christ. You must never be content to leave them just the crumbs from the feast. You must take of your substance and not just of your abundance in order to help them. And you must treat them like guests at your family table.

5. Catholics of the United States, while developing your own legitimate institutions, you also participate in the nation's affairs within the framework of institutions and organizations springing from the nation's common history and from your common concern. This you do hand in hand with your fellow citizens of every creed and confession. Unity among you in all such endeavors is essential, under the leadership of your bishops, for deepening, proclaiming and effectively promoting the truth among man, his dignity and his inalienable rights, the truth such as the Church receives it in revelation and such as she ceaselessly develops it in her social teaching in the light of the Gospel. These shared convictions, however, are not a ready-made model for society (cf. *Octogesima Adveniens*, 42). It is principally the task of lay people to put them into practice in concrete projects, to define priorities and to develop models that are suitable for promoting man's real good. The Second Vatican Council's pastoral constitution *Gaudium et Spes*, tells us that

> lay people should seek from priests light and spiritual strength. Let the people not imagine that their pastors are always such experts, that to every problem which arises, however complicated, they can readily give a concrete solution, or even that such is their mission. Rather, enlightened by Christian wisdom and giving close attention to the teaching authority of the Church, let the lay people assume their own distinctive role (*Gaudium et Spes*, 43).

6. In order to bring this undertaking to a successful conclusion, fresh spiritual and moral energy drawn from the inexhaustible divine source is needed. This energy does not develop easily. The life style of many members of our rich and permissive societies is easy, and so is the life style of increasing groups inside the poorer countries. As I said last year to the plenary assembly of the Pontifical Commission Justice and Peace, "Christians will want to be in the vanguard in favoring ways of life that decisively break with the frenzy of consumerism, exhausting and joyless" (Nov. 11, 1978). It is not a question of slowing down progress, for there is no human progress when everything conspires to give full reign to the instincts of self-interest, sex and power. We must find a simple way of living. For it is not right that the standard of living of the rich countries should seek to maintain itself by draining off a great part of the reserves of energy and raw materials that are meant to serve the whole of humanity. For readiness to create a greater and more equitable solidarity between peoples is the first condition for peace.

Catholics of the United States, and all you citizens of the United States, you have such a tradition of spiritual generosity, industry, simplicity and sacrifice that you cannot fail to heed this call today for a new enthusiasm and a fresh determination.

It is in joyful simplicity of a life inspired by the Gospel and the Gospel's spirit of fraternal sharing that you will find the best remedy for sour criticism, paralyzing doubt and the temptation to make money the principal means and indeed the very measure of advancement.

7. On various occasions, I have referred to the gospel parable of the rich man and Lazarus. "Once there was a rich man who dressed in purple and linen and feasted splendidly every day. At his gate lay a beggar named Lazarus who was covered with sores. Lazarus longed to eat the scraps that fell from the rich man's table" (Lk 16:19). Both the rich man and the beggar died and were carried before Abraham, and there judgment was rendered on their conduct. And the Scripture tells us that Lazarus found consolation, but that the rich man found torment. Was the rich man condemned because he had riches, because he abounded in earthly possessions, because he "dressed in purple linen and feasted splendidly every day?" No, I would say that it was not for this reason. The rich man was condemned because he did not pay attention to the other man. Because he failed to take notice of Lazarus, the person who sat at his door and who longed to eat the scraps from his table. Nowhere does Christ condemn the mere possession of earthly goods as such. Instead, he pronounces very harsh words against those who use their possessions in a selfish way, without paying attention to the needs of others. The Sermon on the Mount begins with the words: "Blessed are the poor in spirit." And at the end of the account of the Last Judgment as found in St. Matthew's Gospel, Jesus speaks the words that we all know well: "I was hungry and you gave me no food, I was thirsty and you gave me no drink. I was away from home and you gave me no welcome, naked and you gave me no clothing. I was ill and in prison and you did not come and comfort me" (Mt 25:42-43).

The parable of the rich man and Lazarus must always be present in our memory; it must form our conscience. Christ demands openness from the rich, the affluent, the economically advanced; openness to the poor, the underdeveloped and the disadvantaged. Christ demands an openness that is more than benign attention, more than token actions or halfhearted efforts that leave the poor as destitute as before or even more so.

All of humanity must think of the parable of the rich man and the beggar. Humanity must translate it into contemporary terms of economy and politics, in terms of all human rights, in terms of relations between the First, Second and Third Worlds. We cannot stand idly by when thousands of human beings are dying of hunger. Nor can we remain indifferent when the rights of the human spirit are trampled upon, when violence is done to the human conscience in matters of truth, religion and cultural creativity.

We cannot stand idly by, enjoying our own riches and freedom if, in any place, the Lazarus of the twentieth century stands at our doors. In the light of the parable of Christ, riches and freedom mean a special responsibility. Riches and freedom create a special obligation. And so, in the name of the solidarity that binds all together in a common humanity, I again proclaim the dignity of every human person; the rich man and Lazarus are both human beings, both of them equally created in the image and likeness of God, both of them equally redeemed by Christ, at a great price, the price of "the precious blood of Christ" (1 Pt 1:19).

8. Brothers and sisters in Christ, with deep conviction and affection I repeat to you the words that I addressed to the world when I took up my apostolic ministry in the service of all men and women: "Do not be afraid. Open wide the doors for Christ. To his saving power open the boundaries of states, economic and political systems, the vast fields of culture, civilization and development. Do not be afraid. Christ knows what is in man; he alone knows it" (Oct. 22, 1978).

As I said to you at the beginning, Christ is our justice and our peace, and all our works of justice and peace draw from this source the irreplaceable energy and light for the great task before us. As we resolutely commit ourselves to the service of all the needs of the individuals and of the peoples—for Christ urges us to do so—we shall nevertheless remind ourselves that the Church's mission is not limited to this witness to social fruitfulness of the Gospel. Along this road that leads the Church to man, she does not offer, in the matter of justice and peace, only the earthly fruits of the Gospel; she brings to man—to every person—their very source: Jesus Christ himself, our justice and our peace.

The Address at Edmonton

POPE JOHN PAUL II

September 17, 1984

I will hear what the Lord God has to say, / a voice that speaks of peace. / Mercy and faithfulness have met; / justice and peace have embraced (Pss 84; 85:8, 10).

Dear Brothers and Sisters in Christ,

1. These are words of today's liturgy, taken from the Responsorial Psalm. The God of the Covenant is a God of peace. Peace on earth is a good that belongs to his Kingdom and to his salvation. This good is obtained in justice and faithfulness to the divine commandments. This good, which is peace, is promised to us in different spheres: as the interior good of our conscience, as the good of our human living together, and finally as a social and international good.

This last meaning was above all what Paul VI had in mind when he wrote these memorable words: "The new name for peace is development." And he wrote these words in the encyclical *Populorum Progressio* (No. 87).

2. Today we come together here in Edmonton to make this theme of the development or progress of peoples the principal object of our meditations and prayers in the Eucharistic Sacrifice. In this Eucharistic community is gathered first of all the whole Church of the Archdiocese of Edmonton. And I wish indeed to greet this church with its pastor, Archbishop MacNeil, as well as the Eparchy of Edmonton of the Ukrainians, together with Bishop Savaryn and Bishop Greschuk. I also acknowledge with deep gratitude the presence of the large group of faithful from Saskatchewan, who have brought their crosses to be blessed. I likewise embrace in the love of Christ Jesus our Lord all the pilgrims and visitors. The refugees from Central America, Southeast Asia and Eastern Europe have a special place in my heart.

I wish to greet all those who have come from other dioceses of Alberta, from Grouard-McLennan, Calgary and St. Paul; also from British Columbia and the Northwest Territory, as well as visitors from the United States. Likewise I greet each ethnic and cultural group including the German-speaking Ukrainians, Italians, Portuguese, Spanish, Lithuanian, Slovak, Bohemian, Croatian, Hungarian, Polish, Filipinos, Chinese, Koreans and Vietnamese. To all of you who are here today, grace and peace in Jesus Christ, the Son of God and Savior of the world.

Considering our theme, I think that in a certain sense all Canada shares in this meeting at Edmonton. If the theme was proposed by the local community, it was certainly done so with a thought towards the whole society for which the cause of the development of peoples is a question of greatest importance and social and international responsibility. Especially since this "development" or "progress" is the new name for "peace."

Judgment to the Son

3. The liturgy leads us to consider this important theme, first of all, as it is presented in the twenty-fifth chapter of Saint Matthew's Gospel.

We have listened today to the Gospel about the final judgment with the same emotion as always. This passage touches some of the most fundamental questions of our faith and morality. These two fields are strictly linked to each other. Perhaps no other passage in the Gospel speaks of their relationship in such a convincing way.

Our faith in Jesus Christ finds here a kind of final expression: The "Father judges no one, but has given all judgment to the Son" (Jn 5:22). In today's Gospel Christ stands before us as our Judge. He has a special right to make this judgment: indeed he became one of us, our brother. This brotherhood with the human race—and at the same time his brotherhood with every single person—has led him to the cross and the Resurrection. Thus he judges in the name of his solidarity with each person and likewise in the name of our solidarity with him, who is our Brother and Redeemer and whom we discover in every human being: "I was hungry . . . I was thirsty . . . I was a stranger . . . naked . . . sick . . . in prison . . ." (Mt 25:35-36).

And those called to judgment—on his right hand and on his left—will ask: When and where? When and where have we seen you like this? When and where have we done what you said? Or: When and where have we not done it?

The answer: "Truly, I say to you, as you did it to one of the least of these my brethren, you did it to me" (Mt 25:40). And, on the contrary: "As you did it not to one of the least of these, you did it not to me" (Mt 25:45).

Injustice and Evil

4. "To one of the least of these my brethren." Thus: to man, to an individual human being in need.

Yet, the Second Vatican Council, following the whole of Tradition, warns us not to stop at an "individualistic" interpretation of Christian ethics, since Christian ethics also has its social dimension. The human person lives in a community, in society. And with the community he shares hunger and thirst and sickness and malnutrition and misery and all the deficiencies that result therefrom. In his or her own person the human being is meant to experience the needs of others.

So it is that Christ the Judge speaks of "one of the least of the brethren," and at the same time he is speaking of each and of all.

Yes. He is speaking of the whole universal dimension of injustice and evil. He is speaking of what today we are accustomed to call the North-South contrast. Hence not only East-West, but also North-South: the increasingly wealthier North, and the increasingly poorer South.

Yes, the South—becoming always poorer; and the North—becoming always richer. Richer too in the resources of weapons with which the superpowers and blocs can mutually threaten each other. And they threaten each other—such an argument also exists—in order not to destroy each other.

This is a separate dimension—and according to the opinion of many it is the dimension in the forefront—of the deadly threat which hangs over the modern world, which deserves separate attention.

Nevertheless, in the light of Christ's words, this poor South will judge the rich North. And the poor people and poor nations—poor in different ways, not only lacking food, but also deprived of freedom and other human rights—will judge those people who take these goods away from them, amassing to themselves the imperialistic monopoly of economic and political supremacy at the expense of others.

The Final Judgment

5. The Gospel of today's liturgy is very rich in content. It is relevant to the different spheres of injustice and human evil. In the midst of each of these situations stands Christ himself, and as Redeemer and Judge he says: "You did it to me," "you did it not to me."

Nevertheless he wishes, in this final judgment—which is constantly in preparation and which in a certain sense is constantly present—to bear witness first of all to the good that has been done.

And here also that significant expression of the teaching of the Church takes a start, whose principal formulation became the encyclical *Populorum Progressio*. What was the inner concern of Paul VI and the universal Church became a dynamic action and a loud appeal that echoes to this day:

> It is not just a matter of eliminating hunger, or even of reducing poverty. The struggle against destitution, though urgent and necessary, is not enough. It is a question, rather, of building a world where every man, no matter what his race, religion or nationality, can live a fully human life, freed from servitude imposed on him by other men or by natural forces; a world where freedom is not an empty word and where the poor man Lazarus can sit down at the same table with the rich man (No. 47).

Yes, "development" is the new name for peace. Peace is necessary; it is an imperative of our time. And so is this development or progress: the progress of all the disadvantaged.

Link between Justice and Peace

6. Today we pray in this spirit. Today's liturgy emphasizes very clearly the link between justice and peace.

Look at the first reading from Isaiah: "There will be poured on us the spirit from above . . . Integrity will bring peace, justice give lasting security. My people will live in a peaceful home, in safe houses, quiet dwellings" (Is 32:15, 17-18).

This was written by the prophet centuries before Christ. How lasting and unchanging are the desires of individuals and peoples!

And later on, after Christ, the apostle Paul writes in the letter to the Philippians: "And the peace of God, which passes all understanding, will keep your hearts and your minds in Christ Jesus" (Phil 4:7).

Yet the condition for such peace is human behavior in every dimension of existence. Hence, Saint Paul continues: "Fill your minds with everything that is true, everything that is noble, everything that is good and pure, everything that we love and honor, and everything that can be thought virtuous or worthy of praise. Keep doing all the things that you learned from me and have been taught by me and have heard or seen that I do. Then the God of peace will be with you" (Phil 4:8-9).

Progress of Peoples

7. Today we are praying in Canada, in the city of Edmonton, for the progress of peoples. Hence, according to the words of Pope Paul VI, we are praying for peace because we are praying for what constitutes its contemporary meaning. The words of the prophet Isaiah and of the Apostle to the Gentiles indicate the same thing. This is what we are praying for as we celebrate this Eucharist and share in it.

May our prayer pierce the heavens! May the God of peace be with us!

May the God of peace be with us! This cry brings with it the whole drama of our age, the whole threat. The nuclear threat? Certainly!

But even more: the whole threat of injustice, the threat coming from the rigid structures of those systems which man is not able to pass through—those systems which do not open themselves so as to permit themselves to go out towards man, to go out towards the development of peoples, to go out towards justice, with all its requirements, and towards peace.

Is the global balance not perhaps ever increasing—the global balance of what we "have not done for one of the least of the brethren"? For millions of the least of the brethren? For billions?

This must also be said here, in Canada, which is as vast as a continent. And at the same time here, from this very place, it must likewise be said to all people of good will, and to all groups, communities, organizations, institutions, nations and governments, that everything we "have done" and what we will still do, what we will plan and will do with ever greater energy and determination—all of this really matters.

And the balance is increasing and must increase of what we "have done" for one person, for millions, for billions: the balance of good in human history.

The judgment spoken of in today's Gospel is constantly being prepared and is already taking place: What you did for one . . . for millions . . . for billions, "you did it to me"!

May the God of peace be with us, here in Canada and everywhere.

May justice and peace embrace (cf. Pss 84; 85:10) once again at the end of the second millennium which prepares us for the coming of Christ, in glory. Amen.

Thank you very much for your participation. I should express my deep gratitude for the whole celebration of your faith in Edmonton, above all for the Archdiocese of Edmonton and the archdiocese of this region, including some parts of Saskatchewan. I thank you for yesterday's reception along the streets. It was wonderful, and especially to the groups singing and dancing which met me during the day. And now I thank you with all my heart for this interreligious prayer.

We are looking and working toward the unity of Christians, but we are looking also to the non-Christian religions, to the people who believe in God, who seek him as it is possible for everyone. And with all of them we unite ourselves going towards our common destiny, for this destiny is God himself. The Second Vatican Council deepened our conviction that all men and women of humanity are brothers and sisters, that we are all created by the same Creator, the same God our Father. We are all redeemed by the same Christ Jesus, Son of

God; and God, his Spirit, the Holy Spirit, is working in the souls of every one of us, and that is this divine dimension of human existence. We are more and more discovering this divine dimension of human existence and we seek how to give expression to God. This interreligious prayer was an example, and I thank you for this solemn Eucharist we just finished celebrating here at Edmonton. I thank you for your participation, for all the different preparations. With you I thank Providence for the sun and for the wind. I thank you for your prayers and for the marvelous songs of your choir. Thank you very much for your orchestra. With the same gratitude I repeat my welcome to all the groups, to all the ethnic groups.

And to all of you I repeat: praised, praised be God the Father, our Father, the Most Holy Trinity, Father, Son and Holy Spirit, for ever and ever. Thank you very much.

The Address at Newfoundland

POPE JOHN PAUL II

September 12, 1984

Dear Brothers and Sisters, dear People of Newfoundland,

1. It was from their fishing boats on the Sea of Galilee that Jesus called Simon Peter and James and John to share his mission. As the Gospel reminds us, Jesus spent much of his time in the ordinary circumstances of daily life, sharing the hopes and hardships of the people. This is why I am immensely pleased to be with you, the members of the fishing community. I extend a special greeting to you, Archbishop Penney, and to those of you who are the spiritual leaders of the other churches and communions represented here. The joyful event that unites us is the blessing of the fishing fleet here at Flatrock.

It is in this context that I have come today to express my solidarity with you, and *to profess with you faith in our Lord Jesus Christ*. This faith of ours, in the Eternal Son of God made man, offers an uplifting message for the whole human community. Our faith in Jesus Christ, true God and true Man, opens up before us a vision of great hope and, at the same time, it speaks to all of us about Christ's commandment to love and serve one another.

In Pain and Hope

2. Long before they settled on these shores, Europeans fished these banks. From fishing villages along these shores, Europeans fished these banks. From fishing villages along these coasts you and your ancestors have set out in all kinds of weather to wrest a living from the sea, often at the risk of your lives. Your wives and families have shared the uncertainty and fear that your way of life involves. In Christian pain and hope they have mourned the loss of many loved ones that did not return. As a Newfoundland poet wrote:

> It took the sea a thousand years, / a thousand years to trace / the granite features of this cliff, / in crag and scarp and base. / It took the sea an hour one night, / an hour of storm to place / the sculpture of these granite seams / upon a woman's face.

Changing Conditions

3. Today your lives are touched by another kind of insecurity, coming not from the sea but from the changed conditions in the fishing industry and in the world economy. Not even Canada with its immense natural resources and limited population has escaped the effects of worldwide economic uncertainty. Here in Newfoundland, even more than in other parts of Canada, you feel the heavy burden of unemployment, which has settled like a blight on the hopes of so many, especially the young, who experience in their own lives how the absence of rewarding employment affects the many aspects of their existence and of society, destroying prospects for the future, affecting the livelihood of families and disturbing the social fabric of the community.

In my encyclical, *Laborem Exercens*, I have emphasized "the fact that human work is a key, probably the essential key, to the whole social question" (No. 3). Men and women are meant to contribute by their work to the building up of the human community, and so to realize their full human stature as co-creators with God and co-builders of his Kingdom. Prolonged failure to find meaningful employment represents an affront to the dignity of the individual, for which no social assistance can fully compensate. The human costs of such unemployment, especially the havoc it brings to family life, have frequently been deplored by the Canadian bishops. I join with them in appealing to those in positions of responsibility, and to all involved, to work together to find appropriate solutions to the problems at hand, including a restructuring of the economy, so that human needs be put before mere financial gain. The social doctrine of the Church requires us to emphasize the primacy of the human person in the productive process, the primacy of people over things.

A Cruel Paradox

4. Canada has been called the breadbasket of the world, and it was one of the world's largest exporters of fish before the recent recession. It is a cruel paradox that many of you who could be engaged in the production of food are in financial distress here, while at the same time hunger, chronic malnutrition and the threat of starvation afflict millions of people elsewhere in the world.

With careful stewardship, the sea will continue to offer its harvest. However, during the last few years the means of processing and distributing food have become more technically sophisticated. The fishing industry has also been concentrated more and more in the hands of fewer and fewer people. Around the globe more and more small or family fishing concerns lose their financial independence to the larger and capital intensive enterprises. Large industrial fishing companies run the risk of losing contact with the fishermen and their personal and family needs. They are exposed to the temptation of responding only to the forces of the marketplace, thus lacking at times sufficient financial incentive to maintain production. Such a development would put the security and distribution of the world's food supply into ever greater jeopardy, if food production becomes controlled by the profit motive of a few rather than by the needs of the many.

Current Situation

5. The current economic situation, especially with regard to fishing, demands courageous decisions in order to overcome all negative consequences. Our Christian view of man and what constitutes his good must be the guiding principles in looking for alternate solutions. The promotion of cooperatives of fishermen, collective agreements between workers and management, some form of joint ownership or partnership—these are some of the possible solutions that would aim at ensuring that the workers have a voice in the decison-making affecting their own lives and the lives of their families.

In a world of growing interdependence, the responsible stewardship of all the earth's resources, and especially food, requires long-range planning at the different levels of government, in cooperation with industry. It also requires effective international agreements on trade. It must take into account the problem of food-aid and aid to development, and be responsive to those in need.

Your Christian Lives

6. My dear friends: hard work and a strong sense of family and community have sustained you in the past in your upright Christian lives. Above all, your faith in Jesus Christ and the hope that it generates in you are at the basis of all your aspirations for a better future. For this reason, in the efforts and struggles of daily living you can say with Saint Paul: "To this end we toil and strive, because we have our hope set on the living God" (1 Tm 4:10).

Together with your spiritual leaders gathered here with me, I pray for all of you and your families. May God our Father grant success to the work of your hands. May his divine Son, our Lord Jesus Christ, who multiplied the loaves and fishes to feed the hungry multitudes, expand the horizon of your fraternal concern to embrace all his brothers and sisters. May the Holy Spirit live in your hearts and fill you with his peace, today and forever.

Let us never forget, dear people of Newfoundland, the values that Christ taught from Peter's boat on the Sea of Galilee and throughout all his life. And let us heed the words of the apostle Paul: "Let everything you do be done in love" (1 Cor 16:14).

II

STATEMENTS OF THE UNITED STATES CATHOLIC BISHOPS

Introduction to Program of Social Reconstruction and a Pastoral Letter

The statements on economic questions which the American bishops have released over the years inevitably reflect the situation of the Catholic community in the United States. That situation does not exactly parallel the situation in which Catholicism has found itself either in Europe or Latin America. Until recently the overwhelming majority of American Catholics were part of the working class. So, unlike the Fribourg Union and Leo XIII, the American bishops were never faced with the task of trying to preserve the status of wealthy Catholics while responding to the legitimate claims of laborers. They were more free to associate the Church with the workers' struggle. Further, American unionism never adopted the strongly socialist (and sometimes antireligious) outlook that marked the labor movement in Europe. While there was some hesitation to become directly involved in unionization prior to *Rerum Novarum*, the link between American Catholicism and the burgeoning unions grew close once the Pope gave the green light.

The union movement gained strength after World War I. The war itself was partially responsible. Women and children had entered the work force as never before as a result of military conscription, and now the nation faced the problem of finding employment for returning soldiers. These factors combined with others to intensify labor strife in the United States.

Because so many of their people were profoundly affected by this strife, the American bishops felt compelled to address social issues. Their *Program of Social Reconstruction* issued on Lincoln's birthday in 1919 and the *Pastoral Letter* released the following September apply the principles of *Rerum Novarum* for the first time in a thorough manner to the American scene. The bishops do not offer any comprehensive theological justification for their recommendations, nor do they attempt to create any specific social model. However, they do present some general teachings that have served as a foundation for future social involvement by American Catholics.

Though the bishops insist that unions must live up to their part in labor contracts, the major emphasis in the *Program of Social Reconstruction* and the relevant section of the *Pastoral Letter* affirm the workers' right to organize. The *Program* asserts that employers may never question this right again. The bishops also make it clear that they do not believe conditions in the United States are as bad as in Europe. Hence the social institutions of America will not require European-style radical surgery. Despite their criticism of specific abuses, the bishops display a sense of hope about the American economic system. They echo Leo XIII's strong rejection of socialist economic models, expressing the belief that such models are neither feasible nor desirable in America.

The closest the American bishops come to proposing an economic model is their endorsement of some worker copartnership in industrial decision-making and some form of worker ownership. The *Program of Social Reconstruction* is the stronger of the two documents on these points: "the full possibilities of increased production will not be realized as long as the majority of the workers remain mere wage earners. The majority must somehow become owners, or at least in part, of the instruments of production. They can be enabled to reach this stage gradually through cooperative productive societies and copartnership arrangements."

Program of Social Reconstruction

Issued by the Administrative Committee
of the National Catholic War Council

February 12, 1919

Foreword

The ending of the Great War has brought peace. But the only safeguard of peace is social justice and a contented people. The deep unrest so emphatically and so widely voiced throughout the world is the most serious menace to the future peace of every nation and of the entire world. Great problems face us. They cannot be put aside; they must be met and solved with justice to all.

In the hope of stating the lines that will best guide us in our right solution the following pronouncement is issued by the Administrative Committee of the National Catholic War Council. Its practical applications are, of course, subject to discussion, but all its essential declarations are based upon the principles of charity and justice that have always been held and taught by the Catholic Church, while its practical proposals are merely an adaptation of those principles and that traditional teaching to the social and industrial conditions and needs of our own time.

Peter J. Muldoon, Chairman,
Bishop of Rockford
Joseph Schrembs, Bishop of
Toledo
Patrick J. Hayes, Bishop of
Tagaste
William T. Russell, Bishop of
Charleston

1. *Reconstruction* has of late been so tiresomely reiterated, not to say violently abused, that it has become to many of us a word of aversion. Politicians, social students, labor leaders, businessmen, charity workers, clergymen, and various other social groups have contributed their quota of spoken words and printed pages to the discussion of the subject; yet the majority of us still find ourselves rather bewildered and helpless. We are unable to say what parts of our social system imperatively need reconstruction; how much of that which is imperatively necessary is likely to be seriously undertaken; or what specific methods and measures are best suited to realize that amount of reconstruction which is at once imperatively necessary and immediately feasible.

2. Nevertheless, it is worthwhile to review briefly some of the more important statements and proposals that have been made by various social groups and classes. Probably the most notable declaration from a Catholic source is that contained in a pastoral letter written by Cardinal Bourne several months ago.

> It is admitted on all hands that a new order of things, new social conditions, new relations between the different sections in which society is divided, will arise as a consequence of the destruction of the formerly existing conditions. . . . The very foundations of political and social life, of our economic system, of morals and religion are being sharply scrutinized, and this not only by a few writers and speakers, but by a very large number of people in every class of life, especially among the workers.

3. The cardinal's special reference to the action of labor was undoubtedly suggested by the now famous Social Reconstruction Program of the British Labor Party. This document was drawn up about one year ago, and is generally understood to be the work of the noted economist and Fabian socialist, Mr. Sidney Webb. Unquestionably, it is the most comprehensive and coherent program that has yet appeared on the industrial phase of reconstruction. In brief it sets up four pillars of the new social order:

(a) The enforcement by law of a national minimum of leisure, health, education, and subsistence;

(b) The democratic control of industry, which means the nationalization of all monopolistic industries and possibly of other industries, sometime in the future, if that course be found advisable;

(c) A revolution in national finance; that is, a system of taxation which will compel capital to pay for the war, leaving undisturbed the national minimum of welfare for the masses;

(d) Use of the surplus wealth of the nation for the common good; that is, to provide capital, governmental industries, and funds for social, educational, and artistic progress.

4. This program may properly be described as one of immediate radical reforms, leading ultimately to complete socialism. Evidently this outcome cannot be approved by Catholics.

American Labor

5. Through its Committee on Reconstruction, the American Federation of Labor has issued a lengthy program of reform proposals and demands which may be grouped under the three heads of trade union action, labor legislation, and general industrial and social legislation. The principal demands under the first head are: the legally guaranteed rights of the workers to organize and to carry on the normal activities of trade unions; a living wage; no reduction in present scales of wages; the right of labor to fix its hours of work; the eight-hour day; equal pay for equal work by the two sexes; exclusive reliance by labor on trade-union effort to maintain fair wages; establishment of cooperative stores; and no organization of a political party by the workers. Labor laws demanded are: prohibition of wage working by children under 16 years of age; abolition of private employment agencies; prohibition of all immigration for two years; and vocational education which will fit the young for life in an industrial society. By implication both the eight-hour day and the living wage are declared to be subjects for trade-union action, not for legislation. Among the measures of general social legislation recommended are: a special tax on "usable land" not cultivated by the owner, and taxes on land values which would make the holding of idle land unprofitable; government housing; government ownership and operation of docks, wharves, and water powers; taxes on excess profits, incomes, and inheritances; and limitation of the power of the courts to declare laws unconstitutional.

6. While this program is more practical and more moderate and reasonable than that of the British Labor Congress, its proposal for taxing land into use could easily involve confiscation. On the other hand, it does not give sufficient consideration to the case of the weaker sections of the working class, those for whom trade-union action is not practically adequate; nor does it demand or imply that the workers should ever aspire to become owners as well as users of the instruments of production.

British Quaker Employers

7. Probably the most definite and comprehensive statement from the opposite industrial class was put forth several months ago by a group of 20 Quaker employers in Great Britain. In outline their program is as follows: a family living wage for all male employees and a secondary wage in excess of this for workers having special skill, training, physical strength, responsibility for human life; the right of labor to organize, to bargain collectively with the employer, and to participate in the industrial part of business management; serious and practical measures to reduce the volume and hardship of unemployment; provisions of such working conditions as will safeguard health, physical integrity, and morals; the reduction so far as practicable of profits and interest until both the basic and the secondary wages have been paid, and transfer to the community of the greater part of surplus profits.

8. The spirit and conception of responsibility that permeate every item of the program are reflected in this statement:

> We would ask all employers to consider very carefully whether their style of living and personal expenditure are restricted to what is needed in order to insure the efficient performance of their functions in society. More than this is waste, and is, moreover, a great cause of class divisions.

American Employers

9. The only formal statements on the subject of social reconstruction that have yet come to our attention from an important group of American employers, are a declaration of principles and certain proposals by the National Chamber of Commerce. The declaration of principles was made at a convention of the organization, in Atlantic City, December 6, 1918. Beyond a general commendation of peaceful and friendly relations between employers and employees, it included nothing of importance on the labor phase of reconstruction. It condemned government operation and ownership of railroads, telegraphs, and telephones, and demanded more moderate taxes and a modification of the Sherman Anti-Trust Law. More recently the executive officials of the chamber have submitted to a referendum vote of its membership a statement, "with a view to furnishing a basis on which American industry can build a national labor program." The main specific proposals in this statement are: recognition of the right of workers to organize; adequate representation of both parties in the determination of employment conditions; a decent home and proper social conditions; no reduction in wages until all other costs of production have been brought down to the lowest possible level; and a system of national employment offices. Inasmuch as this organization represents more employers than any other association in the country, the vote of its members on these proposals will be of the greatest significance.

Interdenominational

10. In Great Britain an organization known as the Interdenominational Conference of Social Service Unions, comprising ten religious bodies, including Catholics, spent more than a year formulating a statement of social reconstruction. (See the summary and analysis contained in the *Catholic Social Year Book* for 1918.) This statement deals with principles, evils, and remedies. Presuming that Christianity provides indispensable guiding principles and powerful motives of social reform, it lays down the basic proposition that every human being is of inestimable worth, and that legislation should recognize persons as more sacred than property; therefore, the state should enforce a minimum living wage; enable the worker to obtain some control of industrial conditions; supplement private initiative in providing decent housing; prevent the occurrence of unemployment; safeguard the right of the laborer and his family to a reasonable amount of rest and recreation; remove those industrial and social conditions which hinder marriage and encourage an unnatural restriction of families, and afford ample opportunity for education of all children industrially, culturally, religiously, and morally. On the other hand, rights imply duties, and the individual is obliged to respect the rights of others, to cultivate self-control, to recognize that labor is the law of life, and that wealth is a trust. Finally, the statement points out that all social reform must take as its end and guide the maintenance of pure and wholesome family life.

11. Such in barest outline are the main propositions and principles of this remarkable program. The text contains adequate exposition of the development and application of all these points, and concrete specifications of the methods and measures by which the aims and principles may be brought into effect. In the latter respect the statement is not liable to the fatal objection that is frequently and fairly urged against the reform pronouncements of religious bodies: that they are abstract, platitudinous, and usually harmless. The statement of the Interdenominational Conference points out specific remedies for the evils that it describes; specific measures, legislative and other, by which the principles may be realized in actual life. Especially practical and valuable for Catholics are the explanations and modifications supplied by the *Year Book* of the Catholic Social Guild.

No Profound Change

12. It is not to be expected that as many or as great social changes will take place in the United States as in Europe. Neither our habits of thinking nor our ordinary ways of life have undergone a profound disturbance. The hackneyed phrase: "Things will never again be the same after the war," has a much more concrete and deeply felt meaning among the European peoples. Their minds are fully adjusted to the conviction and expectation that these words will come true. In the second place, the devastation, the loss of capital and of men, the changes in individual relations, and the increase in the activities of government have been much greater in Europe than in the United States. Moreover, our superior natural advantages and resources, the better industrial and social condition of our working classes still constitute an obstacle to anything like revolutionary changes. It is significant that no social group in America, not even among the wage earners, has produced such a fundamental and radical program of reconstruction as the Labor Party of Great Britain.

A Practical Program

13. No attempt will be made in these pages to formulate a comprehensive scheme of reconstruction. Such an undertaking would be a waste of time as regards immediate needs and purposes, for no important group or section of the American people is ready to consider a program of this magnitude. Attention will, therefore, be confined to those reforms that seem to be desirable and also obtainable within a reasonable time, and to a few general principles which should become a guide to more distant developments. A statement thus circumscribed will not merely present the objects that we wish to see attained, but will also serve as an imperative call to action. It will keep before our minds the necessity for translating our faith into works. In the statements of immediate proposals we shall start, wherever possible, from those governmental agencies and legislative measures which have been to some extent in operation during the war. These come before us with the prestige of experience and should therefore receive first consideration in any program that aims to be at once practical and persuasive.

14. The first problem in the process of reconstruction is the industrial replacement of the discharged soldiers and sailors. The majority of these will undoubtedly return to their previous occupations. However, a very large number of them will either find their previous places closed to them, or will be eager to consider the possibility of more attractive employments. The most important single measure for meeting this situation that has yet been suggested is the placement of such men on farms. Several months ago Secretary Lane recommended to Congress that returning soldiers and sailors should be given the opportunity to work at good wages upon some part of the millions upon millions of acres of arid, swamp, and cut-over timber lands, in order to prepare them for cultivation. President Wilson in his annual address to Congress endorsed the proposal. As fast as this preliminary task has been performed, the men should be assisted by government loans to establish themselves as farmers, either as owners or as tenants having long-time leases. It is essential that both the work of preparation and the subsequent settlement of the land should be effected by groups or colonies, not by men living independently of one another and in depressing isolation. A plan of this sort is already in operation in England. The importance of the project as an item of any social reform program is obvious. It would afford employment to thousands upon thousands, would greatly increase the number of farm owners and independent farmers, and would tend to lower the cost of living by increasing the amount of agricultural products. If it is to assume any considerable proportions it must be carried out by the governments of the United States and of the several states. Should it be undertaken by these authorities and operated on a systematic and generous scale, it would easily become one of the most beneficial reform measures that has ever been attempted.

Employment Service

15. The reinstatement of the soldiers and sailors in urban industries will no doubt be facilitated by the United States Employment Service. This agency has attained a fair degree of development and efficiency during the war. Unfortunately there is some danger that it will go out of existence or be greatly weakened at the end of the period of demobilization. It is the obvious duty of Congress to continue and strengthen this important institution. The problem of unemployment is with us always. Its solution requires the cooperation of many agencies, and the use of many methods; but the primary and indispensable instrument is a national system of labor exchanges, acting in harmony with state, municipal, and private employment bureaus.

Women War Workers

16. One of the most important problems of readjustment is that created by the presence in industry of immense numbers of women who have taken the places of men during the war. Mere justice, to say nothing of chivalry, dictates that these women should not be compelled to suffer any greater loss or inconvenience than is absolutely necessary; for their services to the nation they have been second only to the services of the men whose places they were called upon to fill. One general principle is clear: no female worker should remain in any occupation that is harmful to health or morals. Women should disappear as quickly as possible from such tasks as conducting and guarding streetcars, cleaning locomotives, and a great number of other activities for which conditions of life and their physique render them unfit. Another general principle is that the proportion of women in industry ought to be kept within the smallest practical limits. If we have an efficient national employment service, if a goodly number of the returned soldiers and sailors are placed on the land, and if wages and the demand for goods are kept up to the level which is easily attainable, all female workers who are displaced from tasks that they have been performing only since the beginning of the war will be able to find suitable employments in other parts of the industrial field, or in those domestic occupations which sorely need their presence. Those women who are engaged at the same tasks as men should receive equal pay for equal amounts and qualities of work.

War Labor Board

17. One of the most beneficial governmental organizations of the war is the National War Labor Board. Upon the basis of a few fundamental principles, unanimously adopted by the representatives of labor, capital, and the public, it has prevented innumerable strikes and raised wages to decent levels in many different industries throughout the country. Its main guiding principles have been a family living wage for all male adult laborers; recognition of the right of labor to organize and to deal with employers through its chosen representatives; and no coercion of nonunion laborers by members of the union. The War Labor Board ought to be continued in existence by Congress, and endowed with all the power for effective action that it can possess under the federal constitution. The principles, methods, machinery, and results of this institution constitute a definite and far-reaching gain for social justice. No part of this advantage should be lost or given up in time of peace.

Wage Rates

18. The general level of wages attained during the war should not be lowered. In a few industries, especially some directly and peculiarly connected with the carrying on of war, wages have reached a plane upon which they cannot possibly continue for this grade of occupations. But the number of workers in this situation is an extremely small proportion of the entire wage-earning population. The overwhelming majority should not be compelled or suffered to undergo any reduction in their rates of remuneration, for two reasons: first, because the average rate of pay has not increased faster than the cost of living; second, because a considerable majority of the wage earners of the United States, both men and women, were not receiving living wages when prices began to rise in 1915. In that year, according to Lauck and Sydenstricker, whose work is the most comprehensive on the subject, four-fifths of the heads of families obtained less than eight hundred dollars, while two-thirds of the female wage earners were paid less than four hundred dollars. Even if the prices of goods should fall to the level on which they were in 1915, something that cannot be hoped for within five years, the average present rates of wages would not exceed the equivalent of a decent livelihood in the case of the vast majority. The exceptional instances to the contrary are practically all among the skilled workers. Therefore, wages on the whole should not be reduced even when the cost of living recedes from its present high level.

19. Even if the great majority of workers were now in receipt of more than living wages, there are no good reasons why rates of pay should be lowered. After all, a living wage is not necessarily the full measure of justice. All the Catholic authorities on the subject explicitly declare that this is only the minimum of justice. In a country as rich as ours, there are very few cases in which it is possible to prove that the worker would be getting more than that to which he has a right if he were paid something in excess of this ethical minimum. Why, then, should we assume that this is the normal share of almost the whole laboring population? Since our industrial resources and instrumentalities are sufficient to provide more than a living wage for a very large proportion of the workers, why should we acquiesce in a theory which denies them this measure of the comforts of life? Such a policy is not only of very questionable morality, but is unsound economically. The large demand for goods which is created and maintained by high rates of wages and high purchasing power by the masses is the surest guarantee of a continuous and general operation of industrial establishments. It is the most effective instrument of prosperity for labor and capital alike. The principal beneficiaries of a general reduction of wages would be the less efficient among the capitalists, and the more comfortable sections of the consumers. The wage earners would lose more in remuneration than they would gain from whatever fall in prices occurred as a direct result of the fall in wages. On grounds both of justice and sound economics, we should give our hearty support to all legitimate efforts made by labor to resist general wage reductions.

Housing for Working Classes

20. Housing projects for war workers which have been completed, or almost completed by the government of the United States, have cost some forty million dollars, and are found in 11 cities. While the federal government cannot continue this work in time of peace, the example and precedent that it has set, and the experience and knowledge that it has developed, should not be forthwith neglected and lost. The great cities in which congestion and other forms of bad housing are disgracefully apparent ought to take up and continue the work, at least to such an extent as will remove the worst features of a social condition that is a menace at once to industrial efficiency, civil health, good morals, and religion.

Cost of Living

21. During the war the cost of living has risen at least 75 percent above the level of 1913. Some check has been placed upon the upward trend by government fixing of prices in the case of bread and coal and a few other commodities. Even if we believe it desirable, we cannot ask that the government continue this action after the articles of peace have been signed; for neither public opinion nor Congress is ready for such a revolutionary policy. If the extortionate practices of monopoly were prevented by adequate laws and adequate law enforcement, prices would automatically be kept at as low a level as that to which they might be brought by direct government determination. Just what laws, in addition to those already on the statute books, are necessary to abolish monopolistic extortion is a question of detail that need not be considered here. In passing, it may be noted that government competition with monopolies that cannot be effectively restrained by the ordinary antitrust laws deserves more serious consideration than it has yet received.

22. More important and more effective than any government regulation of prices would be the establishment of cooperative stores. The enormous toll taken from industry by the various classes of middlemen is now fully realized. The astonishing difference between the price received by the producer and that paid by the consumer has become a scandal of our industrial system. The obvious and direct means of reducing this discrepancy and abolishing unnecessary middlemen is the operation of retail and wholesale mercantile concerns under the ownership and management of the consumers. This is no Utopian scheme. It has been successfully carried out in England and Scotland through the Rochdale system. Very few serious efforts of this kind have been made in this country because our people have not felt the need of these cooperative enterprises as keenly as the European working classes, and because we have been too impatient and too individualistic to make the necessary sacrifices and to be content with moderate benefits and gradual progress. Nevertheless, our superior energy, initiative, and commercial capacity will enable us, once we set about the task earnestly, even to surpass what has been done in England and Scotland.

23. In addition to reducing the cost of living, the cooperative stores would train our working people and consumers generally in habits of saving, in careful expenditure, in business methods, and in the capacity for cooperation. When the working classes have learned to make the sacrifices and to exercise the patience required by the ownership and operation of cooperative stores, they will be equipped to undertake a great variety of tasks and projects which benefit the community immediately, and all its constituent members ultimately.

They will then realize the folly of excessive selfishness and senseless individualism. Until they have acquired this knowledge, training, and capacity, desirable extensions of governmental action in industry will not be attended by a normal amount of success. No machinery of government can operate automatically, and no official and bureaucratic administration of such machinery can ever be a substitute for intelligent interest and cooperation by the individuals of the community.

Legal Minimum

24. Turning now from those agencies and laws that have been put in operation during the war to the general subject of labor legislation and problems, we are glad to note that there is no longer any serious objection urged by impartial persons against the legal minimum wage. The several states should enact laws providing for the establishment of wage rates that will be at least sufficient for the decent maintenance of a family, in the case of all male adults, and adequate to the decent individual support of female workers. In the beginning the minimum wages for male workers should suffice only for the present needs of the family, but they should be gradually raised until they are adequate to meet future needs as well. That is, they should be ultimately high enough to make possible that amount of saving which is necessary to protect the worker and his family against sickness, accidents, invalidity, and old age.

Social Insurance

25. Until this level of legal minimum wages is reached, the worker stands in need of the device of insurance. The state should make comprehensive provision for insurance against illness, invalidity, unemployment, and old age. So far as possible the insurance fund should be raised by a levy on industry, as is now done in the case of accident compensation. The industry in which a man is employed should provide with all that is necessary to meet all the needs of his entire life. Therefore, any contribution to the insurance fund from the general revenues of the state should be only slight and temporary. For the same reason no contribution should be exacted from any worker who is not getting a higher wage than is required to meet the present needs of himself and family. Those who are below that level can make such a contribution only at the expense of their present welfare. Finally, the administration of the insurance laws should be such as to interfere as little as possible with the individual freedom of the worker and his family. Any insurance scheme, or any administrative method, that tends to separate the workers into a distinct and dependent class, that offends against their domestic privacy and independence, or that threatens individual self-reliance and self-respect, should not be tolerated. The ideal to be kept in mind is a condition in which all the workers would themselves have the income and the responsibility of providing for all the needs and contingencies of life, both present and future. Hence, all forms of state insurance should be regarded as merely a lesser evil, and should be so organized and administered as to hasten the coming of the normal condition.

26. The life insurance offered to soldiers and sailors during the war should be continued, so far as the enlisted men are concerned. It is very doubtful whether the time has yet arrived when public opinion would sanction the extension of general life insurance by the government to all classes of the community.

27. The establishment and maintenance of municipal health inspection in all schools, public and private, is now pretty generally recognized as of great importance and benefit. Municipal clinics where the poorer classes could obtain the advantage of medical treatment by specialists at a reasonable cost would likewise seem to have become a necessity. A vast amount of unnecessary sickness and suffering exists among the poor and the lower middle classes because they cannot afford the advantages of any other treatment except that provided by the general practitioner. Every effort should be made to supply wage earners and their families with specialized medical care through development of group medicine. Free medical care should be given only to those who cannot afford to pay.

Labor Participation

28. The right of labor to organize and to deal with employers through representatives has been asserted above in connection with the discussion of the War Labor Board. It is to be hoped that this right will never again be called in question by any considerable number of employers. In addition to this, labor ought gradually to receive greater representation in what the English group of Quaker employers have called the "industrial" part of business management—"the control of processes and machinery; nature of product; engagement and dismissal of employees; hours of work, rates of pay, bonuses, etc.; welfare work; shop discipline; relations with trade unions." The establishment of shop committees, working wherever possible with the trade union, is the method suggested by this group of employers for giving the employees the proper share of industrial management. There can be no doubt that a frank adoption of these means and ends by employers would not only promote the welfare of the workers, but vastly improve the relations between them and their employers, and increase the efficiency and productiveness of each establishment.

29. There is no need here to emphasize the importance of safety and sanitation in work places, as this is pretty generally recognized by legislation. What is required is an extension and strengthening of many of the existing statutes, and a better administration and enforcement of such laws everywhere.

Vocational Training

30. The need of industrial, or as it has come to be more generally called, vocational training, is now universally acknowledged. In the interest of the nation, as well as in that of the workers themselves, this training should be made substantially universal. While we cannot now discuss the subject in any detail, we do wish to set down two general observations. First, the vocational training should be offered in such forms and conditions as not to deprive the children of the working classes of at least the elements of a cultural education. A healthy democracy cannot tolerate a purely industrial or trade education for any class of its citizens. We do not want to have the children of the wage earners put into a special class in which they are marked as outside the sphere of opportunities for culture. The second observation is that the system of vocational training should not operate so as to weaken in any degree our parochial schools or any other class of private schools. Indeed, the opportunities of the system should be extended to all qualified private schools on exactly the same basis as to public schools. We want neither class divisions in education nor a state monopoly of education.

Child Labor

31. The question of education naturally suggests the subject of child labor. Public opinion in the majority of the states of our country has set its face inflexibly against the continuous employment of children in industry before the age of 16 years. Within a reasonably short time all of our states, except some of the stagnant ones, will have laws providing for this reasonable standard. The education of public opinion must continue, but inasmuch as the process is slow, the abolition of child labor in certain sections seems unlikely to be brought about by the legislatures of those states, and since the Keating-Owen Act has been declared unconstitutional, there seems to be no device by which this reproach to our country can be removed except that of taxing child labor out of existence. This method is embodied in an amendment to the Federal Revenue Bill which would impose a tax of ten percent on all goods made by children.

32. Probably the foregoing proposals comprise everything that is likely to have practical value in a program of immediate social reconstruction for America. Substantially all of these methods, laws, and recommendations have been recognized in principle by the United States during the war, or have been endorsed by important social and industrial groups and organizations. Therefore, they are objects that we can set before the people with good hope of obtaining a sympathetic and practical response. Were they all realized, a great step would have been taken in the direction of social justice. When they are all put into operation, the way will be easy and obvious to still greater and more beneficial results.

Fundamental Reforms

33. Despite the practical and immediate character of the present statement, we cannot entirely neglect the question of ultimate aims and a systematic program; for other groups are busy issuing such systematic pronouncements, and we all need something of the kind as a philosophical foundation and as a satisfaction to our natural desire for comprehensive statements.

34. It seems clear that the present industrial system is destined to last for a long time in its main outlines. That is to say, private ownership of capital is not likely to be supplanted by a collectivist organization of industry at a date sufficiently near to justify any present action based on the hypothesis of its arrival. This forecast we recognize as not only extremely probable, but as highly desirable; for, other objections apart, Socialism would mean bureaucracy, political tyranny, the helplessness of the individual as a factor in the ordering of his own life, and in general social inefficiency and decadence.

Defects of Present System

35. Nevertheless, the present system stands in grievous need of considerable modifications and improvement. Its main defects are three: Enormous inefficiency and waste in the production and distribution of commodities; insufficient incomes for the great majority of wage earners, and unnecessarily large incomes for a small minority of privileged capitalists. Inefficiency in the production and distribution of goods would be in great measure abolished by the reforms that have been outlined in the foregoing pages. Production would be greatly increased by universal living wages, by adequate industrial education, and by harmonious relations between labor and capital on the basis of adequate participation by the former in all the industrial aspects of business management. The wastes of commodity distribution could be practically all eliminated by cooperative mercantile establishments, and cooperative selling and marketing associations.

Copartnership

36. Nevertheless, the full possibilities of increased production will not be realized so long as the majority of the workers remain mere wage earners. The majority must somehow become owners, or at least in part, of the instruments of production. They can be enabled to reach this stage gradually through cooperative productive societies and copartnership arrangements. In the former, the workers own and manage the industries themselves; in the latter they own a substantial part of the corporate stock and exercise a reasonable share in the management. However slow the attainments of these ends, they will have to be reached before we can have a thoroughly efficient system of production, or an industrial and social order that will be secure from the danger of revolution. It is to be noted that this particular modification of the existing order, though far-reaching and involving to a great extent the abolition of the wage system, would not mean the abolition of private ownership. The instruments of production would still be owned by individuals, not by the state.

Increased Incomes

37. The second great evil, that of insufficient income for the majority, can be removed only by providing the workers with more income. This means not only universal living wages, but the opportunity of obtaining something more than that amount for all who are willing to work hard and faithfully. All the other measures for labor betterment recommended in the preceding pages would likewise contribute directly or indirectly to a more just distribution of wealth in the interest of the laborer.

New Spirit Needed

38. For the third evil mentioned above, excessive gains by a small minority of privileged capitalists, the main remedies are prevention of monopolistic control of commodities, adequate government regulation of such public service monopolies as will remain under private operation, and heavy taxation of incomes, excess profits, and inheritances. The precise methods by which genuine competition may be restored and maintained among businesses that are naturally competitive cannot be discussed here; but the principle is clear that human beings cannot be trusted with the immense opportunities for oppression and extortion that go with the possession of monopoly power. That the owners of public service monopolies should be restricted by law to a fair or average return on their actual investment, has long been a recognized principle of the courts, the legislatures, and public opinion. It is a principle which should be applied to competitive enterprises likewise, with the qualification that something more than the average rate of return should be allowed to men who exhibit exceptional efficiency. However, good public policy, as well as equity, demands that these exceptional businessmen share the fruits of their efficiency with the consumer in the form of lower prices. The man who utilizes his ability to produce cheaper than his competitors for the purpose of exacting from the public as high a price for his product as is necessary for the least efficient businessman is a menace rather than a benefit to industry and society.

39. Our immense war debt constitutes a particular reason why incomes and excess profits should continue to be heavily taxed. In this way two important ends will be attained: the poor will be relieved of injurious tax burdens, and the small class of privileged capitalists will be compelled to return a part of their unearned gains to society.

A Christian View

40. "Society," said Pope Leo XIII, "can be healed in no other way than by a return to Christian life and Christian institutions." The truth of these words is more widely perceived today than when they were written, more than 27 years ago. Changes in our economic and political systems will have only partial and feeble efficiency if they be not reinforced by the Christian view of work and wealth. Neither the moderate reforms advocated in this paper nor any other program of betterment or reconstruction will prove reasonably effective without a reform in the spirit of both labor and capital. The laborer must come to realize that he owes his employer and society an honest day's work in return for a fair wage, and that conditions cannot be substantially improved until he roots out the desire to get a maximum of return for a minimum of service. The capitalist must likewise get a new viewpoint. He needs to learn the long-forgotten truth that wealth is stewardship, that profit making is not the basic justification of business enterprise, and that there are such things as fair profits, fair interest, and fair prices. Above and before all, he must cultivate and strengthen within his mind the truth which many of his class have begun to grasp for the first time during the present war; namely, that the laborer is a human being, not merely an instrument of production; and that the laborer's right to a decent livelihood is the first moral charge upon industry. The employer has a right to get a reasonable living out of his business, but he has no right to interest on his investment until his employees have obtained at least living wages. This is the human and Christian, in contrast to the purely commercial and pagan, ethics of industry.

Pastoral Letter

Issued by the Roman Catholic Hierarchy of the United States

September 26, 1919

Selections*

* * *

X. Industrial Relations

146. In 1891, Pope Leo XIII published his encyclical *Rerum Novarum*, a document which shows the insight of that great pontiff into the industrial conditions of the time, and his wisdom in pointing out the principles needed for the solving of economic problems.

> That the spirit of revolutionary change which has long been disturbing the nations of the world, should have passed beyond the sphere of politics and made its influence felt in the cognate sphere of practical economics, is not surprising. The elements of the conflict now raging are unmistakable, in the vast expansion of industrial pursuits and the marvelous discoveries of science; in the changed relations between masters and workmen; in the enormous fortunes of some few individuals, and the utter poverty of the masses; in the increased self-reliance and closer mutual combination of the working classes; as also, finally, in the prevailing moral degeneracy. The momentous gravity of the state of things now obtaining fills every mind with painful apprehension; wise men are discussing it; practical men are proposing schemes; popular meetings, legislatures, and rulers of nations are all busied with it—and actually there is no question that has taken a deeper hold on the public mind.

147. How fully these statements apply to our present situation, must be clear to all who have noted the course of events during the year just elapsed. The war indeed has sharpened the issues and intensified the conflict that rages in the world of industry; but the elements, the parties, and their respective attitudes are practically unchanged. Unchanged also are the principles which must be applied, if order is to be restored and placed on such a permanent basis that our people

*Editor's Note: Deleted material in this document is indicated in the text by the symbol * * *.

may continue their peaceful pursuits without dread of further disturbance. So far as men are willing to accept those principles as the common ground on which all parties may meet and adjust their several claims, there is hope of a settlement without the more radical measures which the situation seemed but lately to be forcing on public authority. But in any event, the agitation of the last few months should convince us that something more is needed than temporary arrangements or local readjustments. The atmosphere must be cleared so that, however great the difficulties which presently block the way, men of good will may not, through erroneous preconceptions, go stumbling on from one detail to another, thus adding confusion to darkness of counsel.

Nature of the Social Question

148. "It is the opinion of some," says Pope Leo XIII, "and the error is already very common, that the social question is merely an economic one, whereas in point of fact, it is first of all a moral and religious matter, and for that reason its settlement is to be sought mainly in the moral law and the pronouncements of religion."[83] These words are as pertinent and their teaching as necessary today as they were 19 years ago. Their meaning, substantially, has been reaffirmed by Pope Benedict XV in his recent statement that "without justice and charity there will be no social progress." The fact that men are striving for what they consider to be their rights, puts their dispute on a moral basis; and wherever justice may lie, whichever of the opposing claims may have the better foundation, it is justice that all demand.

149. In the prosecution of their respective claims, the parties have, apparently disregarded the fact that the people as a whole have a prior claim. The great number of unnecessary strikes which have occurred within the last few months is evidence that justice has been widely violated as regards the rights and needs of the public. To assume that the only rights involved in an industrial dispute are those of capital and labor, is a radical error. It leads, practically, to the conclusion that at any time and for an indefinite period, even the most necessary products can be withheld from the general use until the controversy is settled. In fact, while it lasts, millions of persons are compelled to suffer hardship for want of goods and services which they require for reasonable living. The first step, therefore, toward correcting the evil is to insist that the rights of the community shall prevail, and that no individual claim conflicting with those rights shall be valid.

---

[83] Apostolic letter, *Graves de communi,* Jan. 18, 1901.

150. Among those rights is that which entitles the people to order and tranquillity as the necessary conditions for social existence. Industrial disturbance invariably spreads beyond the sphere in which it originates, and interferes, more or less seriously, with other occupations. The whole economic system is so compacted together and its parts are so dependent one upon the other, that the failure of a single element, especially, if this be of vital importance, must affect all the rest. The disorder which ensues is an injustice inflicted upon the community; and the wrong is the greater because, usually, there is no redress. Those who are responsible for it pursue their own ends without regard for moral consequences and, in some cases, with no concern for the provisions of law. When such a temper asserts itself, indignation is aroused throughout the country and the authorities are urged to take action. This, under given circumstances, may be the only possible course; but, as experience shows, it does not eradicate the evil. A further diagnosis is needed. The causes of industrial trouble are generally known, as are also the various phases through which it develops and the positions which the several parties assume. The more serious problem is to ascertain why, in such conditions, men fail to see their obligations to one another and to the public, or seeing them, refuse to fulfill them except under threat and compulsion.

Mutual Obligations

151. "The great mistake in regard to the matter now under consideration is to take up with the notion that class is naturally hostile to class, and that the wealthy and the workingmen are intended by nature to live in mutual conflict."[84] On the contrary, as Pope Leo adds,

> Each needs the other: Capital cannot do without Labor, nor Labor without Capital. Religion is a powerful agency in drawing the rich and the breadwinner together, by reminding each class of its duties to the other and especially of the obligation of justice. Religion teaches the laboring man and the artisan to carry out honestly and fairly all equitable agreements freely arranged, to refrain from injuring person or property, from using violence and creating disorder. It teaches the owner and employer that the laborer is not their bondsman, that in every man they must respect his dignity and worth as a man and as a Christian; that labor is not a thing to be ashamed of, if we listen to right reason and to Christian philosophy; but is an honorable calling, enabling a man to sustain his life in a way upright and creditable; and that it is shameful and inhuman to treat men like

[84] *Rerum Novarum.*

> chattels, as means for making money, or as machines for grinding out work.

The moral value of man and the dignity of human labor are cardinal points in this whole question. Let them be the directive principles in industry, and they will go far toward preventing disputes. But treating the laborer first of all as a man, the employer will make him a better workingman; by respecting his own moral dignity as a man, the laborer will compel the respect of his employer and of the community.

152. The settlement of our industrial problems would offer less difficulty if, while upholding its rights, each party were disposed to meet the other in a friendly spirit. The strict requirements of justice can be fulfilled without creating animosity; in fact, where this arises, it is apt to obscure the whole issue. On the contrary, a manifest desire to win over, rather than drive, the opponent to the acceptance of equitable terms, would facilitate the recognition of claims which are founded in justice. The evidence of such a disposition would break down the barriers of mistrust and set up in their stead the bond of good will. Not an armistice but a conciliation would result; and this would establish all parties in the exercise of their rights and the cheerful performance of their duties.

Respective Rights

153. The right of labor to organize, and the great benefit to be derived from workingmen's associations, were plainly set forth by Pope Leo XIII. In this connection, we would call attention to two rights, one of employees and the other of employers, the violation of which contributes largely to the existing unrest and suffering. The first is the right of the workers to form and maintain the kind of organization that is necessary and that will be most effectual in securing their welfare. The second is the right of employers to the faithful observance by the labor unions of all contracts and agreements. The unreasonableness of denying either of these rights is too obvious to require proof or explanation.

154. A dispute that cannot be adjusted by direct negotiation between the parties concerned should always be submitted to arbitration. Neither employer nor employee may reasonably reject this method on the ground that it does not bring about perfect justice. No human institution is perfect or infallible; even our courts of law are sometimes in error. Like the law court, the tribunal of industrial arbitration provides the nearest approach to justice that is practically attainable; for the only alternative is economic force, and its decisions have no necessary relation to the decrees of justice. They show which party is economically stronger, not which is in the right.

155. The right of labor to a living wage, authoritatively and eloquently reasserted more than a quarter of a century ago by Pope Leo XIII, is happily no longer denied by any considerable number of persons. What is principally needed now is that its content should be adequately defined, and that it should be made universal in practice, through whatever means will be at once legitimate and effective. In particular, it is to be kept in mind that a living wage includes not merely decent maintenance for the present, but also a reasonable provision for such future needs as sickness, invalidity, and old age. Capital likewise has its rights. Among them is the right to "a fair day's work for a fair day's pay," and the right to returns which will be sufficient to stimulate thrift, saving, initiative, enterprise, and all those directive and productive energies which promote social welfare.

Benefits of Labor Unions

156. In his pronouncement on labor,[85] Pope Leo XIII describes the advantages to be derived by both employer and employee from "associations and organizations which draw the two classes more closely together." Such associations are especially needed at the present time. While the labor union or trade union has been, and still is necessary in the struggle of the workers for fair wages and fair conditions of employment, we have to recognize that its history, methods, and objects have made it essentially a militant organization. The time seems now to have arrived when it should be, not supplanted, but supplemented by associations or conferences, composed jointly of employers and employees, which will place emphasis upon the common interests rather than the divergent aims of the two parties, upon cooperation rather than conflict. Through such arrangements, all classes would be greatly benefited. The worker would participate in those matters of industrial management which directly concern him and about which he possesses helpful knowledge; he would acquire an increased sense of personal dignity and personal responsibility, take greater interest and pride in his work, and become more efficient and more contented. The employer would have the benefit of willing cooperation from, and harmonious relations with, his employees. The consumer, in common with employer and employee, would share in the advantages of larger and steadier production. In a word, industry would be carried on as a cooperative enterprise for the common good, and not as a contest between two parties for a restricted product.
157. Deploring the social changes which have divided "society into two widely different castes," of which one "holds power because it holds wealth," while the other is "the needy and powerless multi-

[85] *Rerum Novarum.*

tude," Pope Leo XIII declared that the remedy is "to induce as many as possible of the humbler classes to become owners."[86] This recommendation is in exact accord with the traditional teaching and practice of the Church. When her social influence was greatest, in the later Middle Ages, the prevailing economic system was such that the workers were gradually obtaining a larger share in the ownership of the lands upon which, and the tools with which, they labored. Though the economic arrangements of that time cannot be restored, the underlying principle is of permanent application, and is the only one that will give stability to industrial society. It should be applied to our present system as rapidly as conditions will permit.

158. Whatever may be the industrial and social remedies which will approve themselves to the American people, there is one that, we feel confident, they will never adopt. That is the method of revolution. For it there is neither justification nor excuse under our form of government. Through the ordinary and orderly processes of education, organization, and legislation, all social wrongs can be righted. While these processes may at times seem distressingly slow, they will achieve more in the final result than violence or revolution. The radicalism, and worse than radicalism, of the labor movement in some of the countries of Europe has no lesson for the workers of the United States, except as an example of methods to be detested and avoided.

159. Pope Benedict has recently expressed a desire that the people should study the great encyclicals on the social question of his predecessor, Leo XIII. We heartily commend this advice to the faithful and, indeed, to all the people of the United States. They will find in these documents the practical wisdom which the experience of centuries has stored up in the Holy See and, moreover, that solicitude for the welfare of mankind which fitly characterizes the head of the Catholic Church.

* * *

---

[86] *Rerum Novarum.*

Introduction to Five Depression-Era Statements

The severe economic problems of the Depression years led the American bishops to prepare several statements on economic issues. Some are brief and concentrate on a few specific questions such as unemployment. Others cover a range of issues and try to provide a biblical and theological framework for Catholic reflection on the nation's problems. The papal encyclicals influenced these documents, *Rerum Novarum* to some extent, *Quadragesimo Anno* more directly. The last of them, the 1940 statement called *Church and Social Order*, represents the most detailed commentary the American bishops have offered to date on economic matters.

A number of points in these five documents deserve mention. The bishops' commitment to the just wage and to union organizing has not wavered. Some internal battles within the union movement have surfaced, though, and the bishops warn Catholic workers against contributing to labor strife. They also express some concern about Communist influence on American labor. Throughout these documents, there is a clear rejection of the Communist option and even of more moderate forms of Socialism. While the bishops have strong words for economic theory that exaggerates individualism, they reserve their most strident criticism for theories of the left. They warn in their 1933 statement: "One of the greatest dangers facing us is a blind reaction from our former individualism to a regime of state socialism or state capitalism."

A paramount concern of several of these documents is the growing concentration of wealth that Pius XI so forcefully discussed in *Quadragesimo Anno*. The bishops apply the encyclical's words to the American scene in their 1933 statement, *The Present Crisis*:

> Industry in our country, through the concentration of wealth, has acquired such complete control that independent operation, even on the part of so-called owners and employers, is practically impossible. The tremendous increase in the output of industry during recent years . . . has not ensured the worker the proportionate gain

> to which he is justly entitled. It has, however, vastly increased the incomes of industrialists and capitalists.

The 1937 *Statement on Social Problems* recalls Pius XI's deep uneasiness with the tremendous economic power of those who govern credit and determine its allotment. "This control," the bishops say, "is exercised by those who are not the real owners of wealth but merely the trustees and administrators of invested funds. Responsibility is thus divorced from ownership. Nevertheless, they hold in their hands the very soul of production since they supply its lifeblood and no one can breathe against their will." The 1940 comprehensive document on economic issues makes a similar point: "The two great dangers which society faces in the present state of economic organization are, first, the concentration of ownership and control of wealth and, second, its anonymous character which results from some of the existing business and corporation law, whereby responsibility toward society is greatly impaired if not completely ignored."

Having spoken of existing economic difficulties, the bishops face the need to suggest some solutions. They make it clear that the Church prescribes no set model of economic organization. Both the 1933 and 1940 statements, however, support many of the ideas associated with the organic model of the Fribourg Union and the early social encyclicals. The 1940 statement even calls for guilds or a corporate system. These proposals found little support, even among Catholics. Perhaps the bishops were relying too much on an imported social model instead of working with indigenous American political and economic concepts.

These five documents reveal as little tolerance for Socialism as the 1919 statements. They even shy away from the clear support for worker copartnership in industrial decision-making and for forms of worker ownership that appears in the *Program of Social Reconstruction*. The bishops may have felt that such proposals were too close to Socialism and that mention of them might be taken as episcopal support for more radical factions within the American labor movement. Whatever the reason, the omission is conspicuous.

On a more positive note, the bishops suggest that government must play a significant mediating role in America's economy. The problems will not be solved, justice will not be enhanced, by the simple unrestrained dynamics of the market. The 1933 *Present Crisis* insists that an important function of government is to "assist in the organization of the various economic groups." The 1940 statement goes even farther: "In the application of the principles of social justice, an important instrument . . . is governmental authority." Through exercise of this authority the state

> must so regulate the responsibility of property that the burden of providing for the common good be equitably distributed. It must

> furthermore establish such conditions through legal enactment and administration policy that wealth itself can be distributed so each individual member of society may surely and justly come into possession of the material goods necessary for his own livelihood.

The bishops also urge an enhanced role for government in social welfare schemes such as unemployment compensation and Social Security. They are definitely on the same general track as the New Deal reforms in these documents.

However, the bishops' endorsement of state intervention in economic life is not without explicit qualification. The principle of subsidiarity must remain a guide for the application of state power. The state should primarily facilitate the work of smaller groups and take over only when it appears no one else can do the job effectively. The 1937 statement carries a warning about the "tendency to place too much reliance on government to accomplish our economic salvation."

There are a few other points the bishops make in these five documents that have some continuing relevance: tax reform, the disastrous economic consequences of the arms race (in the 1931 statement), and the need to deal with the economic problems of the agricultural sector and to make rural life more attractive. In addressing these three issues, the bishops of the 1930s raise a prophetic voice.

Statement on Unemployment

Issued by the Administrative Board of the
National Catholic Welfare Conference

November 12, 1930

1. Again the United States is suffering the tragedy of millions of men and women who need work, who want work, and who can find no work to do. May God give the country his wisdom and grace to throw off this yoke of suffering, unlike famine only in that men themselves inflict it in the midst of plenty.

2. The workless must indeed be cared for. We thank the men and women, both lay and religious, in our institutions, organizations, and parishes who give food to the hungry, clothe the naked, harbor the harborless during this lengthening year of unemployment. We thank those also who either directly or indirectly, through either money or supplies, make it possible for them to care for the poor who flock to them. God will reward them. There can be no respite in this generosity. More and more money and goods will be needed, it seems certain, to meet during the cold of the coming winter only the call for alms from the poorest of the poor.

3. More than temporary alms is necessary. Justice should be done. This unemployment returning again to plague us after so many repetitions during the century past is a sign of deep failure in our country. Unemployment is the great peacetime physical tragedy of the nineteenth and twentieth centuries, and both in its cause and in the imprint it leaves upon those who inflict it, those who permit it, and those who are its victims, it is one of the great moral tragedies of our time. The failure is not due to lack of intelligence nor any more to ignorance. It is due to lack of good will. It is due to neglect of Christ.

4. We call upon Catholics, and we ask all, to do more than give alms and more even than take measures to provide work and reduce the present army of the unemployed. Both are imperative. People are suffering, and we are obliged to help them. But our country needs, now and permanently, such a change of heart as will, intelligently and with determination, so organize and distribute our work and wealth that no one need lack for any long time the security of being able to earn an adequate living for himself and for those dependent upon him.

5. Cooperation of Catholics in their organizations and as individuals with the federal, state, and city efforts to reduce unemployment is most commendable. They have already done much. We ask them to do still more. But let them also look to the long-time, deeper-seated, and harder task of allowing the likeness of the Savior of the world to shine through our country's economic institutions. Let them begin with their own work and wealth, and their own relations to property, to employees, to employers, to customers, to their corporation and organization associates. Let the spirit of Christ shine there.

6. In a world based in its work and wealth upon the neglect of Christ's teachings, there is, of course, a limit and a boundary to what Catholics of the best of spirit may do. This is not said to discourage or suggest excuses for inaction. The limit must be further extended; the boundary stretched to the utmost. We are ever under the call to do more and more and as one tries the best he can to live his Catholic morals, to try also to remold the institutions that surround work, ownership, and trade to the image of the Savior of the world.

7. To this purpose we commend particularly Pope Leo's great encyclical *On the Condition of Labor*, now nearly 40 years with us, the bishops' *Program of Social Reconstruction* issued shortly after the war, and the passages on industrial relations in the last joint pastoral letter of the American bishops. They give a guide, even in many details, to the remaking in Christ's likeness of the property relations and working life of our times. Catholics should read and study these three. We invite all to read and study them.

8. And as a proof of their practical value both in this period of unemployment and at all other times, we quote briefly from one of them:

> A living wage is not necessarily the full measure of justice. All the Catholic authorities on the subject explicitly declare that this is only the *minimum* of justice. In a country as rich as ours, there are very few cases in which it is possible to prove that the worker would be getting more than that to which he has a right if he were paid something in excess of this ethical minimum. Since our industrial resources and instrumentalities are sufficient to provide more than a living wage for a very large proportion of the workers, why should we acquiesce in a theory which denies them this measure of the comforts of life? Such a policy is not only of very questionable morality, but is unsound economically. The large demand for goods which is created and maintained by high rates of wages and high purchasing power by the masses is the surest guarantee of a continuous and general operation of industrial establishments. It is the most effective instrument of prosperity for labor and capital alike.

9. Had this passage been heeded during the dozen years since it was written, it would in itself have gone far to prevent the calamity we now undergo. "The human and Christian, in contrast to the purely commercial and pagan, ethics of industry," to quote again, will both cure our country of our present malady and prevent its cruel recurrence.

10. We add our earnest appeal for the use of what is the most efficacious of means—prayer. Pray daily that the needy may be relieved;

that the suffering and the consequent moral tragedies may be lessened; that a greater energy may enter into the hearts of all to build a social structure which in far greater measure than the present will voice practically the teachings of Christ and his Church, and bring a larger measure of justice unto men.

Statement on Economic Crisis

Issued by the Administrative Board of the
National Catholic Welfare Conference

November 12, 1931

1. Urged by the charity of Christ, of whose Church we are the shepherds, we seek always to extend to the multitude that spiritual food which alone sustains the life of the soul and all that the soul means to man, both here and hereafter. To the multitude we seek also to give that material food essential to the life and well-being of the individual, of the family, of all society. In this day of worldwide depression and of hardship, we voice our deep paternal sympathy for those millions of Americans of whatever creed or race, who, victims of the present industrial crisis, must rely on their more fortunate brethren for food, clothing, and shelter.

2. We urge the reading, the study, and the application to everyday business, occupational, and social life, of the encyclical of our Holy Father, Pius XI, *On the Reconstruction of the Social Order*. In keeping with the recommendations of the Holy Father, we have enlisted the services of our clergy and laity in a "crusade of charity," either in cooperation with approved relief agencies or independently of them, as varying local conditions suggest.

3. Since we are all bound together as brothers in Christ, it is our duty to insist that the wealthy are obligated in conscience to contribute for the relief of those who suffer, and the more so because the system under which they suffer has yielded wealth to others.

4. While cooperating in these private efforts, we are convinced, because of the vastness of the number suffering, that federal and state appropriations for relief in some form will become necessary.

5. Our economic system should be so improved that the laboring man, suddenly thrown out of employment, would not be deprived of sustenance during a period of severe business depression.

6. We deem it our duty also to quote the Holy Father on the relationships of armament to the present crisis:

7. "The unbridled race for armaments is on the one hand the effect of the rivalry among nations and on the other the cause of the withdrawal of enormous sums from the public wealth and hence not the smallest of contributors to the current extraordinary crisis."

8. The unemployment crisis is deep-rooted in the avarice of human nature which for a century and more has caused disorganization of the processes of production and distribution. This has run its course through unlimited individual and organized competition and is climaxed now by an ineffective economic rule. We ask a living wage for the family; a proper proportion between the wages of the different kinds of workers; an ample sufficiency for all. We ask for wages that will provide employment to the greatest extent possible; and for an equitable sharing of the goods produced so abundantly by industry.

9. And to avoid unjust and inequitable wage reductions, we ask for joint conferences of employers and their associations and labor and their unions, supplemented and assisted by government. Indeed all economic life needs such common counsel to deal with the present depression. Through such common counsel and organization, industry may proceed, animated by a sense of justice and good will to all. Thus will it care for the common good; meet the desire to solve a great problem of the present age; properly use the material resources and talents God has given us; and secure an equitable distribution of the income and wealth of our country and the world.

10. Only on these lines will the problem of how best to form a system of unemployment insurance, reserves, and old-age pensions be successfully worked out. There is dire need that our country and all its citizens bring the competence of every element, versed in the complexities of our industrial and social life to the solution of this great crisis and the avoidance of its like in the future. There is supreme need that our country be guided and enlightened in all these things by the full teaching of Christ.

11. The present crisis should urge everyone to careful thought and courageous action. We urge Catholic organizations to study the social teaching of the Church so as to help prepare Catholics to take their full part in this great task of our times. Fidelity to the teachings of Christ and of his Church, both as individuals and as a social body, is the foundation on which sure and permanent social justice and happiness must be built. What we seek, here as elsewhere, is a fuller measure of the Kingdom of God on earth as it is in Heaven.

Present Crisis

Issued with the Authorization of the
American Hierarchy

April 25, 1933

Selections*

*   *   *

Part One
Crucial Years

1. We are passing through crucial years. Hope is the mark of the present moment. We pray that almighty God may give us back our moral, social, and economic life purified and in all ways bettered by the fires through which it has passed. The tragic trials we have endured, which no human power could avert or arrest, have left us nothing on which to lean but the providence of God. Every thoughtful man has had at least a glimpse of the supernatural background upon which the world of material things reposes and to which it must adjust itself if we are not to have over and over again a repetition of these bewildering experiences. It would be a crowning tragedy if we were to learn no lesson from them, if we were to go back to the condition of things out of which the present crisis issued and after a new era of plenty, endure again a new agony. Our most urgent need is God's blessing upon the world and especially upon our own country. We summon all men of good will to pray for that blessing, and, by their works of unselfishness to deserve it, and to advance the commonweal.

2. We have been witness of a great social and political catastrophe, the causes of which are not to be found in one place or in one nation, but in all places and among all peoples, and the effects of which are devastating and worldwide. Through the mysterious and just dispensations of Divine Providence, the world has been shaken to its very foundations as a consequence of the World War. While the human mind can never measure adequately the monstrous evils which have followed in its wake, we must thank God that it did not overthrow

*Editor's Note: Deleted material in this document is indicated in the text by the symbol * * *.

the entire structure of European civilization and the culture of all the Christian centuries.

Universal Distress

3. Of the evils that have encompassed us, Pope Pius XI, with world vision, said a year ago:

> From the Flood on, it would be hard to find spiritual and material distress so deep, so universal, as that which we are now experiencing; even the greatest scourges that left indelible traces in the lives and memories of peoples, struck only one nation at a time. Now, on the contrary, the whole of humanity is held bound by the financial and economic crisis. . . . There is no people, there is no state, no society or family, which in one way or another, directly or indirectly, to a greater or lesser extent, does not feel the repercussion.[1]

Sacrifices of Our People

4. Our people, accustomed to standards of living and comforts not enjoyed by other nations, have been called upon to endure grievous hardships. We can speak only words of praise of the long-suffering and disciplined spirit of our Catholic people during the four years of our economic and moral crisis. Their sufferings, their privations, their generosity, especially that shown by the poor to those still poorer, will fill an inspiring page of our history. Noble sacrifices have been made by them to support from their almost exhausted funds our Catholic schools and institutions of charity and our many works of religion.

Alleged Causes of Depression

5. When considering the causes of the general distress, we hear many lament the material destruction wrought by the World War; the loss of our foreign markets, the extremes of inflation, and the depths of depression; the orgy of speculation and the consequent wiping out of vast fortunes; the collapse of credit; unlimited mass production, disturbing the balance of population between the rural districts and industrial centers; the inexcusable extravagance of government expenditures; and the national crime of maintaining armaments beyond all reasonable limits.

6. Many, having a materialistic attitude toward life, and therefore without a true moral sense of their obligations, object to any restriction of competition, even that which degrades the dignity of human

---

[1] *Caritate Christi Compulsi.*

labor and ignores every principle of justice. Others resent opposition to monopolies and dictatorship in the economic world, and regard as an infringement of their rights any interference with their powerful corporations, and mergers, or with lobbies, which have sought to corrupt and to control the state.

7. Some, with even greater moral callousness, do not hesitate to array the nations one against the other, if thereby their personal power and riches be increased. In the language of Pope Pius, they permit a social order "which spurns no less the laws of nature than those of God."[2]

Greed

8. In tracing the remote causes of the present misery of mankind, we must listen to him who as a loving father views from an eminence all the nations of the world. Quoting St. Paul, our Holy Father says:

> "The desire of money is the root of all evil." Is it not that lust of earthly goods that the pagan poet called with righteous scorn "the accursed hunger for gold," is it not that sordid egoism which too often regulates the mutual relations of individuals and society, is it not, in fine, greed, whatever be its species and form, that has brought the world to a pass we all see and deplore? From greed arises mutual distrust that casts a blight on all human beings; from greed arises envy, which makes a man consider the advantages of another as losses to himself; from greed arises narrow individualism, which orders and subordinates everything to its own advantage without taking account of others, on the contrary, cruelly trampling underfoot all rights of others. Hence the disorder and inequality from which arises the accumulation of the wealth of nations in the hands of a small group of individuals who manipulate the market of the world at their own caprice to the immense harm of the masses.[3]

9. A worse condition has been brought about, as the Holy Father says: "In our days not alone is wealth accumulated, but immense power and despotic economic domination is concentrated in the hands of the few, and those few are frequently not the owners but only the trustees and directors of invested funds, who administer them at their good pleasure.

10. "This power becomes particularly irresistible when exercised by those who, because they hold and control money, are able also to govern credit and determine its allotment, for that reason supplying, so to speak, the lifeblood to the entire economic body, and grasping,

---

[2] *Quadragesimo Anno.*
[3] *Caritate Christi Compulsi.*

as it were, in their hands the very soul of production, so that no one dare breathe against their will. . . .

11. "This concentration of power has led to a threefold struggle for domination. First, there is the struggle for dictatorship in the economic sphere itself; then, the fierce battle to acquire control of the state, so that its resources and authority may be abused in the economic struggles. Finally, the clash between states themselves."

12. The pontiff continues to outline the deplorable conditions existing:

> Free competition is dead. Economic dictatorship has taken its place. Unbridled ambition for domination has succeeded the desire for gain; the whole economic life has become hard, cruel, and relentless in a ghastly measure. Furthermore, the intermingling and scandalous confusing of the duties and offices of civil authority and of economics have produced crying evils and have gone so far as to degrade the majesty of the state. The state, which should be the supreme arbiter, ruling in kingly fashion far above all party contention, intent only upon justice and the common good, has become instead a slave, bound over to the service of human passion and greed.[4]

13. And still the worst is to be told—"the ruin of souls." Our Holy Father says that today "the conditions of social and economic life are such that vast multitudes of men can only with great difficulty pay attention to that one thing necessary, namely, their eternal salvation."[5] In the language of St. Paul, "as they liked not to have God in their knowledge, God delivered them up to a reprobate sense."[6]

Our Conditions

14. If we apply to our own country the weighty words of His Holiness we find that, in common with other nations, we have brought about our present unhappy conditions by divorcing education, industry, politics, business, and economics from morality and religion, and by ignoring for long decades the innate dignity of man and trampling on his human rights. We have failed to realize that these rights are supreme so far as the purpose of human society is concerned; that they include the right of the individual to life, and also to the means of a normal, healthy life of mind and body, so long as man is willing to do his part: that they include likewise his rights as a social being, which rights should ensure sufficient means to provide for himself and his family. And, when speaking of man as a social being, we mean men, women, and children, the husband and wife—in a word, the human family.

---

[4] *Quadragesimo Anno.*
[5] Ibid.
[6] Rom 1:28.

An Industrial Nation

15. That we are an industrial nation is our public boast. Industry is considered to be of more importance than the moral welfare of man. The lord of all is industry. "Save Industry!" is the cry. "Put big business on its feet and all will be well, as it was in the past!"
16. Industry in our country, through the concentration of wealth, has acquired such complete control that independent operation, even on the part of so-called owners and employers, is practically impossible. The tremendous increase in the output of industry during recent years, due to the natural resources of our country, to inventions, and to machinery, especially to the giant machines, has made some enormously rich, has brought many comforts, and has abolished much drudgery, but it has not ensured the worker the proportionate gain to which he is justly entitled. It has, however, vastly increased the incomes of industrialists and capitalists.

False Philosophy

17. The social philosophy prevailing during recent centuries has carried human society far from its safe moorings. That philosophy—if, indeed, it be worthy of the name—which has ruled governments, groups, and individuals for the past 300 years has not taken as its guide the moral law, has not considered the rights of man. Money, not man, has been the supreme consideration and the justifying end. That philosophy has aroused opposition and has given rise to errors and exaggerations that are anti-Catholic and anti-Christian.
18. That same demoralizing philosophy defended, and defends today, unrestrained individual economic freedom and the economic dictatorship that has succeeded it. That philosophy permits individuals, corporations, and nations to accumulate as much wealth as they can, according to the unfair methods of modern business, and to use such accumulated wealth as they see fit. It honors and proclaims as sovereign rulers of economic empires men who have succeeded in amassing unjustly these fabulous fortunes.
19. That philosophy has broken down or forbidden the establishment of protective organizations. It has broken down or forbidden an organized economic life to administer the production of wealth and its distribution in accordance with social justice and the interdependence of economic relations. It has denied government its right to guard justice and the common good. It has given greed a free hand.
20. That philosophy denied and denies, in reality, the oneness and the solidarity of mankind. In its light, wealth, business, and the power that material prosperity gives, are in themselves supreme ends. Human rights must be sacrificed to those ends, and humanity itself must become the mere instrument in the production of wealth, not the

master controlling it. Such a philosophy has always been and will ever be false and unchristian in principle and application. It has literally taken God out of the world.

Communism

21. This extreme of individualism has led to the extreme of Communism. We rightly fear its spread in our country and see an especial menace in its insidious presentation of fundamental truths for its own destructive ends. The brotherhood of man is loudly proclaimed; energetic protest is made against injustice done the working classes; the abuses of the capitalistic system are vigorously condemned; it is insisted that man shall not exploit his fellow man, nor class dominate class, but that all shall be dedicated to a life of service.

22. A program of social reform couched in such language and with such aims and purposes is unassailable because it is distinctively Christian in origin and purport, but in the hands of the Communists it is merely a snare to allure those who are oppressed by the prevailing economic maladjustment into accepting the iniquitous social and religious tenets of Lenin and Stalin. There is very grave and subtle danger of infection from Communism. Special efforts are being made to win the Negroes, who are the victims of injustice. The Communists have world vision. They have as their objective a world war on God and the complete destruction of all supernatural and even natural religion. They believe it necessary to inaugurate a merciless class warfare, and they insist, in theory at least, on the complete abolition of ownership of private property.

23. It is a strange paradox that many who condemn strongly the propaganda of the Red and the Communist are significantly silent when learned but misguided writers tell us there is no God; when scoffing university professors destroy in the youth of our land belief in God and in the supernatural; when they tell us that man is the plaything of preordained causes; that conscience and sin are myths; that the brotherhood of men, and consequently of nations, is a baseless dream; that morality does not rest upon the immutable and eternal law of God, but is merely a convention of man, subject to the changing conditions of society; that a man's obligations to his fellow man are such only as he is forced to accept by the taxing or police power of the state—in a word, that they are silent when all these destructive forces are preparing the future leaders of Communism in America.

Inevitable Consequences

24. If, under the plea of Liberalism, encouragement or even tolerance be given to the many radical doctrines proposed by teachers, writers, and agitators; if no attempt be made to drag out into the open the secret propaganda that is being carried on; if no consideration be given to the evil consequences that must necessarily follow the divorce of education and economics from morality and religion, what can be expected but that the very foundations upon which our whole social structure rests should be undermined?

25. Is it not inevitable that in our professional, business, and industrial life the sad effects of this divorce should be evident—that among our lawyers, physicians, teachers, writers, industrialists, and businessmen there is to be found too generally an unmoral and unchristian view of life? This is a terrible indictment which must be laid, at least remotely, at the door of irreligious or nonreligious education and unmoral, or immoral, economics.

26. Insofar as governments, institutions of learning, the press, the theater, and other opinion-forming agencies have been indifferent to or have rejected morality and religion, in that measure have they degenerated. This has been said a thousand times, and yet how far are we from the happy condition which would make all these forces realize the necessity of religion and the obligation of working under its ennobling influence!

* * *

The Farm Problem

40. For long years the pivotal importance of restoring the purchasing power of those immediately engaged in agriculture, and of developing the farm as the source of the nation's supply of food and clothing has not been recognized. We have failed to acknowledge that six million farms have provided the widest diffusion of privately owned productive property in the United States, as well as the widest diffusion of self-employed families, in contrast to the regimented employment of men in factories and in urban industries generally. Because of our unsound agricultural policy there has been a movement of our rural population to the great industrial centers that is revolutionary in character; there has been serious interference with the economic independence and self-employment of our people, and hundreds of thousands of farm families have been driven from the position of owners and independent tillers of the soil to that of tenants and day laborers on industrialized farms. As a consequence, there has been a serious disturbance of the balance of population between our cities and our rural districts. While during the Depression there has been a movement back to the land, there is no assurance of its permanency.

41. Perhaps the great majority of those living in our cities have not realized that the farm problem is a serious integral part of the national problem; that there can be no permanent restoration of industry on a national scale until the purchasing power of more than thirty million Americans living on the land is materially increased; that the concentration of wealth in the hands of the few has all but crushed agriculture, and has so drained the farm that the farmer finds it increasingly difficult to wrest a decent living from the land; that wheat has been selling at the lowest price in 300 years; that the wheels of industry in our cities are clogged in no small measure because agriculture lies prostrate.

42. These are among the problems to which the president and the Congress are now devoting their energy and attention. Much may be accomplished by legislation; but nothing that Congress or the president can do will offer a final solution unless it be accompanied by a revival among the people at large of a firm resolve that any solution, whatever its character, must be an expression of the Christian conception of justice and fair dealing. Business, whether big or little, banking, whether national or international, capital in its relations with labor, and labor in its relations with capital, must all be made to feel that any departure from the Christian code of morals will bring on those who are guilty universal censure and reprobation.

Unemployment

43. Unemployment has been our greatest problem in the economic crisis. It has taken from the willing worker the means of earning a livelihood, deprived him of his purchasing power, and made him an object of charity.

44. In a country so marvelously blessed as ours no man should find it impossible to exercise the right given him by nature to earn his bread in the sweat of his brow. In no part of the globe has nature been more lavish in providing all that men need for their comfort, their well-being, and their prosperity. Rich and fertile soil, varied climatic conditions, mineral resources in abundance, have given opportunity to a people industrious and inventive to provide better and higher standards of living for themselves and their families. The spirit of self-reliance and independence which is almost universal among the people of our country found expression, whenever possible, in an effort to make provision against the uncertainties of illness and old age. The universality of savings banks and building and loan societies gives abundant evidence of the general spirit of thrift and self-helpfulness and of a desire for economic independence.

45. But, on the other hand, and in spite of these tendencies and efforts among the great mass of the people, the wealth of the nation gradually flowed into the hands of the few. Capitalists and industrialists, driven by greed, monopolized the sources of wealth and gained control of the products and profits made possible by the progress of technological science, to their own enrichment and to the impoverishment and enslavement of the masses. These few, in order to increase their riches and power, have made the machine a curse rather than the blessing it should be, to lighten the toil and shorten the hours of the worker. Being content with a minimum of profit to ensure employment for all and to permit all to share the comforts produced by the machine is far from the thought of these financial magnates, who have been made by our modern economic system, as Pope Pius XI says, "hard, cruel, and relentless in a ghastly measure."[10]

46. His Holiness lays down the principle that in the restoration of the economic world capital should be allowed a reasonable interest only on the amount invested. "In [the] future a just share only of the fruits of production [should] be permitted to accumulate in the hands of the wealthy."[11] If at this moment that principle were accepted by the small group of capitalists and industrialists, perhaps not even a hundred men, who control the financial destinies of our country, if they were to agree to cooperate with the government and with the masses whom they have so wronged, and to have it written into our legislation that capital in the future shall receive a fair return on its investments, and nothing more, it would go far toward setting in motion the wheels of industry and solving the problem of unemployment.

Unemployment and Old Age Pensions

47. Closely connected with this question are the problems of unemployment insurance and old-age pensions. In principle, we should in times of prosperity provide for days of adversity. This is applicable to industry, to the individual, to the family, to the state, and to the nation. This form of insurance should be provided by the employer, the employee, and the government. But in making such provision, the movement of industry and the consequent discharge of workers or their transfer from place to place, with all the loss and hardship that this implies, should be taken into account.

48. This, however, is a duty belonging to normal times. Sunk in the depths of depression as our people have been for nearly four years, this is not the time to make actual provision for old-age and unemployment pensions. It would be unjust to attempt to force such measures by legislation. Our first concern is to terminate the existing depression. Employment is our first consideration, not insurance against unemployment or old age. Employment can be increased: first, by making drastic cuts in the overhead expenses of industry, by the

---

[10] *Quadragesimo Anno.*
[11] Ibid.

elimination of bonuses and unreasonably high salaries of officials, by the reduction of excessive taxation, which is a hindrance to the resumption of business; and, second, by increasing the wages of workers, thereby putting money in circulation and causing a demand for the normal products of industry. There is a vicious circle. On the one hand, the employer, especially the small producer, cannot afford to pay a just family wage, considering that he is in competition with those who have no conscience and who do not hesitate to make use of the most inhuman methods in conducting business; and, on the other hand, the reduced scale of wages paid to the ordinary worker does not allow him to purchase the bare necessaries of life, to say nothing of creating a normal demand for the products of industry. We wish to lay special emphasis here on the necessity of higher, that is to say, just wages for the average worker, not only to restore prosperity, but principally because of the moral question involved.

Part Two
Remedies

Restore Christ

49. By turning away from Christ, and by rejecting the principles of life and conduct he laid down, human society and human governments necessarily lost sight of the dignity and the rights of man, which, because they were once realized in Christian states, still remain an ideal and a hope even in places where Christianity is merely a tradition. The extent of the denial of Christ in our own country is shocking to the Christian sense. There can be no hope for the restoration of human society without restoring Christ, without striving to accord to man the dignity that he, as God, conferred on every human being. This must be the starting point.

The Authority of Christ

50. The authority of Christ must be acknowledged. Truly God and truly man, he is the supreme Ruler of the world, of our country, of our states, cities, and communities. Tribute is due him not only by individuals and groups, but officially by governments and by the Church. This authority of Christ is from without; it is not within each individual. Moral upheavals, chaos, and ruin have come upon the Christian world because individuals, differing on a thousand points, first presumed to make Christ responsible for their judgments, which made him a contradiction and an absurdity, then, logically, denied his divinity and rejected his authority.

Authority Rejected

51. A lamentable sequel to the rejection of the authority of Christ is that authority as a moral force, binding the conscience of men before God and the world, is ignored practically everywhere except in the Catholic Church. Parental authority, as a consequence, carries with it little if any weight. The authority of the state as having its source in God, through the natural law, is derided as a medieval invention. Catholics are often treated with pity because their Church maintains steadfastly the principle of authority; because that Church by a moral force still binds consciences in the court of man and in the court of God; because that Church still faithfully and untiringly carries out the commission given by Christ:

> All power is given to me in Heaven and in earth. Going, therefore, teach ye all nations . . . teaching them to observe all things whatsoever I have commanded you; and behold, I am with you all days, even to the consummation of the world.[12]

Effects

52. An unhappy result of the rejection of the principle of authority is that individuals seek to be a law unto themselves. Caprice and emotion determine their judgment of right and wrong. What they like is right; what they dislike is wrong. They presume to act on the anarchistic principle that everyone has the right, as is said, "to lead his own life." They do not regard it as an obligation to inquire: Did the divine Christ determine anything in this matter, or has any delegated authority of Christ a right to determine what should be done or left undone? The authority of the state is accepted as a police power, not as one imposing a moral obligation.

53. When we consider that for many decades this sad condition has been growing more general in our country, need we wonder that capitalists, industrialists, and business and professional men are not governed by the moral law, and, fearing only the police power of the state, will attempt anything clandestinely that will advance their private interests, provided they are personally secure from exposure or punishment?

Restore Authority

54. We are demanding a new order, and we are ready to make many changes in the hope of bettering our economic and financial condi-

---

[12]Mt 28:18-20.

tions; but we must remember that no legislation can be enacted that will not be circumvented, and no new order will long endure, unless there be a moral force binding our citizens. That moral force must have its source in Christ. The recognition of the authority of Christ is essential for the restoration not only of the moral but also of the economic order.

Restore International Confidence

55. The fear and mistrust of nations should be abolished. International conferences, the breaking down of tariff barriers, legislation, inflation of credit and currency, may help; but only Christian charity will destroy the suspicion, fear, and mistrust of nations. As the individual life should be governed by charity, which means love of God and neighbor, so should groups and the nations be governed by Christian charity.

Moral Force of Right

56. The real guarantee of peace among nations is love and forbearance, based on the Christian principle of the brotherhood of man. Charity will labor always for peace; it will seek to settle all matters in dispute between nations by arbitration; it will strive to have all the nations work as members of a family, not as enemies trying to ensnare one another. Charity will make it clear that as justice demands self-defense for the individual, so it also insists that national defense is lawful for national preservation against the aggressor, and also for the restoration of order within its own confines. Charity will condemn as fiendish criminals all those who promote strife between nations in order to acquire individual or national riches. Charity will labor that justice be not violated by exhausting the treasury of a nation and imposing an excessive tax burden upon a people for the building of armaments, which always make war more likely. Charity will, in the thought of Benedict XV, make the moral force of right take the place of the material force of arms, and "set up in the place of armies a court of arbitration."[13]

World Justice, Charity, and Order

57. Pope Pius XI, in condemning the unbridled race for supremacy in armaments, pleads with the bishops of the world to "employ every means at your disposal, through preaching and through the press, to enlighten men's minds and to incline their hearts to the require-

---

[13]Letter to the heads of states engaged in war, August 1, 1917.

ments of right reason, and even more to the law of Christ."[14] We desire world justice, world charity, and world order; but we must realize that the selfishness, rivalry, suspicion, intrigue, and hatred of nations are working against these three great aims. It is our duty to pray for peace and to work for peace, and to pray and to labor that our powerful country may lead all the nations of the world to see the folly of armaments, as they are being augmented by the nations today.

Study

58. Our priests and selected groups of the laity, members of the professions, employers, and leaders of trade and labor unions should study most carefully the plan for the restoration of the social order outlined by our Holy Father, whose voice is the voice of the living representative of Christ upon earth. With providential foresight and more than worldly wisdom he has definitely pointed out the way to the true Christian social order.

Study Groups

59. Our Catholic economists, sociologists, and moralists have dealt with many of the questions which are of especial interest today. Their work, which is deserving of high commendation, should be made to reach a wider circle of readers. The Catholic press and Catholic societies should look on the dissemination of sound social and economic teaching as a primary and essential part of the apostolate.

60. Many subjects mentioned in our statement are in need of fuller and more detailed discussion, and these discussions should be made available to wider circles of readers through periodicals and pamphlets. There are other questions which, though treated by Catholic writers, should be restated, owing to their importance today. Such questions are: international peace; world court of arbitration; disarmament; war debts; remission of war debts; the morality of holding companies; injustices of corporations; absentee control; the inflation of stock; dishonest stock promotion; overcapitalization; the true and fictitious value of securities; the immoral transactions of the stock market; deceptive advertising; security of bank deposits; fair interest rates; credit unions; consumers' cooperatives; labor unions; the sound administration of building and loan associations; unjust foreclosures; honest banking; bankruptcy; gambling; last wills and testaments and unjust will contests; unjust chattel mortgages; bribery; price fixing; the minimum wage; the fair price; farmers' marketing cooperatives; the nature and requirements of an organized economic order; distribution of ownership; the moral implications of the new interdepen-

---

[14] Apostolic letter, *Nova Impendet*.

dence of economic life; monopolies. These and many other questions receiving public attention can advantageously be studied by leagues, societies, and groups, according to their capacity, but naturally the emphasis will be placed on the moral aspect, which is the supreme concern of the Church. The position of the Church will have an irresistible appeal if stated in simple, forceful language and in an attractive manner. Her concern is the salvation of souls. Her duty is to speak, in season and out of season, where there is a moral question at stake.

Public Opinion

61. It is our duty as Catholic citizens to share with others the priceless riches of the supernatural treasury of which the Church has been the custodian during all the Christian centuries. True love of neighbor should impel us to influence public opinion. Many may not accept the whole position of the Catholic Church, but thinking and informed men and women cannot fail to be impressed with her teaching on all questions affecting the commonweal, and especially those engaging the attention of the public mind today.

Defense against Hostile Legislation

62. In our study and in our endeavor to form public opinion, we must keep ever in mind what Leo XIII and Pius XI have taught—that the social question is not merely an economic one, but that it is, first of all, a moral and religious question. Governments may not realize that they are failing to promote their own best interests when they fail to regard moral and religious truth, the spiritual and temporal welfare of man, the moral value, therefore, of man and the fullness of his life as a social being, as the preeminent ends they should serve. What a sad spectacle to the world that the governments of Mexico, Spain, and Russia should not only reject moral forces, but should become hard and cruel tyrants, persecuting religion. Conditions in these countries and the suffering of our brothers in the faith are deserving of our serious study. Our daily prayers should be offered that the hand of the persecutor may be stayed.

63. "No man," wrote Leo XIII,

> may outrage with impunity that human dignity which God himself treats with reverence. . . . Nay more; a man has here no power over himself. To consent to any treatment which is calculated to defeat the end and purpose of his being is beyond his right; he cannot give up his soul to servitude; for it is not man's own rights which are here in question, but the rights of God, most sacred and inviolable.[15]

---

[15]*Rerum Novarum*.

Governments must safeguard these rights and all groups must respect them. All legislation must be framed according to them. Economics, industrialism, taxation, all use of things of the world must be regulated by them.

Our Duty to Voting

64. In our form of government the obligation of bringing about a reform of the social order rests upon citizens, who by their votes give a mandate to legislators and executives. This makes evident a civic duty, and for us Catholics it is also a religious one governed by the virtue of piety; that is, a certain filial piety toward our country which impels us to promote the reform of the social order by voting for competent and conscientious men of high moral principles.

Battle for Justice

65. A few individuals, or even several well-meaning corporate entities, owing to unrestrained competition and the rejection of moral principles by their competitors, permitting the "survival of those only who are strongest, which often means those who fight most relentlessly, who pay least heed to the dictates of conscience,"[16] cannot of themselves change a system that is inherently wrong. In a word, because these comparatively few men of conscience cannot do the immoral things and resort to the base and inhuman methods which their competitors in the economic world, without any moral sense, consider merely good modern business, they are helpless of themselves to bring about a reform. They need the militant support of all right-thinking and moral men to fight and to win the battle for justice.
66. It is, as Pius XI reminds us,

> the primary duty of the state and of all good citizens to abolish conflict between classes with divergent interests, and thus foster and promote harmony among the various ranks of society. . . . Just as the unity of human society cannot be built upon class warfare, so the proper ordering of economic affairs cannot be left to free competition alone.[17]

67. All, therefore, who are governed by justice must continue to do the most they can to influence public opinion in order to secure a general recognition of the rights of man. Our Catholic scholars should do everything possible to promote a serious study of this question.

---

[16]*Quadragesimo Anno.*
[17]Ibid.

Rights of Workingman

68. The workingman is entitled to a family wage, which must be an amount sufficient not only to support husband, wife, and children in frugal and decent comfort, but to provide against sickness, unemployment, infirmity, and old age. His right to organize must not be interfered with. His right to an equitable share in the profits, as a wage earner, must receive due consideration. His right to bequeath and to inherit, and his right to employment under normal moral conditions, should be assured.

69. Social justice, working in behalf of the common good, requires that the masses not possessing property rise to a degree of ownership. The chasm between owners—the relatively few—and nonowners—the vast majority—must be bridged by a distribution of ownership through thrift and a real sharing of profits, not merely a profit sharing in name. Profit sharing through stock ownership, or through partnership contracts, in our large corporations has in too many instances proved either disastrous or of little value to employees laboring under the disadvantage of being minority stockholders. Indeed, as Pius XI says,[18] the time seems to have come when the wage contract should itself be somewhat modified by a contract of partnership. This, however, should be a measure of true partnership.

70. We are reminded here by Pius XI of two important truths. Speaking of St. Paul's teaching,[19] "if any man will not work, neither let him eat," His Holiness says, first, "In no sense does he teach that labor is the sole title which gives a right to a living or to profits,"[20] and, second, that an equitable share of the profits of industry should be given to both capital and labor. Labor and trades unions offer one means of obtaining justice in wages and salaries. The normal working of such organizations, whether singly or as a federation of unions, should be to promote the general welfare and to insure for all workers, whether skilled or unskilled, maximum employment, adequate remuneration, the protection of their rights as men and as citizens, and security against accident and indigence.

Capital and Labor Friends

71. Our study should make us grasp fully the principle, clearly stated in the *Quadragesimo Anno*, that as labor should not seize, if it were in a position to do so, all the profits, neither should capital. Capital and labor need each other. They should be friends. They should, as brothers, sit down together at the council table. Unlimited, reckless, im-

---

[18] Ibid.
[19] 2 Thes 3:10.
[20] *Quadragesimo Anno.*

moral competition and economic dictatorship will continue until this is done. Capital and labor should be convinced that greed is a vice, and that a just division of profits can and should be a virtue. Capital and labor should work for the common welfare and for their mutual interest should encourage all workers to organize. Unions, embracing all groups of workers, should be governed by good sense. They should endeavor to distribute opportunity to the workers of every class. They should always seek competent and disinterested advisers, that their organizations may ever be characterized by sanity. The individual or personal and social aspect of labor should be well understood. There should be mutual harmony and mutual support. "Unless, above all, brains, capital, and labor combine together for common effort, man's toil cannot produce due fruit."[21]

Large Corporations and Moral Principles

72. We must recognize that the big corporation has its place, and that, as Pius XI says, "much that was formerly done by small bodies can nowadays be accomplished only by large corporations."[22] They need, however, to reform; they need the fullest publicity given in a language that the ordinary man can understand. The study of our Catholic scholars should put forth concrete plans that will insist upon the rigorous application of moral principles to big corporations. These plans of reform should place limitations on them, so that the rights of smaller units and bodies will be fully protected. Such small units have not only a right to exist but are necessary. They should not be crushed by supercorporations and mergers that fancy it is their right to absorb them. The plans formulated by our scholars should provide, as Pope Pius XI suggests, a graded hierarchical order between various subsidiary organizations. While the big corporations serve a useful purpose, their intolerable abuses, especially their clandestine manipulation of trust funds and earned surplus, must cease if we are to restore the social and economic order. Smaller units of business and production should be encouraged all over the country. Local communities should take a pride in them. The law should protect them, and the courts should safeguard them.

73. Today, as in the past, there is a tendency to place too much reliance on government to accomplish our economic salvation. This trend arises from the very individualism that was long dominant. Greed destroyed economic organization and prevented government from protecting justice and promoting the common good. Greed enslaved governments. Now that the whirlwind is being reaped, peo-

---

[21]Ibid.
[22]Ibid.

ples are relying almost solely on government to bring a measure of justice and order out of chaos. One of the greatest dangers facing us is a blind reaction from our former individualism to a regime of state socialism or state capitalism.

Government Cooperation

74. Government in the fulfillment of its functions should assist in the organization of the various economic groups. These organized groups, without injustice to themselves, but seeking always the common good, can be so constituted as to fulfill properly their own function of production and the distribution of their services. Such an organization of the various economic groups along the lines of their separate industries and fields of endeavor should embrace representatives of every element in the economic group. Imbued with justice, with love for the common good, and with social charity, such an organized economic life can free the state from the danger it faces of becoming an all-engrossing and all-enveloping power. As Pope Pius XI says:

> The aim of social legislation must be the reestablishment of vocational groups. . . . The state should leave to these smaller groups the settlement of business of minor importance. It will thus carry out with greater freedom, power, and success the tasks belonging to it, because it alone can effectively accomplish these, directing, watching, stimulating, and restraining as circumstances suggest or necessity demands.[23]

But government, to quote again, should not "arrogate to itself functions which can be performed efficiently by smaller and lower bodies"—bodies that would comprise the organized and autonomous economic life.

Tax Reform

75. Our Catholic scholars, economists, and moralists should study our crushing burden of taxation, which is, in itself, an indictment of government and of our economic system. Legislators have a serious responsibility whenever they impose taxes. The general welfare of the people should always be kept in mind in performing this duty. To impose taxes unjustly or in a reckless manner or in the interest of special groups or according to the immoral practice of trading votes, too common among legislators, must be regarded as a violation of the oath of office and the betrayal of a sacred trust. Taxation is unjust that favors the strong rather than the weak, the rich rather than the

---

[23] Ibid.

poor. Legislators and men in political life who in imposing taxes sacrifice the general welfare of the people in order to advance their own interests and to continue in office deserve the severest censure.

Fearless Condemnation Necessary

76. Excessive taxation has been a serious hindrance to the revival of business. Patriotic citizens should fearlessly condemn the extravagant expenditure of the people's money by government agencies and bureaucracies. In recent years the cost of government has mounted to staggering proportions, even though the average income of our citizens has been greatly reduced or practically wiped out. This tremendous increase in government expenditures has not brought any corresponding gain to our people.

Interest in Public Expenditures

77. In our country, where the responsibility of selecting honest and competent officials and of forming opinion devolves upon the citizens, it is all the more important that thoughtful and informed men become tax-conscious, that they realize that there will be a day of accounting for endless bond issues, and that they exercise their influence to the utmost to arouse and to sustain in the people at large an intelligent interest in public expenditures.

Intelligible Statement of Tax Methods

78. In the simplest language possible taxation, which ultimately is passed on in great measure to the laboring and trades classes, should be explained to the people. Citizens should be interested in knowing how their money is being spent. They should be informed to what an extent taxation increases the price of the very necessaries of life. Studies on this vital subject should be put out in the most popular form. Public opinion should continue to demand that expenditures by the government for nonessentials be eliminated; that our educational system be simplified; that bureaucracies be limited; that the injustice of favoring special groups at public expense should cease; also, that a clear and simple statement of the cost of government be made available to all our citizens.

79. We venture to speak on this subject, which may seem to transgress our province, because of the grave injustice that is done to the ordinary taxpayer, the workingman, those who have put most of the earnings of a lifetime into modest homes, and to the farmers who have suffered from the iniquities of officials imposing unnecessary taxes.

* * *

Back to the Land

91. The unemployment and destitution of today are the consequence of a revolution in agriculture and industry, which commenced a century and a half ago, when machine power took the place of man power. The machine produced the factory and the factory the great industrial cities. These cities are now overcrowded, and, because of the increasing perfection in technological methods, they are becoming less and less capable of supporting their teeming populations. In addition, the city crushed men's souls as well as their bodies. It deprived them of the material comforts and the necessaries of life, and it made them an easy prey for radicals, who set before them the vision of a new order and a new world, replete with material happiness and advantages. This new order could be attained only through the adoption of a materialistic philosophy in which there was no place for God or religion.
92. One hope for relief in the universal misery of the present lies in the reversal of the policy which produced the factory and the factory system. This reversal, without depriving men of the benefits of industrial progress, would reinstate them as independent home owners in rural communities. Such a change in the living conditions of millions of people would be a revolution, but some radical adjustment in restoring the balance between rural and urban population is imperative if our country is to survive and if our civilization is not to disappear.
93. A necessary preliminary or condition to such a comprehensive change in the living conditions of millions of people would be a revision of the ideas and standards which make country life appear less desirable than city life. This must be accomplished through religion. The Catholic Church has demonstrated, times without number, that it can place rural civilization on an attractive and permanent basis. In rural Catholic communities the people found the source and center of their activities in their parish church, and, under the guidance of their pastors, and through the tender ministrations of the religious orders of men and women, they were immune to the soul-destroying teachings of radicals, atheists, Socialists, and Communists. The reconstruction of rural civilization is not merely a means to protect millions against the poverty, the excitement, and the corruption of cities, not merely an escape from the grinding economic inequalities imposed by the machine age, it is an imperative duty to see that our people shall have homes if the moral and spiritual values of life are to be conserved and if the race is to be saved from extinction.
94. Already many millions of people have felt the logic of the situation and have returned to the land, not as refugees but as pioneers of a new and healthier civilization. This movement should be fostered and encouraged. Its possibilities are illimitable. If carried to a suc-

cessful issue it would work a transformation in our entire civilization, but it is a movement that demands careful planning and sustained effort. It would require the best thought and the concerted labor of federal and state agencies, the good will of industrial leaders, and the cooperation of the Church. It is one scheme that will indubitably make a rich return for whatever outlay of effort or money it may entail in the happiness and security it will bestow on millions who are now homeless and destitute.

95. To speak of its benefits to religion is unnecessary. The very economic forces surrounding the farmer protect the unity of marriage and foster its permanence against birth control and divorce. Crowded industrial centers, on the contrary, especially in the congested districts of our large cities, promote the idea of restricted families and an unwholesome moral life in the divine institution of the home. As Pope Pius XI says, "the present economic regime, and above all the disgraceful housing conditions, prove obstacles to the family tie and family life."[24]

Spirit of the Gospel

96. Grave as are the problems of the present, and dark as the economic outlook may now appear, there is no reason why Catholics should not face the future with confidence and courage. We are the bearers of a great tradition, the tradition of religious, moral, and spiritual discipline, which commenced with the preaching of the Gospel and which gave to Europe and the world a new and more perfect culture and civilization. That culture did not develop as a result of legislative enactments or social and political upheavals, but because men and women took into their souls the spirit of the Gospel and because in their lives they gave a practical exemplification of the teachings of Christ. The greatest revolution in the institutional life of humanity was that which was wrought when those who professed to follow Christ lived the life of earnest and devout Christians. It was because those followers of Christ made faith the paramount influence in life and conduct, and Christian charity the source and goal of all effort that autocracy was dethroned and that mankind came to enjoy the benefits of freedom of conscience and of civil and political liberty, and it was because those who believed that all men without distinction of Jew or Greek, bond or free, are all one in Christ,[25] that the curse of chattel slavery vanished from the world.

97. The social implications of the teaching of Christ have made and are now making an irresistible appeal to the inarticulate but powerful

---

[24]Ibid.
[25]Gal 3:28.

masses of the disinherited. The institutions of society are no longer looked on as means to sustain the arrogance, the luxury and pride of a favored few. Change can be effected as it has been effected by the bomb, the rifle, and the torch, but such change means increased suffering and greater misery; or it can be brought about, without detriment to our heritage of Christianity and civilization, if those who believe in Christ enter with Christ on the road of humility and renunciation. The real authors of violent and bloody revolution in our times are not the radicals and Communists, but the callous and autocratic possessors of wealth and power who use their position and their riches to oppress their fellows. It is the duty of Catholics to be mindful of their obligations, as bearers of the great Christian tradition, to be courageous in rebuking tyranny, luxury, and sordid egotism, and above all to be exemplary in their effort to make their deeds and lives reflect the faith they profess.

Prayer

98. We have insisted that Christ be given his rightful place in the nation and in the hearts of individuals. This must be done through prayer. Our hearts and minds must be lifted up to God to acknowledge his sovereignty over the universe, his divine plan for all his creatures, the eternal destiny of man, and his dependence upon Divine Providence. The mystery of God's government of men and of nations must be proclaimed. We must pour forth our hearts in humble supplication for our personal needs, for the needs of the Church, and for the needs of our country, our state, and our community.

99. It was heartening to the people of our country, and an example to the world, that our president on the morning of his inauguration bowed down in humble prayer, begging God's blessing on his administration, asking Divine Providence to protect every individual of the nation, and to grant him guidance during the years of his tremendous responsibility. The first bishop of the United States, Archbishop Carroll of Baltimore, by writing his beautiful prayer for our civil rulers, has given us an example that should still inspire us. The virtue of patriotism should make us pray daily for our country and for all who govern it.

Jubilee Year

100. During the present Jubilee Year declared by our Holy Father we are observing the nineteen hundredth anniversary of the death of the Divine Savior of the world. It is a year of prayer and a year of penitential practices. The Lord Christ is anxious to save all. We need but to turn to him in earnest, humble prayer, with the firm purpose of carrying out his injunctions. In the words of Pope Pius XI,[26]

> Let us stimulate ourselves to prayer, to penitence for the sins committed by us, having in mind in our prayers and acts of expiation not only our eternal salvation, but also that of all mankind, led astray by so many errors, torn by so many discords and so much hostility, laboring under so many miseries, and fearful of so many dangers. Oh, may the Most Merciful Lord bring it about that the Holy Year . . . will bring peace to souls, to the Church that liberty everywhere due her, to all peoples concord and true prosperity.

101. During the Jubilee Year our Holy Father urges as many of his children as can throughout the world to go to Rome to gain the jubilee indulgence. Under normal circumstances the number of pilgrims would have been extraordinary. Notwithstanding the present adverse conditions, many of the faithful will at the cost of real sacrifice visit the Eternal City to kneel at the feet of the Common Father of Christendom. May the Jubilee Year bring great blessings to America!

102. May we ever watch and pray that Christ abide in us and we in him. May the Church ever prosper, and may our country in returning to prosperity realize that the Lord Christ is its greatest need!

Given at Washington, in conference, on the twenty-sixth day of April, 1933

Edward J. Hanna, Chairman, Archbishop of San Francisco
John T. McNicholas, Archbishop of Cincinnati
John G. Murray, Treasurer, Archbishop of St. Paul
Joseph Schrembs, Bishop of Cleveland
Hugh C. Boyle, Bishop of Pittsburgh
John F. Noll, Secretary, Bishop of Fort Wayne
Thomas F. Lillis, Vice-Chairman, Bishop of Kansas City

[26]Promulgation of the Extraordinary Holy Year for the Nineteenth Century of the Redemption of Mankind.

Statement on Social Problems

A Statement Issued by the Administrative Board of the National Catholic Welfare Conference

November 28, 1937

1. For generations the social purpose of property has been too much disregarded and self-interest has increasingly dominated social and economic life. Selfish interests or private profit rather than social well-being has succeeded in large measure in controlling the policies of governments, in directing finance and industry, and in subjecting labor policies to its own ends. Although an essentially disorganizing principle, it has unwarrantably claimed to be the sole organizing force in society, the guarantee of social order, and the cure for social ills. But the half-truths and half-solutions which this extreme individualism has begotten in the social order are now discredited in the minds of thoughtful men.

2. Nearly 50 years ago the voice of Pope Leo XIII pleaded with governments, with capital, and industry to abolish economic injustice and to establish in industry working conditions befitting the dignity of man, as well as sufficiency of income for family life and old age.

3. Since the close of the World War, economic evils have increased. Social injustice, oblivious to the need of providing self-respecting employment to millions, has embittered the jobless and the poor throughout the world. In many it has aroused the spirit of defiance and revolt.

4. It is to be deplored that the unrest caused by evils already grave and disturbing should be further increased by designing agitators or by cunning propagandists whose immediate interest is to create turmoil, bitterness, class conflict, and thus hasten a "revolutionary situation." Calmness, accuracy of statement, and prudent restraint are highly desirable qualities in every discussion of grievances and remedies.

5. Irresponsible doctrinaries have seized upon worldwide discontent and capitalized it. Adroitly, they have presented some fundamental truths of the Gospel of Christ as if they were the first to expound them. They condemn abuses which Christ condemned and which the Catholic Church has been condemning for nineteen hundred years. The false promises of Communism inspire a crusading spirit, a contagious hysteria. It appeals to personal sacrifice and captures the adventurous spirit of youth. It masquerades as the champion of the downtrodden, as the archenemy of capitalistic abuses, and as the redeemer of the poor and working classes.

6. In our country Communist leaders see three things in their favor: first, a sizable army of propagandists among left wing professors, teachers, and intellectuals; second, the very real dangers to our financial and economic structure; third, the growing articulate discontent among the masses of the people. Unhampered by any fixed moral principles, Communists would hasten the collapse of the structure of our government, calculating that they will be the beneficiaries as the leaders of the new order. If for the moment they are keeping their activities largely undercover, it is because they are biding their time, awaiting the hoped-for collapse. Meanwhile by arraying class against class, and by tactics of boring from within other organized groups they seek to further the destructive ends of Communism. Traditional and constitutional America means nothing to them. They use the liberty guaranteed by the Constitution to erect a new system of government which will deny that liberty which they now misuse. They are willing to use any means to attain their end. Their present restraint is expediency. Their delay is strategy.

7. Many of the promoters of organizations calling themselves peace and youth movements, sponsors of stage and screen entertainment, and so-called crusaders for democracy, especially those upholding the Communism of Spain and refusing to condemn the Bolshevism of Russia are, consciously or unconsciously, propagandists and agents of Communism. They constitute part of the United or Popular Front. The trickery of Communists, as Pius XI points out, knows no bounds. They try perfidiously "to worm their way even into professedly Catholic and religious organizations."

8. Pope Pius XI has challenged the attention of all groups who have had any part in this injustice and calls for a reconstruction of the social order. He advocates no dictatorship either of the right or the left. He seeks no governmental bureaucracy. He desires to see the guild system reestablished in a manner adapted to modern problems and conditions. Neither unrestrained competition nor monopoly nor class conflict nor ubiquitous governmental control provides a sound remedy. Social well-being can be attained best by vocational groups ordering their own economic life under the guidance and encouragement of government. An unjust economic system, he has demonstrated, has had much to do with the rapid spread of the world's social cancer—Atheistic Communism. His voice is for peace as against war between capital and labor. For labor, he has fearlessly demanded recognition of its right to organize, just wages, healthy and humane working conditions, and security for sickness and old age. The truest friend of the poor and laboring man in the world today is Pope Pius XI.

9. Labor has the right and should be accorded recognition of the right to establish its own organizations, to bargain collectively, to choose freely its own representatives. It has its just claims to a reasonable living wage, to healthful working conditions, to security of employment without unfair discrimination. It may enforce its just demands by effective means, but these must always be consonant with the rights of others, the dictates of conscience, and God's laws.

10. Labor should not incur the charge of countenancing coercion and injustice. It is not only unwise but immoral and reprehensible to use physical violence either against fellow employees or against property. It is both dishonest and destructive of genuine progress for labor to violate contracts freely and honorably negotiated and accepted.

11. Not only should labor reject the philosophy as well as the political and economic system of Communism but it should energetically repudiate such tendencies amongst those who undertake to be organizers of labor, thus eliminating any danger of Communist leadership or domination.

12. There are many honorable employers whose motives and purposes are dictated by justice and charity. They should be commended. What is needed is more widespread and profound study of the social problems, with mutual collaboration by both employers and employees in the solution thereof.

13. Pius XI calls attention to the tremendous economic power exercised by those who hold and control money and are able therefore to govern credit and determine its allotment. This control moreover is exercised by those who are not the real owners of wealth but merely the trustees and administrators of invested funds. Responsibility is thus divorced from ownership. Nevertheless, they hold in their hands the very soul of production since they supply its lifeblood and no one can breathe against their will.

14. The increasing ratio of debt to total wealth has also had its influence in lessening the responsibility and advantage which should attach to the ownership of property. It makes for insecurity. Its relationship moreover to the cost of living or a reasonable price level needs careful inquiry. Further study should be given, likewise, to the whole intricate problem of money and credit so that such evils as exist in the present system may be brought to light and suitable remedies introduced.

15. Another method of destroying the liberty of the people, although it begins by lauding democracy and proclaiming freedom, is to establish the dictatorship of an absolutist state. Referring to this totalitarian state, Pope Pius XI in *Quadragesimo Anno* asserts:

> It is feared that the new syndical and corporative institution possesses an excessively bureaucratic and political character, and that, notwithstanding the general advantages referred to above, it risks serving particular political aims rather than contributing to the initiation of a better social order (p. 30).

This kind of state is contrary to the letter and spirit of the American Constitution.

16. It first gives to the people many services; and then it assumes a multiplicity of functions which no normal civil government should attempt to discharge. Gradually the totalitarian state assumes the responsibility and function of the capitalist, the industrialist, the agriculturist, the merchant, and the employer. All this inevitably leads, not to a free state, but to a slave state. The tendency of our time is to make more and more demands on government. Citizens and groups should not ask the government to do for them what they can do for themselves. Sound social policy requires government to encourage citizens to assume as much personal responsibility as possible.

17. The poor and the laboring classes should resist the tendency to set up the omnipotent state. Their chief economic defense is organization. The traditional and ideal Christian society is not an individualistic but an organic society in which the individual, through the instrumentality of his group, works for himself, his group, and the entire social body.

18. It is deplorable that in our country an internecine conflict has broken out between two large organized bodies of workers. Continuance of the struggle can only mean increased suffering and hardship for workers themselves. It is gratifying that conferences looking to conciliation have been initiated; and for the well-being of workers, employers, and the entire people it is earnestly to be desired that these conferences will continue in a spirit of give and take, thereby providing the basis for harmony and lasting peace.

19. It is essential that labor unions be governed by the principles of Christian brotherhood, justice, and fair play. They should embrace all groups of workers. While seeking to promote their own interests they should be guided by sound judgment, have regard for the common economic good, respect property rights, prove themselves worthy of the confidence of every community, and thus perform their rightful function in protecting the legitimate interests of their members and in giving strength and stability to the nation.

Statement on Church and Social Order

A Statement Issued by the Administrative Board and Assistant Bishops of the National Catholic Welfare Conference

February 7, 1940

Introduction

1. With sublime pathos Pope Pius XII in his first encyclical letter pleads with the peoples of the world to turn from the destructive ways of hatred and conflict to the healing ways of charity and peace.[1] He reminds a forgetful world of the universality of divine love; he reconsecrates the whole human family to the sacred heart of the Divine Redeemer; and, summoning men to return to Christ, he re-echoes the entreaty raised so often by his predecessors: "Behold your King" (Jn 19:14).

2. To reenthrone Christ in the minds and hearts of men; to reestablish his kingship in human society; to impregnate the laws and institutions, the aspirations and final purposes of all nations with his spirit, is the supreme hope and purpose of our Holy Father.

> Perhaps—God grant—one may hope (with Pope Pius XII), that this hour of direct need may bring a change of outlook and sentiment to those many who, till now, have walked with blind faith along the path of popular modern errors unconscious of the treacherous and insecure ground on which they trod. Perhaps the many who have not grasped the importance of the educational and pastoral mission of the Church will now understand better her warnings, scouted in the false security of the past. No defense of Christianity could be more effective than the present straits. From the immense vortex of error and anti-Christian movements there has come forth a crop of such poignant disasters as to constitute a condemnation surpassing in its conclusiveness any merely theoretical refutation.[2]

3. With all our hearts we thank him for his guidance and with such strength as we possess we emulate his example. We reaffirm the primacy of our Lord Jesus Christ,

> Who is the image of the invisible God, the first-born of every creature: For in him were all things created in Heaven and on earth,

[1]This statement was made by the administrative board for the American bishops.
[2]*Summi Pontificatus* (NCWC edition, 1939), pp. 11-12.

> visible and invisible. . . . And he is before all, and by him all things consist. . . . Because in him it hath well pleased the Father, that all fullness should dwell (Col 1:15-19).

4. The peace which all right-minded men so earnestly desire, must be based upon a comprehensive program of restoring Christ to his true and proper place in human society. We must bring God back into government; we must bring God back into education; we must bring God back into economic life; we must bring God back indeed into all life, private and public, individual and social. The truth of God, the law of God, the justice, mercy, and charity of God, must, by conscious effort and willing submission, be made to permeate all our social intercourse and all our public relations.

5. In the midst of human society, God has set his Church as "the pillar and ground of truth." To the Church Christ has given the divine mission to teach all things whatsoever he has commanded. The divine mandate permits no curtailment of the law no matter how diverse the circumstances and conditions under which man lives and works, nor any compromise with the full measure of its application to human conduct. The obligation comprehends the actions of man in his private and public life as an individual and as a member of human society.

6. Man is not an isolated individual living in a social vacuum, but a social being destined to live and work out his salvation in association with his fellow beings. He is a member of a community and he has, in consequence, duties of commutative justice and duties of social justice and duties of charity which emerge from this relationship. On no other foundations can man build a right social order or create that good society which is desired so ardently by the great mass of mankind.

7. Inasmuch as the right and duty of the Church to teach the fullness of the moral law and in particular "to deal authoritatively with social and economic problems" (p. 14),[3] are challenged in some quarters or are too frequently misunderstood in others, we judge it wise and opportune to reaffirm the jurisdiction of the Church as the teacher of the entire moral law and more particularly as it applies to man's economic and social conduct in business, industry, and trade. To make our pronouncements authentic and to interpret truly the mind of the Church, we follow closely the teachings of our late lamented pontiff, Pope Pius XI.

8. First, let it be made clear that the Church is concerned only with the moral aspects of trade and industry and does not enter the field

---

[3] All citations, unless otherwise mentioned, are from the encyclical *Forty Years After (Quadragesimo Anno)* of Pope Pius XI (NCWC edition, 1931).

of business in matters that are purely material or technical. The Church is not concerned with the accuracy of economic surveys or the resultant data, nor with the problems of scientific organization, production, cost accounting, transportation, marketing, and a multitude of similar activities. To pass judgment on their aptitude and merits is a technical problem proper to economic science and business administration. For such the Church has neither the equipment nor the authorization. We frankly declare that it would be unwise on her part to discuss their operation except insofar as a moral interest might be involved (p. 14).

9. The Church does not prescribe any particular form of technical economic organization of society just as she does not prescribe any particular political organization of the state.[4] Pius XI makes this clear in his encyclical letter *Quadragesimo Anno* where he states:

> It is hardly necessary to note that what Leo XIII taught concerning the form of political government can, in due measure, be applied also to vocational groups. Here, too, men may choose whatever form they please, providing that both justice and the common good be taken into account (p. 28).

10. From the Sacred Scripture we learn that "the earth is the Lord's and the fullness thereof" (Ps 24:1). No absolute or unlimited ownership therefore can be claimed by man as if he were free to follow his own selfish interests without regard to the necessity of others. The moral law teaches that he has indeed a right to private property but, as Pope Leo XIII points out, "the earth, even though divided among private owners, ceases not thereby to administer to the needs of all."[5]

11. Man is truly the steward of his possessions in the sight of God and has therefore definite responsibilities both of justice and charity toward his fellow man with respect to the use he makes of his property.

12. From Divine Revelation we learn that physical labor was decreed by God even after the fall of man for the good of body and soul (p. 42). The laborer is worthy of his hire. If, however, human labor is treated as a mere commodity to be bought and sold in the open market at the lowest price, then it ceases to fulfill its proper function in society. What a sad perversion of the wholesome plan of Divine Providence that "dead matter leaves the factory ennobled and transformed, where men are corrupted and degraded" (p. 43).

13. From Divine Revelation we learn moreover that each human being has an infinitely precious personality. Pius XI in his encyclical *Divini Redemptoris* sets forth this truth with clarity, force, and beauty:

---

[4]Cf., *Divini Redemptoris* (NCWC edition, 1937), p. 24, par. 32.
[5]*On the Condition of Labor (Rerum Novarum)* (Paulist Press, 1937), p. 7.

> Man has a spiritual and immortal soul. He is a person, marvelously endowed by his creator with gifts of body and mind. He is a true 'microcosm' as the ancients said, a world in miniature, with a value far surpassing that of the vast inanimate cosmos. God alone is his last end, in this life and the next. By sanctifying grace he is raised to the dignity of a son of God, and incorporated into the Kingdom of God in the mystical Body of Christ. In consequence he has been endowed by God with many and varied prerogatives: the right to life, to bodily integrity; to the necessary means of existence; the right to tend towards his ultimate goal in the path marked out for him by God; the right of association and the right to possess and use property (p. 19).

14. Man cannot in consequence be treated as a mere chattel but rather with dignity and respect as a child of God. His labor is not a thing to be ashamed of, but an honorable calling, whereby he achieves a necessary livelihood and fulfills the divine plan of an earthly economy.
15. Because these are moral principles and spiritual truths, jurisdiction in expounding their full scope and obligation belongs to the Church which Christ established as the teacher of men in this world. We in our capacity as shepherds of the flock of Christ cannot be unmindful of our duties in these matters. "Take heed to yourselves," says the apostle, "and to the whole flock, wherein the Holy Ghost hath placed you bishops, to rule the Church of God" (Acts 20:28).
16. It is an unfortunate fact that large numbers of workingmen have become alienated from religion. This is true even of Catholics in some of the older countries. In other words of the Supreme Pontiff it has become the great scandal of the modern world. No matter how we explain the defection, the fact remains that Christian truth and principles of conduct have become greatly obscured "so that we are confronted with a world which in large measure has almost fallen back into paganism" (p. 46).
17. To bring back those who have suffered loss of faith and with it the loss even of earthly hope and charity, it is necessary to reestablish the sound principles of Christian social teaching. To make our progress sure and effective we must recruit and train leaders from within the various ranks of society who know the mentality and aspirations of their respective classes and who with kindly fraternal charity will be able to win both their minds and their hearts. "Undoubtedly," as Pius XI says,

> the first and immediate apostles of the workingmen must themselves be workingmen, while the apostles of the industrial and commercial world should themselves be employers and merchants. It is your chief duty, venerable brethren, and that of your clergy, to seek diligently, to select prudently, and train fittingly these lay apostles, amongst workingmen and amongst employers (p. 46).

18. In existing circumstances the obligation of the Church is manifest. Who can deny the close relationship between economic injustice and a long train of evils, physical, social, and moral? Unfair wages due to a greed for excessive profits and insecurity due to false and immoral economic principles lead directly to undernourishment, bad housing, inadequate clothing, and indirectly to irregular family relations, child delinquency, and crime. Excessively long hours of work in some industrial areas and in some industrial processes create dangers to life and limb, impair the health of workingmen, and impoverish whole families through infection, disease, and premature death. Because human beings and not animated machines toil in industry, therefore the Church cannot abdicate her right and duty to speak out in defense of the rights of human personality nor fail to declare uncompromisingly the moral obligations of industrial and economic life.

19. Today most controversy concerns itself with these questions: (1) ownership, (2) property and labor, (3) security, (4) wages, (5) establishment of social order. We shall here present the Catholic doctrine regulating these matters and in doing so we shall follow the exposition given by our late chief pastor of souls, Pope Pius XI, in his celebrated encyclicals.

I. Ownership

20. The Church has always defended the right to own private property and also to bequeath and to inherit it. We have vindicated this right even to the point of being falsely accused of favoring the rich against the poor. The Church teaches that the right to own property is based on the natural law of which God himself is the author. By the law of nature man must provide for himself and his family and he can fully discharge this obligation only if there exists an established system of private ownership (p. 16).

21. It is essential to remember that ownership has a twofold aspect, the one affecting the individual, the other affecting society. To deny the individual character and aspect of ownership leads to some form of socialism or collective ownership; to deny the social character or aspect of ownership leads to selfish individualism or that form of exaggerated liberalism which repudiates duties and ends in complete irresponsibility to other persons and to the common good.

22. The two great dangers which society faces in the present state of economic organization are, first, the concentration of ownership and control of wealth and, second, its anonymous character which results from some of the existing business and corporation law, whereby responsibility toward society is greatly impaired if not completely ignored. The civil authority, in view of these dangers, must so regulate the responsibility of property that the burden of providing for the common good be equitably distributed. It must furthermore establish such conditions through legal enactment and administration policy that wealth itself can be distributed so each individual member of society may surely and justly come into possession of the material goods necessary for his own livelihood. It is not, however, the government alone which has this responsibility, as will become clear from the further considerations to be noted. Pius XI states:

> It follows from the twofold character of ownership, which we have termed individual and social, that men must take into account in this matter not only their own advantage but also the common good. To define in detail these duties, when the need occurs and when the natural law does not do so, is the function of the government. Provided that the natural and divine law be observed, the public authority, in view of the common good, may specify more accurately what is licit for property owners in the use of their possession (p. 17).

23. In the application of the principles of social justice, an important instrument, therefore, is governmental authority. As Pius XI asserts, the civil authority has the obligation to adjust "ownership to meet the needs of the public good," and by so doing "it acts not as an enemy, but as the friend of private owners (p. 17)."

II. Property and Labor

24. Manifestly, if every man worked either on his own land or with his own tools and in his own business, there would be no labor problem. Self-employment, however, is not the characteristic of our present economic organization. With the advent of machine industry and especially with the development of mass production there has developed an intensification of the individualistic spirit, creating new problems for labor.

25. It is freely admitted that modern industry requires considerable concentration of capital, but it is not admitted that concentration of ownership and control is consequently necessary or beneficial to the common good. The concentration of capital, however, with mass employment, does create a new and more impersonal relationship between capital and labor. The problem is one of providing equitably for the distribution of income between those who supply capital and those who supply labor.

26. In too many instances an undue portion of the income has been claimed by those who have ownership or control of capital, whilst those on the other hand who have only their labor to invest have been forced to accept working conditions which are unreasonable and wages which are unfair. This condition arises from the fact that labor policies have been dictated by false principles in the interests of the owners or capitalists. Second, it arises from the fact that labor frequently has had no voice in the regulation or the adjustment of these problems. Labor can have no effective voice as long as it is unorganized. To protect its rights it must be free to bargain collectively through its own chosen representatives. If labor when unorganized is dissatisfied, the only alternative is to cease work and thus undergo the great hardships which follow unemployment.

27. To remedy the situation, it is necessary to adopt right principles for the distribution of the income of industry. These principles must be both economically sound and morally just. The principle that labor should be compensated to such extent only that it remains physically efficient and capable of reproducing itself in new generations of workingmen, is a vicious principle, devoid of all respect for human dignity and opposed to all sense of social responsibility. It is true that this principle was never widely held in theory, but it has been frequently applied in practice. One such application is found in the policy that labor should be compensated solely according to the principle of supply and demand. This reduces labor to the position of a commodity and makes the workingman accept the fluctuating price in a labor market irrespective of the needs of himself and family. Neither present sufficiency of income nor security for the future play a part in determining his wage standard according to this immoral theory and practice. Such theory or practice is antisocial and anti-Christian, for it denies both social responsibility and the claims of Christian ethics and in their place substitutes the principles of selfishness and force.

28. New developments in the organization of labor under the great impetus which has been given by recent legislation and governmental policy, make it opportune to point out that the principle of force and domination is equally wrong if exercised by labor under certain conditions by means of a monopoly control. To defend in principle or to adopt in practice the theory that the net result belongs to labor and that capital shall receive only sufficient to replace itself is an invasion of the rights of property. This is only a more subtle form of the contention that all means of production should be socialized. Clearly all such proposals disregard the contribution which the owner of property makes in the process of production and are palpably unjust.

29. It is not, however, the excessive claims of labor on the income from industry which constitute the most immediate problem in labor relations today, but rather the abuse of power which not infrequently results in violence, riot, and disorder. Employers at times abuse their economic power by discriminating unfairly against unions, by establishing lockouts, by importing from outside the community strikebreakers who are furnished with arms, and by provoking in other ways ill feeling which precipitates violent disorder. Employees on their part allow themselves at times to be misled by men of evil principles so as to engage in the criminal use of violence both against persons and property. Leo XIII in his encyclical *Rerum Novarum* spares neither group in his denunciation of such immoral conduct. He calls upon the public authority to protect and defend vigorously the rights of all, forestalling preferably the rise of disorder by eliminating the economic abuse from which this disorder springs (pp. 12-24).

30. False principles generate false policies and as a consequence there grows and develops a false economic system which sins both against the true interests of human society and against the true principles of Christian morality. Pius XI insists that owners and employers may not hire working people exclusively for their own benefit and profit, nor divert all economic life to their own will, but must guard social justice, the human dignity of labor, the social nature of economic life, and the interest of the common good (p. 32).

31. The far-reaching need of social justice and its demands are seen from the following words of the Sovereign Pontiff Pope Pius XI:

> Now, not every kind of distribution of wealth and property amongst men is such that it can at all, and still less can adequately, attain the end intended by God. Wealth, therefore, which is constantly being augmented by social and economic progress, must be so distributed amongst the various individuals and classes of society that the common good of all, of which Leo XIII spoke, be thereby promoted. In other words, the good of the whole community must be safeguarded (p. 20).

III. Security

32. Our present economic order rests upon the sanctity of private property. Private property, however, is not well distributed at present among the members of human society. While it is dangerous to exaggerate the disproportion between those who possess adequate property and those who constitute the proletariat or the propertyless, nevertheless, it is certainly within the bounds of truth to state that the existing situation constitutes a grave social evil. Private property in the judgment of many thoughtful men tends to become less and less the characteristic note of our present society. If the majority of our citizens possess insufficient private property to be independent of a wage income for even a short period of time, then there is grave danger to the entire social fabric. Social stability rests upon this basis of individual ownership of property. There should be more of it and not less of it, if our existing economic system is to remain secure.

33. The lack of sufficient private property leads to various forms of insecurity. This insecurity not only leads to the creation of a strong social tension expressing itself in social disorder, but is also contrary to the prescriptions of Christian morality. There can be no question but that in our country we possess adequate resources both in respect to raw materials, technical, or scientific skill, and mechanical equipment sufficient to provide both a high standard of living and also comprehensive security for all classes of society. Workingmen should be made secure against unemployment, sickness, accident, old age, and death. The first line of defense against these hazards should be the possession of sufficient private property to provide reasonable security. Industry, therefore, should provide not merely a living wage for the moment but also a saving wage for the future against sickness, old age, death, and unemployment. Individual industries alone, however, cannot in each single case achieve this objective without invoking the principle of social insurance. Some form of government subsidy granted by the entire citizenship through legislative provision seems to be a necessary part of such a program.

34. We cannot overlook the fact that an important factor making for insecurity is the "immense power and despotic economic domination which is concentrated in the hands of a few and that those few are frequently not the owners, but only the trustees and directors of invested funds, who administer them at their good pleasure (p. 32)." Pope Pius XI then singles out one group in an especial manner as exercising this domination and despotic power.

> This power [he states] becomes particularly irresistible when exercised by those who, because they hold and control money, are able also to govern credit and determine its allotment, for that reason supplying, so to speak, the lifeblood to the entire economic body, and grasping as it were in their hands the very soul of production, so that no one dare breathe against their will (pp. 32-33).

35. That there exists a serious problem from the standpoint of security for workingmen is clearly manifest from the present state of unemployment and the present huge demands on government for public relief against dire poverty. Very significantly our present Holy Father Pius XII writes in his letter addressed specifically to the American hierarchy:

> May it also be brought about that each and every able-bodied man may receive an equal opportunity for work in order to earn the daily bread for himself and his own. We deeply lament the lot of those—and their number in the United States is large indeed—who, though robust, capable, and willing, cannot have the work for which they are anxiously searching. May the wisdom of the governing powers, a far-seeing generosity on the part of the employers, together with the speedy reestablishment of more favorable conditions, effect the realization of these reasonable hopes to the advantage of all.[6]

---

[6] *To the Church in the United States (Sertum Laetitiae)* (NCWC edition, 1939), p. 18.

36. We do not wish to imply that individual employers as a class are willfully responsible for this present state of insecurity but we do claim that a system which tolerates such insecurity is both economically unsound and also inconsistent with the demands of social justice and social charity. Security of the workingmen therefore, as against unemployment, old age, sickness, accident, and death, must be frankly accepted as a social responsibility of industry jointly with society. The distribution of the burden justly between the various groups must be determined, first, through mutual council and honest agreement between the employers and the employees, and second, through the regulation of government acting in its sovereign capacity as promoter of the common good.

37. Not all responsibility rests upon the government. In truth a large measure of responsibility rests upon the proper collaboration of employers and employees or of property owners and wage earners. The economic system itself and the principles which guide its executives must help to achieve security by establishing a fair distribution of income between capital and labor. It must strive to establish an equilibrium between farm income and city income. If the rate of wages (not the annual income) of the industrial worker in the city is out of balance with the rate of returns of the farmer in the country, then there is bound to be unemployment and insecurity. Hence the duty of both groups is to work for a just balance between themselves instead of encouraging selfishness and greed which defeat the interest of both, and violate the principles of morality.

38. The same can be said of the various classes of industrial labor. Here also there must be a balance between various groups both organized and unorganized. Unless this be true the economic system cannot function smoothly and there will inevitably be unemployment, because the one class of workingmen cannot buy the high-priced products of the other class of workingmen with their limited income. If skilled laborers, who, through rigid organization, have a monopoly control of their craft, raise their rate of hourly wages too high, they do not gain their advantage exclusively from the wealthy but from the poor also, in terms of excessive prices. Higher wages as a rule should come out of excessive profits and not out of increased prices.

39. Heartening indeed are the beginnings toward the greater security of the people that have already been made through legislative enactment and public policy. The immediate benefits of these laws to working people may be small and some modifications perhaps desirable, but it is highly gratifying that the principle upon which they rest has become a part of our national policy.

IV. Wages

40. In view of the fact that at present many industrial workers and also farm laborers do not possess sufficient private property to provide either a present livelihood or security for the future, the problem of wages assumes outstanding importance. At the outset it is necessary to state that the wage contract itself is not unjust nor in itself vicious as some theorists have falsely contended (p. 22). It is, of course, true that a contract between employers and employees would serve the purpose of individual and social welfare more effectively if it were modified by some form of partnership which would permit a graduated share in the ownership and profits of business and also some voice in its management. It is not intended that labor should assume responsibility for the direction of business, beyond its own competency or legitimate interest; nor has labor a right to demand dominating control over the distribution of profits. To set up such claims would amount to an infringement on the rights of property. Labor has, however, certain definite rights which have been frequently ignored or largely discounted.

41. The first claim of labor, which takes priority over any claim of the owners to profits, respects the right to a living wage. By the term *living wage* we understand a wage sufficient not merely for the decent support of the workingman himself but also of his family. A wage so low that it must be supplemented by the wage of wife and mother or by the children of the family before it can provide adequate food, clothing, and shelter together with essential spiritual and cultural needs cannot be regarded as a living wage.

42. Furthermore, a living wage means sufficient income to meet not merely the present necessities of life but those of unemployment, sickness, death, and old age as well. In other words, a saving wage constitutes an essential part of the definition of a living wage.

43. In the effort to establish a criterion or standard of measurement of wages, it is necessary to consider not only the needs of the workingman but also the state of the business or industry in which he labors. Pope Pius XI states clearly that "it is unjust to demand wages so high that an employer cannot pay them without ruin, and without consequent distress amongst the working people themselves" (p. 21). Bad management, want of enterprise, or out-of-date methods do not constitute a just reason for reducing the wages of workingmen. It still remains true that a living wage constitutes the first charge on industry. If a business is prevented by unfair competition from paying a living wage, and if such competition reduces prices to such a level that decent and just wages cannot be paid, then those responsible are guilty of wrongdoing and sin grievously against moral principles as well as against the common good. The remedy lies, first, in the adequate organization of both employers and employees in their own proper associations and in their joint action; second, in adequate regulation and supervision by the state through proper legislative enactment.

44. No criterion or standard of wages, however, can be determined independently of price. A scale of wages too low, no less than a scale excessively high causes unemployment (p. 25). Likewise a scale of prices too low no less than a scale of prices too high leads to unemployment. Both create hardship and throw the economic system out of its proper equilibrium causing unemployment for the community and hardship even for the individual who is employed, for he must pay too high a price in view of his wages or he receives too low a wage in view of prices. What is needed is a reasonable relationship and a harmonious proportion. Pope Pius XI states:

> Where this harmonious proportion is kept, man's various economic activities combine and unite into one single organism and become members of a common body, lending each other mutual help and service. For then only will the economic and social organism be soundly established and attain its end, when it secures for all and each those goods which the wealth and resources of nature, technical achievement, and the social organization of economic affairs can give. These goods should be sufficient to supply all needs and an honest livelihood, and to uplift men to that high level of prosperity and culture which, provided it be used with prudence, is not only no hindrance but is of singular help to virtue (p. 25).

45. Wages are an essential element in the determination of prices. In the final analysis the cost of raw materials cannot be segregated from wage costs, for the production costs of raw materials presupposes a multiplicity of wage costs as a component element. If wages continuously change, then there must be a continuous change in prices, unless it is assumed that all wage changes will affect only the profits of owners. As a matter of fact they do not. The economic organization might function just as easily on one price level as another, but it cannot function well if the price level is frequently changing. Rapid or frequent fluctuations disturb the harmonious proportions between income and prices not only for owners and employers but also for the workingmen themselves.

46. This consideration is no argument against a necessary increase of wages whenever and wherever the wages are inadequate to provide a decent living. But it is an argument in favor of attaining a relative degree of stability in the price level as soon as commutative justice and social justice permit. A cogent reason for aspiring to such a condition of stability is the higher interest of the family as against the single or unmarried workingman or employee. The single man benefits more from a wage increase than does the family man if the end result is an increase in prices. The family man is penalized in multiple fashion with every increase in prices. Stability in the price level, therefore, and even a reduction in prices as a secular trend is desirable as one means of distributing our national income more widely and more effectively for the common good. Such a long-range policy will supplement the benefits of an increased family wage in view of increased family burdens as recommended by Pius XI.

47. We do not wish to imply that a universal increase of wages will automatically solve our problem of unemployment and idle factories. Some wage increases come not out of the profits of the wealthy but out of the increased prices for the poor. The first requirement, therefore, is that the lowest paid workingman be the first to receive an increase of wages and simultaneously that prices be not raised but excessive profits be reduced. The ultimate aim, therefore, must be a reasonable relationship between different wages and a reasonable relationship between the prices obtained for the products of the various economic groups (p. 25).

48. Because economic society has not followed the moral laws of justice and charity, the principles of interdependence have been violated and we have precipitated unemployment with all its consequent hardships and misery. To withhold just and reasonable wages from the workingman has injured him directly and immediately, but it has also injured the common good and the interests of the very owners of property. Their factories, their commercial establishments, and their equipment have frequently stood idle as a result. Unless workingmen as a class have sufficient income to purchase their share of the goods which our economic system is capable of producing, the markets will automatically be closed to the sale of goods, and idle factories and unemployment are the disastrous result.

V. Establishment of Social Order

49. It would be unreasonable to expect that an economic system which has been predicated upon false principles and which has been operative over many decades could be reorganized suddenly or with the easy gesture of hasty legislation and new administrative policy. We face a problem which requires for its solution intellectual vision, moral integrity, and persevering effort. Many leaders both in the field of management and in the field of labor must first be convinced that economic laws and moral laws are in harmony and not in conflict with one another. No one section of human society can be grievously injured without that injury reacting harmfully in the final analysis upon all other sections of society.

50. The remedy for our problems is not so simple as some would have us think. The solution is to be found in clear thinking and in a right conscience. Relying upon God's providence we dare not be pessimistic but at the same time we frankly recognize that a full restoration to a Christian social order is a matter of steady growth and not a sudden transition.

51. There are two attitudes which represent extreme positions respecting our economic and social order. The one attitude is espoused by those who reject any and every kind of economic planning or organization. They constitute the group of extreme individualists or the so-called school of economic liberalism. They want no interference whatsoever with the individual either from the government or from the social pressure of group organizations. They will tolerate no restrictions upon individual initiative or personal enterprise. They are liberal only to the extent that they wish to be liberated from all social responsibility. They call it free enterprise but the freedom is for those who possess great resources and dominating strength rather than for the weak or those who depend simply on their own labor for their well-being.

52. They oppose all efforts to establish collective bargaining by organized labor and they resent the action of government in enacting laws which make such collective bargaining obligatory. If there is to be any social planning, they will do it themselves without the collaboration of labor, consumers, or the government. They want the government to be restricted to the function of a policeman or umpire in enforcing private contracts but not to be entrusted with the responsibility of promoting justice and the common good.

53. The second group reject totally this attitude of the individualists and rush to the opposite extreme. These latter desire to socialize all resources or establish a state collectivity. Either all property, as in pure Communism, or at least all productive property as in Socialism, should be owned in their theory by the community or by the state. The state or the community thereupon will engage through its bureaus and agencies in developing an elaborate system of national economic planning. The hope, impractical as that method may be, is to make provision for the needs of all citizens so that there will be no surplus and no deficiency. This system would ignore human nature and human rights as flagrantly as the afore-mentioned group of individualists. In fact, experience indicates that where this system has been tried human beings are victimized in a manner and to an extent even more disastrous. Persecution is the logical and inevitable result of such economic dictatorship.

54. Between these two extremes there is a *via media* completely consistent with Christian morality and with sound economic principles. It is manifestly impossible to expect good economic order if wages, prices, working conditions, and the public good are left to chance or to the haphazard methods of so-called free enterprise. "Free competition, however," says Pope Pius XI, "though within certain limits is just and productive of good results, but it cannot be the ruling principle of the economic world." Economic supremacy, he continues, can still less assume this function of a true and effective guiding principle, "for this is a headstrong and vehement power, which, if it is to prove beneficial to mankind, needs to be curbed strongly and ruled with prudence" (p. 29).

55. The true remedy will be found according to the mind of Pope Pius XI in accomplishing two reforms in our social order. In the first place, there must be reestablished some form of guild or vocational groups which will bind men together in society according to their respective occupations, thus creating a moral unity. Second, there must be a reform of morals and a profound renewal of the Christian spirit which must precede the social reconstruction.

56. The social organism has been dismembered and broken up into fragments each seeking its own selfish interests instead of the common good of all. Until the organic nature of society is again recognized and reestablished through vocational groups or guilds, either one of two things must happen. The state must assume all responsibility, that is, become an absolute economic dictatorship or else the individual remains helpless, defenseless, and completely overpowered by those who enjoy economic supremacy.

57. Not only must the moral principles of justice and charity be recognized and accepted by members of society, but the social and economic system itself must be so organized that these principles can freely function and become truly operative. Hence the need of a guild or corporative system which will establish sound prosperity and which respects the proper hierarchic structure of society.[7] Not only must employers and employees be organized singly and jointly but their organizations must be impregnated with Christian moral and social principles or else their work will be sterile or even productive of new disorders.

58. When we speak of the establishment of a right social order, we understand thereby a reform in the concept and organization of the state respecting its responsibility for public welfare; second, a reform in other fundamental social institutions; and third, and quite emphatically, a reform or correction of morals.

59. "When we speak of the reform of the social order," says Pius XI, "it is principally the state we have in mind." The state cannot do all things nor may we hope for salvation from its intervention alone. In fact, the state has been encumbered with all the burdens once borne by associations now extinct. The distinctive function of the state inconsequence has become submerged and its authority overwhelmed by an infinity of affairs and duties (p. 26).

---

[7] *Divini Redemptoris* (NCWC edition, 1937), p. 21, par. 32.

60. The state, however, cannot be relegated to the position of a mere policeman or umpire. It has the responsibility of providing for the common good. On the other hand it may not and should not become totalitarian in attempting to fulfill all social functions in the way of economic planning and direction. It should leave to the smaller vocational groups the settlement of business of lesser importance. It will then be free effectively to accomplish its real function of "directing, watching, stimulating, and restraining, as circumstances suggest or necessity demands" (p. 26).

61. The primary duty of the state and of all good citizens is to abolish conflict between classes with divergent interests. This may at first sight appear to be purely negative. There is, however, a positive responsibility to foster and promote harmony between the various ranks of society and that by specific means. "The aim of social legislation," says Pope Pius XI, "must therefore be the reestablishment of vocational groups" (p. 27).

62. The remedy for the class conflict which makes the labor market an arena where the two armies are engaged in combat, is to be found precisely in the reintegration of the social body by means of vocational groups, "which bind men together not according to the position they occupy in the labor market, but according to the diverse functions which they exercise in society" (p. 27). The chief qualifications of these vocational groups or guilds, as noted by Pius XI, are that they are autonomous, embrace whole industries and professions, are federated with other constituent groups, possess the right of free organization, assembly, and vote, and that they should dedicate themselves to the common good and with governmental protection and assistance function in the establishment of justice and the general welfare in economic life.

63. The state itself in the manner described above and the existing free organizations of economic life should prepare the way for the ideal type of vocational groups or that same corporative economic system of which the pope so frequently speaks, which he so ardently desired to see realized and toward which rightly conducted activities of these organizations can lead (p. 28).

64. The second reform is of equal importance; it is first in the logical order but simultaneous in the order of time. "Nowadays," states Pius XI, "the conditions of social and economic life are such that vast multitudes of men can only with great difficulty pay attention to that one thing necessary, namely, their eternal salvation" (p. 40). There grows in consequence a disorderly affection of the soul, having its source in original sin but aggravated by the present unhappy social conditions. This leads to an unquenchable thirst for riches and temporal possessions, and prompted by this greed for gain there develops a fever of speculation unrestrained by any scruple in committing the gravest injustices against others. The civil authority which might have mitigated the evil failed lamentably in the enforcement of the moral law and the spirit of rationalism already in the ascendant accentuated the evil by giving free rein to an economic science devoid of moral principles (p. 42).

65. The remedy in the spiritual order is a frank and sincere return to the teaching of the Gospel. God must once more be recognized as the supreme end of all created activity; and all created goods as the instruments under God for the attainment of our final destiny. "Seek ye first the Kingdom of God and his justice and all things else will be added unto you" (Mt 6:33).

66. Unfortunately there has been a tendency among too many to dissociate the virtue of justice from the virtue of charity, with the result that life has been made even more selfish and heartless. Charity is no substitute for justice, but it cannot be ignored or derided without failing utterly to comprehend its meaning and its potent influence in regulating and sublimating our social relations and responsibilities. We need justice without doubt or equivocation, but we also need charity if we are to put our lives in harmony with God's plan and promote that spirit of benevolence which will lift the burdens not only from the backs but also from the souls of men.

67. We understand well that a right social order with a lasting and comprehensive peace cannot be achieved solely through improvement in the economic sphere. The present Holy Father states this clearly in his first encyclical letter:

> For true though it is that the evils from which mankind suffers today come in part from economic instability and from the struggle of interests regarding a more equal distribution of the goods which God has given man as a means of sustenance and progress, it is not less true that their root is deeper and more intrinsic, belonging to the sphere of religious belief and moral convictions which have been perverted by the progressive alienation of the people from that unity of doctrine, faith, customs, and morals which once was promoted by the tireless and beneficent work of the Church. If it is to have any effect, the reeducation of mankind must be, above all things, spiritual and religious. Hence, it must proceed from Christ as from its indispensable foundation; must be actuated by justice and crowned by charity.[8]

68. Our economic life then must be reorganized not on the disintegrating principles of individualism but on the constructive principle of social and moral unity among the members of human society. In conformity with Christian principles, economic power must be subordinated to human welfare, both individual and social; social incoherence and class conflict must be replaced by corporate unity and organic function; ruthless competition must give way to just and

---

[8] *Summi Pontificatus* (NCWC edition, 1939), pp. 33, 34.

reasonable state regulations; sordid selfishness must be superseded by social justice and charity. Then only can there be a true and rational social order; then only can we eliminate the twin evils of insufficiency and insecurity, and establish the divine plan of a brotherhood of man under the fatherhood of God.

69. "In the recognition of the royal prerogatives of Christ and in the return of individuals and of society to the law of his truth and of his love lies the only way to salvation."[9]

70. Well-nigh 50 years have passed since the farsighted Pope Leo XIII stated the Catholic principles of social justice for the modern world. His successors have reaffirmed and elaborated upon them. On numerous occasions, individually and collectively, the bishops of the United States have not only stressed their importance but have formulated practical programs for their effective application to conditions in this country.

71. In giving renewed emphasis to these principles, we urge our people again to give them earnest study, so that they may come to know and love the way of justice; and to strengthen themselves spiritually, through prayer and the sacraments, that they may ever follow it. So doing by God's grace they will, as a leaven in society, fulfill their appointed role in the establishment of the Kingdom of God among men.

Given at Washington, D.C.,
Ash Wednesday, February 7,
1940

Samuel A. Stritch, Chairman, Archbishop of Chicago
John Gregory Murray, Archbishop of St. Paul
Joseph F. Rummel, Archbishop of New Orleans
John Mark Gannon, Bishop of Erie
Hugh C. Boyle, Bishop of Pittsburgh
Francis C. Kelly, Bishop of Oklahoma City-Tulsa
John B. Peterson, Bishop of Manchester
Edwin V. O'Hara, Bishop of Kansas City
John A. Duffy, Bishop of Buffalo
Edward F. Hoban, Bishop of Rockford

[9]Ibid., p. 10.

Emmet M. Walsh, Bishop of Charleston
Karl J. Alter, Bishop of Toledo
Charles Hubert LeBlond, Bishop of St. Joseph
Francis P. Keough, Bishop of Providence
Walter A. Foery, Bishop of Syracuse
Bartholomew J. Eustace, Bishop of Camden

Introduction to Five Postwar Statements

The years following World War II brought new prosperity to the United States, especially to the working classes that included the majority of Catholics. The New Deal reforms and the successes of the unionization effort, both of which the American hierarchy supported, began to pay dividends. However, new problems that demanded attention also surfaced.

For the first time, the bishops extended their concern beyond the boundaries of American Catholicism. Earlier episcopal statements on economics offered comfort to a Catholic population suffering various degrees of economic deprivation. Now, however, the bishops were urging newly affluent Catholics to reciprocate by joining in a concerted effort to aid the remaining poor in the United States, many of whom were not part of the Catholic community. The creation of the Campaign for Human Development illustrates the new thrust. Not all Catholics, now increasingly part of the *have* population of America, have welcomed this continuing but now redirected concern for the plight of the poor.

The postwar documents were definitely influenced by the spirit of their period. The first two, in many ways the most comprehensive theological and philosophical statements on economics the bishops have made, reflect the quiet, optimistic ethos of the Eisenhower years. The 1953 statement picks up on several themes that remain prominent in Catholic teaching. It affirms the Incarnation, so important to John Paul II's thinking, as an important theological foundation for understanding religious responsibilities in the economic sphere. There is also a section on the profound relationship between labor and human dignity—again a theme strongly present in John Paul's writings, especially *Laborem Exercens*. Work, the bishops say, enables us "to share in the creative work of God." Both *Laborem Exercens* and the Canadian bishops' statement give this cocreatorship motif a pivotal place in their theological reflections on economics.

The 1953 and 1960 statements emphasize liberty and the sense of personal responsibility it implies. No other document on economics from Rome or Washington assigns the same importance to these twin values. Both statements celebrate liberty and personal responsibility as central to the American experience in general and to our economic system in particular. The opening sentence of the 1960 statement captures their spirit well: "The history and achievements of America stand as a monument to the personal responsibility of free men." Catholics committed to democratic Capitalism as the system most able to provide justice for the greatest number will certainly find strong support for their position in these two documents.

As regards other issues, the 1960 statement reaffirms the principle of subsidiarity. The 1953 statement emphasizes the primacy of personal, inner transformation over mere social and economic reform, though the bishops certainly see the latter as important: "Economic and social reform, to be effective, must be preceded by personal reform."

Obviously, these documents predate both the discovery of widespread poverty in the United States and the call to international economic responsibility that began with John XXIII and the II Vatican Council and continued with Paul VI, the 1971 Synod and John Paul II. It is doubtful that the American bishops will ever write again on moral responsibility in economic affairs as they did in 1953 and 1960. The whole concept of sinful social structures to which the Synods of 1971 and 1974 gave voice had not yet penetrated Catholic consciousness in this country.

The civil rights movement of the sixties and the social activism triggered by the discovery of continuing widespread racism and poverty in America has forced the bishops to move away from uncritical praise for American institutions. Without abandoning the American political ideal or the capitalist system integral to it, they have reminded Catholics of the need to come to grips with these deep-seated social blights. The 1966 and 1970 statements both address racism and poverty in the body politic. The Church has pressed the case of European immigrants for economic justice, the bishops say. Now it is time that Catholics turn their attention to the problems of the Black, Hispanic, and Indian minorities.

The 1966 statement is primarily a list of specific suggestions for the betterment of conditions in which minority people live. While the document is not strong on theory, the shift in focus it represents from preoccupation with the needs of Catholic workers (overwhelmingly white) is extremely important. The statement marks a new posture for the American bishops, not unlike the one Leo XIII took. Defense of the poor may now mean speaking words of judgment to important elements of the Catholic community.

The brief 1970 document launching the Campaign for Human Development reiterates the 1966 statement's deep concern about poverty. Such poverty cannot be tolerated in the midst of great wealth.

> Poverty in the United States is a cruel anachronism today. At a time when most Americans enjoy unparalleled material bounty, it is

> unthinkable that some Americans should still be condemned to live out their lives within the 'hellish circle' of want. If we close our eyes to the continuing existence of poverty in our nation, we are vulnerable to the accusation of spiritual blindness and moral insensitivity.

This document, influenced by the thought of Paul VI, moves the Church in America toward realizing the need to change sinful social structures that keep the poor in a condition of dependency. The bishops know that the self-help projects to be funded by the Campaign will be a drop in the bucket. Ultimately our national economic structures require adjustment. It is their hope, however, that these projects will break the dependency cycle for some and, more importantly, serve as a catalyst for a much broader national attack on this dehumanizing cycle.

The recession of the seventies brought American consciousness of economic reality to yet another stage. Naive optimism had certainly vanished, but now it was no longer the alleviation of poverty among minorities that concerned the bishops. Scores of people who had *made it* were now unemployed or underemployed. Looking back to that period from the perspective of the eighties, we can see the problems that surfaced at this time were merely the tip of the iceberg. We have had to face the possibility that the American economic system might no longer grow to bring every citizen up to a decent standard of living. Americans might have to make some hard choices. Though the American economy recovered from the recession, many of the structural problems it revealed have not been solved.

The 1975 document serves as an introductory reflection on how Catholics might approach these continuing economic dilemmas. It gives a summary of the basic principles that must be applied, including viewing economic sustainability as a right, measuring economic success more by the distribution of wealth than by its accumulation, acknowledging every person's right to employment, holding government responsible for providing employment when the private sector cannot do so, and accepting the need for broad participation in decisions about economic development. All these principles show the influence of the teachings of the II Vatican Council, John XXIII, and Paul VI. The bishops also recognize important new problems such as inflation. Finally, they are sensitive to the powerful link between the distribution of wealth and societal power. "The distribution of income and wealth are important since they influence and even determine our society's distribution of economic power. Catholic social teaching has condemned gross inequality in the distribution of material goods. Our country cannot continue to ignore this important measure of economic justice."

Two final points should be made about all five postwar documents. First, none of them appeals to natural law as a basis for analyzing economic issues. This is consistent with a growing movement away from a reliance on natural law argumentation. This trend is visible in Vatican documents since the II Vatican Council as well as in American ones. Second, like the Depression-era documents, none of these statements repeats the call for shared decision-making and shared ownership that were stressed in the 1919 *Program of Social Reconstruction*. This theme seems to have fallen by the wayside in American episcopal thinking on economic justice.

The dip in national prosperity that first appeared in the mid-seventies will likely accelerate, spurring the bishops to further reflection on the economy in light of Catholic social thought. They will inevitably challenge American Catholics, who have steadily assumed more prominent roles in political and economic decision-making. The bishops' prophetic voice likely will remain a source of tension in the Church in America as they continue to speak out on behalf of the poor, not only in this country but throughout the world.

A Statement on Man's Dignity

A Statement Issued by the NCWC
Administrative Board in the Name of the
Bishops of the United States

November 21, 1953

1. Every man knows instinctively that he is, somehow, a superior being. He knows he is superior to the land he tills, the machine he operates, or the animals which are at his service. Even when unable to define this superiority in terms of "honor" and "dignity," if a man enjoys the fruits of his nobility, he is content and accepts that status as his due; lacking honor and dignity for any cause, a man is restless, depressed, even rebellious because something proper to him, as a man, is withheld or denied.

2. The Catholic Church has always taught and defended the natural dignity of every human being. She has preached the burden of individual responsibility and has insisted upon the importance of personal conscience. She has reminded mankind that there is a great division between "things" and "men." She has never forgotten that "things were made for men" and that "men were made for God."

3. In thus holding up a mirror to men that they may see their own greatness and realize their personal dignity, the Catholic Church has taught that man's true honor is from God, has been enhanced spiritually by Divine Grace, and is preserved without degradation only when the honor and dignity of God himself are first maintained.

4. Often in times past men have failed to live up to the honor of their state. They have degraded their dignity in many ways. But, always till now, violence and vice, injustice and oppression or any other assaults on human dignity were recognized as abominations and were so abhorred. It has remained for our day to attempt to disregard human personality and to fortify such disregard with the force of legislation or the approbation of custom, as if a man were only a "thing." The present has been described as a rationally established inhumanity working with all the expedients of administrative and mechanical techniques. Our Holy Father, Pope Pius XII, in his 1952 Christmas allocution, gave warning of the attempted mechanization of mankind and protested the stripping of personality from men by legal or social devices. The bishops of the United States, conscious of the growing depersonalization of man, reaffirm man's essential dignity and reassert the rights which flow from it.

Roots of Human Dignity

5. Man's essential worth derives from a threefold source: from the fact of his creation, from the mode of his existence, and from the nobility of his destiny.

6. The mere fact that any creature exists at all requires the creative and sustaining power of God. When God exercises this power to summon any possible reality into actual existence, that reality is thereby sealed with value from within. Such a dignity man shares with the animal and material world around him.

7. But his special type of existence confers on man a special claim to honor. Though immersed in a universe of fleeting and random sensations, he is endowed with an intellect able to pierce the flux of passing images and discover beneath them enduring patterns of truth. Though subjected to the pressures of his environment, and a prey to unthinking appetites, he is endowed with a self-determining will capable of choosing wisely within the framework of law.

8. Intellect and will, then, are man's distinctive adornments. It is their distinctive role to allow a finite creature to grasp truth consciously and to choose goodness freely, and thus to mirror the Infinite Creator who is conscious Truth and absolute Goodness.

9. Man's natural honor, however, has been enhanced by grace, conferred at creation, lost through sin, but restored through the incarnation and redemption of our Lord and Savior, Jesus Christ. When the Son of God took human flesh as an instrument of salvation, all human flesh was honored by his association with it. Through his death and resurrection Christ demonstrated the role and destiny, the honor and dignity of every man for whom he lived and suffered. Since those days of Christ on earth, no man lives by his body alone, nor by the natural powers of his soul alone; every man is sanctified, made holy, made more worthy and more honorable by the enjoyment of the special spiritual life which flows from the cross, or by the possibility that this life will one day be his, to raise him above the limitations of nature, to honor him in unending union with the God who became man.

10. Such is the triple fountain of man's dignity. To the extent these truths cease to energize the sense of reverence in every man, assaults upon the majesty of the human person must increase and intensify. Heedless that his nature has God for its origin and destiny, and reason and revelation for its divinely commissioned guide, man will do what no other creature can—he will deny his true nature and will destroy all that is good within himself.

Man's Dignity and the Body

11. Such a process of degradation is viciously at work in our own country, where the deification of the flesh continues to enlist new devotees. Through its liturgy of advertisement, entertainment, and literature, this cult bids fair to corrode our national sense of decency. When reason abdicates its sovereignty over bodily energies, their purpose is destroyed; and, by a sort of instinctive vengeance, they themselves become destroyers. Like wild animals, these energies are hard to tame, and remain dangerous even when tamed. But whatever lawful use an animal may serve, it is not wisdom for man to accept as his master the lion who seeks to devour him.

12. The Catholic Church, however, has never failed to accord the human body an immense measure of honor. She affirms that it was originally created by God; in one instance actually assumed by him; in every instance meant to be on earth his special temple, and destined eventually to rejoin the soul in his beatific presence. Whatever is uncompromising in her teaching about the body stems from her realism on two points: the body, though good, is not the highest good; and the undisciplined body is notoriously bad.

13. Other sacrileges against personality flow from errors less crude perhaps, but hardly less injurious. Such are some prevailing misconceptions about society, liberty, economics, labor, and education.

Man's Dignity and Society

14. The practical social theory of the last century enthroned the individual but not the person. An individual can be a thing: as for instance an individual tree; but in virtue of his rational soul, a person is more than a thing. Yet the depersonalized view of man gained ascendancy, and generated a society which was a crisscross of individual egotisms, and in which each man sought his own.

15. Against this error our century has seen a reaction which has sought to overcome the isolation of man from man by imposing upon rebellious individuals a pattern of compulsory and all-embracing state organization, with unlimited power in the hands of the civil government. Hence Socialism in its various guises has appeared as forcible organization imposed upon the confusion which resulted from false concepts of human freedom.

16. The Christian concept of man, however, is that he is both personal and social. As a person he has rights independent of the state; as a member of society he has social obligations. Parents and society contribute to the making of a man, hence man is indebted to the social order. At the same time, since his soul comes not from society but from God, a man has rights which no society may violate. The state is a creature of man, but man is a creature of God; hence the state exists for man, not man for the state.

Man's Dignity and Liberty

17. The Christian view, then, avoids the opposing extremes of individualism and collectivism, both of which are grounded on false concepts of liberty—either the unfettered liberty of individualism, which gives the "individual" the right to ignore society; or the unfettered liberty of dictatorship, which gives the government the right to ignore the person by absorbing him into a race or class, thus destroying his freedom of choice. The false liberty of individualism wrecks society by defining freedom as individual license; the false liberty of dictatorship wrecks humanity by defining freedom as the right of a dictator to nullify the person—a right which he claims to derive from social necessity.

18. Concerning the results of such false notions of liberty, Leo XIII issued these warnings:

> The true liberty of human society does not consist in every man doing what he pleases, for this would simply end in turmoil and confusion, and bring on the overthrow of the state . . . likewise, liberty does not consist in the power of those in authority to lay unreasonable and capricious demands upon their subjects, a course which would be equally criminal, and would lead to the ruin of the commonwealth.

19. Liberty in political life may be described as the condition in which the individual finds himself unhampered in the discharge of his duties and in the exercise of his rights. Liberty, however, is something more than a political phenomenon as tyrannical dictatorship contends; it is more than an economic phenomenon as some disciples of free enterprise maintain. It is something more mature than that dream of rights without responsibilities which historic liberalism envisioned; it is certainly different from that terrorism of responsibilities without rights which Communism imposes. It is something wiser than free thought, and something freer than dictated thought. For freedom has its roots in man's spiritual nature. It does not arise out of any social organization, or any constitution, or any party, but out of the soul of man. Hence to the whole tradition of the Western world, liberty does not come essentially from improved conditions of living, either political or economic, but is rather the spring out of which better conditions must flow. A free spirit creates free institutions; a slave spirit permits the creation of tyrannical ones.

Man's Dignity and Economics

20. Closely connected with freedom and human dignity is the right of private property. On the question of private property the aforementioned misconceptions of liberty beget two other extremes: first the belief that a man's right to property is absolute, and that he may do with it what he pleases, without regard for the moral law or social justice, and, second, the reactionary error of Communism, which denies all personal rights and lodges all property in the hands of the state.
21. The Christian position maintains that the right to property is personal, while the use of property is also social. Unrestrained Capitalism makes its mistake by divorcing property rights from social use; Communism hits wide of the mark by considering social use apart from personal rights.
22. Much of our economic restlessness, however, is the festering of man's wounded dignity. Karl Marx himself was perceptive enough to see that "Democracy is based on the principle of the sovereign worth of the individual, which, in turn, is based on the dream of Christianity that man has an immortal soul" (*Marx-Engels Historical-Critical Edition*, Karl Marx Institute, Moscow, vol. I, no. 1, p. 590).
23. Ignoring the testimony of both reason and revelation and believing the "dream" to be only a dream, modern men have tended to concentrate almost exclusively on economic security and to pursue it at times with the fervor of religious devotion.
24. Often the hope is voiced that man will turn to the cultivation of the spirit after all his economic needs are supplied. We are reminded of the delusion of Jean Jacques Rousseau that man, good in himself, has been corrupted only by society. Marxism, changing the formula, gives the same false primacy to external circumstances—man's goodness will depend upon the economic system under which he lives. But the exclusive dependence on economic security and social reform to right the wrongs of mankind is by no means confined to Marxism. It affects the thought of great masses of men who reject the fundamental tenets of Marxism.
25. While we have deep sympathy with all people in their craving for economic security and while we acknowledge the evils, individual and spiritual as well as social, which often flourish in a society when many are forced to live in conditions of degrading poverty, yet we cannot refrain from pointing out the fact that man's goodness is from within. It depends upon man's personal convictions and upon his efforts aided by God's grace. Economic and social reform, to be effective, must be preceded by personal reform. The perfection of a society may not be measured by the moral goodness of the individuals who

compose it; but the goodness of a society cannot rise above the goodness of its members.

26. The position of the Church relative to the economic order is based on the principle that the rights man possesses as an individual and the function he fulfills in society are inseparable. Many of the rights of the individual depend upon the function he fulfills in society. Capital and labor from this point of view are related and made inseparable by the common good of society. This is a prime principle of social justice. The right of the capitalist to his business and to his profits and interest, and the right of the laborer to his wages and his union, are both conditioned by their service to the common good.

Man's Dignity and Labor

27. It is only in the light of the spiritual worth of man that the dignity and importance of labor become evident. Labor is not something detached from the rest of life. Economically, it is bound up with capital as a copartner in production. Socially, it is bound up with leisure as an avenue to cultural enrichment. Spiritually, it is bound up with the soul's development and with salvation. The worker is not a hand, as individualistic Capitalism contends; not a stomach to be fed by commissars, as Communism thinks; but a person who through his labor establishes three relations: with God, with his neighbor, and with the whole natural world.

28. First of all, work unites us to God not only by its ascetic character and through the discipline it imposes on man by subjugating his lower passions to order and reason, but principally because, through the intention of the worker, the material universe is brought back again to God.

29. Second, labor is also the bond uniting man to man, a kind of school of social service, a base of human solidarity, a testimonial to man's insufficiency without his neighbor. In working with others, man ratifies his social dependence and performs an act of natural charity, because he helps create utility for others and thus promotes the happiness of his fellow men. The Catholic view, it will be noted here, adds that labor must always be used, not to dissociate ourselves from our neighbor, but to unite us with him. The greater the material advancement of any country, therefore, the more energetic should be its spirit of neighborliness.

30. Finally, work unites us with nature. It does this by enabling us to share in the creative work of God and by making each of us, in the language of St. Paul, "a helper of God." God, the supreme artist, has communicated artistic causality to men, so that they can now make things and shape events to the image and likeness of their own ideas. The marriage of man's intelligence and will with the material world and the natural forces with which he is surrounded becomes a fruitful union, and from them is generated a culture.

Man's Dignity and Education

31. In transmitting culture from generation to generation, it is the purpose of education to safeguard and develop the dignity of man. At the end of the eighteenth century our first president spoke of religion and morality as indispensable supports of political prosperity. At the end of the nineteenth century our highest court declared that "The reasons presented affirm and reaffirm that this is a religious nation." What is true of our political prosperity and our nation is true as well of our Western culture in general. Yet everywhere modern education is being drained of moral content through the movement which is known as secularism. It has been well said that the education of the soul is the soul of education. Therefore when education tries to thrive in a religious and moral vacuum, and does not aspire to impart a set of principles and a hierarchy of values, it degenerates into a dead and deadening juxtaposition of facts.
32. And even worse. For though it tries to thrive in such a vacuum, education can never really be neutral in practice. It has been truly said that "men must be governed by God or they will be ruled by tyrants." Similarly, education must inculcate a religious and moral outlook, or it will inculcate a materialistic one. And there is no word for dignity in the vocabulary of materialism.

Conclusion

33. Every day in Holy Mass, Almighty God is addressed as he who wondrously established the dignity of man, and restored it more wondrously still. Only by regaining our reverence for God can we of America in the twentieth century rediscover both our own value and the solid basis on which it rests. We must at the same time expend every effort to see that this dignity is reflected in our sense of decency, made aware of itself by education, nurtured by society, guarded by the state, stabilized by private ownership, and exercised through creative activity.
34. The alternative is increasing chaos. The words of a contemporary historian of culture may serve to summarize the issues at stake:

> Unless we find a way to restore the contact between the life of society and the life of the spirit, our civilization will be destroyed by forces which it has had the knowledge to create but not the wisdom to control.

Signed by the members of the Administrative Board, National Catholic Welfare Conference, in the names of the bishops of the United States

Edward Cardinal Mooney, Archbishop of Detroit

Samuel Cardinal Stritch, Archbishop of Chicago

Francis Cardinal Spellman, Archbishop of New York

James Francis Cardinal McIntyre, Archbishop of Los Angeles

John J. Mitty, Archbishop of San Francisco

Richard J. Cushing, Archbishop of Boston

Patrick A. O'Boyle, Archbishop of Washington

John F. O'Hara, Archbishop of Philadelphia

Karl J. Alter, Archbishop of Cincinnati

John F. Noll, Bishop of Fort Wayne

Michael J. Ready, Bishop of Columbus

Emmet M. Walsh, Coadjutor Bishop of Youngstown

Thomas K. Gorman, Coadjutor Bishop of Dallas

Matthew F. Brady, Bishop of Manchester

A Statement on Personal Responsibility

A Statement Issued by the Catholic Bishops of the United States

November 20, 1960

1. The history and achievements of America stand as a monument to the personal responsibility of free men. Our institutions and our industry, the fruit of the American sense of responsibility, have in the past inspired, guided, and helped many other nations of the world. If our future is to be worthy of our past, if the fruit of America's promise is not to wither before it has reached full maturity, our present preeminent need is to reaffirm the sense of individual obligation, to place clearly before ourselves the foundation on which personal responsibility rests, to determine the causes of its decay and to seek the means by which it can be revived.

2. The foremost signs of the decline of personal responsibility are to be found in the family. Marriage, a sacred and binding contract, all too often is considered merely as an arbitrary arrangement to satisfy the instinct of pleasure. The failure of parents to fulfill their responsibilities, as revealed in the frequency of divorce, desertion, and broken homes, is a national disgrace. Any delinquency of parents may well be reflected in the delinquency of youth, which is now commonly considered our greatest national domestic problem.

Personal Responsibility and Industry

3. Equally conspicuous is the evidence of decline in the sense of responsibility within our industrial organization and in our general economic life. At a time when so much depends upon the soundness of our economy and upon our ability to produce to meet the needs of a rapidly developing world, we have been faced by a frequent lack of truly responsible leadership, both on the part of management and of labor. Among the evident instances of the breakdown of personal responsibility most deplorable has been the widespread cynical reaction to the recent revelation of dishonesty, waste, and malfeasance in industrial relations.

4. Although personal responsibility and initiative have been our national characteristics, explaining in large measure our country's progress in human welfare, yet pressures are growing for a constantly greater reliance on the collectivity rather than on the individual. An inordinate demand for benefits, most easily secured by the pressures of organization, has led an evergrowing number of our people to relinquish their rights and to abdicate their responsibilities. This concession creates a widening spiral of increasing demands and pressures with a further infringement on personal freedom and responsibility. The result is the condition recently noted by our Holy Father: "Modern man sees that the sphere in which he can think for himself, act on his own initiative, exercise his responsibilities, and affirm and enrich his personality is in many cases restricted to an excessive degree" (Letter of July 12, 1960, to the "Semaine Sociale" in Grenoble). Intensive socialization can achieve mass benefits, but man and morality can be seriously hurt in the process.

5. This tendency to delegate excessive responsibility to an organization is discernible also in the realm of international affairs. Some manifest no sense of personal responsibility in the affairs of the international community. On the other hand, many citizens seem to feel that our mere adherence to the United Nations absolves us from further responsibility in the international order and that decisions made by the United Nations, regardless of their objective value, are always to be regarded as morally right. Admitting the undoubted value of a policy of supporting the United Nations and recognizing the genuine contribution it has made in many areas, we must understand clearly that the citizens of this country, and of all countries, have a responsibility to judge and to evaluate the United Nations' deliberations and decisions according to objective norms of morality universally binding. This involves also the duty of citizens to make proper representation of such judgment to their respective governments.

Rejection of Personal Responsibility

6. However varied the above-mentioned evils, ranging from the single act of wrongdoing to the moral laxity of the mass mind, the root cause is the same—the rejection of personal responsibility. This is a moral evil, as are all the major ills that beset the present world. As such their cure is largely within the power of individual persons. A godly society is the work of godly men. Even the most universal evil and the threatened mechanization of man can be made to yield before the just and determined will of individual persons.

7. Our Holy Father has pointed out the capacity of the individual in the face of such problems.

> Does it follow that the process of socialization is impossible to control and that, increasing constantly in its breadth and depth, it will one day surely reduce men to the role of automatons? Certainly not. For socialization is not the result of forces of nature acting according to determinism that cannot be changed. It is the work of man, of a free being conscious of and responsible for his acts (Letter of July 12, 1960, to "Semaine Sociale" in Grenoble).

8. In our national life we have experienced the truth of this statement. Our progress has been achieved chiefly according to the measure of individual commitment to responsibility. The heroes of our history have not been blind forces but stouthearted persons; our worthy national goals have been achieved not as a result of environment but by men who made their environment. A strong and responsible nation is fashioned by responsible persons, not group pressures. As Pope Pius XII stated: "The people live from the fullness of the life of the men who make it up; each of them in his place and in the manner proper to him is a person conscious of his own convictions" (Christmas Message, 1944).

9. What is personal responsibility in the context of man's relation to the world? It presupposes the acceptance of one's dignity as a son of God in whatever environment he may be placed and the acknowledgement of binding moral law. It requires the free and deliberate acceptance of one's obligations in the position he occupies—in the family, in the Church, in the corporation, in the labor union, in the nation, in the family of nations. It demands the rule of conscience, not self-satisfaction. It recognizes that every deliberate action of the human person has a relationship with his creator and his purpose in creating the world. It affirms that every human action a man performs derives its significance from that relationship and makes him a cooperator with his creator in forwarding the Kingdom of God. It is a solemn profession that consequently every product of his mind and his hand, every bounty wrung from the earth is to serve that high purpose. As man, bearing the image of his creator, is the brother of every other human person, his noblest work is to bring to his fellow man the blessings of the destiny intended for him by God.

10. It must be emphasized, especially in these times, that the freedom innate in man, as well as the social nature he enjoys, demands as a correlative the fullest personal responsibility. "Therefore every one of us will render an account for himself to God" (Rom 14:12). The marvelous inventiveness of the human mind, conquering space and making each man a neighbor of every other human being on earth, gives urgency to this twofold need: to maintain one's freedom by using it according to the limits and norms of rightful authority; to use it also according to his social nature and the needs of his fellow man.

> For you have been called to liberty, brethren; only do not use liberty as an occasion for sensuality but by charity serve one another. For the whole law is fulfilled in one word, "Thou shalt love thy neighbor as thyself" (Gal 5:13-14).

The social pressures of today's complex life do not excuse from, but rather create a demand for, a greater exercise of personal responsibility. No man can be neutral in a moral cause. By his creation he is born to be committed to the cause of God. The more difficult the situation the more imperative the need for such a commitment.

11. If we are to restore man to his sense of personal responsibility and to the acceptance of life as a mission, we must understand more clearly the moral causes which have undermined men's sense of responsibility.

12. First among these causes has been the marked decline in the force of religious convictions. Washington warned the American people that they should indulge with caution the supposition that national morality could exist without religion. In spite of the much discussed increase of church membership it cannot be doubted that for a long time religious influences have been losing their vigor among the American people, with a debilitating effect in consequence on both public and private life.

13. As a result of this decline of religious convictions the grasp on moral principles has been greatly weakened. Through a faulty concept of morality, modern man has come to imagine that sudden and drastic changes in situations change principles; that principles no longer control situations, but rather that situations shape principles. Inevitably this type of "situational ethics" denies all unchanging principles and makes futile all moral judgments on which the sense of responsibility rests. The need which the world faces is the acceptance of an objective norm of morality, and hence of conduct.

14. This decline in religious belief and moral conviction leaves modern man blind to his immutable spiritual nature. Thus, wittingly or unwittingly, he aligns himself with the forces of materialism among whose tenets there is no room for the concept of personal responsibility.

15. Finally, the social ideals and purposes of modern man, due to the declining influence of religious and moral convictions and to the triumph of the material, tend in many subtle ways to efface the sense of responsibility. As a people we seem to be moving more deeply into a sensate culture. There is an excessive preoccupation with material security at the expense of spiritual well-being. Uniformity of thought and supine loyalty to the organization, whether it be the industrial corporation, the labor union, or the political party, are too often encouraged and rewarded. The organizational man, cloaked in a sort of anonymity, rather than the responsible individual, is favored and advanced. The preparation for this condition is found even in the field of education, where emphasis is placed on adapting oneself to the thinking of the group. The pattern is so prevalent that some psychologists consider juvenile delinquency as a revolt, just for the sake of rebellion, against a stifling uniformity that fails to challenge the individuality of the student.

16. The correction of these basically moral evils and the restoration of a vigorous sense of personal responsibility belong primarily to the field of religion. The development of a truly Christian character is primarily the task of religion, although its inculcation is of vital concern to the state. It is the function of religion to teach man his unique dignity as a son of God and brother of Christ. Pope Pius XII explicitly stated this in describing the function of the Church:

> Always and everywhere, by unceasingly adapting herself to the circumstances of time and place, she seeks to model persons, individuals, and, as far as possible, all individuals according to the laws of Christ, thus attaining the moral basis for social life. The object of the Church is man, naturally good, imbued, ennobled, and strengthened by the truth and grace of Christ (September 19, 1955).

Religion Promotes Responsibility

17. Deepened religious convictions will bolster and reactivate the sense of personal responsibility. We must seek to enlarge the area of personal autonomy to protect the human personality from a greater encroachment on its freedom and responsibility. The individual person must assume as his proud right the accomplishment of whatever he can for himself and for others, especially those of his family, and herein lies the importance of the Christian home. The same principle of responsibility must be consistently applied to every level of action. Pope Pius XI explicitly emphasized this principle of subsidiarity in the *Quadragesimo Anno* published in 1931:

> Just as one cannot take away from individuals and transfer to the community the tasks they are capable of accomplishing by themselves, thus it would also be an injustice—and at the same time a harmful disturbance of the social order—if one were to remove from groups of lower rank functions they can exercise themselves and entrust them to a wider collectivity of higher rank. The natural objective of any intervention in social matters is to assist the members of the social body and not to destroy or absorb them.

18. Even when man enters into associations, as he must to achieve the goals which lie beyond his individual capacity, he should remember their purpose is in relation to his freedom and responsibility. In this respect, the Holy Father stated:

> But this is to be done on the condition that each of these institutions remains within its own sphere of responsibility; that it be offered to, not imposed upon, the free choice of mankind. They must under no circumstances look upon themselves as an end making their members an instrument of their activity (Letter of July 12, 1960, to "Semaine Sociale" in Grenoble).

19. A fresh evocation of the principle and practice of personal responsibility can revivify our society and help to stem the seemingly inexorable march toward the automation of human beings and the steady loss of that freedom which is man's distinctive attribute. It will cure the mental lethargy and inertia which permit organizations to usurp, mainly by default, the rights of their members. It will stimulate a self-reliance which will automatically restore the balance between freedom and security. It will reject unwarranted pressure from groups that seek unjustly to aggrandize their power and will restrict them to their lawful ends. It will see in all business ventures of whatever size a means of serving others as well as self. It will have an immediate effect in every sphere of life—in the home, in the office, as well as in the workshop, in the factory, in our schools, in our cultural groups.

Individual Responsibility

20. An effective response to a call for personal responsibility need not wait for a mass movement. The response belongs to the individual person, as our Holy Father indicated:

> Fully conscious of what is at stake, moved by his apostolic zeal, he then makes a personal engagement with these communities that surround him, the result of a free and justified choice of careful thought about himself, his destiny, and the world (Letter of July 12, 1960, to "Semaine Sociale" in Grenoble).

Such a response by a representative number, given only in the silent sanctuary of the heart, will begin to have its leavening effect. Our appeal for action is made directly to our Catholic fellow citizens, but it reaches out also to all Americans who face the same problems as ourselves.

21. Before it is too late, we must revive in our midst and present to the world the ideals that have been the real source of national greatness. For America will fulfill its destiny when we have achieved that spiritual maturity, described by Pope Pius XII, as men,

> established in their inviolable integrity as images of God; men proud of their personal dignity and of their wholesome freedom; men justly jealous of their equality with their fellow creatures in all that concerns the most intimate depths of human dignity; men solidly attached to their land and their tradition (Pope Pius XII, February 20, 1946).

Signed by members of the Administrative Board, National Catholic Welfare Conference, in the name of the bishops of the United States

Francis Cardinal Spellman,
Archbishop of New York

James Francis Cardinal McIntyre,
Archbishop of Los Angeles

Richard Cardinal Cushing,
Archbishop of Boston

Aloisius Cardinal Muench,
Roman Curia

Albert Cardinal Meyer,
Archbishop of Chicago

Karl J. Alter, Archbishop of
Cincinnati, Chairman

Joseph E. Ritter, Archbishop of
St. Louis

Patrick A. O'Boyle, Archbishop
of Washington

Leo Binz, Archbishop of
Dubuque

William O. Brady, Archbishop of
St. Paul

Joseph M. Gilmore, Bishop of
Helena

Joseph T. McGucken, Bishop of
Sacramento

Lawrence J. Shehan, Bishop of
Bridgeport

Allen J. Babcock, Bishop of
Grand Rapids

Albert R. Zuroweste, Bishop of
Belleville

Pastoral Statement on Race Relations and Poverty

A Statement Issued by the National Conference of Catholic Bishops

November 19, 1966

1. The pastoral concern of the bishops of the United States goes to the poor in our midst, particularly to those who have felt the heavy burden of discrimination. This means, in our day, racial discrimination.

2. These are turbulent days, marked by severe social strains and civic clashes. We are grateful that much progress in civil rights legislation has been made in recent years. Laws have been passed to eliminate discrimination in our nation and to open voting to all. We urge the vigorous use of all legal means to assure their prompt implementation.

3. Comprehensive programs to eradicate poverty have been begun. We ask for strong and continuing support for them and constant efforts to improve them. However, the great task of changing the hearts of men on the subject of equal rights for all requires more than laws and programs. It needs above all a true sense of neighborliness, based upon a religiously inspired conviction that all men are equal before God and that all should be welcomed in our midst.

4. We note with sorrow that civil strife is an everpresent danger. There have been riots in our cities. Racial antagonism has been fostered and continues to be fostered under many emotionally charged and irrational slogans. Moreover, we are still confronted with the depressing problems of poverty, joblessness, and urban and rural slums.

Suffering Minorities

5. As American citizens, we deplore the fact that such conditions exist in a nation so endowed with wealth. As Christian leaders, we must repeat the constant refrain of recent popes and of Vatican Council II, that material goods are held in stewardship for the welfare of all men. Destitution and degrading, avoidable poverty hurt family life, blight the promise of youth, and lead to a bitter harvest of sickness, delinquency, and crime.

6. The problem of poverty is inflicted particularly upon minority groups in our society. The Negro, the Spanish-speaking, and the Indian suffer inordinately under this burden. Nearly half the members of these groups live in poverty. Their unemployment rate is double the national average. They are far more likely than others to be condemned to urban or rural slums.

7. While there are many causes of poverty, most are connected with past or present discrimination. Hence, we affirm once again, as we did in our statement of 1958 and our letter of 1963, and on many occasions in the pronouncements of Vatican Council II, that discrimination based on race, language, religion, or national origins is contrary to right reason and to Christian teaching.

8. We are all the children of God. We share the same rights before God and man. All men of good will desire that the doors of opportunity be opened equally to all who are their brothers under one eternal Father.

9. These statements of principles are so clear and so widely accepted that it is not necessary to dwell upon them here. Our present concern is to reduce principles to action, ideals to programs. In light of these considerations, we respectfully propose the following pastoral suggestions. While these are general in nature, it is our hope that they can be translated, in our cities and throughout our nation, into specific and workable social programs.

10. First, in the current discussion of racial tensions slogans have at times taken the place of reasonable dialogue. We ask that dialogue replace slogans. It would be tragic were our nation to suffer a deepening of the cleavages along racial or economic lines, with shouted epithets of hate replacing reasoned discourse.

11. Since the aggrieved in our nation are mostly the poor and the members of minority groups, it is the clear duty of those who have jobs and status to talk openly and freely to those who have been less fortunate. We must learn, and learn firsthand, what it is to be a poor Negro, a neglected Spanish-American, or a disfranchised Indian.

Beginning of Solution

12. Open discussion of these problems is the beginning of their solution. It is our hope that all our Catholic people will join with their Christian and Jewish brothers, and indeed with all men of good will, in common projects which affirm and realize the dignity of all men.

13. Second, we ask that a concentrated attack upon poverty be mounted upon many fronts. This is a complex problem and its solutions are equally complex. There is work that can be done by individuals, by religious groups, and by the community organizations.

14. Other aspects of this problem require a strong governmental intervention at appropriate levels. We wish to suggest certain objectives that seem to us paramount at this time and which require adaptation to different places in their application.

15. Foremost among these is the quality of education given to the poor. The poorly educated child and the school dropout face life with almost insuperable handicaps in our society. Communities should be concerned about the quality of teachers, schools, guidance programs, and the supplementary aids needed by all children.

16. Adult education is also a great necessity. Citizens in every city, and in our rural areas, should examine critically the type of education afforded to the poor at all age levels and act decisively to make educational opportunities equal for all.

17. Next, we should be concerned with the type and quality of assistance available to poor families. Where welfare relief is necessary, it should be given in a context that favors family stability and respects the human dignity of those who cannot earn their living. Such programs should help maintain the father in the home and be joined, where need be, with training facilities to enable the unemployed to secure gainful work. These programs should offer incentives to part-time or temporary employment, often refused today because of regulations that penalize such efforts.

18. A key concern is job opportunity. This problem has two main facets: realistic training joined with proper motivation and the willingness of employers to hire and promote without discrimination. Unions likewise should open their membership rolls to all without discrimination. We especially compliment those employers and unions which have agreed to take affirmative actions to secure a fully integrated working force. Such open attitudes best express the Christian response to racial discrimination.

Problem of Housing

19. Finally, there is the problem of adequate housing. Millions of Americans live in overcrowded substandard homes. Under such conditions, it is difficult to promote sound family life, to encourage education, or to bring about stable, peaceful neighborhoods.

20. Our citizens, our civic groups, and our churches should be eager to use the opportunities they now have to promote low-cost housing for the poor, to build well-planned public housing units, and to rehabilitate rundown neighborhoods.

21. But this is only part of the task. As our nation becomes increasingly suburban, industry and service occupations are expanding far more rapidly in the suburbs than in our inner cities. We cannot hope to solve the problem of joblessness in our cities if men and women are denied the opportunity of living near possible places where work is available.

22. While the issue of fair housing has been the source of grave tensions in some parts of our nation, conditions have noticeably improved in certain areas. We urge support for sound programs to assure equal housing opportunities for all, without discrimination based on race, creed, or color. Here is a unique chance for responsible dialogue, for learning from successes and from failures, and thus constructing harmonious communities in every part of our nation.

23. We ask these steps out of our pastoral concern for all who are in need. In this world, under God's providence, our nation has been cast into a position of world leadership. This stems in part from our economic and military power, but it is also a recognition of certain unique elements in our democracy. More than most peoples in recorded history, we have striven to make all men equal under law.

24. Today the world watches us anxiously, as it reads of racial struggles and tensions and learns about poverty in an affluent society. If men elsewhere become disillusioned with our democracy, they are offered the choice of another powerful system which also promises equality, but at the sacrifice of basic freedoms.

25. Ours is a fateful choice, one which can decide the destiny, not merely of this American nation, but possibly of the entire world. In this instance at least, what is morally right is a political imperative. Prayerfully, we commend these thoughts to our Catholic people and to all our fellow citizens who share our hopes.

Resolution on the Campaign for Human Development

A Resolution Adopted by the National Conference of Catholic Bishops

November 1970

Christians are concerned not only with man's eternal destiny but also with his temporal well-being. Indeed, the two can hardly be separated. A sufficiency of the goods of the earth is essential for the realization of human spiritual potential. Poverty freely embraced is a virtue; poverty imposed by external circumstances is a calamity and, in many cases, a scandal.

Concern for God's poor has often been voiced by the Church. In declaring that "the joys and the hopes, the griefs and the anxieties of the men of this age, especially those who are poor or in any way afflicted, these too are the joys and hopes, the griefs and anxieties of the followers of Christ" (*Gaudium et Spes*, 1), the Second Vatican Council expressed an enduring Christian insight.

This insight has been acted upon in many concrete ways by the Catholic community in the United States. Concern for the poor has been a hallmark of American Catholicism. Catholic charities, hospitals, homes for the aged, schools—these and many other programs and institutions bear witness to the practical commitment of the Catholics of our country to meeting the needs of the poor.

In our time, however, it has become apparent that merely to alleviate the suffering of the poor, while essential, is not enough. Determined efforts are needed, as His Holiness Pope Paul VI has said, to "break the hellish circle of poverty"—to eradicate the conditions which impose poverty and trap generation after generation in an agonizing cycle of dependency and despair. In our time the legitimate aspirations of the poor for self-determination cannot be ignored.

Poverty in the United States is a cruel anachronism today. At a time when most Americans enjoy unparalleled material bounty, it is unthinkable that some Americans should still be condemned to live out their lives within the "hellish circle" of want. If we close our eyes to the continuing existence of poverty in our nation, we are vulnerable to the accusation of spiritual blindness and moral insensitivity.

A year ago, responding to these challenges, we committed ourselves to a nationwide effort to attack the root causes of poverty in our society. This effort is the Campaign for Human Development. It will reach its climax this year on November 22 in a collection to be taken up in churches throughout the nation.

We do not imagine that the funds obtained by the Campaign for Human Development will by themselves be sufficient to eliminate poverty in our country. We are convinced, however, that these funds, used creatively as seed money to assist self-help programs of many kinds, can and will make a significant contribution to solving the problem. We are anxious to listen to and work with the poor themselves in developing such programs.

A second major goal of the Campaign for Human Development is educational. The poor have not chosen poverty. Poverty is the result of circumstances over which the poor themselves have little or no control. We hope through the Campaign for Human Development to impress these facts on the nonpoor and to effect in them a conversion of heart, a growth in compassion and sensitivity to the needs of their brothers in want.

We appeal, then, to our Catholic people and to all Americans to recommit themselves to the service of the poor. In particular we appeal for their generosity on November 22. In this Thanksgiving season, as we bring to mind once more God's unbounded generosity, we call upon Americans to reflect that generosity in their own lives by a renewed outpouring of concern for his poor.

The Economy: Human Dimensions

A Statement Issued by the
Catholic Bishops of the United States

November 20, 1975

This unemployment returning again to plague us after so many repetitions during the century past is a sign of deep failure in our country. Unemployment is the great peacetime physical tragedy of the nineteenth and twentieth centuries, and both in its cause and in the imprint it leaves upon those who inflict it, those who permit it, and those who are its victims, it is one of the great moral tragedies of our time.

The Bishops of the United States,
Unemployment, 1930.

1. This was the judgment of our predecessors as they responded to the economic crisis of 1930. As pastors, teachers, and leaders, we recall and emphasize their words as our country faces important economic, social, and moral decisions in the midst of the highest unemployment since the 1930s.

I. The Church's Concern

2. Despite recent hopeful signs, the economy is only slowly and painfully recovering from the recent recession, the worst since World War II. We are deeply concerned that this recovery may lack the strength or duration to alleviate the suffering of many of the victims of the recession, especially the unemployed. It is the moral, human, and social consequences of our troubled economy which concern us and their impact on families, the elderly, and children. We hope in these limited reflections to give voice to some of the concerns of the poor and working people of our land.

3. We are keenly aware of the worldwide dimensions of the problem and the complexity of these issues of economic policy. Our concern, however, is not with technical fiscal matters, particular economic theories, or political programs, but rather the moral aspects of economic policy and the impact of these policies on people. Our economic life must reflect broad values of social justice and human rights.

II. The Church's Teaching

4. Our own rich heritage of Catholic teaching offers important direction and insight. Most importantly, we are guided by the concern for the poor and afflicted shown by Jesus, who came to "bring good news to the poor, to proclaim liberty to captives, new sight to the blind, and to set the downtrodden free" (Lk 4:18). In addition, the social encyclicals of the popes and documents of the Second Vatican Council and the Synod of Bishops defend the basic human right to useful employment, just wages, and decent working conditions as well as the right of workers to organize and bargain collectively. They condemn unemployment, maldistribution of resources, and other forms of economic injustice and call for the creation of useful work experiences and new forms of industrial organization enabling workers to share in decision-making, increased production, and even ownership. Again and again they point out the interrelation of economics and ethics, urging that economic activity be guided by social morality.
5. Catholic teaching on economic issues flows from the Church's commitment to human rights and human dignity. This living tradition articulates a number of principles which are useful in evaluating our current economic situation. Without attempting to set down an all-inclusive list, we draw the following principles from the social teachings of the Church and ask that policymakers and citizens ponder their implications.

(a) Economic activity should be governed by justice and be carried out within the limits of morality. It must serve people's needs.[1]

(b) The right to have a share of earthly goods sufficient for oneself and one's family belongs to everyone.[2]

(c) Economic prosperity is to be assessed not so much from the sum total of goods and wealth possessed as from the distribution of goods according to norms of justice.[3]

(d) Opportunities to work must be provided for those who are able and willing to work. Every person has the right to useful employment, to just wages, and to adequate assistance in case of real need.[4]

---

[1]Vatican II, *The Church in the Modern World*, 64; John XXIII, *Mater et Magistra*, 38-39.
[2]Vatican II, *The Church in the Modern World*, 69.
[3]John XXIII, *Mater et Magistra*, 73.
[4]Pius XI, *On the Reconstruction of the Social Order*, 74; John XXIII, *Pacem in Terris*, 11, 18; Vatican II, *The Church in the Modern World*, 67; Paul VI, *A Call to Action*, 6.

(e) Economic development must not be left to the sole judgment of a few persons or groups possessing excessive economic power, or to the political community alone. On the contrary, at every level the largest possible number of people should have an active share in directing that development.[5]

(f) A just and equitable system of taxation requires assessment according to ability to pay.[6]

(g) Government must play a role in the economic activity of its citizens. Indeed, it should promote in a suitable manner the production of a sufficient supply of material goods. Moreover, it should safeguard the rights of all citizens, and help them find opportunities for employment.[7]

6. These are not new principles. They are drawn directly from the teachings of the Church, but they have critical relevance at this time of economic distress. Under current conditions, many of these principles are being consistently violated.

III. Dimensions of the Economic Situation

7. In these reflections we wish to examine briefly the dimensions of our economic problems in three areas: unemployment, inflation, and distribution of wealth and income.

A. Unemployment

8. In October, government figures show eight million persons were unemployed, representing 8.6 percent of the work force.[8] Millions of other persons have given up seeking work out of discouragement or are in part-time jobs although they desire full-time work. Taking this into account, the actual level of unemployment in our country is over 12 percent. It is estimated that twenty million people will be jobless at some time this year, and that one-third of all Americans will suffer the traumatic experience of unemployment within their families.

9. The official unemployment rate does more than underestimate the true extent of joblessness. It also masks the inequitable distribution of unemployment. The figures for October indicate that minor-

---

[5]Vatican II, *The Church in the Modern World*, 65.
[6]John XXIII, *Mater et Magistra*, 132.
[7]John XXIII, *Mater et Magistra*, 20; Vatican II, *The Church in the Modern World*, 67, 70.
[8]The Employment Situation: October 1975; U.S. Department of Labor, Bureau of Labor Statistics; November 7, 1975.

ities, blue collar workers, young people, and women bear a disproportionate share of the burdens of joblessness.[9]

10. These realities clearly indicate that the nation's commitment to genuine full employment has been seriously eroded, if not abandoned. Since World War II, unemployment has been substantial, persistent, and drifting upward. In fact, when joblessness rose dramatically during the latest recession, it took the form of an acute and visible crisis, superimposed on a long-term unemployment problem which has persisted for decades.

11. The costs of this tragic underutilization of our country's human resources are enormous. In economic terms, these high levels of unemployment cost literally hundreds of billions of dollars in lost productivity and tens of billions of dollars in lost revenue and increased expenses for all levels of government.

12. As lamentable as these financial costs are, the social and human impact is far more deplorable. In our society, persons without a job lose a key measure of their place in society and a source of individual fulfillment; they often feel that there is no productive role for them. Many minority youth may grow up without meaningful job experiences and come to accept a life of dependency. Unemployment frequently leads to higher rates of crime, drug addiction, and alcoholism. It is reflected in higher rates of mental illness as well as rising social tensions. The idleness, fear, and financial insecurity resulting from unemployment can undermine confidence, erode family relationships, dull the spirit, and destroy dreams and hopes. One can hardly bear to contemplate the disappointment of a family which has made the slow and painful climb up the economic ladder and has been pushed down once again into poverty and dependence by the loss of a job.

13. The current levels of unemployment are unacceptable and their tremendous human costs are intolerable. Unemployment represents a vast and tragic waste of our human and material resources. We are disturbed not only by the present levels of joblessness, but also by official government projections of massive unemployment for the rest of this decade. We sincerely hope that these figures do not represent resignation to the human and economic waste implied in these rates of unemployment. As a society, we cannot accept the notion that some will have jobs and income while others will be told to wait a

---

[9]Department of Labor figures for October 1975 indicate:
(a) One out of five teenagers were jobless.
(b) Over 11 percent of all blue collar workers were out of work.
(c) 14.2 percent of all minority persons were unemployed.
(d) Nearly 40 percent of all minority teenagers were jobless.
(e) One hundred thirty-four of our 150 major urban areas were officially listed as areas of substantial subemployment.

few years and to subsist on welfare in the interim. For work is more than a way to earn a living. It represents a deep human need, desired not only for income but also for the sense of worth which it provides the individual.

B. Inflation

14. There are those who insist that we must tolerate high levels of unemployment for some, in order to avoid ruinous inflation for all. Although we are deeply concerned about inflation, we reject such a policy as not grounded in justice. In recent years, our country has experienced very high levels of inflation. During this past year, there has been some reduction in inflation, but there are already signs of its renewal, spurred by large increases in food and fuel prices.

15. Inflation weakens the economic stability of our society and erodes the economic security of our citizens. Its impact is most severe on those who live on fixed incomes and the very poor. The double distress of inflation and recession has led to a painful decline in real income for large numbers of people in recent years. Clearly, steps must be taken to limit inflation and its impact.

16. However, low unemployment and high inflation are not inevitable partners, as history and the experience of other industrialized countries bear out. Policymakers should seek and use measures to combat inflation which do not rely upon high rates of joblessness. For many of our fellow citizens, the major protection against inflation is a decent job at decent wages.

C. Distribution of Income and Wealth

17. Within our country, vast disparities of income and wealth remain. The richest 20 percent of our people receive more income than the bottom 60 percent combined. In the area of ownership, the disparities are even more apparent. The top one-fifth of all families own more than three-fourths of all the privately held wealth in the United States, while over one-half of our families control less than seven percent of the wealth.

18. The distribution of income and wealth are important since they influence and even determine our society's distribution of economic power. Catholic social teaching has condemned gross inequality in the distribution of material goods. Our country cannot continue to ignore this important measure of economic justice.

IV. Policy Directions

19. Fundamentally, our nation must provide jobs for those who can and should work and a decent income for those who cannot. An effective national commitment to full employment is needed to protect the basic human right to useful employment for all Americans. It ought to guarantee, through appropriate mechanisms, that no one seeking work would be denied an opportunity to earn a livelihood. Full employment is the foundation of a just economic policy; it should not be sacrificed for other political and economic goals. We would support sound and creative programs of public service employment to relieve joblessness and to meet the vital social needs of our people (housing, transportation, education, health care, recreation, etc.).

20. The burden and hardship of these difficult times must not fall most heavily on the most vulnerable: the poor, the elderly, the unemployed, young people, and workers of modest income. We support efforts to improve our unemployment compensation system and to provide adequate assistance to the victims of the recession. Efforts to eliminate or curtail needed services and help must be strongly opposed.

21. We continue to support a decent income policy for those who are unable to work because of sickness, age, disability, or other good reason. Our present welfare system should be reformed to serve our country and those in need more effectively.

22. Renewed efforts are required to reform our economic life. We ask the private and public sectors to join together to plan and provide better for our future, to promote fairness in taxation, to halt the destructive impact of inflation, and to distribute more evenly the burdens and opportunities of our society. We also ask that consideration be given to a more efficacious use of the land, the nation's primary resource, in order to provide gainful employment for more people. We should also explore the impact of technology and endeavor to preserve the small family farm and other approaches to economic life which provide substantial and productive employment for people. It is not enough to point up the issues in our economy and to propose solutions to our national problems while accepting uncritically the presupposition of an economic system based in large part upon unlimited and unrestrained profit.

23. We pledge our best efforts in support of these goals. We call on local parishes, dioceses, Catholic institutions and organizations to undertake education and action programs on issues of economic justice. We renew our commitment to assist the needy and victims of economic turmoil through programs of financial assistance and active participation in the dialogue over the formulation and implementation of just economic policies. We call on our people to pray for our country in this time of need and to participate in the difficult decisions which can still fulfill the promise of our land.

24. Working together with renewed vision and commitment, our country has the productive capacity and human and material resources to provide adequately for the needs of our people. We take this opportunity to renew the challenge of our fellow bishops of 45 years ago:

> Our country needs, now and permanently, such a change of heart as will, intelligently and with determination, so organize and distribute our work and wealth that no one need lack for any long time the security of being able to earn an adequate living for himself and for those dependent upon him (The Bishops of the United States, *Unemployment*, 1930).

Appendix

25. In adopting this resolution, the bishops sought to link this effort to a major statement issued in 1919 on similar matters. Entitled, "The Bishops' Program of Social Reconstruction," the statement called for: minimum wage legislation; unemployment insurance and protection against sickness and old age; minimum age limit for working children; legal enforcement of the right of labor to organize; a national employment service; public housing; and a long term-program of increasing wages.

26. It also urged: prevention of excessive profits and incomes through regulation of public utilities and progressive taxes on inheritance, income, and excess profits; participation of labor in management; a wider distribution of ownership through cooperative enterprises and worker ownership in the stock of corporations; and effective control of monopolies even by the method of government competition if that should prove necessary.

27. Most of these proposals have been enacted. Partial progress has been made toward others. The 1919 statement provides a historical framework for the current resolution and evidences a longstanding concern for economic justice on the part of the Catholic community in this country.

APPENDIX

Introduction to Ethical Choices and Political Challenges

The Canadian episcopal conference's statement on economic justice contains some of the most challenging remarks that Catholic leaders have directed to the Church in North America. Pope John Paul II's virtual endorsement of the statement's major perspectives has added weight to what had been a controversial document even in Canadian Catholic circles.

The history of Catholicism in Canada parallels that of the Church in America in many ways. However, it has had some experiences, especially with forms of Socialism, that are different from the American experience and relevant to any discussion of religion and economics. Hopefully, exposure to this document will result in greater collaboration between Canadian and American Catholics in confronting economic disparities on this continent and abroad.

Ethical Choices and Political Challenges

Ethical Reflections on the Future of Canada's Socioeconomic Order

CANADIAN CONFERENCE OF CATHOLIC BISHOPS

December 13, 1983

Introduction*

Mr. Chairman, members of the Royal Commission on the Economic Union and Development Prospects for Canada, we welcome this opportunity to present our concerns regarding the current realities and future prospects of Canada's economy. As representatives of the Canadian Conference of Catholic Bishops (CCCB), we believe that there are some important ethical priorities to be addressed with respect to Canada's social and economic order at this particular moment in history.

Your commission, as we understand it, has been given the mandate to study and make recommendations regarding the future of Canada's economic order in relation to changing world conditions. In your terms of reference, it is recognized "that significant changes are occurring in the world economy, particularly in the sphere of industrial activity, the utilization of natural resources, and the movement of capital within and among countries." These changes have resulted in new global economic conditions affecting the political economies of all countries. In this context, your commission has been charged with the responsibility of identifying the challenges, prospects, and implications of these new global conditions for Canada's own political economy. This entails an identification of national goals and policies that may, in turn, require changes in Canada's economic and political structures. Also implicit here is a recognition that basic decisions on goals and priorities involve value choices about the kind of society we want to build in the future.

In recent years, we have attempted to stimulate ethical reflections on these major concerns through a series of social teaching documents. Perhaps the best known example is the New Year statement

*At the request of the President and the Executive Committee, Bishop De Roo and Bishop Drainville represented the Canadian Conference of Catholic Bishops in the actual presentation of this brief to the Macdonald Commission, December 13th, 1983.

of our Social Affairs Commission, *Ethical Reflections on the Economic Crisis,* which drew upon the insights developed by Pope John Paul II's encyclical, *Laborem Exercens.* In addition, the CCCB has issued several related social teaching documents including: *From Words to Action* (1976); *A Society to Be Transformed* (1977); *Witness to Justice: A Society to Be Transformed* (1979); and *Unemployment: the Human Costs* (1980); plus a series of Labor Day Messages on questions of social and economic justice. Taken together, these documents constitute an ongoing process of ethical reflection on Canada's socioeconomic order. At the same time, the CCCB participates in collaboration with other Canadian churches in a variety of research, education and action projects concerned with social and economic justice in this country.**

In addition, a particular pastoral methodology is generally used in the formulation of our ethical reflections, (*From Words to Action,* CCCB, 1976, 9; *A Society to Be Transformed,* CCCB, 1977, p. 9; *Witness to Justice: A Society to Be Transformed,* CCCB, 1979). This pastoral methodology involves a number of steps: (a) being present with and listening to the experiences of the poor, the marginalized, the oppressed in our society (e.g., the unemployed, the working poor, the welfare poor, exploited workers, native peoples, the elderly, the handicapped, small producers, racial and cultural minorities, etc.); (b) developing a critical analysis of the economic, political, and social structures that cause human suffering; (c) making judgments in the light of gospel principles and the social teachings of the Church concerning social values and priorities; (d) stimulating creative thought and action regarding alternative visions and models for social and economic development; and (e) acting in solidarity with popular groups in their struggles to transform economic, political, and social structures that cause social and economic injustices.

Our purpose here is to continue this process of ethical reflections in terms of several themes and topics that relate to the mandate of your commission and the nature of your inquiry. In accordance with the first phase of your inquiry, we have divided our submission into three parts. In part one, we will attempt to clarify the "perspective" from which we speak about our socioeconomic order. In part two, we will identify some of the major "problems" of our socioeconomic order from the standpoint of our ethical perspective. In part three, we will attempt to outline some of the basic "challenges" to be faced regarding the future of Canada's economy. In the final analysis, the

---

**These ecumenical projects include Project North, the GATT-Fly Project, the Task Force on Churches and Corporate Responsibility, the Interchurch Committee on Human Rights in Latin America, Ten Days for World Development, PLURA and the Interchurch Committee on Refugees.

fundamental question before us is what kind of society and people do we want to become.

It should be noted that it is not our intention here to make moral judgments in a dogmatic or authoritarian fashion. Moral principles are themselves universally valid. But their application to concrete situations allows for a diversity of options. Our primary concern here is to stimulate serious public discussion about some major ethical issues regarding the future development of our economy and society.

I. Perspective

Our first task is to clarify the perspective from which we speak about the economic order of our society. As bishops, we do not claim to be technical experts in economic matters. Our primary role is to be moral teachers in society. In this capacity, we attempt to view economic and social realities primarily from the perspective of the gospel message of Jesus Christ and his concern for the poor, the marginalized, and the oppressed (*From Words to Action*, CCCB, 1976, 9). From this perspective, we believe there are fundamental ethical questions to be raised about the values and priorities that govern any socioeconomic order. Thus, we have a responsibility to stimulate ethical reflections on the values, priorities, and structures of this country's socioeconomic order.

In recent years, we have tried to stimulate some critical ethical reflections on Canada's economy through various social statements, working instruments, and education projects. Our experience to date, however, indicates that this is not always an easy endeavor. Ethics and economics have become separate disciplines in the historic evolution of liberal Capitalism itself. The emphasis on economistic and mechanistic approaches has managed to drain the moral content out of economics as a discipline over the past century or more (*A Society to Be Transformed*, CCCB, 1977, p. 6; *Laborem Exercens, On Human Work*, John Paul II, 1981, 7). As a result, serious ethical discourse about the Canadian economy rarely occurs in our culture and society.

The Roman Catholic Church, through almost a century of social teaching, has consistently maintained that there is an ethical order to be followed in the organization of an economy. This is evident, for example, in the writings of Pope John Paul II. In Catholic social teaching, the value and dignity of the human person lies at the center of an economy based on justice. This means, in turn, that all persons in a given society should have the right of common access to, and use of, the goods produced by the economy (*Laborem Exercens*, 14). In this context, peoples are meant to be the agents of their own history. Through their labor, workers are to be the subject not the object of production. In turn, "capital" and "technology" are seen as the instruments of production (*Laborem Exercens*, 12, 13). It follows, therefore, that people in general, and human labor in particular, take priority over both capital and technology in an economic order based on justice.

In general, this is the perspective from which we have attempted to stimulate some ethical reflections on the Canadian economy. This ethical perspective, in turn, is rooted in several major themes and principles developed in the Scriptures and the social teachings of the Church.

Subjects of Creation

According to the Scriptures, all persons are made in the image of God. Thus, the human person is meant to be the subject of creation and the subject of a given economy. As subjects of creation, all persons have certain inalienable rights. Of primary importance is the right to life and all that makes for a more fully human life such as adequate food, clothing, shelter, employment, health care, education, and effective participation in decisions affecting their lives (*Gaudium et Spes, Church in the Modern World*, II Vatican Council, 26; *Pacem in Terris, Peace on Earth*, John XXIII, 1963, 8-26). As subjects of creation, all persons are also entrusted with the responsibility of being co-creators of the earth and stewards for the sake of present and future generations (Gn 1, 2). This means, in turn, that the human person is meant to be the co-creator of an economy and the subject of production.

Primary Purpose

Throughout the Scriptures, the earth is understood to be God's gift for present and future generations of humanity (Gn 1, 2; Pss 8, 19, 104). The resources of the earth are to be developed for God's intended purpose, namely, to equitably serve the needs of all people for a more fully human life. This is the "universal purpose of created things" (*Gaudium et Spes*, 69). It follows, therefore, that the primary purpose of a socioeconomic order should be to develop its resources to serve the common good, namely, the basic life needs of all its people for food, clothing, shelter, education, employment, health care. And, "all other rights whatsoever, including those of property and free commerce, are to be subordinated to this principle." (*Populorum Progressio, On the Development of Peoples*, Paul VI, 1967, 22; *Laborem Exercens*, 14).

Integral Development

The primary purpose of an economy should be reflected in its models of development. From this perspective, models of development cannot be limited to mere economic growth (*Populorum Progressio*, 14). To be authentic, development must be integral, encompassing the social, economic, cultural, and spiritual needs of the whole person. Integral development, therefore, encompasses both the personal and the communal dimensions of human dwelling. To be certain, economic growth can be an important dimension of economic development of a society or community. However, economic strategies aimed at maximizing private profits and consumption, or technological growth designed to maintain power and domination, constitute distorted models of "development" and hence must be resisted.

Priority of Labor

The value and dignity of human work has a special significance in God's plan for creation. It is through the activity of work that people are able to exercise their creative spirit, realize their human dignity, and participate in the development of their society (*Unemployment: The Human Costs*, CCCB, 1980, 5). In this context, working people are to be viewed as the subjects not the objects of production in a given economy. Human labor, therefore, should not be treated as a commodity to be bought and sold in the marketplace (*Laborem Exercens*, 7). On the contrary, human labor must be the subject of production, taking precedence over both capital and technology in the production process (*Laborem Exercens*, 12). In effect, the basic rights of working people take priority over the maximization of profits and the accumulation of machines in an economic order (*Ethical Reflections on the Economic Crisis*, CCCB, 1983). This is the priority of labor principle.

Priority of the Poor

The needs and rights of the poor, the afflicted, the marginalized, and the oppressed are given special attention in God's plan for creation (*From Words to Action*, 4). Throughout his ministry, for example, Jesus repeatedly identified with the plight of the poor and the outcasts of society (e.g., Phil 2: 6-8; Lk 6: 20-21). He also took a critical attitude towards the accumulation of wealth and power that comes through the exploitation of others (e.g., Lk 16: 13-15, 12: 16-21; Mk 4:19). This has become known as "the preferential option for the poor" in the Scriptures. In a given economic order, the needs of the poor take priority over the wants of the rich (*Ethical Reflections on the Economic Crisis*). This does not, in turn, simply mean more handouts for the poor. It calls, instead, for an equitable redistribution of wealth and power among peoples and regions (*From Words to Action*, 3; *A Society to Be Transformed, Unemployment: The Human Costs*, 13).

Means of Production

In the Church's social teachings, capital and technology are understood to be the means or instruments of production (*Laborem Exercens,* 12). In an economy, therefore, capital and technology should be used for humanly constructive purposes, namely, the integral development of peoples. At the same time, the means of production should not be owned in opposition to human labor or owned for the sake of owning them (*Laborem Exercens,* 14). Legal title does not confer absolute ownership. The only title to their ownership is that they serve the basic needs of all people, especially human labor and needs of the poor. There is, in other words, a "social mortgage" on the means of production (John Paul II, Mexico). Capital and technology must be used for constructive rather than destructive purposes in the development of peoples.

Effective Participation

As subjects of creation, all peoples have rights to self-determination, to define their own future, and to effectively participate in decisions affecting their lives (*Populorum Progressio; Justice in the World,* World Synod of Bishops, 1971, 16, 17). This is essential if working people, the poor, and the marginalized are going to exercise their rights to be subjects of their own history. This means, for example, that working people, as subjects of production, should have an effective and meaningful role to play in social and economic planning regarding the use of capital and technology. Effective participation in these kinds of decision-making processes is a basic part of being human. It is essential for an integral model of development (*Justice in the World,* 1, 13-19). In effect, the participation of the marginalized takes precedence over an order which excludes them (*Ethical Reflections on the Economic Crisis*).

Self-Reliance

Integral development also requires an emphasis on more self-reliant models of development. An economy that is largely organized to provide for external interests and dependent on externally controlled means of production, cannot serve the basic needs of its own population (*Populorum Progressio,* 58). Through self-reliance, peoples' energies are directed towards developing local resources to serve the basic human needs (*Justice in the World,* 1, 13-19). This requires, in turn, that local communities identify their basic needs, assess their human and material resources, and acquire communal control over the necessary means of production. In this way, people can be empowered to organize their economy to serve their own basic needs.

Moreover, self-reliant development is rooted in the sociocultural heritage of the people themselves.

Responsible Stewardship

As subjects of creation, people are also called to be responsible stewards of natural resources in a socioeconomic order (*Northern Development: At What Cost?*, CCCB, 1975, 19-24; *From Words to Action*, 6). The resources of planet earth are not limitless. The abuse and waste of finite resources affects the health and well-being of present and future generations. Indeed, nature should not be treated coldly and calculatedly as merely a storehouse of commodities (Ps 104). In our times, humanity must learn to organize socioeconomic systems in such a way that nature remains sufficiently balanced and human needs are adequately satisfied (i.e, ecodevelopment). This means finding ways of using capital and technology in partnership and harmony with nature. In this context, consideration needs to be given to sustainable models of development based on renewable as well as nonrenewable resources.

Global Solidarity

The global realities of interdependence in the modern world call for new forms of solidarity between peoples throughout the world (*Laborem Exercens, Populorum Progressio*, 43 ff). The structural causes of poverty and oppression in the Third World, for example, are linked to the international economic order dominated by affluent and powerful nation states of the First World. The fact that four-fifths of the earth's population is expected to survive on one-fifth of the world's resources can no longer be ignored nor tolerated. What is required is the cultivation of new forms of solidarity—with and among working and nonworking peoples—with and among the poor and oppressed peoples of the world—in the building of a new international economic order. This is the principle of universal solidarity. As such, it guards against any narrow nationalistic chauvinism in developing the economies of nation states.

These, then, are some of the major principles involved in the ethical ordering of an economy and society. Taken together, these moral themes and principles provide an ongoing challenge to all institutions in our society—governments, businesses, labor unions, community organizations, religious institutions, and others. The state, however, has a particularly important role to play in assuring that this ethical order is achieved in the organization and operations of an economy. Indeed, the state has a major responsibility to ensure that the whole economy itself lives up to the criteria of this ethical order (*Laborem Exercens*, 18). This means that the state has the responsibility to intervene in the operations of an economy to ensure that basic human rights and moral principles are realized (*Laborem Exercens*, 18). In order to do so, the state must be able to stand aside from the particular interests of power elites and act on behalf of the common good (*Octogesima Adveniens*, Eightieth Anniversary of *Rerum Novarum*, Paul VI, 1971, 46), with special concern for the poor and powerless groups of society.

II. Problem

Our second task is to identify some of the major problems to be faced concerning the future of Canada's socioeconomic order. In our most recent social statements, we have emphasized that the current economic recession is symptomatic of a deeper structural crisis that is taking place in the international system of industrial Capitalism itself (*Ethical Reflections on the Economic Crisis*). As Pope John Paul II has noted, industrial societies are moving from a relatively benevolent to a more rigid stage of Capitalism that holds forth the prospect of a grim future (*Laborem Exercens*, 1). These changes, as we shall see, reveal a deepening moral crisis which deserves serious attention regarding the future of our socioeconomic order.

As many observers have noted, basic changes are taking place in the structure of both "capital" and "technology" that will have profound social consequences. Today, transnational corporations and banks can move capital from one country or region to another, taking advantage of cheaper labor conditions, lower corporate taxes, and reduced environmental standards. As a result, transnationals can shift their operations anywhere in the world on almost a momentary basis, thereby outflanking both workers' demands and labor unions. At the same time, the introduction of automation and computers to the production process has meant that human work is rapidly being replaced by machines on the assembly line and in administrative centers. As a result, the workerless factory and the automated office may well be among the chief characteristics of this new industrial age. All of this points to a continuing social crisis of permanent or structural unemployment.

In effect, "capital" has become fully transnationalized while "technology" has become capital-intensive. And both have become increasingly concentrated in fewer centers of power. At the same time, these structural changes have created a new global economic environment. The international movement of capital, for example, has restored laissez-faire competition on a global basis as nation states compete with one another for investment by transnational corporations and banks. The new technological rationalization of production has dramatically altered the division of labor between countries and within countries. These new economic conditions, in turn, have served to heighten global tensions—East and West, North and South—thereby contributing to the escalating nuclear arms race and the increasing militarization of national economies (especially in the Third World).

In this new global environment, it appears that nation states like Canada (and its provinces) are being compelled to restructure their economies for the "tough new world of competition." Indeed, Canada finds itself in a somewhat vulnerable position, given such structural problems as high levels of foreign ownership and economic dependency on the United States. In the short term, federal and provincial governments are attempting to restore the profitability and competitiveness of certain industries and provide a much more favorable climate for the private investment of capital and technology. In the long term, both sets of governments are attempting to restructure Canada's economy for the hi-tech computer age of the 1990s, with the private sector being designated as the engine for economic development. And, in order to become more competitive in world markets, the strategy for the eighties, appears to be that of retooling Canadian industries with new technologies, creating new forms of hi-tech industries, initiating new megaresource development projects, and phasing out many labor intensive industries.

Under these new conditions, capital and technology are being reasserted as the dominant organizing principles of our socioeconomic order. These structural changes, in turn, will have profound social consequences. From the perspective discussed above (part one), our society seems to be faced with a deepening moral crisis. The following are some of the signs of this moral disorder in our economy today.

Massive Unemployment

The current structural crisis has generated the highest levels of unemployment in this country since the Great Depression of the 1930s. The official unemployment statistics, combined with the numbers of discouraged workers (those who have given up looking for work) and the numbers of underemployed workers (part-time workers seeking full-time employment) means that well over two million people are being deprived of an adequate family or personal income. Moreover, long range forecasts indicate that this pattern will not substantially change for the remainder of this decade. Indeed, the rapid introduction of labor saving technologies has intensified the crisis. As a result, there seems to be a growing cynical resignation to the continuing realities of high unemployment in our society.[1]

---

[1]Concerning the official unemployment statistics, observers have pointed out the rate calculated by Statistics Canada understates the real extent of unemployment in the country. The methodology used arbitrarily excludes

Social Deprivation

The adoption of monetarist policies has resulted in a series of major cutbacks in social spending at both federal and provincial levels. This includes reductions in revenue for hospitals, public services, education, social agencies, environmental protection, and foreign aid. The introduction of extra billing and user fees for medicare in several provinces further magnifies the problem. If this trend continues, it will likely result in the dismantling of the social welfare apparatus that was gradually put in place following the Second World War. Despite safety net provisions, the main victims of these social cutbacks are still the poorest sectors of the population, including the elderly, people on welfare, the working poor, and the unemployed. Moreover, the current trends towards privatization indicate the possibility of reverting to a system where basic social services are made available to people on the basis of their ability to pay.[2]

Labor Devaluation

The structural crisis has had a major impact on most working people. Wage restraint programs, suspension of collective bargaining rights, and withdrawal of job security provisions have taken their toll, largely on public sector workers. In the private sector, plant shutdowns and layoffs, the deskilling of workers in certain industries, and the general streamlining of the labor force for a hi-tech future have had major social consequences. Under conditions of high unem-

---

hundreds of thousands of Canadians from the "labor force" category. A study by the Social Planning Council of Metropolitan Toronto for example, estimates that in May, 1983, there were 470,000 discouraged workers plus another 427,000 part-time workers seeking full employment who simply do not appear in the official unemployment statistics. In effect, there are over two and a half million unemployed or underemployed people in this country, representing 20 percent of Canada's "labor force." For an examination of the methodology used by governments to understate the dimensions of labor supply and hence the quantity of unemployment, see Stanley Moses, "Labor Supply Concepts: the Political Economy of Conceptual Change," in *The Annals, American Academy of Political and Social Science*, March 1975.

[2]For data on poverty in Canada, see for example: David P. Ross, *The Canadian Fact Book on Poverty* (Ottawa: Canadian Council on Social Development) 1983; David P. Ross, *The Working Poor: Wage Earners and the Failure of Income Securities Policies* (Toronto: Lorimer), 1981.

For an analysis of the eroding social security programs see for example: Allan Moscovitch, "The Rise and Decline of the Canadian Welfare State," in *Perception*, vol. 6, no. 2, 1982; Angelo Djao, *Inequality and Social Policy*. (Toronto: Wiley) 1983.

See also, Randy Sykes, "Privatization" in *C.U.P.E Facts*, vol. 5, no. 3, 1983; Tony Wohlfarth, "Cutbacks—Provincial Style" in *C.U.P.E. Facts*, vol. 5, no. 8, 1983.

ployment, nonworking people have little choice but to price themselves back into the labor market by accepting lower wages and working conditions. As a result, human labor is being further reduced to a commodity, having little or no significance beyond its economic function in the system.[3]

Increasing Marginalization

The introduction of computers and robots in industries and offices has begun to create what may become a new class of people, namely, the so-called "techno-peasants." These are the men and women who are being shut out or marginalized by their functional illiteracy in the new technologies. The most affected are expected to be workers in manufacturing, agriculture, and resource industries. Indeed, it is the middle classes which are most vulnerable to increasing marginalization, due to the new technologies. The upward social mobility of the postwar years is rapidly giving way to the new trend of downward social mobility for many people. This is likely to contribute to an enlargement of the sectors of poverty and powerlessness in our society.[4]

Economic Disparities

There are also signs that economic disparities between classes and regions are growing. In recent years, personal income taxes have been steadily rising while corporate income taxes have been declining as part of economic strategies to attract more private investment. Since lower income Canadians pay a proportionately larger percentage of their income in taxes than wealthier Canadians, the inequalities between social classes is likely to widen further. At the same time, the contin-

---

[3]For an examination and analysis of the phenomenon of labor devaluation see: John Paul II, *Laborem Exercens*, Part II, no. 7 and Part III, nos. 11-15, 1981; John Paul II, Address to Business People and Economic Managers, "Man and His Values are the Principle and Aim of Economics," in *L'Osservatore Romano*, 20 June, 1983; Gregory Baum, *The Priority of Labor*, (New York: Paulist Press) 1982; Canadian Conference of Catholic Bishops, "Unemployment: The Human Costs," January, 1980; Harry Braverman, *Labor and Monopoly Capital: The Degradation of Work in the Twentieth Century*, (New York: Monthly Review Press) 1974; Walter Johnson, ed., *Working in Canada* (Montreal, Black Rose Books) 1975.

See also John Paul II, Address to Members of the Trilateral Commission, "It is not Possible to Separate Technology from Ethics," in *L'Osservatore Romano*, 25 April 1983; David F. Noble, "Present Tense Technology," Parts I and II in, *Democracy*, vol. 3, nos. 2 and 3, 1983; Patricia McDermott, "The New Demeaning of Work" in *Canadian Dimension*, December 1981.

[4]See for example, Ed Finn, "Decline of the Middle Class," in *C.U.P.E. Facts*, vol 5 no. 9, 1983; and Bob Kittner, "The Declining Middle," in *The Atlantic Monthly*, July 1983.

uing centralization of job producing industries in the major metropolitan centers has further aggravated economic disparities between regions. Indeed, the highest rates of unemployment and plant closures, plus some of the sharpest cutbacks in social services, are occurring in the poorer regions of the country. Moreover, renewed reliance on the "trickle-down" mechanism for income distribution through the private sector will likely accentuate these disparities.[5]

Economic Dislocation

The structural crisis has also intensified the concentration of economic power in the hands of a small number of large corporations exercising monopoly control over key sectors of the economy. As a result, many small businesses and small producers (e.g., farmers and fisherpeople) have been forced out of the market. This is evident by the large number of farm bankruptcies, plant shutdowns, small business closures, and the disruption of one-industry towns. In this kind of economic climate, capital and technology tend to become further concentrated in the hands of few transnational enterprises. Under these conditions of excessive competition, only the "strong" are able to survive while the "weak" are eliminated from the market and participation in society.[6]

Export Orientation

A major part of the restructuring of Canada's economy is the retooling of Canadian industries and the streamlining of both resource and industrial sectors for competition in world markets. This trend serves to intensify the export-orientation of our economy. As a result, greater emphasis is placed on organizing our economy to serve external mar-

---

[5]For information on current tax measures see, Marc Lalonde, *Budget Papers*, Ottawa, April 19, 1983, p. 25 ff. Observers have pointed out that while business will receive an estimated $905 million in tax reductions in 1983 and $955 in 1984, an increasing proportion of the tax burden will be transferred to working families. The inequitable tax system maintains a lower top marginal tax rate. The effect is to elevate more Canadians living below the poverty line to the status of taxpayers. At the same time, affluent Canadians are now able to avoid paying taxes on the inflation portion of capital gains made from shares in Canadian corporations.

See also the study prepared for the National Anti-Poverty Organization by Ernie S. Lightman, *Canada's Tax System and the Poor*, Ottawa, 1984.

[6]For documentation on corporate concentration see for example: Peter C. Newman, *The Canadian Establishment*, vol. II, the Acquisitors, Appendix: "The Take Over Record, 1975-1981." (Toronto, McClelland and Stewart) 1981. For an example of concentration in the agricultural sector, see, GATT-Fly, "Canada's Agricultural Marketing Board: A Clearer View," Part II, June 1983.

ket interests rather than producing for the basic needs of our own population. Thus, for example, even as a major food producing nation, Canada is importing an increasing amount of basic food products. In other words, our country is becoming more and more dependent on other countries for the basic food needs of our population. Moreover, increased emphasis on export orientation serves to perpetuate the economic dependency of Third World countries on global markets.[7]

Militarization Trends

Canada's economy has certainly not been immune to the escalating arms race. In recent years, military spending on the part of the federal government has significantly increased to maintain NATO commitments while social spending has steadily declined. The testing of the cruise missile in Canada is a further symbol of this trend toward militarization. Even more disturbing is the retooling of Canadian industries for the production of military products. While a number of Canadian companies are already engaged in nuclear and conventional arms production under the U.S.-Canada Defense Sharing Agreement, more industries are being lured into military production due to weak market conditions elsewhere. As a result, the Canadian economy becomes more closely linked to the arms race.[8]

---

[7]For a general discussion of this problem see for example: GATT-Fly, "The Limitations of the Trade Issue," July 1973. For an analysis of the food trade issue, see for example: GATT-Fly, "Canada's Food Trade—By Bread Alone?", August 1978; GATT-Fly, "Canada's Food—The Road to Self-Reliance," September 1979.

[8]For an analysis of the politics and the economics of the arms race in Canada, see for example, Ernie Reigehr and Simon Rosenblum, eds., *Canada and the Nuclear Arms Race*, (Toronto: Lorimer) 1983; Carole Giangrande, *The Nuclear North: The People, the Regions and the Arms Race*. (Toronto: Anansi) 1983.

For an example of a detailed proposal for "boosting" the economy through increased production of armaments by Canadian industry see the report prepared for Bob Runciman, M.P.P. (Ontario). "The Armaments Industry," (Toronto: Legislative Research Service), March 1983.

For an analysis of the arms race and the factors sustaining it, see for example, Johan Galtung, "The War System," in *Essays in Peace Research*, vol. IV (Copenhagen: C. Ejlers) 1975—.

For an ethical perspective on these issues, see for example: the submissions by the Canadian Conference of Catholic Bishops and the Canadian Council of Churches to House of Commons Standing Committee on External Affairs and National Defense. *Minutes of Proceedings and Evidence*, Issue No. 57, February 16, 1982; Canadian Church Leaders, "Brief on Peace and Disarmament," presented to the Prime Minister, December 14, 1982. See also, National Conference of Catholic Bishops, "The Challenge of Peace: A Pastoral Letter on War and Peace," May 1983, (Washington: United States Catholic Conference) 1983.

Ecological Damage

In order to attract private investment, some governments have lowered environmental standards or decreased their monitoring activities regarding pollution control. In some regions of the country, renewable resources like forests and fish are directly affected by the lack of environmental regulation. In other regions, the storage of radioactive wastes from uranium mines and nuclear plants poses a serious environmental threat to communities and a potential health hazard for workers. At the same time, new industrial technologies continue to generate pollution-causing materials which have a damaging effect on the air, lakes, rivers, and waters. The acid rain issue is the most obvious example. Indeed, the apparent unwillingness of governments and agencies in the United States to enter into agreements with Canada on effective acid rain control is a disturbing sign of the times.[9]

Social Breakdown

Finally, there are growing signs of social breakdown. Underneath the continuing unemployment crisis, for example, lies a deepening human and social tragedy. Indeed, the experience of unemployment generates a sense of alienation and powerlessness that comes from a loss of personal identity and self-worth. These personal traumas tend to translate into social crises such as increasing alcoholism, suicides, family breakdown, vandalism, crime, racism, and street violence. A dramatic illustration is the number of suicide pacts among young people over the past year who see no hope for the future. Moreover, the personal insecurities associated with unemployment are creating a climate of social fear and passive acceptance of these new realities.[10]

---

[9]For an assessment of geological disposal of high-level radioactive waste see for example, the Task Force on the Churches and Corporate Responsibility, "Policy Formation on Aspects of Canada's Nuclear Wastes," a brief to the Atomic Energy Control Board, June 1982.

For an introduction to the acid rain problem, see for example, Pollution Probe, *Acid Rain Primer*, Toronto, 1982.

For a theological reflection on the ecological crisis, see for example, the special issues on "Ecologie et théologie" in *Foi et Vie*, nos. 5 and 6, 1974; Rosemary Ruether, "The Biblical Vision of the Ecological Crisis," in *Christian Century*, 22 November 1978; and Douglas Hall, *The Steward: A Biblical Symbol Come of Age*, (New York; Friendship Press) 1982.

[10]See for example, Harry MacKay, "Social Impact of Unemployment," in *Perception*, vol 6, no. 5, 1983. For a systematic study on the set of relationships between unemployment and social pathologies (disease, mental illness, suicide and crime) see, Harvey Brenner, *Estimating the Social*

Taken together, these are some of the disturbing signs of the times emerging in this new industrial age. To us, they indicate a deepening moral disorder in our society.

In the midst of the present structural crisis, capital and technology are being reasserted as the dominant organizing principles of our socioeconomic order. Under these new conditions, governments and other institutions are being called upon to reorganize their economic strategies and social programs. The social consequences, as we have seen, appear to be a series of assaults on the human dignity of a substantial number of people in this country. The primary victims of this assault are workers, the unemployed, the poor, and the growing number of marginalized people. Today these trends are evident in Canada as a whole and in each of the provinces.

It should be clearly understood that we are not taking a stand against progress or technology *per se*. On the contrary, modern advances in the development of capital and technology could be used to greatly enhance the development of peoples here in Canada and throughout the world. The critical question, however, is who controls these instruments and how will they be used. Unless communities and working people have effective control over both capital and technology, the tendency is for them to become "destructive forces" rather than "constructive instruments" in economic development. Under these conditions, the human person becomes more and more redundant and a victim of impersonal economic forces. This is the central problem of our times. It is first, and foremost, a moral or ethical problem in the structural order of our economy and society.

III. Challenge

Our third task is to identify the basic challenge which we see emerging with respect to the future of Canada's socioeconomic order. Given our perspective (part one) and our analysis of the problem (part two), we believe the fundamental challenge involves a combination of moral vision and political will. The primary task, in our view, is not simply a question of how governments can better manage the economy in the new hi-tech industrial age. It is not a question of how to make people adjust, accommodate, adapt, retrain, relocate, and lower their expectations. What we are facing are some basic structural problems in our economy that reveal a moral disorder in our society.

Costs of National Economic Policy, A Study Prepared for the Use of the Joint Economic Committee, Congress of the United States (Washington, D.C.: Government Printing Office), 1976. For a recent Canadian study, see, Sharon Kirsh, *Unemployment: Its Impact on Body and Soul*, Canadian Mental Health Association, Toronto, 1983.

The challenge before us, therefore, is to search for alternative visions and models for the future development of our socioeconomic order in the new industrial age. As emphasized above, the basic social contradiction of our times is the structural domination of capital and technology over people, over labor, over communities. What is required is a radical inversion of these structural relationships. In other words, ways must be found for people to exercise more effective control over both capital and technology so that they may become constructive instruments of creation by serving the basic needs of people and communities. This requires, in turn, that efforts be made to stimulate social imagination concerning alternative economic visions and models.

There are, of course, some built-in problems in our culture and society which limit our capacities for social imagination. For example, the restricted ideological choice between two systems, either Capitalism or Communism, tends to stifle social imagination (*A Society to Be Transformed*, p. 6-9). At the same time, the dominant forces of transnational capital and technology largely dictate what is desirable and feasible, thereby limiting the capacities of nations and peoples to develop viable options. In addition, social imagination is further hampered by the kind of technological rationality that prevails in our culture today. This is the kind of reasoning that avoids fundamental questions by reducing everything to factual and quantifiable knowledge through a technical means-ends process. Finally, the continued problems of personal selfishness, possessive individualism, pursuit of narrow self-interest and collective greed prevent some people from developing a capacity for creative social imagination.

It is essential that people find ways of breaking out of these dominant modes of thought and develop new ways of thinking about social and economic alternatives (*A Society to Be Transformed*, p. 8). We believe that the moral principles outlined above (part one), provide some guide posts for thinking about alternative visions and models. At this point, we do not intend to put forward detailed proposals or strategies. Our primary concern is to stimulate more creative thinking about social and economic alternatives. We do, however, have several questions, comments, and suggestions to share with you regarding alternative directions.

Moral Purpose

First, what can be done to develop a clear statement of purpose regarding Canada's socioeconomic order that reflects basic moral principles? From our perspective, the primary purpose of our socioeconomic order should be to develop our resources to serve the basic needs of all people for a more fully human life in this country. This includes such basic life needs as adequate food, clothing, housing, education, employment, health care, energy. It also means putting an emphasis on the integral development of peoples, the value and dignity of human work, the preferential option for the poor and the marginalized, and the priority of labor. What can be done to develop a process that leads towards a consensus on these and related principles as the foundation stone of our economy?

Social Goals

Second, what can be done to develop a new set of social goals that adequately reflect these basic purposes and principles? From our perspective, this involves a renewed national commitment to full employment with an emphasis on permanent and meaningful jobs, new patterns of work, with adequate personal or family income. It also entails a fresh commitment to the development of more meaningful and effective forms of providing basic social services (e.g., education, health care, social security benefits, etc.). These social objectives, in turn, require a commitment to finding new and more effective ways of redistributing wealth and power among both people and regions in this country. What can be done to develop a consensus around these and related social goals for the future development of this country?

Empower the Powerless

Third, what can be done to empower the poor and the marginalized to play a more meaningful and effective role in shaping the future development of our socioeconomic order? Across this country, there are working and nonworking people, men and women, in communities—small farmers, fisherpeople, factory workers, forestry workers, miners, native people, office workers, people on welfare, public service workers, small businesspeople, and many others—who have a creative and dynamic contribution to make in shaping the social and economic future of this country. A clear social commitment is required to enable these people to truly become subjects of production and subjects of their own history. What steps can be taken to develop or redistribute resources and means for production in order to achieve this objective?

Economic Planning

Fourth, what can be done to develop more participatory and effective forms of economic planning for the future development of our society? From our perspective, a new approach to both centralized and decentralized planning may be required. The new economic forces of transnational capital/technology mean that nation states must engage in centralized planning in order to ensure the realization of the common good and basic moral principles (*Laborem Exercens*, 17, 18). This may require the nationalization of key sectors of Canada's economy. Yet, experience has shown too that nationalization does not, in and of itself, guarantee popular participation in economic planning. Thus, decentralized forms of economic planning and decision-making also are required to ensure the participation of workers, the poor, and the marginalized. What steps can be taken to develop this kind of approach to economic planning in this country?

Economic Strategies

Fifth, what can be done to develop new economic strategies based on integral, self-reliant, models of development? As a country, we are blessed with an abundance of resources required to serve the basic needs of all our people for food, clothing, housing, employment, education, health care, energy and related needs. A new commitment, however, is needed to break the bonds of dependency and develop new economic strategies based on self-reliance. At one level, this means increasing the self-sufficiency of our industries to manufacture our natural resources as finished products for markets. At another level, it means increasing the capacities of local communities and regions to design models of economic development to serve the basic needs of their communities. What steps can be taken to make these kinds of self-reliant economic strategies a priority in this country?

Social Ownership

Sixth, what can be done to promote new forms of social ownership and control by communities and workers in our society? Indeed, the road to self-reliance itself requires new forms of ownership and control over the means of production. If communities are going to develop their resources to serve basic human and social needs, it is essential that they have effective control over the kinds of capital and technology required to achieve these objectives. If working people are going to exercise their right to become subjects of production, then new forms of worker controlled industries need to be developed. Across the country, there are a few significant experiments in community and worker controlled enterprises that may offer some insights into the problems and possibilities to be faced. What steps can be taken to put a priority on stimulating new forms of social ownership and control by communities and workers?

Social Production

Seventh, what can be done to design more sustainable and socially useful forms of production and development? This means, for example, giving serious attention to developing forms of industrial production that make greater use of renewable energy sources (e.g., electricity, sun, wind, methane, tidal power, etc.) rather than maintaining sole dependence on nonrenewable energy (e.g., oil, gas, coal, etc.). It also means developing strategies to assist workers and industries involved in military production to redirect their energies into more socially useful forms of production. These social objectives, along with corresponding conversion strategies, need to be given serious attention in future economic planning. What steps can be taken now to design and implement more sustainable and socially useful forms of production for the future?

Global Solidarity

Eighth, what can be done to develop economic strategies in the context of global solidarity? Given the international realities of economic interdependence today, any significant changes in Canada's economic strategies are bound to have an effect on working people in other countries. This is especially critical for the poor countries of the Third World. It is important, therefore, to establish new forms of consultation, not only with the countries affected but especially with the workers in relevant industries. If, for example, specific strategies were proposed to strengthen the textile and clothing sectors of our economy, then direct consultations should take place with the workers in related South East Asian industries that would be affected by such changes. What steps, therefore, could be taken to ensure that this kind of global solidarity is actualized in the process of developing new economic strategies?

These are some of the fundamental challenges, Mr. Chairman, facing the future of Canada's socioeconomic order. Taken together, these challenges involve basic value choices about what kind of nation and people we want to become. As a country, we have the resources, the capital, the technology and above all else, the aspirations and skills of working men and women required to build an alternative economic future. Yet, the people of this country have seldom been challenged to envision and develop alternatives to the dominant economic model that governs our society. What is required, in the long run, is a dynamic public process designed to stimulate social imagination, develop alternative models, and forge a new cultural vision in this country.

We hope and pray that your commission will be able to play a significant role in initiating this kind of dynamic public process. For our part, we will continue to do whatever we can to generate critical awareness in local Christian communities. For the present structural crisis constitutes a crucial turning point in our history. It is imperative that conscious decisions be taken now to forge a human economy and a true community for the sake of future generations.

Abbreviations Used in the Index

AE	Address at Edmonton (1984) p. 353
AN	Address at Newfoundland (1984) p. 359
CHD	Resolution on the Campaign for Human Development (1970) p. 467
CM	Christmas Messages (1940, 1941, 1942) p. 94, p. 97, p. 100
CSO	Statement on Church and Social Order (1940) p. 425
DES	Introduction: Five Depression-Era Statements, p. 390
ECPC	Ethical Choices and Political Challenges (1983) p. 480
EHD	The Economy: Human Dimensions (1975) p. 469
EN	Evangelii Nuntiandi (1975) p. 265
GS	Gaudium et Spes (1965) p. 173
JW	Justice in the World (1971) p. 249
LE	Laborem Exercens (1981) p. 290
MD	Statement on Man's Dignity (1953) p. 448
MM	Mater et Magistra (1961) p. 114
OA	Octogesima Adveniens (1971) p. 224
OP	On Pilgrimage: Address at the UN (1979) p. 342
PC	Present Crisis (1933) p. 398
PL	Pastoral Letter (Sept. 26, 1919) p. 384
PP	Populorum Progressio (1967) p. 203
PT	Pacem in Terris (1963) p. 150
QA	Quadragesimo Anno (1931) p. 44
RH	Redemptor Hominis (1979) p. 279
RN	Rerum Novarum (1891) p. 13
RRP	Pastoral Statement on Race Relations and Poverty (1966) p. 463
SEC	Statement on Economic Crisis (1931) p. 396
SPR	Statement on Personal Responsibility (1960) p. 456
SR	Program of Social Reconstruction (1919) p. 367
SS	Special Sensitivity: Address at Yankee Stadium (1979) p. 348
SSP	Statement on Social Problems (1937) p. 421
SU	Statement on Unemployment (1930) p. 393

Index

About the Editors

Father John T. Pawlikowski, OSM, Ph.D., is Professor of Social Ethics at the Catholic Theological Union in Chicago, where he has taught since 1968. He is the author of several books on Christian-Jewish relations and on social ethics, including *Christ in the Light of the Christian-Jewish Dialogue*. He coedited a volume of biblical reflections on the National Conference of Catholic Bishops' 1983 pastoral statement, *The Challenge of Peace*. In 1981, Fr. Pawlikowski served as theological advisor in developing the NCCB's *Reflections on the Energy Crisis*. He has worked very extensively in the area of ethics and economics and is associated with the Center for Ethics and Corporate Policy. Fr. Pawlikowski will contribute a chapter on modern Catholic teaching on the economy to a forthcoming volume on Christianity and Capitalism.

David M. Byers, Ph.D., has written and edited a number of books, including *In the Name of Peace*, a compendium of the American hierarchy's statements on war and peace before 1983. He presently staffs several committees of the National Conference of Catholic Bishops related to evangelization, the missions, and the relationship of religion and science.

Design
Mack Rowe Visual Communications, Ltd.; Alexandria, Va.

Typeface
Palatino and Palatino Semi-bold

Typography
VIP Systems, Inc.; Alexandria, Va.